Introducing Criminological Thinking

Maps, Theories, and Understanding

Jon Heidt
University of the Fraser Valley

Johannes P. Wheeldon
Norwich University

Los Angeles | London | New Delhi
Singapore | Washington DC

Los Angeles | London | New Delhi
Singapore | Washington DC

FOR INFORMATION:

SAGE Publications, Inc.
2455 Teller Road
Thousand Oaks, California 91320
E-mail: order@sagepub.com

SAGE Publications Ltd.
1 Oliver's Yard
55 City Road
London EC1Y 1SP
United Kingdom

SAGE Publications India Pvt. Ltd.
B 1/I 1 Mohan Cooperative Industrial Area
Mathura Road, New Delhi 110 044
India

SAGE Publications Asia-Pacific Pte. Ltd.
3 Church Street
#10-04 Samsung Hub
Singapore 049483

Acquisitions Editor: Jerry Westby
Editorial Assistant: Laura Kirkhuff
Project Editor: Veronica Stapleton Hooper
Copy Editor: Shannon Kelly
Typesetter: C&M Digitals (P) Ltd.
Proofreader: Susan Schon
Indexer: Sheila Bodell
Cover Designer: Janet Kiesel
Marketing Manager: Terra Schultz

Printed in the United States of America

A catalog record of this book is available from the Library of Congress.

ISBN: 9781483333892

This book is printed on acid-free paper.

SFI   Certified Sourcing
www.sfiprogram.org
SFI-00453

14 15 16 17 18 10 9 8 7 6 5 4 3 2 1

SAGE was founded in 1965 by Sara Miller McCune to support the dissemination of usable knowledge by publishing innovative and high-quality research and teaching content. Today, we publish more than 750 journals, including those of more than 300 learned societies, more than 800 new books per year, and a growing range of library products including archives, data, case studies, reports, conference highlights, and video. SAGE remains majority-owned by our founder, and after Sara's lifetime will become owned by a charitable trust that secures our continued independence.

Los Angeles | London | Washington DC | New Delhi | Singapore | Boston

Brief Contents

Detailed Contents

Preface

This book is about theories that explain criminal behavior, criminal acts, crime rates, the activities of the criminal justice system (and its agents), and the origins of the criminal law. These ideas come from many different fields and are all in some way interrelated. Criminologists still do not fully understand how these levels interact.

This book was inspired by some modern developments in criminology. In recent years, many leading criminologists have suggested that the field is not making adequate progress in developing knowledge and encouraging theory growth (Laub, 2004; Weisburd & Piquero, 2008; Young, 2011). We hope that in some small way this book can help to stimulate theory growth by offering a new way of thinking about criminological theories.

My own experiences with learning about and teaching criminological theories for the past 15 years have obviously influenced the content of this book. The first of these goes back to my undergraduate years during the late 1990s and my first experience taking a theory course. I am not proud to admit to this, but I put off taking this course until my very last semester. This was, in part, because I was intimidated by what others had told me about theory courses. According to my fellow students, theory was boring, difficult, and had no use in the real world. I had a completely different experience in the course. It all made sense to me. And it made everything else I had been studying make more sense.

A year later, in 2001, I entered the MA program in the School of Criminology at Simon Fraser University in British Columbia, Canada. Upon being accepted, I had no clear idea of what project I was going to undertake. Luckily, this problem worked itself out during the first semester after I took the required theory course with Dr. Robert M. Gordon. I discovered that a person could actually write an entire thesis about theory. Later, I was accepted into the PhD program at SFU and carried the work even further in a dissertation.

My first experience teaching theory did not go well. In fact, it is not a stretch to call it an unmitigated disaster. It was an evening class at a small local college. The majority of my students were obviously not excited for a three-hour theory course from 7:00 to 10:00 p.m. Go figure.

I must admit that for the first three weeks of the course, I felt lost. I showed up and lectured on the material for three hours with a break in the middle. I told some funny jokes. Unfortunately, this was not enough. A few weeks in, I discovered that I had a possible mutiny on my hands. The students thought that the material was boring and that I was unapproachable. One student even created an anonymous e-mail account so they could share their true feelings about how much they didn't like the course (and me). How the hell did other professors do this? It didn't seem that hard before I tried it!!

After all this, I was crushed. I started to wonder if I had made a terrible mistake moving 2,000 miles from my home to pursue graduate studies in Canada with the hopes of being a teacher. It was at that moment that I decided I had to radically revise the course; I couldn't give up yet. I switched everything to make the lectures more interactive. I added debates, examples of criminal justice issues in the news, personal stories, and short movie clips with discussion questions to illustrate concepts in the theories; I did everything I could think of. Every week I went in and did my best impression of Socrates, constantly probing and provoking the students to think and analyze in any way I could. In short, this is how I became a teacher.

And then something miraculous happened. The class turned around. Some students still didn't like it, but over half seemed at least mildly interested. One student (who would later go on to pursue several degrees in criminology) approached me and said that he couldn't watch movies in the same way after taking my class. He told me his friends and family would get annoyed because he constantly talked about how the theories he was learning applied to the movie being viewed (this is a great thing to hear as a teacher . . . my apologies to his friends and family).

Perhaps the most important event that relates to this book being in existence was meeting my friend and co-author Dr. Johannes Wheeldon. Johannes (or, as I call him, "Jo") came to SFU a few years after I did. Jo was already very accomplished before he entered graduate school. He had wide-ranging knowledge about numerous topics, and, before even taking course work, he seemed to have a command of theory and methods. I was impressed.

Jo and I became fast colleagues and even faster friends. We attended conferences, published papers, and spent many days (and evenings) discussing criminal justice and theories of human behavior. Jo proved to be an academic juggernaut; he sped through the SFU PhD program at a breakneck pace and published several articles and a book in the first few years of his career.

During the last year of my PhD, I received an e-mail message from Jo. He had just finished publishing a book about conceptual maps and research methods and mentioned that he had another idea for a book involving theories. Since I had written my PhD dissertation about criminological theories and used some mapping techniques in the process, this collaboration seemed like a perfect fit…and presto, the book was born! (I will omit any dull discussion about the blood, sweat, and tears that were poured into writing.)

Writing a book is a humbling experience. It gives a person an idea about how little they actually know. It also makes one appreciate how difficult writing a book must have been before computers, the Internet, e-mail, and digital technology. This contribution has benefited from the insights of many. We hope we have fairly presented these views and hope this work helps students, instructors, and researchers to think about criminological theory and thought in new and important ways.

Acknowledgments

One incurs many debts during the writing of a book. We are horrified that we might overlook someone who helped us along the way because there were so many different people, including mentors, colleagues, friends, and family. We would like to thank Dr. Celia Winkler, Dr. Rob Balch at the University of Montana, and faculty members at Simon Fraser University, including Dr. Robert M. Gordon, Dr. Simon Verdun-Jones, Dr. Brian Burtch, Dr. Eric Beauregard, Dr. Barry Cartwright, Dr. Neil Boyd, the late Dr. Liz Elliott, and Dr. Curt Griffiths, to whom we both owe a special debt. Dr. David G. Wagner greatly influenced this work, as did our colleagues at University of the Fraser Valley, Washington State University, and Norwich University.

We would like to acknowledge the contributions of students from our theory courses at UFV and Norwich University as they helped to inform our thinking and approach to the subject. The book also benefited from the insights of students who were part of a postsecondary correctional education program offered by Walla Walla Community College. The seven-step model and some of the exercises were developed and refined with the input of these students. Finally, we would like to acknowledge the contributions of the Sage team, including Jerry Westby, Veronica Hooper, and especially Shannon Kelly.

Publisher's Acknowledgments

Sage wishes to acknowledge the following peer reviewers for their editorial insight and guidance.

Kevin M. Beaver, Florida State University

Paul Becker, University of Dayton

Deborah Baskin, California State University, Los Angeles

Michael A. Cretacci, Buffalo State College

Venessa Garcia, Kean University

Arina Gertseva, Washington State University

Lisa Graziano, California State University, Los Angeles

Jennifer Grimes, Indiana State University

Gale Iles, University of Tennessee-Chattanooga

David Mackey, Plymouth State University

Lisa R. Muftic, Sam Houston State University

Christopher W. Mullins, Southern Illinois University, Carbondale

Cassandra L. Reyes, West Chester University

Miyuki Fukushima Tedor, Cleveland State University

Scott Vollum, James Madison University

Jennifer Wareham, Wayne State University

Tracey Woodard, University of North Florida

For Raegan, who is my best friend, colleague, and advisor all rolled into one,
and for my daughter, Kate, who provided me with extra motivation to finish this project on time.

-jmh

For Liz, Maggie, and Trevor, who remind me every day what really matters.

-jpw

PART I

Introduction to Criminological Thinking

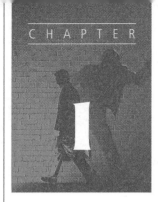

CHAPTER

I

Basic Principles of Theorizing and Mapping

 ## Chapter Overview and Objectives

This chapter introduces some of the ways in which people understand crime and criminological theory. It introduces our approach and presents the core elements of criminological theories. Using visual methods such as maps, graphs, and diagrams, we show readers how to "see" elements of theory. These methods can help students learn key theories and summarize important criminological research. An underlying premise of this book is that a clear understanding of criminological theories and their related research is helpful when designing and implementing criminal justice policies and practices.

To introduce basic elements of criminological thinking, we present some important definitional terms and outline differences between criminological perspectives and specific theories of crime and criminality. Key to our presentation of theory is what we call the seven-step approach to criminological thinking. This chapter will also provide an introduction to the use of visual maps and outline the approach taken in the remainder of the book. This includes the introduction of various criminological perspectives drawn from biology, psychology, and sociology, along with critical and integrated accounts.

By the end of the chapter, readers should be able to:

- Define criminological thinking
- Identify some challenges for criminological theories
- Differentiate between theories, correlations, and criminological perspectives
- Identify key differences between mind maps and concept maps and explain how they can be used to study criminological theory
- Present the seven steps of criminological thinking

What Is Criminological Thinking?
What Is Criminological Theory?

Criminological thinking refers to the ways in which people understand and consider crime and criminological theory. As we shall see, there are numerous ways to understand crime. This variety of criminological perspectives can help broaden one's view of the world but also complicate efforts to manage and control crime. In our experience learning about and later teaching these myriad criminological theories, we have found that theory is a subject that can be difficult and demanding for students. Like research methods, theory involves acquiring a new vocabulary and the ability to connect different strands of related content into a coherent framework of understanding.

People often have negative preconceptions about the word *theory*; this negativity often extends to courses involving criminological theory. Authors of other criminological theory texts have made this point with some regularity. For example, several editions of Williams and McShane's (1994, 1999) *Criminological Theory* textbook opened with the following quote: "Most people immediately rebel when threatened with their first exposure to theory" (1999, p. 1). And in their leading criminological theory textbook, Akers and Sellers suggest that

> to many students, criminal justice practitioners, and other people, theory has a bad name. In their minds, the word *theory* means an irrelevant antonym of *fact*. Facts are real, whereas theories seem to involve no more than impractical mental gymnastics. Theories are just fanciful ideas that have little to do with what motivates people. (2013, p. 1)

We believe that these negative preconceptions about theories obstruct the learning process. It seems useful to point out early on that everyone uses theories on a daily basis and everyone has their own theories about criminal behavior and crime. In other words, theorizing about crime and criminals is not a process engaged in exclusively by criminological theorists. Rather, laypeople, undergraduates, criminal justice system practitioners, and policymakers also take part in this theorizing process on some level. As will be demonstrated throughout this book, these ideas matter and affect the "real world."

This text also attempts to clarify some of the other problems that are common for those trying to understand **criminological theory**. One issue is that terms are often used interchangeably, inconsistently, or unclearly. For example, *theory* has been used to refer to a philosophy or approach, such as Marxist theory; a group of theories, such as learning theory; and specific explanations, such as Merton's strain theory (Cohen, 1989; Wagner, 1984; Williams & McShane, 2014). In addition, terms that refer to elements that comprise a theory—such as *assumptions, assertions, propositions, axioms,* and *postulates*—are also used inconsistently by many social scientists. Unfortunately, criminologists are no exception. Another issue is that the problem focus, scope, and level of explanation of many criminological theories are unclear and used in contradictory or inconsistent ways (Bernard & Snipes, 1996; Short, 1985; Wagner, 1984).

We suggest that this confusion arises partly from the interdisciplinary nature of criminology. However, the variety of disciplines that inform criminological thinking, including biology, psychology, sociology, economics, political science, and geography, among others, should be seen as a strength, and not as a weakness. Each of these areas has contributed ideas to the field and emphasizes different factors and variables. The challenge for students, researchers, and educators is that, all too often, theories do not make clear which criminological problems and level of explanation they address. As we shall see, this lack of uniformity has created problems for criminologists who attempt to test, evaluate, and integrate existing theories. Most important to us is the fact that this also often creates problems for students who are trying to learn and understand criminological theories.

Visual Techniques and Criminological Theory

In this text, we hope to address some of the difficulties discussed above by using various visual techniques to help students "see" difficult connections and relationships between theories and research. While maps are no substitution for reading (and re-reading) this text and other materials, we believe that visual methods can be a useful way to identify, organize, and reinforce conceptual relationships. There are many useful theory texts; few use visual diagrams to their full potential, however. In a world in which people are spending an increasing amount of time staring at screens and engaging visually with their phones, computers, and various forms of entertainment and social media, we believe it is time to make more and better use of visual methods to learn and to teach (Burruss, 2009). Again, this is no substitute for reading about, discussing, and studying the theories. Instead, our goal is to appeal to different learning styles by employing a variety of pedagogical techniques.

Our approach involves the use of a combination of concept maps, mind maps, and other visual diagrams to illustrate various aspects of and relationships between theories. More specifically, visual methods will be used to explain elements and concepts that comprise various criminological theories, demonstrate relationships between theories and their underlying philosophies or meta-theories, and describe changes in theories over time. Use of these visual methods can also be applied in more practical ways. For example, visual methods can be used to clarify the role of research in testing, revising, and validating criminological theories or to help illustrate the relationship between criminological theory and criminal justice system practices. Some students also use the mapping approach described in this chapter to improve their study habits and to help them remember the theories and their concepts. We predict that you will find your own style.

In general, maps can be used in a number of ways to teach criminological theories (Burruss, 2009), and we favor a broad approach to their definition and use (Wheeldon & Faubert, 2009). In addition to the variety of diagrams we use, efforts have also been made to incorporate mapping techniques into exercises designed to help students learn and remember the theories more effectively. To help get you started, here are a few tips. Let's start with the difference between a concept map and a mind map. A **concept map** can be defined as a hierarchical graphical tool for organizing and representing the relationship between different concepts. First presented by Novak (1981), this approach was usefully expanded and developed in the seminal book *Learning How to Learn* (Novak & Gowin, 1984). Concept maps include unique concepts, usually enclosed in circles or boxes. Traditionally, concept maps require labeled nodes denoting concepts and lines demonstrating how independent concepts are linked to form meaningful propositions and claims about the theme (Wheeldon & Åhlberg, 2012). One example is presented in Figure 1.1.

A great deal of information is summarized in Figure 1.1. First, we have to remember that criminological theories are simply ideas. More specifically, they are the ways in which people understand and explain crime. Everyone has theories. The difference between the theories of laypeople and

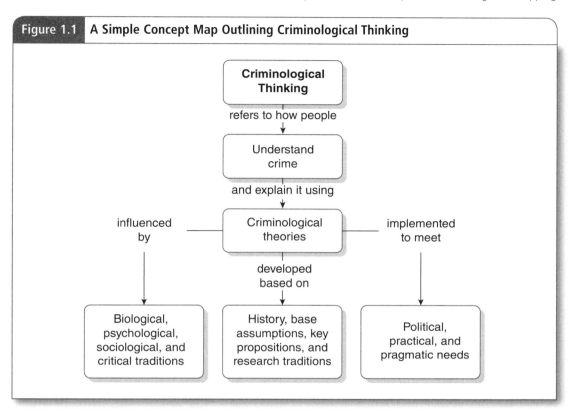

Figure 1.1 **A Simple Concept Map Outlining Criminological Thinking**

criminologists is that criminologists often question their own assumptions about crime and criminals and attempt to test and refine their theories through research and testing. Most laypeople do not have the time, inclination, or resources to partake in such activities. However, it is important to note that many people change their views on crime and the criminal justice system as they progress through life's different stages.

The figure also points out that all criminological theories have histories, base assumptions, and key propositions and are situated within research traditions or particular perspectives. We must also remember that theories are designed to meet a variety of political, practical, and pragmatic needs. In other words, ideas matter because they inform or provide the logic for practices and policies in the criminal justice system. Sometimes this influence is implied and less obvious, but it is always there.

A **mind map** is a diagram used to represent ideas that are linked to and arranged around a key word or idea. First described by Buzan (1974), mind maps have been further defined and developed and are embraced as a tool to help organize ideas and brainstorm complex concepts. Mind maps are structurally more flexible and often less formal than concept maps. They offer a means to represent associations in a variety of ways. This may include the use of images, pictures, colors, or bolded lines (Buzan, 1997). A key focus in mind maps is that they represent an individual's personal style and can therefore be unique. We think mind maps can be used to help students organize or present information, while concept maps do a better job of demonstrating relationships and linkages between specific propositions. Either approach to mapping might be used in each step of criminological thinking or as a way for you to review the main concepts of a theory. We hope as you work your way through the book, you will experiment to discover which approach works best for you. Figure 1.2 provides a mind map of some of the uses of mind maps for criminological thinking, beginning with a central idea and building outward.

Figure 1.2 suggests at least four ways mind maps can be used to assist criminological thinking and provides a number of examples. Presented visually, this information can be quickly scanned and reviewed. Hopefully, you can see that there are important differences between mind maps and concept maps. While we discuss this in more detail later in this chapter, Figure 1.3 suggests some of these structural differences.

In general, mind maps are less formal than concept maps. Concept maps are often arranged in a hierarchical fashion, while mind maps use a more free-flowing tree structure. One way to see the differences between the two is that mind maps might be more useful for understanding abstract ideas (e.g., philosophies and perspectives) or for brainstorming, whereas concept maps might be more useful for understanding policies and/or more formal ideas, such as testable theories and criminal justice practices.

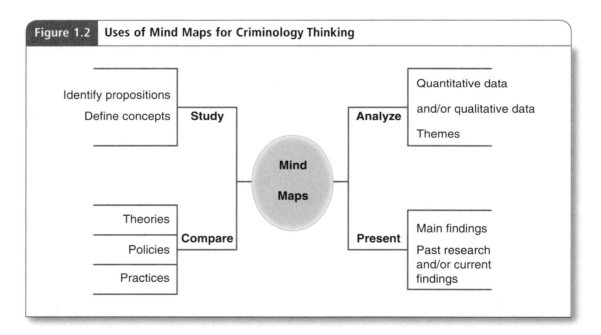

Figure 1.2 Uses of Mind Maps for Criminology Thinking

 ## Seven Steps to Understanding Criminological Thinking

To help clear up the confusion that can arise from the interdisciplinary nature of criminology, we have developed an approach that we use throughout the text to help explain the various aspects of criminological theories. Inspired by Firebaugh (2008), we offer seven key steps for criminological thinking to

Figure 1.3	Differences Between Concept and Mind Maps

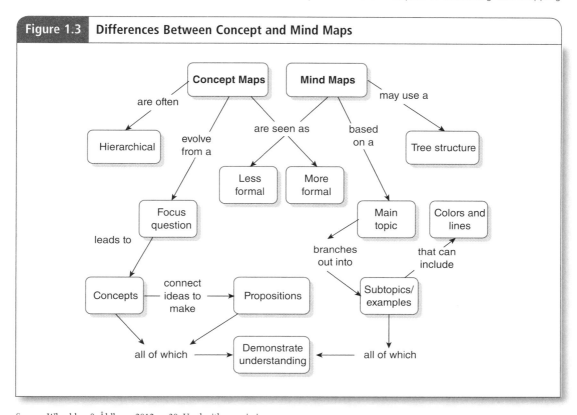

Source: Wheeldon & Åhlberg, 2012, p. 30. Used with permission.

guide our approach. This approach will be discussed in more detail in the next chapter and will be applied throughout the text. For now, let's look at how each step can be connected to criminological theory in general. The seven steps are depicted in Figure 1.4.

First, as we discussed earlier, ideas and theories about crime all have their own internal histories and are often connected to and influenced by history in a more general sense. In other words, key influences include not only intellectual and academic developments but also wider social and historical events that were occurring in society when the theory surfaced. This being the case, a key aspect to understanding a theory is to understand the historical, social, and intellectual context in which it arose. Second, theories always make assumptions about the nature of the crime and social reality (Wagner, 1984). In fact, we cannot theorize if we do not make assumptions about reality. These assumptions often determine the nature of the theory that is being produced. We will discuss specific types of assumptions in Chapter 2.

Third, it is important to understand what the theory is trying to explain, or its scope. Theories often explain different phenomena (e.g., crime rates versus criminal behavior), are posed at different levels of explanation (e.g., micro or macro), and sometimes focus on explaining different aspects of crime (e.g., general criminal/deviant behavior, chronic offending, and white-collar crime). It is important to be clear about these dimensions. Fourth, in order to understand a theory, one must be

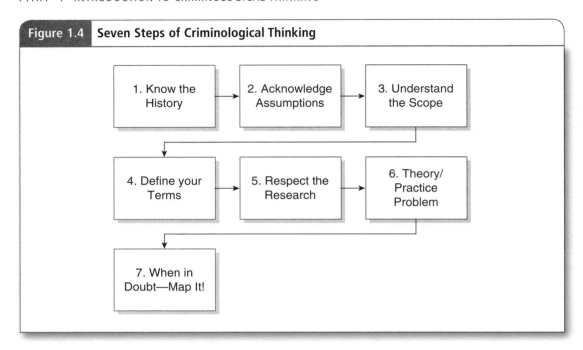

Figure 1.4   **Seven Steps of Criminological Thinking**

familiar with its key concepts and propositions, so it is important to clearly define one's terms. Fifth, theories grow and develop through research, so it is important to have a basic understanding of the research that has been conducted on the different theories. Therefore, in each chapter we will identify the preferred research methods and techniques used by theorists in the different areas. In addition to this, we will briefly discuss several key or classic examples of research and focus on one research exemplar in each area.

Sixth, as mentioned above, it is important to understand the political, pragmatic, and practical ramifications of different theories. To that end, we will spend some time in each chapter explaining how the theories have been translated into policy and practice. In other words, how do these ideas affect the real world? Finally, it should be pointed out that at various points you may feel overwhelmed by information. If this happens, don't panic! As we have mentioned, mapping can be quite useful for organizing your thoughts and learning the material. So, we have step seven of our approach: When in doubt—map it!

Major Orientations and Organization of the Book

There are a variety of different ways to classify criminological theories. For example, one can catego-rize theories by perspective or school of thought (e.g., learning, strain, and control or classical and positivist theories); historically; or by discipline (biological, psychological, or sociological). In this text, we have chosen to present theories based on their level of explanation and disciplinary emphasis. Our hope is to illustrate how ideas from the different levels fit with each other. Therefore, we have divided this book into several different units, each containing different chapters. Part 1, which you are reading now, provides introductory material about the nature of criminological theory and theorizing in criminology. So far, we have described some of the issues and problems in criminological theory and have presented the basics of concept and mind mapping. Chapter 2 also lays out in detail our seven-step approach to understanding criminological theory and describes some of the earlier developments important to understanding the origins of criminology. These include the spiritualistic and demonological explanations, the emergence of the classical school, and the origins of the positivist school of criminology.

Later units are broken down by level of explanation. Part 2 covers the individual difference theories that have emerged from biology and psychology. The first chapter in Part 2, Chapter 3, discusses the theoretical contributions from early biological positivism and some more modern examples of biological theories in criminology. Psychological personality and trait theories are covered in Chapter 4. Again, some early examples of psychological positivism are covered, but we also consider some of the more recent contributions from psychology that have informed modern criminological theories.

Part 3 reviews the micro and process-oriented theories from psychology, social psychology, and sociology. These theories seek to uncover the processes that lead one to become involved in criminal behavior. All of these theories have extensive histories that can be traced back to explanations offered by psychological learning theorists, the work of Emile Durkheim, and contributions from the Chicago school. Chapter 5 covers learning and de-individuation theories from psychology. These theories focus less on individual-level factors and more on environmental, learning, and situational elements that may produce crime. The theories covered in the next three chapters originated in the discipline of sociology. Chapter 6 discusses the branch of theories that emerged from Sutherland's (1949) differential association theory. These theories examine the effects that peer relationships and social learning have on criminal behavior.

Part 3 continues with Chapter 7, which describes the social control theories. This set of theories was greatly influenced by Durkheim's (1895/1938) notions of social control. These theories are also particularly relevant to understanding how youth become involved with crime and why families are important to understanding typical criminal behavior. This being the case, we examine how these theories inform family and school programs geared toward preventing involvement with criminal activity. Labeling theories, also known as societal reaction theories, are the subject of Chapter 8. These theories grew out of early work done in the area of symbolic interactionism and focus on explaining how the labeling process affects future behavior and how this may lead to more serious criminal behavior.

The counterparts to the process theories, the structural theories, are examined in Part 4. These theories were influenced by sociology, ecology, and urban studies. Chapter 9 covers the social disorganization theories. These theories emerged from the work of the Chicago school of sociology and represent the beginnings of American criminology. Chapter 10 describes the contributions of strain theorists to the study of crime. Like the control theorists, strain theorists are heavily indebted to the work of Durkheim (1897/1965), especially his notion of anomie.

Part 5 opens with Chapter 11, which shifts the focus to the criminal law and criminal justice system with a review of the critical or conflict theories in criminology. While these theories offer explanations for criminal behavior, they emphasize the role of the law in determining what is defined as crime and the role of criminal justice system officials in deciding who is considered criminal. This chapter also examines the important contributions of feminism to the study of crime. We consider not only why males commit more crime than females, but also why this explanation is more complex than differences in levels of testosterone between males and females. Part 5 continues with Chapter 12 consists of a review of the rational choice, economic, and deterrence theories. These theories are based on the idea that criminal behavior is a rational choice, and they focus on understanding various aspects of the criminal act with the hope of learning how to prevent crime.

Part 6 will bring us up to date and review the modern, integrated theories in criminology. Chapter 13 discusses the attempts at theory integration in criminology. Integration has been a controversial topic in criminology, and we devote a portion of this chapter to considering why this is the case. In addition, several approaches to integration are examined and assessed, and we see what impact these approaches have had (or may have) on criminal justice practice and policy. Chapter 14 examines the contributions of the biosocial approach to criminology. Biosocial criminologists focus primarily on biological aspects of criminal behavior; however, they also attempt to account for some environmental and social factors that give rise to crime. Chapter 15 covers the developmental and life course (DLC) theories. These theories are very different than the previous ones because they look at how criminal behavior changes over the life course. This approach requires a reexamination of the different levels of explanation and draws upon a variety of different disciplines and fields, which makes life course theories integrative in nature. The concluding chapter sums up the current state of criminological theory and offers some of our thoughts on how to proceed with theory building in criminology.

Think You Get It?

Make a simple visual map of criminological thinking and criminological theory. How could you use visual maps to help you review material, study for a test or midterms, and/or better understand criminological theory?

Conclusion and Review Questions

This chapter has focused on the building blocks for understanding criminological thinking. This requires understanding the seven steps presented above. These include understanding the history of a theory, acknowledging the assumptions, defining key terms and concepts, and respecting existing research. In addition, we have shown that understanding criminological policy and practice requires more than the recitation of key theoretical precepts. By examining the theory–practice problem, students can appreciate how abstract theories can become used, abused, or, more often, ignored.

Finally, we have tried to present the value of visualizing relevant terms, constructs, and debates and outlined at least two approaches to mapping that may be helpful. Concept maps can be useful to show formal and specific relationships between different ideas, while mind maps can help to see the problem in more general or abstract ways. We suggest that students employ both as they read this text and find their own style.

CHAPTER REVIEW

1. In your own words, define criminological thinking.
2. Identify some challenges for criminological theories. How can they be addressed?
3. How are concept maps and mind maps similar and different?
4. How can each type of map be used to study criminological theory?
5. Make your own map of the seven steps of criminological thinking.

CHAPTER

2

The Seven-Step Model and Early Explanations of Criminality

 ## Chapter Overview and Objectives

In this chapter, we present the seven-step model to criminological thinking. In addition to explaining each step and providing examples, we also introduce some key terms that are essential starting points to understanding criminological theory. Finally, we present quantitative and qualitative research traditions and give examples of each. To appreciate contemporary criminological theories, it is useful to understand some of the early explanations of crime and criminal behavior. In this chapter, we show you how to apply the seven-step model to spiritualistic/demonological explanations, the classical school of criminology, and the positivist school. Figure 2.1 provides some early explanations for crime and criminal behavior.

By the end of the chapter, readers should be able to:

- Present and explain the seven-step model to criminological thinking
- List the three main assumptions of human nature explored in this chapter
- Explain the shift from early approaches to explaining crime to more "scientific" approaches
- Compare and contrast quantitative and qualitative research in criminology
- Define key terms such as *causation*, *correlation*, *proposition*, and *falsifiability*

 ## The Seven Steps to Understanding Criminological Thinking

As introduced in Chapter 1, we have organized various aspects of what we call criminological thinking using a seven-step model. Figure 2.2 is a depiction of this model.

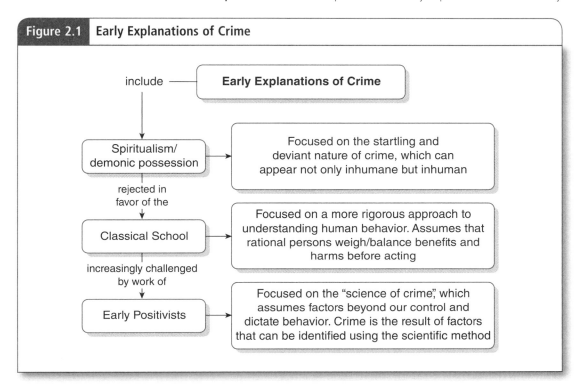

Figure 2.1   Early Explanations of Crime

Step One: Know the History

As discussed above, the interdisciplinary nature of criminology has complicated the use of common terms. This is related to both history and the assumptions that sometimes arise from differing perspectives on that history. While a full recounting of the historical twists and turns in the development of criminological theory is not possible in these pages, exploring some of the historical context surrounding the development of theory is important. The historical period in which specific theories emerged can help us to understand the issues being confronted at the time and how different interactions between theorists and researchers led to the further development of various criminological theories. For now, we will look at a few examples of how history and some of the early criminological theories are connected.

Spiritualistic Explanations: The Demons Made Me Do It

Since the earliest days of human civilization, antisocial and criminal acts have been associated with demonic possession or other evil supernatural forces. Indeed, the horrific nature of some crimes makes it easy to assume that those who commit these crimes are not only inhumane, but also inhuman. The idea that crime was a consequence of demonic possession also led to a variety of purifying rituals—these included physical torture, burning, mutilation, and a whole host of other assaults on the body designed to either drive out the demons or allow the evil spirits to escape the

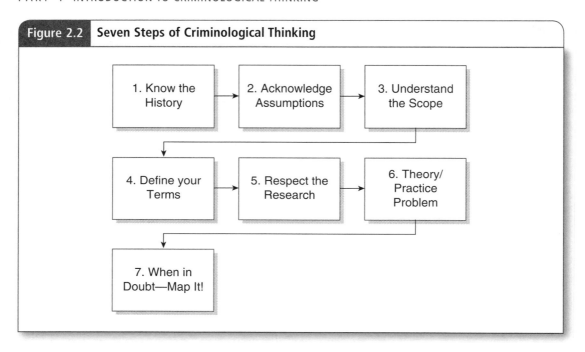

Figure 2.2   Seven Steps of Criminological Thinking

1. Know the History
2. Acknowledge Assumptions
3. Understand the Scope
4. Define your Terms
5. Respect the Research
6. Theory/ Practice Problem
7. When in Doubt—Map It!

body and the soul to be saved. Today, such practices are not a feature of American criminal justice, but there remains a view that retribution is a worthy goal of penal policy and that harsh punishment can be justified based on biblical notions of an "eye for an eye." Of some interest is how the role of religion in penal policy has changed over time. Based on a 50-state survey, prison chaplains reported that

> America's state penitentiaries are a bustle of religious activity. More than seven-in-ten (73%) state prison chaplains say that efforts by inmates to proselytize or convert other inmates are either very common (31%) or somewhat common (43%). About three-quarters of the chaplains say that a lot (26%) or some (51%) religious switching occurs among inmates in the prisons where they work. Many chaplains report growth from religious switching in the numbers of Muslims and Protestant Christians, in particular. (Pew, 2012, p. 11).

At first blush, demonological or spiritualistic explanations of crime and criminality may seem outdated and antiquated. However, it is important to bear in mind that versions of these older explanations of criminality are still embraced by many people in modern society. For example, serial killers, mass murderers, sex offenders, and terrorists are often characterized as "monsters," and some imply their behavior is thought to be unexplainable except in terms of pure evil. Against these simplistic ideas, the philosophical basis for our modern criminal justice system and some important explanations of crime emerged during the Enlightenment in Western Europe. A different and more complex view of human behavior emerged in place of the brutal approach to penal policies of the 17th century.

The Classical School: Maximizing Pleasure and Choosing Crime

The classical school emerged in the 18th century and focused primarily on preventing criminal acts rather than on explaining or understanding criminality or criminal behavior. In other words, classical school philosophers were not particularly interested in why certain people committed crime and which characteristics or factors influenced the decision to commit crime. Cesare Beccaria and Jeremy Bentham are the two most well-known classical school philosophers, and their writings laid the groundwork for the criminal justice system in modern Western society. These scholars agreed that in order to control behavior, society needs a clearly defined set of laws and punishments, a fair legal process, and prisons for those who violate the laws (Lilly, Cullen, & Ball, 2011). Both claimed that there were three important aspects of punishment: severity, certainty, and celerity, or swiftness. In order for punishment to deter potential criminals, these three elements had to be correctly calibrated to specific criminal acts.

According to the classical school theorists, in order to prevent crime and achieve deterrence, a number of conditions must be met. First, the punishment should be calibrated at the appropriate **severity** level. In other words, the punishment must fit the crime and should be comparable to the harm caused by the crime. Second, the chance of being detected must have a high level of **certainty**, or the offender must perceive that he or she is likely to be caught and punished. Third, the punishment should take place shortly after the act or behavior, so the level of **celerity**, or **swiftness**, should be high. Both Beccaria and Bentham agreed that the severity of punishment was much less important than certainty and celerity. In fact, they specifically cautioned against ratcheting up the severity of punishments to unreasonable levels, suggesting that this would eventually cause a backlash in society and a loss of faith in the criminal justice system (Williams & McShane, 2010). Interestingly, many of the deterrence principles offered by Becarria and Bentham have been supported by more modern research on rewards and punishments in psychological learning theory.

By the end of the 18th century, the penal system of Europe had changed drastically, with various forms of incarceration gradually replacing the "theatre of horror." Historian Michael Ignatieff explores how:

> It came to be considered just, reasonable, and humane to immure prisoners in solitary cells, clothe them in uniforms, regiment their day to the cadence of the clock, and "improve" their minds with dosages of scripture and hard labor. Between 1770 and 1840 this form of carceral discipline "directed at the mind" replaced a cluster of punishments directed at the body—whipping, branding, the stocks, and public hanging. (1978, p. xiii)

From the 1920s to the 1970s, the justice system concerned itself with trying to reform, remake, and restructure the lives of offenders and make them into good, honest, law-abiding citizens. Moreover, since World War II, the justice system has also been seen as part of efforts to socially rehabilitate those in conflict with the law (Griffiths, 2010). For example, in the place of long sentences, probation officers have employed a variety of techniques commonly associated with social work, including group work, community work, task-centered work, family therapy, and behavioral programs. By the 1960s, this progressive approach to penal practice

> was the exemplar, the paradigm of the welfarist approach to dealing with crime and offenders. It emphasised rehabilitation, resettlement, individualised social case-work, re-integration—a social welfare approach to social problems. The problem of crime was

understood as a problem of individuals and families in need of help and support, of communities that were disorganised and disadvantaged. The focus of attention was not the crime itself—the instant offence being a matter of mostly legal concern—but instead the personal and social problems that underlay criminal behavior. Crime was a presenting symptom, a trigger for intervention, rather than the focal point for the probation officer's action. (Garland, 1997, p. 3)

The irony is that despite the recognition 200 years ago of the limitations of severe and overly punitive approaches to punishment, there remains support for a return to punishment based not on deterrence but instead on retribution.

Since the 1970s, the United States has begun to rely upon harsher punishments to control crime. This approach has, for the most part, been quite unsuccessful except to reinforce social inequities and racial injustice (Austin & Irwin, 1997; Messner & Rosenfeld, 2001; Western, 2006). Even today, many have lost faith in the ability of the criminal justice system to reduce crime; the hope now is to keep it at a tolerable level (Garland, 2001). The focus on managing crime, increasing punishments, and reducing rehabilitative efforts has gained a foothold throughout North America and the United Kingdom, despite evidence that it does not reduce crime, cut criminal justice costs, or promote rehabilitation and reintegration.

In Chapter 12, we will return to a more detailed review of the classical school and modern theories based on its ideas when we discuss deterrence, rational choice, and economic theories of criminal behavior. For now, we will turn to the origins of the scientific approach to understanding crime, often referred to as the positivist school of criminology.

Positivist Criminology: A Science of Crime?

Positivist criminology emerged after the classical school and also influenced the functioning of the criminal justice system. As mentioned previously, classical explanations attributed crime to free will and choices made by offenders. Positivism, on the other hand, suggests that certain characteristics may make some people more prone to committing crime than others. **Positivist theories** are deterministic and are rooted in the scientific method; positivists assume that factors beyond our control dictate our behavior. These theories may attempt to explain criminality, criminal behavior, or crime rates and are not particularly concerned with understanding the dynamics and situational aspects of specific types of crime or criminal acts.

The origins of the positivist approach in the social sciences can be traced to the work of Auguste Comte, a 19th century French philosopher (Williams & McShane, 2014). In fact, he coined the term *positivism* and is often credited as the original founder of the discipline of sociology (Bohm & Vogel, 2011). Comte dismissed the notions of free will espoused by Enlightenment and classical school scholars and advocated studying social phenomena using testable hypotheses, careful classification, and a systematic approach based on the natural sciences (Williams & McShane, 2014). He believed that the scientific elite would be best equipped to design governmental policies and dictate how the "inferior classes" (i.e., anyone who was not an intellectual) should live their lives (Bohm & Vogel, 2011).

We will return to the positivist school in more detail in Chapter 2 when we discuss the biological theories; for now, let's think about the importance of history. One way to understand the relevance of history is to consider how criminological theories have developed. This may be related to the social context of a period, prevalent views of society at the time, and/or key historical events that may have served to inspire or otherwise influence theorists. Another aspect discussed in later chapters relates to how research findings, interactions between researchers, and even personal feuds and professional rivalries have shaped different criminological theories. We have discussed some of this in relation to the classical and positivist schools of thought in criminology. Figure 2.3 provides one view of how theories might be affected or influenced by social context and history.

Next, we will consider how differing assumptions have impacted the variety of perspectives found in criminology.

Step Two: Acknowledge Assumptions

All criminological theories make a number of assumptions about human nature, behavior, society, and reality (Agnew, 2011). **Assumptions** refer to things that we take for granted as true about people and our world. To clearly understand criminological theories, it is necessary to be familiar with the key assumptions that characterize the different criminological theories. As we have seen, the classical and positivist schools of thought emerged from a debate over the free will assumption. Do people have free will or is their behavior determined by factors beyond their control? Other, more complex theories make different assumptions about various aspects of reality. For now, we will look closer at three assumptions that criminologists (and people in general) make about human nature.

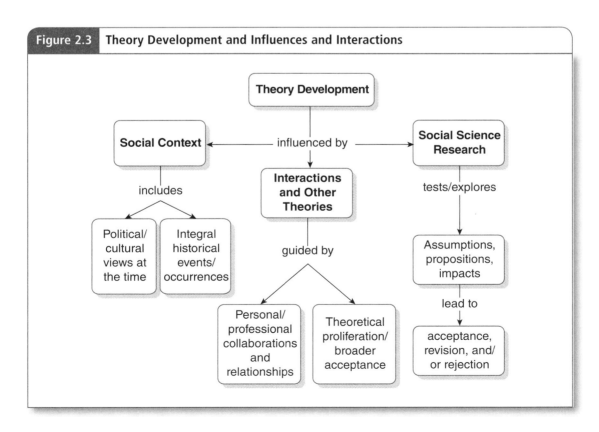

Figure 2.3   **Theory Development and Influences and Interactions**

First, as discussed above, classical school theorists make a number of assertions relating to human nature and human behavior. They believe that people have **free will** and are responsible for their own decision making. Further, they claim that people are **hedonistic** in the sense that they seek pleasure and avoid pain. Finally, classical school thought asserts that people are **rational** and can anticipate outcomes, weigh and balance options, and act in their own self-interest. The classical school took for granted that people will commit crime if proper laws and regulations are not in place. In other words, people seek to maximize pleasure and minimize pain. Originally developed by Jeremy Bentham, a 19th century Jurist, this approach is associated with **utilitarianism** and relies on what is known as the **hedonistic calculus**. The central principle of the approach is summarized in the following passage:

> Nature has placed mankind under the governance of two sovereign masters, pain and pleasure. It is for them alone to point out what we ought to do, as well as to determine what we shall do. On the one hand the standard of right and wrong, on the other the chain of causes and effects, are fastened to their throne. They govern us in all we do, in all we say, in all we think. (Bentham, 1789, p. 11)

In other words, when presented with a choice, people weigh out the pleasure and pain associated with the consequences of the different choices. Based on this calculation, people will act to maximize their own pleasure or happiness. This approach can also be connected to Thomas Hobbes (Williams & McShane, 2010; Lilly et al., 2011). Both Bentham and Hobbes would agree that man's natural state is inherently selfish and that we require laws and regulations to prevent a "war of all against all." If a person assumes that people are naturally pleasure-seeking and need to be kept in line, he or she will likely be very concerned with properly administering punishments to deter people from committing crime. Of course, this is not the only view of human nature.

Second, some theories, including many positivist theories, claim that a person is a blank slate, or *tabula rasa*. This assumption suggests that people are born without any sort of inherent nature and instead are completely shaped by their environment. People who believe in a *tabula rasa* conception of human nature fall clearly on the side of nurture in the nature–nurture debate. The term *tabula rasa* can be traced all the way back to the writings of Aristotle. However, the term is most closely associated with the writings of John Locke, a social and political philosopher (Agnew, 2011; Bohm & Vogel, 2011). If a person agrees that humans are empty vessels whose behavior is shaped by experience, it is more likely that he or she will support the use of social programs or rehabilitation to deal with crime.

Third, other theories assume that people are naturally social or altruistic. According to some theorists, people are socially concerned actors who wish to help others and avoid harming them. This is because people tend to value social ties and do not want to risk losing them. Many sociological theorists believe that human behavior is inherently social. This assumption is also associated with the writings of Jean-Jacques Rousseau, who assumed that humans were inherently good but corrupted by negative influences from society and societal pressures (Agnew, 2011). If a person assumes that people are inherently altruistic and that social forces corrupt individuals, then one might focus on how societal norms, pressures, and power allow some harmful behavior to continue yet define other harmful behavior as criminal.

One contentious issue in the study of crime relates to assumptions made concerning human agency. In other words, do people have free will or are their behaviors determined by factors beyond their control? The answer to this question drastically alters the way in which a criminologist studies crime and criminality and illustrates the basic conflict between the classical and positivist schools of thought (Agnew, 2011). On the one hand, the classical school, believers in the concepts of deterrence and rational thought, and economics theorists all assume that people have free will and are rational actors, so they tend to focus on studying criminal acts over criminal behavior. On the other hand, positivist criminologists assume that human behavior (including criminal behavior) is determined by biological, psychological, social or physical-environmental factors, or a combination of all three. This illustrates how our assumptions about the nature of the actor dictates the method or approach we use to studying crime and criminals (Agnew, 2011).

The assumption of free will versus determinism also illustrates a fundamental tension in our criminal justice system. The notion of deterrence, the judicial process, offender culpability, and individual rights are based on classical school notions. However, other aspects of our criminal justice, such as rehabilitation and treatment, parole and probation, and the use of experts to help with the problem of crime, are clearly a product of the positivist or scientific approach to crime.

A third key assumption crucial to understanding criminological theories concerns the nature of society. In other words, is society characterized more by consensus or conflict? The key question here is, how much attention should criminologists pay to the formation of the criminal law? On the one hand, consensus theorists assume that most people in society agree on which acts should be legal and illegal. On the other hand, conflict theorists assert that the criminal law represents the interests of different competing groups in society. There is some disagreement among conflict theorists as to how many groups are involved in this process. In other words, is it more accurate to think in terms of rich versus poor or in terms of numerous groups pursuing their own interests and competing against one another?

We will revisit these questions in Chapter 11 when we discuss the conflict and critical theories in criminology in more detail. For now, it should be clear how making these different assumptions could affect the nature of theory being proposed and even the policies and practices that emerge. Consider the following table and see if you can determine what policy or programs might result from the assumptions listed.

Student Exercise 1

Assumption About Human Nature	Criminological Orientation	Justice Policy and/or Program Examples?
Naturally pleasure-seeking	Focus on controlling behavior through environment and/or punishment	
Naturally social	Focus on the benefits of social solutions to crime	
Naturally altruistic	Focus on the corrupting influence of societal norms and pressures	

Step Three: Understand the Problem Focus, Scope, and Level of Explanation

Problem focus (or explanatory domain), scope, and level of explanation are important aspects of criminological thinking. Unfortunately, in many social scientific theories these dimensions are unclear or are left unstated, and the same can be said of most criminological theories (Messner, Krohn, & Liska, 1989; Messner & Rosenfeld, 2001; Wagner, 1984). This oversight can lead to serious problems in criminology because criminological theories have varying scopes, are posed at many different levels of explanation, and may address several explanatory domains. The lack of understanding and consistency in this area explains why criminological theories have developed slowly and why there have been so many difficulties associated with integrating different theories (Bernard & Snipes, 1996; Messner, Krohn, & Liska, 1989; Short, 1985). To avoid this confusion, the meaning of scope, level of explanation, and problem focus will be clearly specified below.

Different criminological theories seek to explain different types of phenomena. In criminology, there are several different **explanatory domains** or **problem foci**. Criminologists generally seem to agree that criminological theories focus upon four different aspects of crime (Akers, 2009; Brantingham & Brantingham, 1984; Bernard, Snipes, & Gerould, 2010; Miller, Schreck, & Tewksbury, 2011; Sutherland & Cressey, 1974). Most criminological theories focus on explaining criminal behavior (or criminality), criminal acts, or crime rates. Some theories may also attempt to explain the formation and activities of the criminal law and the criminal justice system. In some cases, theories may attempt to address more than one of the four aspects.

Scope refers to how much the theory can explain and is more specific than problem focus. For example, some theories claim to be general theories that can explain all forms of criminal behavior, but other theories are much more specific and focus on explaining one particular type of crime. Some also argue that the causes of elite or "suite" crime (e.g., white-collar, corporate, and political crime) are different from common or "street" crime (e.g., theft, robbery, burglary, and assault). Still others argue that victimless crimes (e.g., drug use, prostitution, and illegal gambling) cannot be explained by factors that are commonly associated with more violent or victimful crimes (e.g., theft, assault, robbery, burglary, and murder). When reading about and attempting to apply various criminological theories, it is important to think about the scope of the theory and consider what it is attempting to explain.

Another important aspect of a theory is its **level of explanation**, which is sometimes referred to as level of abstraction or level of analysis (Bernard et al., 2010). Some criminologists differentiate between micro-, macro-, and meso-level theories. Micro-level theories explain how specific people or groups of people become criminals, whereas macro-level theories explain how the social structure can affect crime (Short, 1985). Meso-level (or bridging) theories fall somewhere in the middle of micro- and macro-level theories (Williams & McShane, 2010).

Another method of classifying theories based on levels of explanation (also called levels of analysis) involves distinguishing between theories that focus upon **individual differences** that lead to crime and theories that emphasize the **social structural factors** and **social processes** that lead to crime (Akers, 2009; Bernard et al., 2010). In other words, some people may have biological or psychological characteristics (e.g., impulsivity or a lack of empathy) that make them more prone to behaving criminally. However, it is obvious that not every criminal has biological or psychological problems because, in many cases, crime seems more related to social factors. For example, a person may be under financial stress because of socioeconomic status or may have more opportunities to commit crime because of the neighborhood he or she inhabits (both structural factors). In addition, a person's peer group may be involved in crime or the person may simply lack the strong social ties that might prevent him or her from committing crime (both social processes).

Problem focus, scope, and level of explanation may also be connected to a theory's disciplinary origins and criminological perspective. For example, psychological learning theories focus primarily on explaining individual criminality, while rational choice theories are more concerned with explaining the dynamics of criminal acts. Sociological theories, such as strain theory or social learning theory, tend to emphasize social structures and processes. Critical or conflict theories are concerned with understanding how criminal laws are formed and how the activities of the criminal justice system may affect crime and criminal behavior (Bernard et al., 2010).

At this point, it should be clear that while they are all different dimensions of a theory, scope, level of explanation, and problem focus/explanatory domain are all connected to one another in various ways. Figure 2.4 provides one way to see these various elements together.

Step Four: Define Terms and Concepts

The French philosopher Voltaire once stated, "If you would converse with me, define your terms." Before discussing the elements within the different theories, it is important to clarify what we are talking about when we use the word *theory*. **Theories** refer to specific explanations of criminality/ criminal behavior, crime/criminal acts, crime rates, and/or the behaviors of the criminal law/criminal justice system. Theories can be tested and falsified, but they can never be proved fully (Popper, 1962). We can never fully verify theories because we may uncover new facts that fail to support the theory or we may test the theory with new or different data and find that it is much less accurate or useful than previously believed.

Good theories should be straightforward and easy to understand. This means that all other things being equal, we prefer simple theories to more complex ones primarily because simple theories are easier to test and refute. If we know a theory is simple, yet people have failed to refute it, this means that it must be a strong theory. This guiding principle is sometimes referred to as Occam's

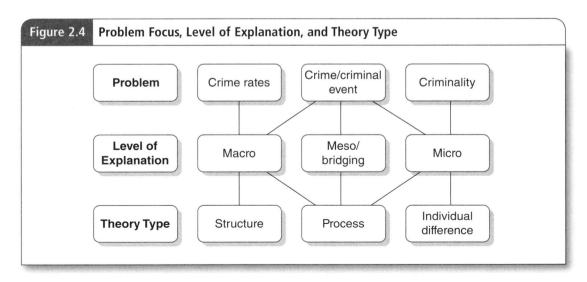

Figure 2.4   Problem Focus, Level of Explanation, and Theory Type

razor. This principle suggests that if two theories explain a phenomenon equally well, we prefer the theory that does it by using the fewest concepts and least complex relationships (Palys, 1997). Let's consider an example.

The basis for Charles Darwin's theory of evolution is natural selection, or the idea that in order for an organism to survive in its environment, it must adapt. Darwin showed that, over time, previous adaptations change future generations. Thus, although some traits have a genetic basis, they can change over time. The theory, of course, is controversial to some. It shouldn't be. The theory does not deny the possibility that some sort of Creator exists, since such a question is beyond the scope of the theory. Natural selection simply serves as the best explanation for what we observe happening in nature. It is based on four key propositions. **Propositions** refer to the key statements of the theory in question (Robinson, 2004, p. 19). For the theory of natural selection (see Figure 14.2), propositions might include the following:

- Within a given species, more individuals are produced by reproduction than can survive within the constraints (e.g., food supply) imposed by the species' environment.
- The disparity between the number of individuals produced by reproduction and the number that can survive creates a struggle for existence (http://www.open.edu/openlearn/nature-environment/natural-history/evolution-through-natural-selection/content-section-2).
- Individuals within a species show variation, and those with advantageous characteristics have a greater probability of survival and reproduction.
- When advantageous characteristics that promote survival are inherited by offspring, individuals possessing those characteristics will become more common in the population over successive generations.

If propositions refer to the key sentences in a theory, **concepts** refer to the key ideas within the propositions. One issue that we will discuss in later chapters is the importance of consistency and precision with regard to our definitions. Concepts ought to be defined in ways that allow others to both understand and clearly measure them. In other words, clarity in criminological thinking is to be praised. However, sometimes overly simplistic definitions obscure or overlook the complexity of criminal events and societal responses to them. To understand the relationship between propositions and concepts, let's consider natural selection again. Based on the above propositions, some key concepts might include struggle, variation, inheritance, and survival.

The main difference between this theory and its competitors is that natural selection is falsifiable. **Falsifiability** means it is possible to refute a central claim made by a theory. We will look at falsifiability in greater detail later; for now we will stick with natural selection. How could this theory be falsified? One way is by looking to the fossil record. As we know a great deal about how various animals (including humans) have changed over time, we can easily look back to see how well the idea of adaptation holds up. The British scientist J. B. S. Haldane, when asked what would constitute evidence against evolution, famously said, "Fossil rabbits in the Precambrian." The joke for those of you who are not geologists is that the Precambrian era comprises the geologic timeframe prior to 600 million years ago, when from an evolutionary point of view rabbits did not exist. While nothing like rabbit fossils have ever been found in this era, it is possible that evolution could be disproved by such a discovery. This is what makes evolution falsifiable and distinct from other explanations such as intelligent design or creationism. While there are plenty of gaps in the fossil record, no fossils have yet been found that disprove evolutionary theory. As such, evolution remains the best theory of explanation we have for the diversity of life on earth.

In addition to being falsifiable, good theories should also uncover new puzzles or problems for researchers to solve. A theory does not have to explain everything; it is just as important to open up new areas of research and help push knowledge in the field further. In other words, a good theory should lead to more research studies (Kuhn, 1962). Theories should also be able to make sense of the existing facts that are known about the phenomenon or phenomena in question (Williams & McShane, 2010). Again, evolutionary theory scores high in both of these categories; this is why it is so widely accepted by scientists. Evolutionary theory is relevant to all organisms from amoebae to humans to blue whales, and it has succeeded in making sense of data that, at first, seemed to be unrelated to it. For example, Gregor Mendel's research on genetics came about at roughly the same time, in the mid-1800s. However, the integration of Darwin's and Mendel's work, referred to as the modern synthesis, did not take place until the early part of the 20th century.

A final point that needs to be made is that theories are composed of statements that explain a relationship between two or more concepts (Thornberry, 1989). As discussed above, theories contain explanatory statements called propositions from which key concepts are identified. Both concepts and propositions must be testable and falsifiable in order to evaluate a theory. Figure 2.5 presents some of the traditional components of theory.

While theories may be very specific, criminological perspectives tend to be more abstract. Perspectives, sometimes called meta-theories or paradigms, are general approaches or underlying philosophies that inform our theories. The classical and positivist schools are early examples of criminological perspectives. Examples of prominent perspectives in modern criminology include psychodynamic, learning, labeling/societal reaction, control, anomie, rational choice/economic/deterrence, critical/conflict, biosocial, and developmental and life-course approaches.

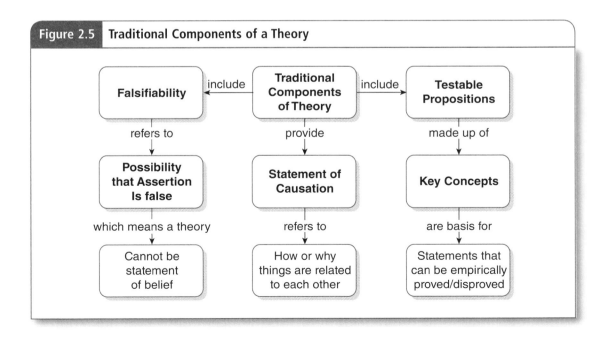

Figure 2.5   Traditional Components of a Theory

Criminological perspectives do not explain specific things. Instead, they provide a list of guidelines and direct the theorist to important aspects of the problem. A person's preferred criminological perspective may determine some of the core assumptions that person makes about the phenomenon he or she is trying to explain. Given that all theories are built on different assumptions, it is important to discuss the key assumptions that characterize criminology. In many cases, these can be connected to criminology's complicated history.

Step Five: Respect the Research

To understand the importance of criminological research, it is necessary to understand basic differences in research traditions. **Qualitative research** refers to the gathering, analysis, interpretation, and presentation of narrative information in order to establish concepts and build theories (Teddlie & Tashakkori, 2009, p. 6). Qualitative research was very much at the heart of early studies of crime, including the ethnographic and interview research that formed part of what is known as the Chicago school (Shaw, 1930; Sutherland & Conwell, 1937). During the 1920s and 1930s, researchers at the University of Chicago undertook numerous qualitative studies of crime and deviance. These researchers viewed the city of Chicago as a sort of social laboratory and focused on understanding how the urban landscape related to social problems such as crime (Adler & Adler, 1987).

Today, there are calls for a renewed focus on qualitative research to understand issues such as offender decision making, social networks, and the ways in which social processes shape criminal events. According to Miller (2005), although many criminological areas of interest have received limited attention from qualitative researchers, they offer promise for future investigations. This includes the use of life history narratives to understand pathways to offending and desistance from crime (Daly, 1992; Giordano, Cherkovich, & Rudolf, 2002; Maruna, 2001; Moore, 1991; Sampson & Laub, 2003) as well as research on organizational processes and decision making within criminal justice and other relevant institutions. The benefit of qualitative analysis is that it can provide a means to focus more deeply on individual cases and context-specific realities.

In criminology, it is far more common for researchers to employ quantitative methods. **Quantitative research** can be described as the techniques associated with the gathering, analysis, interpretation, and presentation of numerical information (Teddlie & Tashakkori, 2009, p. 5). Through clearly defined dependent and independent variables, quantitative research relies upon **hypothesis testing** to evaluate theories. This requires that researchers understand the differences between propositions, concepts, independent and dependent variables, and correlation versus causation. Ideally, theories are stated formally in propositions. As discussed above, propositions are statements that explain the relationships between key concepts within the theory. When the theory is tested, the key concepts are measured with variables. Concepts are words or phrases that represent something abstract in the world (Bohm & Vogel, 2011). The goal of a theory is to explain how two or more concepts are related to each other. Examples of popular criminological concepts include differential association, strain, and social bonds.

A central tool in quantitative research is the variable. In simple terms, a **variable** is a measure of an abstract concept that has variation in the real world. **Independent** (or treatment) variables exert some kind of influence on **dependent** (or test) variables. As we discussed earlier, criminologists are primarily interested in explaining criminal acts, criminal behavior, or crime rates, and it is important to recognize that independent variables must precede the dependent variable in order to test their effects (Bernard & Snipes, 1996; Bernard et al., 2011). Quantitative techniques focus on numeric data and seek to test whether, and to what extent, some variables influence criminal acts, criminal behavior, or crime rates. If a connection is found between variables, this relationship may be the result of a direct cause-and-effect relationship, or **causal** relationship. It may also be the result of a **correlation**. A correlation may allow for an increased probability that one variable will affect another but is not always based on an ironclad direct relationship.

One way to think about causation and correlation is to consider cigarette smoking. Public health messages often imply that everyone who smokes gets cancer; this suggests a direct cause and effect relationship. It is more accurate to say that smoking increases your risk of getting cancer. If the first statement were true, all smokers would eventually get cancer. While smoking causes numerous other health problems in society and is not a good habit to acquire, it is only correlated with cancer (Wheeldon & Åhlberg, 2012, pp. 44–45). Obviously, there are genetic and other environmental factors (e.g., toxins in food, water, and air) that play a role in cancer.

While a correlation does not equal causation, there may be cases in which the sheer number of correlations found in study after study makes it prudent to concede that a causal explanation may exist. For now, it is useful to explain the differences between causation and correlation. In order to establish a causal relationship between two variables, we need a logical basis for our suggested relationship. This is often referred to as the **criteria of causation**, and its aspects can be summarized as follows: (1) There is a reason to suspect that the independent variable affected the dependent variable; (2) it can be established that one variable came before the other; and (3) it can be assumed that some outside (or spurious) variable is not having an impact on our observation. These aspects are outlined in Figure 2.6.

It is important to remain skeptical about casual relationships in criminology. It is far more common and useful to consider the strength of various correlations. A correlation refers to when variables vary systematically and in relation to one another. There are two types of correlations. For example, **direct (or positive) correlations** refer to situations in which increases in the independent variable cause increases in the dependent variable. For example, one might claim that crime (the dependent

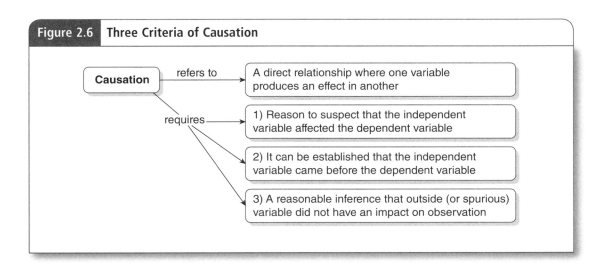

Figure 2.6 **Three Criteria of Causation**

Causation — refers to → A direct relationship where one variable produces an effect in another

Causation — requires →
1) Reason to suspect that the independent variable affected the dependent variable
2) It can be established that the independent variable came before the dependent variable
3) A reasonable inference that outside (or spurious) variable did not have an impact on observation

variable) increases with level of poverty or deprivation (the independent variable). This statement may or may not be true. To test this idea, we could examine crime and unemployment rates to see if a pattern can be observed. **Inverse** (or **negative**) **correlations** refer to when an increase in the independent variable results in a decrease in the dependent variable. Quantitative research has uncovered four main correlates of crime, as presented in Figure 2.7.

While these correlates can be challenged, they remain persistent features of criminological thinking. This is because over a long period of time, criminological research has consistently shown that a relationship between these variables and crime exists. Nevertheless, research has complicated simplistic conclusions about how crime is connected to age, gender, class, and ethnicity. Let's look at one of the most complicated issues in criminal justice: the question of race and ethnicity.

It is no secret that the American justice system has a race problem. In general, ethnic minorities are overrepresented in the prison system. Numeric analysis suggests Asian Americans are likely to commit crimes at a lower rate than white Americans and that African Americans are more involved in crime (Mosher, Miethe, & Hart, 2011; Roberts & Gabor, 1990; Rushton, 1985, 1988). In 2005, about 8% of black males age 25 to 29 were in state or federal prison, compared to 2.6% of Hispanic males and 1.1% of white males in the same age group (Harrison & Beck, 2006). Does this mean African Americans commit more crime? No. The problem is that numeric analyses like these tend to gloss over key details and important questions. For example, what kinds of harm are considered crimes? What crimes does the criminal justice system tend to focus on? Which neighborhoods do police patrol most frequently? What role does institutionalized racism play in who gets charged?

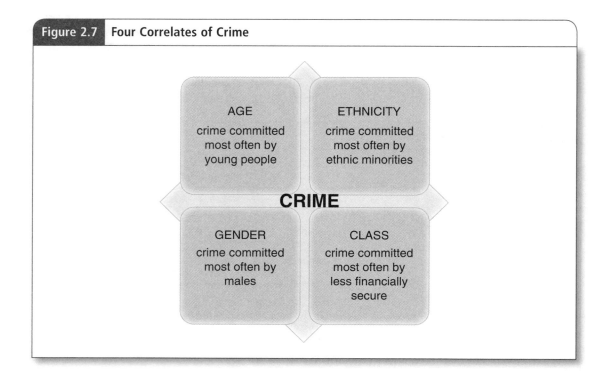

Figure 2.7   Four Correlates of Crime

AGE
crime committed most often by young people

ETHNICITY
crime committed most often by ethnic minorities

CRIME

GENDER
crime committed most often by males

CLASS
crime committed most often by less financially secure

In a review of misdemeanor marijuana arrests in New York City between 1989 and 2000, a major study by Harcourt and Ludwig (2007) found that the pattern of arrests disproportionately targeted the African American and Hispanic populations. African Americans and Hispanics arrested were nearly twice as likely as their white counterparts to be detained before arraignment and convicted, and they were at least three times more likely to be sentenced to additional jail time (Harcourt & Ludwig, 2007, p. 165). This study showed that the pattern of misdemeanor marijuana arrests in New York City since the introduction of broken windows policing in 1994 disproportionately targeted African Americans and Hispanics in relation to their representation in the resident population.

Another study on the same topic provides a useful way to visualize the disparate treatment faced by minorities. Harry Levine's research demonstrates how, since 1995, New York City arrested and jailed more people for possessing marijuana than any other city in the world. Based on interviews with police officers, public defenders, legal aid and private attorneys, assistant district attorneys, and individuals arrested for possessing marijuana, Levine explored changes in enforcement tactics and their consequences during this period. For example, Levine and Small (2008) report that although whites are more prevalent users of marijuana, based on data drawn from the US Department of Health and Human Services (2005), they were less likely than other ethnicities to be arrested during the period investigated by the researchers. Figure 2.8 provides a useful example of simplistic attempts to link crime and ethnicity. This example illustrates that law enforcement tactics may change over time and that crime rates may vary based on these changes (e.g., who gets arrested and why).

Another issue is the question of what we define as a crime. At the time of the writing of this book, despite the massive fraud that resulted in the largest economic downturn in two generations, not one individual from the largest banks and firms on Wall Street had been charged for the events that led up to the financial crisis. This is despite reports from the Federal Bureau of Investigation (FBI) as far back as 2005 suggesting that at least 26 different states had significant mortgage fraud problems, including inflated appraisals, fake supporting loan documentation, and collusion among third-party brokers and those from the mortgage industry (FBI, 2005). As we shall see later in this book, sometimes questions of formal justice are really questions of political expedience, dominant ideology, and/or bureaucratic inertia.

Today, many states, including New York, Colorado, and Washington, appear to be pulling back from the all-out "war on drugs" assault in favor of decriminalization, a focus on evidence-based treatment programs, and the increasing use of drug courts. The National Institute of Justice (NIJ) reports that in 2011 more than 2,600 drug courts were in operation in the United States. These courts use a less adversarial approach than other courts and rely upon multidisciplinary teams to deliver more specific and responsive programming and treatment (NIJ, 2012).

The above examples also suggest a useful way to understand causation and correlation. Rates of criminal behavior may be consistently reported as higher among one group of people. However, this does not mean that this group is somehow more criminal than others. Just because we know two variables are correlated with each another does not mean that one directly causes the other (Wikstrom, 2008). This is a major logical fallacy and one that must be resisted. Another example may be useful. It is well established that there is an inverse correlation between crime and age. In other words, as people get older, they tend to commit less crime. So, does growing old cause people to commit less crime?

Consider all of the factors associated with growing older that may make people less inclined to engage in criminal conduct. It may be that age is simply the best way to capture a whole range of

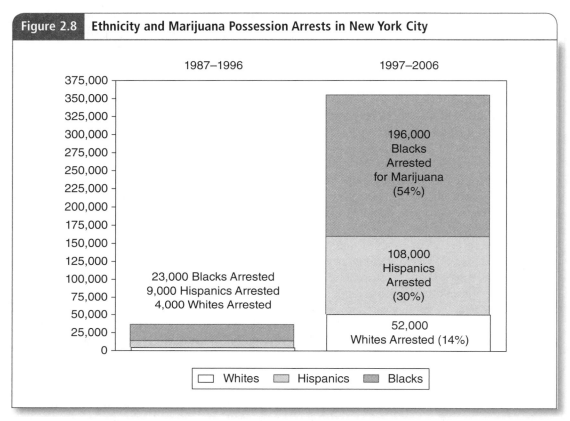

Figure 2.8   Ethnicity and Marijuana Possession Arrests in New York City

Source: New York State Division of Criminal Justice Services, Computerized Criminal History system. Cited in Levine, Harry G. & Small, Deborah Peterson (2008). *Marijuana Arrest Crusade: Racial Bias and Police Policy in New York City, 1997 to 2007.* New York Civil Liberties Union: NY, NY.

changing behaviors that make one less likely to engage in criminal behavior. While it is true that younger people commit crime more often than older people, this does not mean all youth are criminals. In other words, while age is correlated with crime, it cannot perfectly predict involvement in crime over the life cycle of offenders (Gottfredson & Hirschi, 1990).

The complications inherent in explaining the reasons or underlying causes and consequences of youth crime have led some researchers to consider how to combine quantitative theory testing with a qualitative technique that focuses on refining specific aspects of the theory (Laub & Sampson, 2004). For this reason, there has been increasing interest in **mixed methods** in criminology (Agnew, 2011; Maruna, 2010) to combine the clarity of numbers and statistics with the nuance of narrative perspective (Wheeldon & Åhlberg, 2012). Yet, as we will see, other challenges exist. One major issue for researchers attempting to test, revise, validate, or rebuild existing theories is that some theories are much more difficult to understand than others. When theories suggest clear relationships between concepts and variables, either quantitative or qualitative (or perhaps both) techniques can be used. However, when the statements of relationships are embedded within a theorist's writing and are not expressed clearly as propositions, they can prove difficult to test, verify, and further explore.

No matter which research approach is used to test or explore a theory, too often researchers fail to consider counterevidence. All credible research acknowledges limitations and explores counterevidence. In this text, we hope to offer examples of quantitative, qualitative, and mixed-methods research to showcase high-quality research that considers criminological theories from a variety of perspectives. We also agree with the sentiment that the complex features of crime and social control cannot be understood through simple quantitative and cost–benefit analyses alone. It is essential that we renew the "criminological imagination" by exploring criminological theories based on clearly stated assumptions, concepts, and propositions. This must always include research limitations, counterevidence, and an acknowledgment of the researcher's own role in the research process. It must also account for the ways in which theories are linked to the policies developed for and practices employed by those working in the criminal justice system.

Step Six: Recognize the Theory–Practice Problem

Throughout the text, we will offer some discussion on the practical ways various theoretical approaches have influenced the administration of the justice system and its policies, programs, and practices. In the last three decades, criminology has too often ignored the complexities of various theories in favor of more simplistic accounts that fit within the administrative needs of agencies and the sound bites of politicians. As we have explored elsewhere (Wheeldon & Heidt, 2007), this results in either incoherent and/or inconsistent applications of a criminological theory on the one hand, or the development of new approaches that are generally ignored by policymakers on the other hand.

It is important to acknowledge that the relationship between criminology and the criminal justice system has also had an impact on the theories produced by criminologists. There is empirical evidence to suggest that the needs of the criminal justice system and the current political climate can impact the nature of criminological knowledge. Politics may also be relevant in the sense that the government provides a great deal of funding for criminological research. This has led some to suggest that current researchers are driven by governmental assumptions about crime rather than by the input of criminological scholars and their peers (Savelsberg, King, & Cleveland, 2002). Figure 2.9 outlines some emergent considerations for criminological theory.

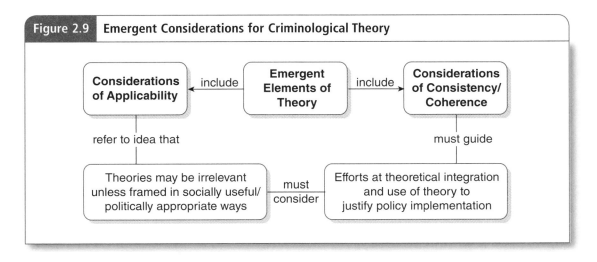

Figure 2.9 **Emergent Considerations for Criminological Theory**

Step Seven: When in Doubt—Map It!

As you have no doubt noticed, we have used a number of visual maps and diagrams so far to help augment the text and to provide another way to see the concepts and relationships we have discussed. Our use of these visual approaches is based on the growing recognition that many students learn in different ways. Different learning styles require different teaching approaches, but by building visual examples and exercises into the text we hope visual learners and nonvisual learners will take the opportunity to map out what they are reading, use maps to prepare for tests and exams, and perhaps even consider how maps could be used to explore criminological theory in more detail.

Throughout this text, we will use both concept maps and mind maps to illustrate various aspects of criminological theories. These diagrams will be used in several different ways later in the book. For example, they will be used to demonstrate relationships between variables within theories, to explain the relationship between theory and research, to clarify the historical development of theories, and to show how theories themselves are interconnected and how they may be integrated with each other. In many cases, we have tried to incorporate mapping into exercises designed to help students learn and remember the theories more effectively.

A Research Example: Classical Criminology and Deterrence Theory

Throughout this text, we will provide research examples of how theories have been explored, concepts conceptualized, and findings presented. Our first such example borrows from the useful discussion by Miller, Schreck, and Tewksbury (2011, pp. 24–27) on four approaches to research on deterrence.

You may recall that classical school criminologists make a number of assumptions about human nature. The first is that people have free will and choose for themselves what to do. The second is that

Figure 2.10	Seven Steps of the Classical School
Seven Steps	**The Classical School**
1. Know the History	Originated during the Enlightenment (ca. 1700–1800) as a reaction to brutal punishment regimes imposed by the church
2. Acknowledge Assumptions	Humans are rational, have free will, and are hedonistic; behavior must be regulated through laws
3. Problem Focus, Scope, and Level of Explanation	Criminal acts committed by individuals; amount of punishment required to control behavior
4. Key Terms and Concepts	Hedonistic (or hedonic) calculus and deterrence
5. Respect the Research	N/A (see later rational theories for examples)
6. Theory/Practice	Formal methods of social control, including legal codes, prisons, determinate sentencing
7. Mapping the Theory	See Figure 2.11

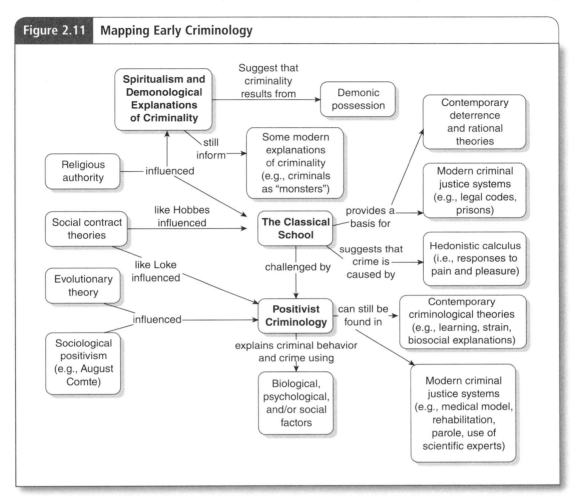

Figure 2.11   Mapping Early Criminology

people are hedonistic, in the sense that they seek pleasure and avoid pain. Third and finally, classical school criminologists believe people are rational and can anticipate outcomes, weigh and balance options, and act in their own self-interest.

It is relatively easy to see the problems with these assumptions. For example, do people always choose what to do? Are people ever compelled by urges they cannot control? Consider motives such as greed, revenge, need, anger, lust, jealousy, thrill seeking, and vanity. Are these always just mere expressions of free will? One might also ask whether a person's choices can be controlled by fear of punishment. This would require that a person know the existing penal codes and sentencing guidelines and have the ability to estimate the likelihood of apprehension, thus perhaps leading that person to conclude that the risk of punishment was not worth the short-term gain associated with committing crime.

A core assumption is that the more **certain**, **swift**, and **severe** the punishment, the greater its ability to control criminal behavior. While research into deterrence supports many of the assumptions made by classical theorists, some aspects of this perspective appear stronger than others (Robinson, 2004). An oft-cited passage from an interview with the influential Alfred Blumstein challenges assumptions about the utility of increasing punishment:

> Research on deterrence has consistently supported the position that sentence "severity" (that is, the time served) has less of a deterrent effect than sentence "certainty" (the probability of going to prison). Thus, from the deterrence consideration, there is clear preference for increasing certainty, even if it becomes necessary to do so at the expense of severity. (1995, pp. 10–13)

Miller, Schreck, and Tewksbury (2011, pp. 24–27) provide some useful discussion on deterrence research based on assumptions and principles drawn from the classical school. We have adapted and added to this discussion and present Figure 2.12 as a useful way to visualize approaches, research examples, and relevant findings on deterrence.

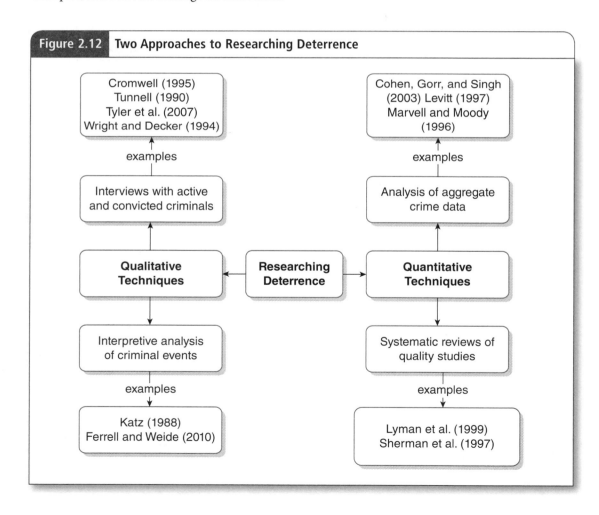

Figure 2.12 **Two Approaches to Researching Deterrence**

One approach to researching deterrence is based on *qualitative research.* As you may recall, qualitative research is based on narrative information and attempting to describe individual experiences rather than positing generalizable findings. Based on **interviews** with 60 incarcerated repeat property offenders, Tunnell (1990) demonstrated how few respondents within his sample considered prison an effective deterrent. He reports that the most common responses explaining the lack of deterrent effects on their actions were that the criminals thought they would not get caught and thought that if they were caught they would be incapacitated for a relatively short time.

Other studies have come out of the Australian Reintegrative Shaming Experiments (RISE), conducted by Tyler, Sherman, Strang, Barnes, and Woods (2007). In one example, longitudinal data drawn from before and after interviews was used by researchers to explore how attitudes to offending were affected by exposure to the normal court-based procedural justice mechanisms on the one hand, and to participation in restorative justice (RJ) conferences on the other hand. The paper concludes that exposure to RJ conferences affected people's orientations toward the law, and, as a result, led people to view the law as more legitimate and to believe that breaking the law in the future would create further problems for them. This is a growing area of interest. In Chapter 13, we will return to John Braithwaite's reintegrative shaming theory.

Qualitative research has in some ways challenged the idea that deterrence is based solely on punishment. It also complicates the way we think about rationality and the process by which people consider others, weigh and balance consequences, and view the justice system itself. For example, based on studies involving burglars, the major risk identified by those interviewed was not severe punishment from the criminal justice system. Instead, researchers consistently found being discovered by the occupants of the residence in question was viewed as the major risk and/or concern (Cromwell, 1995; Wright & Decker, 1994). This research provides a window into understanding how those involved with criminal behavior view their crimes.

Other interesting qualitative studies involve more interpretative approaches to meaning. This includes the work of Katz (1988), who analyzed descriptions of several hundred criminal acts of vandalism, theft, robbery, and murder. In many of these cases, deterrence, as traditionally defined, did not account for the sensual appeal of homicide, shoplifting, and armed robbery, nor did the fact that those committing the crimes were reacting and retaliating to actual or perceived insults and humiliations. In a different example that confronts the complexity of understanding deterrence, Ferrell and Weide (2010) explored contemporary graffiti as a social and cultural artifact of the urban environment. Using interpretive approaches and mapping where graffiti occurs, they suggest that where graffiti appears in the city is essential to understanding its meaning. The relationship between artist, location, and audience, they argue, may challenge simplistic models of crime and crime control.

Another way to approach researching deterrence is based on *quantitative research.* As discussed previously, quantitative researchers focus on the analysis of numeric information and attempt to generalize their findings rather than describe individual experiences. This research approach may be undertaken in a variety of ways, but it must contend with the basic problem that correlates for crime deterrence must attempt to measure the likelihood that a crime that would have occurred absent an intervention or intervening factor *did not* occur (Robinson, 2004). Nevertheless, a variety of studies have been undertaken.

One popular approach is based on an **analysis of aggregate crime data**, which refers to data or data sets that have been combined together. These large data sets can assist to uncover correlations that may be more common than the individual experiences catalogued and considered by qualitative researchers. Some examples of findings using this approach include those of Levitt (1997) and Marvell and Moody (1996), who show how increased police presence leads to reductions in street crime. Attempts to measure the effects of police interventions suggest that while these interventions reduce drug dealing during periods of active enforcement, levels return to baseline once the interventions cease (Cohen, Gorr, & Singh, 2003).

One of the more recent efforts at establishing criminological knowledge is based on **systematic reviews**. These comprehensive literature reviews focus on a single question and try to identify, appraise, select, and synthesize all high-quality research evidence relevant to that question. In this way, evidence is established by relying on a variety of high-quality, peer-reviewed data gathered by independent researchers. The roots of this approach come from the medical field and its use of randomized controlled trials to identify effective treatments for disease. By challenging accepted practice and replacing assumptions with rigorous study, evidence-based medicine has led to improved health outcomes and reduced costs. Systematic reviews of high-quality, randomized, controlled trials are crucial to evidence-based practices, and their use is becoming increasingly important in criminology.

One important contribution is that of Sherman et al. (1998). They reviewed more than 500 justice programs and practices to assess what was working, what wasn't, and what needed more research. Although the focus of this analysis was on crime prevention, some practices can be connected to deterrence as well. Practices found to deter crime included extra police patrols in high-crime areas, monitoring of high-risk repeat offenders, and on-scene arrests of domestic violence suspects. Practices shown not to deter crime (and in some cases make the problem worse) included boot camps for juveniles, scared straight programs, and youth-focused drug awareness programs organized through the Drug Abuse Resistance Education (DARE) program. The findings related to DARE have been tested and validated by others using similar methodologies (Lyman et al., 1999).

Despite these findings, the authors are cautious to suggest that these conclusions are provisional—like all research (Sherman et al., 1998). Clearly, there are questions regarding what works in one geographic area or cultural setting. Another important question that lies at the heart of classical criminology and contemporary research on deterrence is the following: Will the same sanction influence all potential criminals in the same way? Because offenders are individuals with their own histories, experiences, and outlooks, these sorts of sweeping generalizations about deterring crime are difficult to make. Instead, it may be better to focus on how interventions vary in their effectiveness with regard to different crimes and criminals. To address these questions, we need to know more about what biological and psychological processes affect individuals and their decision making. As outlined in Chapters 3 and 4, biological and psychological theories consider the role of individuals and personalities in understanding crime, especially in the context of human development and cognition.

Think You Get It?

Follow the instructions below to make a concept map and a mind map. First, make your own concept map of the seven steps to criminological thinking. In your map, list the key questions to consider in each step. Next, make a mind map of the main differences between quantitative and qualitative research.

Constructing a Concept Map

1. Select 6 to 8 concepts related to the topic you selected. These should be ideas from this chapter. Present these concepts first in a table.

2. Think about this analogy before you begin to map: Concepts can be seen as islands, while linking words are like bridges. These linking words should include arrowheads to show the direction of the relationship between one concept and another.

3. Begin your map by starting with classical criminology near the top of the page. Use the concepts in your table and appropriate linking words and arrows to make a full proposition or claim that can be understood through your map.

4. Because many of the concepts you identified from the chapter are likely connected in one way or another, build new propositions using other concepts and linking words.

Making a Mind Map

1. Start in the middle of the page and write the main topic of interest in a small circle.

2. Draw lines outward and write the name of each of the connected themes.

3. Now write an important idea or aspect as discussed in the chapter that is connected to each theme.

4. Write other words, ideas, or concepts that are connected to your first idea and continue to build your map outward.

5. Use color, the thickness of lines, boxes, or pictures and graphics to make your map unique and expressive.

Conclusion and Review Questions

This chapter has examined the seven-step model in some detail to explain how it is useful for understanding developments in criminological theories. First, we discussed some of the earliest explanations of criminal behavior based on spiritualism or the demonological approach. The model was then applied directly to the classical and positivist approaches to criminology to illustrate the various steps in the model.

Those who study deterrence are increasingly aware of the complications of trying to apply a one-size-fits-all approach to the problem of crime by preventing it before the fact or punishing it afterward. While some approaches to deterrence align with assumptions made by classical school philosophy, others do not. This may be a function of how we understand the relationship between individuals, crime, and approaches to crime prevention.

CHAPTER REVIEW

1. Present the seven steps of criminological thinking and provide two relevant issues for each step.

2. List the three main assumptions of human nature explored in this chapter and explain how they can be connected to our current criminal justice system.

3. What are two early approaches to explaining crime? How are they relevant today?

4. Compare and contrast quantitative and qualitative research in criminology and provide examples of research that rely upon these two approaches.

5. Define key terms such as *theory*, *causation*, *correlation*, *proposition*, and *falsifiability*.

PART II

Individual Difference Theories

CHAPTER

3

Biological Positivist Theories

 ## Chapter Overview and Objectives

In this chapter, we introduce the theories offered by biological positivism. These theories focus on individual characteristics that are inherited and present at birth, such as biological and mental traits. Lombroso, Ferri, and Garofalo (known collectively as "the Italian Positivists") attempted to explore these characteristics by applying the scientific method to the study of criminality. While the simplistic measurement of physical characteristics employed by early biological positivists failed to uncover the ultimate cause of crime, this work led to other, more nuanced approaches, suggesting that there are biological precursors that may make some people more prone to committing crime. Figure 3.1 provides a general overview of the approach we take in this chapter.

By the end of the chapter, readers should be able to:

- Understand the assumptions made by biological positivist theories
- Acknowledge the historical period in which these theories emerged
- Be aware of the level of explanation, problem focus, and scope of biological positivist theories
- Consider the historical and social context that gave rise to the biological positivist theories
- Explain the practical approaches and programs suggested by biological positivist theories

The Biological Positivist Tradition

As discussed in the previous chapter, in criminology and the other social sciences (e.g., sociology, psychology, and economics), **positivism** refers to the application of the scientific method to explain human behavior. Early criminological positivists were primarily biological theorists who sought to explain criminality by identifying physical characteristics and genetic differences that distinguish criminals from noncriminals. However, later theorists started to use psychological and social factors

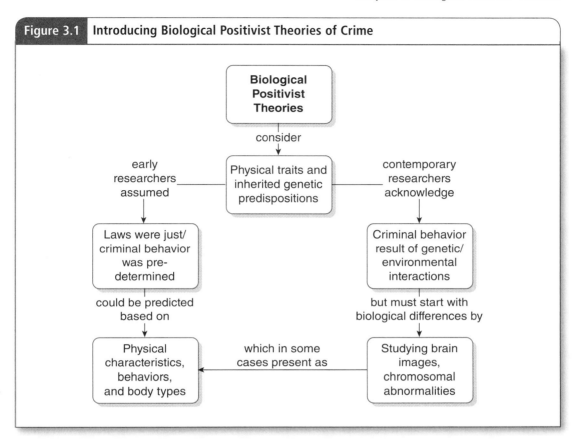

Figure 3.1   Introducing Biological Positivist Theories of Crime

to explain criminal behavior and, in some cases, to identify potential delinquents and criminals. These theorists are referred to as psychological positivists and social or sociological positivists, respectively. In this chapter, we will discuss some of the earlier contributions from biological positivists, but we also explore contributions from psychological positivism, sociological positivists, and more modern biological and biosocial theories in subsequent chapters.

As you read this chapter, consider . . . there is increasing evidence that taking repeated blows to the head can lead to degenerative brain disease. This is not new information, of course. Forty years ago, researchers found that taking punch after punch as a boxer can lead to boxer's dementia. Today, large-scale studies on combat veterans' brains show that repetitive head trauma from improvised explosive devices could be doing the same to soldiers. Further, professional athletes from both the National Football League and National Hockey League have filed class action lawsuits against the leagues. These former players are requesting that a fund be set up for those who experience the

(Continued)

(Continued)

negative side effects of repeated concussions. As you read this chapter, consider what concerns this raises for criminologists and criminal justice system practitioners. What are the implications for the wider society?

Seven Steps of Criminological Thinking

In every chapter, we present seven steps to understanding a theory or an approach to the study of crime. Figure 3.2 outlines the seven steps of criminological thinking.

History and Social Context of Biological Positivism

The origins of the positivist approach, the field of criminology, and really all of the social sciences can be traced back to the Enlightenment, or Age of Reason. This era was characterized by a collection of political, philosophical, and religious upheavals that occurred during the 17th and 18th centuries (Rafter, 2008). During the Late Middle Ages (ca. 14th century to 16th century), people begin to challenge the authority of the Catholic Church and the monarchies in Europe. Spurred by the invention of the printing press, many discovered philosophy and literature, shared new ideas, and rediscovered old ideas. The Renaissance, in part, was driven by a desire to study and better understand nature. The printing press and increased availability of books led to higher rates of literacy and more reading, which had a twofold effect. First, people begin to read key texts (e.g., the Bible) on their own instead of relying upon translations from church and government officials. Second, increased reading among the populace contributed to the proliferation of competing philosophies and ideas that caused people to question society and existing political hierarchies.

Of course, history rarely proceeds along a simple linear timeline, and some disagreement exists among scholars as to how and why the Renaissance occurred and as to what were the specific years of

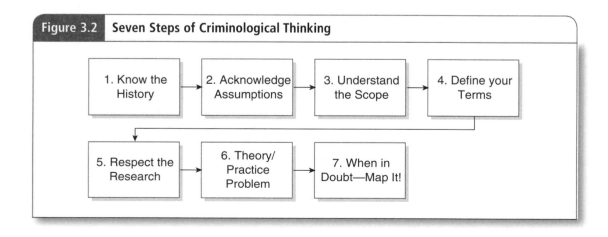

Figure 3.2   Seven Steps of Criminological Thinking

1. Know the History
2. Acknowledge Assumptions
3. Understand the Scope
4. Define your Terms
5. Respect the Research
6. Theory/Practice Problem
7. When in Doubt—Map It!

the Enlightenment. Most, however, agree that the Enlightenment occurred toward the end of the Renaissance during the 17th century and continued into the 18th century. During this period, advances in medicine and science took place, there was an interest in reason and the rationality of man, and a newfound interest in establishing laws, legal systems, and individual rights.

The Enlightenment saw the emergence of the classical school, which viewed man as rational and possessing free will. Legal systems were built on the assumption that people acted to maximize their own pleasure and must be deterred from doing so by social control through laws and regulations. Enlightenment philosophers also offered many reforms to the existing system of justice, including imprisonment, clear legal codes, and clearly defined punishments designed to deter future criminal behavior by fitting the punishment to the crime. The basis for classical school thinking was covered in Chapter 1, and we will also revisit some of these ideas in Chapter 12 to understand how they laid the groundwork for modern theories based on deterrence and economics.

The approach embraced by biological positivists must be seen as a reaction to the free will perspective endorsed by classical school thinkers. This new interest in science gave rise to the three key forerunners to the early biological theories of criminal behavior. First, the early psychiatric work on moral insanity had an impact on biological positivism. These researchers were attempting to further explain how free will functioned and what caused some people to commit evil acts (Rafter, 2008).

Second, the emergence of physiognomy and phrenology preceded Lombroso's work on the criminal man (Savitz, Turner, & Dickman, 1977). **Physiognomy** refers to the belief that behavior can be predicted through a person's physical appearance. Swiss scholar and theologian Johann Kaspar Lavater was one of the pioneers in this area, and his work on physiognomy received almost as much praise as Lombroso's work (Bernard, Snipes, & Gerould, 2010). **Phrenology** refers to a system of reading the bumps on a person's head in order to learn things about his or her character. Viennese physician Franz Joseph Gall and his student Johann Gaspar Spurzheim are considered the main founders of this field (Rafter, 2008). While phrenology may sound quite silly to us and has proved to be scientifically lacking, it grew into a well-developed field (Savitz, Turner, & Dickman, 1977). It offered an explanation of criminal behavior when most were explaining crime through reference to evil or demonic possession. Further, in an era dominated by an extremely retributivist approach to crime, phrenologists were some of the early proponents of rehabilitation and treatment (Rafter, 2008).

Third, the emerging evolutionary perspective had a huge impact on the early biological positivists. This included not only the work of Darwin, but other evolutionary theorists such as Jean-Baptiste Lamarck, Herbert Spencer, and Francis Galton (Rafter, 2008). Gregor Mendel's work on genetics was also quite important to some of the early positivist studies of criminal behavior—in particular, those based on genetic inheritance, such as the family studies of Dugdale (1895) and Goddard (1913).

In 1871, Lombroso proposed his theory of atavistic man, which was very well received, especially in the United States where it became quite popular. At first, his ideas competed with phrenology over which theory best explained criminality, but Lombroso's theory and approach were embraced due to a variety of historical and social factors. Lombroso received support from the American Institute of Criminal Law and Criminology. This influential organization devoted more attention to his research, and his work was translated and distributed (Savitz, Turner, & Dickman, 1977).

In general, evolutionary and biological theories received much more support than other environmental theories (Taylor, Walton, & Young, 1973; Rafter, 1997). Lombroso also gained credibility by using Darwin's evolutionary theory to explain criminality. Evolutionary theory was quite popular at the time, especially in the United States. Finally, as others have also pointed out, Lombroso was responsible for popularizing the medical model in the criminal justice system (Rafter, 2008). This approach viewed offenders as being sick or mentally ill rather than evil or morally lacking and said that they needed treatment rather than just punishment.

For better or for worse, this opened the door for experts to come in and "solve" the problem of crime. As a result, the state and the criminal justice system could exert far greater control over the populace. Lombroso's theory offered a justification for imprisoning offenders beyond standard retributive goals (Taylor, Walton, & Young, 1973). While this may seem like a progressive shift on its face, some have contended that the retributivist system was actually more humane because the brutal punishments were administered quickly and efficiently without drawn-out trials and indeterminate periods of imprisonment for rehabilitative purposes (Foucault, 1977; Newman, 1983).

Assumptions of Biological Positivist Theories

Biological positivists assume that basic human nature is primal and instinctive and must be held in check through socialization. Thus, these theorists view humans as being naturally self-interested and hedonistic. This view is sometimes referred to as a Hobbesian assumption; the belief here is that a strong authority is required to protect people from themselves and others. This is based on an evolutionary view of humans: People are animals and are subject to the same natural laws as animals.

Biological drives and characteristics are viewed as being very important to understanding human behavior. As mentioned previously, the positivist approach must be seen as a reaction against the free will doctrine offered by classical school philosophers. In an oft-cited passage, one of the founders of positivist criminology contrasts his approach against that of the classical school:

> We speak two different languages. For us, the experimental (i.e., inductive) method is the key to all knowledge; to them everything derives from logical deductions and traditional opinion. For them, facts should give place to syllogisms; for us the fact governs and no reasoning can occur without starting from facts, for them science needs only paper, pen and ink and the rest comes from a brain stuffed with more or less abundant reading of books made with the same ingredients. For us, science requires spending a long time in examining the facts one by one, evaluating them, reducing them to a common denominator, extracting the central idea from them. For them a syllogism or an anecdote suffices to demolish a myriad of facts gathered through years of observation and analysis; for us the reverse is true. (Ferri, 1917, p. 244)

Taylor, Walton, and Young (1973) have outlined the basics of the positivist approach. First, positivists believe that human behavior can be measured and quantified. Their hope is to discover causal laws like the physical sciences—through the measurement of phenomena. Second, positivist theorists strive for scientific objectivity or neutrality. Third, there is a belief in the determinism of behavior or the notion that human behavior is predictable and can be predicted based on some set of causal factors.

Biological positivists believe that there is a consensus in society with regard to laws and norms and that this corresponds to the needs of the system (Young, 1981). According to the positivist view, society consists of mostly "normal" people who represent the consensus. Deviants are perceived as the minority and exist at the margins of society (Taylor, Walton, & Young, 1973). This is a very binary approach to society in that it is a very black-and-white view of the world: Criminal law determines what is right and wrong, and people caught violating criminal law are assumed to be in the wrong.

Problem Focus, Scope, and Level of Explanation of Biological Positivist Theories

The problem focus of these early biological theories is clearly on individual criminality and criminal behavior. Crime rates, the origins of criminal law, and activities of the criminal justice system are not key concerns in these theories. Instead, "This theory admits that biological, physiological, psychological and social influences all contribute to the creation of the criminal but that it is in the *individual* that the fundamental predisposition to crime is situated" (Young, 1981, p. 267). As noted in this quotation, there are different varieties of positivism, but the focus here is on the biological and physiological variety.

The scope of biological positivist theories is surprisingly broad. For various reasons, most people assume that violent criminal behavior has a stronger genetic link than nonviolent criminal behavior. However, twin and adoption studies have indicated a much stronger genetic link to petty crime as opposed to aggressive and violent crime (Anderson, 2007; Raine, 1993; Robinson & Beaver, 2008). This implies that biological factors may help make sense of aspects of both petty and violent crime. Indeed, there could even be a biological connection to white-collar crime. However, nearly every modern biologist would readily admit that the interaction between genes and environment must be examined. The level of explanation of these theories is clearly micro and individualistic since the theories focus on explaining individual criminality. As opposed to structural theories that consider broad or macro contexts, these theories focus on individual differences (Bernard & Snipes, 1996).

Key Terms and Concepts in Biological Positivist Theories

The Atavistic Man

Cesare Lombroso was a medical doctor who studied crime and is considered by many to be the father of modern criminology (Lilly et al., 2011). More specifically, he is credited with founding the field of criminal anthropology (Rafter, 2008). After studying medicine in Italy and Austria, he worked in a mental institution and then as a military physician. In 1876 he became a legal professor at the University of Turin. This was also the year in which he published his pioneering book titled *Criminal Man*. Lombroso laid out his theory in five different editions of this book over a period spanning more than 20 years (1876, 1878, 1884, 1889, and 1897). Over this time, he made constant modifications to his theory, and, in later editions, more social and sociological factors were taken into account. Lombroso's explanation of criminality was based on evolutionary theory and suggested that criminals were less evolved than other people. He claimed to have come to this revelation while looking at the skull of an Italian brigand named Villella (Rafter, 2008). He describes this moment in the following passage:

> This was not merely an idea, but a flash of inspiration. At the sight of that skull, I seemed to see all of a sudden, lighted up as a vast plain under a flaming sky, the problem of the nature of the criminal—an atavistic being who reproduces in his person the ferocious instincts of primitive humanity and inferior animals. Thus were explained anatomically the enormous jaws, high cheekbones, prominent superciliary arches, solitary lines in the palms, extreme

size of the orbits, handle-shaped or sessile ears found in criminals, savages and apes, insensitivity to pain, extremely acute sight, tattooing, excessive idleness, love of orgies, and the irresistible craving for evil for its own sake, the desire not only to extinguish life in the victim, but to mutilate the corpse, tear its flesh and drink its blood. (Lombroso, 1876, as cited in Taylor, Walton, & Young, 1973, p. 41)

Over the course of his career, Lombroso measured and catalogued the physical characteristics of a variety of populations, including normal people, the mentally ill, soldiers, and criminals. He compared his findings and discovered correlations between certain individual characteristics (many of them physical) and criminality. Lombroso suggested that criminals had stigmata or markers that could be easily observed (Gibson & Rafter, 2006). A complete list of these markers is presented in Table 3.1.

Today, many of these correlations between physical and behavioral characteristics appear to be ridiculous. However, some of these aspects, such as insensitivity to pain, lack of remorse, and lack of impulse control, are widely researched in modern criminology.

Lombroso used his findings to propose an elaborate classification system that evolved with each successive edition of his book. As mentioned previously, his primary contention was that many criminals, roughly 30% of them, were evolutionary throwbacks or born criminals. He said that these people were simply born this way and claimed that in many cases, moral insanity and epilepsy occurred alongside and were often connected to this type of criminality. For Lombroso, many people were not born criminals but were criminals of passion. These criminals committed crime in the heat of the moment or because of political views. This would include political revolutionaries or husbands who killed in the heat of passion because of an unfaithful wife (Gibson & Rafter, 2006). Later, Lombroso posited the existence of insane or mentally defective criminals. These were people who committed crime because they had low intelligence, were alcoholic, or had a hysterical and excitable personality.

In the final editions of *Criminal Man*, Lombroso refined the notion of occasional criminals, another broad classification, and identified several subtypes. Occasional criminals had no criminal traits but committed crime because of various situational and social factors. Pseudocriminals were minor offenders who were either implicated in crime indirectly or committed crime that was based on legal technicalities. Criminaloids were those who committed crime because of easily available opportunities. Habitual criminals became involved in crime because they lacked a solid education and

Table 3.1   Lombroso's Markers of Criminality

Features	Height/Weight/Skin/Eyes	Other Characteristics
Smaller, deformed skulls	Taller than average	Tattoos and piercings
Crooked noses	Heavier than average	Insensitivity to pain
Sloping foreheads	Dark skin	Lack of remorse
Large ears/protruding jaws	Dark eyes	Little control over passions such as drinking, gambling, sex urges

upbringing or were socially or materially deprived in some way (Gibson & Rafter, 2006). Figure 3.3 is a visual depiction of Lombroso's classification system.

A Theory of Natural Crime

The work of Raffaele Garofalo (1914) represents another important contribution to early biological positivism (Miller et al., 2011). Garofalo's ideas are based heavily on social Darwinism but are much less biologically oriented than those of his predecessor (Bohm & Vogel, 2011; Lilly et al., 2011). He proposed a universal definition of natural crime. Further, he suggested that society was similar to an organism and that crime was like a disease.

Much of Garofalo's (1914) work focused on the proper methods of dealing with crime and suggested practical approaches to reducing crime. He thought that criminals needed to be separated (or quarantined) and treated in order for their "disease" not to spread. If they proved untreatable, he believed criminals should be permanently incarcerated, exiled, or put to death. Garofalo believed that criminal offenses violated the two important moral sentiments of probity and pity. Probity

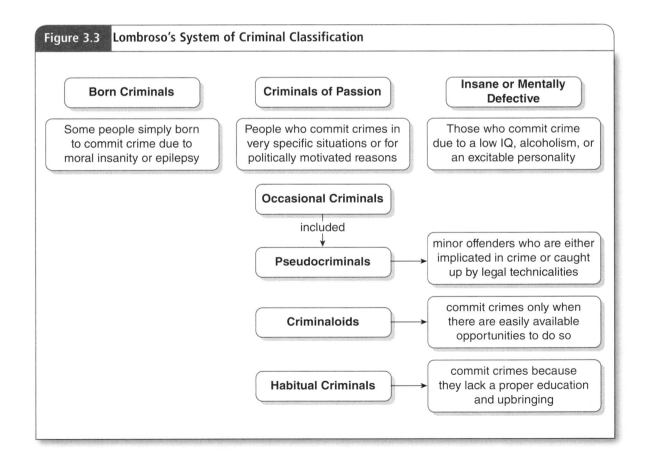

Figure 3.3   Lombroso's System of Criminal Classification

Born Criminals
Some people simply born to commit crime due to moral insanity or epilepsy

Criminals of Passion
People who commit crimes in very specific situations or for politically motivated reasons

Insane or Mentally Defective
Those who commit crime due to a low IQ, alcoholism, or an excitable personality

Occasional Criminals
included
↓
Pseudocriminals → minor offenders who are either implicated in crime or caught up by legal technicalities

Criminaloids → commit crimes only when there are easily available opportunities to do so

Habitual Criminals → commit crimes because they lack a proper education and upbringing

referred to our feelings about the property rights of others (i.e., property crime) while pity referred to our revulsion to the suffering of others (i.e., crimes against the person) (Taylor, Walton, & Young, 1973).

Body Types and Criminality

Lombroso's work and the work of the other Italian Positivists fell into disrepute during the 1920s and 1930s when sociological approaches to criminal behavior began to become popular. However, some researchers still maintained an interest in body type and further explored its relationship to temperament. Kretschmer (1925) identified three body types: the pyknic, or fat, which he thought was correlated to depression; the asthenic, or skinny, which he believed was connected to schizophrenia; and the athletic, which was also correlated with schizophrenia.

Building on Kretschmer's (1925) work, William Sheldon (1940, 1942) identified three types of physique, which he called somatotypes, and three related styles of temperament. **Endomorphs** are soft, round, and have a tendency to put on fat. They have a viscerotonic temperament that includes characteristics such as being laid back, easygoing, sociable, and generally extroverted. **Ectomorphs** tend to be linear, fragile, and have small, slight builds. They tend to be highly intelligent, are often plagued by ailments and allergies, and are generally introverted; their temperament is referred to as cerebrotonic. **Mesomorphs** have heavy bone and muscle development, large wrists, and larger bodies. They are active, dynamic, assertive, and aggressive; this is referred to as the somotonic temperament. Some people might refer to them as alpha males.

According to Sheldon (1949), the mesomorphic body type and somotonic temperament was most likely to produce criminal behavior. While it may sound overly simplistic, several criminologists have used Sheldon's somatotypes as a component of more complex integrated theories (Glueck & Glueck, 1950; Wilson & Herrnstein, 1985). Figure 3.4 provides one way to view these body types.

An Early Biosocial Theory of Criminality

Enrico Ferri, a student of Lombroso, did much to refine and elaborate upon Lombroso's theory and can also be seen as an early forerunner to modern biosocial approaches to crime. In his work *Criminal Sociology* (1896), Ferri proposed a classification that was based on Lombroso's findings and coined the term *born criminal*, which Lombroso used in later editions of *Criminal Man*. He also presented a theory that attempted to account for anthropological, physical, and social factors that gave rise to criminality and crime. Anthropological (or individual) factors explained basic criminality in people and were divided into three subtypes: organic constitutional factors, which included physical factors identified by Lombroso; mental constitutional factors, such as intelligence, disposition, and moral sense; and personal characteristics, such as race, age, sex, social status, and educational level (Ferri, 1896).

Ferri also focused on how environmental factors might influence crime. These included factors such as the climate, season, time of year, weather, and temperature in which the crime was committed. Social factors were macro variables that might influence rates of criminality. These included structural aspects such as population density, family conditions, educational opportunities, and activities/policies of legal systems. Ferri (1896) was careful to point out that it was important to understand and clarify how these various levels of explanation interacted and affected one another. Figure 3.5 offers one way to see these interactions.

Figure 3.4	Sheldon's Somatotypes

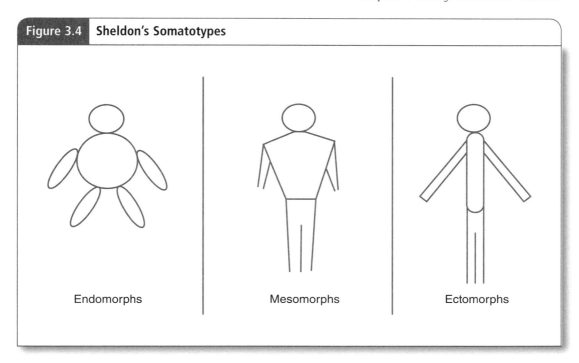

Endomorphs   Mesomorphs   Ectomorphs

Source: Copyright Edward P. Kardas, 2014. Used with permission.

The propositions that can be derived from biological positivism can be summarized as follows:

Theorist	Proposition
Lombroso (1876)	There are physical differences between criminals and noncriminals.
Lombroso (1876); Glueck & Glueck (1950); Sheldon (1949)	Criminal behavior varies with body type and size.
Ferri (1896); Lombroso (1876)	Criminal behavior is related to low intelligence or IQ.

Like Ferri, the work of more recent biological and biosocial criminologists such as Jeffery, Mednick, Ellis, Walsh, Raine, and others involves examining the interactions between biological precursors and environmental factors. As we will explore, to date modern biosocial theories have made very little use of existing sociological explanations of criminal behavior. This offers the potential for a range of new approaches to better predict criminality and study how best to mitigate the biological

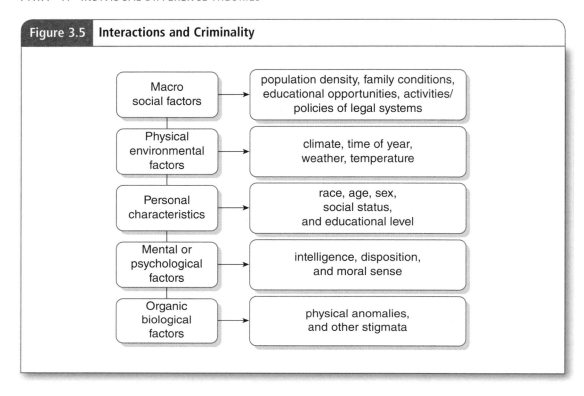

Figure 3.5 Interactions and Criminality

Macro social factors → population density, family conditions, educational opportunities, activities/policies of legal systems

Physical environmental factors → climate, time of year, weather, temperature

Personal characteristics → race, age, sex, social status, and educational level

Mental or psychological factors → intelligence, disposition, and moral sense

Organic biological factors → physical anomalies, and other stigmata

predisposition toward a life of crime. As we will illustrate in later chapters, this also offers an opportunity to integrate theories across levels and between disciplines.

Research on Biological Positivist Theories

Research on a biological basis for crime has been a long-standing enterprise. From the measurement of skulls (phrenology) to the elaborate classification systems created by Lombroso (criminal anthropology), biological approaches to the study of crime have been both praised and maligned. While it is common to dismiss early biological positivist research, understanding the problems with past approaches is essential to thinking about how best to test and examine theories today. One way to view the role of biology and crime is to consider family, twin, and adoption studies. Studies such as these represent attempts to estimate the effect of familial relationships and the role of genetic influences on a host of behaviors.

One branch of biological positivism exists in the family and genealogical studies of Dugdale (1895) and Goddard (1913). Dugdale's study of the Juke family occurred very early; in fact, it predated Darwin's evolutionary theory. The Juke family exhibited a great deal of criminality over successive generations (approximately 50% of the members studied were criminals). In addition, many of the Jukes were involved in prostitution, were very poor, and suffered from innate depravity.

Dugdale (1895) believed that these characteristics were inherited but also thought that the environment could affect heredity. More important, he believed that criminality could actually be passed down through families.

Goddard (1913) examined the Kallikaks in a longitudinal study of two families fathered by the same man (in Goddard's words, "an upstanding man"). The mother of one family was a Quaker woman; the mother of the other family was (again, in Goddard's words) a "tavern wench." Members of the former family produced very little criminality, while members of the latter exhibited a great deal of criminality (Robinson & Beaver, 2008). Goddard disagreed with Dugdale's (1895) finding of inherited criminality. Instead he argued that

> so far as the Jukes family is concerned, there is nothing that proves the hereditary character of any crime, pauperism, or prostitution that was found. . . . The formerly much discussed question of the hereditary character of crime received no solution from the Jukes family, but in the light of present-day knowledge of the sciences of criminology and biology, there is every reason to conclude that criminals are made, not born. The best material out of which to make criminals, and perhaps the material from which they are most frequently made, is feeblemindedness. (1913, pp. 53–54)

As this quote implies, Goddard's (1913) research laid the groundwork for further research connecting intelligence and IQ to criminality that continues to this day. A problem for family studies is the inability to separate the genetic and environmental sources of variation. Thus, family studies are complicated by the question of whether nature or nurture is the stronger predictor of behavior. Therefore, given this complication, this section will focus on two other research designs that are better equipped to test for genetic effects.

As described above, Lombroso did a great deal of research while formulating his theory of criminality and his criminal classification scheme. However, there are several examples of more formal attempts to test his theory. For instance, Charles Goring (1913) published a large research study intended to refute "the superstition of Lombrosianism" (Rafter, 2008, p. 13). Goring was an English prison medical officer, and, like Lombroso, he used his position to take physical measurements (e.g., head size, color of eyes, and facial features) of 3,000 English convicts (Akers & Sellers, 2013). He then compared the measurements of the inmates to a control group of undergraduate students, soldiers, professors, and hospital patients. Notably, Goring used new statistical techniques to test theories pioneered by Francis Galton and his students, including Karl Pearson (Rafter, 2008).

Goring's (1913) research indicated that there were no clear statistical differences between the inmates and the other subjects, and he found that criminals could not be distinguished from civilians on the basis of physical characteristics identified by Lombroso. However, he did still believe that criminals were born with certain inherited criminal traits and that they were inferior to normal people. He conceded some environmental and social factors were involved, but he felt that these were much less important than inherited characteristics (Bernard, Snipes, & Gerould, 2010). Criminals were found to be shorter and skinnier on average than law-abiding citizens and seemed to have lower levels of intelligence or IQ on average. Goring's research also indicated that this finding varied based on frequency and length of imprisonment (Bernard, Snipes, & Gerould, 2010).

A few decades later, Ernest Hooton, a well-known anthropologist and professor at Harvard, conducted a massive study of 17,000 subjects in eight US states (Lilly et al., 2011). Hooton (1939) attempted to provide support for Lombroso's theory and attacked many of Goring's (1913) methods and conclusions (Akers & Sellers, 2013). Like Goring, Hooton measured the physical characteristics of numerous inmates from a variety of correctional institutions (e.g., prisons, reformatories, and county jails). He compared the convict group to a control group of college students, hospital and mental patients, firemen, and policemen (Akers & Sellers, 2013).

Unfortunately, Hooton's methods were problematic, and his research assistants did not always take reliable measurements. Further, much of his analysis was based on ethnic and racial stereotypes. He thought he had found evidence that certain races were prone to committing particular types of crime. This is inherently problematic because it disregards the fact that his sample only contained those who had been caught and convicted of crimes (Rafter, 2008). In addition, this is an example of a tautology, or circular reasoning. In other words, the proposition stating that there were physical differences between criminals and noncriminals was never tested. In Hooton's mind, he knew the results before testing his theory, and he assumed his theory was correct (Akers & Sellers, 2013).

This is a clear inversion of the scientific method; the assumption of physical differences between criminals and noncriminals led Hooton to search for and find these differences. Again, he never really tested his theory—instead he *merely looked for evidence to support it*. When research amounts to cherry-picking evidence that supports one's own view or ideological starting point, scholarship suffers. Because of these shortcomings in his research, Hooton became a very controversial figure, as his methods and conclusions were regularly attacked by his fellow academics. Later in his career, he distanced himself from academia because of the poor reception to his work and turned instead to practical matters of concern involving the government and business (Rafter, 2008).

The fascination with constitutional factors and criminal behavior did not die with Hooton's research. Hooton had a well-known student by the name of William Sheldon who would go on to develop theories involving body type that we discussed earlier (Rafter, 2008). He also had two colleagues at Harvard by the name of Sheldon and Eleanor Glueck—one of the early husband and wife criminology teams. The Gluecks included some of these ideas in their multifactor theory of criminal behavior that was presented in *Unraveling Juvenile Delinquency*. The Gluecks (1950) were attempting to produce a multifactor theory of criminal behavior that combined Hooton's and Sheldon's ideas about constitutional factors and body types and more sociological explanations about family interactions.

Another approach involved studying twins separated at birth to disentangle the effects of biology and the environment. To further explain, it is easy to control for biology if both individuals are genetically identical. This method attempted to examine whether a given trait could be **heritable** or inherited. Monozygotic (MZ), or identical, twins are genetically identical, having 100% of their genes in common with one another. Conversely, dizygotic (DZ), or fraternal, twins are less genetically alike than MZ twins and are in fact no more alike genetically than siblings who are not twins.

One way to compare the behavior of twins is by measuring **concordance rates** among traits. Concordance rates refer to the likelihood that one twin will develop a trait similar to another twin, and they are expressed in percentages. Anderson explains the notion of concordance in the following passage:

> If the concordance for a certain trait in monozygotic twins is determined to be 70%, then this means the chance of the other twin developing the trait is 70%. If we compare the concordance

rates for a specific trait between monozygotic (MZ) and dizygotic (DZ) twins—for example, if the trait is 70% in MZ twins but only 5% in DZ twins—then it would appear to have a heritable component. The twins who are genetically identical are much more likely to share the same trait than the twins who are not genetically identical. Therefore, the trait relates to genetics. If concordance rates were 70% in both MZ and DZ twins, then it would be an environmental effect, as the fact that MZ twins are genetically identical does not appear to make any difference. (2007, p. 92)

In other words, we assess the extent to which genetic factors are responsible for behavior by comparing the concordance between the different types of twins and the traits they possess.

In a review of 13 twin studies conducted up to 1993, Raine (2002) reports that although the studies vary widely in terms of age, sex, country of origin, and sample size, identical twins are twice as likely to have both engaged in criminal activity than fraternal twins (Raine, 1993). Additional twin studies by Slutske and her colleagues (1997) suggest that antisocial and aggressive behavior is far more likely in identical twins relative to fraternal twins, a finding that has been supported elsewhere (Eley, Lichtenstein, & Stevenson, 1999).

Adoption studies provide another way to understand the possible role of biology. They have some advantages over twin studies because they better address the problem of genetic versus environmental influences (i.e., nature versus nurture). For example, by examining offspring separated from their criminal, biological parents early in life and sent to other families, researchers can better assess whether these offspring will grow up to become criminal at greater rates than foster children whose biological parents were not criminal. This allows researchers to examine whether the influence of genetics or the social environment has more of an impact on behavior.

Mednick and his colleagues (1977) have conducted what are probably the most well-known studies of adoption and criminal behavior. This branch of research has helped give rise to the contemporary biosocial approach to criminal behavior and will be discussed in more detail in Chapter 14. Nearly all of the adoption studies conducted in Denmark, Sweden, and the United States suggest a genetic basis to criminal behavior (Raine, 1993). While there may be some question about whether less violent delinquency or more violent behavior is more commonly a function of genetic predisposition, it is difficult to ignore biology after reviewing the existing literature. Clearly, some biological traits make people more prone to criminal behavior, but criminal behavior also requires opportunities. Further, problematic traits thought to lead to crime (e.g., aggression, impulsivity) are always mediated through one's social environment.

Going beyond the question of whether criminality is heritable (and the result of certain genetic predispositions) or a function of one's socialization or upbringing, another recent approach looks at how brains develop as a result of chromosomal abnormalities. For example, XYY syndrome is characterized by an extra copy of the Y chromosome in each of a male's cells. XYY syndrome is associated with an increased risk of learning disabilities and delayed development of speech and language skills. Delayed development of motor skills (such as sitting and walking), weak muscle tone (hypotonia), severe acne, hand tremors or other involuntary movements (motor tics), and behavioral and emotional difficulties are also possible. This chromosomal change occurs as a random event during the formation of sperm cells. An error in cell division can result in sperm cells with an extra copy of the Y chromosome, and a child may have an extra Y chromosome in each of the body's cells.

In a recent cohort study (Stochholm, Bojesen, Jensen, Juul, & Gravholt, 2012), 161 men diagnosed with XYY syndrome were matched against others at risk and by age to examine rates of criminal convictions in Denmark between 1976 and 2006. The researchers found the incidence of convictions was much higher among men with XYY syndrome compared to controls in all crime types except drug-related crimes and traffic offenses. This incidence remained increased for certain crime types (e.g., sexual abuse, arson) even when adjusted for socioeconomic variables such as education, fatherhood, retirement, and cohabitation.

This study builds on older research suggesting that males with similar chromosomal abnormalities tend to have more difficulties at school, to be more mentally immature, to be more impulsive than their siblings, and to have more difficulty in forming relationships with others (Nielsen & Christensen, 1978). Many believe the direct causal connections between XYY syndrome and criminality have not been empirically proved. However, it is still important to be familiar with the controversy created by this research. In later chapters, we will discuss modern parallels to this phenomenon, including the use of the connection between criminality and the so-called warrior gene in recent high-profile court cases.

Another important development in this area is the recognition of the dangers of prenatal alcohol consumption by pregnant mothers. Fetal alcohol spectrum disorder (FASD) is a nondiagnostic term that covers a range of related birth defects resulting from prenatal alcohol exposure. Under this umbrella term are several diagnostic terms such as fetal alcohol syndrome (FAS), partial fetal alcohol syndrome (pFAS), alcohol-related neurodevelopmental disorder (ARND), and alcohol-related birth defects (ARBD). In practice, these may include physical, neurological, and psychological impairments, and those with FASD can present significant challenges for the criminal justice system.

While FASD is the most common form of preventable brain damage to infants in the Western world, the brain damage that results from prenatal exposure to alcohol is irreversible and results in lifelong challenges in learning, behavior, employment, and socialization (Fast & Conroy, 2004). Cases of partial and full FASD have been correlated to an increased incidence of comorbid neuropsychiatric disorders, including attention deficit hyperactivity disorder, learning disabilities, developmental disorders, anger, and social skill problems (Burd, Klug, Martsolf, & Kerbeshian, 2003).

Perhaps the most interesting research in this area is the result of significant advances in brain imaging techniques over the past two decades. A number of studies focused on brain imaging of violent and psychopathic populations have been undertaken (Raine, 1993; Raine & Buchsbaum, 1996; Henry & Moffitt, 1997). Reviews of these studies suggest that violent offenders have structural and functional deficits to the frontal lobe (located behind the forehead) and the temporal lobe (located near the ears). Subsequent research appears to confirm the idea that abnormal functioning of the frontal and temporal regions may predispose one to crime (Intrator et al., 1997; Kuruoglu et al., 1996; Seidenwurm et al., 1997; Soderstrom et al., 2000).

Practical Ramifications of Biological Positivism: The Good, the Bad, and the Ugly?

The Good: The positivists offered "progressive reforms" to the criminal justice system. More specifically, positivists suggested that rather than merely punishing criminals, we should attempt to treat them and rehabilitate them. This stemmed from embracing the medical model that views criminals as sick and criminality as similar to a disease (Rafter, 2008). Thus, our system started to change and new practices were introduced. These include rehabilitation programs, parole, probation, and the recognition of the social lives and experiences of those in conflict with the law. This opened up the criminal justice system to experts such as treatment specialists, probation workers, psychiatrists, social workers, psychologists, criminologists, and others who often sought to help offenders with their problems (Taylor, Walton, & Young, 1973).

The Bad: Some have argued that this emphasis on institutional control through the application of the scientific method had negative consequences for society (Taylor, Walton, & Young, 1973; Foucault, 1977). The individualistic form of biological positivism we have been discussing here lends itself well to political manipulation because it can shift the blame from the society and system to the individual. For example, biological positivists characterize criminals as possessing some characteristic that makes them commit crime. This focus on individual characteristics ensures that any environmental issues or social inequalities that help breed crime are ignored: If we hold the individual responsible, we don't have to change society.

The Ugly: Darwin's cousin Francis Galton introduced the term *eugenics* in his book *Inquiries Into Human Faculty and Its Development* (1883) (Rafter, 2008). This term was based on work he did on inheritance of traits. He only advocated for positive eugenics, or the practice of encouraging fit people to have more children (Anderson, 2007). Negative eugenics was co-opted for political purposes by reformers in the United States, Britain, Canada, and Germany; by the early 20th century, this movement had become very popular. Reformers suggested everything from work colonies to compulsory sterilization for the "unfit" (Anderson, 2007). The unfit were defined as whomever society held hostility toward or looked down upon: immigrants, minorities, criminals, the mentally ill, and the mentally challenged, to name a few. The Nazi regime escalated eugenics measures and started to execute the unfit, who they described as being "life unworthy of life" (or *lebensunwertes leben*). Eugenics policies were also used in Stalinist Russia (e.g., T. D. Lysenko's "socialist biology") (Anderson, 2007), and movements continued in Canada and the United States until the 1970s.

Today, there is no question that repeated head trauma and concussions can result in chronic traumatic encephalopathy (CTE). CTE is a neurodegenerative disease that can cause depression, cognitive impairments, dementia, Parkinsonism, and erratic behavior. This disease can also lead to aggressive and violent behavior. Several high-profile athletes (e.g., Chris Benoit, Junior Seau, and Jovan Belcher), have recently committed violent crimes as a result of their injuries. If indeed this group of people and others who have suffered brain injury present a danger to society, the criminal justice system must respond. However, given the problems with past biological approaches in criminology, any response must be carefully considered.

Think You Get It?

Make a concept map or mind map of the main biological terms and concepts and the results of criminological research in this area. Use the instructions in Chapter 2 or make your own visual map. Based on the information in this chapter, which biological explanations appear to be the most important for the study of crime?

Figure 3.6	Seven Steps of Biological Positivism
Seven Steps	**Biological Positivism**
1. Know the History	Emerged after the Enlightenment (ca. 1800–1900) as a reaction to the classical school; influenced by increasing popularity of science and evolutionary theory
2. Acknowledge Assumptions	The struggle for survival ensures that humans are naturally selfish; biological factors determine behavior; people are naturally conflict oriented but society is characterized by consensus
3. Problem Focus, Scope, and Level of Explanation	Focus on explaining criminality using individual differences (e.g., physical characteristics, body type, and intelligence)
4. Key Terms and Concepts	Criminals are atavistic men or evolutionary throwbacks; somatotypes; criminal behavior related to intelligence
5. Respect the Research	Family inheritance and genetic studies; criminality seems to run in families
6. Theory/Practice	Medical model, scientific experts, indeterminate sentences
7. Mapping the Theory	See Figure 3.7

Criticisms of Biological Positivist Theories

There are a number of criticisms levied against the biological positivist approach to criminology. The first of these involves the assumption that the criminal law is always right and those that break the law are always wrong. This appears to be a binary approach to society and the law. In some ways, categories of individuals (criminals and noncriminals) are essential; however, these approaches tend to accept without question or critical reflection the idea that the law always defines right and wrong. One issue that flows from this underlying assumption is that it allows the scientific authority ascribed to biological approaches to be used by racist-nationalists or other authoritarian regimes for their own political or ideological ends. The specter of Nazi Germany, Stalinism, and the existence of eugenics-based movements and their resulting policies (e.g., forced sterilization and euthanasia) can take on the appearance of a culturally or politically dominant group defining others as degenerate in one way or another.

Early biological positivist approaches look today like pseudoscience used to privilege the physical characteristics of some groups over others. Social Darwinism, or the application of "survival of the fittest" to human society, presumes a genetic source for a socially defined category of behavior. While thinkers associated with biological positivism brought about a revolution in how to study crime and criminal behavior, in retrospect, their contribution also assisted criminologists to identify some of the problems with simply accepting notions about human nature and the assumptions of the scientific method. For example, the faith in the scientific measurement of phenomena was belied by the problems of quantifying criminal behavior. It is clear that key variables were operationalized and defined for the purposes of

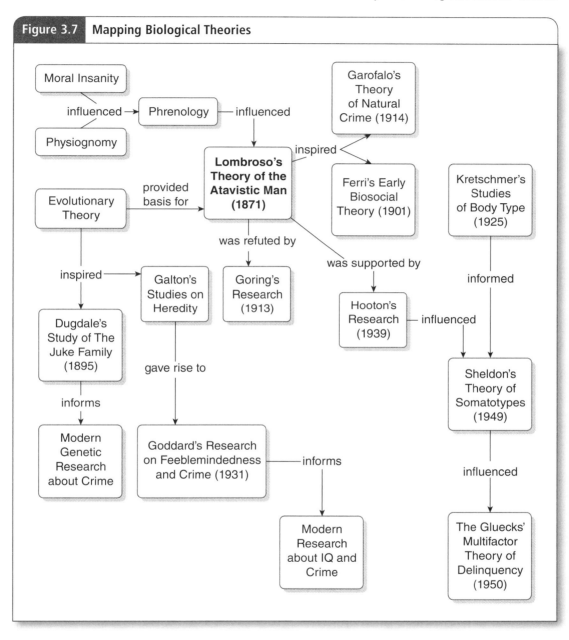

Figure 3.7 **Mapping Biological Theories**

measurement in ways that were inherently problematic. Concepts such as feeblemindedness, inferiority, and even crime all require far more nuance and detail than the early theorists considered.

Other problems were methodological. Research was often based on small or inappropriate samples and failed to contend with the difficulty of operating from an objective, nonbiased vantage point from which to assess society. The problem is that no matter how good our intentions are, humans are in the business of rendering value judgments. Put another way,

> The [experts] must explain what is perceived as unusual in terms of the values associated by their audience as usual. . . . They circumscribe and negate the reality of values different from their own. They do not explain, but merely explain away. (Taylor, Walton, & Young, 1973, p. 33)

The belief that crime must be subject to discoverable causal laws fails to contend with economic and cultural factors. Early biological positivist approaches, with the exception perhaps of Ferri, failed to consider in enough depth the importance of interactions between genetics and environment for human behavior generally and criminal behavior specifically.

Research was also affected by an overreliance on official statistics and definitions of crime. Of course, a basic problem with using official statistics is the dark figure of crime. In other words, we do not catch everyone who violates the law, so not every criminal is correctly defined as such. This problem also interacts with definitions of crime. Again, biological positivists assume that the law defines right and wrong (Taylor, Walton, & Young, 1973). Carried to its logical conclusion, such an uncritical stance on the law and crime allows for horrible atrocities to be defined as normal as long as state definitions define these behaviors as such. Indeed, white-collar and corporate crime have traditionally not been taken very seriously, and many of these behaviors were not even defined as criminal until recently.

Research Example: Rethinking Biology and the Brain

As we discussed above, the advance of brain imaging techniques has changed the potential value of a biological basis for criminal behavior. While it is problematic that the tendency to treat biology as destiny can be used by those in positions of authority to "define" criminals without considering how definitions of crime change over time, efforts to brand all who consider biology and crime to be related as presumptive racists are also misleading. Understanding biology and crime requires first appreciating the role of genetics. One way to consider the problems and potential for biological positivist theories of criminology is to map some of the common misconceptions. Figure 3.8 provides an overview of these misconceptions, which were first presented by Raine (1993) and later reorganized by Robinson (2004).

Of specific interest in this section is the work of Raine (2002). Raine studies antisocial behavior from neuroscientific, developmental, and social perspectives. He and his colleagues focus on risk and protective factors for childhood conduct disorder, reactive and proactive aggression, adult antisocial personality disorder, homicide, and psychopathy. In their lab, Raine and his colleagues focus on structural and functional brain imaging, autonomic and central nervous system psychophysiology, neuroendocrinology, neuropsychology, and x-ray fluorescence. While Raine takes a biosocial perspective to his theorizing that integrates social, psychological, and environmental processes with neurobiological approaches, his research grew out of techniques that we can classify broadly as biological positivist. In the place of measuring skulls or classifying body types like the biological positivists discussed above, Raine's work focuses on identifying and comparing areas of the brain between criminal and noncriminal populations. We will revisit Raine's (1993, 2013) contributions to criminological theory in Chapter 14 when we discuss the biosocial theories of criminal behavior.

The first published brain imaging study of murderers (Raine et al., 1994) involved comparing the scanned brains of 22 murderers who pled not guilty by reason of insanity (or were otherwise found

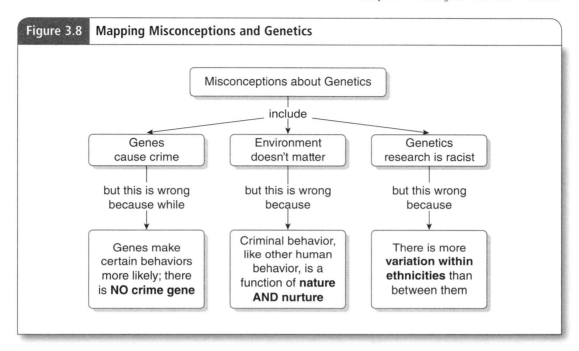

Figure 3.8 Mapping Misconceptions and Genetics

Misconceptions about Genetics

include

| Genes cause crime | Environment doesn't matter | Genetics research is racist |

but this is wrong because while

but this is wrong because

but this wrong because

Genes make certain behaviors more likely; there is **NO crime gene**

Criminal behavior, like other human behavior, is a function of **nature AND nurture**

There is more **variation within ethnicities** than between them

incompetent to stand trial) to the brains of 22 normal controls who were matched with the first group on demographics such as sex and age. The key finding was that the murderers showed significantly poorer functioning of the prefrontal cortex, which is the part of the brain that controls

> deeper and more primitive subconical structures, such as the amygdala, which are thought to give rise to aggressive feelings. Prefrontal damage also encourages risk-taking, irresponsibility, rule breaking, emotional and aggressive outbursts, and argumentative behavior. (Raine, 2002, p. 57)

A recent study used brain scans to look at the anterior cingulate cortex, the part of the brain that is involved in emotion and decision making. Researchers found that if offenders had lower functioning in the anterior cingulate, they were twice as likely to reoffend in the next three years (Aharoni et al., 2013). Another study showed that males with a smaller volume of the amygdala—the part of the brain responsible for emotional responses and that generates feelings such as conscience, remorse, and guilt—were four times as likely to commit an offense in the next three years, even controlling for social background and a past history of violence (Kiehl, 2014).

Another approach looks at reported incidence of head injuries among incarcerated populations. Data suggest that the prevalence of a traumatic brain injury (TBI) in the past may be as high as 10 times that of the general population (Ferguson, Pickelsimer, Corrigan, & Bogner, 2012). In a recent meta-analysis, Farrer et al. (2013) surveyed studies of TBI using a delinquent juvenile sample. The researchers found that approximately 30% of juvenile offenders had sustained a previous brain injury and that the rate of TBIs within the juvenile offender population is significant, suggesting a relationship between TBIs and juvenile criminal behavior.

These developments may also be relevant given reports of the growing problem of criminal behavior in veterans. Elbogen (2012) and colleagues found that 9% of veterans who responded during the research reported an arrest since returning home from military service. While most arrests were associated with nonviolent criminal behavior resulting in incarceration for less than two weeks, those with probable posttraumatic stress disorder (PTSD) or TBI who reported anger/irritability were more likely to be arrested than were other veterans. The findings suggest that a subset of veterans with PTSD and negative affect may be at increased risk of criminal arrest.

> **Now that you've read this chapter** . . . what do head injuries have to do with criminology? Prisoners suffer disproportionately from past traumatic brain injuries. For example, 8.5% of US nonincarcerated adults have a history of traumatic brain injuries (TBI), while approximately 60% of adults in US prisons have had at least one TBI, which is seven times greater than those not incarcerated. Given the large number of individuals in prison who might have been housed in psychiatric facilities in another era, perhaps prisons offer a means to combine prosocial educational opportunities with neuroimaging to explore which parts of the brain are activated during evidence-based rehabilitation.

Conclusion and Review Questions

In this chapter, we reviewed the major theories and ideas offered by the biological positivists. This included a review of the work of the Italian Positivists (i.e., Lombroso, Ferri, and Garofalo) and attempts to further test and refine these insights (e.g., the work of Goring, Hooton, and Sheldon). While in some ways these thinkers revolutionized criminology by introducing and applying the scientific method to the study of criminality, their work also had many shortcomings and negative ramifications. These include an overemphasis on physical characteristics as the ultimate cause of crime and a wholesale adoption of the law as the moral arbiter of right and wrong.

As we have seen, more modern examples of research done in this area include genetics and brain scan studies. While there is no question that different people respond to the world in different ways based on biological differences, the implications of such observations have not been embraced by the criminal justice system. Due to mounting evidence that biological differences matter, we will revisit emerging research later in this text. For now let's review the main concepts and arguments presented in this chapter.

CHAPTER REVIEW

1. List the assumptions made by biological positivist theories.

2. How did the historical period in which these theories emerged shape their early development?

3. What are the problem focus, scope, and level of explanation of these theories?

4. What social and historical factors gave rise to these theories?

5. What practical ramifications did these theories have?

CHAPTER

4

Psychological Positivist Theories

Chapter Overview and Objectives

Like the early biological positivist theories, the psychological positivist theories focus on individual differences or characteristics that can be used to identify criminals. Sometimes this area is also referred to as trait or personality theory. Instead of focusing on physical characteristics or body types, these theories identify personality traits and mental processes that impact behavior. One common starting place is the idea that less intelligent people are more likely to commit crime. Once described as feeblemindedness, stupidity, or dull wittedness, this factor remains a feature of some psychological explanations of criminal behavior. A more recent understanding of personality disorders focuses on specific antisocial behaviors, and there is evidence to suggest certain types of mental illnesses are associated with certain types of crimes. An outstanding issue is how to balance existing tools and assessments to identify serious mental disorders such as psychopathy with the danger posed by their misuse. Figure 4.1 maps some of the key ideas shared by psychological positivist theories. By the end of the chapter, readers should be able to:

- Understand the assumptions and the historical and social context that gave rise to the psychological positivist theories
- Be aware of the level of explanation, problem focus, and scope of psychological positivist theories
- Know the differences between psychopaths and sociopaths and other related disorders (e.g., primary and secondary psychopaths and dyssocial psychopaths)
- Consider how these theories are connected to biological theories
- Be familiar with the practical approaches and programs suggested by psychological positivist theories

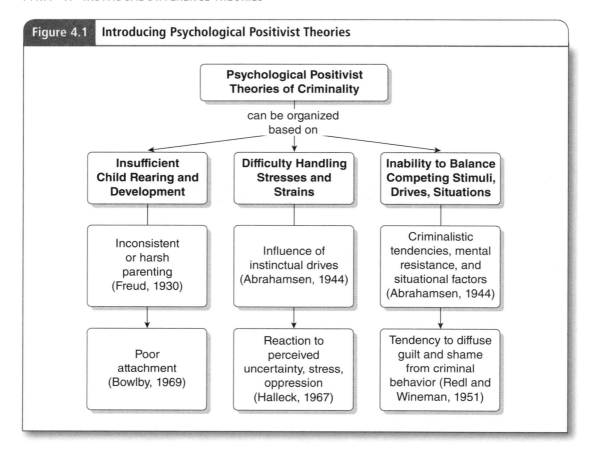

Figure 4.1   Introducing Psychological Positivist Theories

The Psychological Positivist Tradition

Psychological positivist theories have much in common with biological positivist theories in the sense that they use the same positivist approach that emphasizes individual differences to explain criminal behavior. Both emphasize individual-level factors from biology and psychology and attempt to account for some environmental factors. This tradition, along with biological positivism, has contributed to the current biosocial approach in criminology that will be discussed in Chapter 14. Important theorists and researchers in this area that will be discussed in this chapter include Abrahamsen (1944), Aichhorn, (1925), Alexander & Healy (1935), Bowlby (1969), Freud (1920, 1923), Halleck (1967), and Redl and Wineman (1951).

There is no one psychological theory of criminal behavior, and it would be misleading to lump all of these theories into one category, or, for that matter, into one chapter (Bartol & Bartol, 2011). This chapter covers theories that emphasize personality traits and will consider how these traits impact conditioning and learning processes. In Chapter 5, we will examine process-oriented theories from psychology that place less stress on psychological traits and characteristics and more focus on the environment or the situation (Bandura & Walters, 1963, 1977; Zimbardo, 1970, 2007). For now, let's look at personality traits.

Gordon Allport, a well-known psychologist and one of the founders of personality theory, explains the nature of traits in the following passage:

Traits are not observable; they are inferred (as any kind of determining tendency is inferred). Without such an inference the stability and consistency of personal behavior could not possibly be explained. Any specific action is a product of innumerable determinants, not only of traits, but of momentary pressures and specialized influences. But it is the repeated occurrence of actions having the same significance (equivalence of response) following upon a definable range of stimuli having the same personal significance (equivalence of stimuli) that makes necessary the postulation of traits as states of being. Traits are not at all times active, but they are persistent even when latent, and are distinguished by low thresholds of arousal. (as quoted in Eysenck, 1977, p. 8)

According to Allport, one must bear in mind that these traits are unobservable, and thus scientists infer them from behavioral patterns. They are not necessarily the sole determinant of behavior. Carried to its logical conclusion, this implies that personality itself is unobservable. The most commonly examined traits include intelligence, aggression, empathy, and impulsivity. We will review the theories and research associated with these traits in this chapter.

> **As you read this chapter, consider . . .** since 1982, there have been at least 62 mass shootings across the country, and these killings have unfolded in 30 states, from Massachusetts to Hawaii. Twenty-five of these mass shootings have occurred since 2006, and seven of them took place in 2012. For example, Adam Lanza, 20, shot his mother dead at their home then drove to Sandy Hook Elementary School, where he killed 20 children and six adults before committing suicide. James Holmes, 24, shot 12 people in a movie theater during the opening night of *The Dark Knight Rises* and was later arrested outside. Jared Loughner, 22, opened fire outside a Safeway during a constituent meeting with Congresswoman Gabrielle Giffords (D-Ariz.) before he was subdued by bystanders and arrested.
>
> These young, white men all exhibited signs of mental illness and were reported to suffer from paranoid schizophrenia. So is mental illness to blame for mass gun crimes? As you read this chapter, consider this question: If mental illness leads to crime, doesn't that mean that those with a mental illness would commit crimes at a higher rate than others?

Seven Steps of Criminological Thinking

In previous chapters we provided the seven-step map for you. Can you recall the seven steps? Make your own map as you read the next section. Organize the key points as you read, based on each step.

History and Social Context of Psychological Positivism

The impact of psychological positivism in criminology can be traced to three key influences: early work on moral insanity, research on intelligence and feeblemindedness, and Freud's (1920, 1923) psychoanalytical approach. The notion of moral insanity emerged in the 18th century in the work of Benjamin Rush, Philippe Pinel, and James Cowles Prichard (Rafter, 2008). All three identified a specific criminal type: remorseless, impulsive, and morally undeveloped, but otherwise normal.

Rush was a signer of the US Declaration of Independence, a social reformer, and a psychiatrist. His most significant contribution was to redefine behavioral and moral problems as mental diseases rather than relying upon religious explanations that attributed them to sin and demonic possession (Rafter, 2008). Pinel was a French psychiatrist, and he first referred to psychopathy in 1801 in a medical treatise, calling it a "mania without insanity or delusion" (in French, *manie sans de'lire*) (Pichot, 1978). Later, Prichard, an insane asylum physician, coined the term *moral insanity* (Rafter, 2008). This idea was a forerunner of the concept of psychopathy and laid the groundwork for research in that area and in the area of intelligence and crime (Rafter, 2008). These early psychiatrists believed that psychopathy was innate but could be affected by diet and alcohol use.

Robert Hare (1970), the foremost theorist and researcher in psychopathy today, defines psychopathy as a set of symptoms and personality traits. Unlike their feebleminded forerunners, psychopaths were thought to be mentally and intellectually normal but were considered unstable and less responsive to punishment. Therefore, they were unaffected by deterrence. The condition was (and still is) assumed to be hereditary and incurable (Rafter, 1997). The term *psychopathy* originated in an Austrian psychiatric textbook called *The Principles of Medical Psychology*, by Ernst von Feuchtersleben. German experts on psychopathy, such as Richard von Krafft-Ebing and Emil Kraepelin, influenced many American psychiatrists (Rafter, 1997). Psychopathy was further developed and refined in the work of three American psychiatrists: William Healy, Bernard Glueck, and Elizabeth Spaulding (Rafter, 1997).

Healy, a student of Sigmund Freud, referred to psychopathy as "psychic constitutional inferiority" and believed that the condition arose from an inability to exercise self-restraint or self-control. Glueck tried to further define psychopathy, which he equated with criminal behavior, and offered a clinical definition that might be useful for administrative purposes (Rafter, 1997). Spaulding studied female psychopathy and noted the gender differences between psychopaths. Perhaps the popularity of psychopathy in psychiatry can be attributed to professional self-interest. Because of widespread reforms to insane asylums and medicine during the late 19th century, the field of psychiatry was losing influence; one commentator referred to it as "a specialty adrift from mainstream medicine, a backwater" (Rafter, 1997, p. 169). Involvement with the criminal justice system provided an opportunity for new research projects and subjects.

The origins of the theories about intelligence and crime can be traced to the renewed interest in the inheritance of traits that took place during the early 20th century (Rafter, 2008). Research such as Goddard's (1913) study of the Kallikak family, presented in Chapter 3, provided some support for the inheritance of traits such as low intelligence, once called feeblemindedness. In later research, Goddard (1914) suggested that feeblemindedness ran in families and was a cause of crime. However, he did not argue for a genetic basis of criminality (Rafter, 2008). The notion that those of lower intelligence are more likely to commit crime remains a persistent feature of some psychological explanations of criminal behavior (Wilson & Herrnstein, 1985). For example, when one looks at academic achievement between incarcerated and nonincarcerated populations, significant differences can be observed, as outlined in Figure 4.2. However, as Lilly and his colleagues (2011) point out, these differences cannot simply be attributed to IQ.

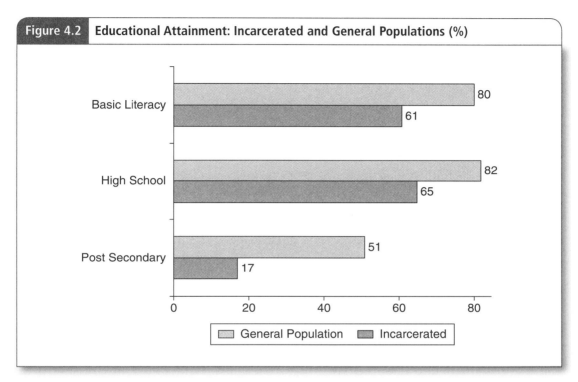

Figure 4.2 Educational Attainment: Incarcerated and General Populations (%)

Source: Adapted from Brazzell et al. (2009).

Psychoanalytic thought was pioneered by Sigmund Freud (1923, 1930) and is still a very influential force in psychology. This approach also gave rise to a variety of criminological theories discussed in later chapters. There are three basic concepts associated with Freud's psychoanalytic approach to personality: the id, the superego, and the ego. The **id** is the instinctual part of human personality and is governed by the pleasure principle, which means that it constantly seeks to maximize pleasure. In other words, the id seeks out stimuli that give us pleasure and instant gratification, such as food and sex (Freud, 1923). The **superego** is the opposite of the id and is sometimes referred to as our conscience. This part of the personality develops as we become socialized and serves as a moral compass since it helps us to tell right from wrong. In some cases, our superego will cause us to experience guilt if we have done something wrong; this helps shape future behavior in socially acceptable ways. The **ego** operates on the reality principle and serves as a sort of mediator or referee between the id and the superego. Our egos help us make acceptable compromises between our id and superego (Freud, 1923).

Think You Get It?

As you are reading this, your id is likely telling you that you could be doing something much more pleasurable (e.g., you could get some delicious, but unhealthy, fast food; or you could go out to pub with some friends for drinks; or, better yet, you could do both!). Your superego might be saying that you had better get your reading done because you will get behind if you do not, which may lead to bad marks, possibly failing out of school, and being forced to deliver pizzas for minimum wage…this would be disappointing to your parents and family. In fact, your superego might argue that you should spend the rest of the night reading to get ahead. Finally, your ego will come in and save the day with a reasonable compromise. Get your reading done, then you can eat something that is reasonably healthy, and then you can go out for a few drinks with some friends—but you can't stay out all night drinking!

As you can see from the example above, interactions between these three aspects of personality are useful for understanding all forms of human behavior and have specific applications to criminal behavior. More specific explanations of criminal behavior can be derived from these insights and will receive more discussion below. In general, Freud's key concepts are presented in Figure 4.3.

Later, Freud's work was developed by some of his well-known students, including Alfred Adler, Carl Jung, Erik Erikson, and Erich Fromm. While these students used many of Freud's central ideas, they made many adjustments to the framework, and, in some cases, they challenged their mentor on

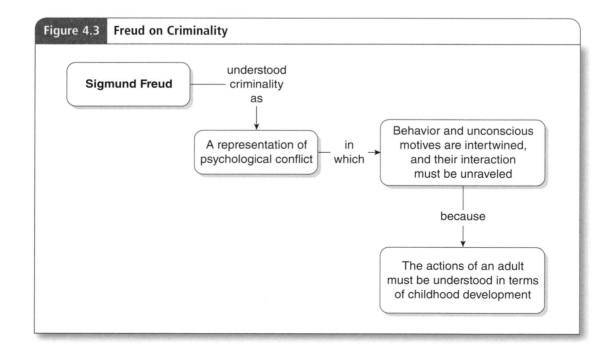

Figure 4.3   Freud on Criminality

certain points. Their work tends to be more humanist and progressive and gives much more consideration to social dynamics (Bohm & Vogel, 2011). The branch created by Freud's students is often referred to as neo-Freudian, or the humanistic-existential approach.

Adler initiated the break with Freud's psychoanalytic thought. He believed that Freud's emphasis on the pleasure principle as a main motivator of human behavior was misguided. He stressed more social aspects that affected the development of human personality (Adler, 1927). Jung (1921), another important neo-Freudian, suggested the traits of extraversion and introversion to describe personality type and interaction style. People with an extraverted personality tend to be more social and outgoing and are at ease, even energized among crowds. Conversely, introverts tend to be more withdrawn and socially isolated, and they tend to prefer solitary activities, such as reading and writing. Fromm (1942) and Erikson (1950) emphasized the importance of the ego, social factors, and later developmental stages in the formation of human personality. Ideas from the neo-Freudians have also found their way into several different explanations of criminal behavior that will be explored later in this chapter.

A last important influence is this area is early work done in experimental psychology. Pavlov's (1897) classical (or respondent) conditioning is particularly important to understanding some psychological positivist theories. Most people are familiar with his famous work involving salivating dogs. In this study, dogs learned to associate two unrelated stimuli because of past experience. Pavlov accomplished this by simply ringing a bell shortly before he fed the dogs every day. Soon, the dogs would salivate after they heard the bell, even without being exposed to food. This indicated that the dogs had learned to associate the ringing bell with food. This early research is particularly important to understanding Eysenck's (1964) theory of the criminal personality, reviewed later in this chapter.

Assumptions of Psychological Positivist Theories

Many of the assumptions made by psychological positivists are similar to those made by biological positivists. This should come as no surprise considering they both rely upon the positivist approach. Like their biological cousins, psychological positivists assume that people are naturally hedonistic and act to maximize their own pleasure. For these early positivists, behavioral motivation was determined by instinctual drives for survival and sex (Abrahamsen, 1944). These ideas originated in evolutionary theory (Darwin, 1859, 1871) and were also embraced in Freud's (1923, 1927) psychoanalytic approach and the approaches of other psychological theorists. In this view, then, people are different only in degree from animals (Einstadter & Henry, 2006).

According to Freud (1930), there are inherent tensions between the individual and society. Humans are designed by evolution to seek pleasure, but when we live in society we are often required to forgo or at least delay pleasure. We do this in exchange for the protection of the group; this is implied in the notion of the social contract (Hobbes, 1651). So, in other words, the law serves to restrict our potential for obtaining pleasure and happiness. Unlike the social contract theorists, Freud (1930) was not concerned with moral questions but rather natural questions; he implies that it is against our nature to live in society.

Like the biological positivist theories, at the core of these theories is the idea that people who commit crime have different thought processes and perceptions of reality (Miller et al., 2011, pp. 63–64). Personality determines motivation, and motivation arises from the instinctual drives mentioned above (Alexander & Healy, 1935). Abrahamsen, an early psychoanalytic theorist interested in crime, explains the relationship like this:

> All our tendencies—social, antisocial or criminal—are linked to our needs and desires, which arise from our instincts (our libido or life force) and which have been approved or disapproved by our ego and superego. Carrying out an antisocial or criminal act, then, depends on how the ego and superego react to instinctual impulses. This reaction again depends on the way these two personality elements have been conditioned by the environment and upon the situation to which the person has been exposed. (1960, p. 36)

Because these are positivist theories, they are clearly deterministic. As discussed in Chapter 2, the positivist approach also carries with it several other important assumptions, such as the notions that human behavior can be studied with pure scientific objectivity and that natural laws can be discovered that can be used to explain and predict human behavior. Psychological positivists also generally believe that personality traits are stable over life, so people do not change over time (Einstadter & Henry, 2006).

Finally, these theories are clearly consensus oriented and uniformly assume that conformity to the law equates to a normal personality (Akers & Sellers, 2013, p. 66). Experts are called upon to evaluate normality in individuals, and the law defines what is normal. In other words, these theorists rarely question the validity of the law, a subject many criminologists consider essential to understanding criminology itself (Einstadter & Henry, 2006).

Problem Focus, Scope, and Level of Explanation of Psychological Positivist Theories

The problem focus of psychological positivist theories is clearly individual criminality. Group dynamics, environmental factors, and situational factors are given little consideration. Most theorists in this area seek to identify a criminal personality that is composed of several traits (Einstadter & Henry, 2006).

Psychological positivist theories have a somewhat limited scope. Early psychoanalytic theorists and researchers were especially interested in juvenile delinquency because they believed that poor parenting practices and early childhood experiences determined whether or not one would become a criminal (Aichhorn, 1925; Alexander & Healy, 1935). Later, interest shifted to chronic or persistent criminals involved with serious and broad ranges of criminal acts. The goal here was to identify a general criminal personality that gives rise to serious criminal behavior and persistent offending. These theories are posed on the micro or individual level; group forms of crime and variations in crime rates are not addressed.

Theories offered by the psychological positivists are not as useful for explaining more common types of crime (e.g., minor theft, vandalism) and occasional minor criminal activity (e.g., drug use). However, they may be used to make sense of some white-collar and corporate crime. The suggestion here is that the corporate and business world may be an ideal environment for psychopaths (Babiak & Hare, 2006).

Key Terms and Concepts in Psychological Positivism

Early Psychoanalytic Explanations of Criminality

Even though the work of Freud has had a massive impact on the field of criminology, he had little to say specifically about criminal behavior. However, a careful reading of psychoanalytic writings about aggression, violence, and criminality reveals several possible pathways to crime. First, Freud (1923) claimed that an overly severe superego could produce increased levels of guilt. In order to relieve this guilt, the individual may commit crime with the intention of being caught and punished. This type of criminality is sometimes referred to as **neurotic offending** (Andrews & Bonta, 2003). This position is summarized by Freud in a footnote from his famous work, *Civilization and Its Discontents*:

> The "unduly or overly indulgent father" is the cause of children's forming an over-severe super-ego, because, under the impression of the love that they receive, they have no other outlet for aggressiveness other than turning it inwards. . . . It can be said, therefore, that a severe conscience arises from the joint operation of two factors: the frustration of instinct and the experience of being loved, which turns the aggressiveness inwards and hands it over to the super-ego. (1930, p. 93)

A second Freudian explanation of criminality involves the notion of deviant self-identification. In this case, the superego develops normally, but the person may develop a positive relationship with a criminal (or someone who commits crime) and may excuse this behavior or even partake in similar activities to eliminate the threat this causes to one's ego. For example, if a person has a good relationship with a parent but the parent happens to be a criminal, the person may redefine the behavior as positive and may even take part in it to reduce the conflict this causes. Individuals who have gone through the process of deviant self-identification are sometimes referred to as **antisocial offenders** (Andrews & Bonta, 2003; Serin et al., 2011).

A third path to delinquency occurs when the ego is weak and fails to control the demands of the id for instant gratification. In this case, the unregulated id dominates the personality and the individual behaves impulsively and hedonistically, with little thought given to the consequences of his or her actions. These people have poor judgment, low impulse control, and often disregard or fail to perceive threats of punishment. These types of offenders are often called the **weak ego type** or **impulsive offenders** (Andrews & Bonta, 2003; Redl & Toch, 1979). The final path to criminality identified by psychoanalytic criminologists is generically referred to as the **psychopathic personality**. In this case, the superego has failed to develop properly, causing a lack of conscience and an inability to feel empathy for others. These offenders tend to be manipulative, egocentric, and guiltless (Andrews & Bonta, 2003; Serin et al., 2011).

Aichhorn's (1925) psychoanalytic theory of juvenile delinquency is one of the earliest direct applications of Freudian theory to criminal behavior. Freud was Aichhorn's teacher and also wrote the foreword to his book, *Wayward Youth*. The theory offered in this text suggests that criminal behavior is the result of an unregulated id and an undeveloped ego or superego. Aichhorn argues that the main cause of ego and superego impairment is problematic parenting practices, including discipline that is excessively harsh, overly lenient, or inconsistent. It is relatively easy to see how this theory extends the basic explanation of criminality offered by the psychoanalytic approach.

Alexander and Healy (1935) offer yet another psychoanalytic explanation of criminal behavior that is very similar to Aichhorn's (1925), although they focus exclusively on male criminal behavior. They agree with Aichhorn that most criminality results from problems with parenting (e.g., excessive or inconsistent discipline and spoiling). However, they also point out that brotherly rivalries, competition with one's parents (i.e., Oedipus complexes), and early childhood deprivations may be related to criminal behavior.

Abrahamsen (1944, 1960) proposed a theory based upon the earlier one offered by Alexander and Healy (1935). However, in his formulation there is less emphasis on juvenile crime. This theory identifies three major factors involved in criminal behavior: criminalistic tendencies, mental resistance, and the situation. Criminalistic tendencies arise from natural instinctual pressures originating in the id linked to survival and sex that are suppressed in noncriminals. These are motivating factors that induce a person to commit crime (Abrahamsen, 1944). Mental resistance is largely derived from the superego and ego, both of which are responsible for controlling the id. One's level of mental resistance may also be affected by social and intellectual factors; these function as insulating factors that prevent a person from committing crime. The situation refers to both external elements (e.g., stress, strain, and pressure to commit crime) and internal factors (e.g., a person's mood and current psychological state). These factors vary based on chance and the way in which an offender interacts with his or her environment (Abrahamsen, 1944).

In later work, Abrahamsen (1960) emphasized the interactive nature of his theory and tried to identify key interactions to understanding criminality based on his earlier attempt to formalize his ideas by suggesting two laws of criminality (Abrahamsen, 1944). These laws are presented in Figure 4.4.

Techniques of Ego Defense

Redl and Wineman's (1951) techniques of ego defense theory is an attempt to specify how the ego and superego function to control behavior. This theory suggests that the superego is responsible for the regulation of morals and ethics, while the ego deals with our responses to formal types of punishment. The logical implication is that, in many cases, the ego is more important in determining criminal behavior than the superego. These theorists go on to point out that some people may develop a "delinquent ego" to deal with the underlying guilt and shame that result from their bad behavior. The delinquent ego may cause the individual to diffuse guilt in five main ways, as presented in Figure 4.5.

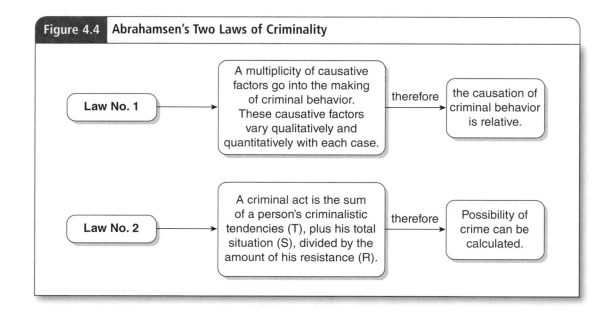

Figure 4.4   Abrahamsen's Two Laws of Criminality

Law No. 1 → A multiplicity of causative factors go into the making of criminal behavior. These causative factors vary qualitatively and quantitatively with each case. → therefore → the causation of criminal behavior is relative.

Law No. 2 → A criminal act is the sum of a person's criminalistic tendencies (T), plus his total situation (S), divided by the amount of his resistance (R). → therefore → Possibility of crime can be calculated.

Figure 4.5	Means to Diffuse Guilt
Category	**Explanation**
Denial	The individual denies that the behavior took place or claims to not remember the act.
Nothing New	The individual points out that others behave in the same unacceptable ways or suggests that it was the result of behavior that occurred in the context of a group.
Poor Me	The individual may say that he or she has been victimized in a similar way.
Eye for an Eye	The individual may claim that the person deserved to be victimized.
Justice	The person might suggest that he or she made things right after the fact.

It is worth noting that this theory resembles several other theories that emerged later in the history of criminology. These include Sykes and Matza's (1957) techniques of neutralization and Bandura's (1990) mechanisms of moral disengagement. We will address both of these theories in subsequent chapters.

A Theory of Oppression and Criminality

As mentioned previously, a number of Freud's followers (sometimes called neo-Freudians), including Adler, Erikson, Fromm, and Maslow, broke with many of his ideas and created their own intellectual movement in psychology known as the humanistic-existential perspective. The general thrust here is that psychoanalytic theory is too concerned with evolutionary motivations based on survival and sex. The fact is that modern human beings are motivated by many different factors. Criminological theories inspired by the humanistic perspective focus much more on social issues that affect psychological functioning, such as feelings of superiority or inferiority (Adler, 1927), or on criminal behavior as the result of the drive for status and respect (Erikson, 1950).

Building on the work of Fromm (1942), Halleck (1967, 1968) attempted to apply some of the humanistic-existential ideas from the neo-Freudians to the study of crime. Halleck (1967) emphasizes the importance of oppression in criminal behavior. According to this theory, there are two types of oppression: objective and subjective. Objective oppression is externally imposed by society and refers to measurable phenomena, such as levels of classicism, racism, sexism, and homophobia. Subjective oppression is internal to the individual and is much more difficult to measure. As levels of oppression (both perceived and real) rise, people look for ways to adapt to the increasing stress created. Crime is but one of the many adaptations to this strain or stress; other adaptions include conformity, activism, and mental illness. It is worth noting that this theory greatly resembles Merton's (1938) strain theory, which we will discuss in Chapter 10.

Attachment Theory

Bowlby's (1969) attachment theory is an example of another theory that makes use of a psycho-analytic approach. In this theory, the development of personality is tied to **maternal attachment**. Bowlby suggested that this first attachment lays the basis for a lasting psychological connectedness between human beings. Healthy attachment early in one's life serves as a model for all future attachments. If this attachment is unhealthy or unstable, personality development is disrupted, causing behavioral problems, including delinquency, crime, and other forms of antisocial behavior.

Attachment theory stimulated a great deal of research. In response to some of these findings, this theory was revised in two important ways. First, it was determined that the primary attachment does not need to be with the mother; a consistent caregiver that meets the child's needs is all that is required. Second, Bowlby (1969) claimed that healthy attachments could not be established after age two, but research has suggested that healthy attachments can be established later (Andrews & Bonta, 2003).

Bowlby's (1969) theory is clearly compatible with the control theories that will be reviewed in Chapter 7. Both focus on family and attachment, and control theorists have drawn upon the attachment research. For example, Hirschi's (1969) theory of social bonding and Gottfredson and Hirschi's (1990) self-control theory both emphasize the effect attachments and socialization have on behavior. Katz (1999, 2002) has noted this compatibility and proposed an integrated control theory based upon it. Farrington (1992) also included ideas from Bowlby's (1969) attachment theory in his developmental integrated cognitive antisocial potential theory, which we will cover in Chapter 15.

A Theory of the Criminal Personality

Eysenck's (1964) theory of the criminal personality combines ideas from classical conditioning theory (Pavlov, 1897) with a hierarchical trait approach based on Jung's (1921) concepts of extraversion and introversion. According to Eysenck's (1964, 1978) theory, people vary on key factors of personality, including extraversion (E), neuroticism (N), and psychoticism (P). Eysenck (1964) argues that E is related to the activity of the neurons located in the reticular activating system (RAS), which is located in the brain. This suggests an underlying biological basis for personality. People with low levels of activity in the RAS region will be extraverts and will seek stimulation, such as going out to parties and pubs and interacting in other social situations. Those with high RAS activity will be introverted and will avoid stimulation by spending time alone, staying at home, and avoiding extended periods of social interaction.

Levels of neuroticism are linked to activity in the autonomic nervous system, which is composed of the sympathetic and parasympathetic nervous systems. The sympathetic and parasympathetic nervous systems help organisms respond to emergencies. The sympathetic system activates processes that help the organism stay vigilant (e.g., increases in heart rate, blood flow, and respiration), while the parasympathetic system helps decrease arousal by bringing the body back to a normal state of functioning. These systems are under the control of structures in the limbic system of the brain (i.e., the hippocampus, amygdala, hypothalamus, and cingulum). People with high levels of neuroticism are sensitive, easily overstimulated, and react poorly to stressful situations. Those who are low in neuroticism are calm, stable, and show lower physiological levels of arousal, even when under stress (Bartol & Bartol, 2011).

In later work, Eysenck (1967) introduced the third key dimension of personality, called psychoticism (P), and explained its importance in understanding criminality (Eysenck, 1978). People high on the P dimension tend to be cold, antisocial, and egocentric. Eysenck said very little about the physiological basis for psychoticism, but other researchers have explored possible connections to brain functioning. The most common finding is that levels of dopamine, a chemical that influences reward-seeking behavior, are important to understanding the P dimension of personality (Lester, 1989).

Because people can vary in these traits, there can be a number of potential personality types. In other words, different combinations of traits produce different personality types. For example, people with low levels of E and N will be easier to condition than the other types, whereas people with high levels of E and N will be more difficult to condition (Eysenck, 1964). Higher levels of N, P, and, to a lesser extent, E appear to be correlated with an increased risk of criminality (Hopkins-Burke, 2005).

Another part of Eysenck's theory deals with the socialization process (Blackburn, 1993). Like psychoanalytic theorists, he believed socially unacceptable impulses and urges are controlled through the formation of a superego or conscience (Blackburn, 1993). This conscience formation takes place when we are young children through parental discipline and punishment; this process is similar to classical conditioning (Bartol & Bartol, 2011). Eysenck goes on to argue that most people are socialized to avoid crime in an almost reflexive way. In other words, they automatically associate the negative aspects of punishment with rule-breaking behavior. Consequently, Eysenck (1964) emphasizes the importance of classical conditioning over instrumental conditioning in understanding criminality. Key propositions of the psychological positivist theories are presented in Figure 4.6.

Figure 4.6	Eight Propositions of Psychoanalytic Theories
Author(s)	**Proposition**
Freud (1920, 1923); Aichhorn (1925); Alexander & Healy (1935)	Criminal behavior results from an overactive id and an underdeveloped superego, conditions that are caused by overly harsh, inconsistent, or unduly lenient parenting practices.
Abrahamsen (1944)	Crime results from the interaction of three sets of factors that include criminalistic tendencies (T), mental resistance (R), and situational factors (S).
Abrahamsen (1944)	Criminalistic tendencies arise from natural instinctual drives based upon survival and sex; mental resistance is determined by the strength of one's ego and superego to regulate behavior.
Redl & Wineman (1951)	The superego is responsible for interpretation of morals and ethics, and the ego controls our responses to formal punishment.
Redl & Wineman (1951)	A delinquent ego will diffuse guilt and shame stemming from criminal behavior by denying, rationalizing, and minimizing an act.
Eysenck (1967)	Criminality results from poor conditioning (or learning); people with high levels of extraversion, neuroticism, and psychoticism are more difficult to condition and do not learn as quickly as those with lower levels of these traits.
Halleck (1967)	The more the offender's behavior is a response to severe oppressive stress, the more unreasonable the criminality.
Halleck (1967)	The more indirect or unrealistic the oppression to which the offender is responding, the more unreasonable the criminality.
Bowlby (1969)	Insecure and insufficient parental attachment leads to increases in behavioral problems and juvenile delinquency.

Everything You Always Wanted to Know About Psychopathy but Were Afraid to Ask

It has been said that psychopaths "know the words, but not the music" (Johns & Quay, 1962, p. 18). To put it differently, psychopaths fail to fully understand the emotional content characteristic of human social interaction. This allows them to manipulate, exploit, and victimize others without being bothered by morals, ethics, or conscience. The origins of the modern conception of the psychopath can be found in the work of Hervey Cleckley (1941) in his well-known book, *The Mask of Sanity*. Cleckley's work was based on his observations of patients at a neuropsychiatric hospital over several years. He found that there were many patients who seemed free of any identifiable mental illness but who exhibited a number of common characteristics. Some of these characteristics included superficial charm, absence of nervousness, dishonesty, insincerity, lack of remorse/shame, poor judgment and learning ability, egocentricity, a lack of affect or emotion, promiscuity, and impulsivity.

The modern notion of psychopathy refers to a constellation of affective, interpersonal, and behavioral characteristics (e.g., egocentricity, impulsivity, irresponsibility, low emotional affect). Hare (1996) further defines psychopaths as "intra-species predators who use manipulation, intimidation, and violence to control others and satisfy their own selfish needs" (p. 94). According to Hare (1996), these people are not necessarily criminals; they are also well suited to become politicians, lawyers, cult leaders, radical political activists, elite businesspeople, and corporate executives.

As described previously, the notion of psychopathy has existed for at least a century (Serin et al., 2011), and some argue that it can be traced back even further (Bobich, 2006; Rafter, 2008). Despite this long history, and numerous revisions and reformulations, there is still a fair amount of confusion around psychopathy. We will try to dispel some of these myths here.

First and foremost, psychopathy is a personality disorder and not a mental disorder. In other words, psychopaths are not considered to be mentally ill. Second, psychopaths are not psychotics; this confusion may stem from references to the slang version of psychotic, or *psycho*. Psychotics may have delusions and hallucinations that may spur their behavior. Schizophrenia is an example of a psychotic disorder. While rare, in popular entertainment the term *psychopathic killers* is used to suggest those who indiscriminately kill everyone they meet. In reality, some psychopaths are law-abiding citizens and manage to channel their aggressive energies in less antisocial ways.

Third, *psychopathy, sociopathy*, and *antisocial personality disorder* are often used interchangeably but are actually distinct terms with different meanings (Babiak and Hare, 2006). Further, in early versions of the *Diagnostic and Statistical Manual of Mental Disorders* (DSM), psychopathy was equivalent to *sociopathic personality disorder*. In 1968, the American Psychological Association tried to coordinate its classification system with that of the World Health Organization and reclassified psychopathy as *antisocial personality* in the DSM-II (Hare, 1970). In later versions of the DSM (III and IV), attempts were made to distinguish psychopathy from *antisocial personality disorder* (APD). It should also be noted that the term *sociopathic personality disorder* is no longer used, but, in some cases, people with APD are referred to as sociopaths (Babiak & Hare, 2006). Unfortunately, this shifting maze of terminology and poorly defined criteria has resulted in further confusion over the term and its use as a classification tool in forensic and legal settings (Hare, 1996; Bobich, 2006).

Some notes about the prevalence of psychopathy and APD will also prove useful in distinguishing the two terms. Psychopaths represent roughly 1% of the general population, and 15% to 25% of the prison population (Hare, 1996). APD is present in 50% to 75% of prisoners and about 6% to 9% of the general population (Samuels, Nestadt, Romanoski, Folstein, & McHugh, 1994). These figures suggest that psychopaths represent a small subset of people with APD. In other words, almost all psychopaths have APD, but only a small subset of those diagnosed with APD would qualify as psychopaths (Hare, 1996).

Fourth, there have been considerable revisions to terminology and to the structure of the checklist itself that have increased confusion. Early on, Hare (1970, pp. 3–8) outlined three categories of psychopaths: the **primary psychopath**, the **secondary or neurotic psychopath**, and the **dyssocial psychopath**. The primary psychopath is the only "true" psychopath, according to Hare. People in this category have identifiable psychological, emotional, cognitive, and biological differences that distinguish them from the general or criminal population. Born with physical differences in the amygdala region of the brain, these individuals exhibit temperamental differences such as impulsivity, cortical underarousal, and fearlessness that lead them to risk-seeking behavior and an inability to internalize social norms (Raine, 1993).

Far more common are what Hare calls the secondary and dyssocial psychopaths. These two categories include a diverse group of antisocial individuals who comprise a large segment of the criminal population. The secondary psychopath commits antisocial or violent acts because of severe emotional problems or inner conflicts. They may be called acting-out neurotics, neurotic delinquents, symptomatic psychopaths, or simply emotionally disturbed offenders. Dyssocial psychopaths display aggressive, antisocial behavior they have *learned* from their subculture. These individuals exhibit personality disorders that are the result of negative sociological factors, such as parental neglect, delinquent peers, poverty, and extremely low or extremely high intelligence (Hare, 1970).

While we will discuss the problems associated with psychopathy as a theory in the proper sense of the word, it is useful to consider some of the terminology and characteristics often associated with psychopathy. Psychopathic traits, according to the Psychopathy Checklist—Revised (PCL-R), are outlined in Figure 4.7.

Figure 4.8 is a word cloud based on the terms in the PCL-R figure.

Figure 4.7	**Psychopathic Traits From the PCL-R**
Glib and superficial charm	Promiscuous sexual behavior
Grandiose sense of self-worth	Early behavior problems
Need for stimulation	Lack of realistic long-term goals
Pathological lying	Impulsivity
Conning and manipulative	Irresponsibility
Lack of remorse or guilt	Failure to accept responsibility for own actions
Shallow affect	Many short-term marital relationships
Callousness and lack of empathy	Juvenile delinquency
Parasitic lifestyle	Revocation of conditional release
Poor behavioral controls	Criminal versatility

Source: Adapted from Hare psychopathy checklist-revised (Pcl-R). (2003). In E. Hickey (Ed.), *Encyclopedia of murder and violent crime.* (p. 214). Thousand Oaks, CA: Sage. Retrieved from http://knowledge.sagepub.com/view/violentcrime/SAGE.xml

Figure 4.8	Psychopathy Checklist Word Cloud

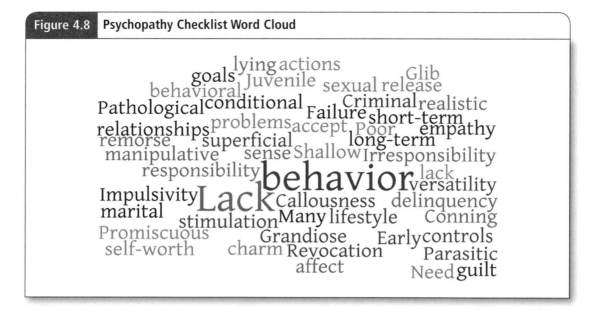

Recent reformulations of the psychopathy checklist have posited a two-facet, four-factor model of psychopathy. One facet deals with personality and assesses affective states (e.g., lack of empathy, lack of remorse, failing to take responsibility for actions) as well as interpersonal interaction style (e.g., superficial charm, deceitful, grandiose sense of self). The second facet deals more directly with social deviance and assesses lifestyle issues (e.g., lacks goals, impulsive, and irresponsible) and antisocial behavior (e.g., poor behavioral control, juvenile antisocial behavior, and antisocial behavior as adult) (Hare, 2003).

Unlike other psychological theories, it is difficult to view psychopathy as a distinct theory. However, a number of models have emerged that attempt to account for the biological origins of the disorder. These models are very complex and highly specialized, but they can be summarized as follows. A number of functional impairments have been found in psychopaths. First, psychopaths seem to have abnormal anxiety levels. Several theorists have suggested that psychopaths have lower levels of anxiety and tend to be manipulative, cunning, and cool under pressure (Blair, 2005). Others claim that psychopaths show heightened anxiety levels and tend to be impulsive, short-sighted, and easy to anger.

Second, psychopaths also seem to exhibit reduced responses to punishment. In other words, they have less fear of punishment and it has less impact (or deterrent effect) on their future behavior. Third, psychopaths seem to have problems processing information with emotional content or that is intended to invoke an emotional response. They have difficulties telling when people are frightened, upset, or sad (Blair, 2005). There is also research indicating that executive functioning may be involved with the violence inhibition mechanism (VIM). Blair (1995) argues that all social animal species (including humans) have a mechanism, the VIM, in the brain that is responsible for mediating the suppression of aggression. The VIM is triggered by nonverbal cues that spark an empathetic response. Blair (1995) also suggests that the VIM may be partly responsible for moral underdevelopment and that dysfunction in this mechanism could be related to psychopathy. These intriguing findings may offer a partial explanation as to why there is such great overlap between impulsivity and psychopathy (Fishbein, 2001).

Other theorists have proposed more general or unified formulations of psychopathy (Bobich, 2006; DeLisi, 2008). For example, Bobich (2006) has proposed a general theory of psychopathy by analyzing the data and findings about psychopathy. From this analysis, three key domains emerged: cognitive, affective, or behavioral. He then organized the findings based on how they fit within the domains and related this back to some of the original psychoanalytic explanations of criminality. The cognitive domain indicated a lack of superego control, the affective domain related to low levels of attachment to others, and the behavioral domain was thought to result from a lack of inhibition.

DeLisi (2008) has claimed that psychopathy has the potential to be a "unified theory" of crime based on several key arguments. First, he suggests that psychopathy captures the negative dimensions associated with antisocial behavior. He also points out that some well-known criminological theories, such as Gottfredson and Hirschi (1990), have parallels with psychopathy. Second, he argues that psychopathy lends itself well to a developmental approach that examines crime over the life course. In other words, findings about psychopathy correspond to findings in developmental research suggesting a small group of persistent and very serious offenders are responsible for a great deal of crime. Third, psychopathy is also compatible with emerging biosocial theories of criminal behavior. DeLisi (2008) falls short in specifying how psychopathy can be considered a theory. A major issue is his failure to offer any assumptions, propositions, or key causal mechanisms that explain how psychopaths become criminals.

Research on Psychological Positivist Theories

Early support for psychoanalytic explanations of criminality was largely clinically based, anecdotal, and often influenced by the researchers' practical experience. For example, Aichhorn was a psychiatrist who also served as a director at an institution for juvenile offenders, and he based many of his observations on interactions at work (Aichhorn, 1925, 1964). The research that inspired Hare's psychopathy checklist emerged from a practitioner's on-the-job experience of dealing with serious offenders at a neuropsychiatric hospital (Cleckley, 1941). In many cases, it is difficult to differentiate research from practice, and there seems to be great overlap between the two.

One of the earliest studies to use psychoanalytic theory was Healy's (1915) work, *The Individual Delinquent*. This study was undertaken at a juvenile psychopathic institute that focused on treatment, and the hope was to uncover insights about treatment and intervention effectiveness. The sample consisted of 1,000 repeat offenders, mostly adolescents who were 15 or 16 years old. Healy (1915) examined a variety of different factors in this study, including family and developmental histories; psychological, social, and environmental factors; and physical and medical characteristics (which we might associate with Lombrosian indicators of criminality). The researchers also performed numerous medical and psychological examinations and conducted in-depth psychoanalytic interviews with the offenders.

The findings indicated the usefulness of a case study approach over a classification or typological approach. The causal process underlying delinquency was found to be quite intricate and to involve numerous factors. Finally, this study advocated further examination of the interactions between the factors (Healy, 1915).

Another important study by Healy and Bronner (1926) involved examining 4,000 young repeat offenders from Boston and Chicago. Factors the researchers looked at included age, sex, heredity, nationality, religion, family life (e.g., poverty, parental neglect), physical characteristics and habits, intelligence, mental illness, and specific offenses. They found that early developmental factors and life experiences were very important to understanding involvement in delinquency. Their findings also indicated that desistance does not depend on any single factor; they suggest that it is the product of the interaction of several factors.

Healy and Bronner (1926) claimed that they could predict with reasonable certainty which delinquents would continue on in their life of crime by using certain mental factors (e.g., intelligence). They also noted that certain community and social factors were important but that their exact effects and interactions with other factors were not well understood. Finally, they also mentioned that the failure rate of treatment is very high and that the low rates of success would not be tolerated in business, industry, or science. However, they did not see treatment as being hopeless or pointless. The following quote is particularly telling:

> With our data showing that for the most part there are no peculiarities in delinquents that set them off as a group, or radically distinguish those who have a good outcome after having started in delinquency, from those that are Failures, and with our knowledge of much that can be modified in external conditions and mental life, the future seems to have great possibilities. We may rationally believe that if a reasonable part of the enthusiasm, energy, and funds devoted to other forms of civic and social improvement, or if a tithe of the present-day genius and ingenuity displayed in invention or that is at the service of banal entertainment were applied to a constructive program for the prevention of delinquency and crime we might have just as large returns as in these other fields. (Healy & Bronner, 1926, p. 224)

These words are just as true today as they were in the 1920s. Other research also appears very relevant to modern concerns about parenting and the development of psychosocial traits that allow people to interact in empathetic and prosocial ways.

Bowlby's (1944) early research focused on juvenile delinquency and maternal attachment. He worked at a child guidance clinic in London and based his study on a sample of 44 juveniles who were referred to the clinic for treatment. The children were evaluated and tested, and then in-depth interviews were conducted separately with the mothers and their children. These results were then compared to a control group of "normal" children. He found that 39% of the delinquent group had experienced maternal separation as opposed to only 5% of the control group of "normal" children (Serin et al., 2011). Further, his findings indicated that 86% of the thieves diagnosed as affectionless psychopaths also had experienced prolonged maternal separation when they were young (Bowlby, 1944).

At this point, it is important to consider how biological and psychological predispositions may interact with the physical and/or social environment to activate certain dormant traits. Eysenck completed numerous studies on the impact of personality characteristics on criminality. He theorized that criminal behavior may be a function of both personality differences (i.e., offenders are more likely to be extroverted, neurotic, and psychotic) and conditioning, in that some individuals are simply more difficult to condition than others. Eysenck (1977; Eysenck & Gudjonsson, 1989) identifies two sources of poor conditioning: personality types (extroverts are more difficult to condition) and physiological factors (in particular, low cortical arousal).

The most common research in this area involves personality assessments of inmates, mental patients, and mental health clients. Based on clinical work done in the 1960s and 1970s with offenders in a forensic psychiatric hospital, Yochelson and Samenow (1976) proposed another approach to understanding criminal personality based on thinking patterns. Trained as psychoanalytic theorists, both Yochelson and Samenow accepted the basic Freudian explanation of criminality but hoped to further explain the characteristics of the criminal personality. First, they believed that criminality was inborn; they rejected the neo-Freudian argument that criminality was the result of deep-seated conflicts in one's personality arising partly from social interactions (Miller, Schreck, & Tewksbury, 2011). Second, they claimed that all offenders exhibit a list of traits and thinking patterns that lead them to get involved with crime; some of these include

> fear of injury and personal insult, anger, pride, concrete rather than abstract thinking, fragmented thinking and behavior (i.e., a mixture of responsibility and irresponsibility . . . an "inconsistent inconsistency"), belief that they are special or unique, susceptibility to suggestibility in group and peer settings, lying, callous, lack of empathy, lack of responsibility and accountability, lack of trust, and super-optimistic. (Yochelson & Samenow, 1976, pp. 251–453)

While this research did point out the importance of thinking patterns in understanding criminality, it contained numerous problems and logical inconsistencies. Yochelson and Samenow (1976) imply that all or most offenders would exhibit the characteristics described in their research. This is quite a grandiose claim to make, especially considering the limitations of their sample. Their study was limited to a very exclusive group of serious offenders imprisoned in a psychiatric hospital, so it is unlikely that the thinking patterns would hold true for all or even most criminals (Lilly et al., 2011). Many of the thinking patterns identified overlap with each other, are highly subjective, or are closer to traits than true thinking patterns. Likewise, the inconsistent use of terminology creates numerous problems when trying to measure concepts and test the theory. Finally, the researchers systematically ignored all social factors in their theory, instead proposing that criminals are insulated, nonsocial creatures that are inwardly controlled by their devious and corrupted minds. They also claimed that offenders are rational and make conscious choices to commit crime while at the same time arguing for the existence of some stable criminal personality that extends across all criminals. This is illogical; one cannot argue for both free will and the existence of some stable criminal mind that controls the actions of all offenders (Lilly et al., 2011). Further, the consensus in psychology and the social sciences more generally is that behavior is a product of the interaction between individual characteristics and environment.

Practical Ramifications of Psychological Positivism

The field of psychology has influenced community corrections in a number of important areas. The most prominent influence relates to the classification of an offender's risk and needs and the development of case management plans and offender supervision strategies based on these classifications (Bonta & Andrews, 1993; Andrews and Bonta, 2003). Another example in this area is the development of different techniques used to interview, assess, and counsel offenders and the strategies used to foster compliance with the basic rules of community supervision. In general, these approaches begin from the same assumption of treatment regimes in early correctional institutions. Offenders were "sick" and had problems; they needed "healing" through therapy and understanding.

While the Freudian approach to rehabilitation was abandoned after the cognitive revolution, the emphasis on thinking patterns still remains. Another way in which the psychological positivist theories live on in the criminal justice system is in the emphasis on risk prediction and actuarial assessments. These are essentially the products of the personality theories described above. Ways of assessing psychopathy include rating scales, interviews, and self-reports (Serin et al., 2011, p. 353). One of the clearest practical ramifications of psychological theories can be found in the Psychopathy Checklist—Revised (PCL-R). This assessment scale was developed over 40 years (Hare, 1970, 1978, 1996, 2003). People are scored on a 20-item scale, and each item is scored out of 3 points, with an overall score ranging from 0–40. A score of 30 denotes a psychopath (Hare, 1996).

While initially used in psychiatric settings, the PCL-R and other risk assessment tools are becoming increasingly common in legal settings and as part of release planning in correctional institutions. Feeley and Simon (1996) have argued that the new emphasis on risk prediction is part of a larger movement in criminal justice system philosophy called "the new penology." This new approach focuses on managing unruly groups through risk assessment rather than on rehabilitating criminals. Other techniques that characterize this approach include selective incapacitation of dangerous and chronic offenders (and an increased reliance upon this), increased penalties for minor crimes such as drug use, and detection of drug use through testing (especially with regard to parole and probation) (see also Harcourt, 2007, for a detailed history of risk and actuarial assessment in criminal justice).

The bureaucratic logic behind the new penology and the risk movement is also readily apparent in our everyday lives. Indeed, some companies have started offering a screening version of the PCL-R for businesses as part of their hiring practices (see Serin et al., 2011). For example, in the article "Executive Psychopaths," the *Harvard Business Review* argues that

> chances are good there's a psychopath on your management team . . . I'm talking about the real thing, the roughly 1% of the population that is certifiably psychopathic. True psychopaths are diagnosed according to very specific clinical criteria, and they're nothing like the popular conception. What stands out about bona fide psychopaths is that they're so hard to spot. They're chameleons. They have a cunning ability to act perfectly normally and indeed to be utterly charming, as they wreak havoc on the lives of the people around them and the companies they inhabit. Many of psychopaths' defining characteristics—their polish, charm, cool decisiveness, and fondness for the fast lane—are easily, and often, mistaken for leadership qualities. That's why they may be singled out for promotion. But along with their charisma come the traits that make psychopaths so destructive: They're cunning, manipulative, untrustworthy, unethical, parasitic, and utterly remorseless. There's nothing they won't do, and no one they won't exploit, to get what they want. (Morse, 2004)

Beyond the boardroom, the use of actuarial methods in the field of crime and punishment is growing. These methods include parole prediction instruments and violent sexual predator scores, racial profiling on the highways, instruments to predict future dangerousness, drug-courier profiles, and Internal Revenue Service computer algorithms to detect tax evaders. One challenge is that without clear guidelines and validated instruments, an overreliance on these tools can amount to placing complex individuals into categories that, while administratively useful, may not be exact (Hacking, 1990). In North America, this has led to judicial concern about the overreliance on other sorts of risk-based assessment (Cole, 2007).

Criticisms of Psychological Positivism

There are a number of general criticisms that can be raised about the psychological positivist theories. First, in many cases, psychological positivists are reductionist in nature, meaning that they assume all criminal behavior can be explained with reference to personality traits. This is a problem because this approach breaks down when we begin to examine differences in crime rates between countries, cities, or even neighborhoods within the same city. If one carries this reasoning to its logical endpoint, the arguments become ridiculous. For example, if all criminal behavior is explained by personality, this implies that levels of personality disorders must be much higher in the United States than in Canada or Sweden because of the disparity in crime rates. This illustrates the problem of cross-level integration: It is very difficult to produce a theory that can both explain individual criminal behavior and address macro-level crime rates (Messner & Rosenfeld, 2001). This is an issue that will be revisited in later chapters.

Other critics argue the practical risk assessment model that the psychological positivistic approach has embraced formalizes subjective moral assumptions (Kemshall, 1995) and leads to a false sense of certainty and to injustices that can be difficult to remedy. In 2011, National Public Radio

Seven Steps	Psychological Positivism
Figure 4.9	**Seven Steps of Psychological Positivism**
1. Know the History	Surfaced during the 19th and 20th centuries alongside the rise of psychiatry and studies of intelligence and IQ
2. Acknowledge Assumptions	Biological instincts produce psychological urges and create abnormal personalities prone to deviance and crime; society is characterized by a consensus, and the law plays a large role in determination of abnormal personality.
3. Problem Focus, Scope, and Level of Explanation	Focus on explaining criminality using individual differences (e.g., abnormal personality and IQ)
4. Key Terms and Concepts	Criminal personality, techniques of ego defense, attachment, and psychopathy
5. Respect the Research	Studies focus on juveniles; identification of traits that compose criminal personality
6. Theory/Practice	Early psychoanalytic treatment in prisons (talk therapy); classification and risk prediction in the criminal justice system (e.g., psychopathy checklist)
7. Mapping the Theory	See Figure 4.10

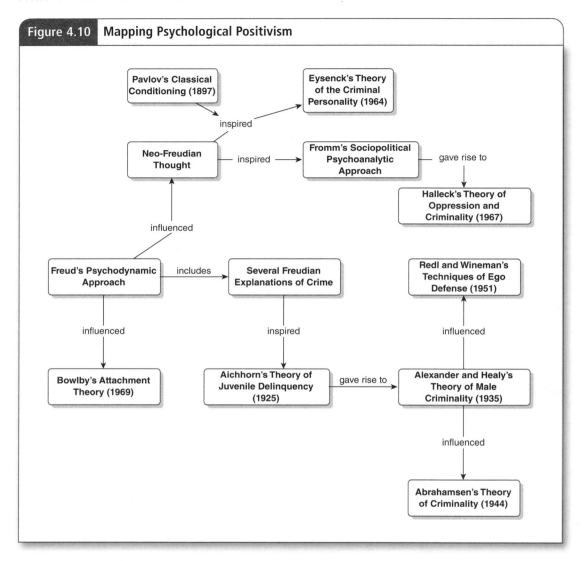

Figure 4.10 **Mapping Psychological Positivism**

(NPR) science correspondent Alix Spiegel reported on the story of Robert Dixon, who is currently in a maximum security prison in Vacaville, California, and is unlikely to ever get parole because of his score on the PCL-R. Spiegel tells the story of the PCL-R's creation and reports that the man who created the test, Robert Hare, has concerns about how it is currently being used in the criminal justice system. Tools that produce results that cannot be replicated, or that make fundamental assumptions that cannot be questioned, allow for ideological or political decisions to be made based on a misrepresentation of scientific tools and processes.

A more specific problem with psychopathy is the tendency of clinical definitions to collapse in tautologies. A **tautology** (sometimes called circular logic) is a classic error of logic. It occurs when a definition is used as an explanation. So, a psychopath can be defined as someone who commits violent crime with no discernible motive. This criminal is not driven by profit and is not protecting his or her reputation, two common motives for crime. In other words, this criminal commits violent crime without any discernible motive, and therefore this criminal is a psychopath. This takes us in a logical circle and explains nothing.

In a similar vein, many diagnostic definitions of antisocial personality disorder in the latest *Diagnostic and Statistical Manual of Mental Disorders* (DSM-V) include repeated acts that are grounds for arrest. Therefore, someone has antisocial personality disorder because they commit antisocial acts. These tautologies have driven American psychiatry since at least the 1970s, and the problems with the validity of the taxonomies of mental illnesses have led the National Institute of Mental Health (NIMH), the world's largest funding agency for research into mental health, to explore new tools and techniques for diagnosis. For example, NIMH has launched the Research Domain Criteria (RDoC) project to transform diagnosis by incorporating genetics, imaging, cognitive science, and other sources of information to lay the foundation for a new classification system (Insel, 2013).[1]

A final issue is that psychological positivist theories also have difficulties making sense of group criminal behavior and antisocial behavior that is conformist in nature. For example, these theories make little sense if one considers examples of group behavior that have resulted in some of the most horrible atrocities of human history, such as the Holocaust and the Rwanda genocides (Dutton et al., 2005; Zimbardo, 1970, 2007). This problem requires that we consider how psychological learning and situational theories can be applied to explain criminal behavior and make sense of some of this problem, as we will explore in the next two chapters.

Research Example: Mental Illness and Crime

Some recent studies have focused on the role of mental illness in crime. For example, studies suggest that as many as three in five prison inmates have some form of mental illness (Fazel & Danesh, 2002). The most commonly associated illnesses are schizophrenia and antisocial personality disorder. On its Web site, the National Institute of Health (NIH) defines **schizophrenia** as

> a chronic, severe, and disabling brain disorder . . . in which those who suffer may hear voices others do not, believe other people are reading their minds, controlling their thoughts, or plotting to harm them. This can terrify people with the illness and make them withdrawn or extremely agitated. People with schizophrenia may not make sense when they talk. They may sit for hours without moving or talking. Sometimes people with schizophrenia seem perfectly fine until they talk about what they are really thinking.

In a study of crime and schizophrenia, Lindqvist and Allebeck (1990) analyzed 790 schizophrenic patients discharged from hospitals in Stockholm, Sweden, in 1971. They compared this to data obtained from the Central Swedish Police Register from 1972 to 1986. They found that the crime rate

---

[1]For more on how the NIH is updating diagnosis beyond the DSM-V, see http://www.nimh.nih.gov/about/director/2013/transforming-diagnosis.shtml.

among male schizophrenics was similar to that found in the general population for males. Among female schizophrenics, the crime rate was twice that of the general female population. However, the rate of minor violent acts was found to be four times higher in the schizophrenics than the general population. This being said, it is important to realize that less than 2% of all people with schizophrenia are arrested for violent crimes (Phillips, Wolf, & Coons, 1988). While antisocial personality disorder is one of the most well-known mental disorders, other mental health issues have been linked to criminal behavior. Johns Hopkins University (2013) offers a detailed breakdown of personality disorders by cluster, as seen in Figure 4.11.

Recent research examining personality disorders and criminal behavior has found a surprising number of mental disorders among the prison population (Fazel & Danesh, 2002). While more than 9 million people are imprisoned worldwide, data on those with serious mental disorders such as psychosis, major depression, and antisocial personality disorder is scarce. (Fazel & Danesh, 2002) undertook a study that involved 62 surveys from 12 countries and included 22,790 prisoners. Key demographics of the sample are listed in Figure 4.12.

Figure 4.11	Clusters of Personality Disorders	
Cluster	**Disorder**	**Description**
A (Odd/ eccentric)	Paranoid personality disorder	Cold, distant, and unable to form close, interpersonal relationships. Often suspicious of their surroundings and project their anger onto others.
A (Odd/ eccentric)	Schizoid personality disorder	Often so absorbed in their own thinking and daydreaming that they exclude themselves from attachment to people and reality.
A (Odd/ eccentric)	Schizotypal personality disorder	Cold, distant, introverted, and have an intense fear of intimacy. People also exhibit disordered thinking, perception, and ineffective communication skills.
B (Dramatic/ erratic)	Borderline personality disorder	Unstable in their perceptions of themselves and have difficulty maintaining stable relationships. Moods may also be inconsistent, but never neutral—reality is always seen in "black and white."
B (Dramatic/ erratic)	Antisocial personality disorder	Casual disregard for the feelings, property, authority, and respect of others. May include violent or aggressive acts involving or targeting other individuals without a sense of remorse or guilt for their actions.
B (Dramatic/ erratic)	Narcissistic personality disorder	Severely inflated feelings of self-worth, grandiosity, and superiority over others. People with narcissistic personality disorder often exploit others who fail to admire them and are overly sensitive to criticism, judgment, and defeat.
B (Dramatic/ erratic)	Histrionic personality disorder	Overly conscious of their appearance and constantly seeking attention. Often behave dramatically in situations that do not warrant this type of reaction. The emotional expressions of such people are often judged as superficial and exaggerated.

Cluster	Disorder	Description
C (Anxious/ inhibited)	Dependent personality disorder	Heavily reliant on others for validation and fulfillment of basic needs. Often unable to properly care for themselves. People with dependent personality disorder lack self-confidence and security and are deficient in making decisions.
C (Anxious/ inhibited)	Avoidant personality disorder	Hypersensitive to rejection and avoid situations with any potential for conflict. Persons with avoidant personality disorder become disturbed by their own social isolation, withdrawal, and inability to form close, interpersonal relationships.
C (Anxious/ inhibited)	Obsessive-compulsive personality disorder	Inflexible to change and have trouble completing tasks and making decisions. Are often uncomfortable in situations beyond their control and find it difficult to maintain positive relationships.

Source: Adapted from Johns Hopkins University (2013).

Figure 4.12	Key Characteristics of Sample	
Mean Age (Years)	29
Gender (Men)	81%
Imprisoned for Violent Offense	26%
Major Depression	10%
Personality Disorder	65%
Antisocial Disorder	47%

Source: Adapted from Fazel & Danesh (2002).

Fazel and Danesh (2002) concluded prisoners were several times more likely than the general population to have psychosis and major depression and about ten times more likely to have antisocial personality disorder.

Based on this work and follow-up research (Fazel & Seewald, 2012), Davison and Janca (2012) tested the association between personality disorder and criminal offending by reviewing recent literature in order to connect personality disorders by clusters with specific types of criminal offenses. Cluster A, B, and C personality disorders were each found to be associated with different types of offenses. Although rates of personality disorder are high in all serious offenders, the role played by personality disorder may be greater in some offenses than others. Davison and Janca argue that frameworks for understanding how a personality disorder may interact with other factors to contribute to offending can assist psychological explorations of crime and criminality. These findings offer an interesting way to consider the role of personality disorders in criminality, as outlined in Figure 4.13.

Figure 4.13	Personality Disorders Most Commonly Associated With Crime	
Cluster	**Personality Disorder**	**Associated With These Crimes**
A (Odd/ eccentric)	Paranoid personality disorder	Robbery Blackmail
A (Odd/ eccentric)	Schizoid personality disorder	Kidnapping Burglary Theft
B (Dramatic/ erratic)	Antisocial personality disorder	Obstruction of justice Firearms offenses Robbery and blackmail Escape and breach Fraud Burglary and theft Violence Murder/suicide
B (Dramatic/ erratic)	Narcissistic personality disorder	Fraud Forgery
C (Anxious/ inhibited)	Dependent personality disorder	Firearms offenses Violence
C (Anxious/ inhibited)	Avoidant personality disorder	Criminal damage Sex offenses
C (Anxious/ inhibited)	Obsessive-compulsive personality disorder	Firearms offenses Sex offenses

Source: Adapted from Davison & Janca (2012).

Now that you've read this chapter. . . consider again mental illness and crime. Between 2006 and 2013, 934 deaths resulted from 146 shootings that matched the FBI's definition of mass shooting. However, these deaths accounted for less than 1% of all gun-related homicides. While the media focuses on mass shootings, 33 Americans are killed every day with a handgun by a family member or an intimate partner. While it may be prudent to expand the federal prohibition on gun ownership by individuals adjudicated as having a serious mental health condition or receiving involuntary outpatient treatment, it is a mistake to blame gun crimes on mental illness. Most people with serious mental illness, even schizophrenia and bipolar disorder, are never violent toward others. According to the Consortium for Risk-Based Firearm Policy, only about 4% of violence in the United States is attributable to mental illness.

Conclusion and Review Questions

Like the early biological positivist theories we explored in Chapter 3, the psychological positivist theories focus upon individual differences or characteristics that can be used to identify criminals. Sometimes this area is also referred to as trait or personality theory. Instead of focusing on physical characteristics or body types, these theories identify personality traits and mental processes that impact behavior. One common starting place was the idea that less intelligent people are more likely to commit crime. Once described as feeblemindedness, stupidity, or dull wittedness, this factor remains a feature of some psychological explanations of criminal behavior. More recent understanding of personality disorders focuses on more specific antisocial behaviors, and there is evidence to suggest certain types of mental illnesses are associated with certain types of crimes. The trouble is how to balance the existing tools of assessment used to identify serious mental disorders such as psychopathy with the danger posed by the misuse of these tools.

CHAPTER REVIEW

1. What are the assumptions made by psychological positivist theories?

2. What kinds of crimes do these theories try to explain?

3. What are the differences between primary, secondary, and dyssocial psychopaths?

4. How have historical and social context influenced psychological positivist theories?

5. What are some of the practical approaches and programs suggested by psychological positivist theories?

PART III

Process Theories

CHAPTER

5

Psychological Process Theories

⬚ Chapter Overview and Objectives

In this chapter, we focus on psychological process theories by reviewing social cognitive and deindividuation theories. We will explore how these psychological theories are relevant to understanding certain types of criminal behavior. An important starting place is the difference between hard and soft determinism (Bandura, 1986). The biological and psychological positivist approaches introduced in previous chapters are associated with hard determinism. This is the idea that behavior is the result of biological or psychological abnormalities or antisocial traits. Psychological process theories assume that whatever individual traits a person may possess, these traits are shaped through environmental influences. These influences may include the family, school, peers, or even the social circumstances or situation. Figure 5.1 provides an overview of these theories. By the end of the chapter, readers should be able to:

- Understand the assumptions made by psychological process theories
- Be aware of the level of explanation, problem focus, and scope of these theories
- Explain the historical and social context that gave rise to these theories
- Compare and contrast research on these theories
- Apply the practical approaches and programs suggested by psychological process theories to the criminal justice system

⬚ The Psychological Process Tradition

It should be noted from the outset that this classification does not appear in most theory texts. However, some have referred to these theories as "process psychology" theories that are closely connected to sociological process theories (Gibbons, 1994). While these theories emerged from the discipline of psychology in the subspecialty of social psychology, they have come to play an important role in explaining some

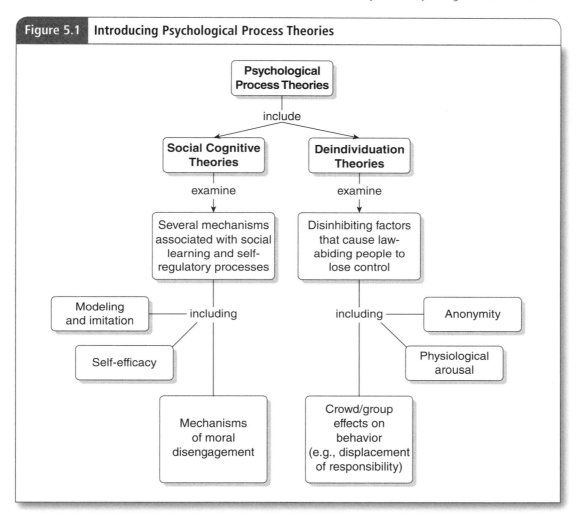

Figure 5.1 **Introducing Psychological Process Theories**

forms of criminal behavior. In general, these theories examine psychological processes that influence some people to behave criminally and/or antisocially. Specifically, they examine how social interaction, group factors, and situational dynamics impact behavior (Bandura & Walters, 1963; Festinger, Pepitone, & Newcomb, 1952; Zimbardo, 1970). In other words, these theories do not attribute criminality to free will, genetic makeup, or personality traits like the other theories we have studied so far (Bohm & Vogel, 2011).

Social cognitive theory is also referred to as social learning theory (Bandura, 2001). Deindividuation theories are sometimes called theories of the situation (Zimbardo, 2007). It is important to realize that while these have similarities, they are not the same theory; they are more accurately viewed as complementary theories. Each theory focuses on temporally distinct phenomena that give rise to social interactions that take on a psychological dimension. Social cognitive theory involves a long-term process and focuses upon the person's learning history. By contrast, deindividuation theory is more of a short-term process that occurs rapidly and is highly sensitive to situational dynamics.

> **As you read this chapter, consider . . .** why do people in groups engage in behavior that is out of character? For example, on September 29, 2013, Alexian Lien and his family were driving on New York City's West Side Highway when they encountered a group of motorcyclists. After Lien's SUV bumped a biker, some of the other motorcyclists surrounded the SUV, dismounted, and approached the vehicle. According to police, others in the group began to damage the vehicle. Lien accelerated to escape, reportedly driving over three motorcycles and a rider named Edwin Mieses Jr., who was critically injured. The motorcyclists chased Lien, and Lien's wife called 911 four times in an 8-minute period. The motorcyclists caught up to Lien and forced the SUV to stop. One individual smashed the windows of the car while others pulled Lien from his SUV and brutally beat him in front of his wife and two-year-old child. The assault lasted about 20 seconds. A video recording posted on YouTube shows a number of bikers gathered around Lien, hitting, kicking, and stomping on him. At one point, one of the motorcyclists beats Lien with a helmet. Can psychological process theories help explain this event?

Seven Steps of Criminological Thinking

History and Social Context of Psychological Process Perspective

The social cognitive and deindividuation theories have a long and overlapping history in the discipline of psychology. The origins of these theories can be traced back to work on crowd behavior carried out by the French social psychologist Gustav Le Bon (1895/1960). Le Bon was born in 1841 and lived during a period in which France was undergoing great turmoil, near constant political strife, and social upheaval. Crowd violence during this period was a fact of life (Merton, 1960). Le Bon witnessed several major crowd events that galvanized a large segment of France's large industrial population. The focus of Le Bon's (1895) pioneering work, *The Crowd*, was to explain how identification with a group could override individual will. His methods were not overly rigorous, and some found the scientific aspects of his work to be lacking:

> His is the method of social philosophers, social psychologists, and social observers, prevalent in his own day and far from absent in ours: the method of using historical anecdotes as a source of ideas under the illusion that the source somehow authenticates the interpretation stemming from them. (Merton, 1960, p. xxxi)

Le Bon was clearly more of a problem finder than a problem solver and more of a social philosopher than a theorist—his ideas were too vague and abstract to be scientifically testable. However, his work did help to uncover new intellectual puzzles for theorists to solve (Kuhn, 1962).

Le Bon identified three basic processes that were crucial to understanding the crowd or mob mentality. First, he said that the anonymity provided by the crowd was important. He claimed that this lifted responsibility and restraint and freed the individual from normal social control. Second, Le Bon (1895) posited a contagion mechanism in which individual interests were sacrificed in favor of collective interest. Third, and most important, he argued that the crowd could make individuals highly suggestible and easily manipulated. He describes this hypnotic effect below:

He is no longer conscious of his acts. In his case, as in the case of the hypnotized subject, at the same time certain faculties are destroyed, others might be brought into a high degree of exaltation. Under the influence of a suggestion, he will undertake the accomplishment of certain acts with irresistible impetuosity. (Le Bon, 1895, p. 31)

According to Le Bon (1895), these processes work in conjunction with each other to extinguish one's individual personality and replace it with a crowd mindset or so-called mob mentality.

Le Bon's work led to a more formal theory of imitation formulated by another French social psychologist named Gabriel Tarde (1903) in his work *The Laws of Imitation*. Tarde was specifically interested in criminal behavior and was quite critical of Lombroso's work on the atavistic criminal that we reviewed in Chapter 1. Tarde claimed there were three laws of imitation: the law of close contact, the law of imitation of superiors by inferiors, and the law of insertion. The **law of close contact** states that the level of intimacy we share with role models influences our behavior. In other words, if the model happens to be a person we have a close relationship with (e.g., a parent, sibling, or close friend), the impact of the observed behavior will be greater. The **law of imitation of superiors by inferiors** simply suggests that we model our behavior on those who have a higher position or more experience than we do. Young people imitate older people, the poor imitate the wealthy, and subordinates tend to imitate people who are in charge. The **law of insertion** contends that new behaviors will either reinforce or replace already established behaviors. For example, e-mail scams have become increasingly common in the last decade or so and are often based on other well-established forms of conning; the computer simply provides a new venue for criminals to ply their trade.

Assumptions of Psychological Process Theories

Both social cognitive and deindividuation theories assume that humans are blank slates and that personality is shaped largely in response to one's environment (Agnew, 2011; Banudra, 1986, 2001; Zimbardo, 2007). The major theorists in this area attest to the plasticity of human nature and our capacity for both good- and bad-natured behavior:

Seen from the social cognitive perspective, human nature is characterized by a vast potentiality that can be fashioned by direct and observational experience into a variety of forms within biological limits. To say that a major distinguishing mark of humans is their endowed plasticity is not to say that they have no nature. . . . The plasticity, which is intrinsic to the nature of humans, depends upon neuropsychological mechanisms and structures that have evolved over time. These advanced neural systems for processing, retaining, and using coded information provide the capacity for the very characteristics that are distinctly human—generative symbolization, forethought, evaluation, self-regulation, reflective self-consciousness, and symbolic communication. (Bandura, 1986, p. 21)

In other words, people capable of both good and evil, and evolution has programmed us to change with different situations and environments to allow us to adapt and survive.

Some psychological process theorists also appear to embrace a conflict assumption regarding the nature of society. Unlike the psychological positivists, psychological process theorists do not see the law as the ultimate determinant of right and wrong or normal and abnormal. Instead, they acknowledge that laws and norms change over time and even from situation to situation. Thus, we can see how a psychological process theorist might view crime, and the formation of law as well. In many cases, the policies and practices of governments, corporate entities, and other bureaucratic structures become the object of analysis (Dutton et al., 2005; Zimbardo, 2007). This conflict orientation is usefully captured in this quote:

> As a general rule, people judge the harmful acts of favored individuals and groups as unintended and prompted by situational circumstances but perceive the harmful acts of the disfavored as intentional and personally initiated. Value orientations of the labelers also influence their judgments of activities that cause harmful effects. . . . Dissident aggression is also judged in large part on the basis of factors external to behavior. Some of these include the perceived legitimacy of the grievances, the appropriateness of the coercive tactics, the professed aims of the dissenters, and the ideological allegiances of the observers (Bandura, 1973). People vary markedly in their perceptions of aggression for social control and social change (Blumenthal, Kuhn, Andrews, & Head, 1972). The more advantaged citizenry tend to view even extreme levels of violence for social control as lawful discharges of duty, whereas disadvantaged members regard such practices as expressions of institutionalized aggression. Conversely, aggression for social change, and even group protest without violence, is judged as violence by patriots of the system but not by dissidents. Thus, in conflicts of power, one person's violence is another person's benevolence. (Bandura, 1977, pp. 199–200)

In one way, these theories are inherently incompatible with other biological or psychological explanations. While they do not deny that these factors are important, psychological process theorists emphasize situational and social factors. This does not absolve people of responsibility for their actions because people choose whom they interact with, and these interactions shape and are shaped by the social environment (Bandura, 1986, 2008; Zimbardo, 2007). In fact, Bandura (1986) goes so far as to argue that he does not view freedom and determinism as being incompatible with each other because the social cognitive perspective acknowledges that people regulate and influence their own behavior. This approach, known as reciprocal determinism, suggests that behavior interacts with cognitive and environmental factors to produce subsequent behavior. In other words, past behavior actually influences future behavior.

Think You Get It?

Following the classical school, new "scientific" or positivist approaches to criminology appeared in the late 1800s and early 1900s and suggested criminal behavior was predetermined. Biological positivists focus on what differences genetic or hereditary variations make in a person's behavior, while psychological positivists look at specific personality traits. Psychological process theories are quite different. While they feel genetics or individual traits may be relevant, psychological process theorists consider social interactions to be essential and recognize the power and influence of situational circumstances. Where do you stand? Are we born good people and then corrupted by an evil society, or are we born evil and then redeemed by a good society? What are the limitations of accepting this either/or proposition? Is it possible, as Zimbardo (2007) suggests, that each of us has the potential to a saint or sinner, altruistic or selfish, gentle or cruel, dominant or submissive, perpetrator or victim, prisoner or guard?

Problem Focus, Scope, and Level of Explanation of Psychological Process Theories

The problem focus of these theories is criminal behavior and, in particular, crime that occurs in the context of the group and in response to influences of the group. This is a somewhat unique problem focus; these theories address gaps left in positivist theories that we reviewed in previous chapters. For instance, positivist theories struggle to explain why biologically and psychologically normal people commit crime. It is important to note that people who have no mental disorders or biological defects commit a great deal of crime. The scope of these theories is quite broad. Some common crimes and forms of minor deviance can be explained based on this theory, as can more serious and unusual types of crime, such as riots, hooliganism, military massacres, and genocides (Dutton et al., 2005; Zimbardo, 2007).

These theories are also applicable to certain forms of white-collar and corporate crime that depend on group dynamics and influence (Bandura, 1997). Psychological process theories are posed at the micro level since they primarily consider how group influences affect individual behavior. However, they still acknowledge that some structural factors are important to consider. For example, Bandura (1986) acknowledges that the incentives that motivate behavior are socially structured to a certain extent; again, the interest is in how this affects individual behavior. In a similar vein, Zimbardo (2007) stresses the importance of understanding how systems and bureaucracies can create bad situations that cause individuals to behave in undesirable or immoral ways.

Key Terms and Concepts in Psychological Process Theories

Early Learning Theories and Criminality

Instrumental learning theories from Thorndike (1898) and later Hull (1943) preceded the emergence of social cognitive theory. These theories stressed that behavior can also be learned from the consequences of behavior as opposed to simple conditioning based on external factors. This theoretical trajectory led to the formation of the Yale school of psychology, which later gave rise to the frustration-aggression hypothesis and early formulations of social learning theory (Dollard, Miller, Doob, Mowrer, & Sears, 1939; Miller & Dollard, 1941). The work of the Yale school was a forerunner to other psychologically based learning theories, such as operant conditioning (Skinner, 1953); social learning theory; and other social cognitive approaches (Bandura & Walters, 1963; Bandura, 1977).

With their frustration-aggression hypothesis, Dollard and his colleagues (1939) were attempting to combine the notion of the pleasure principle offered by Freud with early theories of psychological behaviorism offered by Thorndike (1898) and Hull (1943). There are several key concepts that are crucial to understanding the frustration-aggression hypothesis. First, **aggression** is thought to be a consequence of **frustration**. However, aggression is not always directly observed as response to frustration because people learn to suppress their aggressive impulses through socialization and social interaction (Dollard et al., 1939). Second, aggression results from something called an **instigator**, which is basically a broader version of a stimulus and serves to motivate behavior. Dollard and his colleagues distinguish between instigators and stimuli:

The concept of an instigator is clearly much broader than that of a stimulus; whereas the latter refers only to energy (as physically defined) exerted on a sense-organ, the former refers to any antecedent condition, either observed or inferred, from which the response can be predicted, whether the condition be a stimulus, verbally reported image, idea, or motive or state of deprivation. (1939, p. 3)

Third, the **goal response** is any behavior that terminates the instigator. Fourth, the **reinforcing effect** refers to the recollection of successful goal responses initiating a learning process. Fifth, **frustration** is defined as the denial of a goal response arising from either (1) inaccessible goals or (2) punishment in response to goal-seeking activities. Of course, this has ramifications for criminality, which are described below:

Criminality here is viewed, not as a function of the absolute level of frustration nor of the absolute degree of anticipated punishment, but as a function of the discrepancy between the two. With a low degree of anticipated punishment, criminality does not result if frustration is sufficiently low; likewise given a high degree of frustration, criminality does not result if anticipation of punishment is sufficiently high. But when anticipation of punishment deviates in the downward direction and frustration deviates upward, the magnitude of the resulting discrepancy carries with it a correspondingly increasing expectancy of criminality. (Dollard et al., 1939, p. 141)

Figure 5.2 provides one way to visualize this theory.

In an attempt to further refine the frustration-aggression hypothesis, Miller and Dollard (1941) formulated an early version of social learning theory. There are four key factors important to understanding this theory. First, a **drive** is the motivation to act or a strong stimulus. Drives may be either primary or secondary. *Primary drives* are innate and arise in response to frustration, pain, fatigue, hunger, thirst, cold, and sex. In some cases, these drives are obscured by various social conventions (e.g., delaying sex until marriage). *Secondary drives* are acquired and are learned in response to social interaction. Examples of these include fear, anxiety, social praise, and money. **Response** refers to learned behavior that is the result of drives. **Cues** elicit responses and determine when responses occur. Finally, **rewards** increase response rates through learning. According to Miller and Dollard (1941), behavior is learned through observing others and imitating them based on the perceived consequences of their actions. Behaviors that recur tend to be those that are rewarded with positive forms of reinforcement.

Social Cognitive Theory

Albert Bandura is the main proponent of cognitive theory and its most prominent theorist. He has identified several key mechanisms associated with social learning, including modeling, self-efficacy, and moral disengagement. A number of terms are used interchangeably with **modeling**, and this has the potential to create considerable confusion. Observational learning, imitation, and vicarious learning all refer to the same process (Bartol & Bartol, 2011).

Traditional behaviorists assume that behavior can only be impacted through direct reinforcement. However, Bandura disagreed, saying that

learning would be exceedingly laborious, not to mention hazardous, if people had to rely solely on the effects of their own actions to inform them what to do. Fortunately, most human

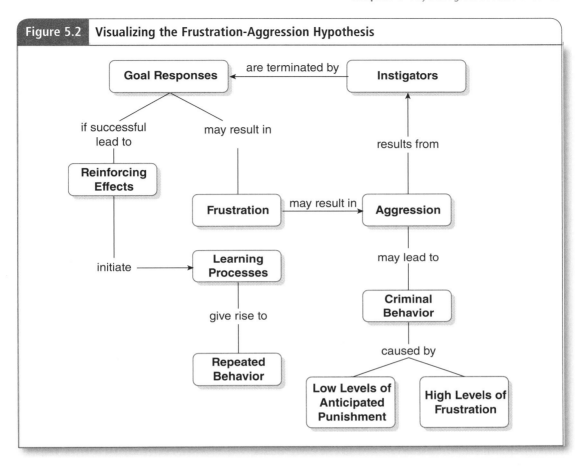

Figure 5.2   Visualizing the Frustration-Aggression Hypothesis

behavior is learned observationally through modeling: from observing others one forms an idea of how new behaviors are performed, and on later occasions this coded information serves as a guide for action. (1977, p. 22)

Building on the work of previous learning theorists, Bandura (1977) claimed that reinforcement could also be vicarious in nature. So, if one observes a model being rewarded or punished, then the observer's behavior may also be affected. Bandura also suggested that the effects of this **vicarious reinforcement** would depend on the characteristics of both the observer and model being observed. For example, does the observer lack confidence or self-esteem? Is the model being observed a close personal friend or a family member of the observer, or just an acquaintance? Does the observer think highly of the model? Does the model occupy a position of high status in the eyes of the observer? Generally, the more positively the observer views the model, the more of an impact the modeled behavior will have.

From his research, Bandura (1977) determined that modeling can occur in three different ways. First, it can occur through a **live model**, which simply means a person observing someone they know performing a behavior. Second, Bandura posited the existence of **verbal modeling**, or modeling that can be accomplished through verbal instruction. Third, he argued in favor of **symbolic modeling,** which occurs through various forms of mass media (e.g., books, TV, and movies). Examples of symbolic models in mass media include television and movie stars, professional musicians and athletes, politicians, and other world leaders. Figure 5.3 provides an overview of modeling.

According to social cognitive theorists, reinforcement is much more important in shaping behavior than punishment (Bandura & Walters, 1963). Given the perennial concern with deterrence and its effectiveness, this is particularly relevant to the study of crime. Bandura and Walters (1963) suggested that verbal or physical punishment will inhibit aggressive behavior in the presence of the punisher. However, too much or overly severe punishment may lead the recipient to transfer his or her aggression to external objects when out of the presence of the agent. The ramifications for punishment and persistent antisocial behavior are described in the following passage:

> We suspect that most persistent antisocial behavior is maintained through substantial intermittent positive reinforcement, which outweighs the inhibitory effect of punishment, expect insofar as the latter leads to changes in the form of antisocial acts designed to maximize the offender's chances of securing further reinforcements. (Bandura & Walters, 1963, p. 213)

Further, for social cognitive theorists, explaining change from antisocial to prosocial behavior is more difficult to explain than persistence of antisocial behavior (Bandura & Walters, 1963).

Figure 5.3	Visualizing Bandura's Modeling Theory

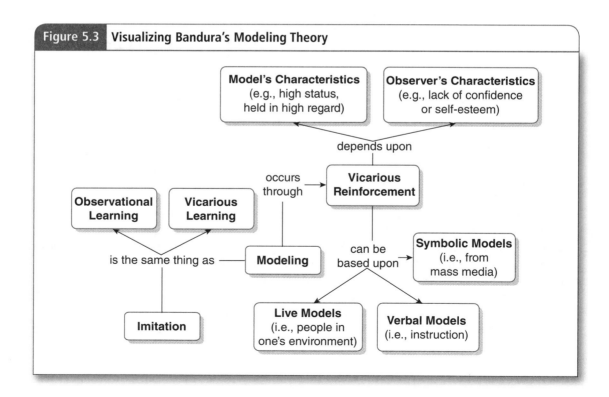

Self-efficacy is another important mechanism in social cognitive theory and is one of the key self-regulatory processes that affect behavior. Self-efficacy is defined as

> the conviction that one can successfully execute the behavior required to produce the [desired] outcomes. . . . The strength of people's convictions in their own effectiveness determines whether they will even try to cope with difficult situations. People fear and avoid threatening situations that they believe themselves unable to handle, whereas they behave affirmatively when they judge themselves capable of handling successfully situations that would otherwise intimidate them. (Bandura, 1977, pp. 79–80)

Other effects of self-efficacy include a reduction in anticipatory fears and inhibitions, expectations of eventual success, and heightened coping efforts. The macro-level counterpart to self-efficacy is collective efficacy. Collective efficacy is particularly relevant to criminology because Sampson and his colleagues developed this concept based on studies on how social disorganization explains differences in neighborhood crime rates. This structural theory will be explained in more depth in Chapter 9.

The next theory of interest is Bandura's (1990) mechanisms of moral disengagement. In this theory, he identifies a number of mechanisms that allow an otherwise normal or "good" person to commit bad acts. This theory clearly not only has parallels with deindividuation theory (because it explains how one's moral inhibitions against certain behaviors are lower) but also greatly resembles Redl and Wineman's (1951) ego defense techniques reviewed in Chapter 4 about psychological positivist theories and Sykes and Matza's (1957) neutralization theory, which will be reviewed in Chapter 7. These theories all argue that people who commit crime develop techniques to diffuse their conscience and lower moral restraints against antisocial and criminal behavior (Maruna & Copes, 2005).

The first mechanism identified by Bandura (1990) is called **moral justification**. This refers to when people justify their actions by redefining the nature of the behavior. For example, killing can be seen as religiously or patriotically redefined as righteous, such as killing in the name of one's god or country. The second mechanism is known as **displacement of responsibility**. In many cases, a person can avoid moral culpability of a bad act by claiming that he or she was just following orders of a higher authority. This is readily apparent in times of war and was at work in the Holocaust in the form of psychologically normal soldiers following commands to kill hundreds of Jews. We can also see this mechanism at work when we examine other atrocities perpetrated by the military, such as the Abu Ghraib prisoner abuse (Zimbardo, 2007).

Diffusion of responsibility is the third mechanism. This occurs when the culpability for the morally problematic act is diffused among a number of people, often through some bureaucratic process. In other words, no one person feels solely responsible as a result of the group decision-making process. Examples of this abound, especially in examples of corporate malfeasance (e.g., the Ford Pinto scandal) (Bandura, 1990). The fourth mechanism is **distorting the consequences of an action**. As the name implies, this involves ignoring, minimizing, distorting, or disbelieving the negative consequences of one's behavior. **Dehumanizing the victim** is the fifth mechanism of moral disengagement and refers to practices designed to remove a perpetrator's empathy by depicting the victims as lower animals or subhuman. This can be achieved through comparisons to lower animals (e.g., the victims are likened to rats, bugs, or other vermin) and through negative labeling (e.g., calling the other group savages, satanic fiends, or using other derogatory racial slang) (Bandura, 1990).

Deindividuation Theory

Deindividuation theorists emphasized and elaborated upon the impact of disinhibiting effects on behavior posited by social cognitive theory. However, their primary inspiration was clearly Le Bon's (1895/1960) writings about crowd and mob mentality. One early effort to derive a theory from these sources was Festinger, Pepitone, and Newcomb's (1952) group deindividuation theory. It should also be noted that Festinger and his colleagues coined the term *deindividuation*.

Deindividuation simply describes the process that occurs in groups in which a person loses his or her individuality and becomes enmeshed in the collective interests of the group. This theory suggests that "under conditions where the member is not individuated in the group, there is likely to occur for the member a reduction of inner restraints against doing various things" (Festinger et al., 1952, p. 382). Deindividuation theorists also argued that individuals have a number of inner restraints restricting behavior that can be diffused under the condition of deindividuation within a group.

Festinger and his colleagues went on to state that some groups (e.g., some racist or activist groups) offer opportunities to satisfy these inner repressed needs and that this makes these groups particularly attractive to some people. They also discuss how groups offer opportunities for individuation and deindividuation. More specifically, they argue that no group can provide both processes at the same time. They stated that groups offering only opportunities for deindividuation tend to be quite unstable (e.g., crowds and other random groups of people). Conversely, groups offering only opportunities for individuation are also not very attractive either. Attractive groups (and, by implication, successful social movements) offer opportunities for both processes at different times (Festinger et al., 1952).

Zimbardo (1970, 2007) specified additional variables associated with the deindividuation process in his extension of the theory offered by Festinger and his colleagues. Some of the key variables identified here include anonymity, displacement of responsibility, physiological arousal, and states of altered consciousness brought on by alcohol and drugs (Zimbardo, 1970). Figure 5.4 provides one way deindividuation can be visualized.

Zimbardo goes on to suggest that deindividuated states cause people to violate social norms and behave in emotional, irrational, and impulsive ways. He also argues that in some cases deindividuated states are tied to larger structures or systemic influences, such as bureaucracy and the chain of command. More specifically, he argues that systems can lay the groundwork for deindividuation because they often encourage mindless deference to authority (Zimbardo, 2007). Figure 5.5 presents an overview of ten key propositions that are of importance in this area.

Research on Psychological Process Theories

Bandura first made a film of one of his young female students beating up a Bobo doll—an inflatable clown-like creature with a weight in the bottom that makes it bob back up when it is knocked down. In the video, Bandura's student punched and kicked the Bobo doll, sat on it, hit with a little hammer, and shouted various aggressive phrases at it. Bandura showed his film to groups of kindergarten children who, as you might predict, liked it a lot. The children then were let out to play with a brand new Bobo doll and a few little hammers while observers sat nearby with pens and clipboards in hand. In mere minutes, the children began to imitate the young lady in the film, hitting, kicking, and even using the hammers on the Bobo doll.

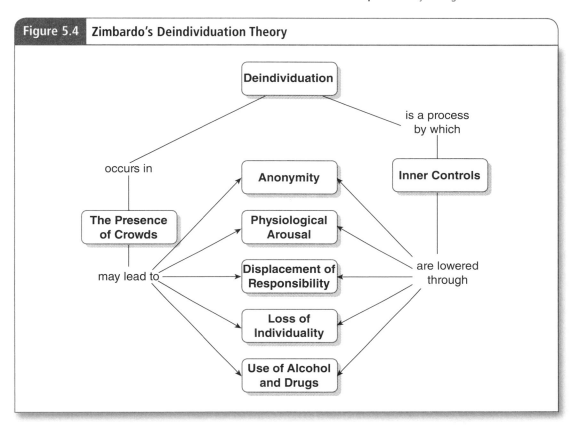

Figure 5.4 Zimbardo's Deindividuation Theory

Figure 5.5 Ten Propositions of Psychological Process Theories

Author	Proposition
Dollard et al., 1939	As anticipation of punishment goes down and frustration goes up, the likelihood of criminality increases.
Miller & Dollard, 1941	Behavior is motivated by drives, learned through imitation, and recurs because of positive reinforcement.
Bandura & Walters, 1963	Antisocial behavior is maintained through substantial intermittent positive reinforcement, which outweighs the inhibitory effects of punishment.
Bandura & Walters, 1963	Punishment is most effective insofar as it leads to changes in antisocial patterns and increases additional pro social reinforcement.
Bandura & Walters, 1963	Persistent antisocial behavior is maintained through substantial intermittent positive reinforcement, which outweighs the inhibitory effect of punishment.

(Continued)

Figure 5.5	(Continued)
Author	**Proposition**
Bandura, 1977	Models held in high esteem and with engaging qualities are more likely to be imitated by others.
Bandura, 1977	Observers with higher self-esteem and confidence will be less affected by modeling.
Bandura, 1990	Moral disengagement from culpability for antisocial behavior can be achieved through a number of techniques, including moral justification, diffusion and displacement of responsibility, distortion of consequences, and dehumanization of the victims.
Festinger et al., 1952	When inner moral restraints are lowered in response to deindividuation, the likelihood of antisocial (and criminal) behavior goes up.
Zimbardo, 1970	In a deindividuated state, anonymity and arousal are heightened, leading individuals to experience a loss of their personal identity that makes them highly susceptible to antisocial influences.

The role and power of imitation should not be underestimated. Bandura did a large number of variations on this study. Responding to criticism that the Bobo dolls were supposed to be hit, he even made a film of the young woman beating up a live clown. When the children went into the other room and found a live clown, they proceeded to punch him, kick him, and even hit him with the little hammers that were provided.

Stanley Milgram (1963, 1974) conducted a famous experiment designed to assess blind obedience. Participants were taken into a room and placed in front of a board of fake controls. They were then told by the experimenter that they were completing a task on learning and that they were to read a list of word pairs to a "learner" and then test the learner on accuracy. The participant read a word and four possible matches. If the learner got the match wrong, the participant was to administer a shock to the learner via a nearby fake control panel (the learners were part of the experiment, and the shock was not real). After each wrong answer, the intensity of the shock increased. The participant was instructed by the experimenter to continue to administer the shocks, stating that it was their duty. As the voltage increased, the learner would begin to complain of pain, yell out in discomfort, and eventually scream that the pain was too much. In the study, 65% of experiment participants administered the experiment's final, and most severe, 450-volt shock.

Participants demonstrated a range of negative emotions about continuing. Some pleaded with the learner, asking the actor to answer questions carefully. Others started to laugh nervously and act strangely in a variety of ways. Some subjects appeared cold, hopeless, somber, or arrogant. Some thought they had killed the learner. Nevertheless, participants continued to obey, discharging the full shock to learners. One man who wanted to abandon the experiment was told the experiment must continue. Instead of challenging the decision of the experimenter, he proceeded, repeating to himself, "It's got to go on, it's got to go on." Only one participant refused to administer shocks past the 300-volt level (Milgram, 1963, 1974).

Milgram's experiment included a number of variations. In one, the learner was not only visible but participants were asked to force the learner's hand to the shock plate so they could deliver the punishment. Less obedience was extracted from subjects in this case. In another variation, participants were instructed to apply whatever voltage they desired for incorrect answers. Participants averaged 83 volts, and only 2.5% of them used the full 450 volts available. This shows most participants were good, average people, not evil individuals. They obeyed only under coercion. In general, more submission was elicited from participants when (1) the authority figure was in close proximity, (2) participants felt they could pass on responsibility to others, and (3) experiments took place under the auspices of a respected organization. The participants, covered by a veil of anonymity, were able to be more aggressive in this situation than they possibly would have in a normal setting.

The role and power of anonymity within deindividuation has been replicated in experiments more connected to criminology than Milgram's original research (Diener, Fraser, Beaman, & Kelem, 1976; Nadler, Goldberg, & Jaffe, 1982). These studies suggest deindividuating conditions cause behavioral changes in undifferentiated individuals but have relatively little effect on the behavior of self-differentiated individuals. Self-differentiated individuals have a more developed sense of self and are less likely to be swayed by group dynamics. Dodd (1985) looked specifically at antisocial and criminal acts among those asked anonymously to explain which acts they would commit if no one would ever find out. Dodd (1985) suggested that his study demonstrated that personal traits and characteristics were not a strong predictor of behavior. Instead, he claimed that in this situation, behavior simply changed from what would be normal for a certain individual to behavior that was not representative of an individual's normal behavior.

Think You Get It?

The role of anonymity was explored in an article about deindividuation and Internet trolling (Bishop, 2013). Trolling is the deliberate use of the Internet to abuse, accuse, or otherwise harass others. Bishop connects trolling to depersonalization, which is characterized by a decreased sense of self-identity (Seigfried, Lovely, & Rogers, 2008) that makes it less likely to view others as worthy of respect (Demetriou & Silke, 2003). Think about a time you witnessed (or participated) in an online insult fest. Did your anonymity matter? What is it about the Internet that can lead some online interactions to get out of hand?

Practical Ramifications of Psychological Process Theories

In his discussion of antisocial aggression, Bandura (1973) argued that the approach to corrections embraced by our criminal justice system is antiquated. Further, he contended that most correctional practices meant to reform are unable to effect meaningful changes in personality. He cited a lack of accountability as one of the prime culprits; recidivism rates are very high, and people generally accept this state of affairs. Internal attempts to evaluate practices are also assumed to be ineffective because the evaluators often have a vested interest in demonstrating success and minimizing failure. Bandura specifies his thoughts on correctional reform in the following passage:

Amelioration of antisocial aggression requires changing not only correctional systems, but also weak psychological theories that prescribe the remedial measures. Interventions must be reoriented from probing for internal malfunctioning to social treatment. By altering social practices in the family and school and changing community influences that foster aggressive behavior, the development of assaultive personalities can largely be prevented. (1973, p. 310)

Bandura (1973) offered several alternative practices based on social cognitive theory. Some of these include institutional remedial systems based on rewards rather than punishments; competency training that offers opportunities to improve intellectual, educational, and/or vocational skills; the development of self-regulatory functions by involving inmates in treatment programs; and encouraging inmates to change their association preferences from antisocial to prosocial groups.

In a similar vein, deindividuation theorists have argued that the modern criminal justice system has a problematic view of human nature and is overly reliant on economic and psychodynamic theories of human behavior involving cost–benefit analyses and individualistic explanations of human behavior (Haney, 2002; Hanson & Yosifon, 2003; Shestowsky & Ross, 2003). Theorists in this area tend to advocate a public health model approach to criminal justice. Zimbardo explains the preferred model:

Most institutions in any society that is invested in an *individualistic* orientation hold up the person as sinner, culpable, afflicted, insane or irrational. Programs of change follow a medical model of dealing only at the individual level of rehabilitation, therapy, re-education, and medical treatments, or punishment and execution. All such programs are doomed to fail if the main causal agent is the situation or system and not the person. . . . We need to adopt a public health model for prevention of evil, of violence, spouse abuse, bullying, prejudice, and more that identifies vectors of social disease to be inoculated against, not dealt with solely at the individual level. A second paradigmatic shift is directed at legal theory to reconsider the extent to which powerful situational and systemic factors must be taken into greater account in sentencing mitigation. (2007, p. viii, italics in original)

Haney (1982, 2002) forcefully argues that our modern system of criminal justice embraces an outdated view informed by individualistic psychology and ignores important psychological research and findings. Deindividuation theorists appeared particularly displeased with the change in criminal justice policy that took place in the 1980s. This change involved increased incarceration and a shift away from the rehabilitative approach to severe punishments. Other problems include a racial disparity in sentencing and excessive instances of incarceration of nonviolent drug offenders (Haney & Zimbardo, 1998).

It should be noted that these commentators offer more than empty critiques and in fact suggest an alternative approach to criminal justice. First, they suggest more consideration be given to situational and contextual effects on human behavior rather than a sole emphasis on a dispositional and individualistic approach. This involves embracing the findings of modern psychology that reveal the importance of social context and interaction in shaping human behavior. Practically, this might involve the increased use of restorative justice approaches and risk assessment that is context sensitive rather than solely focused on individual factors (Haney, 2002).

Figure 5.6	Seven Steps of Psychological Process Theories
Seven Steps	**Psychological Process Theories**
1. Know the History	Emerged during the early 20th century from studies of group behavior and theories of imitation/social learning
2. Acknowledge Assumptions	Humans are blank slates; behavior can be explained through interactions of social context and psychological factors; society is characterized by conflict; laws do not necessarily determine psychological abnormality
3. Problem Focus, Scope, and Level of Explanation	Explain group forms of criminal behavior (e.g., riots, massacres), political, and white-collar crime through social psychological processes
4. Key Terms and Concepts	Frustration-aggression, modeling, self-efficacy, moral disengagement, and deindividuation
5. Respect the Research	Research examines social learning and situational dynamics and how they affect participation in group crime and response to authority
6. Theory/Practice	Cognitive-behavioral therapy in prisons; social solutions to crime involving family and community
7. Mapping the Theory	See Figure 5.7

Criticisms of Psychological Process Theories

Certain aspects of both of these theories remain unproven. One part of social cognitive theory, symbolic learning, has not tested particularly well, and a variety of studies suggest media does not affect behavior in consistent ways. For example, the role of violence in the media on real-world behavior is moderated by numerous factors (Huesmann & Taylor, 2006). In the Bobo doll experiment, some critics have argued that the children were manipulated into responding to the aggressive movie. The children were teased and became frustrated because they could not touch the toys. Many critics believed the experiment was unethical and morally wrong because the children were trained to be aggressive. According to Wortman and Loftus (1992), "How many more of the experiments finding a link between violence on television and aggressive behavior have ethical problems? It is not surprising that the children had long-term implications because of the methods imposed in this experiment" (p. 45).

Likewise, deindividuation was not particularly adept at explaining the willingness to embrace antinormative values. For example, in a meta-analysis of 60 studies on deindividuation, Postmes and Spears (1998) found that the results were better explained by theories that suggested people accept the norms of a group and then act accordingly. Anonymity was still found to be important, as were some of the core tenets of classical deindividuation theory, such as the influence of group norms on individual behavior. Zimbardo (2007) has argued that deindividuation theory is supported by a number of different studies.

Figure 5.7	Mapping Psychological Process Theories

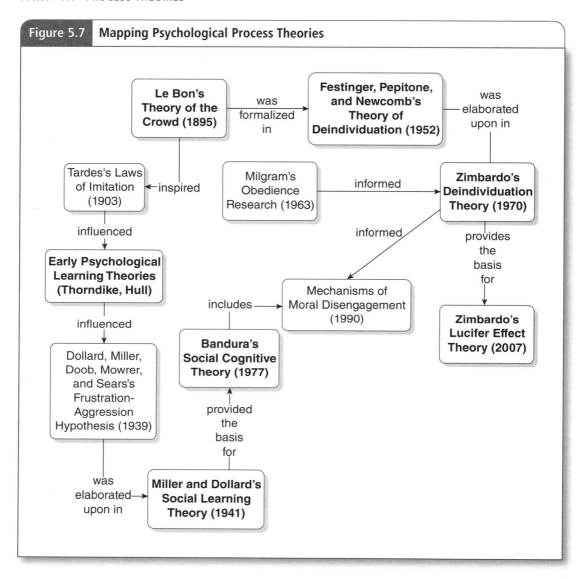

 Research Examples: The Stanford Prison Experiment, Milgram in Liberia, and Police Legitimacy

In previous chapters, we have focused on one research example. However, the import of Milgram's work on anonymity and obedience has had lasting impacts both in criminology and beyond. Milgram's work prompted Zimbardo (1969) to write his initial theory and model of deindividuation. In one of the most famous experiments in criminal justice—and one unlikely to be approved by an institutional review board (IRB) today—Zimbardo created a mock prison environment in the basement of Stanford

University's psychology building. He selected 24 men with no abnormal personality traits and randomly assigned each of them to undertake the role of either a prison guard or a prisoner. Prisoners were made to dress alike in stocking caps and hospital dressing gowns, and they were identified only by a number assigned to them rather than by name. Guards were given uniforms and reflective glasses to hide their faces.

While the experiment was planned to last for two weeks, it was abandoned after only six days because of the sadistic behavior from the guards and signs of depression and extreme stress on the part of the prisoners. Zimbardo attributed this behavior to deindividuation due to immersion within the group, the creation of strong situational dynamics, and the anonymity and diffusion of authority the experiment allowed. Today, Zimbardo continues to use the Stanford Prison Experiment Web site[1] to help those interested to reconsider the experiment in light of the abuse of Iraqi prisoners by US military personnel and private contractors at a prison at Abu Ghraib.

Another example of recent research applicable to criminal justice is behavioral-based games and experiments deigned to explore concepts surrounding legitimacy, destructive obedience, and the role of authorities (Dickson, Gordon, & Huber 2013; Patten, 1977). New research in Liberia suggests that when a legitimate authority instructs them to do so, citizens will make costly contributions to a public good even in the absence of incentives or sanctions. Indeed, citizens may do so even when they know others will not do the same. In Liberia, the site of horrific civil war that left around 150,000 people dead, a cease-fire was implemented in 2003 that a United Nations (UN) mission is attempting to sustain. The UN Security Council extended the peacekeeping mandate for another year in mid-September 2013. In deciding to extend the mandate, the council determined that the situation in Liberia continues to constitute a threat to international peace and security in the region.

In Liberia, while abuse of power undermines citizens' support for all types of authority, the consequences of this abuse are especially severe for peace-builders themselves. Peace-builders who abuse their power induce higher rates of cooperation among citizens in the short term. However, citizens who are abused by peace-builders are more likely to disapprove of their presence and to perceive their actions as unfair. If "peace-building is more than a technical exercise in creating political structures but an important social-psychological exercise in state legitimation" (Talentino, 2007, p. 167), the process of teaching people how to believe in the institutions of the state can be easily undermined (Blattman, Hartman, & Blair, 2014; Wheeldon, 2010a).

In the United States, legitimacy has also become an issue with regards to proactive police policies, such as stop-and-frisk. Tyler, Fagan, and Geller (2014) suggest the traditional public safety versus individual liberty debate has been complicated by findings that stop-and-frisk undermines public perceptions of police professionalism. Perceived police legitimacy is directly shaped by whether police are viewed as exercising their authority fairly and lawfully. Based on the attitudes and experiences of a stratified random sample of young men ages 18 to 26 from 37 neighborhoods in New York City, the study found that police behavior is a major factor in shaping perceptions of police legitimacy. Young men in this age group made up approximately half of the some 4.4 million involuntary police stops that occurred between 2004 and 2012. The paper concludes that only about one in ten stops resulted in an arrest or citation, and as many as one in five may have been legally insufficient. Tyler, Fagan, and Geller argue tactics such as stop-and-frisk "could poison citizen support for and cooperation" with law enforcement and limit the efforts of police to prevent crime (2014, p. 4).

---

[1]For more, see http://www.prisonexp.org/.

Now that you've read the the chapter . . . how can we understand what happened to Alexian Lien? How do the theories discussed in this chapter connect to this event? A total of 15 people were arrested, 55 motorcycles were confiscated, and 69 summonses were issued in connection with the September 29th event. Eleven suspects have since been charged. Sources have reported a total of five off-duty officers were originally present on the West Side Highway and that at least two saw the assault. NYPD ten-year veteran and undercover detective Wojciech Braszczok surrendered to authorities. He and the other co-accused face up to 25 years on the top charge of first-degree gang assault.

Conclusion and Review Questions

In this chapter, we have explored the social cognitive and deindividuation theories and have considered how they are relevant to explaining crime and criminal behavior. These theories offer a different view of offenders from that of the positivist theories reviewed in the previous two chapters. In these theories, great importance is placed on social factors and situational dynamics rather than relying solely on physical characteristics and personality traits to explain criminality. This area has yielded some very well-known research studies, including Bandura, Ross, and Ross's (1961, 1963) Bobo doll experiments, Milgram's (1963, 1974) obedience experiments, and Zimbardo's (1971) Stanford Prison Experiment. These theories advocate criminal justice system reform based on a public health model that encourages reform systems and subsystems responsible for dealing with aggression, antisocial, and criminal behavior.

CHAPTER REVIEW

1. What assumptions are made by psychological process theories?

2. What is the level of explanation, problem focus, and scope of these theories?

3. Explain the historical and social context that gave rise to these process theories.

4. Compare and contrast research on psychological process theories. What are some examples of important research on these theories?

5. How have psychological process theories been applied to the criminal justice system?

CHAPTER

6

Differential Association and Social Learning Theories

Chapter Overview and Objectives

In this chapter, we explore differential association and social learning theories of criminal behavior. Building on the psychological process theories introduced in Chapter 5, and with the recognition of the important role played by socialization, these theories focus explicitly on the family, school, peers, and the longer-term processes by which people develop, acquire, and integrate social norms into their own personal actions and inactions. Of specific interest in this chapter are differential association (Sutherland, 1942), lower-class focal concerns (Miller, 1958), social learning theory (Burgess & Akers, 1966; Akers, 1998), subculture of violence theory (Wolfgang & Ferracuti, 1967), and the so-called code of the street (Anderson, 1999).

In criminology, differential association and social learning theories seek to describe the process of criminal and delinquent socialization, and they specifically focus on how criminal behavior is observed, learned, and executed. One question is whether families or peers play the most important role in delinquent behavior. For social learning theorists, a renewed focus on the role of modeling and interacting with others has led to a more developed theory of learning. Often applied to a variety of social interactions to explain how people learn the values, attitudes, techniques, and motives for criminal behavior, social learning theory remains one of the most tested and supported theories in criminology and has significant practical implications for social and criminal justice policy.

By the end of this chapter, readers should be able to:

- Understand the history of and assumptions made by differential association and social learning perspectives
- Be familiar with the problem focus, scope, and level of explanation of the differential association and social learning theories
- Appreciate the complexity of causality and how it relates to the social sciences and criminology

- Consider how these learning explanations could be more fully integrated with biological and psychological theories
- Explain the practical implications of differential association and social learning theories in the criminal justice system and wider society

The Differential Association and Social Learning Tradition

The differential association and social learning theories attribute criminal behavior to improper socialization and delinquent peers. This set of theories makes use of sociological and psychological concepts to explain why some people commit crime. One central theme of these theories is that one's environment is crucial to understanding learning patterns. According to these theorists, people learn to behave criminally by "hanging out with the wrong crowd." A strong and consistent finding in criminology is the role of delinquent peer associations in subsequent criminality (Andrews & Bonta, 2003).

Like the psychological process theories reviewed in the last chapter, these theories also have their roots in the work of Gabriel Tarde's (1903) three laws of imitation. Edwin Sutherland's nine propositions of differential association include the ideas of Tarde, but Sutherland expanded on them and was much more specific. In contrast to others in the learning perspective, Ronald Akers used a social-psychological approach, including the concept of reinforcement, which increases or decreases the

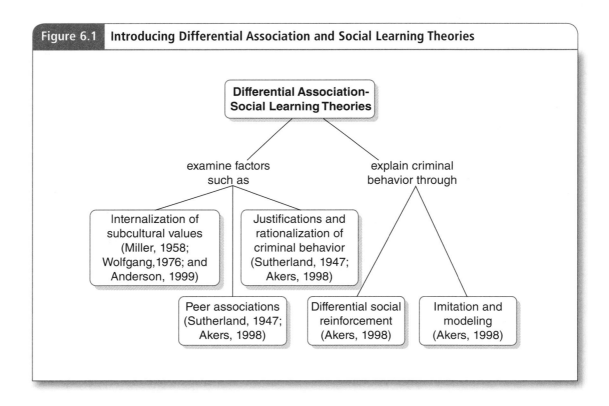

Figure 6.1   Introducing Differential Association and Social Learning Theories

strength of a behavior. In addition, he later incorporated some aspects of modeling and imitation first proposed by Albert Bandura that were discussed in the previous chapter.

> **As you read this chapter, consider . . .** three Delaware day care workers were arrested in 2012 after they were accused of forcing toddlers to fight each other while recording the fights on a camera phone. Police said one child could be heard crying, saying, "He's pinching me," and a day care worker responded, "No pinching, only punching." As you read through this chapter, consider how this experience might affect these kids.

Seven Steps of Criminological Thinking

History and Social Context of Differential Association and Social Learning Perspective

Differential association and social learning theories can be connected to the symbolic-interactionist approach developed by Charles Horton Cooley and George Herbert Mead, and later by W. I. Thomas (Lilly et al., 2011). **Symbolic interactionism** refers to the idea that people form opinions of themselves based upon how other people treat and react to them. This approach is also important to understanding labeling theory and will be revisited in Chapter 8. For now, we will focus on a common and important starting point for this trajectory.

Differential association emerged in the 1930s as a product of the Chicago school. The Chicago school refers to the first sociology department, which was founded in the University of Chicago in 1892. The Chicago school researchers were quite rigorous and supported their theories with both quantitative and qualitative forms of research. They claimed that the city was a "microcosm of humanity" and thought of cities as social laboratories that warranted study and observation (Williams & McShane, 2010). The influential years of the Chicago school spanned from the late 19th century until the 1950s. The school was especially dominant between World War I and the end of the Great Depression; these were periods of great growth and societal change.

Of specific interest to criminologists is the work that took place during the 1920s and 1930s, often referred to as social disorganization theory (Shaw & McKay, 1942/1969). Members of the Chicago school observed that historical transformations had changed how society functioned. Some of these changes also affected the prevalence of crime and societal attitudes about criminals. For example, during this period cities grew rapidly from massive waves of European immigrants, African Americans fleeing the post–Civil War South, and an influx of displaced farm workers as smaller family farms became less common (Lilly et al., 2011). The intensified population shift from a rural, homogeneous, agrarian community to a vast, heterogeneous, industrial metropolis had many social consequences. The influx of new inhabitants and greater mixing of ethnicities in American cities led to conflicts between older, more established residents and the recent immigrants. In many cases, the immigrant groups were blamed for increasing levels of crime (Williams & McShane, 2010).

Edwin Sutherland, founder of differential association theory, was one of the key figures in the Chicago school and had a great impact on the field of criminology. He was heavily influenced by criminological work done in the Chicago school and the ways in which social disorganization and cultural transmission impacted neighborhoods. These themes were explored through the Chicago school based on immigration studies of the Polish community in the city (Lutters & Ackerman, 1996). The central idea of social disorganization theory is that the environment of the city, dramatically different from that of the agricultural communities of most immigrants, actually acts as a force to render the structures, relationships, and norms of an immigrant's homeland irrelevant to his or her new living situation. With their traditional social structures in flux, immigrants had to radically restructure those relationships to fit the new environment or abandon them altogether and rebuild based on new, adopted norms. As a result, certain neighborhoods were more prone to crime than others. Shaw and McKay (1969) argued that pro-criminal values are transmitted from generation to generation in a process called cultural transmission.

Thorsten Sellin's (1938) culture conflict theory also had a great impact on Sutherland's future work. Sellin proposed two forms of cultural conflict through his theory—primary and secondary. **Primary conflict** refers to conflicts that arise between a recent immigrant's culture and the wider culture. For example, many cultures around the world have radically different views of masculinity and femininity when compared to common attitudes in North American culture. In some cultures, men are dominant and are expected to defend family honor; women are expected to be submissive. This sometimes results in "honor killings" in which males kill female relatives because they are believed to have dishonored their family (Williams & McShane, 2010). While such a practice may be condoned in some cultures, it is obviously not in line with Western norms of equality and justice.

Another type of conflict, **secondary conflict**, can arise within some groups that develop cultures of their own with values that differ from those of the wider culture. Most people would refer to these groups as subcultures (Williams & McShane, 2010). Subcultures will be explored later in the chapter. For now, the main point is that members of the Chicago school were interested in how the transition in all aspects of social life—vocational, religious, and familial—impacted neighborhoods and crime rates. This interest was based on what researchers were observing in neighborhoods in Chicago. This focus led to research on social patterns, and, as we shall see, remains a part of theories considered relevant today.

Assumptions of Differential Association and Social Learning Theories

Theories in this area all share a *tabula rasa* ("blank slate") conception of human nature. In other words, people are essentially products of their learning histories and interactions with others. People may be different from one another in superficial ways, but all people learn to commit crime (or obey the law) from observing and interacting with other people. These theories are clearly positivist theories in the sense that they assume that criminals and noncriminals can be distinguished from each other. They are also determinist because they assume that behavior is determined by factors beyond one's control. However, these theories are different from the biological and psychological positivist theories discussed in Chapters 3 and 4 because they focus on social factors that involve interactions and connections with friends, peers, family, and relatives. Social process theories, along with the social structural theories discussed in the next section of this text, are sometimes referred to as examples of sociological positivism.

While many social process theories are consensus oriented and assume that laws emerge from general societal acceptance of definitions of right and wrong, they are not based on a "strong" approach to consensus. In general, differential association and social learning theories typically acknowledge that numerous systems of competing values and norms exist. Some even dispute the nature of specific laws, such as certain forms of drug use and gambling (Williams & McShane, 2010). They all consider learning as a social process that occurs as a function of observing, retaining, and replicating behavior observed in others. As such, these theories emphasize the importance of modeling the behaviors, attitudes, and emotional reactions of others. Now that the key assumptions of differential association and social learning theories have been identified, let's focus on understanding their problem focus, scope, and level of explanation.

Problem Focus, Scope, and Level of Explanation of Differential Association and Social Learning Theories

The problem focus of all of the differential association and social learning theories is criminal behavior. Depending upon the theory, the scope may be quite general and attempt to explain all forms of criminal behavior. However, there are also more specific theories that seek to explain specific types of criminal behavior, such as violence or other subcultural behavior. In general, these specific theories are much less useful for explaining crime committed in isolation and without previous criminal interactions. These theories also tend to downplay the significance of certain biological factors that may affect the learning process, such as impulsivity or insensitivity to pain, as discussed in Chapters 3 and 4. For these theories, the focus is on how interactions influence whether individuals adopt or avoid certain behaviors.

Theories in this area are posed at either the micro or meso level of explanation. On the one hand, Sutherland's (1942) differential association theory and Akers's (1998) social learning theory focus on explaining individual learning histories and would be considered micro-level theories (Williams & McShane, 2010). On the other hand, subcultural theories such as Miller's (1998) focal concerns, Wolfgang and Ferracuti's (1967) theory of subcultural violence, and Anderson's (1995) code of the street consider the importance of structural factors and group norms in criminal behavior. As such, we think they should be considered meso-level theories.

Key Terms and Concepts in Differential Association and Social Learning Theories

Differential Association Theory

The earliest contribution in this area is Edwin Sutherland's differential association theory that was first proposed in 1939 and finalized in 1947. This theory focuses on explaining peer influences among deviant youths as a special mechanism of becoming criminal. Sutherland asserts that when favorable peer experiences with deviance exceed unfavorable experiences with deviance, a person is more likely to engage in unlawful acts. Sutherland (1939) was trying to provide a scientific theory that could explain variations in criminal behavior between individuals. This was, in part, a response to a damning government report that characterized the field of criminology as unscientific and poorly developed (Laub, 2004). As one way of countering these criticisms, Sutherland laid the theory of differential association out in nine propositions. They appear in their original form in Figure 6.2.

Figure 6.2	Propositions of Differential Association

1. Criminal behavior is learned.

2. Criminal behavior is learned in interaction with other persons in a process of communication.

3. The principal part of the learning of criminal behavior occurs within intimate personal groups.

4. When criminal behavior is learned, the learning includes techniques of committing the crime, which are sometimes very complicated, sometimes simple, and the specific direction of motives, drives, rationalizations, and attitudes.

5. The specific direction of motives and drives is learned from definitions of the legal codes as favorable or unfavorable.

6. A person becomes delinquent because of an excess of definitions favorable to violation of law over definitions unfavorable to violation of the law.

7. Differential associations may vary in frequency, duration, priority, and intensity.

8. The process of learning criminal behavior by association with criminal and anti-criminal patterns involves all of the mechanisms that are involved in any other learning.

9. While criminal behavior is an expression of general needs and values, it is not explained by those needs and values, since non-criminal behavior is an expression of the same needs and values.

Source: Adapted from Sutherland & Cressey (1974, pp. 75–77).

It may be useful to further explain these propositions. Basically, the theory claims that one learns the **physical techniques** for committing crime, such as breaking into and hotwiring a car, as well as the **neutralizations** or **rationalizations** used to justify that crime, from other people through social interaction. Intimate personal groups could refer to one's immediate family, close relatives, friends, or peer acquaintances. **Definitions** can be thought of as values or attitudes toward the law. Thus, differential association refers to the interactions that one has with others and how these interactions vary from individual to individual. It is not merely the amount of interactions that matter, but the weight and perceived importance of various experiences (Williams & McShane, 2010). Sutherland believed that learning crime was like learning other kinds of behavior. He did not believe his theory could explain all crime—for example, it excludes most murders, crimes of passion, crimes from emotional stress, irrational and impulsive crimes (Sutherland & Cressey, 1974)—but he believed it could explain many other types of crime.

Sutherland and Cressey (1974) also offered a macro-level counterpart to differential association called differential social organization. Differential social organization refers to areas where there are widespread differential associations encouraging crime. Sutherland used this term because high-crime areas can, in fact, be characterized by some group organization. In some cases, these groups are geared toward criminal activities, and while Sutherland was not trying to explain crime rates per se, he was interested in why some areas had more crime than others (Akers, 1998).

Sutherland's theory gave rise to a number of branches of new theories. One of these branches is sometimes referred to as the subcultural strain theories and includes theories proposed by Cohen (1955) and Cloward and Ohlin (1960). While related to social interaction theories, subcultural strain theories focus more on structural factors that give rise to criminal behavior. We discuss these in greater detail in subsequent chapters. For now, try to visualize differential association, which has been defined as "the process by which one is exposed to normative definitions favorable or unfavorable to illegal or law-abiding behavior" (Akers, 1997, p. 64). According to Sutherland, merely associating with criminals is not enough for a person to adopt criminal definitions. Instead, the content and pattern of the learning and interaction is important. Figure 6.3 provides one way to visualize differential association.

Differential association suggested new ways to think about how people learned behaviors. Building on this work, other theoretical developments emphasized the acquisition of criminal values as the central cause of criminal behavior.

| Figure 6.3 | **Visualizing Differential Association** |

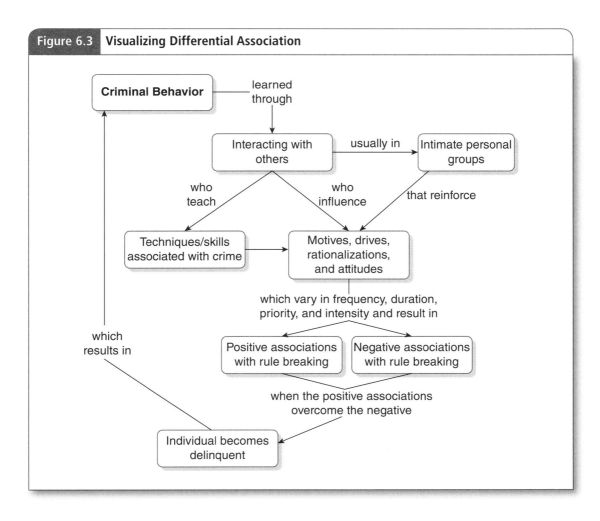

The Theory of Lower-Class Focal Concerns

Influenced by the Chicago school, subcultural learning theories emphasized cultural and learning factors. An early example of a theory in this branch is Miller's (1958) **theory of lower-class focal concerns**. This theory emerged from ethnographic research conducted by Miller in lower-class communities in the Boston area. Miller (1958) argued that a separate lower-class culture exists, and thus the scope of the theory is "law violating acts committed by members of adolescent street corner groups in lower-class communities" (1958, p. 1). This theory suggests that there are particular values or focal concerns that distinguish lower-class culture from middle- and upper-class culture. These differences can explain the motivation for criminal behavior because, according to the theory, lower-class communities have values that encourage people to break the law and an inability to deal with the practical consequences of these values, be they legal or interpersonal. According to this theory, there are six key values that distinguish the cultural system of the lower-class community from the wider middle-class culture: toughness, smartness, excitement, trouble, fate, and autonomy. These are presented in Figure 6.4.

There is great deal of importance placed upon being a "tough guy" and not being viewed by others as soft. **Toughness** is the first focal concern and encompasses both physical prowess and mental and emotional control. Miller (1958) speculates that this is partly a product of the proliferation of female-headed households in the lower classes. This has created an almost obsessive concern with displays of masculinity and machismo. Interestingly, this theme is echoed in other subcultural

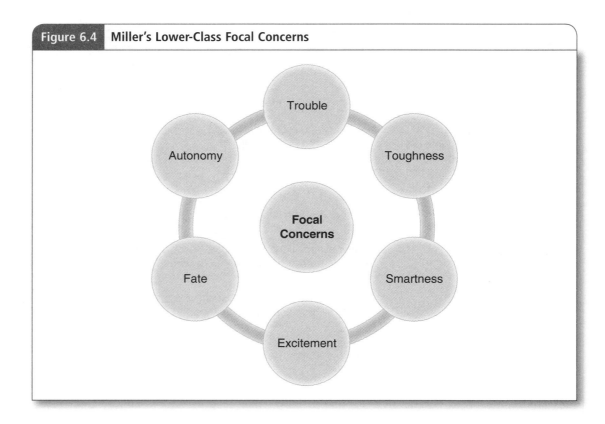

Figure 6.4   Miller's Lower-Class Focal Concerns

theories discussed later in this chapter (Anderson, 1999). The second focal concern, **smartness**, refers not to book learning or education but instead to "street smarts." The ability to both con people out of material goods and to see through scams is valued. **Trouble**, the third focal concern, is one's ability to deal with legal and interpersonal problems. For example, for younger males this may refer to issues that arise from drinking and sex.

According to Miller (1958), the emphasis on **excitement** arises because the lives of lower-class people can be quite monotonous. Great value is placed on "thrills," or risk-taking. The notion of **fate** is also an important focal concern of the lower classes. Miller argues that many lower-class people see themselves as having very little control over their own destinies. This leads to a variety of behavior associated with the lower classes, including a fascination with gambling or playing the lottery. Finally, having **autonomy** over oneself is a major concern in the lower classes. While this may sound like the polar opposite of fate, it refers to exerting control over situations and taking charge when possible. During his research, Miller (1958) noted that people in the lower classes are concerned with "not being pushed around" or manipulated by other people, especially authority figures.

It is important to understand that following these values does not always cause one to run afoul of the law, but the likelihood of crime rises because illegal solutions are often seen as normal. For example, if a gang member is conned, then the expectation is that there will be a demonstration of toughness to ensure that person is not conned again in the future. Subcultural theories remained a hot topic in criminology for several years. However, by the 1960s, interest had waned considerably because of new interest in labeling theory (Miller et al., 2011). During the late 1960s, there was a resurgence of interest in subcultural theories.

Subculture of Violence Theory

Wolfgang and Ferracuti's (1967) subculture of violence theory is an interdisciplinary attempt to explain how the use of violence becomes normal in certain subcultures. Instead of the specific lower-class subculture as suggested by Miller (1958), this theory views subcultures as overlapping with the dominant culture. The scope here is limited to group or subcultural criminal behavior involving violence and aggressive behavior. The authors point out that subcultures are often attached to geographic areas and may be smaller—limited to neighborhoods—or may define an entire region, such as the American South (Miller et al., 2011). Whatever its advancements over previous attempts to explain subcultures, Wolfgang and Ferracuti's (1967) theory did not attempt to explain how these subcultures originate.

Wolfgang and Ferracuti (1967) suggested that the use of violence is dictated by situational considerations and is not viewed as unacceptable when used properly. Proper use of violence is defined through differential associations, learning, and modeling. One's conscience or moral values can be overridden and guilt will not be experienced as long as violence is used at the proper time and in accordance with the definitions that have been learned. Their theory draws upon three main sources: culture conflict and differential association, psychological learning theory, and research about homicide and other violent crimes. Figure 6.5 presents the propositions of the theory, and Figure 6.6 is one example of how the theory might be visualized.

The Code of the Street

Another development in understanding how subcultures can be related to crime is Anderson's (1999) so-called code of the street. Anderson was influenced by both Sutherland's (1966/1947)

Figure 6.5	Propositions of Subculture of Violence Theory

1. No subculture can be totally different from or totally in conflict with the society of which it is a part.

2. To establish the existence of a subculture of violence does not require that the actors sharing in these basic value elements should express violence in all situations.

3. The potential to resort or willingness to resort to violence in a variety of situations emphasizes the penetrating and diffusive character of this cultural theme.

4. The subcultural ethos of violence may be shared by all ages in a sub-society, but this ethos is most prominent in a limited age group, ranging from late adolescence to middle age.

5. The counter-norm is nonviolence.

6. The development of favorable attitudes toward, and the use of, violence in a subculture usually involve learned behavior and a process of differential learning, association, or identification.

7. The use of violence in a subculture is not necessarily viewed as illicit conduct and the users therefore do not have to deal with feelings of guilt about their aggression.

Source: Adapted from Wolfgang & Ferracuti (1967, p. 317).

Figure 6.6	Visualizing Violence and Subcultural Learning

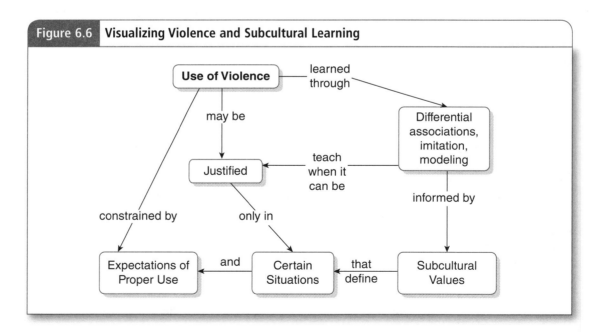

differential association theory and the subcultural theories that followed (Miller, 1958; Wolfgang & Ferracuti, 1967). Anderson's theory is derived from ethnographic research in which he examined both inner-city and middle-class or "well-to-do" neighborhoods in the city of Philadelphia. The scope of the theory is limited to interpersonal violence among inner-city youth. The central thesis is that the rules of civil law have been weakened and replaced with something he calls the code of the street. According to Anderson (1999), most inner-city families are law abiding and try to instill respect for the law in their children. However, some inner-city families are so dysfunctional that they fail to instill positive values. Children are poorly parented and spend a majority of their time on the streets "campaigning for respect" (Lilly et al., 2011, p. 54). These individuals eventually become alienated from society and its institutions, including the police and criminal justice system.

This code often involves obtaining status and respect through displays of violence and aggressive behavior. In other words, if one is disrespected or "dissed," one must respond with aggression and violence. It is also crucial that others do not see one as weak; again, displays of aggression and violence are thought to ensure that one is viewed as strong (Miller et al., 2011). It is important to note that actually committing violence is not integral to the code, but rather one must display a willingness to commit violence. This willingness can be communicated in a variety of ways, including words, phrases, looks, gestures, and postures. Even habits such as personal grooming (e.g., facial hair and hairstyles) and attire, such as clothing and jewelry, can alert others to a potential for violence (Bernard et al., 2010).

Anderson (1999) argues that structural factors have also contributed to the rise of the code. He claims that the desire for respect arises in part because conventional avenues in which one can gain respect are often very limited for people who live in the inner cities. They also face numerous economic barriers, and the opportunities for respectable, well-paying jobs are rare. The code is also thought to affect boys more than girls because of its emphasis on masculinity. The key elements of the code of the street are outlined in Figure 6.7.

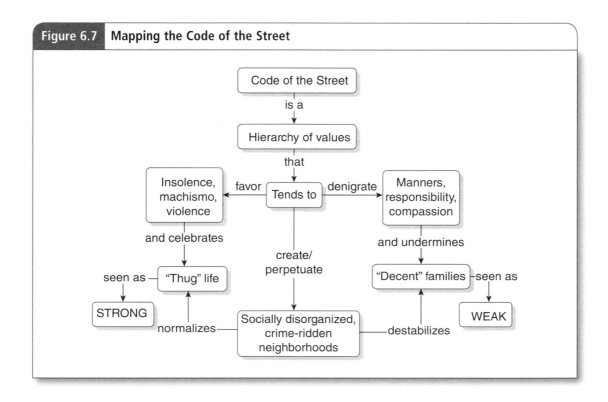

Figure 6.7   Mapping the Code of the Street

Figure 6.8	**Key Propositions in Social Learning Theory**

1. Criminal behavior is learned according to the principles of operant conditioning.

2. Criminal behavior is learned both in nonsocial situations that are reinforcing or discriminative and through social interaction in which the behavior of other persons is reinforcing or discriminative for criminal behavior.

3. The principal part of learning criminal behavior occurs in those groups which comprise the individual's major source of reinforcements.

4. The learning of criminal behavior, including specific techniques, attitudes, and avoidance procedures, is a function of the effective and available reinforcers, and the existing reinforcement contingencies.

5. The specific class of behaviors which are learned and their frequency of occurrence are a function of the reinforcers which are effective and available, and the rules or norms by which these reinforcers are applied.

6. Criminal behavior is a function of norms that are discriminative for criminal behavior, the learning of which takes place when such behavior is more highly reinforced than noncriminal behavior.

7. The strength of criminal behavior is a direct function of the amount, frequency, and probability of its reinforcement.

Source: Adapted from Burgess & Akers, 1966, pp. 128–147.

Akers's Social Learning Theory

Akers's (1966, 1998) social learning theory is one of the most important theories to understand in this chapter. It combines elements of previous theories and research and outlines propositions in useful and testable ways. The theory was originally proposed in an article written by Burgess and Akers in 1966 and was called differential social reinforcement theory, perhaps to avoid confusing it with Bandura's psychological version of social learning theory that emerged around the same time. In later articles, Akers has consistently referred to his theory as social learning theory and has elaborated upon and clarified various aspects of it to counter criticisms leveled by other scholars (Akers, 1998). The theory's key propositions are included in Figure 6.8.

Social learning theory is a complex theory. As such, it is necessary to be familiar with several key concepts and learning mechanisms central to the theory. Burgess and Akers (1966) used several concepts proposed by Sutherland, including differential association and definitions favorable to the violation of law. In order to further explain the learning process described by Sutherland, Burgess and Akers (1966) also incorporated several learning mechanisms from psychological learning theory. According to (1998), the two primary learning mechanisms are differential reinforcement and imitation. **Differential reinforcement** occurs in response to actual or anticipated rewards and punishments that become attached to different forms of behavior. This portion of the theory is derived from Skinner's (1953) operant conditioning theory in psychology. Operant conditioning holds that when behaviors are followed by a reinforcing stimulus, this results in an increased probability that the behaviors will occur in the future. These reinforcements and punishments may be social or nonsocial in nature.

Social reinforcements are considered to be the most important in shaping behavior and refer to the status or praise from peers that may occur in response to criminal or deviant behavior. Nonsocial reinforcement can include the intrinsic pleasurable effects of drug use or the sneaky thrill or adrenaline rush associated with crime. **Imitation** (or **modeling**) refers to observational learning and has its roots in Bandura's social learning theory from psychology. The likelihood of the behavior being modeled by the observer is affected by several factors, including the characteristics of the model, the type of behavior being observed, and the consequences of the behavior seen by the observer (Akers, 1997). Akers (1998) also points out that imitation is much more important to the initial acquisition of novel behavior than in the maintenance of such behavior. The content of the learning is reflected in the definitions (i.e., beliefs and attitudes) that are formed in the learning process. Akers (1998) expands on the concept of definitions to explain exactly how they interact with the learning process and proposes two main types of definitions.

First, there are **general definitions** that provide rules for behavior and are learned during the socialization process. These rules are based upon moral, religious, and conventional norms/values (e.g., it is wrong to kill, it is wrong to steal, one should follow the law). Second, there are **specific definitions**; these can be thought of as exceptions to the rules provided in the general definitions. These might include the idea that it is okay to kill in self-defense, okay to steal food if one is starving, or okay to do drugs because it is a victimless crime. Definitions favorable to crime are acquired through the learning process and correspond to the type of reinforcement they provide. **Positive definitions** encourage criminal behavior and involve some form of positive reinforcement. For example, a person may learn that displays of violence and aggression may secure status and elicit praise or respect from their peers or friends. **Neutralizing definitions** are learned through negative reinforcement and help to justify, excuse, or rationalize criminal behavior. We will return to neutralization in the next chapter. For now let's try to visualize social learning theory. Figure 6.9 provides an example of this.

Akers (1998) has gone further to explain how differential associations affect the learning process over time. Similar to Sutherland's (1966/1947) theory, in social learning theory the notion of differential association refers to interactions with one's intimate personal groups. The impact that differential associations have on behavior is determined by several different factors: frequency, duration, intensity, and priority. First, frequency refers to how consistent interactions are over a period of time. The more often the interactions occur, the more of an effect they will have on behavior. Second, duration is the actual amount of time spent in the interaction. Interactions that stretch over long periods of time will influence behavior more than ones that are short term. Third, some interactions are thought to be more intense or important to the learner. Interactions with high intensity are thought to have more of an impact on the learner. Finally, interactions that occur early in life are said to have higher priority. So, generally, interactions that begin in childhood will have more of an impact than others that occur later in life (Akers, 1997).

Akers (1998) also clarifies the notion of intimate personal groups and claims that one's primary groups, such as family and friends, are most important but that secondary groups, such as acquaintances from work and/or school, also play a role in the learning process. He also points out that the composition of these groups will change throughout one's life. In adolescence, friends are normally met through leisure activities and school; later in life, friends are met through work or through living proximity, and religious activities become more important.

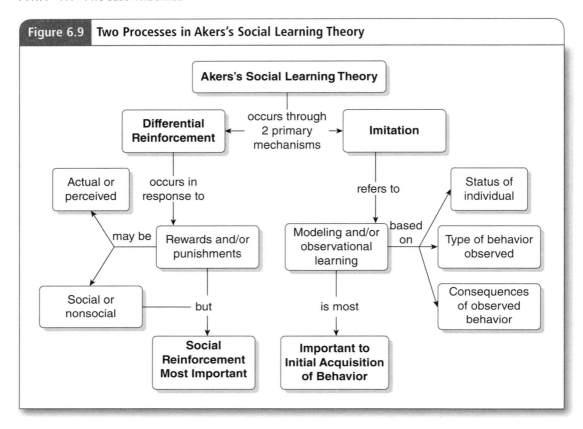

Figure 6.9   Two Processes in Akers's Social Learning Theory

Research on Differential Association and Social Learning Theories

In general, no characteristic of an individual is more likely to predict criminal behavior than the number of delinquent peers an individual identifies as friends (Jang, 1999). The concepts of differential association, definitions, imitation, and differential reinforcement have been explored separately as well as in various combinations in the research literature. Of these social learning concepts, differential association has been examined most frequently and has consistently been shown to be a significant factor in explaining criminal and deviant behaviors (Conway & McCord, 2002; Daigle, Cullen, & Wright, 2007; Losel, Bliesener, & Bender, 2007; Sellers, Cochrane, & Winfree, 2003; Steffensmeier & Ulmer, 2003).

Ron Akers initially explored social learning theory through four studies. These include the Boys Town study, the Iowa study, the elderly drinking study, and the rape and sexual coercion study. The first of these projects is by far the most well-known and cited (Akers & Jensen, 2006). In the Boys Town study, survey data from over 3,000 students in grades 7 through 12 in eight school districts in the Midwest was collected and analyzed. While the majority of the questions focused on substance abuse, the data allowed Akers and his colleagues to test social learning theory in more detail. The research that emerged from the Boys Town study provided overwhelming support for the propositions of social learning. The social learning variables explained both limited alcohol and drug use and affected the probability that adolescents would go on to more serious and significant substance abuse.

Social learning theory has remained one of the core criminological paradigms over the last four decades. Further, a large body of scholarship has emerged testing various propositions specified by the theory. For example, Cao (2004) suggests that social learning theory has "received empirical support" and that whether "tested alone, or with other criminological theories," the perspective's "main arguments are largely supported" (2004, p. 97). Pratt, Cullen, Sellers, and Thomas Winfree (2010) point out that numerous quantitative studies have synthesized the existing research on predictors of crime, recidivism, and institutional misconduct and found that variables identified by social learning theory—antisocial attitudes and antisocial peer/parental associations—are among the strongest predictors of offending behavior (Andrews & Bonta, 2003; Gendreau, Goggin, & Law, 1997; Gendreau, Little, & Goggin, 1996).

The research literature has consistently found that there is a strong relationship between childhood experiences of violence in the family and early childhood aggression. Hotton (2003) examined childhood aggression and found that exposure to violence in the home was significantly related to aggressive behavior among children. The study used data from the National Longitudinal Survey of Children and Youth (NLSCY), developed by Human Resources Development Canada and Statistics Canada. Hotton found that approximately 32% of children exposed to violence were considered highly aggressive, compared with 16% of children not exposed. The study also revealed that hostile and ineffective parenting practices were related to higher levels of child aggression.

While exposure to violence in the family may be a stronger predictor of aggression in childhood, peer influences appear to be more important in adolescence. Research on adolescent aggression has shown that exposure to violent or delinquent peers is a stronger predictor of violence among adolescents than the influence of family. Daigle et al. (2007) examined gender differences in the predictors of juvenile delinquency. The study used data from the National Longitudinal Survey of Adolescent Health (Add Health), a school-based panel study of adolescents in grades 7 to 12 in the United States between 1994 and 1996. The study found that the factors that predicted delinquency were similar for both boys and girls and that the most significant predictor for both was the number of delinquent peers they interacted with. Negative peer associations, then, appear to be better predictors of delinquency and aggression in adolescence than negative family experiences.

Practical Ramifications of Social Learning Theory

Crime prevention policies are rarely designed with social learning theory in mind (Lilly et al., 2011). However, social learning theory has impacted the world of criminal justice policy and practice in a variety of ways. As presented above, the main tenet of social learning theory is that deviant and criminal conduct is learned and maintained through associations with family and, more important, peer networks. Based on this logic, it follows that antisocial behavior could be modified "to the extent that one is able to manipulate those same processes or the environmental contingencies that impinge on them" (Akers & Sellers, 2004, p. 101). From this perspective, policymakers should focus on developing and implementing preventive and rehabilitative programs that use social learning variables to change behavior in a positive way. Examples of programs guided by social learning principles include behavioral modification, delinquency prevention, peer counseling, and even gang interventions. One goal of these programs is to provide positive experiences and role models for offenders, especially younger offenders, in the hopes of diminishing the likelihood of future criminal or delinquent behavior.

Mentoring programs are probably the best example of how social learning theories can be integrated into policy. When organized through regular meetings over an extended period of time, these programs can foster positive relationships between adults and juveniles that aid in addressing at-risk behavior. Such behavior might include poor school performance, substance abuse, associating with delinquent peers, and dropping out of school. Based on a meta-analysis of 55 peer-mentoring evaluations, Dubois and his colleagues (2002) found mentoring was most successful when programs adopted a range of theory-based and empirically based "best practices" to guide relationships between mentors and mentees. Summarized by Small (2008), best practice includes frequent contacts of an hour or more, relationships lasting one year or longer, regular participation in moderate to highly structured and well-organized activities, a willingness to discuss personal relationships and social issues, and developing relationships with key persons in the youth's life, especially parents.

Another area in which the application of social learning principles has been particularly popular is in the area of correctional treatment (Andrews & Bonta, 2003; Ross & Ross, 1995). Most forms of rehabilitation in prison rely partly upon concepts provided by social learning theory and other cognitive-behavioral learning theories from psychology. Again, some have argued that these cognitive-behavioral theories are compatible with social learning theory because all emphasize learning mechanisms (Akers, 1998). The notion that associations with delinquent or criminal peers are important in determining risk of further criminal behavior is a recurring theme in many correctional treatment programs.

Figure 6.10	Seven Steps of Differential Association and Social Learning Theories
Seven Steps	**Differential Association and Social Learning Theories**
1. Know the History	Foundations located in symbolic interactionist perspective and formulation of differential association theories in the mid-20th century, alongside Chicago school theories of social disorganization
2. Acknowledge Assumptions	Humans are blank slates; example of social positivism (i.e., behavior determined by social factors); "weak" consensus theories that acknowledge differences in norms and values in society
3. Problem Focus, Scope, and Level of Explanation	Subcultural and group criminal behavior; general theories that address many forms of crime; focus on social processes that give rise to criminal behavior
4. Key Terms and Concepts	Differential association, social learning, and subculture of violence
5. Respect the Research	Studies focus on peer influences and other social processes that explain deviant and criminal behavior
6. Theory/Practice	Social solutions to crime, including peer mentoring programs, gang interventions, and cognitive-behavioral therapy in prisons
7. Mapping the Theory	See Figure 6.11

Figure 6.11 Mapping Learning: From the Chicago School to the Code of the Street

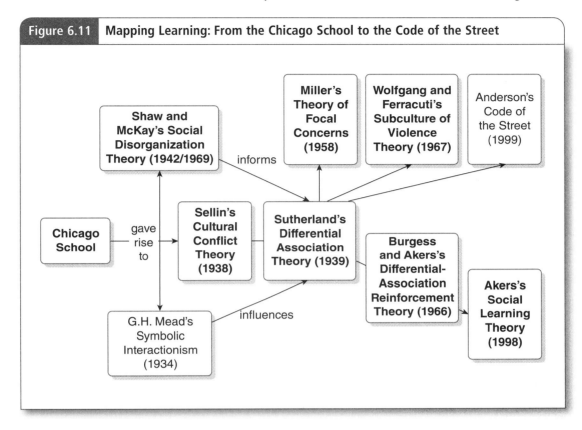

Think You Get It?

These theories should remind us of how key people, experiences, and times have shaped who we are today. A life history interview involves gathering data about an individual to "paint a picture" of who that person is. Instead of a random collection of facts, this approach seeks to compile an account of the person's life story, including important themes in the person's life that reflect the development of his or her personality and relationships with others. Review the key concepts in social learning theory. Think back to your own life and create a mind map that explores key experiences and times in which you learned from either your parents or peers. Below are some ideas to get you started.

- List people who would be examples of high-priority/intensity/duration/frequent influences in your life when you were younger (family members, teachers, babysitters, friends, etc.).
- Give examples of several different sources of social and nonsocial reinforcement in your own life.
- What is your earliest memory of learning that something was "good" or "bad?"

Criticisms of Social Learning Theory

While social learning theory is important in criminological thinking, it has been criticized based on its central thesis. Essentially, social learning theory suggests that increased associations with deviant peers increase the likelihood that one will adopt attitudes and values favorable to criminal conduct. The issue, based on our discussion of causation above, is the temporal ordering of the adoption of deviant attitudes and behaviors and the association with other deviant peers. We might think of it as the chicken and the egg problem. Do young people with deviant attitudes learn them through peer association, or do they seek out peers with similar attitudes? Put another way: Where do antisocial attitudes come from?

Gottfredson and Hirschi speculate on the origins of deviant attitudes in the following passage:

Individuals with low self-control do not tend to make good friends. They are unreliable, untrustworthy, selfish, and thoughtless. They may, however, be fun to be with; they are certainly more risk taking, more adventuresome, and reckless than their counterparts. It follows that self-control is a major factor in determining membership in adolescent peer groups and in determining the quality of the relationships among the members of such groups. We would expect those children who devote considerable time to the peer group to be more likely to be delinquent. We would also expect those children with close relationships within a peer group to be less likely to be delinquent. (1990, pp. 157–158)

The problem is that the cause of the delinquency, from a critic's point of view, is not associations with deviant peers. Instead, delinquent behavior or attitudes favorable to it are established *before* group contact (Akers & Sellers, 2004). From this perspective, it could be said that some individuals seek out similar peers, simplified as "birds of a feather tend to flock together." While Lilly et al. (2011) report Akers's reply as "if you lie down with dogs, you get up with fleas," witticisms don't quite settle the issue.

Subsequent research, however, seems to address some of these issues. For example, in a study of illicit drug users and nonusers, Kandel and Davies (1991) found that more frequent drug users were more likely to have closer relationships with their drug-using peers than nonusers had with their conventional peers. In addition, while not all adolescents are influenced to the same degree by their peer associations, delinquents do form close relationships with one another, and these relationships do facilitate the onset and persistence of delinquency (Haynie, 2001). Critics have also pointed out that social learning theory does not account for individual differences or opportunity structures. Further, beyond treatment and rehabilitation, this theory offers little advice for how to control and prevent crime (Jeffery, 1990). Some have also argued that it is difficult to operationalize (Matsueda, 1988). Akers (1998) has responded to some of these criticisms by further explaining how to operationalize variables.

 ## Research Example: Meta-Analysis and Social Learning Theory

Learning theories are based on symbolic interactionism, or the idea that we take meaning from how we perceive the numerous interactions in our life. Social learning theory emphasizes the "reciprocal interaction between cognitive, behavioral, and environmental determinants" of human behavior (Bandura, 1977, p. vii). As a general theory of crime and criminality, Akers's version of social learning theory has very successful and has been used in research to explain a diverse array of criminal behaviors. The theory, as proposed by Akers (1998), is centered on the idea that learning processes produce both conforming and deviant behavior. These arise based on social structures, interactions, and situations. In short,

> The probability that persons will engage in criminal and deviant behavior is increased and the probability of their conforming to the norm is decreased when they differentially associate with others who commit criminal behavior and espouse definitions favorable to it, are relatively more exposed in-person or symbolically to salient criminal/deviant models, define it as desirable or justified in a situation discriminative for the behavior, and have received in the past and anticipate in the current or future situation relatively greater reward than punishment for the behavior. (Akers, 1998, p. 50)

The conceptualization of social learning theory embodies within it four fundamental premises: differential association, definitions, differential reinforcement, and imitation (Akers & Sellers, 2004). These can be complicated to test. One trend in criminology is using research approaches and statistical techniques drawn from medicine and education to test the strength of different theories, based on their propositions. As we saw in Chapter 1, a systematic review undertakes a comprehensive literature review that focuses on a single question to identify, appraise, select, and synthesize all high-quality research evidence relevant to that question (Wheeldon & Åhlberg, 2012). These rigorous reviews have become the basis for a number of other meta-analyses that attempt to synthesize and summarize many different research findings in a consistent and coherent way.

A recent rigorous attempt to assess the propositions outlined by social learning theory was conducted by Pratt and his colleagues (2010). Their approach involved including in the analysis all studies measuring social learning variables that were published in the leading criminal justice/criminology journals from 1974 to 2003. This resulted in the consideration of 133 studies. The concepts of interest in this study included peers' behaviors, parents' behaviors, others' behaviors, peers' attitudes, parents' attitudes, others' attitudes, peer reactions, parental reactions, others' reactions, and number of admired models witnessed. By controlling for variables normally associated with competing criminological theories, Pratt and colleagues concluded that

> social learning theory has performed rather well. Empirical support for its key propositions is not unqualified, and it is unlikely to unseat all theoretical contenders. Even so, the results of our meta-analysis clearly show that it deserves its status as one of the core perspectives in criminology. (2010, p. 710)

One way to visualize the results of this study is to map the core concepts based on the effect size of predictor variables on the outcome variable of crime/deviance. In the simplest terms, **effect size** is a measure of the strength of the relationship between two variables. Based on the results from Pratt and his colleagues' (2010) examination of social learning theory, we have organized three predictor variables from highest to lowest based on their relative effect size in Figure 6.12.

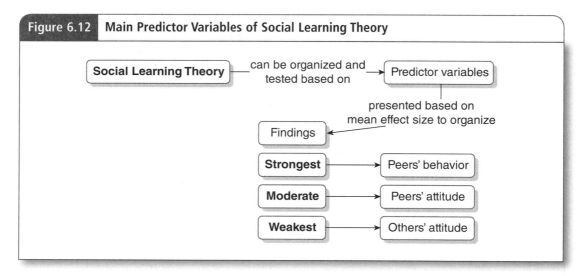

Figure 6.12   Main Predictor Variables of Social Learning Theory

Social Learning Theory — can be organized and tested based on → Predictor variables

presented based on mean effect size to organize

Findings

Strongest → Peers' behavior

Moderate → Peers' attitude

Weakest → Others' attitude

Now that you've read this chapter . . . think back to the day care workers who were encouraging toddlers to fight each other. What is the danger of this approach to childcare? The three women were charged with assault, endangering the welfare of a child, reckless endangering, and conspiracy for the incident. How does this behavior connect to the work of Albert Bandura and his famous Bobo doll studies?

Conclusion and Review Questions

This chapter has explored differential association and social learning theories that describe and explain the social processes that play a role in understanding criminal behavior. Social process theories make use of psychological concepts and findings, especially those from social psychology and the study of personality. In criminology, differential association and social learning theories seek to describe the process of criminal and delinquent socialization and specifically how criminal behavior is observed, learned, and executed. In general, criminologists who embrace social process theories focus on how people interpret and define their social reality and the meanings they attach to it through various sorts of interactions. Often applied to a variety of social interactions to explain how people learn the values, attitudes, techniques, and motives for criminal behavior, social learning theory remains one of the most tested and supported theories in criminology and has significant practical implications for social and criminal justice policy.

CHAPTER REVIEW

1. How did the history of and assumptions made by differential association and social learning perspectives impact on their development?

2. What aspects of criminality do differential association and social learning theories attempt to explain?

3. Does having delinquent peers always result in criminality? How does this statement connect to the differences between causation and correlation?

4. How might the biological and psychological theories explored earlier be integrated within learning theories?

5. What are some practical implications of differential association and social learning theories in the criminal justice system and wider society?

CHAPTER

7

Control Theories

 ## Chapter Overview and Objectives

As discussed in the previous chapter, differential association and social learning theories focus on how various aspects of culture and societal norms are transmitted and how individuals *learn* these norms (Akers, 1998). By contrast, control theories focus on how proper socialization keeps people in line and how misbehavior can be *controlled* (Nye, 1958). In this chapter, we examine a number of theories connected to the control perspective. Unlike social learning theorists, social control theorists see crime not as something which people are influenced to commit but as the natural way of being and the direct consequence of the failure to instill proper values, control our own self-interest, and ensure that socialization includes the fear of consequences for failing to abide by rules, laws, and social norms. Figure 7.1 outlines the control theories covered in this chapter. By the end of the chapter, readers should be able to:

- Understand the relevance of the historical period in which control theories emerged
- Explain the core assumption about human nature that informs control theories
- Be aware of the level of explanation, problem focus, and scope of these theories
- Present the four aspects of Hirschi's social bonding theory
- Consider how school-based or community-based programs can be connected to the perspectives discussed in this chapter
- Evaluate the empirical status of control theories based on existing research

The Control Tradition

Control theories all share a Hobbesian assumption about human nature that says people act in ways that will maximize their own pleasure and self-interest. Since people are not naturally altruistic, our normal urges must be suppressed and controlled. While each varies in its focus, control theories view the interactions between family and friends as predictors of why most people *do not* commit crime. Parents who monitor, recognize, and punish bad behavior allow their children to develop the

128

| Figure 7.1 | **Introducing Control Theories** |

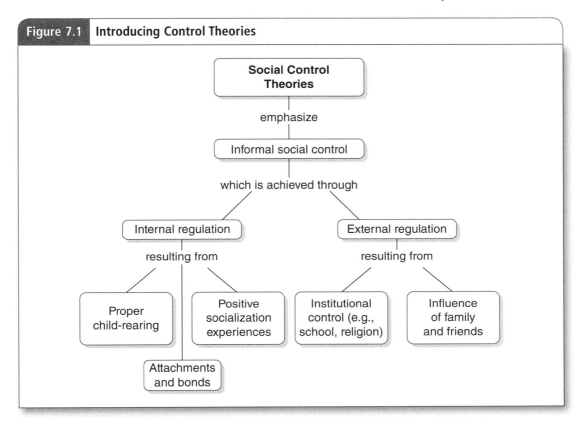

ability to control their urges, interact in prosocial ways, and avoid negative life outcomes and criminal lifestyles (Pratt & Cullen, 2005).

As you read this chapter, consider . . . should juveniles be tried as adults? Who is responsible for the conduct of a 16-year-old? A Texas teenager named Ethan Couch faced criminal prosecution and civil lawsuits from victims' families after he killed four people. Couch had THC, Valium, muscle relaxants, and three times the legal adult limit of alcohol in his system when the vehicle he was driving flipped, grievously injuring one of his passengers and killing four people on the side of the road. *The Dallas Morning News* reported that Couch pled guilty to intoxication manslaughter in juvenile court. State District Judge Jean Boyd sentenced him to 10 years' probation and no jail time. As part of the order, Couch attended therapy sessions for driving drunk and his family covered the cost of an expensive lock-down residential treatment facility. Later it was revealed that Couch's parents, while not abusive, were neglectful and had failed to hold him responsible for his behavior. As you read this chapter, consider what a social control theorist might suggest occurred in this case. Should parents be held legally responsible for the actions of their children?

Seven Steps of Criminological Thinking

History and Social Context of the Control Perspective

While symbolic interactionism is an important starting point for differential association and social learning theories, control theories originated in the work of Emile Durkheim (1938/1895, 1965/1897). Durkheim (1938/1895) argued that crime was a normal part of society. Like Hobbes and the scholars from the classical school, Durkheim assumed that people are naturally self-interested and require outside control. Crime as an essential fact of life characterizes all societies in all locations and time periods. In fact, according to Durkheim, crime is functional and actually serves a purpose—including indicating the moral boundaries of acceptable behavior. Further, societies without crime would likely be quite abnormal. For example, a completely crime-free society may indicate that the society is overly permissive and acts are legal that perhaps should be against the law. The absence of criminal prosecution in a society may also suggest high levels of social disorder (i.e., minor criminal acts are tolerated by the authorities because of the prevalence of very serious criminal acts) (Durkheim, 1938/1895).

Durkheim's (1951 [1897]) concept of anomie is also important to understand control theories. While we will revisit this idea in more depth later when we discuss strain theories, for now we will focus on how it applies to control theories. **Anomie** originates when there is a disjuncture between individual and collective values in society. This results in widespread confusion over what constitutes proper behavior. In other words, the connection between individual and social interests becomes unclear or nonexistent. Society eventually becomes less cohesive, and social controls, such as attachments between people, start to break down. The lack of connections between individuals and society "frees people up" to commit crime and engage in other types of unacceptable or undesirable behaviors. Anomie tends to surface during times of great social and historical change (Durkheim, 1951). The shift in American society at the mid-point of the 20th century offers a useful way to understand social change.

The 1950s are often recalled as a time of extreme conformity and the ideal of the "perfect nuclear family." This is reflected in TV shows such as *Leave it to Beaver* and *Father Knows Best*; gender roles were well defined and authority figures enjoyed unparalleled influence. This approach to social organization in North America was contested as a result of attitudinal shifts in the 1960s and 1970s. Challenging authority became stylish, and traditional gender roles were questioned as women began pursuing higher education in greater numbers and demanding equal treatment in the workplace. Men began to wear their hair long and sport jewelry, and the development of birth control loosened norms around sex. Another development was the increased use of drugs and alcohol among young people. Marijuana and LSD use became more mainstream and normal. Social activism and antiwar protests became more common as reports from Vietnam challenged official government accounts. This social conflict was reflected in music of this period, starting with Elvis and the Beatles, and later the Doors and Led Zeppelin.

In some ways, the development of control theories might be seen as a reaction to the perceived moral permissiveness often ascribed to the 1960s (Williams & McShane, 2010; Lilly et al., 2011). According to crime statistics, the number of crimes committed in the United States escalated significantly from 1960 through 1971. While this increase was due in part to the incorporation of crime data from Alaska and Hawaii, it is more often attributed to the criminalization of the civil rights movement and various student protests and to the government's responses, which often involved the criminal justice system. This era involved an inherent tension between the rise of groups who sought recognition for their views and the inability of the traditional political process to accommodate these groups. However, control theories were also influenced by the thinking of Durkheim, who was writing about the nature of control long before the rise of sex, drugs, and rock 'n' roll.

Control theories were also influenced by the work of the Chicago school, specifically later research done by Shaw and McKay (1969). Early control theorists such as Reiss, Nye, and Reckless were members of the Chicago school and elaborated upon Shaw and McKay's early control research, which itself had grown out of the social disorganization tradition. These theories also have parallels with the psychological theories of Sigmund Freud. As discussed in Chapter 2, the socialization process is essential to understanding how people internalize norms and how those norms influence behavior (Miller et al., 2011). While socialization is achieved primarily through family processes and interactions (Lilly et al., 2011), other institutions are also important. These may include schools and religious institutions (Miller et al., 2011).

One can see these sociological and psychological influences reflected in most versions of control theory. More specifically, control theories typically distinguish between internal factors that control a person (e.g., personality aspects and conscience from proper socialization keeps a person in line) and external factors, such as relationships and stakes in society that restrain a person from delinquent or criminal behavior. For control theorists, both are keys to understanding how behavior is controlled. The speculation made by most control theorists is that people with well-developed internal controls do not need external controls. For many, not engaging in crime is a result of an internal moral code and not the result of a fear of criminal sanction. Modern control theories can be traced back to early control theorists who proposed that personal and social controls such as relationships, commitments, values, norms, and beliefs discouraged them from breaking the law. For example, Albert Reiss (1951) asserted that the failure of primary groups such as the family to provide reinforcement for nondelinquent roles and values was crucial to the explanation of the growing "delinquency" of the period.

Assumptions of Control Theories

Like the differential association and social learning theories, control theories are all clearly positivist and determinist. They believe that criminals and noncriminals can be distinguished from each other and that people's behavior is influenced by factors beyond their control. Further, they also believe that behavior can be studied scientifically and measured in various ways.

Control theories assume people act in ways that will maximize their own pleasure and self-interest. This implies that behavior requires control and regulation. This idea can be connected to the classical school of criminology in which behaviors are seen as the result of a rational calculation that focuses on maximizing pleasure while minimizing pain. As noted earlier, Durkheim also assumed that people required external control to properly regulate their behavior.

Unlike differential association and social learning theories, control theories assume that laws emerge based on the agreement of society as a whole. Although some control theorists concede a human's natural impulses for pleasure inevitably conflict with society's interests, laws are thought to represent a product of widespread agreement about what should be legal and illegal. Consequently, the control perspective assumes that there is a societal consensus as to what constitutes crime (Williams & McShane, 2010). This consensus assumption is also found in the writings of Durkheim (1938, 1951).

Problem Focus, Scope, and Level of Explanation of Control Theories

The problem focus of control theories can be difficult to grasp for some students. One could argue that control theories are actually attempting to explain conformist or law-abiding behavior rather than deviant or criminal behavior. However, this group of theories seeks to explain how control fails or breaks down, allowing delinquent and criminal behavior to result. It may be best to see these theories as primarily interested in explaining how criminal behavior occurs. Juvenile delinquency is a common area of interest, although some control theories address adult crime as well. While these theories can be applied to many victimful and victimless crimes, they have difficulties accounting for white-collar crime, political crimes, and corporate crime. In addition, control theories struggle to explain crime committed by middle-class, suburban youth—especially if financial security is assumed to be a reliable indicator for strong familial ties and role models. Control theories are primarily micro-level theories (Williams & McShane, 2010). They focus on explaining individual criminal behaviors and pay very little attention to the group dynamics of criminal behaviors.

Key Terms and Concepts in Control Theories

Personality-Oriented Control Theory

Reiss's (1951) personality-oriented control theory is one of the earliest examples in the control trajectory. Reiss was not attempting to explain juvenile delinquency but instead was trying to develop an instrument that would predict recidivism among delinquents. The data used to initially formulate the theory were found in official juvenile court records from Cook County (including the city of Chicago) in Illinois.

Reiss began by defining social control as "the ability of social groups or institutions to make norms or rules effective" (1951, p. 196). Similar to differential association theory, this theory assumes that one's primary groups, such as immediate family and friends, have the biggest impact on that person's behavior. He argued control is weakened in families because of divorce or when a child is raised outside of his or her natural family, and this control would be lower in juveniles raised in institutional settings.

Reiss (1951) provided three statements that suggested when delinquency was most likely to occur. The first two of these statements were individually oriented and used concepts that were drawn out of psychoanalytic theories about personality development; the third statement focused more on social factors that give rise to delinquency. First, delinquency is more likely to occur when there is a relative absence of internalized rules or norms governing behavior. In other words, the socialization process is unsuccessful or is only partly successful, resulting in a lack of internalized control. This could occur because the person lacks external socialization, or the process of being socialized could be disrupted by certain personality characteristics (e.g., impulsivity or a lack of empathy).

Second, Reiss (1951) claimed that delinquency is more likely to occur when there is a breakdown in previously established controls. This can occur for a number of different reasons (e.g., a sudden change in one's environment or a traumatic event). Here the cause is external, but it affects internal functioning of the individual. Third, delinquency is more likely to occur when there is a relative absence of social rules or techniques for enforcing such behavior in the social groups of which the person is a member. In this case, the cause is clearly external and usually results in the removal or lifting of external forms of control (Reiss, 1951, p. 204).

This theory also identified two key aspects of control that give rise to conformity: acceptance and submission. **Acceptance** is akin to the internal component of control. In other words, a person accepts the rules because he or she has internalized the rules and believes them to be right. **Submission** is similar to the external aspect of control. People submit because they fear the consequences, such as arrest or punishment, of not following a norm or law. Thus, the socialization process may be unsuccessful, or only partly successful, when it results in a lack of internalized control. This could occur because the person lacks external socialization, or the process of being socialized could be disrupted by certain personality characteristics, such as impulsivity or a lack of empathy. However, a person with little internalized control can still be held in check by fear of punishment and other consequences (i.e., deterrence). Reiss's theory is summarized in Figure 7.2.

The Family-Focused Theory

An extension or elaboration of Reiss's (1951) control theory can be found in Nye's (1958) later formulation called family-focused theory. Nye (1958) tested his theory using self-report data from three

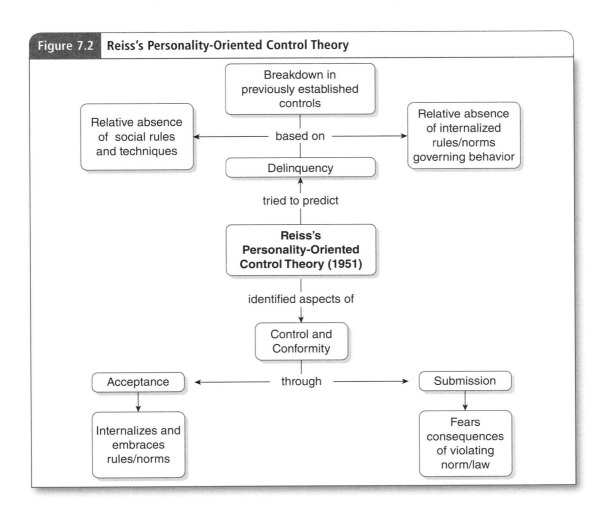

Figure 7.2 **Reiss's Personality-Oriented Control Theory**

towns in the state of Washington (Bernard et al., 2010) and claimed that delinquency is a multicausal process that involves personality and subcultural and social factors. Nye (1958) emphasized explaining conformity and suggested two types of external control (Lilly et al., 2011).

First, there is the **direct control** that is exerted through norms and laws in society. Like Reiss (1951), Nye says we follow norms and laws because we fear the consequences of not doing so. However, Nye was careful to point out that an overemphasis on direct control, especially from parents, can create problems:

> It is postulated that as direct controls become too pervasive, it becomes impossible for an adolescent to function as a member of his peer groups; his needs, therefore, are not being met in institutional behavior and more are met through delinquent behavior, despite close parental control. (1958, p. 156)

Indirect control refers to control that is exerted informally through one's attachments. For example, if a teenage boy is closely attached to his parents, he may refrain from crime because he does not want to disappoint them or let them down.

Nye (1958) also points out that control can be exerted internally through one's conscience or moral compass, and he referred to this as **internalized control**. Finally, he claims that the availability of alternative means to goals also serves to control behavior. A person could be relatively low on the other three dimensions of control, but if there are other **alternatives** available to satisfy that person's goals, there will be no need to become involved in crime. For example, most teenage males crave excitement, and crime sometimes satisfies this need. However, if the person in question becomes involved in other activities that satisfy the need for thrills, such as sports or other outdoor activities, there will be no (or less) need to commit crime (Nye, 1958, pp. 6–8).

Differences in male and female levels of criminality are explained by the differing levels of family control generally applied to each gender, with lower levels of direct control applied to boys compared to girls. According to Nye (1958), girls are subject to more restrictive parental policies that limit the activities of their peer groups, leading to fewer opportunities for delinquency and crime. Interestingly, when the levels of direct control are lifted, rates of female delinquency are comparable to male levels (Nye, 1958, pp. 98–99). One could further argue that during the era of this research, boys were typically encouraged to be more independent and self-reliant than girls. It is not hard to see how these differences in monitoring and expectations would have encouraged family attachments to take hold more effectively for girls than boys. Nye's theory is depicted in Figure 7.3.

Containment Theory

Reckless's (1961) containment theory is unique when compared with other control theories because it examines both motivational and control factors associated with criminal behavior. Containment theory is a middle-range theory that seeks to explain both property (e.g., theft, robbery, and burglary) and personal crime (e.g., murder, assault, and rape). Reckless noted that the scope of his theory did not extend to subcultural crimes or crimes that result from mental illness, organic impairments, neurotic mechanisms (e.g., compulsive shoplifting or arsonists), and most forms of organized crime.

The central proposition in containment theory asserts that criminal behavior occurs when a person experiences various external pushes or internal pulls (e.g., motivating factors) to commit crime and when one's external and internal containment (e.g., control factors) is weak (Reckless, 1973).

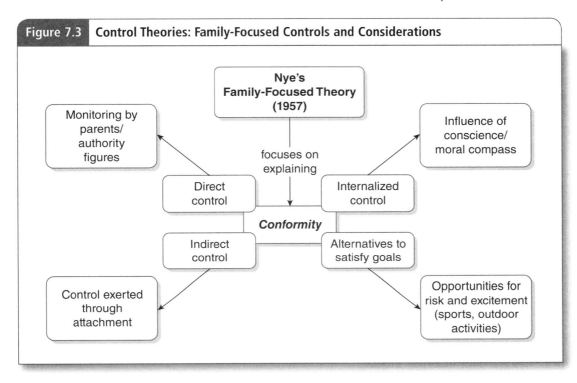

Figure 7.3   Control Theories: Family-Focused Controls and Considerations

Nye's
Family-Focused Theory
(1957)

focuses on
explaining

Monitoring by
parents/
authority
figures

Direct
control

Internalized
control

Influence of
conscience/
moral compass

Conformity

Indirect
control

Alternatives to
satisfy goals

Control exerted
through
attachment

Opportunities for
risk and excitement
(sports, outdoor
activities)

Internal pushes refer to mental and situational states that all people experience. Examples of internal pushes include drives, motives, restlessness, disappointments, rebellion, hostility, and feelings of inferiority. **External pulls** include environmental and social factors that pressure one to engage in crime. Poverty or deprivation, limited opportunities, conflict/discord, and advertising/propaganda are common examples of external pulls (Reckless, 1973). A central proposition in containment theory is that if a person has a strong inner and outer containment, he or she can resist the pushes and pulls.

The idea of inner containment is similar to the notion of internal control suggested by Reiss (1951) and Nye (1958). Consequently, the concept of inner containment (like internal control) is heavily reliant upon Freudian concepts and psychoanalytic notions. According to Reckless (1973), **inner containment** consists of self-concept, self-control, ego strength, a well-developed superego, high frustration tolerance, and an elevated sense of responsibility. He argued that self-concept is particularly important to the theory. This was really the downfall of the theory because subsequent empirical research failed to support the importance of self-concept (Akers, 1997). **Outer containment** is similar to the notion of social control and includes things such as effective supervision and discipline, reasonable sets of social expectations that guide behavior acceptance, identity, and belongingness (Reckless, 1973). In the following passage, Reckless describes one way to visualize his theory:

In a vertical order, the pressures and pulls of the environment are at the top of or the side of the containing structure, while the pushes are below the inner containment. If the individual has weak outer containment, the pressures and pulls will have to be handled by the inner control system. If the outer buffer of the individual is relatively strong and effective, the individual's inner defense does not play such a critical role. Likewise, if the person's inner controls are not equal to ordinary pushes, an effective outer defense may help hold him within bounds. If inner defenses are in good working order, the outer structure does not have to come to the rescue of the person. (1973, p. 56)

Think You Get It?

Using the paragraph above, create a map that outlines Reckless's theory. One approach would be to list key concepts and use his description to connect them. Exchange your map with a colleague. How are they the same and how are they different? Do you both agree on what the key concepts are?

The Techniques of Neutralization

In place of the sole focus on predicting behavior (Reiss, 1951), some theorists began to examine the role that offenders play in freeing themselves up to commit crime. In other words, how does a person decide to adopt criminal values that loosen social control? The exemplar of this activity is Sykes and Matza's (1957) techniques of neutralization. These theorists attempted to further explain the rationalizations that allow criminal behavior to occur. While many textbooks classify neutralization theory as a control theory, it might also be seen as connected to differential association theory. As we shall see below, the theory proposed by Sykes and Matza (1957) emerged as an elaboration of a core proposition from Sutherland's differential association theory, and it serves as a good example of the ways in which theories cross simplistic boundaries.

Sykes and Matza (1957) attempted to further explain the rationalizations that allow criminal behavior to occur based on proposition four from Sutherland's differential association theory (Akers, 1997, 1998). This proposition, as you may recall, stated that

> when criminal behavior is learned, the learning includes techniques of committing the crime, which are sometimes very complicated, sometimes simple and the specific direction of motives, drives, rationalizations, and attitudes (Sutherland & Cressey, 1974, pp. 80–82)

Through their theory, Sykes and Matza (1957) suggested that there are a variety of neutralizations that "free" people to adopt alternative or nonconformist values and partake in criminal behavior. They outlined five main techniques of neutralization used by people when they decided to participate in crime.

First, one may **deny responsibility** for the criminal act. In this case, the offender argues that he or she was not really responsible for the behavior or that the behavior was beyond his or her control. For example, the person may say that he or she became involved in crime because of "hanging out with the wrong crowd" or because of a bad childhood. Second, there is **denial of injury**, in which one claims that the criminal act caused no real harm to the victim. This is perhaps one of the most common methods and probably has been used by everyone at some time or another. For example, when we say downloading music or movies is all right because we are not directly hurting anyone, we are denying injury. Of course, others apply this logic to more serious crimes, such as burglary or theft. **Denial of victim** takes place when the offender claims that the victim was "asking for it" or that there was no actual victim. The offender might claim that the assault victim disrespected the offender and therefore deserved to be assaulted.

Condemnation of the condemners refers to when the offender says that other people do the same things he or she is doing and fail to get into trouble. For example, someone who evades paying taxes may claim that wealthy people do similar things but never get caught because they have better lawyers and accountants. **Appeal to higher loyalties** is when the offender claims that he or she was obeying a higher power or law in committing the crime. In these cases, the act sometimes takes on a "noble" quality. For example, a man accused of assault may claim that the victim insulted his wife so the person deserved to be attacked. Lilly et al. (2011, p. 104) provide a useful diagram outlining neutralization strategies and slogans, which we have adapted in Figure 7.4.

Theory of Social Bonding

The most well-known control theory is perhaps Hirschi's (1969) theory of social bonding. This theory integrated and expanded upon a number of ideas that had appeared in earlier formulations in

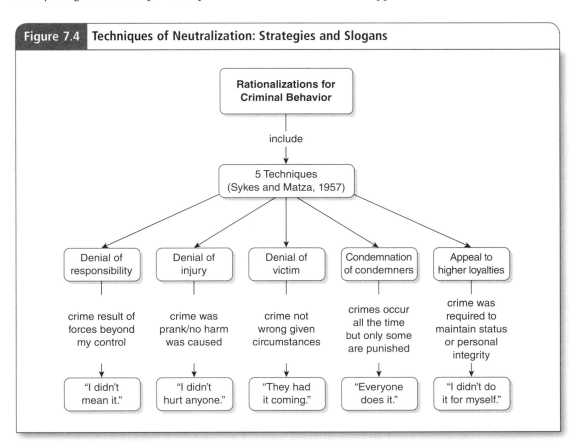

Figure 7.4   Techniques of Neutralization: Strategies and Slogans

the control program. Hirschi (1969) offered an important model that demonstrated how to test his theory. This strategy for advancing criminological knowledge included defining theories clearly, deriving testable propositions, measuring the theories' variables and design studies to assess these propositions empirically, and supporting or rejecting the extant theories based on the resulting data (Pratt et al., 2010, p. 765).

The central proposition in Hirschi's theory states that delinquency results from weak social bonds. Social bonds consist of four interrelated elements or strands. **Attachments** are the connections one has to other people. Most important is the relationship a person has with his or her parents; however, relationships with other family members, relatives, teachers, coaches, caregivers, authority figures, and other community members are also important. Hirschi (1969) claims that this element of the bond plays the largest role in preventing a person from partaking in criminal behavior (Bernard et al., 2010). **Commitment** refers to one's stakes in conformity (Toby, 1957). In other words, how much does a person have invested in society and its institutions, such as family, education, and religion? There is an inherently selfish aspect in this element of the bond; our commitment to society is measured by how much we benefit from being invested in these institutions (Miller et al., 2011). A woman might be committed to society because she has a great job that pays well; however, she is only committed because the job provides wealth, status, and access to other material possessions.

Involvement is simply the amount of time that is consumed by legitimate activities. If a person is going to school, plays on the soccer team, and participates in the debate team, that person has very little time for illegitimate activities. This part of the bond can be reflected in the expression "idle hands are the devil's workshop." **Belief** refers to one's internalization of the laws and other social norms. This is the clear consensus aspect of the theory because it implies that there is a common set of norms in society (including some parts of the law) that are being violated (Hirschi, 1969, p. 23). Important questions here include the following: Does the person believe in the law? Does the person believe that authorities should be respected? Does the person feel an obligation to behave properly?

Social bonding theory can be visualized in a number of ways. Figure 7.5 provides one approach.

Low Self-Control Theory

Hirschi's (1969) social bonding theory dominated the area of control theory for many years after it was initially proposed and has had a massive impact on criminology as a whole. It has been the focus of countless studies and still remains one of the most cited theories in criminology. Somewhat surprisingly, Hirschi seemed to change his position in 1990 when he proposed his new explanation of criminal behavior with Michael Gottfredson in their controversial book, *A General Theory of Crime*.

Gottfredson and Hirschi (1990) started out by stating that they were "disappointed" in the ability of mainstream criminology to produce a satisfying theory of crime that was consistent with the facts known about crime. In order to remedy this, they returned to the insights of the classical school scholars and embraced a hedonistic explanation of criminal activity. However, as you might remember from Chapter 2, the classical school theorists were not attempting to explain criminality but rather were interested in forming a theory about deterrence and criminal law and were more interested in explaining criminal acts. In this theory, crime is defined as "acts of force or fraud undertaken in the pursuit of self-interest" (Gottfredson & Hirschi, 1990, p. 15).

Not wishing to completely abandon their positivistic roots, Gottfredson and Hirschi (1990) produced a theory focused on explaining criminality by examining the characteristics of criminal events. They found that criminal acts tend to be impulsive, poorly planned, and risky and that they usually

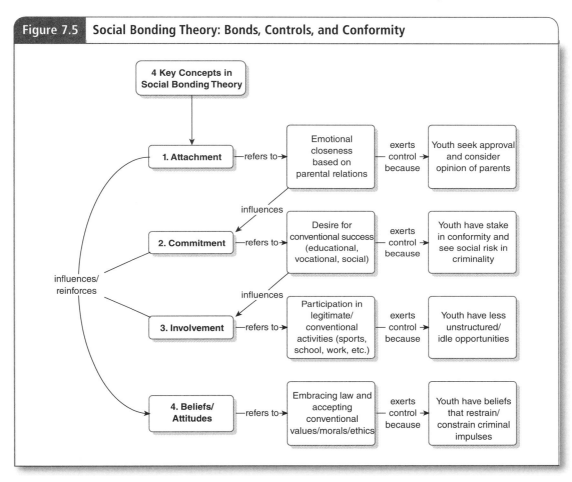

Figure 7.5   Social Bonding Theory: Bonds, Controls, and Conformity

provide instant gratification. Gottfredson and Hirschi (1990) claimed that offenders likely share these characteristics, and therefore their acts are merely a reflection of their inner control mechanisms. Further, they noted that there are behaviors that are theoretical equivalents of crime (e.g., drinking, smoking, promiscuous sex, and gambling) because they deliver some form of immediate gratification. In other words, crime and its theoretical equivalents are thought to be the result of the same underlying problem: low self-control. Low self-control is defined as "the tendency to avoid acts whose long-term costs exceed their momentary advantages" (Hirschi & Gottfredson, 1994, p. 3).

According to Gottfredson and Hirschi (1990), low self-control is a stable, natural, unsocialized state and is directly associated with a lack or absence of socialization. The primary source of socialization is effective child-rearing; however, they also mentioned that socialization can be achieved through school experiences and the discipline associated with the educational process. They do acknowledge that some personality traits (e.g., impulsivity, lack of empathy, and low intelligence) may make this socialization process more difficult but claim that effective socialization can overcome any constellation of problematic traits.

This explanation is really a theory of hedonistic criminality. Indeed, it seems that Gottfredson and Hirschi (1990) argue that every crime is hedonistic. This emphasis is discussed in the following passage:

> The object of the offense is clearly pleasurable, and universally so. Engaging in the act, however, entails some risk of social, legal, and/or natural sanctions. Whereas the pleasure attained by the act is direct, obvious, and immediate, the pains risked by it are not obvious, or direct, and are in any event at greater remove from it. It follows that though there will be little variability among people in their ability to see the pleasures of crime, there will considerable variability in their ability to calculate potential pains. But the problem goes further than this: whereas the pleasures of crime are reasonably equally distributed over the population, this is not true for the pains. Everyone appreciates money; not everyone dreads parental anger or disappointment upon learning that the money was stolen. (Gottfredson and Hirschi, 1990, p. 95)

Questions always arise as to the relationship between Hirschi's (1969) social bonding theory and Gottfredson and Hirschi's (1990) low self-control theory; this question was left unaddressed until recently. In many cases, researchers interpreted the more recent formulation as a theory about traits, and efforts were undertaken to construct measures of self-control (Grasmick, Tittle, Bursik, Arneklev, 1993; Gibbs & Giever, 1995). Further, many interpreted the more recent theory (Gottfredson and Hirschi, 1990) as a reversal of Hirschi's (1969) original position. However, both Hirschi (2004) and Gottfredson (2006) have suggested that these are misinterpretations of their theory. Instead, they argue that social control and self-control are essentially the same thing. Hirschi stated that

> self-control becomes the tendency to consider the full range of potential costs of a particular act. This moves the focus from the long-term implications of the act to its broader and often contemporaneous implications. With this new definition, we need not impute knowledge of distant outcomes to persons in position to possess such information. Children need not know the health implications of smoking or the income implications of truancy, if these implications are known to those whose opinion they value. (2004, p. 543)

It seems clear that this situation has not yet been resolved. But despite its controversial nature and numerous misinterpretations, this theory has had a considerable impact on criminology.

Research on Control Theories

Social bonding theory is one of the most widely tested theories in criminology, with well over 100 published scholarly articles testing its key aspects (Akers & Sellers, 2013). The theory asserts that one's social bonds to family and school are a major predictor of delinquent behavior. Many studies have concluded that the kinds of informal social control mechanisms specified by social bond theory are important to our understanding of criminal behavior (Laub, Sampson, & Allen, 2001). Research in this area has found a strong relationship between parental attachment and lower levels of delinquency. This suggests that providing support to parents in the form of parenting skills training could be an effective step toward addressing youth crime by building strong bonds between parents and children (Farrington & Welsh, 2007; Greenwood, 2006; Kumpfer & Alvarado, 2003). In recent years, questions have emerged about the ability of the theory to function as a stand-alone approach to understanding juvenile delinquency (Lilly et al., 2011).

The research presented by Hirschi (1969) in *Causes of Delinquency* generally supported his theory. He offered empirical research that tested and supported the theory using data obtained from the Richmond Youth Study. This study examined 4,000 students at 11 junior and senior high schools in Contra Costa County, California. Self-report data was obtained through a questionnaire administered to the students. School and police records were also used as a data source (Hirschi, 1969). However, future research efforts yielded somewhat weak support for the theory. This is especially true in the case of the concepts of involvement and belief (Bernard et al., 2010; Williams & McShane, 2010).

One issue is that much of the research seems to rely upon self-report data, and thus the theory may be better at explaining minor or less serious forms of crime because people tend to omit serious crimes when completing questionnaires. Finally, the theory also seemed to break down when subjected to testing involving longitudinal rather than cross-sectional data (Agnew, 1991). Cross-sectional data examines one point in a person's life while longitudinal data tracks a person over their life course (Williams & McShane, 2010). Akers and Sellers have suggested that the magnitude of the relationships between bonds and offending is moderate at best (2004, p. 122). As discussed later, there are questions about how best to define and operationalize the four bonds identified by Hirschi in 1969.

Gottfredson and Hirschi's (1990) general theory was based on a reexamination of the age–crime curve. The age–crime curve suggests that criminal activity peaks in the teenage years, with most criminals (about 70%) desisting by their 30s (Moffitt, 1993). Observed in detail by David Farrington, criminal activity begins to increase in early adolescence, peaks in the late teenage years, and declines steeply from the mid-20s and thereafter (1986, pp. 192–195). Farrington argued that the age–crime curve reflects decreasing parental controls and a peaking of peer influence in the adolescent years, which leads to increased criminal activity. Then family and community ties and controls reemerge as people age, and these factors are associated with reduced criminal behavior. We will revisit the notion of the age–crime curve in later chapters. Figure 7.6 provides an overview of the age–crime curve.

According to Gottfredson and Hirschi (1990), the age–crime curve is invariant across race and gender, applies to all types of crimes, and is identical across societies, cultures, and periods of history. In fact, they actually compared data associated with the age–crime curve from the United States in the 1990s to Goring's findings about age and crime in England and Wales during the 1840s. Surprisingly, the distribution of criminals by age was almost identical for the two time periods.

Gottfredson and Hirschi (1990) then attempted to use their theory to explain findings about the importance of peer groups, schools, and work to crime in other areas of criminological theory. They claimed that the connection between peer groups and crime was not well explained by learning theories such as differential association theory. Rather, they argued that individuals in delinquent peer groups have low self-control. Further, these **low self-control** individuals also tend to have similar interests in risk-taking and gratifying activities, many of which overlap with various forms of crime (e.g., underage drinking, joyriding, minor theft, vandalism, and drug use). They also argued that people with low self-control have problems in school not because they are negatively labeled but rather because school is structured to reward high levels of self-control. This explains why many criminals do poorly in school.

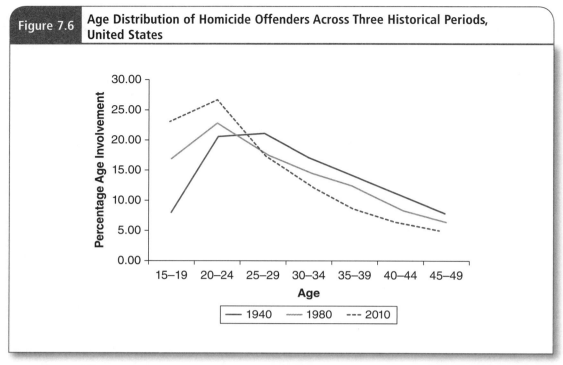

Figure 7.6 Age Distribution of Homicide Offenders Across Three Historical Periods, United States

Source: Ulmer & Steffensmeier (2014, 383). Used with permission.

Numerous studies exist about the relationship between low self-control and criminal behavior, many of which provide some support for the theory (Burton, Cullen, Evans, Alarid, & Dunaway, 1998; Pratt & Cullen, 2000; Higgins, 2004). For example, Chapple (2005) used child and young adult data from the National Longitudinal Survey of Youth (NLSY) to test this self-control theory. In addition, she was able to hold constant other well-known correlates of criminal behavior, such as sex, age, poverty, and race. Self-control was measured through parental assessment and with reference to the Behavioral Problem Index (BPI), a well-validated index from the developmental literature. In accordance with Gottfredson and Hirschi's (1990) theory, Chapple (2005) found that self-control predicted peer rejection in early adolescence and subsequent membership in delinquent peer groups. However, she also found that peer rejection completely mediated the effect of self-control on delinquency; this conflicts with predictions offered by self-control theory.

Recent research reported by Moffitt (2012) examines self-control based on the Dunedin Multidisciplinary Health & Development Study, ongoing since 1972–1973. This study is designed to assess the development and well-being of a general sample of New Zealanders. Individuals were studied at birth (1972–1973) and followed up on and assessed at the age of 3 when the longitudinal study was established. Since then, participants have been assessed every 2 years until the age of 15, then at ages 18 (1990–1991), 21 (1993–1994), 26 (1998–1999), 32 (2003–2005), and 38 (2010–2012). Moffitt and her colleagues examined how well children's self-control predicts real-world outcomes after children reach adulthood. Data were first gathered from reports made by parents, teachers, and researcher-observers. These data were then combined into a composite measure. By controlling for socioeconomic advantage and IQ, this approach compared the measure of self-control of children at ages 3, 5, 7, 9, and 11 with the health, wealth, and criminal activities of these children as adults. The findings can be divided into three main focus areas.

In terms of health, childhood self-control predicted the number of adult health problems. The higher the self-control, the lower the number of health problems. Lower self-control was associated with elevated risks of substance abuse and substance dependence. Childhood self-control also appears to be connected to financial planning, money management, and other indicators of wealth, such as home ownership and investment funds. Overall, poor self-control was a stronger predictor of financial difficulties than social class or IQ. Finally, based on analysis of court convictions in Australia and New Zealand, children with low self-control were significantly more likely to be convicted of a criminal offense as adults, again after accounting for social class and IQ (Moffitt, 2012).

Practical Ramifications of Control Theories

It is debatable as to whether or not social control theories have directly influenced criminal justice policy. Many measures that social control theorists would support were in existence long before the idea of social control surfaced. Advice offered by control theory often seems to correspond to "common sense" advice about how to properly socialize children (Williams & McShane, 2010). However, it still seems important to identify programs and practices that correspond to the logic offered by social control theories. In a sense, this provides support for the theories.

After reading about the history and description of the control perspective, it should be obvious that control theorists would support efforts to strengthen institutions such as the family (Gottfredson & Hirschi, 1995). Control theorists assert that the role of the parent is paramount to the bonding of young people to the family. This bond is seen as fundamental to diminishing a child's propensity for delinquent involvement. The research discussed above provides an evidentiary basis for family-based programs targeting early childhood development being effective in preventing subsequent youth delinquency and adult criminality. Dr. Fraser Mustard, the late child development advocate, once stated that

> if you want a highly competent population with limited behavior problems and no violence, then you don't have any choice but to invest in early childhood development. . . . Since parents have the dominant effect on a child, you want to make damn certain you give parents every opportunity to be good. (Rushowy, 2007, p. A1)

Beyond the family, schools and religion are thought to play prominent roles in the socialization of young people; effective socialization acts as an insulating factor against crime. School can provide support to young people that they may not be receiving elsewhere. Based on these observations, Sprott, Jenkins, and Doob (2005) advised that it is antithetical for schools to implement zero-tolerance policies that only serve to further exclude and isolate young people who have acted violently and sever their ties to the school. They argue students deemed to be at risk or delinquent should receive greater support from the school, not less. This would suggest policies promoting school cohesion and bonding young people to their schools should be favored, including, for example, school-based restorative justice programming (Morrison, 2007). Of course, schools are not the only places in which people can be socialized. Extracurricular activities, such as 4-H, Boy/Girl Scouts, organized sports, language clubs, or debate teams, may also discourage delinquent and/or criminal behavior (Bernard et al., 2010; Williams & McShane, 2010).

Despite the conservative edge of the control theories, modern right-wing efforts to strengthen punishment and increase imprisonment would not be supported by most control theorists. However, proponents of control theory are universally pessimistic and caution that rehabilitation programs advocated by many liberals are also likely doomed to fail (Gottfredson & Hirschi, 1995). In addition to supporting families and schools, control theorists support efforts to prevent crimes before they happen. Further, they also acknowledge that because serious crimes are so uncommon, they should not be the focus of crime prevention efforts. Instead, they argue, attempts should be made to reduce and discourage the commission of minor crimes that often lead to more serious crimes.

Think You Get It?

Review the discussion of low self-control in this chapter. Why does this theory sound appealing as an explanation for criminal behavior? How is this theory connected to social control?

Figure 7.7	Seven Steps of Control Theories	
Seven Steps	**Control Theories**
1. Know the History	Emerged during the 1950s and 1960s; influenced by Durkheim's work on social control and early Chicago school research
2. Acknowledge Assumptions	Humans are naturally selfish and hedonistic; example of social positivism (i.e., behavior must be controlled by social factors); consensus oriented (i.e., laws represent widespread agreement as to what should be illegal)
3. Problem Focus, Scope, and Level of Explanation	Role of the family and other social attachments in regulating behavior; seek to explain why people obey the law rather than commit crime
4. Key Terms and Concepts	Containment, attachment, bonding techniques of neutralization, and self-control
5. Respect the Research	Research on how families and other social institutions (e.g., school, religion) regulate behavior
6. Theory/Practice	Strengthen families and other social institutions to encourage informal social control; extracurricular activities to keep juveniles busy and out of trouble
7. Mapping the Theory	See Figure 7.8

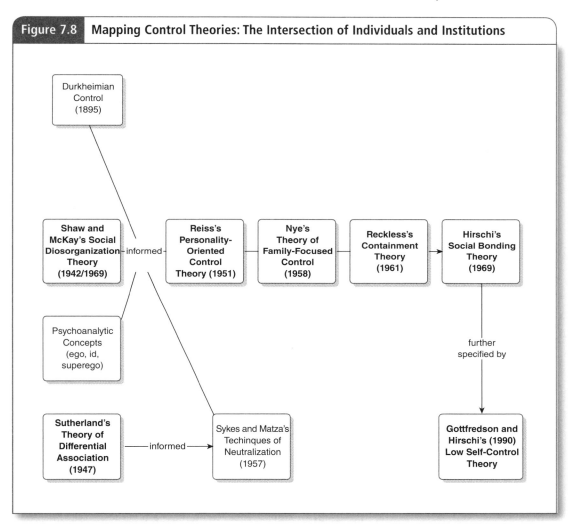

Figure 7.8 | **Mapping Control Theories: The Intersection of Individuals and Institutions**

Durkheimian Control (1895)

Shaw and McKay's Social Diosorganization Theory (1942/1969) —informed— Reiss's Personality-Oriented Control Theory (1951) → Nye's Theory of Family-Focused Control (1958) → Reckless's Containment Theory (1961) → Hirschi's Social Bonding Theory (1969)

Psychoanalytic Concepts (ego, id, superego)

Sutherland's Theory of Differential Association (1947) —informed→ Sykes and Matza's Techinques of Neutralization (1957)

further specified by

Gottfredson and Hirschi's (1990) Low Self-Control Theory

 ## Criticisms of Control Theories: The Complexity of Causation

Few doubt that a strong family and effective parenting are important to childhood development. Thus, it is surprising that the empirical support for social bonding theory is not a bit stronger (Robinson, 2004). One problem is based on the research about social learning theory. According to social bonding theory, delinquent behavior as a result of poor socialization would lead to association with delinquent peers. However, attachment to delinquent peers has been shown to encourage delinquent behavior, not the other way round.

Another issue identified by Lilly et al. (2011) is the persistent attempt to present social bonding theory as a stand-alone explanation for all juvenile delinquency with little regard for how other factors may impact the observed relationship. While lacking modesty about one's theoretical contribution is hardly unique, in Hirschi's case, subsequent research has provided a more nuanced view of how bonds may be affected by larger forces in society. An important example relates to how real and perceived racial discrimination may undermine social bonds and shape criminality for ethnic minorities (Unnever, Cullen, Mathers, McClure, & Allison, 2009).

Another issue is the paternalistic undertones that underlie the social control tradition. For example, Gottfredson and Hirschi (1990) find the traditional roles of women and men to be crucial to the development of children. They seem to feel that if society could regain traditional American values, with the woman staying at home, the husband working during the day, and the children disciplined by both parents, criminality would decrease. While most would agree that stable families and effective parenting reduce crime, the notion that the rise in criminality is a result of women working outside the home is both overly simplistic and insulting to women. Additionally, having one parent stay at home is not a realistic option for many people in the current economic climate of modern society.

Research Example: Social Bonding Theory Through Life Histories

A unique study applied Hirschi's bonding theory to a qualitative study of homeless male substance users from New Haven, Connecticut (Hartwell, 2003). As discussed above, Hirschi's (1969) social bond theory emphasizes absent social attachments among juvenile delinquents. Yet the theory also offers a useful framework to examine the lives of homeless substance users because of the interrelatedness of the elements of social bonding. Elements of interest to Hartwell (2003) included attachment to families; commitment to social norms and institutions (e.g., school, employment); involvement in activities; and the belief that these things are important. Her findings offer a rich view of the consequences for these men of what Hartwell calls an "initial non-normative or attenuated social bond" (2003, p. 499). Common narrative findings using illustrative quotes from Hartwell's study (2003, pp. 481–496) are presented in Figure 7.9 on page 146. We have organized them chronologically from bottom left to top right based on Hirschi's original four elements—attachment, commitment, involvement, beliefs—which are reconceived in the figure as themes.

Instead of insisting on social bonds as the primary predictor for juvenile delinquency, this example connects early experiences, structure, and processes over the lifetimes of a vulnerable population. While the retrospective self-reports from homeless, substance-abusing men presented here cannot be generalized, consistent patterns emerged based on social bonding theory that may offer a means to revisit this theory in the future. By examining the relationship between social bonds, delinquency, and substance abuse over a person's lifetime, new research may assist to connect the interrelatedness of the elements of social bonding theory (Hirschi, 1969).

Figure 7.9 A Narrative Map: Social Bonding and Subsequent Substance Abuse

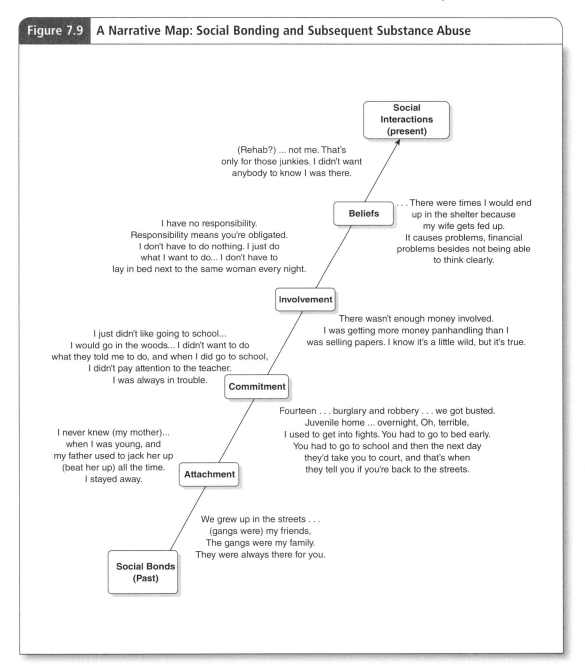

Now that you've read the chapter, consider . . . should juveniles be tried as adults? Who is responsible for the consequences of a drunken 16-year-old? Ethan Couch drove drunk and killed a disabled motorist and three Good Samaritans. He was described in testimony as a spoiled teen from a rich but dysfunctional family. G. Dick Miller, a consulting clinical psychologist, testified Couch suffered from "affluenza." He suggested that though Couch's rich but distant and dysfunctional parents stunted his development, Couch could be turned around with treatment and no contact with his parents. Miller suggested Couch's parents should share part of the blame for the crash because they never set limits for the boy and gave him everything he wanted. How would social control theorists react to Miller's defense? What do you think?

Conclusion and Review Questions

This chapter has explored a number of theories that can be seen as part of the social control tradition. For control theorists, the focus on the family as the most important intimate group for youth has had profound implications for understanding criminological thinking. While research has not supported all of the propositions put forward by control theorists, few doubt the importance of family structures. Social control theory focuses on how the absence of close relationships with conventional others can free individuals from social constraints, thereby allowing them to engage in delinquency. Despite a lack of empirical support for some of these theories, they remain popular in criminology.

CHAPTER REVIEW

1. Discuss how the relevant history influenced control theories. Provide two examples.

2. What is the core assumption about human nature that informs control theories? What are some of the challenges of embracing this view?

3. Consider the quotes presented in Figure 7.9. How could you connect these quotes to the four aspects of Hirschi's social bonding theory?

4. In your opinion, what are the strongest arguments for social bonding theory? Provide an example of a school-based or community-based program that can be connected to the perspectives discussed in this chapter.

5. How could the micro-explanations from Part 1 be more fully integrated with process theories? Create a map connecting one or more aspects from Part 1 with one or more of the theories from Part 3.

Labeling Theories

⬚ Chapter Overview and Objectives

Labeling theories focus on labels and how they affect people's behavior. These theories are also known as societal reaction theories because they focus on reactions from society, and the criminal justice system in particular. In the examination of the social processes that give rise to crime and deviance, labeling theorists ask different questions. These include the following: What kind of behavior is considered deviant? Who considers the behavior deviant? What is the behavior deviating from? Why is this behavior considered deviant? (Taylor, Walton, & Young, 1973). These theories also consider the origins of the criminal law and criminal justice system practices. An important distinction in labeling theories is made between primary deviance and secondary deviance. Primary deviance is rule-breaking behavior that is carried out by people who see themselves, and are seen by others, as conformist. Labeling occurs when this behavior is applied in a way that becomes part of that individual's identity. This labeling may lead to secondary deviance, or rule-breaking behavior that would not have otherwise occurred. Labeling theories are interested in how the internalization of labels helps to maintain criminal behavior over time. Thus, while labeling doesn't explain the original deviant act, these theories may be useful for explaining why criminals continue to commit crime. Figure 8.1 provides an overview of labeling theories.

By the end of the chapter, readers should be able to:

- Understand the assumptions made by labeling theories
- Be aware of the level of explanation, problem focus, and scope of labeling theories
- Know the differences between the traditional positivist approach and the naturalistic approach
- Understand the difference between soft and hard determinism
- Consider the relationship between these theories and other criminological process theories and how labeling theories can provide practical approaches and programs connected to the justice system

| Figure 8.1 | An Overview of Labeling Theories |

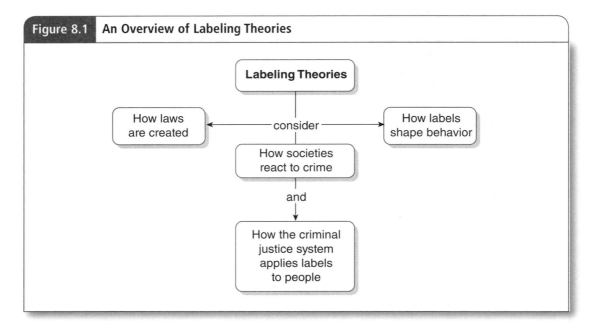

The Labeling Tradition

The development of labeling theories can be traced to the emergence of social behaviorism, and especially the perspective of symbolic interactionism. Many of these developments were connected to scholars associated with the University of Chicago, such as Charles Horton Cooley, George Herbert Mead, and Herbert Blumer. Symbolic interactionism was also impacted by work done in the field of psychology. The work of American pragmatists such as John Dewey and William James was particularly important to the development of symbolic interactionism and labeling theory. As a philosophical approach, pragmatism relies upon the experimental method, democracy, and Darwinism (Mead, 1934, p. x). In criminology, Mead's symbolic interactionism integrated Dewey's view that meaningful knowledge arose from an active adaptation of the human organism to its environment. It also considered James's view of truth, which is *"only the expedient in the way of our thinking, just as 'the right' is only the expedient in the way of our behaving"* (James, 1907, p. 106). Thus, truth is a function of social interactions that guide how people define their lives. This observation influenced the ethnographic work at the University of Chicago and led to numerous studies of crime and deviance in the 1930s that are now viewed as foundational research in criminology.

As you read this chapter, consider...outside a Walmart supercenter in Alabama, two people were forced to wear signs that read, "I am a thief, I stole from Walmart." Attalla City Judge Kenneth Robertson Jr. ordered the two people to wear the signs for four hours each day during two successive Saturdays to avoid a 60-day jail sentence. Judges aren't the only ones embracing this approach.

Parents of some teens are choosing public humiliation as punishment for their children. For example, a 15-year-old was made to stand on a busy Florida street corner wearing a sign that said, "I sneak boys in at 3 a.m. and disrespect my parents and grandparents." As you read through the chapter, consider what labeling theorists might have to say about this approach to punishment.

Seven Steps of Criminological Thinking

History and Social Context of Labeling Theory

It may come as a surprise to learn that early symbolic interactionists were influenced by the work of Charles Darwin, the founder of evolutionary theory. This is not to say that these theories have a biological basis. Instead, early symbolic interactionists were inspired by the observational methods and naturalistic approach used by Darwin (Cooley, 1902; Mead, 1934; Blumer, 1969). The origins of symbolic interactionism are often credited to the work of Charles Horton Cooley and his friend and colleague George Herbert Mead (Lilly et al., 2011). Cooley's central argument is that individuals and society are inextricably linked to one another:

> If we accept the evolutionary point of view we are led to see the relation between society and the individual as an organic relation. That is, we see that the individual is not separable from the human whole, but a living member of it, deriving his life from the whole through social and hereditary transmission as truly as if men were literally one body. He cannot cut himself off; the strands of hereditary and education are woven into all his being. And on the other hand, the social whole is in some degree dependent upon each individual, because each contributes something to the common life that no one else can contribute. Thus we have, in a broad sense of the word, an "organism" or living whole made up of differentiated members, each of which has a special function. (1902, p. 35–36)

This quote asserts that humans are part of society, so, therefore, if we are to study human behavior, we must also consider humans' relationship to society.

Cooley (1902) introduced several important concepts that laid the groundwork for later symbolic interactionism and labeling theories. First, he pointed to the importance of the ego or self, which he referred to as the "I." He borrowed this idea from psychologist William James, but Cooley emphasized the social aspects of the self. Cooley (1902, p. 184) also posited the existence of the "looking-glass self," which consisted of three principal elements, depicted in Figure 8.2 on page 152.

In other words, we form opinions about ourselves based on reactions from others and our perceptions of their feelings and thoughts about us.

Mead (1934) built on the ideas offered by Cooley and developed an approach known as social behaviorism. He embraced the idea of a social self or "I" offered by Cooley and elaborated upon this by adding the concept of "me." According to Mead, the "I" is the creative part of the self that is responsible for creative or novel behavior, whereas the "me" is the learning or experiential part of the self. The self is conceptualized as an adaptive and iterative process that will vary based on social context. Therefore, the self emerges through social interaction and creates meaning based upon this that will

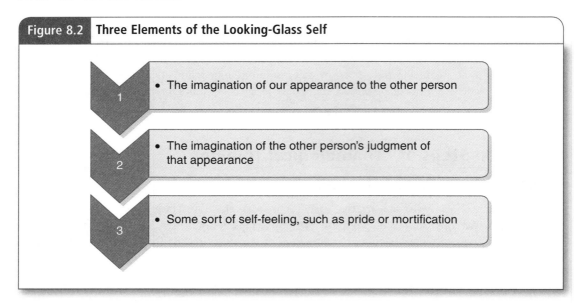

Figure 8.2   Three Elements of the Looking-Glass Self

1
- The imagination of our appearance to the other person

2
- The imagination of the other person's judgment of that appearance

3
- Some sort of self-feeling, such as pride or mortification

influence future behavior. Blumer (1969) extended Mead's (1934) notions of social behaviorism and is credited with coining the term *symbolic interactionism*. He was also a member of the Chicago school of sociology and is connected to the emergence of the social disorganization and differential association theories discussed in previous chapters. According to Blumer (1969, p. 2), symbolic interactionism rests on three premises.

As outlined in Figure 8.3, the first premise is that humans act toward things on the basis of the meanings that the things have for them. As a consequence of this, we treat people differently when we know things about them because we attach meaning to those things. For example, some people may treat a woman differently if they become aware that she is a mother. This status or role grants moms a measure of respect; some people will act more protectively toward mothers or may assume that mothers are more mature than other single females. The second premise is that associations arise from our social interactions with other people, such as relatives, authority figures, friends, and peers. The third and final premise states that these meanings are modified through an interpretative process used in different ways by different people. All people react to events in their lives, but the meanings of these events will change over time.

Labeling theories started to become popular in criminology during the 1960s. This period of history was a time of great social change and was characterized by a variety of social and political movements. These developments gave rise to the civil rights movement that demanded equal rights for minorities and the women's movement that pushed for greater recognition, rights, and respect for women. These events also laid the foundations for other progressive movements that would emerge in the later part of the 1960s and early 1970s. A common point of agreement among all of these movements was a tendency to question the dominant norms of society. In many cases, this involved questioning the activities of the government. It should come as no surprise that this spirit was reflected in criminology, and especially in its theories. Labeling theorists began to question the

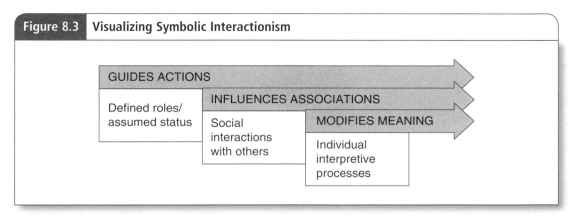

Figure 8.3 | Visualizing Symbolic Interactionism

GUIDES ACTIONS

Defined roles/
assumed status

INFLUENCES ASSOCIATIONS

Social
interactions
with others

MODIFIES MEANING

Individual
interpretive
processes

activities of the criminal justice system and examine how these actions affected future criminal behavior. This sparked interest in the study of the law, the police, and courts and correctional systems that later critical and radical theorists would develop.

Assumptions of Labeling Theories

Labeling theorists view humans as active subjects who shape their own destinies (Matza, 1969). Similar to other sociological theorists, these theorists assume that the individual is inextricably linked to society and is not separable from the human whole (Cooley, 1902). In other words, society is more than just a collection of individual actors. The notion of the "self" implies that humans are reflexive, thinking creatures; this is what distinguishes humans from other animals. Humans are able to reflect on their own behavior and reactions from other people. Indeed, the "self" emerges through social interactions and changes over time (Mead, 1934).

As mentioned previously, labeling theorists embrace a naturalistic approach to studying crime. This approach is much different from the positivist approach assumed by other theories that we have discussed. Matza summarizes this naturalistic approach in the following passage:

> Naturalism, as the very term implies, is the philosophical view that strives *to remain true to the phenomenon under study or scrutiny.* For naturalism, the phenomenon being scrutinized is considered to be an object or subject depending on its nature—not the philosophical preconceptions of a researcher. . . . So conceived, naturalism stands against all forms of philosophical generalization. Its loyalty is *to the world* with whatever measure of variety or universality happens to inhere in it. Naturalism does not and cannot commit itself to eternal preconceptions regarding the nature of phenomena. Consequently, it does not and cannot commit itself to any single preferred method for engaging and scrutinizing phenomena. (1969, p. 5)

This quotation can be interpreted as a call to broaden the focus of criminological inquiry and is a clear break with the early positivist approach. Matza (1969) also accused positivist criminologists of not being true to the phenomenon they were studying. More specifically, he charged that researchers were overcommitted to a purely positivistic approach based on the natural sciences. Unfortunately, humans cannot be studied in the same way we study inanimate objects or even other animals. After all, humans react and often know when they're being observed and studied; they may also adjust their behavior if they think it will benefit them.

The naturalist approach and the unique view of human nature found in labeling theories demand an alternative to a purely deterministic assumption or one that assumes humans have complete free will. Matza (1964) referred to this new assumption as soft determinism; some have also referred to it as soft free will (Williams & McShane, 2014). This view acknowledges that humans make choices, but these choices are not free choices, rather they are constrained by various biological, psychological, and environmental factors (Robinson & Beaver, 2008, pp. 49–50). This assumption has become very influential in other areas of criminological theory, including most of the theories discussed in later chapters of this text. As mentioned previously, labeling theorists are also interactionist in their approach; this is based on the work of Cooley (1902) and Mead (1934). Lemert discusses the interactionist approach below:

> More careful analysis tells us that interaction is not a theory or explanation at all, but rather it is a condition of inquiry which amounts to a confession of open-minded ignorance about how factors work together. The interactional approach was valuable as a necessary methodological step away from reified and particularistic theories of the causation of human behavior held by nineteenth-century writers (e.g., instinct theory). Properly used, it corrects and supplements purely static or structural analysis but does not abolish the significance of social forms and structures as limiting factors in human behavior. (1951, p. 11)

Labeling theorists assume that conflict characterizes society more so than consensus (Williams & McShane, 2014). In the following passage, Blumer attempts to answer the question of what holds society together:

> It is held that conflict between values or the disintegration of values creates disunity, disorder, and instability. This conception of human society becomes subject to great modification if we think of society as consisting of the fitting together of acts to form joint action. Such alignment may take place for any number of reasons, depending on the situations calling for joint action, and need not involve, or spring from, the sharing of common values. The participants may fit their act to one another in orderly joint actions on the basis of compromise, out of duress, because they may use one another in achieving their respective ends, because it is the sensible thing to do, or out of sheer necessity. This is particularly likely to be true in our modern complex societies with their diversity in composition, lines of interest, in their respective worlds of concern. In very large measure, society becomes the formation of workable relations. To seek to encompass, analyze and understand the life of a society on the assumption that the existence of society depends on the sharing of common values can lead to a strained treatment, gross misrepresentation, and faulty lines of interpretation. (1969, p. 76)

The conflict orientation is also readily apparent in labeling theories because these were the earliest efforts to focus on how societal reaction, criminal law, and the criminal justice system could sometimes contribute to crime (Becker, 1963; Matza, 1969). Because of this focus, these theories laid the groundwork for conflict or critical theories, which will be discussed in Chapter 11 (Taylor et al., 1973). The conflict orientation is outlined in Figure 8.4.

| Figure 8.4 | **Mapping Key Conflict Assumptions** |

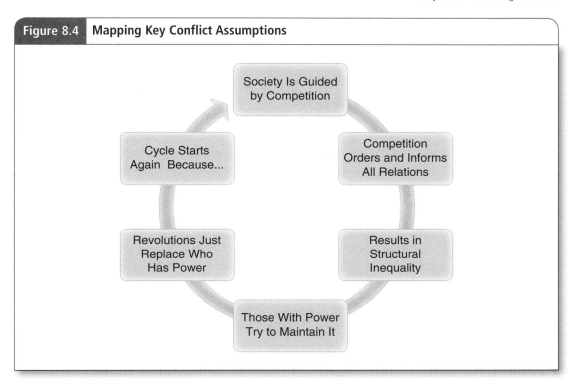

Problem Focus, Scope, and Level of Explanation of Labeling Theories

Like the other social process theories, the central problem focus of the labeling theories is criminal behavior. However, as described previously, these theories take a much different approach to explaining criminal behavior than do traditional positivist theories. A major difference is that labeling theorists reject the notion that criminals and noncriminals differ in any meaningful way. Labeling theorists would argue that the major difference is that criminals have been caught and labeled (Tannenbaum 1938; Lemert, 1951; Becker, 1963; Matza, 1969). In other words, the positivist search for a key characteristic that causes people to commit crime is a pointless endeavor. If we only consider truly heinous crimes such as serial/mass murder, pedophilia, and rape, this idea may seem far-fetched and unbelievable. However, we need to bear in mind that the overwhelming majority of criminal acts are minor crimes (Felson, 2005). Further, it is important to realize that most people do become involved with crime at some point in their lives, usually during their teenage years. In other words, some delinquent behavior during adolescence is, in fact, normative and normal and not perverse and pathological (Moffitt, 1993).

According to Becker (1963), there are two dimensions to deviant behavior. We must determine not only if the individual is breaking a rule or not (i.e., is the individual conforming or deviant?) but we must also consider the perception and reaction of others to the individual in question. Based on these dimensions, several categories emerge. There are people who obey rules and those who are perceived by others as obeying the rules; these people are called conformists. There are also people who break the rules and who others perceive as breaking the rules; these people are called deviants. The remaining two categories are of most interest to labeling theorists. There are falsely accused deviants who are perceived as rule-breaking when, in reality, they are not. Finally, secret deviance occurs "behind closed doors" and therefore is not perceived as a departure from the norm. Becker (1963) argues that these categories are important because these distinctions are not often made and this causes problems when trying to explain criminal behavior. This is because we have an incomplete, and possibly distorted, picture of who commits crime, as Becker's (1963) example illustrates.

The scope of labeling theories extends to most forms of crime, including street crime (e.g., theft, burglary, robbery); victimless crime (e.g., drug use, prostitution); and white-collar crime. These theories can also be useful in explaining serious crime and chronic offending. However, these theories are unable to explain how the initial deviation occurs; they only explain why people keep committing crime. This is not necessarily a problem; these theories merely start further down the causal chain than other positivist theories that focus on explaining the origins of criminal behavior. According to labeling theorists, the causes of the original criminal act are usually much different from the reasons why one continues to commit crime (Lemert, 1951).

Labeling theories are posed at the micro level of explanation and are, at heart, social process theories (Robinson & Beaver, 2008). This is because they seek to uncover the processes by which criminal behavior is maintained over a period of time. However, they also identify some structural factors that may be associated with criminal behavior. For example, many labeling theorists spend a great deal of time discussing the origins of criminal law in order to understand how particular acts are defined as crime (Lemert, 1951; Becker, 1963; Matza, 1969; Schur, 1973). However, these structural aspects are a secondary concern; the primary focus is clearly on the processes associated with criminal behavior. The structural aspects introduced by these theories are more fully developed in the conflict theories that will be discussed in Chapter 11.

Key Terms and Concepts of Labeling Theories

The Dramatization of Evil

Frank Tannenbaum was a history professor who proposed an early example of labeling theory. He was also a former convict who had spent time in Blackwell Island Prison in New York for his role in labor protests (Yeager, 2011). Tannenbaum (1938) suggested that the tendency of positivists to attribute crime to individual factors was problematic when it came to controlling delinquency because most delinquency occurs in groups. So, the key to understanding and dealing with criminal behavior is to clarify the group dynamics around it. Drawing upon early Chicago school research on gangs (Thrasher, 1927), Tannenbaum (1938) sought to explain how youth become involved with delinquency and how this leads to more serious adult criminal behavior. He pointed out that criminal behavior is often preceded by problems in school, such as truancy, poor performance, and conflicts with teachers and other students. In many cases, those with issues in school find themselves in groups of friends who are having similar issues; these "play groups" are often the forerunners to gangs. In the early stages, these groups are not necessarily based around delinquent activities, and, in fact, nondelinquent activities may have the same meaning as delinquent activities. In other words, the delinquent activities may just be part of the child's day and may be defined as harmless fun.

According to Tannenbaum (1938), the gang starts to compete with other institutions (e.g., school and the family) for the child's allegiance. Eventually a conflict develops between the child and society because of the reaction to the activities of the gang. The act eliciting the reaction may not even be criminal (e.g., making too much noise), but the situation may escalate to more serious behavior and an arrest may occur. This initial singling out of a child or group of children is referred to as the *dramatization of evil*. Tannenbaum describes this labeling process below:

> The process of making the criminal, therefore, is a process of tagging, defining, identifying, segregating, describing, emphasizing, making conscious and self-conscious; it becomes a way of stimulating, suggesting, emphasizing, and evoking the very traits that are complained of. If the theory of relation of response to stimulus has any meaning, the entire process of dealing with the young delinquent is mischievous in so far as it identifies him to himself or the environment as a delinquent person. The person becomes the thing they are accused of being. (1938, pp. 19–20)

The tag or label causes the person to feel isolated, and this pushes him or her further into groups of people who have been similarly treated. This gives rise to criminal subcultures that are very difficult to control.

A Theory of Secondary Deviation

Edwin Lemert (1951) offered another important labeling theory. Lemert (1951) distinguished between two types of deviance: primary and secondary. **Primary deviation** refers to acts that are committed before the label is given and internalized by the individual. The reasons behind committing the act may stem from a variety of factors. For example, the person may have some biological characteristic that makes him or her more prone to problematic behavior, or the person may be put in a situation that elicits deviant or criminal behavior (e.g., "heat of the moment" crime). In these cases, the person has not defined himself or herself as deviant and is, for the most part, law-abiding and conformist.

Secondary deviation occurs when deviant acts are repetitive and of high social visibility. These acts elicit a severe societal reaction, and this identification is incorporated into the "me" of the actor. In other words, the self of the person becomes redefined, and that person begins to see himself or herself in a new role, that of the criminal or deviant. In effect, the deviant or criminal role becomes integrated within the person's personality. Secondary deviation is a defensive reaction to negative reaction from society that causes personality and behavioral changes. Lemert (1951) argued that these changes could be seen in styles of dress, speech, bearing, and mannerisms.

Master Status and Deviance

Howard Becker's (1963) labeling theory is another classical statement of the labeling process. Becker loved jazz and played in many bars and clubs. During this time, the jazz scene was associated with a great deal of underground drug use, especially marijuana use. Becker used the experiences and connections he had in this scene as a basis for his theory. In his theory, he argued that we must acknowledge that human behavior develops in an orderly sequence and that the importance of different variables changes over time. In other words, some personality trait may be important to explaining drug use, but this is no guarantee that every person with the trait will use drugs. For the behavior to manifest itself, opportunities and social-environmental factors must be present at the right time. For example, a person who is impulsive (a trait associated with drug use) may experiment with drugs but may never become a regular user because that person doesn't have regular access to the drug.

According to Becker (1963), a key factor to understanding deviant behavior is the process of being caught and branded as a deviant or criminal. In his work, he drew upon sociologist Everett Hughes's (1945) distinction between master and auxiliary status traits to clarify how others view deviant behavior. **Master status** is a person's defining trait or characteristic; auxiliary status refers to traits that are expected to accompany master status. Being a doctor is a good example of master status; this label often defines an individual's personality and carries with it a number of expectations. For example, even in modern society, doctors are often expected to be male, older, white, and intelligent; these are common auxiliary status traits applied to doctors. Becker (1963) claimed that a deviant or criminal identity is also an illustration of master status. In other words, people often jump to conclusions if they find out someone is a convict. They may assume the person is morally bankrupt or untrustworthy, even if the crime is unrelated to such characteristics.

Committing one criminal act, being apprehended, and then labeled can completely redefine one's personality. The labeling process may also influence society's perception of the person, thereby causing negative social reactions to the individual. This may lead to a self-fulfilling prophecy in which labels previously acquired may alter one's future behavior and produce more deviance. Negative perceptions and expectations held by other people may cause the deviant to be exiled from conventional groups, leading to social isolation. The social isolation often leads to further involvement in the criminal sub-culture because other legitimate avenues for employment and social interaction have been cut off. Involvement in these criminal groups leads to learning more criminal techniques and justifications for the behavior.

> **Think You Get It?**
>
> List three ways people acquire labels in life. Are they always deserved? How might the act of label-ing be connected to crime? Is it true that people live up to what we expect of them? Is the notion of a self-fulfilling prophecy accurate? Could we have a criminal justice system in which labels are meaningless?

Research on Labeling Theories

Research about labeling theory has traditionally been qualitative in nature because of the anti-positivistic and deterministic emphasis associated with early theorists in this area. Simple questionnaires, personality assessments, and surveys, often associated with quantitative research, were viewed as inexact techniques to examine the nature of social reality. Instead, labeling theorists preferred interviewing and content analysis as research techniques. In some cases, these methods were combined with a more general ethnographic approach to produce a well-rounded picture of the group being studied (see, for example, Becker, 1963, and Young, 1971). More recent research has applied quantitative research techniques to examine questions of parental labeling (Matsueda, 1992); the gender gap in offending (Bartusch & Matsueda, 1996); and the role of official interventions (Bernburg & Krohn, 2003; Chiricos, Barrick, & Bales, 2007).

An essential starting place is the research of Howard Becker, introduced above. His book *Outsiders: Studies in the Sociology of Deviance* (1963) focused on the emergence of marijuana law and the drug-using subculture. He was particularly interested in understanding the process of becoming a marijuana user. Becker defined deviance as a matter of the definition of "normal" among a certain group at a certain time. Thus, deviance is a matter of opinion, not a defined universal state. Social groups make rules or operate based on certain norms. Deviating from those norms makes one an "outsider." According to Becker (1963), when the label of outsider is successfully applied, an individual may start to be seen as a deviant. He claims that this may propel an individual along the criminal path if the label has, first, been applied to an individual and, second, accepted by that individual.

Many assume that acquiring a deviant identity is always bad, but there may be status in living outside the rules of the group. While labeling influences social interactions, it also may open doors. There is status associated with rule-breaking. From "bad boys" to punk rockers, outsiders get attention simply because they refuse to comply with the dominant group's norms or because they have been labeled as someone who doesn't "fit into" mainstream society. The problem here is that treating outsiders as deviant may deny them the ability to interact socially with other nondeviants, and this may serve to further isolate them from the rest of society. As a result of this process, individuals must create a new group identity for themselves and find other ways to interact. Instead of encouraging a person to change his or her ways using informal methods, the process of labeling a person deviant maintains the same deviant behaviors that the labeler was attempting to change.

Young's (1971) study of drug users living in the Notting Hill section of London is an example of an ethnographic study based, in part, on labeling theories. Notting Hill was an area populated by younger, lower-class people, many of whom were part of the bohemian or hippie lifestyle. Young lived in this area for a period of time and established some close ties with other residents. In addition to his research, Young (1971) presented a discussion of the types of drugs commonly used in this area, along with a comparison of their physiological effects and sociopolitical histories. Like Becker (1963) and several other researchers, he also presented evidence suggesting users learn how to acclimate themselves to the high of various drugs. In other words, the physiological effects of drugs are mediated by individual perception, social expectations, and norms.

The research focused on the media portrayals of people in this area and how this reporting shaped police views about the situation. The police came to see the hippies as lazy, unstable, sexually promiscuous drug addicts who did nothing productive for society. Young (1971) claimed that this reaction, and the resulting treatment, changed drug-use patterns in the area; the social norm shifted from occasional to habitual use. As a result, drug use became something that connected people in the area and was a way of asserting their individuality. Nonusers were viewed with distrust, and this served to further isolate people in the area from larger society. Young called this process a *deviancy amplification spiral.* Eventually, this was represented symbolically in the bohemian/hippie subculture as longer hair and more outlandish clothes became more common.

In more recent years, labeling has also been reimagined as a process associated with structural disadvantage. Bernburg and Krohn (2003) showed that police or juvenile justice involvement in early adolescence increases the likelihood of criminal activity in early adulthood, even when one controls for previous offending, parental poverty, and school ability. Using a revised labeling approach, their quantitative analysis demonstrated that official interventions have both direct and indirect effects that increase the probability of involvement in subsequent delinquency and deviance. In line with traditional labeling theories, they conclude that interventions may trigger exclusionary processes that have negative consequences for conventional opportunities.

Another application of labeling illustrates the stigma of guilt between two populations of convicted felons in Florida. Chiricos, Barrick, and Bales (2007) hypothesized that receiving a felony label would increase the likelihood of recidivism. Their study was based on a unique design comparing those who were found guilty and convicted through a traditional procedure with those found guilty but not labeled criminal and sentenced to probation, based on the discretion of a judge. While those in the first group were more likely to be labeled criminal, members of the second group lost no civil rights and were able to lawfully claim they had not been convicted of a felony. Reconviction data for 95,919 men and women who were either adjudicated or had adjudication withheld show that those formally labeled were significantly more likely to reoffend in two years than those who were not. The researchers found that labeling effects are stronger for women, whites, and those who reach the age of 30 years without a prior conviction.

Labeling is also an important part of Elijah Anderson's (1999) research about the code of the street, which was reviewed in Chapter 6. Anderson notes that the labels associated with "decent" and "street" families amount to evaluative judgments made about local residents in disadvantaged communities. The labeling that results can confer status on certain individuals, groups, or families. Of some concern is the recognition that formal sanction from the criminal justice system may not carry with it the stigma it once did. For example, in the context of some disadvantaged inner-city communities, official labelers and labels have less legitimacy. In some communities, an arrest has become a normal and expected ritual of male adolescence. Based on retrospective personal interviews with 20 minority youth (aged 18 to 20) from high-poverty urban neighborhoods, Hirschfield (2008) argues juvenile arrest typically carries little stigma and does little discernible harm to self-concept or social relationships. Instead of seeing labeling as a result of official interventions in individual terms, mass criminalization of inner-city African American youth has exacted collective costs in terms of social exclusion. These policies may have ironically created the conditions by which labels once assumed to be negative now have cache or status.

Practical Ramifications of Labeling Theories

Labeling theorists have offered some important revisions to crime control policy and practice. These suggestions are sometimes collectively referred to as the four Ds: decriminalization, due process, deinstitutionalization, and diversion. First, the theorists suggested that victimless crimes (e.g., drug use and prostitution) and juvenile status offenses (e.g., underage drinking and smoking) be removed from the criminal code. The goal of this would be to limit criminal records to people who are clearly dangerous or violent. Second, they claimed that due process should be afforded to all defendants. This demand was a reaction to the institutionalized racism that, in their view, characterizes the criminal justice system (Lilly et al., 2011). Third, labeling theorists also argued in favor of deinstitutionalization. In other words, they felt that less people should be locked up in prisons, primarily because of the stigma attached to a criminal record. As we are all well aware, being sent to prison can negatively impact one's attachments to society and future job prospects, making it extremely difficult to reintegrate back into society (Lilly et al., 2011).

The fourth and final suggestion offered by labeling theorists was increased use of diversion programs. The goal of diversion programs is to steer less serious offenders, especially young offenders, away from the criminal justice system and into penalties based on restitution (e.g., composing written apologies to victims); community improvement efforts (e.g., cleaning up garbage and graffiti); and job-skills training programs.[1] Much to the surprise of labeling theorists, use of diversion programs did not reduce the number of people in the system but rather increased it. In an ironic twist, more and more people came under the control of the criminal justice system through a phenomenon known as **net-widening** (Cohen, 1985). In other words, the use of diversion programs merely served to widen the net of the criminal justice system.

Another, more general recommendation of labeling theorists is simply leaving the kids alone whenever possible. Schur (1973) suggested an approach to juvenile justice known as radical nonintervention. He claimed that the juvenile court system often subscribes to a vague and confusing definition of delinquency, sets arbitrary penalties, and disguises punishment as treatment. Rather than forcing individuals to adjust, Schur (1973) suggests that society should acknowledge a wide range of diversity and refrain from criminalizing behaviors that are not dangerous to the general public.[2]

Figure 8.5	Seven Steps of Labeling Theories
Seven Steps	**Labeling Theories**
1. Know the History	Gained popularity in the 1960s at a time of social upheaval when many were questioning traditional norms (gender/ethnicity)
2. Acknowledge Assumptions	Social interactionism key to learning; conflict in society inevitable
3. Problem Focus, Scope, and Level of Explanation	Most forms of crime; focus on processes by which criminal behavior is maintained over time
4. Terms and Concepts	Role of delinquency in groups; primary/secondary deviance; master status
5. Respect the Research	Results are mixed but overall recognition that labeling is often a process associated with structural disadvantage
6. Theory/Practice	Decriminalization, due process, deinstitutionalization, and diversion
7. Mapping the Theory	See Figure 8.6

 ## Criticisms of Labeling Theories

Despite the intuitive sense and historical importance of labeling theory, it has been the subject of a number of critiques. As discussed earlier, labeling theory doesn't explain the origins of criminal acts, only the consequences of official reactions to those acts. The focus is on the behavior that follows after the labeling, and critics suggest the theory is willfully blind to the motivations that underlie the

---

[1]For more, see http://www.efrypeelhalton.ca/adult/divrsn_prgrm.html and https://www.ncjrs.gov/html/ojjdp/9909–3/div.html.

[2]For more, see https://www.ncjrs.gov/App/Publications/abstract.aspx?ID=11309.

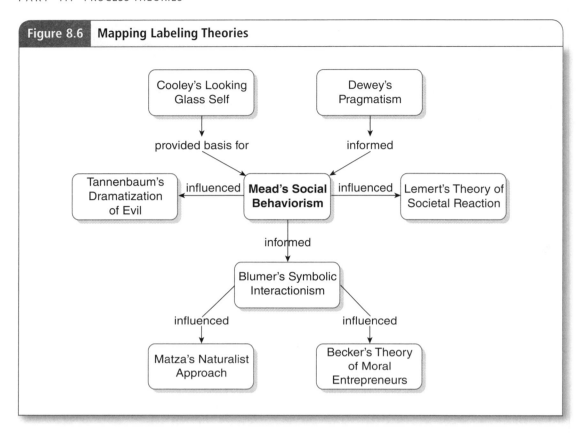

Figure 8.6 **Mapping Labeling Theories**

original antisocial behavior. Labeling theory has also been criticized for its focus on a relatively limited range of behaviors. Extremely common forms of everyday crime, such as property crime, are missing from the analysis.

As these theories are unable to explain why people originally commit crime, they might best be seen as part of a larger, more systematic explanation of criminal behavior. In fact, some labeling theorists have suggested that these explanations should not be called theories. Becker elaborates upon this view in the following passage:

> I never thought the original statements by myself and others warranted being called theories, at least not fully articulated theories they are criticized now for *not* being. A number of authors complained that labeling theory neither provides an etiological explanation of deviance nor tells how the people who commit deviant acts come to do that—and especially why *they* do it while others around them do not. Sometimes critics suggest that a theory was proposed, but that it was wrong. Thus some thought the theory attempted to explain deviance by the responses others made to it. After one was labelled deviant, according to this paraphrase, then one began to do deviant things, but not before. You can easily dispose of

that theory by referring to the facts of everyday experience. . . . The original proponents of the position, however, did not propose solutions to the etiological question. They had more modest aims. They wanted to enlarge the area taken into consideration in the study of deviant phenomena by including the activities of others than the allegedly deviant actor. They supposed, of course, that when they did that, and as new sources of variance were included in the calculation, all the questions that students of deviance conventionally looked at would take on a different cast. (1963, p. 178)

In other words, the main goal of labeling theorists was to enlarge the perspective of criminologists by shifting the focus to how criminal justice processes and societal reactions may contribute to crime.

Another, more complex critique is that, in some cases, labeling theorists seem to imply that the person labeled as deviant is passive and plays little or no role in the process. This suggests that meaning and action arise not from a negotiation between the self and others but instead simply as a result of the judgment of others. This critique may be relevant in two ways. First, there is the issue of people who refuse to accept the labels assigned to them. This is implied in both Anderson's (1999) and Hirschfield's (2008) work. What happens when labels assumed by some to be negative are twisted to become associated with status or even perhaps a cultural norm? This represents the rejection of the judgment of others.

The opposite issue is to what extent labeling can actually serve a purpose. For example, reintegrative shaming suggests the shame one feels at being identified as responsible for a harmful action can "work" to reform and reduce future deviant behavior (Braithwaite, 2001). While this is very different from attempting to force one to feel shame, there may be occasions where the application of the label can result in a decrease in deviant behavior. This represents the internal acceptance of the judgment of others that one feels some responsibility for or perhaps connection to. Labeling does not seem to be able to address either of these critiques.

 ## Research Example: Saints, Roughnecks, Labels, and Arrests

William Chambliss's 1973 study, known as the Saints and the Roughnecks, is a classic example of research that highlights the role of labels. In this study, Chambliss focused on two groups of students from Hanibal High School and observed their behavior over two years. One group composed of eight teenagers was referred to as the Saints. These kids came from middle-class homes, did well in school, and held positions in school government. They also engaged in delinquent behavior such as truancy, drinking, wild driving, petty theft, and vandalism. The Saints were well dressed, well mannered, and had nice cars, and thus they were able to avoid the deviant label. Chambliss stated not one Saint was officially arrested for any misdeed during the 2 years he observed them. The police viewed these boys as the good kids and leaders of the youth in the community. If these boys were pulled over, they were polite and respectful, and usually the police let them off with a warning (Chambliss, 1973, p. 26).

The six subjects from the other group, called the Roughnecks, all came from lower-class households. The Roughnecks were constantly in trouble with police, even though their rates of delinquency were about equal to that of the Saints. Chambliss reported that the Roughnecks engaged in three main types of delinquency: theft, drinking, and fighting. Community members perceived that this group of kids was delinquent, referred to the Roughnecks as a gang, and reacted as though the behavior of the Roughnecks was a problem. Chambliss asks why the community, the school, and the police reacted to the Saints as though they were good, upstanding, nondelinquent youths with bright futures but to the Roughnecks as though they were tough criminals who were headed for trouble. Why did the Roughnecks and the Saints follow such different career paths after high school—paths which, by and large, lived up to the expectations of the community? Chambliss (1973) suggested that members of the community were ignorant of the array of delinquent acts that characterized the Saints' behavior and were much better informed about the Roughnecks' involvement in delinquency. He concluded that social class and societal labeling led to one group being defined as delinquent and that this label shaped the subsequent futures of those in this group. This selective perception and processing and the punishment of some kinds of criminality and not others means that

> visible, poor, nonmobile, outspoken, undiplomatic "tough" kids will be noticed, whether their actions are seriously delinquent or not. Other kids, who have established a reputation for being bright (even though underachieving), disciplined and involved in respectable activities, who are mobile and monied, will be invisible when they deviate from sanctioned activities. . . . They'll sow their wild oats—perhaps even wider and thicker than their lower-class cohorts—but they won't be noticed. When it's time to leave adolescence most will follow the expected path, settling into the ways of the middle class, remembering fondly the delinquent but unnoticed fling of their youth. The Roughnecks and others like them may turn around, too. It is more likely that their noticeable deviance will have been so reinforced by police and community that their lives will be effectively channeled into careers consistent with their adolescent background. (Chambliss, 1973, p. 31)

> **Now that you've read this chapter . . .** think back to the attempts by the judge to change behavior by forcing those convicted of a crime to stand outside a business with a placard, or by the parents who required their teen to stand at an intersection holding a sign outlining the teen's bad behavior. While some seem convinced of the value of these methods, the theorists discussed in this chapter might be less supportive. Why might labeling theorists suggest this approach is limited in effectiveness? What problems might it lead to?

Conclusion and Review Questions

Labeling theories focus on how the internalization of labels may maintain criminal behavior over time. For many, there is an intuitive truth to labeling theory, and, for most people, at least some of the sentiments ring true. However, when tested empirically, this group of theories tends to perform rather poorly (Lilly et al., 2011). Despite this, some contemporary theorists have suggested that labeling-like effects may be important to understanding criminal behavior (Laub & Sampson, 2004; Moffitt, 1993). It is clear that labeling theories cannot explain the emergence of criminal behavior; however, they are useful for understanding why people continue committing crime. They also offer a way to think about the dangers of placing people into categories. These theories force us to consider that in some cases our treatment of others may influence how they see themselves.

CHAPTER REVIEW

1. What are the differences between the approach used by labeling theorists and those used by other social process theorists?

2. What is master status and how does it apply to the labeling process?

3. Describe the relationship between symbolic interactionism and labeling theory.

4. What is the dramatization of evil? What is the difference between primary and secondary deviance?

5. What are the four Ds?

PART IV

Structural Theories

CHAPTER

9

Social Disorganization Theories

 ## Chapter Overview and Objectives

In this chapter, we examine the first major branch of structural explanations, often referred to as social disorganization theories. We have all heard that there are good and bad areas of a city or town. While simplistic, it is true that crime occurs in some areas more often than it occurs in others. On a different level, some cities have more crime than others. Social disorganization theorists ask why these variations occur.

The notion that certain places tend to produce more crime grew out of the social disorganization tradition started by the Chicago school that was introduced in earlier chapters. This early work examined residential locations of juveniles referred to Chicago courts and suggested that crime was concentrated in particular areas of the city. Further, rates of crime remained relatively stable within different areas despite continual changes in the areas' populations. These observations led Shaw and McKay to conclude that crime was a function of environmental and social dynamics and not necessarily a function of the types of individuals within neighborhoods. As such, social disorganization theories focus on characteristics of neighborhoods, communities, and cities that contribute to variations in crime rates. Figure 9.1 provides an overview of these theories. By the end of this chapter, readers should be able to:

- Understand assumptions made by social disorganization/ecological theorists
- Be aware of the level of explanation, problem focus, and scope of the social disorganization theories
- Know the difference between kinds of people vs. kinds of places theories and the connections between these theories and the social process theories discussed in previous chapters
- Understand the ecological fallacy and how it relates to theories in this area
- Explain the history of social disorganization theories and its relevance to practical approaches and programs suggested by social disorganization/ecological theories

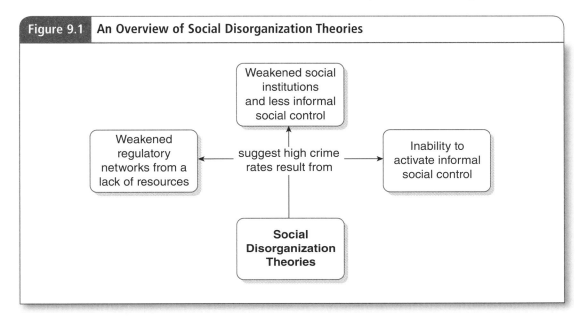

Figure 9.1   **An Overview of Social Disorganization Theories**

 ## The Social Disorganization Tradition

Social disorganization is a theory of crime and criminal activity that links crime rates with neighborhood characteristics. This group of theories makes use of sociological and ecological concepts to understand how certain areas appear to "breed" crime. A core principle of social disorganization theory is that aspects of a community are more important to understanding criminal behavior than individual characteristics (e.g., personality factors or race). In other words, crime is related to the pathology of the neighborhood, not the pathology of the individual.

While the popularity of this tradition waned starting in the 1950s, in recent years it has reemerged to make significant contributions to criminological thinking. Some criminologists have conceptualized this resurgence in interesting terms:

> There is no question that certain aspects of the original Shaw and McKay thesis were problematic. However, despite the appearance of occasional obituaries for the perspective, there has been a significant revitalization of the theory within the last ten years. Admittedly, some criminologists have expressed chagrin at this resurrection . . . [calling it] the "herpes of criminology . . . once you think it's gone for good, the symptoms flair up again." (Bursik and Grasmick, 1993a, p. 30)

It seems clear that not all criminologists view the Chicago school research in a positive light. However, it is still arguably the most influential component of American criminology.

One of these emerging approaches explores social disorganization and behavioral regulation based on structural variations between key groups and social networks. These sources of regulation include primary friendship and kinship relations, secondary group relationships, and the public sphere, which consists of groups and institutions beyond the immediate neighborhood (Bursik & Grasmick, 1993a, 1993b). Another perspective can be found in the work of Robert Sampson, who argues that social disorganization can reduce both the informal resources within a community (social capital) and the ability of citizens to utilize those resources to reduce undesirable behavior (collective efficacy). Sampson, Raudenbusch, and Earls (1997) argues that when communities do not trust their neighbors, they are less likely to believe they can ensure the safety of those who live within their boundaries. When this negative outlook becomes prevalent within communities, it becomes far more difficult to engage residents in efforts to reduce crime.

> **As you read this chapter, consider . . .** how might social disorganization apply to current criminological problems? For example, those released from prison tend to come from a small number of resource-deprived neighborhoods. They come back to neighborhoods that still have the same criminal opportunities and associations that led them to incarceration in the first place. In August 2005, Hurricane Katrina ravaged the Louisiana Gulf Coast. It devastated many of the neighborhoods where ex-prisoners typically resided, and thus those who would have been released to these communities had to go somewhere else. If social disorganization theories are correct, what do you think the impact of moving away from high-crime communities would be on those recently released from prison?

Seven Steps of Criminological Thinking

History and Social Context of Social Disorganization Theories

A central starting point of the Chicago school was research about urban patterning and development that was undertaken during the 1920s and 1930s. While the theories in this area are sometimes referred to as neighborhood effects theories and urban sociology (Sampson, Morenoff, & Gannon-Rowley, 2002), they all trace their origins to the Chicago school studies of social disorganization (Bursik & Grasmick, 1993a; Sampson, 2012) and, specifically, to the work of Shaw and McKay (1969). Members of the Chicago school observed that historical transformations changed how society functioned. Some of these changes also affected the prevalence of crime and societal attitudes about criminals.

As you may recall, it was during this period that cities grew rapidly due to massive waves of European immigrants, African Americans fleeing the post–Civil War South, and an influx of displaced farm workers as smaller family farms became less common (Lilly et al., 2011). The population shift had many social consequences. The influx of new inhabitants and greater mixing of ethnicities in American cities led to conflicts between older, more established residents and recent immigrants. In many cases, the immigrant groups were blamed for increasing levels of crime (Williams & McShane, 2010).

The influences of the Chicago school theorists are difficult to pin down because they drew upon the work of many different scholars from a variety of fields and disciplines to inform their thinking (Park & Burgess, 1921). However, there are a few influences that are particularly important to understanding the theories in this area. Adolphe Quetelet (1831) and André-Michel Guerry (1833) were both statisticians who attempted to find spatial patterns in criminal activities in France and Belgium, respectively (Shaw & Mckay, 1969). Their work gave rise to a field known as moral statistics that analyzed statistics associated with various types of social pathology. This approach can be seen as one of the earliest attempts to understand crime scientifically (Taylor, Walton, & Young, 1973). These moral statisticians, as they are sometimes called, applied this approach to social problems such as rates of divorce, prostitution, mental health, and suicide and helped lay the groundwork for the field of criminology (Sampson, 1986). Like the moral statisticians, social disorganization/ecological theorists seek to explain variations in rates of crime and other urban social problems.

Sociological thinkers such as Emile Durkheim and Georg Simmel also impacted the formation of Chicago school social disorganization theory. First, Durkheim's emphasis on the importance of social institutions (e.g., family, religion, and school) on human behavior was embraced by social disorganization theorists (Park & Burgess, 1921). Second, Simmel's notion of conflict and his views on cities were influential on the thinking of the early members of the Chicago school. Simmel viewed society as a collection of smaller competing groups with different values and interests that frequently clashed with each other (Park & Burgess, 1921).

Chicago school social disorganization theorists also embraced an ecological approach based on research from the animal and plant sciences (Park & Burgess, 1921; Park, Burgess, & MacKenzie, 1925; Park, 1936). They viewed cities as the natural habitat of humans and believed that there were parallels between plant/animal communities and human communities. More specifically, they embraced the notion of "webs of life" or ecosystems. Plants, animals, and even humans must live in an environment of competitive cooperation, thereby forming a natural economy. According to ecologists, this is the definition of a community (Park, 1936). This approach came to be known as human ecology (Park, Burgess, and McKenzie, 1925).

The central idea of the early social disorganization approach is that urban environments are dramatically different from the agricultural communities of most immigrants (Lutters & Ackerman, 1996). As discussed in previous chapters, the environment of the city can act to reinforce the institutions, relationships, and norms of immigrants' homelands. When traditional social structures are in flux, newly arrived immigrants may restructure those relationships to fit the new environment or abandon them altogether. This may lead to a weakening of traditional institutions, such as the family and religion, in urban areas (Shaw, 1969). In addition, many immigrants were forced to live in the poorer sections of the city with other immigrants. In many cases, immigrants from different countries shared little in common with each other; sometimes they did not even share a common language. As a result, certain neighborhoods became more prone to crime than others. Shaw and McKay (1969) argued that procriminal values are transmitted from person to person and generation to generation in a process called cultural transmission. The nature of this transfer is explicitly tied to the places in which people live and the breakdown that characterizes these areas.

Beginning in 1948, ideas about the relationship between people and their environments underwent another shift based on a series of Supreme Court decisions known as the *Restrictive Covenant Cases.* As applied to race, the Supreme Court held that the equal protection clause of the Fourteenth Amendment outlawed judicial enforcement of any agreement barring people from owning real property by a state. Further, the Supreme Court concluded that the enforcement of racial covenants (i.e., racially segregated areas) by federal courts violated the due process clause of the Fifth Amendment. These decisions had the effect of overturning longstanding policies and practices enforcing racial restrictions in housing (Bursik & Webb, 1982). However, until Congress passed the Housing Rights Act in 1968, many informal structures of racial segregation remained in the system. For example, realtors and property owners could still discriminate on the basis of race. Nevertheless, during this period, areas of the city that were once essentially off limits to African Americans became accessible.

These changes in the housing structure allowed new research exploring the relationships between people and places based on reformulations of social disorganization since the 1970s. The roles of social influences, neighborhood characteristics, and especially the intergenerational cultural transmission of norms and expectations have been revisited and strengthened by Robert Sampson and his colleagues (1999).

Assumptions of Social Disorganization Theories

The social disorganization/ecological theories are based upon two main assumptions. The first is that human nature is a *tabula rasa* ("blank slate") and that behavior is shaped by one's social and spatial environment. A well-known Chicago school theorist, Robert Park, explains how human nature is formed:

> For man is not merely an individual with certain native and inherited biological traits, but he is at the same time a person with manners, sentiments and ambitions. It is the social environment to which the person, as distinguished from the individual, responds; and it is these responses of the person to his environment that eventually define his personality and give to the individual a character which can be described in moral terms. (Park et al., 1925, p. 100)

Social disorganization/ecological theorists do not necessarily ignore the importance of biological or individual factors, nor do they deny the potential for people to embrace a hedonistic orientation. They do assume, however, that social factors and the environment play a greater role in determining human behavior.

These theories are positivist and deterministic because they assume that behavior is influenced by social factors. They use a scientific approach based on naturalism and social ecology. **Neighborhood effects** are characteristics thought to be particularly important in shaping human behavior. Chicago school theorists also characterized the city as a social laboratory and viewed it as a natural microcosm of humanity (Park et al., 1925).

These theories assume that society is characterized by some conflict between competing groups within the city. Different groups of people live within cities in relative isolation, and they often have different customs, traditions, and values, as discussed in Chapter 1. Cities may also appear to be organized by class, occupation, and/or race (Park et al., 1925). Charles Darwin's notion of a "struggle for existence" is part of the naturalistic/ecological approach used by this group of theorists, and, thus, the evolutionary struggle is viewed as relevant for social groups within the city (Park, 1936).

Based on the points described above, you might think that these theorists view conflict as common and even normal in society. However, they all agree that society is characterized by much more consensus with regard to norms and laws than conflict (Kornhauser, 1978). In other words, social disorganization theorists acknowledge that some level of conflict is natural in society while embracing the view that law and norms are a result of agreement or consensus.

Problem Focus, Level of Explanation, and Scope of Social Disorganization Theories

The problem focus of the social disorganization theories is crime rates. In other words, these theories examine differences in levels of crime between different neighborhoods, communities, and cities. In addition, these theories also attempt to explain changes in crime rates over time.

To further clarify the role of problem focus in criminological theorizing, Stark (1987) has distinguished between kinds of people and kinds of places theories. *Kinds of people theories* refer to theories that focus on particular traits derived from biology and psychology that may influence crime; these theories are the same thing as the individual difference theories discussed in Chapter 1 of this text (see Bernard & Snipes, 1996). *Kinds of places theories* refer to theories that examine the effects that one's physical and spatial environment have on crime, and they represent one branch of structural theories. In this chapter, the focus is on kinds of places theories and how neighborhood characteristics give rise to higher levels of crime as the level of explanation (Stark, 1987). Therefore, these theories are posed at the macro or structural level because they focus on social, economic, political, and institutional factors that give rise to crime.

The scope of this set of theories is limited primarily to street-level crime. However, these theories can also explain some other serious social problems that plague urban areas, such as mental illness, truancy, juvenile offending, infant mortality, heat wave deaths, and low birth weights (Shaw & McKay, 1969; Sampson, 2012). Elite crime, such as white-collar and corporate crime, and pathological crime (e.g., crime involving mental disorder or serious chronic offending) are not directly addressed.

Key Concepts and Terms of Social Disorganization Theories

The Concentric Zone Model and Social Disorganization Theory

The social disorganization theories can be traced back to Ernest Burgess's concentric zone theory. He based his theory on insights and observations made by Robert Park during the course of his ethnographic research on urban areas. More specifically, Burgess formalized and made testable many of Park's ideas about urban development and applied his theory to the city of Chicago. These theorists were particularly interested in how expansion and growth in the city affected social structure and culture and how this gave rise to new social problems, such as increased crime (Park et al., 1925).

Burgess claimed that the city of Chicago had grown in a concentric ring pattern, similar to a dartboard, and that the city revolved around an area called "the Loop." The Loop was basically the downtown area and central business district and was the central part of the city where one would find skyscrapers, office buildings, department stores, fancy hotels, theaters, the transit hub, and city hall. The next innermost zone, known as the zone-in-transition (ZIT), contained the "slum" or ghetto area, and also some first-generation immigrant colonies or enclaves (e.g., Chinatown and Little Sicily). This area was also being invaded by urban sprawl from the Loop.

Zone 3 was referred to as the zone of workingmen's homes, inhabited by workers likely employed in zone 1 or 2. In addition, some of the more successful second-generation immigrants may also have made it here. The next area, Zone 4, was known as the residential zone. This neighborhood was where one would start to see middle- to high-class apartment buildings and single-family dwellings. Zone 5 was known as the commuter zone. This included areas such as the suburbs and smaller satellite cities approximately 30–60 minutes away from the city center (Park et al., 1925). Figure 9.2 is a visual representation of Burgess's concentric zone model.

Burgess also argued that the expansion that was occurring in certain sections of the city could be explained by using plant ecology. Specifically, he thought the idea of expansion and succession of different sections within the city was particularly important. Much like aggressive plant species can invade one's garden, Burgess believed that the central business district would invade the ZIT. Consequently, property owners in the ZIT would fail to maintain their dwellings because they assumed that wealthy developers from the Loop would buy them out. This made rent cheap in the ZIT, and this attracted the poorest members of the city. Most people living in the ZIT attempted to move out as soon as possible, which created high levels of mobility in the area. This mobility prevented people from establishing solid relationships and a sense of community. Further, many of those left behind were extremely poor, mentally disordered, and/or criminals. This served to destabilize the area, leading to high levels of social disorganization and crime (Park et al., 1925).

It should be obvious by now that the ZIT was of most interest to criminologists. This area was populated by many different racial groups and ethnicities that lacked common connections with each other due to linguistic, cultural, religious, or other differences. The instability produced by this living situation resulted in low levels of social control, which gave rise to more crime and delinquency. It should be noted that this was not directed at any particular culture, ethnicity, or racial group. Shaw and McKay applied Burgess's model directly to the city of Chicago and tested it by measuring rates of juvenile delinquency in the various zones. They examined data over three decades and found that even when racial groups in the ZIT changed, the results were the same. We will return to a discussion of the research conducted by Shaw and McKay later in this chapter.

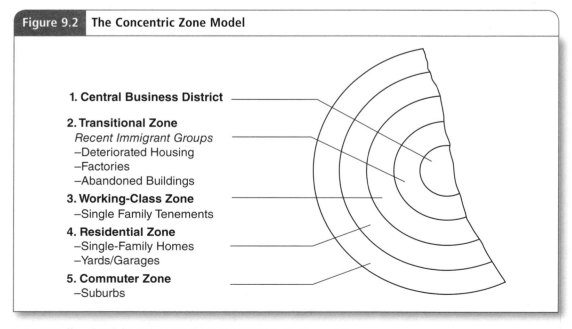

Figure 9.2 | **The Concentric Zone Model**

1. **Central Business District**

2. **Transitional Zone**
   Recent Immigrant Groups
   –Deteriorated Housing
   –Factories
   –Abandoned Buildings

3. **Working-Class Zone**
   –Single Family Tenements

4. **Residential Zone**
   –Single-Family Homes
   –Yards/Garages

5. **Commuter Zone**
   –Suburbs

Source: B. Hoffman (2010), http://www.crimetheory.com. 2/3/10. Used with permission.

In her seminal critique of criminological theories, *Social Sources of Delinquency,* Kornhauser (1978) argued that while Shaw and McKay's underlying theoretical approach was unclear and imprecise, it could still be used to show how neighborhoods exerted or failed to exert informal controls over behavior. Instead of viewing the correlates as the causes of crime in the zones-in-transition, she argued that these factors eroded the levels of social control in these areas and that this was the real cause behind the higher levels of delinquency in certain sections of the city. This macro-level approach offered a means to reinvigorate social disorganization theory based on the notion that communities differ in their ability to regulate behavior. Two major theories emerged in response to Kornhauser's (1978) work: Bursik and Grasmick's (1993a, 1993b) theory of community control and Sampson's theory of collective efficacy.

A Theory of Community Control

Bursik and Grasmick's (1993a, 1993b) theory of community control expands on Kornhauser's (1978) interpretation of social disorganization. Bursik and Grasmick (1993a) clarified the meaning of control and described the importance of institutional and personal networks in regulating behavior. In order to do this, they identified several additional levels of community social control and introduced several new organizational concepts. The first level of control is referred to as **private control**. This is rooted in interpersonal relationships within communities and is exerted informally—for example, through a withdrawal of social support, esteem, and sentiment. The second level of control is known as **parochial control** and refers to informal control arising from institutional sources outside the family, such as schools, churches, and voluntary organizations. These first two levels of control help residents further integrate into their community.

The third level of control, **public control**, "focuses on the community's ability to secure the public goods that are allocated by agencies located outside of the neighborhood" (Bursik & Grasmick, 1993a, p. 17). These resources are thought to take two basic forms: economic resources provided by municipalities and private/public decision-making agencies, and law enforcement resources derived through relationships with the local police department. To further clarify the link between economic deprivation and crime rates, Bursik and Grasmick (1993b) explain that "the effect of economic deprivation on crime and delinquency is, in fact, an indirect one, mediated by the capacity of a neighborhood to solicit human and economic resources from external institutional actors" (p. 279). So, areas with high levels of poverty and low levels of crime can exist as long as they are able to access assistance from outside sources.

According to Bursik and Grasmick (1993a, 1993b), these three aspects of community control are interrelated and slowly emerge as residents interact over time. When community control breaks down or is absent in neighborhoods, levels of crime will rise as word spreads among criminals. This aspect of Bursik and Grasmick's (1993a, 1993b) theory is loosely based on routine activities and opportunity theories that will be discussed further in Chapter 12.

Collective Efficacy Theory

Sampson's theory of collective efficacy is another theory inspired by the Chicago school research. He suggested that **collective efficacy** is the key concept to understanding social disorganization (Sampson, Raudenbush, & Earls, 1997; Sampson, 2012). Another source of inspiration for Sampson's theory was Bandura's (1977) work in psychology, discussed in Chapter 5. Bandura's concept of self-efficacy refers to a person's belief in his or her ability to succeed in life and accomplish his or her goals.

Sampson's collective efficacy theory focuses on the ability of the neighborhood to harness informal social control and prevent crime. In a sense, collective efficacy is the inverse of social disorganization theory. In the following passage, Sampson explains the key elements important to understanding the concept of collective efficacy:

> The concept of collective efficacy draws together two fundamental explanatory mechanisms—*social cohesion* (the "collectivity" part of the concept) and *shared expectations for control* (the "efficacy" part of the concept). (2012, p. 152)

According to Sampson (2012), there are several informal social control strategies that can be used to address crime and delinquency. Examples of these include monitoring groups of children and teens, sharing information about children's behavior, increasing the willingness of residents to intervene in truancy and teens hanging out on street corners, and guarding public spaces from gang and criminal organization exploitation.

In addition to explaining crime and delinquency, Sampson (2012) claimed that, similar to social disorganization, collective efficacy is capable of explaining problems beyond just crime and delinquency rates. Other issues that collective efficacy can shed light on include health-related problems that are linked to one's social environment, including asthma, low birth weight, and even heat wave deaths (Sampson, 2012). Figure 9.3 outlines collective efficacy as a concept.

Taken together, these theories imply a series of testable propositions. Robinson and Beaver (2008, p. 254) summarize the main propositions of the different theories of social disorganization. These are outlined in figure 9.4.

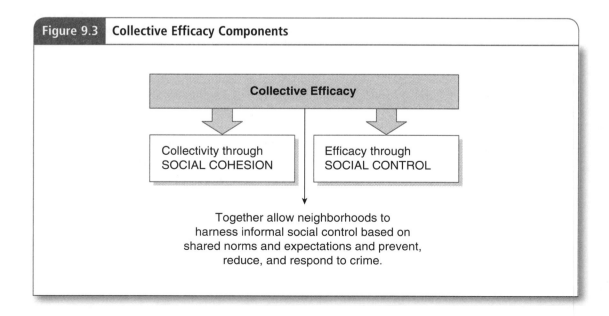

Figure 9.3   Collective Efficacy Components

Collective Efficacy

Collectivity through SOCIAL COHESION

Efficacy through SOCIAL CONTROL

Together allow neighborhoods to harness informal social control based on shared norms and expectations and prevent, reduce, and respond to crime.

Figure 9.4	Conditions of Collective Efficacy
Concept	**Propositions**
Social Disorganization	Poverty, low socioeconomic status, residential mobility, instability or transiency, immigration, racial or ethnic heterogeneity, population density, physical disorder or incivilities, and family disruption or single-parent families are related to high rates of street crime.
Collective Efficacy Informal Social Control	Prosocial networks, supervised teenage peer groups, organizational participation, trust within the neighborhood, and a willingness to engage antisocial or otherwise problematic behavior are linked to low levels of street crime.
Resource Mobilization and Political Influence	Linkages between politically active residents in a neighborhood and networks of association among neighborhood groups are linked to low levels of street crime.

Research on Social Disorganization Theories

Two students of Ernest Burgess, Clifford Shaw and Henry McKay, were the first researchers to test Burgess's concentric zone theory. To do this they used data from Cook County court records of male juvenile delinquency from 1900 to 1906, 1917 to 1923, and 1927 to 1933 (Shaw & McKay, 1942/1969). From these records, they were able to plot patterns of delinquency in the various zones of the city. Just as Burgess predicted, Shaw and McKay found that the highest levels of delinquency were in the ZIT. Their research also indicated that rates of truancy, infant mortality, tuberculosis, and insanity all corresponded to the rates of delinquency and were generally higher in the ZIT. They also found similar patterns of delinquency and the other social problems in Philadelphia, Boston, Richmond, Cincinnati, and Cleveland (Shaw & McKay, 1969). Shaw and McKay (1969) observed that the key institutions in these pathological areas were failing to properly regulate behavior. Schools in these areas were often underfunded, membership in churches was constantly changing, and families were strained and broken apart by poverty. They called this state of institutional breakdown *social disorganization*.

In their original research, Shaw and McKay (1969) identified three key factors that produced social disorganization. First, these neighborhoods are characterized by low economic status and poverty. They have high rates of families on social assistance, low rates of home ownership, and an abundance of low-paying, menial jobs (see also Sampson & Groves, 1989). Second, there were high levels of residential mobility or instability in these areas (Shaw & McKay, 1969). If residents are constantly moving in and out, it is impossible to establish strong relationships among them, thus leading to weakened informal social control. Consequently, institutions such as the family, church, and school, which are commonly responsible for regulating behavior, are weak, ineffective, and sometimes nonexistent.

Third, these communities had high levels of ethnic and cultural heterogeneity (Shaw & McKay, 1969). In other words, in many communities with high levels of social disorganization, the researchers observed there were many small groups of people with radically different cultures, norms, and languages living in the same neighborhood. Given the lack of a common language, these groups were not able to communicate effectively with each other and had little in common culturally, so they failed to understand each other and develop strong relationships. It is important to note that Shaw and McKay were not suggesting that certain races or ethnicities were prone to crime. Rather, they were pointing out that living in these small clusters of racial enclaves prevented residents from developing strong community ties beyond their native groups. Despite attempting some rigorous and thorough research, Shaw and McKay never clearly explained the causal chain between crime and social disorganization (Kornhauser, 1978; Bursik & Grasmick, 1993a, 1993b). This has made it very difficult to disentangle and empirically evaluate their underlying model.

Other researchers have been more successful. By re-analyzing data from the 1982 British Crime Survey (BCS), a survey of 10,905 residents in 238 localities in Great Britain, Sampson and Groves (1989) were able to refine and test Shaw and McKay's (1942/1969) original statement of social disorganization. They then collected data from 1989 on 11,030 residents and compared the results using their theory. The theory was supported in both cases. To test the theory, they also had to operationalize the variables. First, they identified five exogenous sources of social disorganization, three of which Shaw and McKay (1969) had suggested, including economic status, residential mobility, and ethnic/cultural heterogeneity. To these they added two more correlates that were implied in Shaw and McKay's research, namely family disruption, such as high levels of divorce and single-parent families, and urbanization that impedes social interaction and participation (e.g., population density) (Sampson & Groves, 1989).

Second, Sampson and Groves (1989) argued that these factors do not directly influence crime and delinquency; instead, the effects are mediated through other variables known as internal dimensions of social disorganization. In other words, external factors impact the internal dimensions of community life that control crime, such as local friend networks, organizational participation, and the prevalence of unsupervised teenage peer groups (Sampson & Groves, 1989).

In a meta-analysis of 214 studies published between 1960 and 1999, Pratt and Cullen (2005) concluded that social disorganization and resource/economic deprivation theories had the strongest empirical support. Specifically, they found that indicators of concentrated disadvantage, such as racial heterogeneity, poverty, and family disruption, were among the strongest and most stable predictors of crime. The research by Pratt and Cullen (2005) suggests that a focus on social disorganization and resource/economic deprivation theories, and the related policy implications for crime and youth violence reduction, warrant further consideration.

Bursik and Webb's (1982) research on community change patterns was based on a re-analysis of the Chicago school finding of stable delinquency rates in certain sections of Chicago over time, despite changing racial/ethnicities from 1940 to 1950. Bursik and Webb (1982) updated this analysis and examined the patterns from 1950 to 1960 and 1960 to 1970. They found that since 1950, assimilation patterns of some racial and ethnic groups had changed, and these groups were not allowed to properly integrate into society. These patterns were altered by two important Supreme Court cases handed down in 1948, *Shelley v. Kraemer* and *Hurd v. Hodge*. These decisions held that governments could not enforce racial restrictions in housing (Bursik & Webb, 1982).

Once legal restrictions on where African Americans could live were lifted, they began to move into sections of the city occupied by white people. Driven by antipathy and fear, many of the white residents moved out; this phenomenon became known as "white flight." Because of the disruption to the community caused by this sudden residential mobility, delinquency rates rose in these areas from 1950 to 1960. Rates of crime also climbed during this period. Bursik and Webb (1982) concluded that this rise in crime was not a result of having a higher concentration of black residents in these areas but because of the destabilization of the community caused by excessive residential mobility and segregation.

A restabilization and normalization process took place after the "white flight," and this may explain why crime rates declined during the period from 1960 to 1970.

Practical Ramifications of Social Disorganization Theories

Perhaps the most important practical attempt to put the lessons of these theories into practice is a group of social programs collectively referred to as the Chicago Area Project (CAP). Bursik and Grasmick discuss the importance of this project:

> If a Hall of Fame existed for community crime prevention projects, the Chicago Area Project (CAP) would certainly be one of the charter inductees. Not only has it been one of the most widely discussed and controversial programs since its initial organization by Clifford Shaw (with the assistance of Henry McKay) in 1932, but it is also one of the most enduring and currently serves as an umbrella organization for over thirty community associations in Chicago. (1993a, p. 160)

The goal of the CAP is to develop social programs in disorganized areas of Chicago with the intention of reducing crime and disorder. The strategy here is to recruit local citizens to help the neighborhoods to plan community activities (e.g., recreation/camping trips, parent–teacher groups); provide employment options; and manage community resources more effectively. Shaw believed it was particularly important to keep things local. Unless people within a neighborhood who are invested in the community are the ones who administer these programs, important opportunities for change can get lost in government bureaucracy and the unrealistic expectations of those who live and work elsewhere (Shaw & McKay, 1969).

Since the importance of the CAP has been recognized, a growing body of literature has begun to document encouraging lessons about interventions and factors that can contribute to positive changes in communities. While it is too soon to say all programs can work everywhere and 100% of the time, the literature points to promising areas that deserve sustained, careful attention (Fulbright-Anderson & Auspos, 2006). Programs that seem to have considerable merit focus on community-level interventions, such as community building, neighborhood safety, housing, and economic development, and others that focus on individuals, such as youth development, education, social services, and employment.[1]

In general, the research on social disorganization suggests that programs should be physically located in low-income neighborhoods and run by people with ties to the neighborhoods that they serve. This can both provide key services to those with the most needs and build local capacity policy among individuals with ties to those communities. This should serve to strengthen residential bonds and interconnections within neighborhoods.

An essential starting point is programs focused on families, and especially on children. Family preservation programs are short term, intensive, empowerment-model programs that focus not on an individual client but rather on the needs of the entire family. In dozens of states and cities, programs based on the Homebuilders projects funded by the Edna McConnell Clark Foundation have supported at-risk families in partnership with individuals, agencies, and organizations in the community. These programs rely upon social work, mentoring, and community development to promote personal growth and family preservation (Nelson, Landsman, & Deutelman, 1990).

---

1. http://www.chicagoareaproject.org/

Another important lesson that has emerged from social disorganization research is that programs operated by large public bureaucracies should become more neighborhood based and more open to input from the clients and communities they serve. Research suggests that social control is least effective when imposed by outside forces (Fulbright-Anderson & Auspos, 2006). Community controls are strengthened most when informal, community-level networks are voluntarily tied to external bureaucracies and other resources (Figueira-McDonough, 1991). Diverse reform trends in policing, education, and social services all stress more community involvement in public bureaucracies (Chubb & Moe, 1990; Goldstein, 1977; Kamerman & Kahn, 1989). However, recent policies that have resulted in the vast overuse of incarceration have degraded the potential for the very communities who need to develop informal social controls to be able to do so (Rose & Clear, 1998). The overreliance on incarceration as a method of control may hinder the ability of some communities to foster other forms of control because it serves to weaken family and community structures by destroying family structures in certain areas. For example, during the 1980s and 1990s, an alarmingly high percentage of young black males were imprisoned for minor drug and other nonviolent crimes. The sentences they received for these minor offenses were often very long, and, in many cases, these young men had children and other dependent family members. Consequently, many black communities lacked strong male role models and many black children grew up without stable fathers. As this illustrates, the side effects of policies intended to reduce crime by focusing on trying to control individual behavior may in fact exacerbate the very issues they are intended to address.

Figure 9.5	Seven Steps of Social Disorganization Theories
Seven Steps	**Social Disorganization Theories**
1. Know the History	Appeared during the roaring 1920s and mark the early origins of the Chicago school; incorporate aspects of sociological and ecological thought
2. Acknowledge Assumptions	Humans are thought to be blank slates; importance of individualistic factors not denied, but social/environmental factors thought to be of more importance; grounded in a conflict orientation
3. Problem Focus, Scope, and Level of Explanation	Focus on explaining why some neighborhoods have more crime than others (i.e., higher crime rates); structural factors are emphasized
4. Key Terms and Concepts	Social disorganization, community control, and collective efficacy
5. Respect the Research	Applied models of growth/development to Chicago and other cities; measured community participation and poverty to assess how these affected crime rates; examined changes in communities over time
6. Theory/Practice	Large-scale community projects (e.g., Chicago Area Project) involving community building, neighborhood safety, housing, and economic development; localized politics with involvement from residents
7. Mapping the Theory	See Figure 9.6

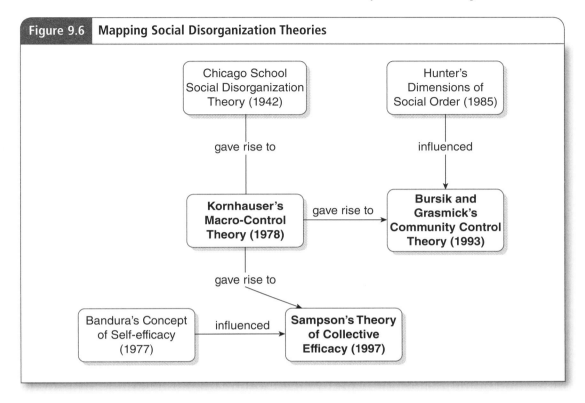

Figure 9.6   Mapping Social Disorganization Theories

Criticisms of Social Disorganization Theories

As Robinson (2004) points out, a problem with social disorganization is built into the name of the theory itself. If we define disorganization to be a problem, then on some level, we may be assuming that organization is natural and normal. This requires that we define what a socially organized community looks like. Is it Mayberry from *The Andy Griffith* show, with white picket fences, clean streets, and affluent families? This kind of thinking can lead to circular reasoning. As Bohm (2001) points out, many tests of social disorganization theory use the concept of social disorganization but then use delinquency and criminality as indicators of social disorganization. We need to ask, what are we measuring? And what are we comparing it to?

Another issue is known as the ecological fallacy (Robinson, 1950). The issue is that one cannot make inferences about individuals based on aggregate-level data. In other words, one cannot make predictions about individual human and criminal behavior based on correlations derived from sources such as official crime statistics. Some have suggested that the ecological fallacy presents problems to not only social disorganization theories but also other social structural theories (Bernard et al., 2010). As a result of this robust critique, social disorganization and other social structural theories began to fall out of favor in the 1950s and lay dormant for several decades. While it is important to be aware of this issue, some have argued that these concerns have been overstated (Sampson, 2012; Stark, 1987).

Stark (1987) argues that cases of the ecological fallacy are somewhat difficult to find and that in most instances they are "transparent examples of spuriousness" (p. 906). Bursik (1988) points out that the notion of the ecological fallacy does not assert that the aggregate or structural level of explanation is inappropriate for all types of theoretical investigation. Most recently, Sampson (2012) has suggested that Robinson's (1950) critique was misleading:

> Robinson's mistake, and that of many readers, was to assume that ecological researchers only cared about individual-level inferences. Rather than arguing against ecological or neighbor-hood-level research, the right message was to make clear the distinction amongst units of analysis and to appropriately frame analytical questions, an early version of what we now call "multilevel" analysis. It follows that if the main goal is to explain *rates of variation* across neighborhoods rather than individual differences, Robinson's critique does not hold. Moreover, worry about the ecological distracted attention from the "individualistic fal-lacy"—the often-evoked and also erroneous assumption that individual-level relations are sufficient to explain collective outcomes. (2012, pp. 39–40)

The confusion over the ecological fallacy illustrates the importance of understanding the level of explanation and problem focus of the theory at hand. Figure 9.7 outlines the ecological fallacy.

A final criticism of social disorganization theory is that it does not go far enough in examining how power differentials in society shape urban development and how this affects crime rates in different sections of the city (Taylor, Walton, & Young, 1978). These theorists do make reference to economic elements, such as when property owners purposely let their buildings fall into disrepair because they plan on selling them to members of the expanding business district, and they recognize the power of political linkages. However, they fail to question how broader questions about political

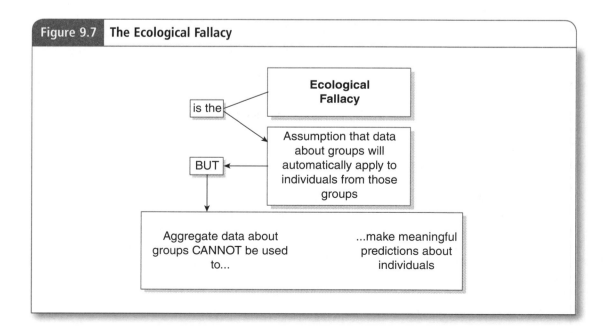

Figure 9.7 The Ecological Fallacy

arrangements influence neighborhood disadvantage and the role wealthy individuals and organizations can play in manipulating the political process to achieve their own ends.

Research Example: Disorganization, Community, and Mixed Methods

A useful example of recent research based on social disorganization is the Project on Human Development in Chicago Neighborhoods (PHDCN), one of the largest projects ever attempted in criminology (http://www.icpsr.umich.edu/icpsrweb/PHDCN/). This project started in 1982 and initially suffered from a great deal of in-fighting and controversy. It took years to develop the proper instruments, reach out to the community, and pilot test the project's approach (Sampson, 2012). The project relied on an interdisciplinary approach to data collection and analysis. The research team was composed of behavioral geneticists, neurobiologists, child psychiatrists, psychologists, sociologists, and criminologists.

The PHDCN was an interdisciplinary study of how families, schools, and neighborhoods affect child and adolescent development. It was designed to advance the understanding of the developmental pathways of both positive and negative human social behaviors. In particular, the project examined the pathways to juvenile delinquency, adult crime, substance abuse, and violence. At the same time, the project also provided a detailed look at the environments in which these social behaviors take place by collecting substantial amounts of data about urban Chicago, including data on its people, institutions, and resources. The PHDCN has resulted in a very important series of research studies; one of these was published in the prestigious journal *Science* (Sampson, Raudenbush, & Earls, 1997). The researchers originally intended to study several cities, but funding and pragmatic concerns forced them to focus only on the city of Chicago (Sampson, 2012).

The design used in this project consisted of two major components. The first was an intensive study of Chicago's neighborhoods, particularly the social, economic, organizational, political, and cultural structures and the dynamic changes that took place in the structures over time. The team obtained raw data by dividing the city of Chicago into neighborhood clusters based on a variety of information, including major geographic boundaries (e.g., railroad tracks, parks, freeways); knowledge of Chicago's local neighborhoods; and cluster analysis of census data (Sampson, 2012, p. 79).

The second component was a series of coordinated longitudinal studies that followed over 6,000 randomly selected children, adolescents, and young adults. The goal was to examine the changing circumstances of their lives and the personal characteristics that might lead these young people toward or away from a variety of antisocial behaviors. This involved extensive interviews of children and their primary caregivers from sampled households. Researchers gathered information about health, temperament, personality, cognitive functioning, ethnic identity, moral development, social competence, exposure to violence, substance abuse, delinquency, family structure and process, and peers. In addition, the team conducted three large-scale community studies to gain a deeper understanding of the neighborhoods involved as a whole (Sampson, 2012).

The Community Survey (CS) assessed all Chicago neighborhoods in the PHDCN, and independent data were collected for each neighborhood. The team interviewed 8,782 individuals 18 and older about the structural and cultural organization of their neighborhoods. They also completed a systematic social observation (SSO) of all the street sections within 80 of the neighborhood clusters. This involved making video and audio recordings of different sections of the city while driving in an SUV and supplementing this with observer logs. The goal was to help orient the researchers to "the sights, sounds, and feel of everyday life" in these areas (Sampson, 2012, p. 90).

Another strategy was the Key Informant Study, which consisted of interviews with approximately 2,800 community leaders from a variety of institutional domains, including business, law enforcement, community organization, education, politics, and religion. Once this data was collected, the PHDCN set about to test various theoretical propositions within social disorganization and collective efficacy. One development was the identification of *intervening mechanisms*. These are mediating variables between the traditional social disorganization variables and crime rates, such as the effect of social disorganization on rates of family disruption and collective efficacy, which, in turn, directly influence crime rates (Sampson & Groves, 1989; Sampson, Raudenbush, & Earls, 1997).

Based on the videotaping and systematic rating of more than 23,000 street segments in Chicago, scales of social and physical disorder for 196 neighborhoods were constructed. Sampson & Raudenbush (1999) produced an alternative interpretation of the link between disorder and crime. More specifically, they suggested that typical activities categorized as social disorder (e.g., soliciting prostitutes and loitering) and incivilities (e.g., painting graffiti) are evidence of either crime or ordinance violations. They viewed these problems as resulting from the same forces as those that produce more serious crimes. In other words, they argued that both disorder and crime are manifestations of the same phenomenon.

To further clarify which phenomena might be relevant, Morenoff, Sampson, and Raudenbush (2001) combined structural characteristics from the 1990 census with a survey of 8,872 Chicago residents in 1995 to predict homicide variations in 1996–1998 across 343 neighborhoods. They found that spatial proximity to homicide, concentrated disadvantage, and low collective efficacy independently predicted increased homicide rates. Their findings also suggested that local organizations, voluntary associations, and friend/kinship networks could promote the collective efficacy of residents and help to achieve social control.

The Longitudinal Cohort Study collected three waves of data over a period of 7 years from a sample of children, adolescents, and young adults and their primary caregivers. Seven randomly selected cohorts of respondents were selected so researchers could study the changing circumstances of their lives and any personal characteristics that might lead them toward or away from a variety of antisocial behaviors. The age cohorts include birth (0), 3, 6, 9, 12, 15, and 18 years. Numerous measures were administered to respondents to gauge various aspects of human development, including individual differences and family, peer, and school influences.

As part of the Longitudinal Cohort Study, 412 infants from the birth cohort and their primary caregivers were studied during wave 1 (1994–1997). Researchers examined the effects of prenatal and postnatal conditions on the health and cognitive functioning of infants in the first year of life. The Infant Assessment Unit also sought to link early developmental processes with the onset of antisocial behavior and to measure the strength of these relationships. The infants received an assessment between the ages of 5 to 7 months in addition to the protocol given to all infants in cohort 0 as part of the Longitudinal Cohort Study. Measures assessed visual recognition and memory, physical health and birth complications, temperament, and family environment. Videotape was used to record the responses of the infant to different types of stimulation as well as to capture interactions between the parent and infant to determine empathic responsiveness of the parent, encouragement and guidance, and overall psychopathology.

Sampson's (2012) book *Great American City* is based on a decade of data collection associated with the PHDCN. In a review, Denton (2013) argues that the book will change thinking among sociologists, demographers, criminologists, and policymakers and set a new research agenda to test the findings from Chicago. She identifies three essential contributions the book makes. The first is methodological and related to how Sampson treats selection bias. Typically this refers to the problem in research design that when people choose to participate in a program, intervention, or project, the results gathered from their participation are problematic since the factors that led them to choose to participate may be more important than the result of the program or intervention. In the context of his research, Sampson takes almost the opposite approach. He argues that "selection is not a 'bias' but rather part and parcel of a dynamic social process—another form of neighborhood effect" (2013, p. 29). Since "selection bias is itself a form of neighborhood effect" (2013, p. 308), the process of selection itself deserves more attention. Thus, in some areas of criminology, this means studying why people choose to participate in a program instead of trying to statistically control for their participation. For Sampson, this means focusing on how the process of moving itself affects individuals, regardless of the neighborhood they wind up in, and how social ties and networks condition that mobility.

During the 7 years between 1995 and 2002, Chicago neighborhoods changed for the better, and they changed more for movers than stayers. But the racial hierarchy remains: Whites gain most, blacks least, and Latinos are in the middle. Sampson concludes these moves connect the places and reproduce the structure of inequality in Chicago. This suggests the focus in criminology on mere individual differences may miss how neighborhood inequality constrains collective efficacy and contributes to crime. Figure 9.8 provides a clear view of how neighborhoods and crime in Chicago are connected.

The second contribution identified by Denton (2013) is the explicit neighborhood-centric analysis. Sampson's approach defines neighborhoods as more than census tracts or groups based on city blocks, and he argues that individual reactions to neighborhood differences become a social mechanism that shapes our other perceptions and behavior both inside and outside the neighborhood. The emphasis is on the places themselves, and their location in the larger matrices of places is based on Sampson's assumption that people are social creatures. This means locations shape the relationships that make people who they are. The first contribution of this work is defining neighborhoods both socially and spatially, which is done by studying the neighborhood itself and the location of the neighborhood within the city. Sampson argues that beyond the focus in contemporary criminology on individual- and micro-level explanations of crime, neighborhoods are very important to understanding how rates of behavior vary across social spaces.

A final contribution from Sampson is the consequences of this spatial reality on collective efficacy. As discussed above, collective efficacy refers to attempts by those in the neighborhood to harness informal social control and prevent crime through communal ties and shared expectations. However, just as people are embedded in relationships to other people, the placement of neighborhoods and the spatial organization of communities within a city matter as well. Sampson demonstrates that associations across neighborhoods in perceptions of disorder, residential stability, crime, and collective efficacy are simultaneously local and connected across the city. This is of significance when considering the racial composition of neighborhoods.

For example, Sampson argues that white neighborhoods with low collective efficacy are most often (60% of the time) located near neighborhoods with high collective efficacy, while Latino

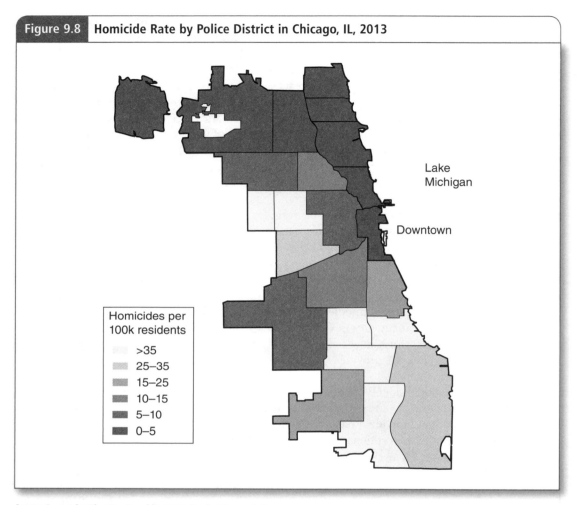

Figure 9.8 Homicide Rate by Police District in Chicago, IL, 2013

Source: Copyright, The New Republic, 2014. Used with permission.

and black neighborhoods with low collective efficacy are near neighborhoods with high collective efficacy only 25% and 20% of the time, respectively. This suggests that even if white neighborhoods are not advantaged or high in collective efficacy, the neighborhoods near them are. As a result, they can still benefit from these collective goods even though they themselves are not contributing.

In sum, Denton (2013) concludes that Sampson's *Great American City* has "the potential to change the intellectual terrain in many, many areas: neighborhood effects research, the meaning of selectivity, collective efficacy, inequality, altruism, civic society, social networks, crime, migration, organizations" (p. 6).

> **Now that you've read this chapter. . .** what do you think? If social disorganization theories are correct, what do you think the impact of moving away from high-crime communities would be on those recently released from prison? Kirk (2009) found that if a parolee moves away from his or her former neighborhood, it substantially reduces the chances of reincarceration. Consider three reasons based on social disorganization theory why this might be so. Should states force those released from prisons to move to new neighborhoods?

⊠ Conclusion and Review Questions

In this chapter, we examined the first major branch of structural explanations. These are often referred to as social disorganization and ecological theories. Social disorganization theorists ask why variations in crime occur in different areas of a city or town. The notion that certain places tend to produce more crime originally grew out of work by the Chicago school. More recent research in Chicago has highlighted the need to examine the intersection between people, places, and crimes through a multidisciplinary lens. As we have seen, there is broad support for these theories, and some interesting policy-based work offers a means to address how and why some crime appears to be a result of the interactions of people in a certain geographical location.

As we will see in the Chapter 12, social disorganization and ecological theories are not the only theories that emphasize the geographic distribution of people, places, and things. For example, opportunity and rational choice models of crime consider how targets, crime, motivated offenders, and capable guardians interact in time and space (Brantingham & Brantingham, 1984; Cohen & Felson, 1979). These theories are more social psychological rather than sociological and focus more on explaining individual behavior without as much of a focus on group dynamics (Bursik, 1988). They also play into the rise of more conservative approaches to crime and crime control, which claim the responsibility for criminality belongs to those committing crime rather than to the society in which these individuals were born, raised, and lived.

CHAPTER REVIEW

1. List some core assumptions made by social disorganization and ecological theorists.

2. What do social disorganization and ecological theories try to explain?

3. Explain the history of social disorganization and ecological theories and its relevance to practical approaches and programs suggested by these theories.

4. How have social disorganization and ecological theories been critiqued in the past? What is the strongest objection to them in your opinion?

5. What does recent research based on social disorganization theory tell us about this approach? Why were multimethod research strategies adopted?

CHAPTER

10

Social Strain and Anomie Theories

 Chapter Overview and Objectives

In this chapter, we turn our attention to social strain and anomie (SSA) theories in criminology. These theories suggest that stressors and pressures in one's life increase the likelihood of criminal behavior for a variety of reasons. Chief among these strains is the emphasis in American culture on materialism, wealth, and consumerism. Social stratification and institutional structures limit upward mobility and create strains and stressors that may produce negative emotions, such as frustration and anger, which can result in impulsive crimes. These emotions may also create longer-term pressures for corrective action, with crime serving as one possible response. Crime may also be used to reduce or escape from strain or to seek revenge against the source of the strain and other related targets. SSA theories acknowledge that only a minority of strained individuals turn to crime. In recent years, these theories have undergone a transformation and have shifted focus from social norms to monetary success and finally to a broad range of goals that are shared by people from all walks of life. Figure 10.1 provides an overview of SSA theories.

By the end of the chapter readers should be able to:

- Understand assumptions made by anomie and social strain theories
- Be aware of the level of explanation, problem focus, and scope of the social strain and anomie theories
- Know the differences between anomie and social disorganization and ecological theories
- Understand the origins of the structural-functionalist tradition and how it relates to theories in this area
- Have knowledge of the practical approaches and programs suggested by anomie theories

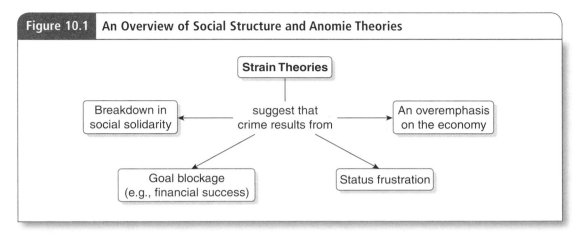

Figure 10.1 An Overview of Social Structure and Anomie Theories

The Social Strain and Anomie Tradition

All SSA theories have emerged from the work of Emile Durkheim and particularly his concept of anomie. He suggested that societal rules as to how people ought to behave were breaking down and causing confusion. This breakdown has the potential to cause problems because, without clearly defined norms, behavior becomes less predictable and people become unsure of what to expect from each other. Subsequent theories focused on the rejection of norms when individuals felt blocked from achieving monetary success or the somewhat broader goal of middle-class status (Merton, 1938).

Many people refer to SSA theories simply as anomie theories or strain theories, and this has created some confusion. Classifying them simply as anomie theories implies that Merton directly adopted all of the ideas attached to Durkheim's concept of anomie; in fact, it is clear that Merton borrowed selectively from Durkheim's thinking on this subject. Further, there is also a branch of psychological research that frequently refers to strain, but these are individualistic forms rather than societal forms of strain. Merton disliked the label of *strain theory* because of its association with these psychological and individualistic explanations of behavior (Cullen & Messner, 2007). In general, these theories can be used to examine structural and cultural factors that explain variations in crime rates from society to society.

As you read this chapter, consider . . . in 2008, the United States suffered a massive financial crisis brought about, in part, by the actions of those working at investment banks. According to Michael Lewis (2014), just as the scale of the problem was being discovered, another issue was undermining the fairness of the entire financial system. High-volume traders were paying for faster access to the stock market. Using speed, technology, and automation, a small group of investors gained an advantage over less technologically savvy investors. In an interview on *60 Minutes*, Michael Lewis stated, "The United States stock market, the most iconic market in global capitalism, is rigged." As you read this chapter, consider the consequences of this finding. What would structural strain theorists suggest is the danger in this story?

Seven Steps of Criminological Thinking

History and Social Context of Social Strain and Anomie Theories

Merton's (1938) classical statement of strain theory emerged in the years following the Great Depression (1929–1939). However, the history of these ideas goes back much further. As discussed in previous chapters, Emile Durkheim was a French thinker who first defined anomie as a normlessness state that characterizes unstable societies. In anomic societies, key institutions such as the family, church, education, and political systems have often broken down or become weakened. According to Durkheim, a breakdown in institutional control may lead to increased levels of deviance, crime, and other social pathologies.

Durkheim believed that one could trace the development of societies along a continuum based on their level of solidarity or connectedness (Beirne & Messerschmidt, 2011). Old-fashioned societies with lower levels of technological development and less industrialization are thought to have **mechanical solidarity**. Members of these societies also tend to think and act in similar ways and have common customs and traditions; society is connected through primary relationships (e.g., ties of kinship and friendship). In these societies, the law tends to be quite repressive and religion plays a great a role in everyday life.

As societies become more technologically advanced and industrialized, they move closer to **organic solidarity**. Customs, traditions, and beliefs in these types of societies tend to be quite diverse; these societies are held together more by contractual relationships than by kinship and friendship ties. The division of labor in these societies becomes more specialized, and law focuses more upon restoring relationships rather than punishing the guilty. Cities and larger urban centers illustrate many of these characteristics. For Durkheim (1938/1895), crime was viewed as a social fact or "a category of facts which present very special characteristics: they consist of manners of acting, thinking, and feeling external to the individual, which are invested with a coercive power by virtue of which they exercise control over him" (p. 52). Some have also argued that fear of crime and chronically high crime rates in Western countries after World War II are contemporary versions of social facts (Liska, Lawrence, & Sanchirico, 1982; Garland, 2001).

Merton's highly influential article titled "Social Structure and Anomie" (1938) was written and published just as the United States was recovering from the Great Depression, which began following the collapse of the stock market on Black Tuesday, October 29th, 1929. While millions of shares of stock were sold off the week before Black Tuesday, the value of most shares fell sharply, leading to financial ruin and panic. Businesses closed, banks failed, and people lost their savings. Millions were out of work, and wages for those still fortunate enough to have jobs fell by about 50%. By 1932, the industrial output of the United States had been cut in half, and more than 90,000 businesses had failed completely. Extreme poverty and hunger were rampant, and many were forced to live in Hoovervilles, or shantytowns, built by homeless Americans who had lost everything. The United States, the land of opportunity, had become the land of desperation (Sutton, 2004).

Despite the extreme hardships experienced during the Great Depression, few wealthy Americans actually suffered. In fact, about 40% of the population was not affected by the fall of the economy or the failing stock market (Bernanke, 1995). It was during this era of desperation and imbalance of power that Merton began to develop his theory of anomie. The disaster of the Great Depression, coupled with increased immigration rates, led Merton to predict that certain groups of people would have a harder time achieving economic success than others. He referred to this goal of wealth as the American Dream. James Truslow Adams, a writer and historian best known for his three-volume history of New England, had earlier coined this term. He suggested life in America

> should be better and richer and fuller for everyone, with opportunity for each according to ability or achievement regardless of social class or circumstances of birth. . . . [It is] a dream of social order in which each man and each woman shall be able to attain to the fullest stature of which they are innately capable, and be recognized by others for what they are, regardless of the fortuitous circumstances of birth or position. (Adams, 1931, pp. 214–215)

Merton recognized that this dream was a powerful force in American society. He also saw that it required access to means, resources, and opportunities not equally available to every member in society. Merton expanded on Durkheim's theory of anomie, or the insecurity felt by a lack of social norms, by focusing on how this failure to attain wealth could lead to deviant and/or criminal behavior. Merton (1938) claimed that "the extreme emphasis upon the accumulation of wealth as a symbol of success in our society militates against the completely effective control of institutionally regulated modes of acquiring a fortune" (p. 59).

This institutional focus was a result of the influence of an approach known as **structural-functionalism**. According to structural-functionalists, society is more than the sum of its parts or just a collection of individuals; different parts of society work together in a systematic fashion and are connected with one another. In this view, society is seen as being similar to an organism or a machine. Even crime is seen as a normal part of society and is viewed as serving important functions, such as uniting people by helping establish the boundaries of acceptable behavior. While many might assume that a crime-free society would be desirable, a structural-functionalist would argue that a society without crime might be indicative of an overly repressive society or a society in a deep state of chaos and lawlessness. As a metatheory or grand theory, structural functionalism is closer to a philosophy or perspective because it is impossible to falsify. Durkheim and Merton are both considered structural-functionalists.

Assumptions of Social Strain and Anomie Theories

Social strain theories all assume that humans are naturally social and altruistic and that society serves to corrupt human nature (Agnew, 2011). This view of human nature can be seen as a reaction to the early forms of biological and psychological explanations found in the work of biological positivists such as Lombroso and Hooton (Merton & Ashley-Montagu, 1940). In the following passage, Merton presents his view of human nature:

> For one thing, it no longer appears so obvious that man is set against society in an unceasing war between biological impulse and social restraint. The image of man as an untamed bundle of impulses begins to look more like a caricature than a portrait. For another, sociological perspectives have increasingly entered into the analysis of behavior deviating from pre-scribed patterns of conduct. For whatever the role of impulses, there still remains the further question of why it is that the frequency of deviant behavior varies within social structures and how it happens that the deviations have different shapes and patterns in different social structures. (1949, p. 185)

This quote raises an interesting issue. Crime cannot be explained by merely referring to untamed impulses because crime varies within the social structure. For example, some countries have more crime than others, some cities have more crime than others, and some neighborhoods have more crime than others. It is difficult to argue that all of this variation is explained by individual differences such as impulsivity or variations in levels of self-control. To put it differently: The United States has a higher crime rate than Sweden, but does this mean that there are more psychopathic or impulsive individuals in the United States? Probably not. Instead, strain theorists would argue this is the result of differences in the social structures of the two countries.

Like social disorganization theories, social strain theories do not claim that biological factors are irrelevant but rather that they are mediated through one's social environment. Since these theories assume social forces shape human nature, it should come as no surprise to find out that anomie theories are also deterministic. Some refer to this approach as *sociological positivism*. Unlike believers in early forms of positivism based on biology and psychology, Merton and Ashley-Montagu (1940) challenged the notion that biological factors could fully explain criminal behavior. The brand of sociological positivism embraced by social strain theorists is different because these theories are concerned with societal level factors that produce crime. In particular, Merton believed that structural and cultural aspects of American society and the economic system of capitalism produced crime.

Social strain theorists view society as being characterized by a consensus over values, norms, and laws. However, according to Merton, one's position in the social structure does influence certain interests and values (Taylor et al., 1973). These theorists imply that there is some conflict between different groups in society that is usually the result of social class and competition that is characteristic of capitalist societies. In Merton's words, "The same social pattern can be dysfunctional for some parts of the social system and functional for other parts" (as cited in Taylor et al., 1973, p. 100). This helps to explain how differing patterns of behavior are produced by one's location in the social structure.

Problem Focus, Scope, and Level of Explanation of Social Strain and Anomie Theories

Social strain and anomie theories focus on explaining structural variations in crime rates. In particular, strain theorists emphasize the criminogenic nature of capitalism (Taylor et al., 1973). Merton's (1938) anomie theory and many of its extensions are not intended to explain criminality or individual criminal behavior (Merton, 1995). Instead, these theories focus on explaining group dynamics of crime and how these relate to larger structural and cultural factors. However, Agnew's (1992) general strain theory (GST) pays much more attention to interpersonal dynamics and individual-level factors while still remaining true to the logic in Merton's (1938) original SSA theory. Because it draws upon the findings of several different branches of research in psychology and social psychology, GST has begun to take on an integrated nature. This being the case, GST will be reviewed in more depth in Chapter 13, which focuses on general and integrated theories.

The scope of Merton's (1938) original strain theory focuses primarily on street-level crime committed for profit; however, other types of crime (e.g., drug use, civil disobedience) and emergence of criminal subcultures are addressed in some cases. He did discuss the phenomenon of white-collar and upper-class crime, but he assumed that this type of crime was much less common than typical lower-class street crime and mentioned that the lower classes were under much more pressure to commit crime (Merton, 1938, p. 190). More recently, these theories have been applied to explain occupational, white-collar, and corporate crime (see Passas, 1990, 2010; Murphy & Robinson, 2008).

Key Terms and Concepts in Social Strain and Anomie Theories

Social Strain Theory

In his 1938 article, "Social Structure and Anomie," Merton proposed his social strain theory. The theory generated numerous studies and is one of the most-cited articles in both criminology and sociology. Social strain theory posits the existence of culturally prescribed goals and institutionally approved or legitimate means in society. According to Merton (1938), the dominant cultural goal in American society is achieving the American Dream (economic success). Again, the underlying idea is that anyone can be successful and socially mobile as long as he or she works hard enough. The legitimate means, or norms, consist of opportunities and attitudes that allow one to become successful in life. These include the access to a good education and the connections necessary to get a good job upon entry into the workforce.

Merton (1938) hypothesized that because of the emphasis on competition in American society (and other capitalist societies), there is a disjuncture between the goals and means. In other words, access to legitimate means is not distributed evenly across all socioeconomic classes in society. Lack of access to the means and the pressure created by the emphasis on economic success breed stress among members of society, leading to higher levels of anomie or normlessness and, ultimately, to higher crime rates.

According to Merton (1938), people adapt to this strain in one of five different ways. First, **conformity** occurs when a person embraces both the cultural goals and the legitimate means to achieve them. This is the only nondeviant adaptation, and Merton (1938) claimed that in a stable society, conformity would be the most common adaptation. The majority of law-abiding citizens with honest jobs could be considered conformists. Second, **innovation** refers to individuals who embrace the cultural goal of economic success but lack access to the legitimate means. These people will eventually turn to illegitimate means (e.g., profit-making crimes, such as theft, burglary, robbery, drug dealing, and other cons) to achieve economic success. Merton never claimed that all criminals came from the lower class but rather that these people were under the most pressure to commit crime:

> Whatever the differential rates of deviant behavior in the several social strata, and we know from many sources that official crime statistics showing higher rates in the lower strata are far from complete or reliable, it appears from our analysis that the greatest pressures toward deviation are exerted upon the lower strata. (1968, p. 198)

The third adaptation is called **ritualism**. Ritualists are people who have abandoned the cultural goals but still adhere to the legitimate means. These people have given up on achieving the American Dream and realize that their jobs will never make them rich, but they still desire the security that comes from having a steady job. Someone who is basically "going through the motions" exemplified by the disillusioned office worker, the typical 9-to-5 retail employee, or the lifetime fast-food worker best illustrates this adaptation.

The fourth mode of adaptation is **retreatism**. According to Merton (1938), this is the least common of the deviant adaptations and results when a person rejects both the cultural goals and legitimate means. Retreatists are in an escapist mode; they have dropped out or given up on society. Examples of this adaptation include chronic alcoholics, drug addicts, and vagrants. However, psychotics, outcasts, commune members, and people who commit suicide also could be included in this category. **Rebellion** is the fifth and final adaptation. Rebels not only reject both the goals and means, but also substitute their own goals and means. In some cases, their activities might result in criminal or deviant behavior (e.g., protests), but these actions are not undertaken for personal profit or gain. Rather, they are often intended to defend some higher principle or greater good. Political dissidents and activists are examples of this mode of adaptation. For example, progressive heroes such as Martin Luther King Jr. and Gandhi would be considered rebels, but there are more negative examples of this adaptation as well (e.g., Osama Bin Laden, white supremacist/militia groups). Merton's strain theory is depicted in Figure 10.2.

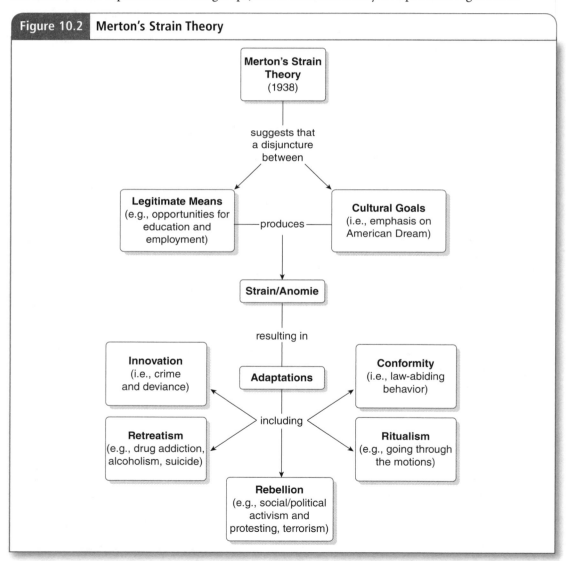

Figure 10.2   Merton's Strain Theory

Murphy and Robinson (2008) attempted to elaborate upon Merton's (1938) strain theory by suggesting a new adaptation called the maximizer. The maximizer utilizes both legitimate and illegitimate means to achieve the cultural goal of the American Dream. Therefore, this adaptation can be viewed as a combination of the conformist and the innovator. Murphy and Robinson also claim that this adaptation is quite common in American society. Further, maximizers are usually not viewed as criminal because they are pursuing the American Dream in a partially legitimate context.

This expansion of Merton's theories of anomie and strain combines both legitimate and illegitimate means of opportunity in pursuit of the American Dream. To illustrate this adaptation, Murphy and Robinson (2008) refer to examples of corporate malfeasance in which normally law-abiding businesspeople knowingly violated regulations or ignored serious issues with their products that resulted in serious harm to the general public (e.g., defects in the engine of the Ford Pinto, efforts to cover up harmful effects of tobacco).

Subcultural Strain Theory

Cohen's (1955) subcultural strain theory is an early extension of Merton's anomie theory intended to explain the genesis of delinquent subcultures. The central principle in this theory is based on Merton's (1938) original theory, but Cohen also incorporates ideas from psychoanalytic theory (Freud, 1920, 1923) and Sutherland's (1939) differential association theory. It is also worth noting that Cohen was a student of both Merton and Sutherland, so it should come as no surprise that Cohen's theory incorporates ideas from both strain and differential association theory. This theory posits that lower-class delinquent subcultures exhibit behavior that is nonutilitarian, malicious, and negativistic:

> This fact is of crucial importance in defining our problem—that much gang stealing has no motivation at all. Even where the value of the object stolen is itself a motivating consideration, the stolen sweets are often sweeter than those acquired by more legitimate and prosaic means. In homelier language stealing for the "hell of it" and apart from the considerations of gain and profit is a valued activity to which attaches glory, prowess and profound satisfaction. There is no accounting in rational and utilitarian terms for the effort expended and the danger run in stealing things which are often discarded, destroyed or casually given away. A group of boys enters a store where each takes a hat, a ball or a light bulb. They then move onto another store where these things are covertly exchanged for like articles. They then move onto other stores to continue the game indefinitely. They steal a basket of peaches, desultorily munch on them, and leave the rest to spoil. They steal clothes they cannot wear and toys they will not use. Unquestionably, most delinquents are from the more "needy" or "underprivileged" classes, and unquestionably many things are stolen because they are intrinsically valued. (Cohen, 1955, p. 25)

In other words, the crime committed by members of the delinquent subculture does not always need to have a clear purpose. Instead, they are engaging in these activities to attain some sort of status among their peers.

In lower-class delinquents, the motivation to steal for status stems from what Cohen (1955) called **status frustration**. He argued that teachers and other authority figures often evaluate lower-class children by using what he called the *middle-class measuring rod*. This term refers to a collection of behaviors and attitudes that Cohen attributed to members of the middle class and includes characteristics such as the ability to delay gratification and set long-term goals. He claimed that since members of the lower classes often lacked these characteristics, their children couldn't possibly live up to the standards that were derived from them. Drawing upon the Freudian concept of **reaction formation**, Cohen (1955) suggested that lower-class youth often redefine goal achievement to include delinquent activities and behaviors. According to Cohen, this is a collective solution to status frustration and lays the groundwork for the genesis of lower-class delinquent subcultures and gangs.

Cohen (1955) also made attempts to address female delinquency and middle-class male delinquency. This is notable because, before Cohen's work, very little effort was made to explain these sorts of crimes. Female delinquency was seen as a form of reaction formation in young girls against the double standards that society held them to during this time period. Cohen argued that many of these delinquent activities revolved around sex and that they could be seen as attempts to establish satisfactory relationships with members of the opposite sex (1955, p. 147). The old maxim of "boys will be boys and girls will be good" holds true here. Some minor forms of criminality and deviance (e.g., vandalism, underage drinking, and sexual activity) are almost expected out of males, but if females behave in similar ways, their actions are viewed as a more severe form of deviance. One could argue that this is still true today in a less extreme sense.

Cohen (1955) viewed middle-class male delinquency as a reaction to being raised primarily by women. These youth sought to exhibit their masculinity through acting out and protesting against female authority. The delinquent activities participated in by middle-class males were geared more toward taking risks and being tough (e.g., joyriding, drag-racing, fighting).

Differential Opportunity Theory

Another attempt to extend Merton's theory into the problem domain of gangs and subcultures can be found in Cloward and Ohlin's (1960) differential opportunity theory. Again, it's worth noting that Cloward was Merton's student while he attended Columbia University and that Ohlin was Sutherland's student at the University of Indiana and obtained his doctorate from the University of Chicago. Consequently, it is easy to detect the influence of differential association and social disorganization in this theory although the central theoretical principles are derived from strain theory. More specifically, Cloward and Ohlin (1960) expand on opportunity structures proposed by Merton. They say that illegitimate opportunities are also limited and shaped by one's social environment, and they offer three types of subcultural adaptations that may emerge. The type of adaptation that emerges is a function of the level of social disorganization.

The notion of subcultural adaptations is an elaboration on the modes of adaptation offered by Merton (1938); they are intended to "denote the *principal orientation* of each form of adaptation" (Cloward & Ohlin, 1960, p. 21). First, there is a **criminal pattern** (based on innovation from Merton); this includes criminal gangs that engage in large criminal enterprises geared toward profit-making activities (e.g., drug dealing, smuggling, and illegal gambling). Members are usually introduced to these subcultures as juveniles and began to learn criminal skills and attitudes favorable to crime at this point. Because interaction and learning are required to pass on criminal trades and skills, levels of social disorganization cannot be too high or these subcultures will not form. Second, Cloward and Ohlin (1960) identify a **conflict pattern**. In these gangs, respect is earned through violence and aggression; crimes for profit might be present but are not emphasized. Members of these gangs usually lack strong relationships with adults and have few role models. This pattern emerges in areas with higher levels of social disorganization and less control over young people.

Figure 10.3	Mapping Differential Opportunity Theory

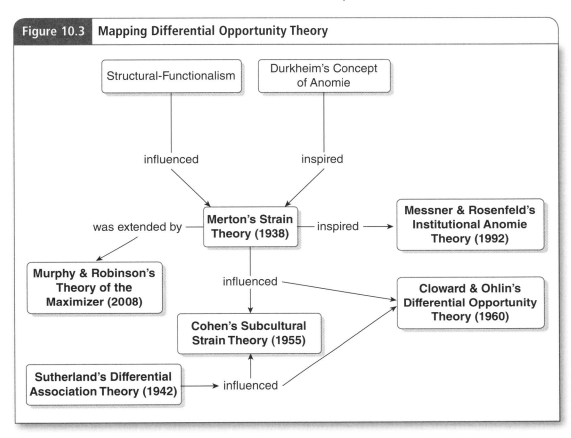

Third, there is a **retreatist pattern** to some gangs. Drugs and drug use are the central focus of groups in this category and this use runs the gamut from alcohol to marijuana to harder drugs. Older members of this subculture teach younger members the techniques required to use and obtain drugs. Profit-making crime is emphasized, but it is much different from that emphasized in the criminal subculture. In these groups, the swindle, the hustle, or the con is preferred; prostitution or dealing drugs to make money or buy drugs are also common. The idea that criminal behavior is learned can be connected to Sutherland's differential association theory and later social learning theories. In several of the adaptations, there are clearly criminal skills being taught and passed down from older to younger members. Subcultural norms are also passed down, including both expectations and rationalizations.

Institutional Strain Theory

Messner and Rosenfeld's (1994) institutional strain theory can be seen as an extension of Merton's (1938) original strain theory. These theorists are particularly interested in the role of the American Dream in producing high crime rates. More specifically, they argue that the emphasis on economic success and the "fetishism" of money has caused very high rates of crime in the United States. It is important to note that, unlike Merton (1938), they do not necessarily view this as an unavoidable by-product of the capitalist system because other capitalist countries (e.g., Canada, Finland, Japan, and Germany) have much lower rates of crime than the United States. Messner and Rosenfeld (2012) believe that social institutions are particularly important to explaining and understanding societal variations in crime rates. **Social institutions** are defined as "relatively stable sets of norms and values, statuses and roles, and groups and organizations that regulate human conduct to meet the needs of society" (Messner & Rosenfeld, 2013, p. 74). This theory focuses specifically on the institutions of economy, polity, education, and family.

Messner and Rosenfeld (2013) go on to claim that the institutional balance of power in the United States is skewed toward the economy because of the American Dream and the overemphasis on economic success. Further, they suggest that the economy has intruded into other social institutions and caused noneconomic institutions to be devalued; this has affected the ability of these institutions to control human behavior. For example, American politics is dominated by lobbying groups and political action committees that use vast sums of money to try to impact electoral outcomes. The idea that politics depends on financial interests over all others undermines the notion that the government is of the people, by the people, and for the people.

The influence of economic interests is also changing how people view education. Increasingly privatized, universities are now run like corporations, constantly trying to cut positions, increase class sizes, and maximize profit, often at the expense of education. Today, many students view college and university as a required stop to get a job and care little about the substance of the education they receive. Even the family has become an arena for economic consumption. As anyone who has had a baby knows, parents are constantly targeted to buy designer baby clothes, high-tech video baby monitors, and even iPad-equipped potty training systems. Children increasingly expect personal cell phones and eschew hand-me-downs, and parents may feel like failures if they cannot buy everything for their children.

To summarize, institutional strain theory attributes high levels of crime in the United States to cultural and social structural aspects of American society. The cultural aspect is the American Dream and the emphasis on economic success, which eventually results in anomie. The structural aspect stems from the dominance of the institution of economy; this dominance has caused other institutions to deteriorate and become less effective in controlling behavior.

Research on Social Strain and Anomie Theories

Research on structural or institutional strain makes use of macro-level data, such as rates of property and violent crime, and homicide rates. These studies, taken as a whole, suggest partial support for institutional anomie theory and the relationship between the economy, poverty, social supports, and some types of crime. However, some analyses of older crime data have failed to support the key proposition that crime is a function of normlessness and the insecurity associated with changing values. For example, Lodhi and Tilly (1973) found that crime rates were actually falling in France during the 1800s. This finding challenges the societal and institutional instability Durkheim reported as central to this era.

More recent research suggests that higher conditions of anomie are associated with higher levels of certain kinds of crime, specifically property crime (Kick & LaFree, 1985). Robinson (2004) also points to a number of studies that suggest while urbanization and industrialization appear to be associated with property crime rates, this is not due to changing norms and values at the societal level. Instead, there is evidence that the strains associated with economic pressures and income inequality may lead to increases in crime when social control institutions meant to regulate behavior (e.g., the family and education) are weak (Jensen, 1996; Messner & Rosenfeld, 2001).

Chamlin and Cochran (1995) examined the effects of poverty and noneconomic measures such as church membership, higher levels of voting participation, and lower levels of divorce on property crime rates in the United States. They concluded the effects of poverty on property crime depend on the strength of noneconomic institutions such as religion, family, and voter participation to mitigate the criminogenic impact of economic deprivation. Maume and Lee (2003) replicated this finding and concluded that noneconomic institutions (i.e., polity, family, and education) mediated the relationship between the economy and violence.

Messner and Rosenfeld (1994) examined the relationship between the economy, measured as economic inequality, and political participation in relation to criminal homicide rates in 45 modern industrialized nations. They found that when social supports were made available to citizens to reduce their reliance on market forces, there was a significant and direct negative effect on homicide rates. This finding has been replicated (Pratt & Godsey, 2003) and applied outside of the United States to examine the interaction effects between economic inequality and homicide rates in societies with weak institutions of social protection. For example, Savolainen (2000) found that nations offering the most generous welfare programs tended to have the lowest levels of economic inequality. Piquero and Piquero (1998) extended this general finding by examining the education component of institutional anomie theory. Based on census data from 50 US states and the District of Columbia, they found that higher percentages of individuals enrolled full time in college reduced the effect of poverty on both crime types.

Other approaches have examined specific countries. For example, an important development includes attempts to test institutional anomie in countries that have undergone large-scale social change. Russia is a good test case. Following the collapse of the USSR in 1991, Russia launched a program of privatization meant to convert the command economy used in socialist systems to a free-market system in which individual actors, rather than state actors, play the most important role in the economy. The challenge was that while legal, political, regulatory, and social institutions are a fundamental part of market economies, these institutions tend to be absent or underdeveloped in formerly communist countries such as Russia. As a result, a number of researchers wanted to explore social change, institutions, and crime in the country. Some research focused on how economic globalization undermined institutional controls designed to limit the power of transnational corporations in Russia. Passas (2000) argued this increased crime rates and, as a result, anomie. Other research examined the effects of poverty, socioeconomic change, and family strength on regional homicide rates. Kim and Pridemore (2005) have concluded that poverty and socioeconomic change are positively and significantly related to the variation of regional homicide rates in Russia.

Strain comes in many forms. While Merton, Cohen, Cloward and Ohlin, and others have explored the disjunction between the desire to achieve the American Dream and the limits imposed by an inequitable class structure, Unnever and his colleagues (2009) explored how criminology missed an important opportunity to explore how systemic racism itself might serve as another sort of strain that leads to increased criminal behavior. While trying to demonstrate the reasons why strain theory should be relegated to the criminological dustbin, Travis Hirschi (1969) inadvertently failed to recognize that his data set contained evidence that "perceived racial discrimination places African American youth at risk for engaging in crime" (Unnever et al., 2009, p. 379). The problematic role of delinquency can be understood based on Cloward and Ohlin's (1960, pp. 113–117) view that delinquency is more likely when youths experience "unjust deprivation."

For example, if discrimination resulted in this sort of deprivation, it could cause these youths to withdraw an attribution of legitimacy from official norms. Cloward and Ohlin stated that "an increase in the visibility of external barriers to the advancement of Negroes heightens their sense of discrimination and justified withdrawal of attributions of legitimacy from conventional rules of conduct" (1960, p. 121). Unnever and his colleagues describe Hirschi's omission in this way:

> Hirschi's laser-like mission to falsify strain theory thus shaped his use of the questions in the Richmond Youth Project and the very specific way in which he tested whether discrimination fostered crime (i.e., in the way predicted by strain theory). This strategic approach, however, meant that Hirschi did not probe to see if other measures of racial discrimination included in the data set might contribute to delinquent involvement. (2009, p. 383)

As a result, criminologists generally ignored racial discrimination as a meaningful risk factor for African American offending.

However, not all research ignored race. For example, one study found that the intersections of race, place, and crime and the role of relative deprivation could lead to people feeling that they were "being taken advantage of" (Blau & Blau, 1982, p. 126). Thus, while the link between race and violent crime was excluded when socioeconomic inequalities were controlled, opportunities for broader research programs to explore how systematic racism may itself be criminogenic were missed. Such a focus might have predicted racial disparities in arrests, imprisonment, and executions in the United States following the civil rights movement. It also could have assisted in the broader recognition that cultural and historical traditions in America supported the strategic regulation and control of marginalized groups through harsh criminal justice practices (Tonry, 2008).

Practical Ramifications of Social Strain and Anomie Theories

During the 1960s, there was a flurry of social programs in the United States, many of which were specifically designed to address the growing crime problem (Moynihan, 1969). Many of the policies offered in this new wave of social solutions to crime were influenced by ideas from social strain theories. In 1959, a committee of politicians and social scientists was asked to develop a theoretical framework to be used in a proposal to secure government funding for a project that involved providing youths with improved social services and opportunities for employment. A by-product of this work was a book titled *Delinquency and Opportunity* (1960) that contained Cloward and Ohlin's influential subcultural-opportunity theory (Lilly et al., 2011). In the following passage, Moynihan discusses the importance of understanding this theory in relation to the social programs it inspired:

> As with most major (or attempted major) social initiatives, the origins of the community action programs of the war on poverty will be found first of all in intellectual history. The record is that a set of ideas are making their way from university lecture rooms and professional journals to the halls of Congress and the statute books of the national government. And in surprisingly short order. That action should originate in thought is nothing unusual, nor is it especially noteworthy, in this or any other time, that this involved the work of professional men pursuing their professions. The speed of the transmission process, however, is apparently new, involving as it would seem to do, the emergence of a professional style in

reform also, and of a cadre of persons in and about American government whose profession is just that. These processes, obviously, are closely linked, and very likely to interact in some ways, but it is the history of the idea that must be first attended. (1969, pp. 6–7)

Cloward and Ohlin's (1960) theory eventually caught the attention of Robert Kennedy, who was the US attorney general during the time. Several important pieces of legislation were passed that were based, in part, on ideas from their book. The first of these acts was the Juvenile Delinquency Prevention and Control Act of 1961. This act funded programs to improve conditions for youth in poorer communities (Vold & Bernard, 1986). Eventually, this was expanded as a part of President Lyndon B. Johnson's war on poverty, and the Economic Opportunity Acts of 1964 and 1967 followed (Moynihan, 1969). These acts also focused on organizing communities and providing enhanced social services.

Perhaps the most well-known program that emerged during this era was the Mobilization for Youth (MFY) Program. This program aimed to improve educational and employment opportunities for young people in poverty-stricken communities. Later, more programs followed that sought to extend opportunities to all residents of the poorer neighborhoods (Lilly et al., 2011; Moynihan, 1969). The underlying logic of the MFY program was very similar to that of the earlier Chicago Area Project (CAP). It assumed high levels of social disorganization characterized these areas and that this disrupted the level of informal social control. However, there was one important philosophical difference between the founders of the CAP and those associated with the development of the MFY program: Many people working in the MFY program thought that there was a need to change the political structures that produced the inequalities (Lilly et al., 2011). Specifically, they thought capitalism had contributed to the increased alienation experienced by the lower-class youth and claimed that this eventually helped to give rise to the increased rate of juvenile gang formation during the 1950s.

This emphasis on challenging the system soon led to disputes between certain MFY workers and city officials. Eventually, the members of the "radicalized" faction of the project started to see reforming the system as the main goal of the program, and they became less concerned with the original goal of integrating members of the lower class into mainstream society (Moynihan, 1969). Local newspapers began to suggest that MFY workers were actually "Commies and commie sympathizers"; the sociological theories that formed the basis for the program became associated with subversive Marxism and communism (Lilly et al., 2011). The war on poverty and programs associated with it were discontinued when the Nixon administration took power in the early 1970s (Vold & Bernard, 1986).

Some scholars have attributed the failure of the MFY program to the political radicalization of its members and their goals (Moynihan, 1969). While this was likely an important factor, it does not effectively explain the larger failure of the Johnson administration's war on poverty. It seems as though that part of the problem was related to the way in which some of the programs were delivered. Some have speculated that government bureaucracies eventually took control and systematically excluded the people they were trying to help. In short, the members of the poverty-stricken communities had no voice of their own; this served to increase levels of alienation and helplessness and caused neighborhood conditions to grow worse. Wildavsky illustrates this array of problems in the following passage:

A recipe for violence: Promise a lot; deliver a little. Lead people to believe they will be much better off, but let there be no dramatic improvement. Try a variety of small programs, each interesting but marginal in impact and severely underfinanced. Avoid any attempted solution remotely comparable in size to the dimensions of the problem you are trying to solve. Have middle-class civil servants hire upper-class student radicals to use lower-class Negroes as a battering ram against the existing local political systems; then complain that people are going around disrupting things and chastise local politicians for not cooperating with those out to do them in. Get some poor people involved in local decision-making, only to discover that there is not enough at stake to be worth bothering about. Feel guilty about what has happened to black people; tell them you are surprised they have not revolted before; express shock and dismay when they follow your advice. Go in for a little force, just enough to anger, not enough to discourage. Feel guilty again; say you are surprised that worse has not happened. Alternate with a little suppression. Mix well, apply a match, and run. (as quoted in Moynihan, 1969, p. ii)

One might ask why these social approaches to crime based on strain theory were suddenly able to have such an impact on criminal justice systems in North America. Moynihan (1969) identified four important developments that help to explain the rise of Johnson's war on poverty legislation (i.e. The Juvenile Delinquency Prevention and Control Act of 1961 and the Economic Opportunity Acts of 1964 and 1967). First, Moynihan (1969) suggested that the emergence of new econometric techniques and theories allowed for an easier management of the economy. This created a surplus of money that could be spent on exploring these social engineering techniques. Second, there was an influx in the recording and use of statistics, which contributed to the growth of the social sciences in general. Third, there was a clear professionalization of the middle class as more and more people started attending university and obtaining post-secondary education. Finally, foundations were expanded, and this provided more funding to undertake social research (Moynihan, 1969).

Figure 10.4	Seven Steps of Strain Theories
Seven Steps	**Strain Theories**
1. Know the History	Emerged in the 1930s during the Great Depression; influenced by Durkheim's notion of anomie and the structural-functionalist approach
2. Acknowledge Assumptions	Assume that humans are naturally altruistic and are corrupted by society and culture; example of sociological positivism that implies a level of conflict in society
3. Problem Focus, Scope, and Level of Explanation	Seek to explain differences in societal-level crime rates; structural and cultural factors are emphasized
4. Key Terms and Concepts	Social strain, subcultural strain, differential opportunity, and institutional strain
5. Respect the Research	Examine connections between crime and the economy (e.g., poverty, industrialization, and urbanization); recent research focuses on how emphasis on economy creates institutional breakdown
6. Theory/Practice	Large-scale social programs meant to change society are supported (e.g., war on poverty, Mobilization for Youth program)
7. Mapping the Theory	See Figure 10.5

Figure 10.5	**Mapping Social Strain and Anomie Theories**

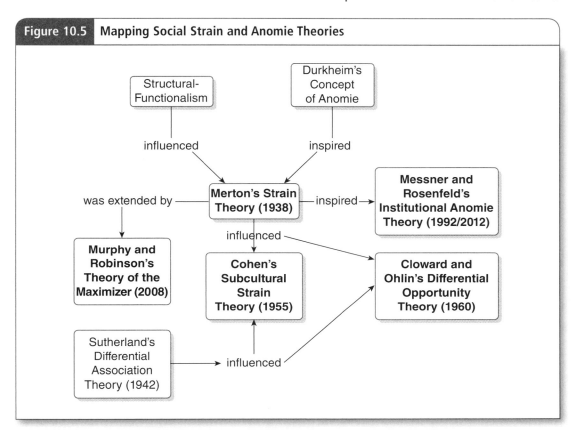

All of these factors created the perfect conditions for the translation of theory into practice. Unfortunately, this also created very high expectations for the programs. When many of these programs proved to be ineffective, the lack of success was attributed to their underlying social logic rather than other factors involving implementation or political issues.

Criticisms of Social Strain and Anomie Theories

Merton's (1938) theory has been the recipient of a variety of different criticisms. Prominent among these is that the underlying goal of the American Dream is far too specific to American society. One might be able to extend this theory to capitalism, but, as mentioned previously, research has demonstrated that there are capitalist societies in which the crime rate is actually quite low. Further, one has to wonder how wider cultural values affects this. Another problem with Merton's (1938) theory is the fact that it fails to explain the differences in male and female involvement in crime. That is, strain would predict higher levels of crime among groups that lack opportunities for economic success. But consider that females have historically been denied opportunities in numerous ways. Women have had trouble accessing the upper tiers of the corporate world, and equal pay for equal work is still not a universal reality. Why aren't criminal justice systems swamped with female criminals who have been denied opportunities? Social strain theories have difficulties addressing this question.

The subcultural strain theories have also received some criticism. For example, some have argued that Cohen's (1955) use of reaction formation did not accurately portray the development of a typical working-class male. According to Kitsuse and Dietrick (1958), working-class children are often eager to assume adult responsibilities. Second, the historical method used by Cohen (1955) does not lend itself to empirical verification and research (Kitsuse & Dietrick, 1959). Finally, others have pointed out that Cohen's (1955) representation of one delinquent subculture was overly simplistic (Downes, 1966).

Critics have also pointed out a number of problems in Cloward and Ohlin's (1960) differential opportunity theory. One major criticism of this theory stems from its typology of subcultural adaptations. The problem here is somewhat obvious; it doesn't take much examination to reveal that very few gangs clearly fit perfectly into one of the categories offered in Cloward and Ohlin's theory. While they are careful to note that their typology only denotes the principal orientation of the gang, the theorists seem to imply that many gangs fit into one subcultural adaptation:

> These shorthand terms simply denote the *principal orientation* of each form of adaptation from the perspective of the dominant social order; although one can find many examples of subcultures that fit accurately into one of these three categories, subcultures frequently appear in somewhat mixed form. Thus members of a predominantly conflict subculture may also on occasion engage in systematic theft; members of a criminal subculture may sometimes do combat in the streets with rival gangs. But this should not obscure the fact that these subcultures tend to exhibit essentially different orientation. (Cloward & Ohlin, 1960, p. 21)

This seems to be more of a problem than the authors acknowledge, and this defect makes their theory very difficult to empirically test (see Empey, 1982, and Short & Strodtbeck, 1965, as cited in Lilly et al., 2011).

🖾 Research Example: Measuring Social Strain

As discussed earlier in this chapter, Messner and Rosenfeld (2013) argue in a new book that social institutions are particularly important to explaining and understanding societal variations in crime rates. Focusing on macro-level crime rates, such as anomie and other structural strain theories, they suggest social institutions are defined as stable sets of norms and values, statuses and roles, and groups and organizations that serve to regulate human behavior and meet the needs of society (Messner & Rosenfeld, 2013). Their most recent book builds on their earlier work outlining institutional anomie theory (Messner & Rosenfeld, 1994; 2001).

Messner and Rosenfeld (2013) posit that the pervasive cultural mandate in the United States to obtain material wealth, combined with a structural anomic imbalance favoring economic interests over all others, leads to high levels of violent crime. They have gone on to claim that the institutional balance of power in the United States is skewed toward the economy because of the American Dream and an overemphasis on economic success. Like Merton (1938), they argue that when the social structure fails to provide sufficient means to achieve valued goals in legitimate ways, illegitimate efforts (often through crime) will increase. Unlike Merton, however, they build on this to argue that this economic focus also undermines other institutions, such as those related to education, the family, and civic and political issues. These institutions, they argue, can regulate the behaviors that otherwise result from the tendency to see all things in economic terms.

One challenge has been how to measure some of the key concepts outlined by Messner and Rosenfeld's theory using macro-level data. For example, concepts such as economic dominance within a society or the effectiveness of noneconomic controls are difficult to directly test (Chamlin and Cochrane, 2007). Messner himself noted that these concepts, like anomie, "defy easy operationalization" (2003, p. 107). While indirect tests have been attempted by combining various variables through structural multivariate models, sometimes simple research designs offer a more direct test of the underlying assumptions of a theory.

Chamlin and Cochrane (2007) reviewed the third wave of the World Values Survey (1995–1997) and identified two questions that appeared related to how those from differing social systems valued the acquisition of material wealth. One question had respondents choose from four options related to a future employment opportunity. The options were good income, job security, friendly colleagues, or feelings of accomplishment, and respondents picked which of those four they would prefer. The second question was even more relevant. Respondents were asked whether less emphasis on money or material success would be a good thing, a bad thing, or would not matter.

By presenting the percentage of those who reported that income was the most important feature of work alongside the percentage of those who felt less emphasis on money or material success would be a good thing, Chamlin and Cochrane sought to directly measure societal-level views that are outlined in institutional strain theory. The findings complicate some of the assumptions of institutional anomie theory. First, Chamlin and Cochrane found that 60% of the sample (26 countries) had a higher percentage of those who felt income was the most important part of work. Second, they noted that nearly 69% of Americans agreed that less emphasis on money or material success would be a good thing. While many assume that rates of violent crime and robbery are much higher in the United States than in other countries, Chamlin and Cochrane (2007) used international crime data to suggest that while violent crime is substantial in the United States, it is not exceptional.

Based on this study, crime is neither a unique feature of American life nor a function of societal views about material wealth and the role of money in society. The authors do hint at an interesting way to further their analysis. Societal-level attitudinal data may offer one way to measure adherence

---

Now that you've read this chapter . . . think back to the pay-for-play scheme whereby high-frequency traders paid for better access and used technology to make billions. In response to the allegations by Lewis and others, New York attorney general Eric Schneiderman described high-frequency technology as "insider trading 2.0." Faster access to the market meant that microseconds of lead time were enough to allow computers to make tens of billions of dollars for a small group of individual traders. By making assessing interest in stocks and making faster trades, these traders could skim off other trades by buying a stock someone else had requested at one price and selling it a higher price before the buyer could react. In response to these discoveries, a small group of former bank employees decided to start their own stock exchange, IEX, that they promised would be fair to all investors. An interesting side note is that these former bank employees all had immigrated to the United States from places such as Canada, Russia, and the United Kingdom. How does this observation connect with social strain theories?

to the American Dream of material success, but it does little to explain how the institutional balances of power or the effectiveness of noneconomic institutional controls might be based on how citizens view the legitimacy of social institutions. Thus, in societies where people accept the legitimacy of civil and social institutions, this may mediate how inequalities within the society are linked with violent crime rates and may shape the interrelationships between "economic institutions, noneconomic institutions, anomie, and serious crime (Chamlin & Cochrane, 2007, p. 59).

Conclusion and Review Questions

In this chapter, we examined social strain and anomie (SSA) theories in criminology. These theories emphasize the importance of social and cultural pressures that increase the likelihood of criminal behavior. These theories emphasize strains created by materialism, wealth, and consumerism. According to strain theorists, upward mobility and financial success are limited by social stratification and institutional structures. This creates frustration and anger, which can eventually lead to deviant and criminal behavior. Crime and deviance may also be used to reduce or escape from strain or to seek revenge against the source of strain and other related targets. In recent years, these theories have focused on a broader range of goals beyond financial success that may be present in society. Questions remain about the role of materialism, wealth, and consumerism in creating and perpetuating crime in America and how individual responses to strains and stressors are associated with criminal behavior.

CHAPTER REVIEW

1. What are the assumptions made by anomie and strain theories?

2. How do history and culture fit into the development of these theories?

3. What is the level of explanation, problem focus, and scope of the anomie theories?

4. What are some differences between anomie and social disorganization/ecological theories?

5. What are some of the practical approaches and programs suggested by anomie theories?

PART V

Theories of Crime and Criminal Justice

Conflict Theories

 ## Chapter Overview and Objectives

This chapter reviews conflict theories in criminology. This set of theories includes a number of approaches, including nonpartisan conflict theory, Marxism, feminism, post-structuralism, and post-modernism. In many cases, these theories are portrayed as being one and the same, and they are often confused with each another. However, each of these approaches takes a unique and sometimes critical view of crime, law, culture, and social control based on an assumption that conflict is a natural part of society. In this chapter, we identify two recurring themes that clarify how these theories are relevant to criminology as a whole.

The first of these themes refers to the fundamental difference between the consensus and conflict views about the role of law and legal institutions in society. The second theme relates to the specific ways in which criminal law, legal codes, punishment, and other forms of social control can result in harm for those with the least power within societies. In sum, conflict theorists take a critical view of society and see it as full of divisions that result in conflict. Instead of true consensus, people are kept in line through overt and covert coercion:

> The shape and character of the legal system in complex societies can be understood as deriving from the conflicts inherent in the structure of these societies which are stratified economically and politically. (Chambliss & Seidman, 1971, p. 3)

So, conflict criminologists often see the criminal justice system and the law as being shaped through political and economic conflicts between people from different socioeconomic classes in society. Figure 11.1 provides an overview of conflict theories.

By the end of the chapter, readers should be able to:

- Understand the assumptions made by conflict theories
- Acknowledge the historical period in which these theories emerged
- Be aware of the level of explanation, problem focus, and scope of conflict theories
- Explain some practical approaches and programs suggested by these theories
- Consider the critiques leveled against conflict theories

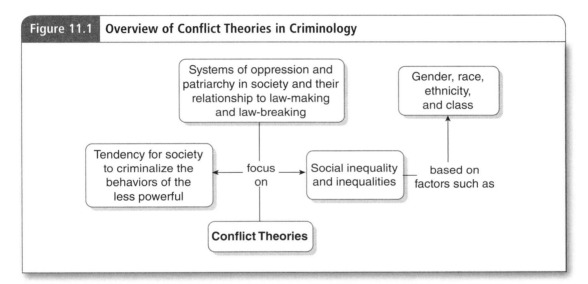

Figure 11.1   Overview of Conflict Theories in Criminology

⬛ The Conflict Tradition

Conflict theories in criminology originated in sociology. The concepts that underlie these theories can be traced to classical sociological theorists such as Karl Marx, Friedrich Engels, Georg Simmel, and Max Weber. The theories emerging from the conflict tradition were also informed by earlier contributions of sociological criminology, including strain, subcultural, and labeling theories (Cohen 1974; Young 1988). Similar to social disorganization and strain theories, conflict theories focus primarily on macro-level structural factors that produce crime. However, unlike other structural theories, conflict theories focus more on explaining the origins of the law and activities of the state and criminal justice system than on criminal behavior. In addition, these theories point out the importance of class, race, gender, and culture to understanding crime (Lynch & Michalowski, 2010).

Many commentators have noted that this area is composed of numerous perspectives and theories, all united by a conflict approach. As mentioned previously, we refer to these as conflict theories because theories in this area are united by a conflict assumption of society. According to this assumption, the criminal justice establishment imposes standards of upper-class morality on the whole of society. The social and economic forces that operate within society also serve to perpetuate crime. The system is designed to separate the powerful from those without power, undermining rights by using divisions including but not limited to structural factors, social hierarchies, financial differences, and gender and racial biases.

As you read this chapter, consider . . . in 2014, the Education Department released a report highlighting the racial disparities in American education. According to the research, African American students of all ages are suspended and expelled at rates three times higher than those of white children, starting at the earliest stages of education. Black children represent 18% of preschool enrollment but 48% of preschool children receiving more than one out-of-school suspension; in comparison, white students represent 43% of preschool enrollment but only 26% of preschool children receiving more than one out-of-school suspension. In addition, while black students represent 16% of student enrollment, they represent 27% of students referred to law enforcement and 31% of students subjected to a school-related arrest. In comparison, white students represent 51% of enrollment, 41% of students referred to law enforcement, and 39% of those arrested. As you read this chapter, consider how conflict theorists might explain this.

Seven Steps of Criminological Thinking

History and Social Context of Conflict Theories

Perhaps the earliest influence on social conflict theory can be found in the Marxist approach. Karl Marx was a radical activist and scholar active during the mid-1800s. After being blacklisted at the University of Berlin for his political views, Marx started a radical newspaper that was eventually shut down by the government. Later, he started another radical journal; it was while working on this project that he met his lifelong friend and collaborator, Friedrich Engels. Engels was from a wealthy family that owned textile mills, and he supported Marx financially throughout his life. Most speculate that he did this at least in part because he realized the importance of Marx's philosophical writings. While Marxist thought has had a huge impact on the field of criminology, Marx himself actually said very little about crime. However, Engels was much more vocal about this subject (Paternoster & Bachman, 2001; Lynch & Michalowski, 2010; Taylor et al., 1973).

The general approach used by Marxists to study society is known as **historical materialism** (also called **dialectical materialism**) (Turner, 2013). A basic tenet of this approach is that society, including crime and justice, can only be fully understood with reference to historical, social, cultural, and political factors (Lynch & Michalowski, 2010). More specifically, this approach emphasizes the importance of the economy to understanding society and its institutions. To clearly understand the conflict theories, one must be familiar with some basic concepts from Marxist thought.

The **mode of production** describes the preferred economic system characterizing a particular society (Lynch & Michalowski, 2010). According to Marx, societies progress through different stages, including slavery, feudalism, capitalism, communism, and socialism, each with its own unique economic system (Turner, 2013). The mode of production consists of the means of production and relations of production. The **means of production** refer to the institutions, tools, machines, and forms of labor associated with the mode of production. The **relations of production** describe the relationships that individuals hold with the economic system or mode of production. Lynch and Michalowski describe the relations of production and how they have varied throughout history:

Every historical period has organized tools and workers into distinctive social systems to accomplish the tasks of production and distribution of goods and services. These different systems have included the feudal manor, the plantation, the private farm, the local factory, and the global corporation. For example, if the mode of production is corporate capitalism, the means of production will be complex machines operated by wage laborers, supervised by salaried white collar employees, within the context of a hierarchical structure that produces profit for stockholders who are not a direct part of the production process. (2010, p. 27)

Some concrete examples may help to further illustrate these concepts. In early stages of capitalism in the United States, the plough, steam engine, and cotton gin were particularly important to the economy and were therefore central to the mode of production (Lynch & Michalowski, 2010). Later, the concept of the assembly line and the invention of automobiles and phones transformed the structure of capitalism. In more recent times, computers, cell phones, and other forms of electronics have become increasingly important. These complex innovations have shaped our modern economy in many ways. It is important to note that modern economies are now very dependent on jobs created by the Internet and associated with electronic devices (e.g., computer programmers, Web site designers, video game developers, and network specialists).

Marx claimed that capitalist systems produce two classes: the bourgeoisie and the proletariat. The **bourgeoisie** refers to the owners of businesses and the means of production, such as bankers, merchants, and businessmen (Turner, 2013). In modern capitalism, this group accounts for roughly 2% -5% of the population and consists of the wealthy members of society, or the elite. Small business owners, or **petty bourgeoisie**, are sometimes distinguished from corporate heads and other large-scale entrepreneurs. The **proletariat** (or workers) represents the rest of society. These people are the salaried employees and hourly wage laborers who sell their labor to support themselves (Lynch & Michalowski, 2010).

Workers are kept in line through the propagation of a *false consciousness*. False consciousness refers to the tendency of the proletariat to adopt the views of elites and accept ideologies that run counter to its members' interests. For example, many people believe that capitalism increases democratic freedom because it allows people to choose one product or service over another. In other words, it seems that people often falsely equate capitalism with greater democracy. While the choices within market economies may appear to ensure broader political freedom, this belief fails to account for the role of media, social conditioning, and other sorts of inequalities in shaping those choices (Wolin, 2008). Does the choice among 70 kinds of breakfast cereal equate to true freedom?

Marx described another chronically unemployed or underemployed group called the **lumpenproletariat**. In modern times, this group is sometimes referred to as the underclass, and some suggest it is composed of chronically homeless people and those living in extreme poverty. People in this group would be prone to behavior such as trash scavenging, dumpster-diving, prostituting, pimping, small-time drug dealing, and other minor forms of crime geared toward making money. This group is also of special interest to criminologists because members of the lumpenproletariat were thought to be prone to crime because of their position in society.

Along with Marx, Max Weber is considered to be one of the founders of the discipline of sociology. Weber also believed that conflict was a natural part of society, but his political views were much less politically extreme than those of Marx. Weber believed that a society could be understood by examining its system of domination. He claimed that those who hold power want members of society to see it as legitimate. Weber referred to legitimized power as **authority**. He argued that legitimate power can be derived from three different sources: charismatic authority, traditional authority, and rational-legal authority (Turner, 2013).

The notion of rational-legal authority is most relevant to the study of crime. The administrative apparatus used for creating and enforcing regulations and statutes in the law is the bureaucracy. Weber argued that in its ideal form a bureaucracy eliminates all irrational, personal, and emotional elements from the decision-making process. As most people are aware, however, in practice this is rarely ever true. By pointing this out, Weber identified the primary arena of conflict in modern society: Who creates laws and who administers them? The answer, of course, is that this is done through political parties that represent particular groups of people. Weber claimed that political parties exist for the purpose of fighting for domination, and to do so they advance their own economic interests and values of the group(s) they represent (Turner, 2013). It should not be hard to see why political domination and the power to create and enforce laws are of interest to criminologists.

Georg Simmel was another important early sociologist who assumed that conflict was a natural a part of society. He was the first to argue that conflict could actually be a productive force that helped people to achieve their goals. More specifically, conflict is viewed as a counterpart of cooperation and social action. In other words, wider social conflict can reinforce integration within social groups (Turner, 2013). Like those of Weber, Simmel's ideas have consequences for the creation and enforcement of laws. Thus, they are of great interest to criminologists, especially those interested in the sociology of law and legal jurisprudence theory.

Until the late 1960s and 1970s, socio-legal studies and legal analyses had been ignored by most mainstream criminologists (Cohen, 1974). During the 1960s and 1970s, however, criminologists realized that it was important to understand the differences between how laws appear on the books versus how they operate in practice (Chambliss, 1964; Chambliss & Seidman, 1971). Through this method of legal analysis, criminologists also begin to explore how the law might be manipulated to further the interests of business elites and other members of the upper classes. Key influences can be found in the work of legal realists such as Pound (1942), Hall (1952), and Skolnick (1966) (Taylor et al.,1973; Michalowski & Bohlander, 1976).

During the social upheaval of the 1960s, the work of Marx and other conflict theorists gained new adherents. This time period was characterized by numerous chaotic events. In the 1960s, the paranoia of McCarthyism had begun to subside, and the stigma attached to Marxism was reduced. This was an era in which a number of social norms were challenged by the civil rights and women's movements. The countercultural movement and the hippies also waged an attack on social norms of the time. Even the music of the period, rock'n'roll, could be viewed as a challenge to dominant social (and sometimes political) norms.

The disillusion associated with the Vietnam War led to the growth of a counterculture that rejected traditional views of society and existing social norms. The assassinations of President John F. Kennedy, Martin Luther King Jr., and several other important US political figures caused increasing chaos, and protests and social activism demonstrated a loss of faith in the government (Lynch & Michalowski, 2010). In some ways, this period was an extremely dark time in American history. However, it was also a time of great social progress as fundamental assumptions about the roles of social organization and social conflict began to be reappraised (Sykes, 1974).

In 1977, a Conference on Critical Legal Studies (CLS) was held in Madison, Wisconsin. This conference brought together a number of law students involved with the civil rights movement, protesters against the Vietnam War, and others who challenged the idea that American law was fundamentally fair and just. Conference participants went on to adapt ideas drawn from Marxist and socialist theories, using them to explain crime and deviance. One observation was that the law and legal practices were used to manage economic power and maintain the status quo in society. The underlying contradiction here is that while many assume that law is the result of democratic decision making or impartial judicial reasoning, the law often appears to favor the powerful and wealthy over the poor and unconnected. This focus has led to critical examinations of legal decisions and issues based on economic contexts and considerations (Michalowski, 2012).

Another variant of critical theory draws on ideas offered by the Frankfurt school, a name associated with scholars from the Institute for Social Research at the University of Frankfurt in Germany. These critical scholars distanced themselves from simplistic and reductionist Marxist approaches that focused on the determinative nature of economic and political structures. Instead, they sought to uncover how social change could result from social struggle. This critical perspective examines the construction of cultural and psychosocial meanings and views these as central to understanding society (Berger & Luckmann, 1966). Some criminologists influenced by critiques based on literary theory suggest that the law is really just a social construction and that nothing is really inherently a criminal act (Cohen, 1974). Instead, societies define certain behaviors as crime for a variety of reasons. In some cases, this has very little to do with the amount of harm caused by the behavior (Robinson & Beaver, 2008). Instead, law is part of a process of domination that actively limits people's ability to distinguish between the present and other possible futures. For example, laws serve as overarching ways to assign moral judgments, but relying on existing laws can lead people to forget or fail to consider other forms of harm that may not be illegal. Despite the differences among critical legal scholars, taken together their contribution is the idea that people should not blindly accept official definitions of crime. Further, they encourage people to consider how crime is socially constructed and guided by the ideology of different people and groups.

As we discussed earlier, conflict theories were also influenced by earlier criminological theories, including strain, subcultural, and labeling theories (Cohen, 1974; Young, 1981, 1988; Lynch & Michalowski, 2010). It is important to keep in mind that some criminologists referred to as mainstream or orthodox criminologists actually have much in common with conflict theorists. For example, Merton's strain theory was essentially a veiled critique of capitalism, and Sutherland coined the term *white-collar crime* and spent a great deal of time studying this phenomenon. As a result, as it did with many others deemed too "political," the FBI monitored these scholars, as well as Ernest Burgess of the Chicago school, during J. Edgar Hoover's tenure (Keen, 1999; Lilly et al., 2011; Taylor et al., 1973).

The conflict approach eventually gained more acceptance in criminology, which led to the emergence of some influential programs at several universities. Sir Leon Radzinowicz, a leading figure in British criminology, describes one episode that raised the profile of the conflict tradition in criminology:

> I do not wish to end this account without mentioning a rather amusing episode. Right in the middle of the Third National (Criminology) Conference, taking place in Cambridge in July 1968, a group of seven young social scientists and criminologists, participants of the Conference, met secretly and decided to establish an independent "National Deviancy Conference" and soon afterwards they duly met in York. At the time, it reminded me a little of naughty schoolboys, playing a nasty game on their stern headmaster. It was not necessary

to go "underground" because we were not in any way opposed to discussing new approaches to the sociology of deviance. (1999, p. 229)

The "naughty schoolboys" included Jock Young, Stan Cohen, and Ian Taylor, all of whom would go on to become well-known and highly influential criminologists. They also established the New Deviancy Conference (NDC), which represented an alternative to the mainstream positivist approach that dominated British criminology (Mooney, 2012).

While these events were occurring in the United Kingdom, the conflict tradition was also emerging in North America. For many years, the center of excellence for research and theorizing in conflict criminology was located at the University of California at Berkeley (Paternoster & Bachman, 2001). The progressive faculty and students at this institution established a new journal for conflict criminologists called *Issues in Criminology* (later changed to *Crime and Social Justice*) and founded the Union of Radical Criminologists (URC) (Michalowski, 2012). Unfortunately, the school was closed down in 1976, in part because of funding issues and administrative conflicts that stemmed from the radical political views held by many members of the department (https://www.socialjusticejournal.org/SJEdits/06Edit-1.html).

In the 1980s, Ian Taylor, one of the founders of the NDC in the United Kingdom, immigrated to Canada after accepting a position at Carleton University in Ottawa. During this decade, he was successful in establishing a strong conflict criminology program that still exists to this day. The conflict tradition later spread to other parts of Canada, including the University of Ontario's Institute of Technology Faculty of Social Sciences and Humanities. While the conflict tradition is well supported in Canada, there is evidence that it is becoming increasingly marginalized by neoliberal government policies (DeKeseredy, 2012).

Assumptions of Conflict Theories

Conflict theorists assume that humans are naturally altruistic because human activity requires social interaction and interdependence. At the same time, one's social environment may serve to accentuate negative characteristics, such as aggression and greed (Einstadter & Henry, 2006). This builds on the thinking of Jean-Jacques Rousseau, who claimed people join together through a social contract for the benefits and necessity of cooperation. However, civilization has its price. According to Rousseau, people are undermined by the tyranny of society, most notably the emergence of private property, which breeds inequality and envy, requiring the creation of law. This broader view is based on a rejection of the idea that some individuals are just "bad apples." Instead, conflict theorists suggest that society is a bad barrel that serves to corrupt otherwise good individuals (Einstadter & Henry, 2006).

Most conflict theorists assume that capitalism is a corrupting force that encourages egoism and distorts human nature (Paternoster & Bachman, 2001). However, other social forces may also corrupt people. The power of patriarchy, complexities of colonialism, and realities of racism all figure in conflict theories. According to this view, humans are both determined and determining. In other words, these theorists do not endorse a pure determinist approach nor do they subscribe to an unrestrained notion of free will (Bohm & Vogel, 2011). Human beings are both products and producers of their environments; they react to and influence their social institutions. However, human nature is also affected by historical and cultural context (Einstadter & Henry, 2006; Young, 1981). According to Lynch and Michalowski,

[The] central tenet of conflict-critical tradition is that crime and justice can only be fully understood when analyzed with respect to the historical, social, and political-economic context within which they occur. (2010, p. 26)

Obviously, the conflict theorists embrace a conflict view of society that is rooted in the works of Marx, Weber, and Simmel. Most conflict theorists assume that while there may be consensus over some laws (e.g., murder, sexual assault), there is much more conflict in society over moral values (Bohm & Vogel, 2011).

Think You Get It?

Make a list of behaviors that people generally agree should be regarded as crimes. Next, consider behaviors that are currently classified as crimes but with less societal consensus. Think about acts that have been recently criminalized and acts that were once crimes but are now legal. Can you think of any acts that are legal but perhaps should be against the law?

Problem Focus, Scope, and Level of Explanation of Conflict Theories

Unlike the positivist theories covered in previous chapters, conflict theories also focus on explaining aspects of the criminal justice system and the criminal law. This could include the origins and enforcement of the criminal law and the activities of the agents of social control (i.e., police, corrections officials, and courts). A conflict theorist might also ask how these institutions have changed over the years and why this has happened (Bernard et al., 2010). In other words, they are not really attempting to explain criminal behavior directly. Rather, they see crime as a reaction to and natural by-product of institutional activities. Quinney describes this new problem focus in the passage below:

Two schools of thought have developed. Some argue that crime is properly studied by examining the offender and his behavior. Others are convinced that the criminal law is the correct object: how it is formulated, enforced and administered. The two need not become deadlocked in polemics. The long overdue interest in criminal definitions happily corrects the absurdities brought about by studying the offender alone; the two approaches actually complement one another. A synthesis of the criminal behavior and criminal definition approaches can provide a new theoretical framework for the study of crime. (1970, p. 4)

Conflict criminologists are not completely disinterested in the problem of criminal behavior. However, as the quote above implies, they believe that criminal behavior cannot be understood without an understanding of how criminal definitions are created.

The scope of conflict theories encompasses street-level crime as well as elite or suite crimes. Crime resulting from individual differences (biological or psychological characteristics) is not directly addressed. Conflict theories are primarily macro oriented and tend to explain micro-level behavior through structural factors. While certain predispositions to crime exist, they are viewed as unimportant in the big picture as the conditions suitable to committing crime are created by structural factors (Paternoster & Bachman, 2001).

Key Terms and Concepts in Conflict Theories

Early Conflict Theories in Criminology

The earliest attempt to apply Marxist ideas to explain crime was undertaken by a Dutch criminologist named Willem Bonger (1916). He argued that the roots of crime lay in the exploitative and alienating conditions of capitalism. Drawing on the work of Rousseau, he argued that capitalism distorts human nature and that crime results from the conditions created by capitalism. According to Bonger (1916), humanity's inherent state of **altruism**, which he defined as concern for the well-being of others, was replaced by **egoism**, in which one is concerned only with one's own selfish desires. He claimed that criminal thoughts emerge because the capitalist system nurtures individual egoism and suppresses one's natural altruistic tendencies. In his view, all individuals in capitalist societies were susceptible to egoism and would be likely to take advantage of others because they were alienated from authentic social relationships. Bonger suggested that it was this alienation that led to crime.

It is important to mention that while Bonger was mainly concerned with structural factors, he also incorporated some psychoanalytic concepts in his formulation. Poverty is seen as the major cause of crime. However, the effects of poverty can be traced to the family structure and parental inability to properly supervise their children. Some have characterized the inclusion of positivist ideas as too radical a departure from the original Marxist canon (Taylor et al., 1973). This does not negate the fact that Bonger (1916) was a pioneer in applying Marxist ideas to explain crime. One ought to also keep in mind that he was working during the early 20th century; the suggestion of a connection between the political economy and crime was a revolutionary idea in this era.

Another early attempt to apply social conflict ideas to crime can be found in the work of George Vold (1958). This theory was heavily influenced by Simmel's ideas about social conflict. Vold moved conflict away from an exclusive emphasis on normative conflicts to include *conflicts of interest.* Thus, within society there are constant struggles to maintain and improve the interest of one's own group against other groups that are attempting to do the same thing. Instead of two main competing groups, as posited in Marxism, Vold's (1958) view is that there are many different competing groups fighting to have their voices heard.

Conflict is not always a bad thing. It can create the conditions for social change, generate group solidarity, and may actually result in increased societal stability (Vold, 1958). In other words, a person will become more committed to his or her group (and its cause) the harder that person has to fight for it. Eventually, the competition generated by this conflict leads to equilibrium in society because each group is forced to compromise part of the time. Bernard and his colleagues elaborate upon the process described by Vold:

> These social interaction processes [between the groups] grind their way through various kinds of uneasy adjustment, to a more or less stable equilibrium of balanced forces, called social order or social organization. Social order, therefore, does not reflect a consensus among the groups, but reflects the uneasy adjustment, one to another, of the many groups of various strengths and different interests. Conflict is thus one of the principal and essential social processes in the functioning of society. (2010, p. 247)

Max Weber's conception of power is also incorporated into Vold's (1958) theory. Vold states that power eventually manifests itself in the legislative process and that this has ramifications for the study of crime. Powerful groups have the power to decide which types of behavior are criminalized. Hence, for Vold, the activities of criminal justice system officials, criminals, and lawmakers are intimately connected to conflicts between different interest groups (Bernard et al., 2010).

Turk's (1969) theory of the criminalization process is another prominent example of conflict theory in criminology. This theory draws upon the conceptual scheme of conflict and authority and seeks to explain how authorities assign the criminal label to particular individuals and why some accept authority while others do not (Turk, 1966). The central argument is that laws represent deeply held social and cultural norms of powerful interest groups (Gibbons, 1979). Turk (1969) also suggested that social and cultural norms vary with age, gender, and race/ethnicity and that these key characteristics determine whether or not one will come into conflict with the law. In addition, less sophisticated subjects (e.g., juveniles) will have a higher likelihood of coming into conflict with the law than sophisticated subjects (e.g., middle-aged businessmen) who can more easily manipulate and circumvent legal norms. Finally, more conflict will be generated when laws are violated that embody the deeply held norms of those in power (Bernard et al., 2010).

Many conflict theorists embrace a Marxist perspective and assume that social class is crucial to understanding crime and the origins of the criminal law. However, building on Weberian thought, Turk (1969) believed that these phenomena could be better explained by examining the exercises of power through the social institutions that dominate everyday life. For Turk, a pluralist conflict model of statuses and norms better explains criminalization. Instead of class, it is the authority vested in groups that control key positions in religious, educational, governmental, and even family relations that matter. Like Vold (1958), Turk (1969) argues that some conflict is beneficial to society. Conflict may encourage society to consider whether the current consensus is justified, or it may help society justify pursuing various reforms. This tension between stasis and change is built on the distinction between cultural norms that set out what behavior is expected and social norms that represent the reality of what happens.

Richard Quinney (1970) proposed another important conflict theory. Like his predecessors, Quinney (1970) stated that authorities define crime and that their definitions often correspond to the interests of groups in authority (e.g., special interest groups and lobbyists). Those who are the least connected to the dominant group(s) are at the greatest risk of having their behavior defined as criminal. Quinney (1970) also makes use of some ideas from Sutherland's differential association theory to clarify how "different segments of society have different normative systems and different patterns of behavior, all of which are learned in their own social and cultural settings" (Bernard et al., 2010, p. 250). Finally, ideas from social constructionism and labeling theory are also incorporated within this theory. Quinney (1970) claims that criminal roles are formed through a labeling process that may give rise to subsequent criminal behavior, and he also points out that our conceptions of crime are constructed through human communication and interaction.

Quinney (1970) argues that certain segments of society are more highly organized (e.g., business elites, labor groups) than others (e.g., the poor, certain racial/ethnic minorities, and other disenfranchised populations). He claims that the probability that a person will violate the law is a function of the level of power and organization of the group with which that person is associated. In other words, groups with less power and organization are the most likely to have their behaviors become the target of criminalization (Bernard et al., 2010). This serves to explain how authorities acquire and maintain their positions. It also has implications for individuals who are caught up in the system.

According to Quinney, criminology should promote harm reduction. Rather than "teaching people a lesson," Quinney and others take the view that punishing criminals simply escalates violence (Wheeldon, 2009). These sentiments form the basis for another well-known criminological contribution from Quinney known as **peacemaking criminology**. In this approach, criminal justice system practitioners reduce harms caused by the system. This is done by employing a variety of programs and practices that focus on resolving conflicts through the active participation of those involved, including victims, offenders, and the broader community. Today, these programs and practices are collectively known as **restorative justice** (RJ) and are of growing interest in modern criminal justice systems. We will return to examples of these programs and the findings from other recent research later in the chapter.

Chambliss and Seidman (1971) proposed a key conflict theory that focuses on the functioning of the criminal justice system. A major influence on this theory arose from the area of legal realism. The legal realist viewpoint suggests that one must focus on the "law-in-action" rather than the "law-on-the-books" (Chambliss and Seidman, 1971, p. 3 & pp. 176–177). These theorists suggested one work from a conflict orientation to better understand how the law and criminal justice system operate in the real world. Consider policing. Few doubt the societal value of police, sheriffs, and the National Guard. However, at various points in history, the police have been used to suppress rights that are today recognized as basic. For example, during the 1960s and 1970s, society witnessed an uptick in antigovernment protests and activism and a reappraisal of the role of police, who were widely seen as pawns that were used to protect systemic racial discrimination.

The theory presented by Chambliss and Seidman (1971) can be summarized as follows. First, they suggest that as society becomes increasingly complex, it becomes more and more repressive. Growing complexity also causes more social stratification, and the elite eventually gain control over other, less powerful groups. Consequently, the elites determine which norms are formalized and made into law (Chambliss & Seidman, 1971). They also draw on Marxist thought claiming that economic stratification occurs alongside social stratification. More simply, wealthy and powerful interest groups manipulate government bureaucracies as a means for maintaining their power. In general, various struggles take place within society among groups with opposite interests. The state and the law are central to perpetuating certain forms of social ordering, and this tends to result in the domination by the ruling class for its own benefit. This inevitably leads to social inequality and social conflict (Chambliss & Seidman, 1971).

Think You Get It?

A man named Ralph worked the 4 p.m.-to-12 a.m. shift in a factory. After coming home from work one night, he decided to work on his car. Ralph had no garage, so he had to work on the car in the street. He was working under the hood of the car when a police officer stopped and asked him what he was doing. After telling the cop that he was working on his car, Ralph was asked to provide his driver's license and registration card. Ralph showed his identification and the cop left. Within five minutes, another policeman showed up and the same routine took place. A few minutes after the second cop left, a third cop stopped and asked Ralph what he was doing. Ralph became angered and told the cop that he was stealing the car. Ralph was then arrested and taken to the police station (Chambliss, 1973, p. 192). How does this case illustrate the formal power of the state? How does this case illustrate the informal power of the state?

The Behavior of the Criminal Law

The interest in social control, the emergence of laws, and the application of punishment was buoyed by developments on the periphery of criminology. For example, the work of sociologist Donald Black (1976, 1984) influenced the critical legal studies movement discussed above. Black's (1976) theory proposed in *The Behavior of Law* also appears to build on the Weberian tradition and incorporates other classical sociological ideas from Marx and Durkheim. This approach presents a view of social control in which law attempts to organize society based on coercive notions of respectability.

In his theory, Black (1976) argues that there are five key dimensions to social life: stratification, morphology, culture, organization, and social control. *Stratification* is a vertical dimension to social life and refers to how important resources (e.g., food, water, land, and money) are distributed among people. This aspect is most easily conceptualized as social class and economic status. The horizontal aspect of social life is called *morphology*. This dimension examines the degree of integration and interaction among people and the division of labor that has emerged in society. *Culture* refers to symbolic aspects of social life and encompasses social notions of what is good, what is true, and what is beautiful (Bernard, Snipes, & Gerould, 2011). Dimensions of culture include religion, science, and art. The capacity for collective action in society is called *organization.* Social control is "the normative aspect of social life, or the definition of deviant and the response to it, such as prohibitions, accusations, punishments, and compensations" (Black, 1976, pp. 1–2). The law is viewed as a governmental form of social control.

Within each of these dimensions, a hypotheses can be formulated about the criminal law (Bernard et al., 2010). For example, like the earlier conflict theorists, Black (1976) claimed that those with more power could use the law to their advantage and that those with less power are often targets of criminalization. Consequently, in societies with high levels of stratification, the law will be susceptible to manipulation. Law is also mediated through organizational levels. These include differences in levels of organization of offenders and victims, and this may lead to discrepancies in how the law is applied. For example, individual behavior is more likely to be labeled as criminal and/or deviant than organizational behavior, so, according to Black (1976), we would expect street criminals to be prosecuted more often than corporations, irrespective of the amount of harm caused.

Criminal offenders exist as status and power seekers, but they face different applications of penal law. Black (1976) argues the law will be used more severely against the poor and uneducated and less severely in situations where other recognized forms of social control (e.g., etiquette, custom, folkways, and ethics) are strong. Thus,

> much crime is moralistic and involves the pursuit of justice. It is a mode of conflict management, possibly a form of punishment, even capital punishment. Viewed in relation to law, it is self-help. To the degree that it defines or responds to the conduct of someone else—the offender—as deviant, crime is social control. (Black, 1984, p. 1)

Black's (1976) theory of law and social control focuses on how one defines another's behavior as deviant, and more on how various disputes are handled. According to this line of thought, variation in the handling of conflicts can be explained sociologically—generally in terms of who holds power and influence and who does not. Black's contribution is in focusing explicitly on the sociology of institutions as well as the types and techniques of social control and the products or results of these efforts.

The New Criminology and Left Realism

The book *The New Criminology: For Social Theory of Deviance* precipitated the resurgence of social theory in criminology. Ian Taylor, Paul Walton, and Jock Young (a.k.a. the naughty schoolboys) argued that theory must account for structural origins of crime, address the social psychology of crime, and revisit the rational elements involved in criminal behavior (Taylor et al., 1973). They combined this with an interest in understanding deviance, including its nature, origin, and outcomes, and the societal reaction to such acts. This book succeeded in leveling a wide-ranging critique against all of the previous criminological theories, yet it failed to achieve its aim of explaining why certain theories thrive while others are ignored (Currie, 1974). Skeptical of positivistic assumptions in any form, the authors did offer a means to understand aspects of traditional criminology not often discussed, including the notion that deviance is by nature remarkable and not simply part of the human character. However, the book was responsible for tearing down more than it erected in its place, and many criminologists were critical of its ultimate contribution (Wheeldon & Heidt, 2007).

In response to some of the criticisms leveled at the "new criminology" of the 1970s, left realism focused on how to develop a coherent theory to guide alternative practical solutions to the problems of crime. By focusing on working-class crime, left realists identified the need for a new, more holistic approach to understanding crime. For example, they pointed out that victims of crime, especially women, minorities, and the working class, lacked a voice in the criminal justice system during this time. A central theory that emerged from the left realist approach is Young's (1987) square of crime, which sought to clarify the interrelationship among the four components of crime: the victim, the offender, the public, and the police. Left realists claim that research concerning the nature of crime must consider all four of these factors and should seek to understand the interactions between them.

Young (1987) claimed that most previous criminological theories only addressed one aspect of crime, resulting in overly simplistic and superficial theories. For example, positivist theories that attempt to explain criminality and criminal behavior focus almost exclusively on offenders and their behaviors. Other theories that draw on the classical school and focus on rationality emphasize the role of criminal opportunities and victims. This represents one side of Young's (1987) square of crime: the parties involved with the criminal act (i.e., offender and victim).

The other side of the square examines the activities of the criminal justice system (e.g., the origins of the law, patterns of arrest among the police) and the public perception of crime. Relations between the public and the police are important because they can influence the public's fear of crime and also its willingness to report crimes to the police. This has ramifications for crime rates and also levels of informal social control (Young, 1987). Finally, relationships between the police and offenders may indirectly influence how the police treat citizens (Young, 1987). For example, innocent members of a criminally stereotyped group may be needlessly stopped and searched, causing frustration with the system. This comes full circle and may change the public's view of the police and other agencies of social control (Young & Matthews, 1992). As we will see later, this view can be connected to the recent backlash against stop-and-frisk policies in New York City.

Feminist Explanations of Criminal Behavior

Another important development is the application of the feminist critique to criminology. Feminism is a set of theories and strategies focused on understanding gender equality and promoting gender empowerment (Williams, 2000). Feminist critiques of the 1970s focused on the failure of criminology to explain criminality because many existing theories seemed to be based on men to the exclusion of women (Pollock, 1999). Gender plays an important role in how we understand social institutions, processes, and relationships. The application of feminism to the field of criminology is based on a critical assessment of the patriarchal principles that govern and maintain the rules of behavior in society.

According to feminist thinkers, the interpretation of right and wrong is defended and defined by a legal system that was created by men and for men. Building on other work that focuses on social order and the power of interactions, feminist criminology views the justice system as a product of widespread **patriarchy**. This is an ordering of society that is based on culturally created notions of masculine and feminine and that favors men over women in positions of authority. For many decades, female crime has been all but ignored by mainstream criminology.

An essential starting point is the important, though flawed, work of Otto Pollak (1950). Pollak identified a number of principles that remain relevant today. He viewed male and female as equally criminal, each with a tendency to engage in different types of crime. He also suggested women were more likely to play an instigator role rather than a direct role in a crime. Finally, he suggested the justice system was likely to treat women more leniently based on their perceived weakness (or the chivalrous nature of men). Today, we would likely describe this finding, if true, as an example of a paternalistic attitude to women. Although it may seem strange to some to suggest our justice system is not harsh enough, there is a view that treating women differently may undermine the equality and fairness of the legal system.

Think You Get It?

Using the National Criminal Justice Reference Service's section on Women and Girls in the Justice System (and the resources available there), test Pollak's principles.

- Do men and women commit crime at the same rate?
- Are women and men likely to commit the same kinds of crime?
- How has the proportion of male and female crime changed in recent decades?
- Is there a chivalry effect in the criminal justice system?

Another important contribution in this area can be found in the work of Freda Adler (1975). Using case studies and interviews, Adler explored the rise in officially recorded crimes by women and demonstrated how traditional notions of masculinity and femininity were changing as a result of larger social forces, particularly the women's liberation movement. By challenging female "passivity," Adler suggested that the increasing formal equality between men and women would create more opportunities for crime. Despite these conclusions, there is little evidence that women who embrace more liberated roles are more likely to offend than more traditionally oriented women. In fact, low rates in aggressive offenses and white-collar crime for women versus men suggest other challenges for Adler's views. Nevertheless, the analysis and debates Adler's work provoked led criminologists to other avenues of research.

For example, Adler's work forced the recognition that just as many theories of crime were based on male offending, offender treatment in correctional facilities also traditionally focused on men to the exclusion of women and girls (Zaplin, 1998). While perhaps justified in numeric terms, this often means programs developed in a generic sense, based on male-centric norms, fail to address the specific needs of female offenders (Covington & Bloom, 2006; Zahn et al., 2009). This one-sidedness is important because today women represent 17% of all offenders under some form of correctional sanction. This requires expanding correctional approaches to account for how gender shapes behavior and life circumstances. Adjustments might include adopting rehabilitation as the essential goal, using multidisciplinary teams when designing and implementing interventions, and emphasizing the importance of gender-specific and culture-specific interventions that are based in theory (Zaplin, 1998, pp. 383–384). Many might argue that both men and women could benefit from these principles; this is but one illustration of why feminist thinking may be important to criminologists.

Besides its potential to inform practice, Adler's work is also relevant to criminological theories. For example, John Hagan's (1989) power-control theory suggests that concepts of delinquency and family structure are linked to assumptions about gender equality. By combining elements of class and power, Hagan identified how levels of patriarchy within households impact the differences in delinquency between daughters and sons. The theoretical model ultimately links parental supervision, particularly differential supervision of daughters and sons by mothers, to power differentials between parents. Hagan (1989) suggests women may work but still face the primary responsibilities for child care. This suggests the home-based concentration of power will continue, and male and female rates of criminality are likely to remain quite different for some time to come. Given that this theory is integrated, we will return to it in Chapter 13 when we discuss recent contributions to integrative theorizing in criminology.

The way in which society constructs gender is also a starting point for Messerschmidt's masculinity hypothesis. According to this view, criminal behavior can be used as an alternative means to achieve masculinity if traditional opportunities are not available. Outlets of successful masculinity include a stable family life, children, success in school, and, most important, occupational achievement, which is often associated with monetary success (Archer, 1994, p. 135).

According to Messerschmidt (1993), society tells men that in order to assert their masculinity they must hold a steady job and bring home a good paycheck. When these traditional means of demonstrating masculinity are stifled or do not exist, criminal behavior and violent behavior are more likely to occur (Messerschmidt, 1993, p. 81). Thus, if a man does poorly in school, at his job, or in his family life, he must seek out alternative "masculine-validating resources" (Messerschmidt, 1993, p. 83). Furthermore, people who have used violence as a way to assert masculinity in the past come to accept violence as an acceptable means to display their manhood. In effect, they become predisposed to using these approaches based on certain situational cues. These norms become regulated and reproduced based on assumptions about gender roles and relationships (Messerschmidt, 2000).

Respect the Research

There are two main obstacles to discussing the research implications of conflict theories. The first is that many conflict theories do not attempt to explain crime directly. Instead, they simply identify social conflict as a basic fact of life and a source of discriminatory treatment, and then they attempt

Figure 11.2	Key Conflict Theories and Propositions
Theorist	**Proposition**
Bonger (1916)	Capitalism breeds egoism in individuals, breaks down family structures, and produces higher levels of crime.
Vold (1958)	Consensus emerges through the conflict of numerous competing groups in society.
Turk (1969)	The norms of less sophisticated and weaker groups in society become the targets of criminalization.
Quinney (1970)	The probability that a person will violate the law is a function of the level of power and organization of the group with which that person is associated.
Chambliss & Seidman (1971)	Societal complexity increases repression and social stratification, consolidating power among societal elites.
Black (1976)	The law is shaped by five dimensions of social life: stratification, morphology, culture, organization, and more general levels of social control.
Young (1987)	Crime is influenced by four factors: offenders, victims, the criminal justice system, and the public.
Messerschmidt (1993)	If traditional methods of displaying masculinity are stifled or nonexistent, crime will be used as an alternative way of asserting manhood.

to catalog and contest the results of this treatment. The second challenge is that among these theorists, there is widespread skepticism about the value of traditional approaches to research. In other words, many conflict researchers assume that knowledge is itself socially constructed, with no independent reality apart from the minds of those who create it. Dominant worldviews are based on the norms of the rich and powerful. According to this view, traditional research efforts tend to privilege the views and orthodoxies of those who have historically held power.

A well-known example of research using a historical perspective derived from Marxist thought is Rusche and Kirchheimer's (1939) study of punishment. This research examined historical shifts and changes in punishment that occurred from the Middle Ages (ca. 14th century) until the early 20th century. In short, Rusche and Kirchheimer found that as labor became more available during the late Middle Ages, punishments became increasingly severe. It was during this period that torture and capital punishment were used most extensively, in some cases for minor crimes. As the ruling classes found that they needed more labor, a shift to imprisonment occurred. In prison, criminals could be put to work, and this could allow the elites to profit off of their labor. Based on their findings, Rusche and Kirchheimer (1939) argued that punishment must be seen as a social phenomenon and not merely as a means of upholding justice and protecting society. Further, they claimed that forms of punishment are shaped by economic factors and often correspond to the prevailing means of production in society at a given time.

Another example of research that draws on some of the earlier conflict theory can be found in Reiman's (1979) classic study, *The Rich Get Richer and the Poor Get Prison.* First published in 1979, it has been updated a number of times based on new and up-to-date criminal justice statistics. Taking an approach influenced by structural Marxist thought, Reiman (1979) argues that the criminal justice system is biased against the poor from start to finish—from the definition of crime through the process of arrest, trial, and sentencing. By showing the disparity between prison terms for white-collar offenders versus offenders convicted of burglary, he demonstrated that the cost of white-collar crime is in the hundreds of billions, far more than the cost of other kinds of crime.

As Reiman (1979) points out, corporate executives rarely end up in jail. He argues that if your goal was not to reduce crime or address the harms caused by those with power and influence but rather to keep a large number of people under some form of state control through prison, probation, or parole, you would develop a system that looks a lot like the one that is currently operating in the United States. If indeed the system is rigged against the poor and powerless, then the consequences of the mass incarceration and disenfranchisement of a large number of African Americans are not an accident. Instead, this outcome is, by design, based on unspoken cultural norms, beliefs, and biases.

A recent approach that explores the intersection of culture and crime is **cultural criminology**. Applied to crime and deviance, cultural criminology places criminality and its control in the context of culture (Hayward, 2012). Cultural criminologists view crime and the institutions of crime control as the products of often-unconscious societal determinations about meaning, and they see the construction of crime and social responses as a culture construction (Ferrell, 1995). One central idea is that crime, violence, and risk are unique in contemporary consumer culture because of the roles market forces play in shaping and ordering society. The result is a set of informal rules that guide moral entrepreneurship, political innovation, and deviance and represents a distinct way to think about crime:

> Cultural criminology thus provides criminologists the opportunity to enhance their own perspectives on crime with insights from other fields, while at the same time providing for their colleagues in cultural studies, the sociology of culture, media studies, and elsewhere invaluable perspectives on crime, criminalization, and their relationship to cultural and political processes. Bending or breaking the boundaries of criminology in order to construct a cultural criminology in this sense undermines contemporary criminology less than it expands and enlivens it. (Ferrell, 1995, pp. 36–37)

One way to consider crime in terms of the societies in which it arises is to expand upon the traditional approaches to research. This involves a focus on understanding the role of culture in the lives of those who are the subjects of criminological research. To address the gap that exists between and among the worlds of the scholars and those of officers, victims, and offenders who inform criminological research, ethnographic and phenomenological research approaches attempt to better capture and analyze another person's lived experiences. This includes understanding similarities and differences in motivations to engage in troublemaking and deviant behavior. It also includes the interactions and sensations associated with engaging in various types of crime (Katz, 1988).

For example, inspired by the movie *Fight Club*, Jackson-Jacobs (2004) explored brawls as a form of ritual. Rather than violent transgressions by an aggressor on a victim, he compares these social interactions to "picking up" someone at a bar and details each step in escalation. While this research connects affluence, masculinity, and emotional distance, it also explores how every step toward inter-personal violence has what appears to be a physiological response among those predisposed to engage in this sort of behavior. It also suggests that our culture makes people want to engage in deviance to relieve the alienation it breeds and as a means to feel like one is in control of one's life. This alienation is described in some detail in the book *Fight Club*, which the movie is based on.

> Man, I see in Fight Club the strongest and smartest men who've ever lived. I see all this poten-tial, and I see it squandered. God damn it, an entire generation pumping gas, waiting tables—slaves with white collars. Advertising has us chasing cars and clothes, working jobs we hate so we can buy shit we don't need. We're the middle children of history, man. No purpose or place. We have no Great War. No Great Depression. Our great war is a spiritual war. Our great depression is our lives. We've all been raised on television to believe that one day we'd all be millionaires, and movie gods, and rock stars, but we won't. We're slowly learning that fact. And we're very, very pissed off. (Ziskin & Fincher, 1999)

This passage provides an example of how one could redefine this brawling behavior as a reaction to the alienation that arises from the false promises offered by the capitalist system.

Jackson-Jacobs (2004, p. 243) suggested that his findings connect to cultural criminology in three important ways. First, the role of the media and films creates expectations for these sorts of events. Part of what makes *Fight Club* powerful is the way it suggests that what lies just beneath our white-collar lives is a desire to prove ourselves using culturally seated notions of masculinity. Second, he says that brawls like the ones he details appear to occur only in affluent cultures where there is a large enough population and a high enough turnover to bring new strangers together. This suggests part of this phenomenon is based on the transient nature of our postmodern capitalist economy. Third, and finally, he suggests the desire to engage in these masculine set pieces is a function of wanting to exert some kind of control and personal responsibility in a culture in which real choices are few and con-strained. For criminology, this means that

> to understand the reality of crime and criminalization, then, a cultural criminology must account not only for the dynamics of criminal subcultures, but for the dynamics of the mass media as well. Today, mediated images of crime and criminal violence wash over us in wave after wave, and in so doing help shape public perceptions and policies in regard to crime. But of course these contemporary cases build on earlier mediated constructions of crime and control. . . . Clearly, then, both the everyday collective practice of criminality and the crimi-nalization of everyday life by the powerful are *cultural enterprises* and must be investigated as such. (Ferrell, 1995, p. 28)

Recognize Practical Ramifications

Many people confuse all conflict approaches with Marxism. This is an error. The policy implica-tions of Marxism involve overthrowing the capitalist system through a massive societal restructuring that will ensure that everyone has what they need, thereby lowering crime rates. However, one can accept the basic thrust of conflict theories regarding the role of power, gender, language, finances, and status without reducing every issue or problem to a question of class warfare. In criminology, the left realist movement of the 1980s and 1990s is often highlighted as an example of an effort to make use of critical theories while using quantitative methods of research. Focusing especially on the working class, minorities, and women (DeKeseredy, Saunders, Schwartz, & Alvi, 1997), left realists recommended the implementation of a number of policies, such as community activities, neighborhood watches, community policing, and dispute resolution centers.

Other conflict theorists favor policies and programs that may also be relevant for the study of crime. Raising the minimum wage, higher taxes on the wealthy to fund education programs, single-payer health care, paid maternal and paternal leave, and policies of family support are seen as ways of improving society and reducing crime. Those interested in feminist critiques argue that it is essential to reform our patriarchal society by ensuring people understand the experience of victims. Recent efforts are apparent in the focus on sexual assault in the military and on the failure of traditional forms of hierarchy to ensure women can safely serve in branches of the armed forces. It may also be relevant to understanding the Supreme Court of Canada's recent decision that found some laws against prostitution to be unconstitutional.

Another, perhaps less outwardly practical, approach is called constitutive criminology (Henry & Milovanovic, 1996) and can be traced back to the work of Foucault (1977) and other postmodern and post-structuralist philosophers. Constitutive criminologists advocate for a more critically reflexive criminology. More specifically, they argue that the field has disregarded and ignored philosophical concerns (Arrigo & Williams, 2006). Policy recommendations include encouraging criminologists to assume an active role in an effort to counter inaccurate and moral-panic-inducing journalism; disputing data, especially the use of official statistics; challenging journalists by providing counterarguments to misleading news stories; and encouraging the use of harm-reduction measures over traditional solutions to crime (e.g., law enforcement, prison, parole, and courts) (Henry & Milovanovic, 1996, p. 214–220).

Together, these efforts led to resurgent interest in older criminological examples, including a return to Sutherland's suggestion to study white-collar criminals, Christie's (1977) ideas of "conflict" as property, Foucault's substitution of penality for penology, and Pepinsky and Quinney's (1991) formulation of peacemaking principles (Henry & Milovanovic, 1996). Contemporary debates, such as efforts to decriminalize and regulate marijuana at the state level, renewed interest in white-collar crime, and the rise in the use of drug courts and other harm reduction approaches, have parallels with critiques offered by conflict criminologists. Again, many of these critiques draw attention to the emphasis on one sort of harm to the exclusion of others and to the need to engage in a more introspective review of the costs of certain policies for the least powerful in society. It is hard to deny the role race has played in American criminal justice.

A recent example that can be used to illustrate some of these points is the controversy over the stop-and-frisk policies in New York City. Stop-and-frisk searches have been an NYPD tool for decades, but recently there has been increased criticism over the number of these stops and, more important, the people targeted for them—overwhelmingly black or Latino males. In August 2013, US district court judge Shira Scheindlin issued her long-awaited opinion finding that the NYPD had violated the Fourth and Fourteenth Amendments due to the way it had conducted stop-and-frisk searches. This decision followed federal class action lawsuits, widespread criticisms, and the observation that these searches resulted in some level of physical force in many cases.

Social researchers have also become involved. Quantitative studies have suggested that the negative impacts of stop-and-frisk searches outweigh any possible utility. One unpublished paper by NYU's Dennis Smith and SUNY Albany's Robert Purtell (2008) found that stop-and-frisk policies have had

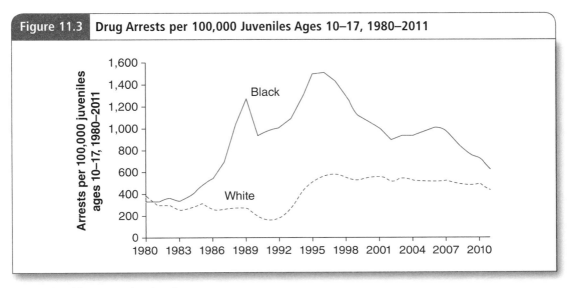

Figure 11.3 | Drug Arrests per 100,000 Juveniles Ages 10–17, 1980–2011

Source: Adapted from Puzzanchera (2013).

no significant effects on rates of assault, rape, or grand larceny. While there was evidence stop-and-frisk laws reduced robbery, burglary, motor vehicle theft, and homicide, Smith and Purtell (2008) noted the diminished returns of these policies on most of the offenses they analyzed. Based on an updated methodology to account for some of the limitations in the Smith and Purtell analysis, Rosenfeld and Fornango (2011) concluded that the stops show few significant effects on precinct robbery and burglary rates. (p. 19) In a recent analysis, Weisburd and Telep (2014) argued that while stop-and-frisk can be seen as an example of hot-spot policing, in the long run, such policies will have unintended negative consequences that will outweigh any short-term benefits.

Qualitative studies have also explored stop-and-frisk to understand the impact of this policy on those who are most often stopped by police. For example, the Morris Justice Project (MJP) has spent more than two years in New York City documenting experiences of policing in a 40-block community near Yankee Stadium. MJP is a collaborative research team comprised of neighborhood residents and representatives from the CUNY Graduate Center, John Jay College, and Pace University Law Center. Together, they have conducted focus groups of local residents. Another project by the VERA Institute of Justice focused on the experiences and perceptions of the young New Yorkers who are most likely to be stopped. Trust in law enforcement among these young people is alarmingly low. This has significant public safety implications, as young people who have been stopped more often are less willing to report crimes, even when they themselves are the victims. In short, stop-and-frisk policies often alienate the communities they are intended to serve.

Criticisms of Conflict Theories

Conflict theories are often very critical of the criminal justice system, but this does not mean that these theories themselves are above critique. One major issue is that conflict theories do not attempt

| Figure 11.4 | The Social Consequences of Stop-and-Frisk in New York City |

8 out of 10 have been stopped more than once in their lifetime.

Some reported **more than 20 stops.**

44% reported being stopped at least nine times in their lifetime.

MOST WERE INVOLVED IN AT LEAST ONE STOP THAT WENT BEYOND A SIMPLE VERBAL INTERACTION WITH THE OFFICER.

70% reported being frisked or searched during at least one stop.

Nearly half reported that officers threatened them and/or used physical force against them.

26% reported police displayed a weapon.

THE VAST MAJORITY BELIEVE THAT, IN GENERAL, THE STOPS THEY'VE EXPERIENCED WERE NOT WARRANTED.

More than 8 out of 10 disagreed with the statement, "The officer had a good reason to talk to me."

Less than a third reported ever being informed by police of the reason they were stopped.

85% said illegal items such as weapons, drugs, or open containers of alcohol were never discovered during a stop they had been involved in.

HALF BELIEVE THE OFFICERS WHO STOPPED THEM WERE BIASED AGAINST THEM.

Source: Fratello, Rengifo, & Trone (2013).

to explain crime but instead try to identify social conflict as a basic fact of life and a source of discriminatory treatment. Likewise, most conflict theories ignore biological and psychological characteristics of behavior that we know are important. Specifically, much of Marxist criminology appears to be in a time warp in that it assumes that the conditions prevailing in Marx's time still exist in the same form

Figure 11.5	Seven Steps of Conflict Theories
Seven Steps	**Conflict Theories**
1. Know the History	Surfaced during the 1960s and 1970s; heavily influenced by Marxist thought; Simmel and Weber also important influences
2. Acknowledge Assumptions	Humans are viewed as altruistic but corrupted by capitalism; rejects social positivist approach in favor of a view that humans are shaped by and shape their own environments; strong conflict assumption (i.e., those in power gain and maintain their position through coercion and exploitation of the weak)
3. Problem Focus, Scope, and Level of Explanation	Focus is on the activities of criminal justice system agents and origins of criminal law; emphasis is on structural factors that influence law-making and law-breaking
4. Key Terms and Concepts	Egoism, conflicts of interest, criminalization process, social constructionism, peacemaking criminology, legal realism, left realism, and feminism
5. Respect the Research	Research examines how economic shifts affect punishment and disparities in sentencing based on social class and how culture shapes views of crime, criminals, and criminality; ethnography and other qualitative analysis are preferred over quantification
6. Theory/Practice	Seek to challenge and upend existing power structures in society; embrace programs and policies such as neighborhood watches, community policing, dispute resolution centers, higher taxes on the wealthy to fund education programs, single-payer health care, and policies of family support
7. Mapping the Theory	See Figure 11.6

today in advanced capitalist societies. Constitutive criminology assumes that changing the way people think and talk about crime can help society better understand it. Others suggest peacemaking criminologists never offer any notion as to how crime rates can be reduced beyond counseling that we should appreciate a criminal's point of view and not be so punitive. While this is not terrible advice, it is of limited use when dealing with crime in practice. Some feminist theories have also been found wanting. They appear to have provided some useful insights, but specific predictions about crime often haven't materialized. The main goal of reforming the patriarchal structure of society will also prove to be difficult simply because there isn't a clear way to do this.

Sometimes it may seem like conflict theories are good at critiquing, complaining, and tearing down, but not very useful in articulating a reasonable alternative. This is a common refrain. Left realism represents an effort to turn these criticisms of criminal justice into practical realities. More specifically, left realists are interested in collaborating with criminal justice system practitioners with the hope of achieving progressive changes within the system. They believe this would be more effective than merely criticizing the system from the confines of academia. However, many critics suggest that the effort to cooperate with criminal justice agencies has ultimately caused left realism

| Figure 11.6 | Mapping Conflict Theories |

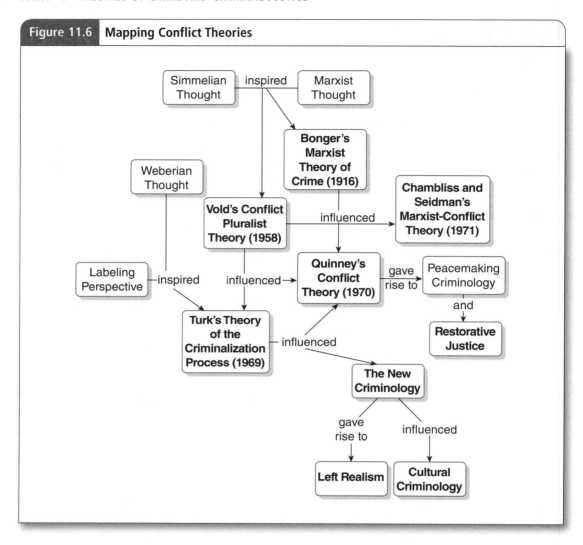

to be captured and co-opted by the state. This is often connected to the rise of Tony Blair and New Labour in the United Kingdom. The phrase "tough on crime and tough on the causes of crime" ultimately served as cover for increasingly punitive policies, and a rise in incarceration rates occurred despite the fact recorded crimes dropped significantly. Some speculate that the lack of a more developed basis for left realism in criminology allowed the state-defined research based on simplistic positivistic assumptions to guide the study of crime and undermine more critically reflexive approaches (Arrigo & Williams, 2006). In other words, the spirit of reform in left realism was lost in practical translation.

One practical outcome that can be seen as a result of the critical theories in criminology is restorative justice. This practical approach is designed to empower the community itself and those involved in a crime to come together and find the best solution. It can allow for a more robust discussion of the harms caused by a deviant or criminal act and generate a more common understanding among participants. As Liz Elliott (2011) argues, too often formal institutions ignore racism, classism, and the need for victims to play an active role in overcoming the fear, shame, and damage associated with crimes. Restorative justice addresses these social justice issues by making the community the primary site of social action.

 ## Research Example: Restorative Justice as a Practical Critique of the Criminal Justice System

An example of the interrelationship between theory, research, and criminal justice practice can be found in the restorative justice approach. Although key principles common to restorative justice originally grew out of practice and tradition before the articulation of peacemaking criminology, these programs cannot be properly understood without reference to key theories presented after the fact. Harms refer here to those damages suffered by the victim of a particular incident, by an offender, and even by communities. This expanding notion provides an important shift in thinking about crime and an expansion in thought about how harm might be addressed (Pepinsky & Quinney, 1991).

The second principle is a desire to foster the role of the community in the neighborhood where the harm occurred. Elliott (2002) has argued that this is important in at least two ways. First, the inclusion of the community in any process to address harm acknowledges the important role the community plays in crime commission and prevention. In addition, by specifically including the community in the process, there is the acceptance of the notion that even those not harmed in a particular case still have an interest in its successful resolution (Elliott, 2002, pp. 462–463). This allows restorative justice to engage community members in a process where they have a meaningful role in the outcome of decisions that matter to them. The third principle is related to the moral potential for restorative justice. By rooting morality in attending to the real needs of actual individuals through processes which are consistent with and reflect community values, restorative justice offers an interesting alternative to the formal justice system. Instead of relying on official definitions of crime that are the product of societies and cultures with problematic histories, involving people and communities in exploring the harms and coming to a collective solution is at once practical and radical.

Pepinsky (1991) suggests critical traditions and feminist traditions inform peacemaking criminology and are related to some of the underlying assumptions that remain within the restorative justice movement today. Based on the critical traditions, there remains a distrust of the state as an impartial arbiter and a desire to locate justice in individual communities in which residents participate in the decision-making process (Einstadter & Henry, 1995; Gibbons, 1994). From the feminist tradition, Pepinsky (1991, p. 310) identifies Kay Harris as an influential thinker who argued that restorative processes should allow those who have suffered harm to participate in the design of an appropriate response.

While the connection between restorative justice and peacemaking criminology has historical pedigree, recent justifications have placed crime at the intersection of individuals, groups, and cultures. In 1999, the Supreme Court of Canada recognized that the concept and principles of restorative justice were still developing. In *R. v. Gladue,* the Court stated that in general terms, restorative justice may be described as an approach to remedying crime in which it is understood that all things are interrelated and that crime disrupts the harmony which existed prior to its occurrence, or at least which it is felt should exist. The appropriateness of a particular sanction is largely determined by the needs of the victims, and the community, as well as the offender. The focus is on the human beings closely affected by the crime. (para. 71)

The number of restorative justice programs, models, and approaches has grown exponentially in the last three decades in the United States and around the world. Still, some critics within and outside the criminal justice system doubt the value of restorative justice projects, and others argue definitional disagreements confound efforts to systematically study outcomes (Wheeldon, 2009b). Those who support these programs have countered that restorative justice may be able to further moral and cognitive development by emphasizing mutual problem-solving, communication, negotiation, compromise, and responsibility (Minor & Morrison, 1996). By creating a means by which people must confront real and difficult dilemmas, "social experiences can promote development . . . when they stimulate our mental processes" (Crain, 1985, p. 126). The idea is that when we are challenged, we develop through an increased competence in balancing conflicting value claims. By exposing individuals to morally formative experiences in which past behavior is called to account, and through mutual conflict resolution, an opportunity for parties to understand and clarify those norms and values can be created (Van Ness & Strong, 1997).

One approach is restorative justice conferences (RJC). Designed to bring together victims, offenders, and communities, RJCs are face-to-face meetings between victims and offenders involved in a crime in which the participants discuss the offense and its consequences and try to resolve the issue. Conducted in the presence of a trained facilitator, RJCs often involve the families and friends of the principle participants and others affected by the crime. For policymakers, there are two main concerns: (1) Do RJCs reduce future offending? and (2) Do RJCs improve victim satisfaction? Figure 11.7 offers a visual map of a recent meta-analysis published by the Campbell Collaboration that sought to answer these questions (Strang, Woods, Sherman, Mayo-Wilson, & Ariel, 2013).

Now that you've read the chapter . . . think about the 2014 report by the Department of Education that explored racial disparities in American education and especially the number of arrests and referrals to law enforcement by race. Now consider what has been called the "school-to-prison pipeline." This national trend occurs when students of color are funneled out of public schools and into the juvenile and criminal justice systems. Many of these children have learning disabilities or histories of poverty, abuse, or neglect, and would benefit from additional educational and counseling services. Instead these students are isolated, punished, and pushed out. What might a conflict theorist suggest is happening here? Why does this trend represent a challenge for the criminal justice system?

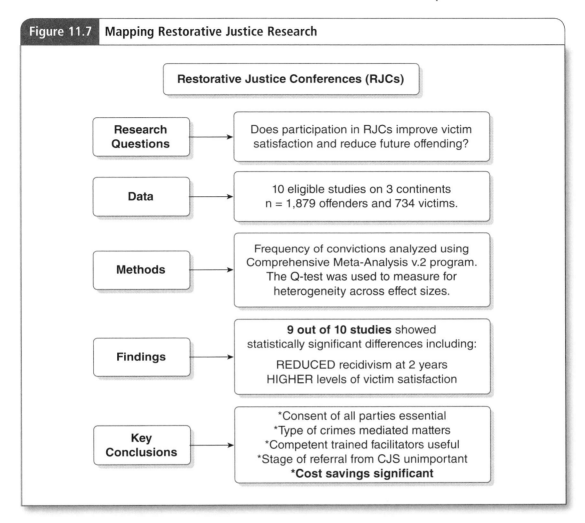

Figure 11.7   Mapping Restorative Justice Research

Restorative Justice Conferences (RJCs)

Research Questions → Does participation in RJCs improve victim satisfaction and reduce future offending?

Data → 10 eligible studies on 3 continents n = 1,879 offenders and 734 victims.

Methods → Frequency of convictions analyzed using Comprehensive Meta-Analysis v.2 program. The Q-test was used to measure for heterogeneity across effect sizes.

Findings → **9 out of 10 studies** showed statistically significant differences including:

REDUCED recidivism at 2 years
HIGHER levels of victim satisfaction

Key Conclusions → *Consent of all parties essential
*Type of crimes mediated matters
*Competent trained facilitators useful
*Stage of referral from CJS unimportant
*Cost savings significant

✖ Conclusion and Review Questions

This chapter reviewed the many different varieties of conflict criminology, including the Marxist and nonpartisan conflict theories and explanations offered by legal theorists, feminists, postmodernists, and post-structuralist thinkers. Conflict theorists take a much different approach to understanding crime than other criminologists because they focus more on understanding the activities of the criminal justice system and the criminal law. The insight derived from this approach is of a different nature than approaches that locate the source of crime solely within the individual, and it offers a different way to understand crime, law, culture, and social control.

We identified two recurring themes that offer one way to understand how these theories are relevant to criminology. The first of these themes refers to the fundamental difference between the consensus and conflict views of the role of law and legal institutions in society. The second theme relates to the specific ways in which criminal law, legal codes, punishment, and other forms of social control can result in harm for those within societies with the least power. While conflict criminologists view the criminal justice system through a political and economic lens, we have tried to suggest some practical ways these theories have influenced the current justice system.

This area of criminological study has yielded some very interesting theories and research findings. Reiman's (1979) research has highlighted differences in the treatment of offenders from different classes, shedding light on an injustice rarely perceived by the general public. Restorative justice takes a radically different approach from that of the traditional criminal justice system and has provided an alternative to the traditional punitive model of justice. Finally, it is interesting to note that the contemporary movement to decriminalize marijuana use, the increased use of drug treatment courts, and efforts to hold white-collar and corporate criminals more accountable are all very compatible with the agendas of the conflict theorists.

CHAPTER REVIEW

1. How are the assumptions made by conflict theories relevant?

2. Why is the historical period in which these theories emerged important?

3. What kinds of criminological issues do conflict theories try to explain?

4. List some practical approaches and programs suggested by conflict theories.

5. Why are the critiques leveled against conflict theories important? How are they limited?

CHAPTER

12

Rational Choice Theories

 ## Chapter Overview and Objectives

Rational choice theories all adhere to the basic logic of the classical school. Recall from earlier chapters that classical school scholars believe that people use a hedonistic calculus to make decisions, and they hold that people act to maximize pleasure and minimize pain. Consequently, these theories take criminal motivation for granted. Instead, the focus is on the dynamics of criminal acts and the structural aspects that create or constrain opportunities to commit crime. Many theories in this area have been heavily influenced by situational crime prevention practices. Further, many of the theories have clear practical ramifications and offer many recommendations for reducing and preventing crime to criminal justice system practitioners. Rational choice theories also fit well with the traditional system of justice as both assume that people are rational decision makers who exercise control over their behavior. Figure 12.1 provides an overview of rational choice theories.

By the end of the chapter, readers should be able to:

- Know the difference between classical, neoclassical, and postclassical perspectives and the assumptions they make about human nature
- Understand that these theories explain criminal acts and crimes rather than criminality, criminal motivation, or criminal behavior
- Be aware of the assumptions, level of explanation, problem focus, and scope of rational choice theories
- Explain what the expected utility principle is and how it has been applied in criminological theories
- Realize the importance of rational choice theories to many policies and practices in the criminal justice system
- Consider the critiques leveled against rational choice theories

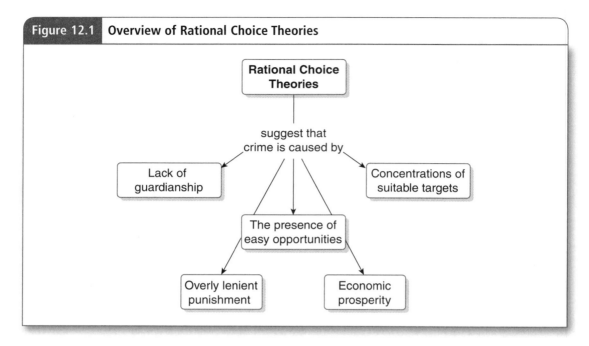

Figure 12.1   Overview of Rational Choice Theories

The Rational Choice Tradition

The rational choice tradition comprises a group of theories known by a variety of names. They have been referred to as deterrence theories, neoclassical theories, environmental criminology, the criminal event perspective, and situational choice theory (Cohen & Felson, 1979; Einstadter & Henry, 2006; Lilly et al., 2011; Meier, Sacco, & Kennedy, 2001; Williams & McShane, 2014). Similar to the conflict tradition, these terms are often used interchangeably to refer to this field of theories as a whole. In reality, there are subtle differences between the various formulations in this area. However, they do share some things in common and can be seen as a set of interrelated theories (Ekblom & Tilley, 2000). As stated previously, these theories generally assume that humans are rational actors with free will.

Economic models of human behavior have greatly influenced these theories. Consequently, several terms from economics have been used to describe theories in this area. For example, some use the term *neoclassical* to refer to those who support punishment as a means to control crime through deterrence. As such, this branch of theories is also sometimes referred to as deterrence theories (Van Den Haag, 1975; J. Q. Wilson, 1975). According to Beirne and Messerschmidt (2011), the neoclassical approach resulted from a compromise between classicism and positivism. In other words, neoclassical theorists still embrace the notion of free will and the view of people as rational decision makers, but they acknowledge that these decisions are shaped by various environmental factors.

Einstadter and Henry (2006) have also identified a branch of deterrence theories called postclassical theories. Postclassical theorists believe that deterrence can be most effectively achieved through adjustments to the physical environment rather than through punishment imposed by the criminal justice system. In other words, why not prevent crime before it happens rather than trying to locate, arrest, convict, imprison, and rehabilitate criminals?

The rational choice theories are sometimes associated with a conservative political ideology that is overly reliant on punishment (Einstadter & Henry, 2006). While this is accurate for some of the earlier deterrence theories, many rational theories do not necessarily take a punitive stance with regard to criminal justice system policy. Despite this grounding in more liberal thought of some of these theorists, others have injected some extreme political commentary into their formulations (Van Den Haag, 1975; J. Q. Wilson, 1975). However, most do not view this political stance as central to the modern version of rational choice theory (Felson, 2002). Theorists in the rational choice tradition also have drawn upon datasets ignored by other theories, including self-report findings and research from the field of victimology (Williams & McShane, 2014).

> **As you read this chapter, consider . . .** how have people's routines and activities changed over the years? For example, how has shopping changed in the last ten years? Consider how the places we shop and our methods of paying have evolved and the consequences this has for crime. Also consider how the things we buy have changed. How have sizes and prices changed? How have shifts in technology both limited and contributed to opportunities for crime?

Seven Steps of Criminological Thinking

History and Social Context of Rational Choice Theories

A number of social, political, and historical events in the late 1970s and 1980s shaped the rational choice theories. As discussed in previous chapters, the decade of the 1950s was a time of relative peace and conformity, but this mood changed in subsequent decades. Numerous social movements characterized the 1960s. This period involved a great deal of political upheaval and change in the United States. People began to question authority and challenge government power, and this trend continued into the 1970s.

Toward the end of the 1970s, the United States experienced an economic crisis. Manufacturing jobs shifted overseas, and this left more people out of work. Huge segments of the population, especially racial minorities, were affected by this loss of blue-collar employment. This was accompanied by a shift to conservative governments in both the United States and the United Kingdom, and these governments offered unequivocal answers to complex social questions regarding social welfare, public housing, and crime control. Conservative politicians such as President Ronald Reagan and Prime Minister Margaret Thatcher enjoyed popular support and an electoral mandate to enact significant social changes. One focus was the criminal justice system. Conservatives had long doubted the penal-welfare approach supported by liberals and progressives. Many conservatives thought that liberals viewed the justice system as a means to offer social support to those who engaged in crime because they lacked adequate opportunities for success. Soon, people from both sides of the political spectrum started to question the ability of the criminal justice system to deal with crime because crime rates had been climbing since the 1950s (Garland, 2001).

Negative reactions to criminal justice system practices were buoyed by some developments in criminal justice research and scholarship. First, the well-known research on correctional interventions undertaken by Martinson (1974) lent support to the idea that the system had failed in its attempts to address the crime problem (Lilly et al., 2011; Miller et al., 2011). The results of this research can be summarized as follows: "With few and isolated exceptions, the rehabilitative efforts that have been reported so far have had no appreciable effect on recidivism" (Martinson, 1974, p. 25). Martinson's conclusions provided the basis for what would later become the "nothing works" doctrine. This cynical approach became tremendously influential in the area of corrections and helped set the stage for cuts to rehabilitation, education, and job-training programs in prisons for years to come. Why did it have such an impact? It provided the perfect justification for cutting programs and funds, which satisfied the fiscal goals of the conservative governments during this era.

Another development can be found in the work of conservative political scientists who waged a devastating attack on the social explanations of crime, such as differential association and strain theory (Laub, 2004). Less than a year after the emergence of the "nothing works" doctrine, James Q. Wilson articulated a new theoretical perspective endorsing a more punitive approach in his seminal work, *Thinking About Crime* (1975). J. Q. Wilson (1975) asserted that society needed to change the way it was dealing with crime. More specifically, he thought that the search for an underlying explanation of crime ought to be abandoned in favor of a concerted effort to control and manage crime. According to Wilson, a different view of criminals and crime control must be adopted if this goal was to be accomplished:

> Wicked people exist. Nothing avails except to set them apart from innocent people. And many people, neither wicked nor innocent, but watchful, dissembling, and calculating of their opportunities, ponder our reaction to wickedness as a cue to what they might profitably do. We have trifled with the wicked, made sport of the innocent, and encouraged the calculators. Justice suffers, and so do we all. (1975, p. 209)

The quote above appears to imply that during the 1950s and 1960s, the criminal justice system had gone "soft" and was no longer punishing people severely enough or with enough certainty. This endorsement of punitive crime control tactics was accompanied by attacks on the use of social programs to help solve crime and other social problems (Van Den Haag, 1975).

All of this activity helped to lay the groundwork for a shift in the practices of the criminal justice system in both the United Kingdom and United States, and to a lesser extent in Canada. Throughout the 1980s and into the 1990s, there was an emphasis on punishment and crime prevention and much less focus on rehabilitation and reintegration. Because of its relationship to the criminal justice system, these changes also affected criminology as a field. While it is accurate that theory often influences criminal justice practice, it is important to remember that the reverse is also true: Criminal justice practices sometimes influence theorizing in criminology.

These developments helped to usher in a return to the logic of the classical school. This was also inspired by the emergence of theories and research in economics about crime (Clarke & Cornish, 1985). The hedonistic calculus suggested by Bentham could be seen as a forerunner to later economic theories of behavior based on the expected utility principle (Akers, 1990).

Other major influences in this area include architectural and urban planning studies focusing on crime prevention. In criminology, there is a longstanding interest in the connections between crime and place. As early as the first half of the 19th century, French scholars were analyzing the distribution of crime across regions with differing ecological and social characteristics (Guerry, 1833; Quetelet, 1831). A century later in the United States, Chicago school sociologists concluded that characteristics of the urban environment are critical to explaining the emergence of crime in specific communities (Burgess, 1925; Thrasher, 1927; Shaw & McKay, 1969). During the 1960s and 1970s, the interest in place and the geographical imagination of criminology began to reemerge (Brantingham & Brantingham, 1993).

Much of this newfound interest was sparked by Jane Jacob's (1961) classic book, *The Life and Death of American Cities*. In this work, she argued that changes in architecture and urban planning triggered by increased urbanization eroded the sense of community in many neighborhoods. Jacobs (1961) claimed that the slum-clearing and urban renewal practices of the 1950s increased crime. She claimed that the older architectural characteristics, such as porches, stoops, and street-level windows, allowed for superior natural surveillance while encouraging bonding between residents. Later scholars, such as Jeffery (1971) and Newman (1972), sought to expand on these ideas and explain how urban planning and architectural ideas applied to preventing and controlling crime. In general, interest in crime and place moved from macro considerations and places like cities, regions, and states to micro considerations that focus on the characteristics of the places themselves (Eck & Weisburd, 1995).

Some types of rational choice theories are also informed by work done in social and human ecology (Felson, 2002). The work of Amos Hawley (1950) was especially influential. He suggested that large-scale changes to people's everyday routines were important to understanding human behavior. Further, he thought it was important to understand how technological changes affected these routines.

Finally, most rational choice theorists draw on research from self-reports and the field of victimology (Felson, 2002). This data is often used to refine theories of criminal acts. After all, victims are a factor in most criminal acts.

Similar to the conflict-theorists, rational choice theorists have congregated at several centers of excellence. For example, many prominent rational choice theorists have been associated with Rutgers University in the United States. Rutgers has a Center on Public Security that focuses on applying many of the ideas from rational choice theory to preventing crime (http://www.rutgerscps.org). Another major center of rational choice theory is located in Canada at Simon Fraser University in the School of Criminology. Particularly influential here are Brantingham and Brantingham's environmental criminology studies and the Institute for Canadian Urban Research Studies (http://www.sfu.ca/criminology/research.html#ICURS). In the United Kingdom, the main hub of this activity is the Home Office Policing and Reducing Crime Unit (Ekblom & Tilley, 2000).

Assumptions of Rational Choice Theories

Like the classical school philosophers, rational choice theorists assume that humans are naturally selfish and seek to maximize their own pleasure. Embracing a naturalist approach, they argue that people make rational choices to commit crime (Agnew, 2011). Felson clarifies this stance below:

> Why should crime be any less specific than the rest of nature? Even if offenders are often generalists over time, they are responsive at any given moment to very precise crime chances. Thus, we must study crime by gathering its details like a naturalist, classifying offense circumstances like a taxonomist, and working out interdependent systems like a physiologist. (2002, p. 167)

Unlike early classical school approaches, most rational choice theorists assume that there is some variation among individuals in their propensity to commit crime.

As implied above, more recent theories in this branch do not assume that people are completely unaffected by outside factors and acknowledge that behavior is not always purely rational. Instead, they embrace the notion of *bounded rationality*, also referred to as soft free will (Einstadter & Henry, 2006; Williams & McShane, 2014). Clarke explains this further in the following passage:

> It is not suggested that decision making will always be fully rational or properly considered. It seems more appropriate to hold to a notion of "limited rationality" in which economic explanations are tempered by psychological factors. . . . For example, people's capacity and willingness to acquire and process information about the risks of crime vary widely. So do their desire for profit and willingness to take risks. Some burglars seem to disregard completely the low probability of being intercepted by police patrols, while others take great care to avoid such an eventuality. (1983, p. 231)

Despite this concession, many rational choice theories still avoid questions about the etiology of crime.

Like earlier classical school formulations, rational choice theories support the notion of a social contract and believe that, by and large, the criminal law represents a societal consensus about crime (Einstadter & Henry, 2006). However, unlike the classical school theorists, rational choice theorists do question the likelihood of deterrence being accomplished solely through punishment. Instead, most of these theorists support crime prevention tactics that attempt to prevent criminal acts before they take place or that manipulate the environment to reduce the number of opportunities for crime (Felson, 2002).

Problem Focus, Scope, and Level of Explanation of Rational Choice Theories

Unlike most criminological theorists, rational choice theorists make little effort to explain individual motivation to commit crime. Instead, they assume that there are motivated offenders and focus on explaining crime rates and other aspects of the criminal event, such as criminal decision making and offender search patterns (Brantingham & Brantingham, 1978; Clarke & Cornish, 1985; Cohen & Felson, 1979). Brantingham and Brantingham clarify this specialized problem focus:

> The criminal-event problem set revolves around the dimensions of discrete criminal events. It involves the study of the temporal and spatial components of crime, for example, when murders or burglaries occur and where. It also involves the technical components of crime, for example, how burglars break into a house and what weapons murderers use. It involves characteristics of offenders and targets. . . . The study of criminal events—that is, of crimes—forms the meeting ground for criminologists and criminal justice scholars. In it are inherent both the intellectual appeal of search for order and pattern (i.e., for prediction and explanation) and the utilitarian policy appeal of control. (1984, p. 20)

Despite this focus, the scope of the rational choice theories is quite broad. These theories focus primarily on explaining property crimes, such as robbery, burglary, and auto theft. However, some can be applied to other forms of crime, such as white-collar and drug crimes (Brantingham & Brantingham, 1993; Felson, 2002).

Rational choice theories have been proposed at the macro and micro levels, and they address structural and process elements of criminal events (Ekblom & Tilley, 2000). For example, routine activities theory attempts to account for structural factors such as technological shifts and changes in people's daily activity patterns that help explain the rising crime rates of the 1960s and 1970s. Several process elements of the criminal event are also addressed by other theories. For example, in their rational choice theory, Clarke and Cornish (1985) attempted to clarify how offenders make decisions to commit crime and the ramifications this has for situational crime prevention tactics. Finally, in the crime pattern theory developed by Brantingham and Brantingham (1984, 1993), the focus is on explaining offender search patterns and how ecological and environmental factors lead to higher crime rates in some areas.

Key Terms and Concepts in Rational Choice Theories

Early Economic and Deterrence Theories

Gary Becker's (1974) economic-deterrence theory of crime is an early example of the shift to economic explanations. This theory uses the **expected-utility principle** from economics to explain criminal behavior (Akers, 1990). It states that offenders will act in ways to maximize their interests based on rational calculation. Recall that Beccaria (1764) and Bentham (1765) claimed that people could be deterred from criminal activity as long as the punishment was certain, appropriately severe, and delivered quickly after the criminal act. Through this application, Becker (1968) attempted to clarify how severity, celerity (or swiftness), and certainty of punishment contribute to deterrence.

Becker's (1968) theory is essentially a pure deterrence theory. He claimed that people generally do not vary in their motivation to commit crime, but instead they vary in their perceived costs and benefits of committing crime. In short, he was trying to specify how offenders respond to the costs of crime imposed by the criminal justice system. Consequently, the emphasis is shifted to examining how criminal justice resources can be most efficiently used to reduce crime. The underlying idea here is quite simple: Behavior can be directly affected through punishments imposed by the criminal justice system. The focus of this theory is much more on punishing crimes than on directly changing offender motivations to commit crime. This theory can be seen as a challenge to most of the sociological theories of criminal behavior, such as differential association and strain theory, that were popular during this time.

In his book *Thinking About Crime*, J. Q. Wilson (1975) took an approach that had much in common with Becker's (1968) earlier economic-deterrence theory. Like Becker (1968), Wilson also embraced a neoclassical, economic approach to classical school deterrence theory. This can be seen as another attempt to further clarify how deterrence functions. J. Q. Wilson (1975) also advocated a return to the examination of the classical school and deterrence principles by arguing that the criminal justice system must make crime more costly by increasing the length of some punishments. He was careful to caution against imposing overly severe sentences, however:

> The more severe the sentence, the greater the bargaining power of the accused, and the greater the likelihood he will be charged with a lesser offense. Extremely long mandatory minimum sentences do not always strengthen the hand of society; they often strengthen the hand of the criminal instead. (J. Q. Wilson, 1975, p. 179)

The underlying theme in J. Q. Wilson's (1975) work is that our efforts to change people, either by providing them opportunities or by rehabilitating them, are likely to be ineffective. He suggests that the only way to reduce the crime rate is to incapacitate repeat offenders by increasing the amount of time they serve.

Wilson and Kelling's (1982) broken windows theory can be seen as an attempt to further refine J. Q. Wilson's (1975) earlier deterrence theory. This theory also incorporates findings from Zimbardo's (1970) deindividuation theory, discussed in Chapter 5. In terms of impact on the criminal justice system, this formulation is perhaps one of the most influential criminological theories ever proposed. According to Wilson and Kelling (1982), areas that exhibit public disorder (e.g., broken windows, graffiti, public drug use and dealing) emit situational cues that attract criminals. These cues send the message that crime is tolerated in the surrounding area, drawing unsavory individuals (e.g., aggressive panhandlers, drunks, addicts, rowdy teenagers, prostitutes, and mentally disturbed individuals) to certain neighborhoods. Law-abiding people also pick up on these cues and move away from and/or avoid these sections of the city. This creates situations conducive to offending, which leads to more criminal opportunities and serves to destabilize certain communities through lowering levels of informal social control. Wilson and Kelling (1982) suggest that police need to increase their visibility in affected areas and aggressively enforce all laws to exert control (i.e., a zero-tolerance approach). In other words, the only way to restore levels of informal social control is to raise levels of formal social control. Figure 12.2 suggests some of the connections between these theories.

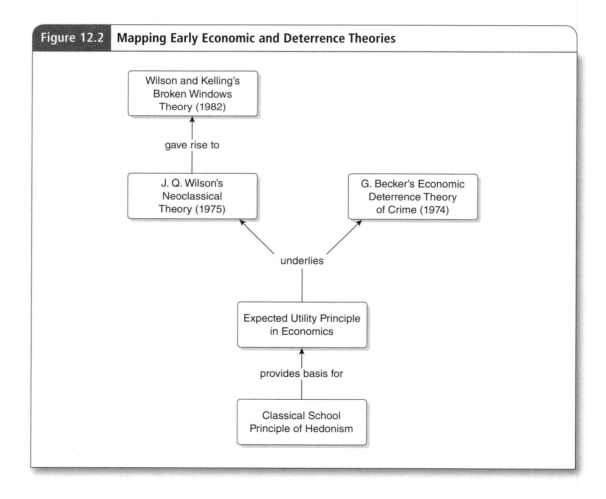

Figure 12.2 Mapping Early Economic and Deterrence Theories

Routine Activities Theory

Another key theory from the rational choice tradition is Cohen and Felson's (1979) routine activities theory. This theory is based upon three principles, as outlined in Figure 12.3. The first principle is drawn directly from classical school logic; the other two are drawn from social ecology and sociology and warrant further discussion.

Building on ideas offered by Durkheim (1938/1895), Cohen and Felson (1979) claimed that large-scale social changes and technological advancements are important to understanding changes in crime rates over time. This is an extension of Durkheim's (1938/1895) modernization thesis, which states that human interaction and the patterning of social activities change as society becomes increasingly industrialized and technological. More specifically, as societies become more modernized, they move away from the mechanical solidarity of rural, agrarian societies (i.e., high social cohesion) and drift toward organic forms of solidarity that characterize more urban, industrialized societies (i.e., less social cohesion) This all changes the way social control functions in society and can impact crime rates.

Felson (1998) also incorporated the work of another sociologist, William Ogburn (1964), to further refine Durkheim's (1938/1895) modernization thesis. Ogburn (1964) suggested that inventions can also cause important social changes and alter patterns of interaction among members of society. This helps to explain how technological shifts affect crime and criminal activity. For example, it seems obvious that some technological advancements, such as computers, have created new opportunities for crime. Some have even suggested that while official crime rates have fallen, the number of crimes committed online has dramatically risen but that this may not be reflected in existing crime statistics. This may change in a fundamental way how people ought to think about crime, law, harm, and societal responses (Hall, 2012). However, in routine activities theory, the concept of inventions does not necessarily refer to "high" technology or new gadgetry; simple inventions (e.g., barbed wire) or nonmaterial inventions

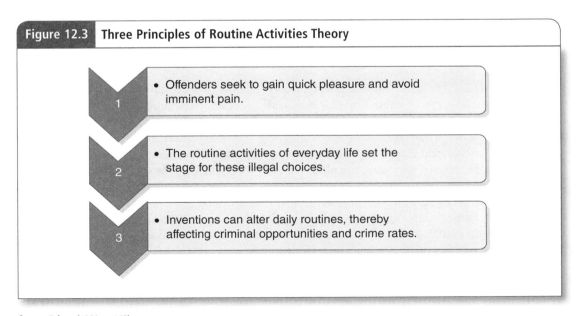

Figure 12.3 | **Three Principles of Routine Activities Theory**

1
- Offenders seek to gain quick pleasure and avoid imminent pain.

2
- The routine activities of everyday life set the stage for these illegal choices.

3
- Inventions can alter daily routines, thereby affecting criminal opportunities and crime rates.

Source: Felson (1998, p. 165).

(e.g., money management techniques and architectural/design changes) can also be crucial to explaining changes in crime rates (Felson, 1998, pp. 167–168).

The core ideas of routine activities theory are also partially derived from the work of Amos Hawley (1950), a well-known social ecologist. Hawley was influenced by some of the early members of the Chicago school, including Robert Park, Ernest Burgess, and Roderick McKenzie. According to Hawley (1950), it is important to realize that functional fluctuations are important to understanding large-scale behavioral changes in groups of organisms. These fluctuations (i.e., an organism's everyday habits involved with moving and securing food) are important because they determine the routine activities of groups of organisms.

From the concept of functional fluctuations, Cohen and Felson proceed to derive a conceptual scheme for analyzing criminal acts:

> We argue that structural changes in routine activity patterns can influence crime rates by affecting the convergence in space and time of the three minimal elements of direct-contact predatory violations: (1) motivated offenders, (2) suitable targets, (3) the absence of capable guardians against a violation. (1979, p. 589)

Based on this framework, Cohen and Felson (1979) argued that the rising crime rates of the 1960s and 1970s could be attributed to societal shifts that occurred after World War II; these changes greatly impacted the routine activities of normal people of this era.

For example, because of advancements in equal rights and the women's movement, many females entered the labor force or decided to pursue higher education during this period. This left many homes unattended during the day, which created many new criminal opportunities and suitable targets. Crime rates also rose as technological advancements reduced the weight and size of high-priced electronic items, such as car radios and television sets. This, of course, also created more suitable targets and better opportunities for crime. If one assumes that people are naturally inclined to commit crime when certain circumstances exist, the focus then shifts to how to constrain the opportunities to participate in crime.

Rational Choice Theory and Crime

Clarke and Cornish's (1985) rational choice theory is another important formulation in the rational choice tradition. This theory emphasizes the similarities of offenders and nonoffenders and suggests that other criminological theories tend to "over-pathologize" crime. Essentially, this is a criticism of the medical model or the idea that criminality is something that needs treatment to be cured. It is also a critique of the sociological theories that attribute crime to poor social conditions and poverty. Like the other theories in this area, economic models of decision making provide the basis for Clarke and Cornish's (1985) formulation. However, it is still appropriate to think of their work as a micro-oriented theory that focuses on explaining criminal acts rather than criminality.

It is true that the assumption of rationality is not testable (see Robinson & Beaver, 2008), but this is not necessarily a requirement since assumptions are merely the basis for theorizing and often cannot be directly tested (Wagner, 1984). In order for a formulation to be considered a theory, the resulting models of criminal decision making just have to be testable and falsifiable, which they are. In addition, there is a wealth of empirical research suggesting that at least some types of crimes involve some planning and deliberation (Cromwell, Olson, & Avery, 1991; Wright & Decker, 1994). The key propositions in rational choice theory (Cornish & Clarke, 2001, p. 24) are outlined in Figure 12.5.

Figure 12.4   Visualizing Routine Activities Theory

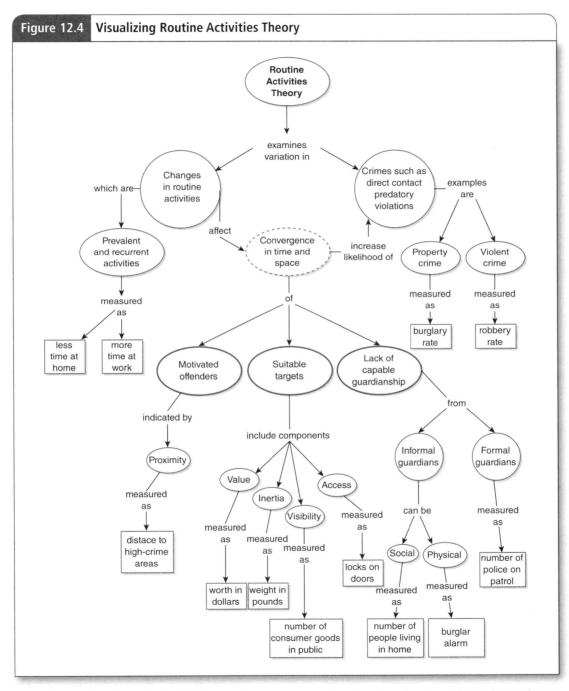

Source: Wheeldon, J., & Burruss, G. W. (2013). Teaching tips: Employing visual techniques to teach. In Criminology and criminal justice classrooms: Notes from the field. *The Criminologist: The Official Newsletter of the American Society of Criminology, 38* (1): 32–34. Retrieved from http://www.asc41.com/Criminologist/2013/2013_Jan-Feb_Criminologist.pdf

Figure 12.5	Propositions in Rational Choice Theory
1	Crimes are purposive and deliberate acts, committed with the intention of benefiting the offender.
2	In seeking to benefit themselves, offenders do not always succeed in making the best decisions because of the risks and uncertainty involved.
3	Offender decision making varies considerably with the nature of the crime.
4	Decisions about becoming involved in particular kinds of crime (involvement decisions) are quite different from those relating to the commission of the specific criminal act (event decisions).
5	Involvement decisions can be divided into three stages—becoming involved for the first time (initiation), continued involvement (habituation), and ceasing to offend (desistance)—that must be separately studied because they are influenced by quite different sets of variables.
6	Event decisions include a sequence of choices made at each stage of the criminal act (e.g., preparation, target selection, commission of the act, escape, and aftermath).

Propositions one and two are derived from classical school thought, which was discussed in Chapter 2. The other propositions require further explanation as they distinguish Clarke and Cornish's (1985, 2001) theory from earlier theories in the rational choice tradition. Proposition three implies that different crimes fulfill different needs, so it makes sense to focus on criminal acts rather than on offenders or criminality. Clarke and Cornish (1985) also suggest that different decision-making models are required for different types of crime.

In the remaining propositions, criminal event decisions are distinguished from criminal involvement decisions. Involvement decisions (i.e., deciding to participate or continuing to participate in criminal activity as well as deciding to desist from it) are thought to have less of a direct influence on the criminal event, whereas event decisions relate to how criminals weigh options to offend based on the characteristics of the criminal opportunity at hand. Background factors, current life circumstances, and situational variables are also thought to affect decisions to participate in criminal activity (Clarke and Cornish, 1985, 2001).

Environmental Criminology and Pattern Theory

Another important branch of theories in this area is often referred to as environmental criminology (Brantingham & Brantingham, 1978, 1984, 1993). This development has its origins in Jeffery's (1971) crime prevention through environmental design approach (CPTED). It is important to note that the underlying theory in CPTED is, in fact, an early deterministic biosocial theory rather than a true deterrence or rational choice theory (Robinson, 1996). However, environmental criminology fuses ideas from CPTED with concepts from routine activities and rational choice theory.

The underlying theory in CPTED is based on Skinner's (1953) operant conditioning principles; however, it emphasizes the interaction between biological factors and factors associated with the physical environment. This approach was influenced heavily by Jacobs' (1961) work on urban planning. Jeffery (1971) builds on these ideas by suggesting that the physical environment plays a role in determining behavior. He claims that simple changes to architecture, lighting, and urban planning can be made to eliminate opportunities for crime and to better control behavior. According to Jeffery (1971), considering opportunities for crime can also help us understand how criminals perceive and interpret their environments.

Brantingham and Brantingham (1978) extended these ideas to explain how criminals choose targets in their model of crime site selection. This theory suggests that a criminal's emotional state is important to understanding how he or she selects crime sites. When emotional involvement is high, searches tend to be simple and brief, whereas low emotional involvement will generate a longer, more calculated and complex search (Brantingham & Brantingham, 1978). They also claim that the environment emits cues or signals that inform motivated offenders which areas are ideal for the commission of crime. More specifically, these cues alert the offender to the opportunities for crime and the risks of apprehension. These cues are interpreted using knowledge acquired from previous experiences or, in some cases, are learned from others in a social context.

Brantingham and Brantingham (1978) also tried to explain how criminals learn from their crimes. They claimed that over time, offenders form mental templates based on experience and social learning derived from a variety of cues. These templates tend to be similar from criminal to criminal, and therefore theories can be created that will make predictions about behavior. For example, there are similarities in the way people perceive distance and conceptualize maps, and many people have consistent day-to-day activity patterns (Brantingham & Brantingham, 1984, pp. 349–358). The implication here is that universal characteristics of criminal templates may be identified and can be used to reduce and prevent criminal opportunities. The geometry of crime represents an extension of the crime site selection model (Brantingham & Brantingham, 1991). In their 1981 book, *Environmental Criminology* (reissued in 1991), Brantingham and Brantingham explain how they accomplished the elaboration:

> These propositions [in the original model] are not spatially specific. They posit that criminals engage in search behavior which may vary in intensity and that criminals use previous knowledge to select targets. The propositions do not describe the spatial characteristics of the search patterns or selection patterns. The model presented in this chapter will attempt to articulate these general propositions spatially. (1991, p. 29)

In this newer formulation, the level of rigor and precision is increased because a potential offender's movement is described with regard to spatial movement patterns. Brantingham and Brantingham also argue that offender searches tend to be short, inexpensive, and easy. This is the first appearance of the "least effort principle," and it can be viewed as an early attempt to introduce a rational choice element into the formulation. In other words, criminals will pursue easy opportunities that don't require a great deal of effort.

According to Brantingham and Brantingham (1991), an offender's perceptions of the world must be considered in order to understand his or her movement patterns. In their revised theory, they also identify basic, complex, selective, and dynamic search patterns. Basic searches account for an offender's home location and search patterns are based solely on this location. Models for more complex searches include the offender's home location as well as frequently visited school, work, and leisure locations. In both basic and complex searches, the theorists assume that there is a uniform distribution of targets. In selective and dynamic searches, it is assumed that targets are distributed unevenly.

These types of searches involve more planning, deliberation, and intention. In other words, the offender has focused on a particular location because the offender knows that targets are concentrated there. Like basic search models, selective search models are based on only the offender's home location. Dynamic searches, like complex searches, account for other frequently visited sites related to school, work, and leisure activities (Brantingham & Brantingham, 1991, pp. 30–47). Figure 12.6 provides one view of search patterns.

The emphasis on the interaction between motivated offenders and suitable targets clearly indicates the influence of Cohen and Felson's (1979) routine activities theory. Further, a great deal of attention is paid to routine activity patterns when attempting to understand how offender searches take place.

Figure 12.6 **Offender Search Patterns**

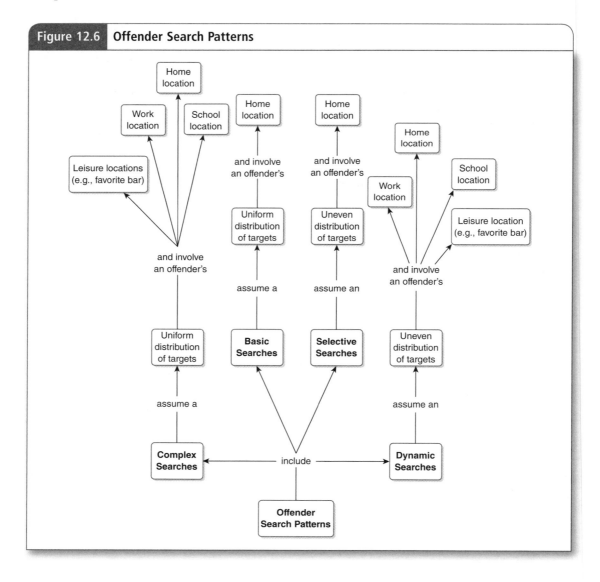

In their crime pattern theory, Brantingham and Brantingham (1984) refined their theory based on ideas offered by other rational choice theories. For example, they point out that targets are not uniformly or randomly distributed throughout cities. Instead, targets are thought to occur in certain patterns, and therefore crime is also thought to occur in some pattern. This idea can be used to help predict the areas in which criminal acts will most likely occur.

To help conceptualize the activity patterns of criminal offenders, Brantingham and Brantingham (1984) introduce several new concepts into their theory that are helpful to understanding the micro-spatial offending patterns of offenders. **Nodes** are hubs of activity that attract people (including offenders) for various reasons. Examples of nodes include centers of work and of leisure activity, such as bars, restaurants, and malls. **Paths** refer to routes (e.g., roads and walkways) that people use to travel between different nodes. The theorists point out that people tend to use the same routes on a daily basis. They describe **edges** as "linear elements not used as paths" that help form boundaries where people tend not to venture (e.g., the street before a bad section of the city, railroads, and other physical boundaries) (1984, p. 359). The space between the nodes is called **activity space**, and a criminal's **awareness space** is the area within visual range of activity space (Brantingham & Brantingham, 2008, p. 84).

Brantingham and Brantingham (1984) suggested that crimes are committed in the vicinity of the criminal's commonly traveled paths and nodes (i.e., awareness space) when suitable opportunities present themselves. This concept can be used to create maps that track offending patterns. Brantingham and Brantingham's (1993) pattern theory helps connect their previous two theories and refines factors that are involved in criminal events. They claim that in order to explain criminal acts, one must consider the process of committing the crime, the offender's template and activities, and the readiness/willingness of the offender to commit crime when the opportunity presents itself. Further, they argue that these factors are arranged on an environmental backcloth, which is "a term used for the variable, ever-changing context that surrounds the daily lives of individuals" (Brantingham & Brantingham, 1993, p. 287).

The environmental backcloth accounts for the changing external environment of individuals (structural elements), while the template focuses on individual decision making. Ideas from rational choice theory and routine activities are incorporated to explain how aspects of the criminal templates are formed (Eck & Weisburd, 1995). Brantingham and Brantingham describe how ideas from routine activities theory are relevant to the template/activity backcloth portion of their pattern theory:

> While forming patterns in the foreground, the event process rests on a general backcloth formed by routine activities (including repeat or routine criminal activities) and on a template that helps identify what a "great" chance is or what a "good" opportunity would be or how to search for chances and opportunities. (1993, p. 269)

These routine activities help shape offenders' patterns of travel throughout the day and affect how their templates are formed (Brantingham & Brantingham, 1993).

The theoretical model of hot spot generation is another attempt to build upon crime pattern theory (Brantingham & Brantingham, 1999). This theory introduces two new concepts: crime generators and crime attractors. **Crime generators** refer to places where people go to engage in non-criminal activities. Offenders may target these areas specifically because of the availability of opportunities and/or because they are within the awareness space of their commonly traveled routes.

These areas include malls, bus stops, subway/skytrain stations, and other places that attract large numbers of people. Slums, "red-light" districts, and drug areas that attract criminals because of an ecological label (i.e., bad reputation) are designated as **crime attractors**. When these areas happen to overlap with other structures that predispose an area to crime (e.g., poverty, traffic arteries, schools, and shops), crime hot spots may be created. The goal of this theory is to specify how a convergence of certain conditions can create high levels of crime within a particular area (Brantingham & Brantingham, 1999).

Research on Rational Choice Theories

There has been no shortage of research on rational choice theories. This shouldn't be surprising given that they focus on very practical concerns and offer concrete ways to reduce crime. Overall, research done on these theories has indicated that they have mixed support. Deterrence researchers have found some deterrent effects, but formal deterrence is not nearly as strong as most people think. Broken windows theory has been wildly successful from a practical point of view, but some have questioned whether or not this approach is really effective. Situational crime prevention tactics and environmental criminology have received more support, but various problems arise when we attempt to control crime through environmental manipulation (e.g., crime displacement).

Skogan's (1990) research provides some empirical support for broken windows theory and justifies the policies derived from it. This study involved residents in 40 neighborhoods in six US cities and examined the links between perceptions of crime and levels of disorder. Skogan found that the two were causally related and that disorder was present before serious crime occurred in the neighborhoods.

Recently, several research studies have questioned the effectiveness of the policies suggested by the broken windows approach. For example, Harcourt (2001) reanalyzed Skogan's (1990) original data and reached very different conclusions. Most important, he found that the support offered by Skogan's (1990) oft-cited study was actually very weak and that there was little reliable evidence to support the logic of the broken windows approach to policing.

As discussed previously, these approaches have played an outsized role in criminology. Rational choice theories have been used to justify increasingly punitive policies and a focus on crime prevention based on the view that crime is inevitable. This influence has been widespread, despite good empirical evidence that has questioned major elements of the model. To address past limitations, Piliavin and his colleagues (1986) tested some components of rational choice theories, such as (1) opportunity/reward based on the frequency of perceived opportunities for crime and (2) risk/cost based on respondents' estimates of being seen, reported, arrested, losing their job, going to prison, or losing friends or family. Using longitudinal data collected between 1975 and 1979, they found some support for the opportunity/reward component of rational choice theories but little for risk/cost. They concluded that decisions to engage in criminal behavior depend far more on personal perceptions of criminal opportunities rather than the fear of criminal punishment or personal losses, even for those at high risk of formal sanction (Piliavin, Gartner, Thornton, & Matsueda, 1986, pp. 116–117). To restate this more simply: Deterrence does not work as well as most people think it does.

These findings can be linked to early research connecting environment and opportunities for crime that emerged from the theory of defensible space offered by architect Oscar Newman (1972). He claimed that the high rates of crime seen in American neighborhoods in public housing units could be attributed to architectural layout and design. In particular, he criticized the huge, inhuman scale of the developments and their stark design, which made it seem that no one cared about them (Clarke, 1997). While initially vilified, Newman had an enormous impact on the design of public housing in many parts of the world. Newman and other architects, such as Richard Gardiner, put forward a wide range of detailed design suggestions to change these conditions and make housing safer (Gardiner, 1978).

A more recent focus has been on the role of facilities and crime. Facilities refer to special-purpose structures, such as high schools, taverns, convenience stores, churches, and apartment buildings. In a useful review of quantitative research, Eck and Weisburd (1995) conclude different types of facilities increase or decrease crime in their immediate environment based on accessibility, management, location, and the population attracted to the facilities in question.

Stahura and Sloan (1988) provided some empirical support for routine activities theory. Their study used 1972 and 1980 crime data from 676 American suburbs to evaluate Cohen and Felson's (1979) routine activities theory. To do this, they operationalized the main concepts of the theory, including criminal motivation (percentage poor, percentage unemployed, percentage black, and percentage youth), criminal opportunities (employment concentration and percentage multiple housing), and levels of guardianship (police employment and expenditure, and percentage of female participation in the labor force). The findings generally supported the routine activities theory model and indicated that key concepts from the theory have direct and/or indirect additive effects on violent and/or property crime rates.

Sherman, Gartin, and Buerger (1989) have provided further support for routine activities theory. They used spatial data analysis to test the basic premise of routine activities theory, or the idea "that criminal events result from likely offenders, suitable targets, and the absence of capable guardians against crime converging non-random in time and space" (Sherman et al., 1989, p. 48). To do this, they analyzed spatial data from police calls to over 115,000 addresses and intersections in Minneapolis throughout a 1-year period. They found that a small number of hot spots were responsible for a majority of the calls. This suggests that certain areas have characteristics that produce and/or attract criminal activity.

There are a few examples of qualitative research that lend credibility to Clarke and Cornish's (1985) rational choice theory and especially their notion of bounded or limited rationality. Cromwell, Olson, and Avary's (1991) ethnographic research about criminal decision-making processes is an exemplar in this area. The researchers conducted interviews with 30 active burglars in the city of Midland, Texas, and went on ride-alongs in which they visited crime sites while the burglars explained how the burglaries took place. They called this technique *staged activity analysis*. The primary purpose of the study was to see whether or not rational choice theory was appropriate for explaining the crime of burglary. Do burglars carefully select their targets and plan their crimes? And if so, how rational is the process?

Subjects were asked to reconstruct their past burglaries as nearly as possible. Cromwell and his associates reported that the burglars in his study employed a three-component decision-making strategy. First, they assume that the site contains something of value. Second, they determine whether or not they can get into the site without a witness seeing them. Third, they consider how difficult it would be to break into the site (e.g., is there a lock or is the door hanging open?). Based on Cromwell and his colleagues' research, it appears that burglars use environmental cues to assess potential risks, including whether the site is occupied, if it is in plain view, and what the degree of difficulty would be in gaining access. The researchers were also interested in the effects of drug use on the decision-making process and how this impacts the rational choice model. They found that drug use and burglary were interrelated. In other words, burglars commit their crimes to obtain money to buy drugs, and they also use drugs to initiate and facilitate the commission of burglaries. In addition, the study attempted to uncover the effects that accomplices have on burglary decisions and examined the fencing strategies used to dispose of the goods from the burglaries.

Cromwell and his colleagues' research also sought to gauge the effect of deterrence in the form of punishment from the criminal justice system. The researchers found that the data obtained in the interviews provided a great deal of support for the postclassical theories. In particular, the burglars seemed to make decisions based on situational dynamics that arose during the burglaries and not in response to threats made by the criminal justice system. The template for crime site selection and decision making offered in the interviews was rational, but offenders often altered the plan based on environmental cues and opportunities. This matches the notion of limited or bounded rationality offered by rational choice theorists and also provides some support to rational choice theories. Like previous researchers, Cromwell and his colleagues (Cromwell, Killinger, Kerper, & Walker, 1985) suggested that burglars tend to be opportunistic rather than purely rational and are easily deterred or displaced from one target site to another. Situational factors, such as the presence of a dog, an alarm system, security hardware, and alert neighbors, may be the most effective deterrents.

There is also substantial empirical evidence supporting the model of crime site selection. For example, Brantingham and Brantingham (1981) tested the plausibility of interrelationship between "the physical distributions of opportunities for crime, transportation flow patterns, and the awareness spaces potential criminals" (p. 89). To do this, they mapped and compared the locations of major paths and landmarks to commercial burglaries in New Westminster, British Columbia. They found that burglaries generally corresponded to the locations of major landmarks and moderately traveled streets; more frequently traveled streets were thought to have higher levels of surveillance that served to deter burglary. Brantingham and Brantingham (1981) concluded that some landmarks and levels of traffic flow could be used to predict where burglaries occur.

The most compelling research in this area is on the role and effectiveness of police practices. This research was part of the 1997 Maryland report to Congress and the establishment of the Campbell Collaborative. The Campbell Collaborative publishes rigorous systematic reviews that seek to find the best ways to address crime and disorder. Perhaps the strongest evidence based on rational choice theories is about hot spot policing. Based on findings that 50% of calls regarding incidents are concentrated in less than 5% of addresses in a city, police can target a sizable amount of crime by focusing on these specific places (Weisburd & Telep, 2010). Drawing on a number of randomized field trials (Braga & Bond, 2008; Braga, 2005; Sherman & Weisburd, 1995; Weisburd & Green, 1995) in areas where hot spot policing was used, crime was found to decrease. Systematic observations confirmed the official crime data results and showed significant reductions in social and physical disorder. We will revisit hot spot policing and some of the critiques that have been made against it in the research exemplar section.

Practical Ramifications of Rational Choice Theories

The notion of rational choice has influenced the development and focus on crime prevention programs. For some, the relationship between criminality and environmental cues and the ability to map types of crime and propensity for crime based on defined geographic markers have provided a useful basis upon which environmental redesign and situational crime prevention (SCP) can be justified. As Phillips (2011) points out, the basic principles behind SCP techniques are not new. Landowners in medieval Britain protected their castles with drawbridges, moats, and lookouts on the castle walls. More basic SCP techniques have been adopted by the general population in the form of locks and bolts. These simple target-hardening measures have been classified into a framework of opportunity-reducing measures as part of the "crime as opportunity" paradigm shift in criminology.

The idea that communities could "design out" crime is not a new one, and this approach has been conceived and implemented in various ways. CPTED generally involves changing the environment to reduce opportunities for crime. It also aims to reduce the fear of crime and increase the aesthetic quality of the environment and the quality of life for law-abiding citizens, especially by eliminating opportunities for crime (Clarke, 1995; Crowe, 1991). CPTED can also shape perceptions of personal crime risks.

Both SCP and CPTED provide useful techniques to block opportunities for crime. Because the decision to offend or not to offend may be influenced more by cues about the perceived risk of being caught than by cues of reward or ease of entry, design-based strategies emphasize enhancing the perceived risk of detection and apprehension. The key is identifying conditions of the physical environment that provide opportunities for or precipitate criminal acts and then altering those conditions (Brantingham & Faust, 1976). The goal is crime prevention. Cornish and Clarke (2003) present 25 opportunity-reducing techniques; these are depicted in Figure 12.7.

In addition, a number of typologies have been developed to classify and compare crime prevention measures. Brantingham and Faust (1976) identified three levels of crime prevention: primary, secondary, and tertiary. **Primary prevention** strategies approach crime reduction by addressing underlying factors that have a general influence and create the conditions amenable to criminal events. These programs respond to large-scale social problems that emerge from economic pressures, a lack of social cohesion, or other physical conditions that promote crime and fear generally (Brantingham, Brantingham, & Taylor, 2005). These programs may include national media campaigns encouraging people to secure their homes, the specification of improved locks on cars, new legislation, or large-scale social programs. Primary prevention might also involve conducting a crime prevention analysis of major municipal projects before construction commences in order to "design out" crime from the outset (Brantingham & Brantingham, 2000, pp. 225–227).

Secondary prevention measures focus more narrowly on individuals, groups, or social conditions or physical settings considered at a high risk of becoming involved in criminal events. Secondary prevention techniques might include specific programs for children with parents who have a history of criminal activity, at-risk youth, and prisoners trying to reintegrate back into the community. Secondary prevention also targets frequently victimized locations and may address the problem by relocating targets to areas where there are other businesses or better visibility (Brantingham & Brantingham, 2000, pp. 227–228).

Tertiary prevention efforts are directed toward crime prevention and include a variety of programs and initiatives that attempt to rehabilitate a frequent crime site or offender. This might include site-specific law enforcement, the physical modification of a repeatedly victimized building, offender rehabilitation programs, or a variety of other measures. Such measures may include assistance for those seeking to exit the sex trade, victim–offender mediation programs, or other restorative or reintegration programs (Brantingham & Brantingham, 2000, pp. 228–231).

Figure 12.7	25 Opportunity-Reducing Techniques			
Increase the Effort	**Increase the Risks**	**Reduce the Rewards**	**Reduce Provocations**	**Remove the Excuses**
1. Harden targets. Immobilizers in cars; anti-robbery screens	6. Extend guardianship. Cocooning; neighborhood watch	11. Conceal targets. Gender-neutral phone directories; off-street parking	16. Reduce frustration and stress. Efficient queuing; soothing lighting	21. Set rules. Rental agreements; hotel registration
2. Control access to facilities. Alley gating; entry phones	7. Assist natural surveillance. Improved street lighting; neighborhood watch hotlines	12. Remove targets. Removable car radios; pre-paid public phone cards	17. Avoid disputes. Fixed cab fares; reduce crowding in pubs	22. Post instructions. "No Parking"; "Private Property"
3. Screen exits. Tickets needed; electronic tags for libraries	8. Reduce anonymity. Taxi driver IDs; "How's My Driving?" signs	13. Identify property. Property marking; vehicle licensing	18. Reduce emotional arousal. Controls on violent porn; prohibit pedophiles working with children	23. Alert conscience. Roadside speed display signs; "Shoplifting Is Stealing" signs
4. Deflect offenders. Street closures in red-light districts; separate toilets for women	9. Utilize place managers. Train employees to prevent crime; support whistle-blowers	14. Disrupt markets. Checks on pawnbrokers; licensed street vendors	19. Neutralize peer pressure. "Idiots Drink and Drive"; "It's OK to Say No"	24. Assist compliance. Litter bins; public lavatories
5. Control tools/weapons. Toughened beer glasses; photos on credit cards	10. Strengthen formal surveillance. Speed cameras; CCTV in town centers	15. Deny benefits. Ink merchandise tags; graffiti cleaning	20. Discourage imitation. Rapid vandalism repair; V chips in TVs	25. Control drugs/alcohol. Breathalyzers in pubs; alcohol-free events

Source: Cornish & Clarke (2003).

Van Dijk and de Waard (1991) built on this model by further delineating the level of crime prevention intervention for offenders, situations, or victims. Originally, Graham & Bennett (1995) suggested a three-part classification for preventative approaches: criminality prevention, situational crime prevention, and community crime prevention. This system has since been revised to include law enforcement prevention, developmental prevention, community-based prevention, and situational prevention (Tonry & Farrington, 1995). Further, it has been applied in Canada through four categories: legal prevention, social prevention, social development programs, and situational prevention (Brantingham, Brantingham, & Taylor, 2005). While these models are descriptively useful, a revised view of prevention based on geospatial understandings of neighborhood crime patterns may better assist police and community decision making.

It also may be useful to consider models that build on the experience of the United Kingdom in the broader use of hot spot mapping techniques to identify the geographic occurrence of specific types of crime (Ratcliffe, 2004). Crime prevention programs consider the geospatial dimension of crime and respond with specified crime prevention initiatives. One way to conceive of how these initiatives might be organized is based on a micro, meso, and macro description of zones of criminality. Considering crime prevention at the neighborhood level, some useful connections can be made between the micro, meso, and macro designation and the primary, secondary, and tertiary levels of crime prevention. Figure 12.8 offers a rudimentary view of this relationship.

At the micro level, crime mapping can assist in identifying hot spots that may be suited to a variety of design and situational interventions based on tertiary prevention. Indeed, Brantingham and Brantingham (1995) have usefully shown how hot spot identification and crime mapping can assist prevention by focusing on crime generators or crime attractors; changing access to hot spots through the introduction of new lighting, barriers, or one-way streets; and providing a basis for more targeted policing efforts (Brantingham & Brantingham, 1995). At the meso level, secondary prevention techniques might be applied. Because secondary prevention focuses on the social conditions or physical settings known to be at high risk of becoming involved in criminal events, the techniques drawn from Clarke and Cornish's (1985) understanding of situational crime prevention may provide practical and cost-effective examples of measures that might be taken.

Through a better understanding of hot spot displacement zones, additional areas can be identified and risks mitigated based on mapped displacement patterns that consider both offender and crime type (Johnson & Bowers, 2004). Once hot spots of crime have been identified, design and situational responses undertaken, and displacement risks assessed and mitigated, the data collected may

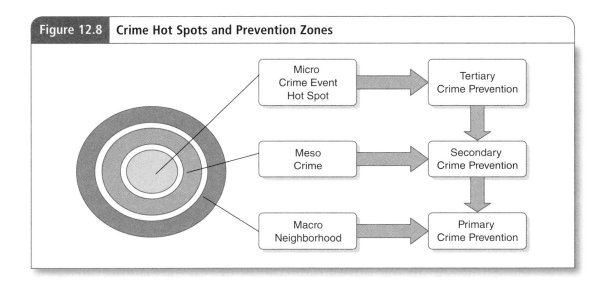

Figure 12.8   Crime Hot Spots and Prevention Zones

provide insight into larger macro social, economic, or cultural factors that create the conditions favorable to crime. While large-scale social problems cannot simply be "designed out," as Newman (1972) appears to suggest, new developments in the United Kingdom suggest that targeting factors such as social cohesion can influence crime conditions in neighborhoods. There is also evidence that the perception of cohesiveness within individual neighborhoods can be an important predictor of various types of recorded crime (Wedlock, 2006).

These findings coincide with conclusions drawn from a variety of other studies, including those from the Home Office in the United Kingdom, authors interested in informal social control through social capital, and even some proponents of the restorative justice movement (Elliott, 2011). But what type of programs can assist to promote social cohesion? Are there levels and types of these kinds of community-centric programs that may be better suited to one neighborhood than another? By better understanding the phenomena of crime and displacement, various crime prevention techniques can be more coherently applied based on geographic crime patterns, and relevant community-centric programs can be designed based on these findings. To be successful, this approach requires an understanding of new developments in crime mapping, design interventions and displacement, the value and limitations of situational crime prevention, and the role of community cohesion in crime prevention.

Figure 12.9	Seven Steps of Rational Theories
Seven Steps	**Rational Theories**
1. Know the History	Came about during the late 1970s and 1980s; rooted in classical school thought; also influenced by economic models of behavior, urban planning, and human ecology
2. Acknowledge Assumptions	Believe humans seek pleasure; embrace "bounded rationality"; conflict is viewed as natural; majority of laws are the result of consensus
3. Problem Focus, Scope, and Level of Explanation	Focus on explaining dynamics of criminal acts and crime rates; little attempt made to explain individual motivation for crime; contain elements of both structural and process theories
4. Key Terms and Concepts	Expected utility principle, neoclassical approach, broken windows theory, postclassical approach, routine activities, crime site selection, geometry of crime, pattern theory
5. Respect the Research	Studies focus on deterrence and its effects on crime rates; also examine how architecture and environmental design affect crime; qualitative research used to understand criminal decision making and processes
6. Theory/Practice	Deterrence, CPTED, and situational crime prevention
7. Mapping the Theory	See Figure 12.10

| Figure 12.10 | **Mapping Deterrence-Rational Choice Theories** |

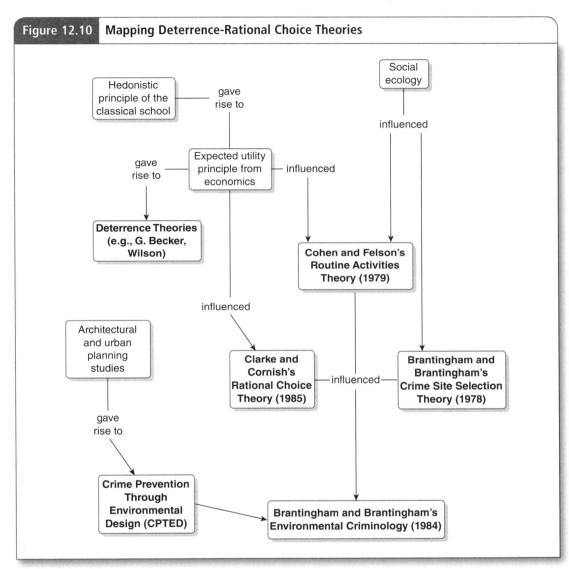

Criticisms of Rational Choice Theories

One challenge to all rational choice models is the difficulties associated with directly observing and measuring another person's thoughts to determine if they are rational. Because of this issue, rational choice theorists have been accused of tautological or circular reasoning (Akers, 1990; Robinson & Beaver, 2008). In a sense, these criticisms are accurate because proponents of rational choice tradition assume that most offenders have some degree of rationality. They also assume everyone defines rationality in the same way. Consider the drug addict, the jilted lover, or the recently fired employee. How can one suggest a form of universal rationality when emotional events may overtake an individual?

Because the rational choice decision model does not adequately explain variance in burglary, a cognitive-behavioral approach may be needed to analyze the burglar's decision-making process in order to design effective crime prevention strategies. Since the theory doesn't explain motivation in any meaningful way, some suggest it is not really a theory with specific propositions (Robinson & Beaver, 2008). This suggests that the rational choice models can only assist in understanding very specific types of crime that involve a degree of rationality (e.g., nonviolent and organized drug dealing, burglary, robbery).

Another critique suggests that early rational choice theories based on deterrence stressed a purely punitive law enforcement approach (Van Den Haag, 1975; E. O. Wilson, 1975). Research has demonstrated that many of these punitive policies have been dismal failures. For example, increases in punishment severity have created a massive prison population in the United States, but there is little evidence that this has led to increases in deterrence (Akers & Sellers, 2013). Further, there is little evidence that this contributed to the crime drop witnessed in the United States and many other Western countries that started in the 1990s (Bernard et al., 2010). The research on deterrence is very clear: In order to be effective, policies must address aspects of deterrence beyond severity; certainty is particularly important (Robinson & Beaver, 2008).

In both the American and Canadian contexts, many of these policies have been shown to be ineffective and misguided (Gendreau, Goggin, & Cullen, 1999; Zimring & Hawkins, 1995). For example, longer prison sentences have been shown to be ineffective in substantially reducing rates of recidivism. Incarceration has been shown to be ineffective as a specific deterrent for all but high-risk, violent offenders. Mass incarceration, or the American "incarceration binge," has failed to reduce the crime rate in any meaningful or direct way (Austin & Irwin, 1997).

In terms of place-based policing, there is the worry that hot spot interventions may simply result in crime moving away temporarily or simply relocating to another area. For example, there is evidence that while police interventions do reduce drug dealing during periods of active enforcement, these levels return to baseline once the intervention ceases (Cohen et al., 2003). While proponents of opportunity reduction and situational crime prevention argue that such concerns are overstated, there is evidence to suggest that in some cases, the activity that is being targeted does just move a short distance away (Jeffery & Zahm, 1993, p. 337). While Barr and Pease (1992) suggested displacement is "an albatross around the neck of purposive crime prevention" (p. 197), we will see below that questions of displacement depend a great deal on how displacement is defined and how benefits and challenges associated with police interventions are measured.

Research Example: Hot Spots, Displacement, and Crime

Can simply employing environmental interventions really prevent crime? For some, the relationship between criminality and environmental cues has provided a useful basis upon which the environmental redesign of hot spots can be justified. Before 2010, many argued that the kinds of interventions suggested by these theories simply shift how, when, and where crime is committed. Displacement theory argues that removing opportunities for crime or seeking to prevent a crime by changing the situation in which it occurs does not actually prevent crime, but merely moves it around.

Felson and Clarke (1998) suggest that there are five main ways that crime is moved around: (1) crime can be moved from one location to another (geographical displacement), (2) crime can be moved from one time to another (temporal displacement), (3) crime can be directed away from one target to another (target displacement), (4) one method of committing crime can be substituted for another (tactical displacement), or (5) one kind of crime can be substituted for another (crime type displacement). In a review of SCP evaluations, Guerrette and Bowers (2009) found that of those studies that did measure displacement, 77% examined spatial displacement, 27% examined target displacement, 15% examined offense displacement, 10% examined tactical displacement, and 5% examined temporal displacement. None of the studies evaluated examined perpetrator displacement, in which individuals who are taken off the street, arrested, or incarcerated are simply replaced by others engaging in the same behavior.

There has been a great deal of discussion about the nature and extent of crime displacement. While examples of displacement exist in some cases, in other cases, research studies have reported that displacement did not occur at all or occurred only to a limited extent. Instead, rational choice theorists claim that displacement occurs only under certain conditions. Although displacement typologies often consider displacement as being negative, there can be some positive effects. For example, a crime may be displaced to a less serious type of crime or to a crime with greater risk, with lower rewards, or that causes less serious damage. In this case, it could be argued that crime has been "deflected" (Barr & Pease, 1990, 1992), and this may represent something of a success since the crime may then produce less harmful effects (Home Office, 1993).

While the phenomenon of displacement is complex, it remains an integral threat to crime prevention and an important consideration. In 1994, Professor Rene B. P. Hesseling, working for the Ministry of Justice in Holland, analyzed available literature on displacement. Twenty of the studies were British studies, sixteen were from the United States, ten were from Holland, and nine were from various countries in the developed world. Thirty-three studies found some form of displacement—mostly quite limited—and no study found complete displacement of crime. More recent analysis revisited the Philadelphia Foot Patrol Experiment and explored the longitudinal deterrent effects of foot patrols in violent crime hot spots Sorg, Haberman, Ratcliffe, & Groff, 2013). The displacement uncovered had decayed during the 3 months after the experiment, and the researchers suggested previously displaced offenders had returned to the original target areas, causing inverse displacement.

While displacement is possible, it is not an inevitable consequence of crime prevention. Further, if displacement does occur, it will be limited in size and scope. This conclusion is supported by other review studies on the topic. While some have found drug dealing to be susceptible to displacement (Caulkins, 1992; Eck, 1993; Rengert, 1990; Sherman, 1990), a study of drug-addicted burglars by Cromwell, Olson, Avary, and Marks (1991) concluded that prevention does not always lead to displacement. Nevertheless, many still assume displacement should be measured (Barnes, 1995) and that new approaches should attempt to formulate models for anticipating and understanding displacement when it occurs (Brantingham & Brantingham, 2003). Brantingham and Brantingham (2003) agreed in principle that when an intervention is put in place, one result may be that crime "will displace the shortest possible distance" into either the current neighborhood or into a surrounding neighborhood with a similar make-up, including a "similar target backcloth" (2003, p. 126). This all changed as the result of research conducted by David Weisburd on hot spot policing.

Over the last two decades, Weisburd and his colleagues have demonstrated that crime tends to cluster in small areas. Weisburd's research on hot spot policing emphasizes the role of place—not people—as the key unit of analysis for crime prediction and prevention. His research, funded by the National Institute of Justice, largely focused on crime in specific cities and showed that crime can drop substantially in small hot spots without rising in other areas. These hot spots of crime allow law enforcement to better concentrate resources in these locations. This challenged displacement theory in two important ways. First, it showed that crime cannot be displaced easily because opportunities for crime are limited in low-crime areas, and offenders are often attached to the area where they perform their routine activities. Recent research in Spain using CCTV cameras supports these findings. By examining police crime data and CCTV incident data, Cerezo (2013) found some crimes were displaced to nearby areas within or close to the city center. These areas happened to have no camera coverage but similar opportunities to commit crimes. The second challenge came from Weisburd and his colleagues (2006) producing evidence to show that the introduction of a crime prevention strategy in a small, high-crime area often creates a "diffusion of benefits" to nearby areas. This work suggests that crime patterns depend not just on criminals but also on policing in key places and other factors, such as the placement of fences, alleys, and other environmental features. Interventions could reduce crime in both the immediate zone around the target area and in other areas adjacent to the target area.

Based on reviews and empirical evidence on crime displacement, one could come to the conclusion that interventions not only work to stop crime in the target area but also provide crime prevention benefits. Weisburd and his colleagues (2006) used observations in the target and catchment areas (where crime was most likely to be displaced to), supplemented by interviews and ethnographic field observations, to suggest that in crime markets involving drugs and prostitution, crime does not simply move around the corner. For his work on hot spots and displacement, Weisburd won the Stockholm Prize in Criminology. This is an international prize sponsored by the Swedish Ministry of Justice and awarded for "outstanding achievements in criminological research or for the application of research results by practitioners for the reduction of crime and the advancement of human rights" (http://www.nij.gov/journals/266/Pages/weisburd.aspx).

Now that you've read this chapter . . . people these days do much more of their shopping online. We even have a new techie holiday called Cyber Monday, which refers to the Monday following Thanksgiving when online retailers offer exceptional bargains. This creates numerous opportunities for cybercrime, but it may limit more traditional crime, such as robberies in mall parking lots.

The items that we buy have clearly changed in the last few decades. A proliferation of electronic gadgets now generates considerable excitement and spurs on our economy. Unfortunately, many of these objects also tend to be highly portable and make great targets for criminals. Laptops, portable gaming systems, and smartphones are small, light, and expensive. What might be the consequences of these developments in consumer culture?

Conclusion and Review Questions

In this chapter, we have explored rational choice theories. These theories all adhere to the basic logic of the classical school and assume rational, free-willed actors attempt to maximize benefits and minimize risk. These theories focus on explaining crimes and criminal acts rather than on criminal motivations.

They also focus on understanding deterrence and the intricacies of how deterrence works, which includes researching what kind of sanctions are best suited to deter criminal activities. In some cases, rational choice theorists recommend changing the environment in which crimes occur in order to influence how those likely to commit crime assess the opportunities to do so. Rational choice theories combine insights from economics, architectural and urban planning theories, behaviorism, and macro sociology in order to understand crime, and thus many of these theories have clear practical ramifications and offer recommendations for reducing and preventing crime to criminal justice system practitioners. While there is an inherent problem in attempting to measure criminal motivation, research has shown how crime and place are connected and how criminal justice interventions can reduce crime and promote crime prevention benefits.

CHAPTER REVIEW

1. What are the differences between classical, neoclassical, and postclassical perspectives and the assumptions they make about human nature?

2. Why do rational choice theories explain criminal acts and crimes rather than criminality, criminal motivation, or criminal behavior?

3. Explain what the expected utility principle is and how it has been applied in criminological theories.

4. Provide some examples of the practical application of rational choice theories in criminology. Why have these theories been so popular?

5. List three critiques leveled against rational choice theories.

PART VI

Integration in Criminology

CHAPTER

13

Integrated and General Theories

 Chapter Overview and Objectives

In this chapter, we turn to integrated and general theories of crime. As you have no doubt noticed, criminology is a field that is overcrowded with theories, approaches, and orientations. Theoretical extensions, cross-fertilization, and integration have advanced our understanding of the causes of crime. These theories also offer a novel way to combine macro or structural theories that focus on crime rates or patterns of crime and meso or process theories that focus on interactions that give rise to crime or lead to desistance. Some of these theories also account for how micro theories of individual differences may affect social processes. These approaches offer a means to create new linkages, which is important when advancing theoretical growth. Different integrated and general theories assume that by combining biological factors, environmental factors, structural factors, education, parental ties, and peer associations, we can better explain why some people engage in criminal behavior while others do not. Figure 13.1 provides an overview of integrated and general theories.

By the end of the chapter, readers should be able to:

- Understand assumptions made by integrated and general theories
- Be aware of the different types of integration and levels of explanation, problem focus, and scope for key integrated and general theories
- List some examples of integrated criminological theories and explain how they build on past theories and research
- Appreciate the complexity of integration and the critiques leveled at some integrative efforts
- Discuss the practical approaches and programs suggested by integrated and general theories

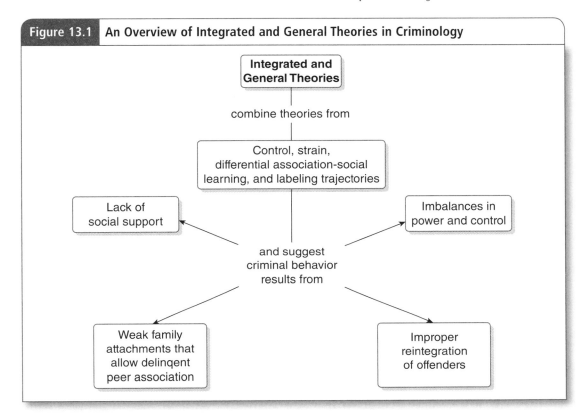

Figure 13.1   **An Overview of Integrated and General Theories in Criminology**

⊠ The Integrative Impulse in Criminology

The integrative tradition is based on the observation that by narrowing down the number of ideas in the field, criminology can do a better job of explaining crime and its consequences. As Barak (1998) puts it, "The need for integration springs from the historical and continued reality in which there are many disciplinary routes to crimes and criminology" (p. 10). This view is based on the notion that complex social phenomena such as crime and punishment cannot be fully understood using a single philosophical stance or theoretical tenet. In addition to severely limiting analysis, such a simplistic approach requires one to ignore more factors than it is possible to consider.

During the 1980s, criminologists began to express concerns about the state of theorizing in criminology (Liska, Messner, & Krohn, 1989). To remedy this, criminological theorists proposed numerous integrated theories of crime and criminal behavior. However, there were earlier, more foundational theories that are examples of this kind of activity. For instance, Merton (1938) and Sutherland (1966/1947) both drew on multiple perspectives and philosophies to formulate their groundbreaking theories. Likewise, the pioneering work of Cohen (1955) and that of Cloward and Ohlin (1960) could be seen as early attempts at theory integration.

Integration has been defined as efforts "to bring parts together into a unified whole" (Liska et al., 1989, p. 1). The notion of a unified whole implies some ordering or establishing of relationships among parts. Thornberry (1989) defines theoretical integration as "the act of combining two or more sets of logically interrelated propositions into one larger set of interrelated propositions . . . in order to provide a more comprehensive explanation of a particular phenomenon" (p. 52). In other words, criminological theory integration may require adopting more integrative knowledge-based frameworks to explain human motivation, social organization, and structural relationships.

> **As you read this chapter, consider . . .** how do reintegration and social support programs go hand in hand? Several of the theories discussed in this chapter raise concerns about properly reintegrating offenders back into society. This is an issue in most criminal justice systems, but it is of special concern in the United States. The high number of people the United States incarcerates creates challenges when these people are released back into the community. How can we effectively reintegrate offenders back into society? What types of social support programs are required? Do these programs need to be tailored specifically to individual criminals, or will a one-size-fits-all approach be possible? As you read this chapter, consider how integrated theories could assist efforts to promote the reintegration of those currently incarcerated.

Seven Steps of Criminological Thinking

History and Social Context of the Integrated and General Theories

Unlike many of the theories that we have covered so far, integrated theories and general theories have a rather brief history in criminology. While many of the theories discussed earlier have integrative aspects (for example, see Cohen, 1955; Cloward & Ohlin, 1960) in the sense that they may use several factors to explain criminal behavior, early integrated theories tend to be somewhat narrow and are perhaps better thought of as an elaboration on or an extension of existing theories (Cullen & Agnew, 2011; Tittle, 1995). Many early integrated theories tended to draw on sociological and social psychological contributions, but very few incorporated biological factors (Robinson & Beaver, 2008).

As discussed in the previous chapter about rational choice theories, the 1980s and 1990s were a time of social and political conservatism. This new mood was also reflected in the field of criminology as the emphasis shifted from explaining and understanding criminal behavior to controlling crime. This sparked interest in deterrence and crime prevention but provided little motivation to propose new and original theories of criminal behavior. Instead, most theories from this era are amalgamations of previous theories and viewpoints. According to Williams and McShane (2014), in criminology even the first decade of the new millennium was characterized by a lack of new and fresh ideas. It isn't clear if this was due to the fact that the creative juices stopped flowing in criminology or because criminologists decided to sit back and take stock of their own work for a few decades. This seems to be more than an isolated opinion, as many criminologists made similar statements during this period (Laub, 2004; Weisburd & Piquero, 2008; Young, 2011). Perhaps it is for some of these reasons that the integrative approach continues to be popular to this day.

The earliest example of a concerted integrative approach can be found in Elliott, Ageton, and Cantor's (1979) strain-control paradigm. As its name suggests, this theory sought to combine the major theories in criminology. While integration may have seemed to be the next logical step in developing criminological theory, Elliott and his associates drew some rather heavy criticism for their work. Some claimed that integrative attempts like Elliott's combined theories that were fundamentally incompatible (Hirschi, 1979). Elliott and his colleagues (Elliott, Huizinga, & Ageton, 1985) responded by stating that the competitive mode of theorizing had failed and went on to lament the extremely low level of explained variance in existing criminological theories.

To resolve some of these controversies, criminologists devoted an entire conference to unraveling the mysteries of integration (Liska, Messner, & Krohn, 1989). This gathering yielded a few useful suggestions, but very little progress was made toward identifying a common or uniform approach to integration. Despite the lack of uniformity in method, several examples of integrated theories emerged during the early 1990s.

It is important to realize that many of these theories were also intended to be general theories of criminal behavior. More recently, criminologists have proposed elaborate integrated theoretical frameworks that seek to integrate theories in unique ways (Agnew, 2005; Farrington, 1992; Moffitt, 1993; Robinson & Beaver, 2008; Sampson & Laub, 1993; Wikstrom & Sampson, 2006). These recent approaches will receive more discussion in the concluding chapters of this text.

Assumptions of Integrated and General Theories

Hirschi (1979) warned that criminologists should be careful when integrating theories. More specifically, he advised that theorists should avoid combining theories with conflicting assumptions. While this may be less of a problem than it has been made out to be, it is important that theorists consider the logical underpinnings of the theories they're combining to ensure that they are compatible. For example, integrating micro theories that assume people maximize pleasure with macro theories that suggest people are naturally altruistic is not logically possible without some justification.

Since integrated theories are, by nature, composed of several constituent theories of human nature, their assumptions are not readily apparent at first glance. Several commentators have recognized that most integrated theories incorporate some learning element (Akers, 1989; Hirschi, 1989). The theories discussed in this chapter draw primarily upon the sociological explanations of criminal behavior, especially learning, strain, control, and labeling (Bohm & Vogel, 2011; Braithwaite, 1989; Tittle, 1995). All of this indicates that most integrated theorists, like learning theorists, assume that human nature is a product of interactions between the individual and the environment (Einstadter & Henry, 2006).

As mentioned in the previous two chapters, most modern theories embrace Matza's (1964) notion of soft determinism, sometimes referred to as soft free will or indeterminism (Agnew, 1995; Williams & McShane, 2014). Recall that this simply means that humans both shape and are shaped by their environment (Agnew, 2011). The integrated theories discussed in this chapter all assume that society is characterized by consensus more than conflict. This consensus is viewed as partial and applies only to some laws of universal agreement (Braithwaite, 1989; Tittle, 1995).

Problem Focus, Scope, and Level of Explanation of Integrated and General Theories

It is important to note that many of the integrated theories reviewed in this chapter are also considered to be general theories of criminal behavior, but some of the more complex theories also attempt to address the dynamics of criminal acts, neighborhood crime levels, and societal crime rates (c.f., Agnew, 2005). Some of these theories also attempt to account for societal reactions to a deviant act in the same fashion as labeling theories (Agnew, 2005; Braithwaite, 1989; Hagan, 1989). Since many of these are also general theories of crime, their scope tends to be quite broad, and they purport to explain many different forms of crime and criminal behavior. Unlike many other criminological theories reviewed up to now, many of these theories do address white-collar crime as well as more common forms of street crime (Agnew, 2005; Braithwaite, 1989; Colvin, 2000; Hagan, 1989; Tittle, 1995).

As mentioned previously, most of the theories in this chapter integrate the sociological explanations of criminal behavior. In other words, they combine the process-oriented and structural theories discussed in previous chapters. Theories that examine individual differences (e.g., self-control, impulsivity, and aggression) and their relationship to criminality receive much less attention (Bernard & Snipes, 1996). However, more recent developmental and life course theories and other integrated approaches pay much more attention to individual differences important to understanding criminal behavior (Farrington, 1992; Moffitt, 1993; Robinson & Beaver, 2008). Developmental and life course theories will be reviewed in Chapter 15.

Key Terms and Concepts in Integrated and General Theories

The theories discussed in this section all illustrate examples of integration; integrated theories, however, are also found in developmental/life course and biosocial research programs, which will be discussed in subsequent chapters. For now, let's focus on types of integration and useful examples of criminological integration. This chapter will review several prominent examples of integrated theories in criminology. Before doing this, the logic behind integrating theories must be clarified and the different types of integration must be discussed. Scholars have identified three different types of integration: conceptual, propositional, and cross-level (also called multilevel) (Bernard & Snipes, 1996; Hirschi, 1979; Liska et al., 1989; Miller et al., 2011). These are outlined in Figure 13.2.

Conceptual Integration

Conceptual integration involves linking concepts from different theories under one overarching theoretical framework (Pearson & Weiner, 1985). The goal is to identify conceptual parallels between

Figure 13.2	Types of Integration and Theoretical Examples	
Type of Integration	**How It Works**	**Example**
Conceptual	Links concepts from different theories under one overarching theoretical framework	Theory of coercion and social support (Colvin, Cullen, & Vander Ven, 2002).
Propositional	Links propositions in a developmental sequence (end to end, side by side, up and down)	Strain-control paradigm (Elliott et al., 1979)
Cross-Level	Links macro/structural and meso/interactional theories	General integrated theory (Agnew, 2005)

different theories in order to justify linking them together. For example, Akers (1990) has suggested that certain variables from his social learning theory correspond to variables specified in strain, control, and rational choice theories. Some argue that this type of theorizing can result in "theoretical mush" and muddies the empirical waters because it blurs the boundaries that exist between theories (Akers, 1989).

Social Support and Coercion Theory

One recent prominent example of conceptual integration is Colvin, Cullen, and Vander Ven's (2002) theory of coercion and social support. According to Colvin and his colleagues (2002), these two simple concepts are capable of uniting all of the major theories in criminology. **Coercion** is defined as a force that motivates one to act because of the anxiety it creates. The source of the coercion can be *interpersonal* (e.g., stemming from relationships, friendships, or family sources) or *structural* (e.g., desperate economic situations, abuses of state power). Coercive controls are also thought to originate in the workplace and filter into family life. The authors also point out that the concept of coercion is rooted in an anomie/strain perspective.

According to Colvin and his colleagues, **social support** refers to "organized networks of human relations" that can be used to assist people in meeting their needs (2002, p. 24). These theorists also identify two types of social support: *instrumental* (e.g., providing advice, guidance, or material/financial assistance) and *expressive* (e.g., providing an outlet for ventilation of emotions and affirmations of one's self-worth and dignity). This portion of the theory is connected to the control approach that was pioneered by members of the Chicago school. The authors claim that levels of social support may come from law-abiding or criminal sources. If law-abiding sources of social support are low, and social support from criminal sources is high, the person may be susceptible to subcultural participation. Clear parallels to the differential association and social learning theories can also be seen here.

Colvin and his colleagues (2002) describe two dimensions of coercion and social support: strength and consistency. *Strength* varies from no coercion to very strong coercion, while *consistency* assesses the regularity of the coercion or support. Inconsistent coercion or social support is thought to breed anger and low self-control, which can later result in predatory criminal behavior. Consistent coercion without social support can result in mental health issues, such as depression and anxiety. Finally, the theorists also argue that there is usually an inverse relationship between coercion and social support. In other words, it is very difficult to provide high levels of social support in a coercive atmosphere (Colvin et al., 2002). This theory is outlined in Figure 13.3.

Propositional Integration

Some scholars have questioned whether or not conceptual integration is really true integration since it involves manipulating words and meanings (Bernard & Snipes, 1996; Liska et al., 1989). Others have suggested that conceptual integration is myopic and incomplete because it often relies upon variables from one discipline or perspective (Robinson & Beaver, 2008). Finally, some have argued that propositions, not concepts, are the true building blocks of theories (Thornberry, 1989).

Hirschi (1979) has identified several different types of propositional integration: end to end, side by side, and up and down. End-to-end (or sequential) integration takes place when propositions are arranged in a developmental sequence. Hirschi further explains that "dependent variables in prior theories become independent variables in subsequent theories" (1979, p. 34). For example, one could argue that weak social bonds in youth set the stage for association with delinquent peer groups.

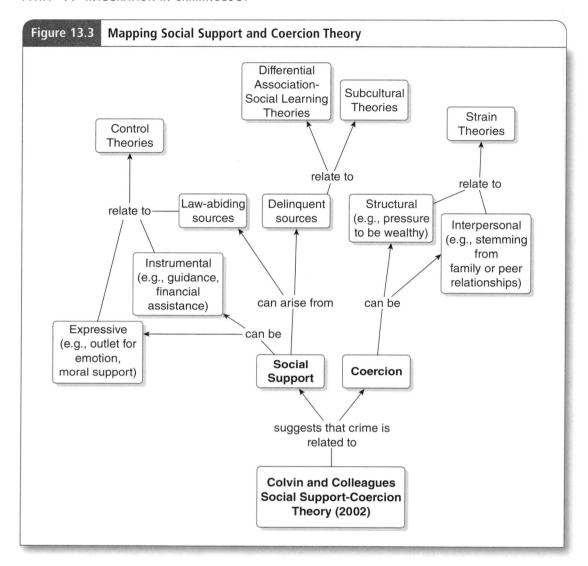

Figure 13.3 Mapping Social Support and Coercion Theory

Side-by-side (or horizontal) integration refers to when an integrated theory connects key propositions from different theories and specifies the cases and situations appropriate for using them (Liska et al., 1989). This allows the theorist to create special theories for different types of criminological phenomena. Identification of typologies that specify how certain theories relate to different criminals is one strategy that is commonly used to create these integrations (Gibbons, 1985; Liska et al., 1989). Another option is to specify interconnections between theories to create integrated explanations for particular types of crime (Tittle, 1995).

Up-and-down (or deductive) integration is when one theory absorbs another because it has more general or abstract propositions. This integration is much more common in the natural sciences and to date has rarely occurred in criminology, but some theories from earlier chapters illustrate this type of integration. Burgess and Akers's (1966) differential reinforcement theory (also referred to as social learning theory and reviewed in Chapter 6) and Black's (1976) behavior of law theory (reviewed in Chapter 11) are examples of up and down integration (Hirschi, 1979).

The Strain-Control Paradigm

Elliott and his associates proposed the earliest example of propositional integration in criminology. Their strain-control paradigm combines ideas from strain theory (Merton, 1938), control theory (Hirschi, 1969), social learning theory (Burgess & Akers, 1966), and social disorganization theory (Shaw & McKay, 1969). This formulation was proposed in a series of integrated propositions that explain how the different aspects of the theories relate to each other. The first proposition suggests that the probability of delinquency is highest if there are control deficiencies early in life. This concept of control is similar to Hirschi's (1969) notion of the social bond, but the elements that compose the bond are different. Elliott and his colleagues identify two aspects of the social bond: integration and attachment. The external component, referred to as integration, describes the attachments one has to other people and society in general. In terms of Hirschi's (1969) social bonding theory, integration is the equivalent of the attachment and involvement strands of the social bond. The internal element is called attachment, and it refers to the internalized aspect of the bond. This element encompasses the concepts of commitment and belief in Hirschi's (1969) theory.

The second proposition states that social disorganization in the home and community can cause strain that can weaken the social bond. If these social connections are disrupted, the natural restraints on behavior are lifted, allowing the individual to partake in delinquency and crime with little to no feelings of guilt. In this theory, strain is conceptualized as it is in Merton's (1938) strain theory and refers to the stress created by the inability to achieve socially defined goals (Elliott et al., 1979, 1985).

The third proposition introduces differential association/social learning theory into the equation and offers two different pathways that may lead to delinquency. In the first pathway, an individual fails to form strong attachments early in life, and this leaves the individual vulnerable to the influences of delinquent peers early in the adolescent years. In the second pathway, an individual has formed strong social bonds, but these bonds are weakened through strain (e.g., an inability to achieve success in school), and the individual is free to associate with delinquent peer groups, which leads to criminal behavior (Elliott et al., 1979, 1985). Figure 13.4 provides one view of this integrated theory.

Cross-Level Integration

Liska and his associates (1989) have elaborated on Hirschi's (1979) original scheme by introducing micro and macro dimensions. These are called cross-level (or multilevel) integrations. Braithwaite's (1989) reintegrative shaming theory, Hagan's (1989) power-control theory, Tittle's (1995) control balance theory, and Agnew's (2005) general integrated theory are all examples of cross-level integrations (Bernard & Snipes, 1996). These theories unite process-level theories, such as social bonding and social learning, with structural theories, such as social disorganization and strain theories. While it is true that Elliot's strain-control paradigm also combines theories from these areas, it does not address macro-level factors that influence crime and instead focuses solely on criminal behavior at the micro

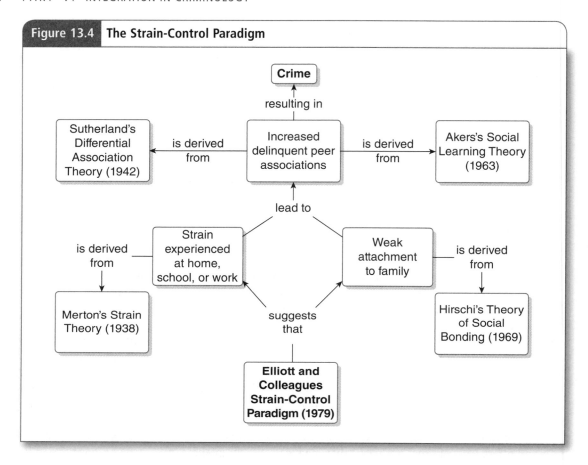

Figure 13.4   The Strain-Control Paradigm

level. Very few theories have been proposed that adequately address all levels of explanation. Most focus on interactions between structural factors and social processes; individual difference theories are usually left out of the equation entirely (for an exception, see Agnew, 2005).

Reintegrative Shaming Theory

Braithwaite (1989) has proposed a theory of reintegrative shaming that is an example of a cross-level, side-by-side integration (Bernard & Snipes, 1996, p. 317; see also Barak, 1998, p. 202). By referencing Dickens's classic tale *Oliver Twist,* Braithwaite illustrates the integrative aspects of his theory:

Let us simplify the relevance of this chapter by imagining Fagin's lair as something of a caricature of a criminal subculture. We need control theory to bring young offenders to the doorstep of the criminal subculture (primary deviance); stigmatization (labeling theory) to open the door; subcultural and learning theory to maintain the lair as a rewarding place for secondary deviants to stay in; and opportunity theory to explain how such criminal subcultures come to exist in the first place. (1989, p. 16)

Braithwaite begins by distinguishing between two types of shaming: reintegrative shaming and disintegrative shaming (or stigmatization). Reintegrative shaming refers to when society shames an offender but then later allows the offender to reenter society with no stigma or label. Disintegrative shaming takes place when society shames to such a degree that it creates a "society of outcasts" (Braithwaite, 1989, p. 55).

At first blush, it might appear that in terms of crime control the latter type of shaming is more desirable; after all, it is easier to keep track of the questionable people if they are all in one place. However, Braithwaite (1989) argues that this is not the case because it serves to lower levels of informal social control due to the offender losing his or her attachments to society. This frees the offender up to take part in the criminal subculture, which also happens to be a repository for knowledge and learning about deviant and criminal behaviors and skills.

Hopefully, by this point it is easy to see how Braithwaite (1989) is combining several theories discussed in previous chapters. Shaming clearly relates to labeling theory, and the consequences of and reactions to negative labeling are explained through control, subcultural, and social learning theories. The theories being combined here are all process oriented, but Braithwaite also introduces macro-level factors into the mix. Interdependency refers to levels of dependency among individuals, while communitarianism measures the extent to which the interdependence encourages group membership and commitment (Braithwaite, 1989). He goes on to argue that higher levels of interdependency and communitarianism produce reintegrative shaming, while lower levels give rise to disintegrative shaming.

To summarize, societies with low levels of communitarianism and interdependency will stigmatize offenders, and this will erode the offenders' bond to wider society and reduce their opportunities for legitimate success in society. When the bond has deteriorated and opportunities are nonexistent, offenders will actively seek out those who will accept them, leading them to criminal subcultures. Braithwaite (1989) concludes that this is why individualistic societies such as the United States have higher crime rates than more communitarian societies such as Japan. Figure 13.5 provides one way to visualize reintegrative shaming theory.

Power-Control Theory

Hagan's (1989) power-control theory is another example of a cross-level, side-by-side integration. Previously introduced in Chapter 11, this theory seeks to explain why males commit so much more crime than females. In order to do this, Hagan (1989) examines micro processes within the family and how they are shaped by structural factors. The class structure of society plays an important role in explaining the variations in offending between males and females. Power in the family is gained through employment outside of the home. Therefore, in patriarchal societies, fathers tend to have more power than mothers. This power differential translates into child-rearing practices as well; in most families, more control is exerted on the behavior of girls than boys. This creates an aversion to risk-taking in females and lower levels of criminal behavior. Hagan (1989) predicts that as more women gain employment outside the home, the rate of female criminality will rise. This theory combines the process-oriented control theory with ideas from Marxist and feminist theory that examine class and gender aspects of criminality.

Control Balance Theory

Tittle's (1995) control balance theory is a side-by-side integration, but it also incorporates aspects of up-and-down integration; Tittle calls this approach *synthetic integration*. The theory accounts for

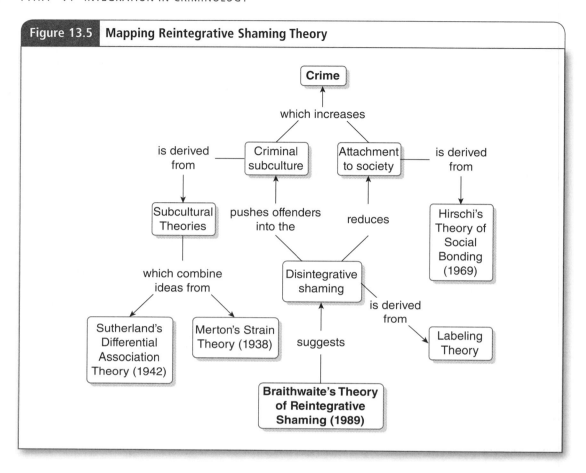

Figure 13.5 Mapping Reintegrative Shaming Theory

both inhibiting and motivating factors that relate to deviant behavior by combining ideas from control, learning, deterrence, and rational choice theories. Tittle (1995) argues that deviance results when individuals experience control imbalances. The notion of control used here applies both to how much control individuals are subject to and how much control they are able exert over themselves. This varies not only between individuals but also from situation to situation.

The type of deviance relates to the type of control balance experienced by the individual. Control deficits create repressive forms of deviance, including predatory, defiant, and submissive behaviors. Predation includes typical property crimes (e.g., theft, robbery, and burglary) as well as more serious crimes (e.g., rape and homicide) that involve physical violence and manipulation. Defiant acts of deviance are illustrated by rebellious acts against social norms and conventions (e.g., curfew violations, vandalism, and political protests). Submissive deviance occurs in response to extreme control deficits and may include a willingness to endure sexual degradation and other humiliating acts.

Control surpluses create autonomous deviance, including exploitative, plunderous, and decadent behaviors. Exploitation is an indirect form of predation that occurs when an individual hires or manipulates others into committing crime for them (e.g., contract killing, some forms of corporate and political crimes). Plunderous behavior includes behavior that is meant to further one's interests at the expense of others (e.g., large-scale pollution, some forms of corporate crime geared toward maximization of profit at societal expense). Decadent forms of deviance are bizarre and irrational. In fact, in many cases these acts don't seem to further the interests of the person committing them. For example, sadistic forms of torture, group sex with children, or even cannibalism illustrate this type of deviance (Bernard et al., 2010). To a certain extent, this makes sense since as a person gains a larger control surplus, that person starts to abuse the power in more extreme ways. While the central focus of this theory is clearly the notion of control balance, Tittle (1995) also tries to account for situational and opportunity-based variables in his theory.

General Strain Theory and Beyond

Robert Agnew (1992) has proposed a general strain theory (GST) that represents an extension of classical strain theory (Merton, 1938). This version of strain theory is formulated at the social psychological level and focuses on how negative relationships pressure people into crime. Recall that other strain theories focus on social structural factors that produce higher crime rates.

According to Agnew (1992), older versions of strain theory were not inaccurate but merely misguided. He claims that while these older theories do identify one important dimension of strain—the inability to achieve one's goals—they ignore other important situations that can induce strain. Agnew (1992) suggests that strain theorists must reconsider the types of goals being referred to in their earlier formulations. More specifically, he asks if they were referring to aspirations (i.e., ideal goals) or expectations (i.e., more realistic goals). In order to clarify these issues, Agnew (1992) draws upon equity/justice and expectations and cites theory literature from social psychology (Berger, Zelditch, Anderson, & Cohen, 1972; Berger, Fisek, Norman, & Wagner, 1983).

The aggression and stress literature from social learning theory (c.f., Bandura, 1973) is also used to expand upon the different types of strain. Agnew (1992) argues that situations that remove or threaten positively valued stimuli also cause strain. For example, the death of a family member or the loss of a boyfriend or girlfriend can cause negative emotions such as anger, which can lead to strain and eventually to crime. The presentation of noxious stimuli (e.g., negative peer or parental relationships, criminal victimization, verbal insults or threats) may also induce strain in individuals. Agnew (1992) is quick to point out that these types of strain often overlap in practice and therefore should not be seen as mutually exclusive.

Later, Agnew (2001) elaborated on GST by specifying the types of strain most likely to lead to crime. This is important because, as most people know, there are many strains in daily life, and most of them do not lead to criminal behavior. First, a strain that is viewed as being high in magnitude is more likely to lead to crime. Agnew offers an illustration of this in the following passage:

> Imagine that you are chatting with a group of acquaintances and someone reacts to a remark you make by stating "you don't know what you're talking about." Now imagine the same situation, but this time someone reacts to your remark by stating "you're an asshole" and shoving you. Both of the reactions are likely to upset you, but I think most people would agree that the second reaction is more likely to lead to crime. (2006, p. 58)

Second, if a strain is seen as unjust, it is more likely to result in crime. For example, if an individual purposely shoves another person, this will be more likely to trigger an aggressive response than if an individual accidentally shoves another person. Third, if the strain is associated with low social control, it increases the likelihood of criminal behavior. For instance, parental rejection is a type of strain that erodes the parent–child relationship; this also lowers levels of attachment and thereby lowers the social control exerted over the individual by that relationship. Fourth, if the strain creates pressure to engage in crime, then criminal behavior is more likely to occur. In some situations, such as bullying, lack of a response could lead to further torment. Given this fact, those who experience the strain of being bullied may be compelled to respond in some criminal way to prevent further abuse (Agnew, 2006).

In recent years, Agnew (2005) also proposed an integrated general theory that incorporates his ideas from GST as well as insights from social control, social learning, labeling, and routine activities theories. Further, it addresses individual differences by considering how personality traits influence other processes involved in crime. This theory clearly is cross-level integration in the sense that it combines key structural factors and social processes with factors derived from individual difference theories (Bernard et al., 2010).

In order to integrate all of these factors, Agnew (2005) introduces several new constructs to organize important concepts from the theories he is incorporating. The central premise of this theory is that criminal behavior occurs when constraints against crime (e.g., external control, stakes in conformity, and internal control) are low and motivations to commit crime (e.g., reinforcement for crime, exposure to criminal models, and beliefs favorable to crime) are high. The notion of constraints is derived from work done by control theorists. External aspects of control are derived primarily from bonding theory (Hirschi, 1969), while internal control aspects are based largely on one's level of self-control (Gottfredson & Hirschi, 1990).

According to Agnew (2005), motivations to commit crime result from internal pushes and external pulls, which are concepts borrowed from Reckless's (1961) containment theory. Pulls or temptations to commit crime are drawn from social learning theory and include reinforcements for crime, exposure to criminal models, and learning beliefs favorable to committing crime. Pushes to commit crime emerge from Agnew's (1992) GST and include situations and/or relationships that block people from achieving important goals, remove positive stimuli, and present noxious stimuli.

Constraints and motivations are assumed to vary based on the situation. Short-term influences include easy opportunities for crime, the presence of authority figures, and provocations to commit crime. These correspond to key variables identified in Cohen and Felson's (1979) routine activities theory. Finally, notions from labeling theory are also incorporated because Agnew (2005) states that attention needs to be paid to how prior criminal behavior may affect subsequent criminal behavior. Further, negative labeling is thought to reduce constraints on crime (informal social control is lowered because criminals are shunned) and raise motivation for crime (because they are exiled, offenders are forced to associate with other offenders).

Agnew (2005) suggests a variety of variables that affect the constraints from and motivations for committing crime. These include impulsivity/low self-control, irritability, negative interactions and bonding experiences, poor school or work performance, and association with delinquent peers. He also organizes these variables based on various life domains, including self, family, school, peers, and employment. For example, factors relating to the self would include personality traits (e.g., low self-control and irritability), factors relating to the family would include levels of parental attachment and family cohesion, and so on. These domains are useful not only as an organizing tool but also for clarifying how variables interact with each other. For instance, irritability may cause problems in caregiver bonding and attachment; this illustrates how individual and process-oriented factors may influence each other. Figure 13.6 offers an overview of strain theories and Agnew's contribution.

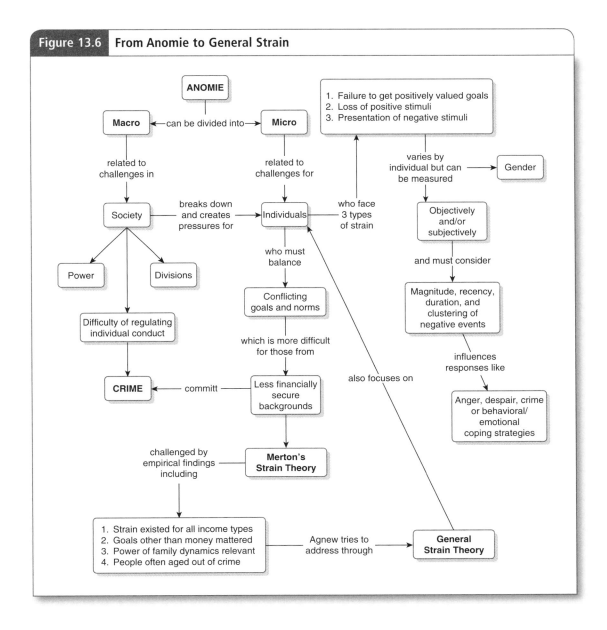

Figure 13.6   From Anomie to General Strain

Research on Integrated and General Theories

Early integrated theories in criminology have generated a substantial amount of research. This ranges from small-scale theory testing (Piquero & Hickman, 1999) to large-scale research studies (e.g., the National Youth Survey Family Study) to more topical investigations of white-collar crime (Murphy & Harris, 2007). Perhaps the earliest example of a research study associated with the integrated and general theories is the National Youth Survey Family Study (NYSFS), which was started in 1976 as the National Youth Survey and renamed in the 1980s.

This study focused on 1,725 adolescents ranging in age from 11 to 17. Initially, researchers interviewed the adolescents as well as a parent, guardian, or caretaker; this was also supplemented with data from official records (Benson, 2002). The participants of the NYSFS were selected using a scientific method meant to obtain a representative sample of the national population. In other words, the results of this study can be generalized to the general US youth population (Benson, 2002). This study followed participants for over 30 years, checking in periodically to examine changes in their feelings and behavior with regard to their career goals, community, family, violence, drug use, and social values. Data from this study has been used to evaluate a number of different theories (e.g., Elliott's strain-control paradigm) and as the basis for analysis in a number of research studies.[1]

Piquero and Hickman (1999) tested control balance theory using survey data gathered from 176 undergraduate students in various criminal courses. The survey included several "offense scenarios," or hypothetical offending situations, along with several questions regarding the participant's response to the situation. Below is an example of a scenario used in this research. This scenario is intended to assess one's level of defiance.

> Bill and Lisa have been dating for six years and have recently gotten engaged. One night in bed, Bill asks Lisa if she would be interested in having another partner join them in bed for fun one evening before they get married as their "last hurrah." At first, Lisa's reaction is one of concern because she begins to think that Bill is getting tired of her. In fact, Lisa's initial reply is "No, I don't think I am ready for that." Over the next few weeks, Bill and Lisa have sex less frequently than they did before. Lisa wonders if his lack of interest is a result of her unwillingness to consider a third partner. Throughout this time period, Lisa thought more about the request and thinks that it actually might be "fun." One Friday night after dinner, Lisa tells Bill that she has reconsidered her position and would actually like to try the threesome. A few nights later at the shore, Bill, Lisa, and another partner engage in sexual activities. (Piquero & Hickman, 1999, p. 326)

After reading these scenarios, respondents were asked to estimate their likelihood of participating in the activities on a scale of 1 to 100. In addition to these questions, participants were also asked about the degree of control they exercised over others and the amount of control to which they were subjected. The questions explored a variety of domains, including school, work, and family life.

Based on this data, the researchers constructed a control balance ratio designed to assess the level of criminal motivation. In addition, they also tried to account for the impact of criminal opportunities and constraints (i.e., perception of deterrence) on behavior. The findings of this study were mixed;

---

[1]For more on the study and the resulting research, see http://www.colorado.edu/ibs/NYSFS/index.html.

control deficits were clearly linked to deviant behavior but not exactly as Tittle (1995) predicted. More specifically, the researchers failed to find consistent links between particular types of deviance and control deficits or surpluses as predicted by the theory (Piquero & Hickman, 1999).

Hagan, Boehnke, and Merkens (2004) tested power-control theory using data from both Canada and Germany. The sample was drawn from families living in Toronto and Berlin that included opposite-sex siblings. According to the theory, gendered notions influence the level of control applied to girls and boys. In male-dominated households, males are given more freedom and females less. Thus, the difference in amount of delinquency depends on how children are raised.

Researchers analyzed 1,232 individuals (616 sibling pairs) ranging in age from 12 to 17. Participants were given a survey in which they were asked about control patterns in their respective families. The survey included questions about division of labor within the families, levels of occupational prestige held by each parent, and levels of juvenile delinquency. The researchers found that families in which the father has a higher-status occupation tend to exert more control on female children versus male children. Not surprisingly, this leads to higher levels of male delinquency in these families.

Power-control theory, as you may recall, suggests that authority in the workplace translates into authority at home. According to the theory, in cases where working mothers have higher-status occupations, parenting styles will be more egalitarian. In this study, the authors predicted that as labor markets became more equitable, parenting practices would follow suit. However, Hagan and his colleagues (2004) found that even in situations where mothers have more power than fathers, there is still substantial and significant evidence that daughters are subjected to higher levels of control, indicating that gender differences in control tend to persist even in cases where the mother and father have equal status in the family. If gender differences in parental styles are linked to gender differences in delinquency, why does male subcultural delinquency persist even when patriarchal, or male-dominated, power structures are increasingly rejected?

Building on Braithwaite's 2001 book, *Restorative Justice and Responsive Regulation,* Murphy and Harris (2007) have attempted to apply reintegrative shaming theory to explain white-collar crime. This study collected data from 652 Australian tax offenders who had been caught and punished for investing in illegal tax avoidance schemes. Respondents in the sample were 25 to 76 years of age, with the vast majority being males, and the survey contained over 200 questions designed to assess participants' attitudes toward the Australian tax system, the Australian Tax Office, and paying taxes. In addition, self-reported tax compliance behavior and experiences with law enforcement officials were examined.

The researchers sought to test several hypotheses based on Braithwaite's (1989) original reintegrative shaming theory. They found that the white-collar criminals were less likely to reoffend if they perceived their treatment as more reintegrative and less stigmatizing. Further, feelings of shame were found to play a significant role in whether or not offenders complied with tax laws in the future. Finally, the results indicated that more research was required to further understand the social and emotional impact of regulation on white-collar offenders.

Murphy and Harris (2007) also point to another example that they claim supports their findings. Michael Wenzel (2006) studied the effectiveness of different types of letters that reminded small-business taxpayers about the requirement to file their quarterly business activity statements with the Australian Taxation Office (ATO). The business owners were all noncompliant taxpayers. Wenzel tested three types of letters. The first was the ATO's standard reminder letter, which outlined the possible penalties and punishments for failing to file relevant statements. The other two letters focused on principles of procedural fairness that shared many commonalities with reintegrative shaming theory.

The first of these procedural justice letters emphasized consideration and respect for tax-payers (i.e. interpersonal fairness), while, at the same time, communicating to the taxpayers that they had not fulfilled their taxation obligations under the tax code, which is broadly consistent with the approach proposed by reintegrative shaming theory. The second letter provided taxpayers with information about their obligations and provided justifications for the ATO's decision to pursue them further (i.e. informational justice). . . . Both the informational and interpersonal letter yielded greater lodgment compliance from individuals compared with the standard ATO letter. It was also found that fewer complaints were made to the ATO from taxpayers who received the informational and interpersonal letters. (Murphy & Harris, 2007, pp. 912–913)

Research by Kurtz, Linnemann, and Green (2013) tests several aspects of differential social support and coercion theory. Recall that in this theory, the development of self-control, delinquent behavior, and mental health results from social interactions that may either be coercive or support-ive. Coercive interactions such as force, direct and indirect intimidation, and violence compel compliance out of fear or anxiety. Such interactions may be employed consistently or erratically. The theory predicts that individuals who are disciplined in an erratic manner will tend to develop strong anger directed toward others and low self-control, and they are likely to become chronic offenders. On the other hand, individuals that receive consistent support will have low anger, high internalized self-control, and strong social bonds, and they will engage in minimal criminal behavior. The authors analyzed data from the 1995 National Survey of Adolescents (NSA) and found support for the role of coercion on delinquent behavior. They also found that youth who report consistent support are likely to display few criminal behaviors, which aligns well with the social support aspect of the theory.

Practical Ramifications of Integrated and General Theories

The central assumption of integrated criminological theories is that different types of crime may require different approaches from the criminal justice system. This pragmatic approach means that integrated theories should offer practical suggestions for those who work within the system. It should come as no shock then that many integrated and general theories offer recommendations that are similar to theories in other chapters of this book. This makes sense; it seems obvious that integrated theories would offer more integrated and potentially practical solutions to crime.

In practice, however, this is difficult. One contribution that these theories have made to the practical world is the realization that no one approach to understanding crime is sufficient. Some integrated theories suggest that justice agencies need to consider how to engage multidisciplinary teams of professionals to properly respond to and address crime. Others suggest punishment-only approaches fail to properly motivate prosocial behavior and ignore the relevance of gender, parenting, and criminal opportunities. For example, Elliott and his colleagues (1985) suggest that there are dif-ferent pathways to crime and that this could affect how we deal with crime in the criminal justice system. By identifying the intersection of delinquent behavior, mental health problems, and drug use on long-range criminal involvement, researchers have a better hope of developing preventative strat-egies to address crime and delinquency before they happen. This indicates that early interventions focused on these behaviors, such as programs for at-risk youth, could prevent criminal behavior in the future. Additionally, those that work with schools could help identify and assist youth who suffer from multiple risk factors.

In addition, recall the research by Murphy and Harris (2007) that attempted an empirical test of Braithwaite's theory of reintegrative shaming by gathering data from tax offenders. Murphy and Harris found that feelings of reintegration/stigmatization experienced during an enforcement event were related to reoffending behavior and that those offenders who felt that their enforcement experience had been reintegrative in nature were less likely to report having evaded their taxes 2 years later. Braithwaite (2009) applies these general principles to the 2008 financial crisis to explain how it might have been prevented. He argues that crime prevention literature suggests repeat victimization and offending are concentrated in time and space and that early intervention to prevent wider inflammation of such hot spots is more effective than enforcement tactics that punish or stigmatize.

Braithwaite (2009) suggests one approach called negative licensing. Distinct from more formal and onerous approaches, such as business accreditation, negative licensing involves a statutory requirement that provides for anyone to practice a particular occupation as long as that person does not breach requirements that relate to unacceptable or unsatisfactory conduct. Braithwaite suggests that by employing negative licensing and empowering agents to walk a beat and kick the tires at financial hot spots (p. 1), so to speak, the ethical culture of business—and especially banks—might be transformed. In 2013, a number of jurisdictions in Australia introduced negative licensing.

Agnew's (1992) general strain theory and the theory of coercion and social support from Colvin and his colleagues (2002) make similar practical suggestions because they all advocate increasing social support in various ways. These theories suggest that developing problem-solving and coping skills, especially in young people, would be effective ways to control crime. Programs that teach parenting skills and anger management skills, and supervised after-school programs, can also address the underlying causes of crime (Agnew, 2005, 2006; Colvin et al., 2002). Agnew's (2005) integrated theory also makes practical recommendations that are compatible with social support theory.

◾ Criticisms of Integrated and General Theories

As mentioned previously, Hirschi (1979) claimed that integration of theories was problematic because in many cases theories have conflicting base assumptions. Later, he added that most integrated theories have not led to an advancement of criminological knowledge. He also criticized the integrated approach more generally for its tendency to attribute ownership of certain variables to certain theories. Rather, he claimed that variables exist independently of theories and that theorists need to more clearly specify their assumptions, propositions, and the causal structures of their theories (Hirschi, 1989). Several commentators have also argued that integration does not really advance criminological knowledge and often obscures connections between variables (Akers, 1989; Hirschi, 1989).

Despite the potential for theory integration, not everyone agrees on the universal worth of the integrationist project. Has the drive toward integration hindered, rather than helped, criminology? One result has been the creation of a subfield of integrationists. Critics of this approach have noted that the integrationists often combine theoretical frameworks without adequately addressing the underlying challenges of this kind of connection. While the relevance of critiques like this should not be dismissed, it might be argued that the social need for better criminological theories requires that attempts be made to promote integration within specific guidelines. In this view, an integrative

Figure 13.7	Seven Steps of Integrated Theories
Seven Steps	**Integrated Theories**
1. Know the History	Came about during the 1980s and 1990s; response to stagnation in theorizing and domination of deterrence-based, rational approaches
2. Acknowledge Assumptions	Humans are blank slates and human nature is a product of interactions between the individual and the environment; embrace soft free will, or indeterminism; laws reflect societal consensus
3. Problem Focus, Scope, and Level of Explanation	These theories typically address several problems, including criminal behavior, criminal acts, crime rates, and the influence of societal reaction; they incorporate individual differences and process and structural factors
4. Key Terms and Concepts	Conceptual, propositional, and cross-level integration; social support and coercion; strain-control paradigm; reintegrative shaming; power-control theory; control balance theory; general strain theory; constraints and motivations for crime
5. Respect the Research	Large-scale surveys tracking youth offending patterns; more attention paid to white-collar forms of crime
6. Theory/Practice	Provision of support and nonstigmatizing, nonpunitive interventions to prevent young offending; use of multidisciplinary teams to provide solutions for crime
7. Mapping the Theory	See Figure 13.8

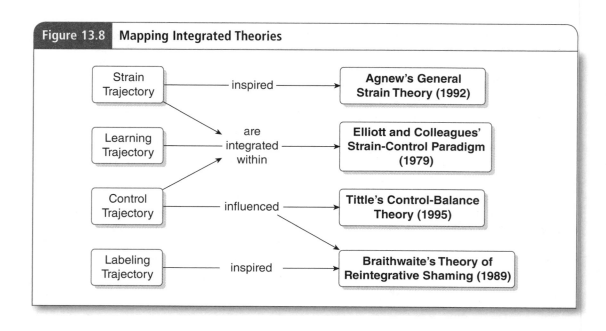

Figure 13.8   Mapping Integrated Theories

approach would draw strength from established methods, findings, theories, and bodies of knowledge while treating seriously competing interests of theoretical integrity with practical necessity (Wheeldon & Heidt, 2008). One approach outline could organize integrative efforts based on the life course development literature.

A significant challenge inherent in any integrative project is the tendency to pick and choose elements of one's favorite theories, while disregarding other crucial elements. Integration cannot be seen as simply creating mere abstraction in a grand theory where concepts are simply grouped within concepts. While producing a "general" or "unified" theory to which people either conform or do not conform may be tempting, an individual can be both the cause and consequence of society, and deviancy may be both subjective and diachronic (Barak, 1998, p. 189). Indeed, most existing integrations only incorporate factors from one or two disciplines. This can lead to theories that are not properly researched or constructed (Lilly et al., 2011), which undermines integrated theories and may harm their credibility.

Research Example: General Strain and Social Support

Tittle, Broidy, and Gertz (2008) attempted a test of Agnew's (1992) general strain theory. As discussed above, strain theory extends a micro-level application of earlier efforts and integrates strain notions with other mainstream theories by identifying factors that can affect the link between strain and crime. Agnew identifies a number of variables, including social support and criminal peer association, and argues that emotions, particularly anger, allow strain to express itself in unconventional ways (Agnew, 1992, pp. 71–74). In addition, Tittle and his colleagues examined whether social support makes it more or less likely strain will emerge. Social supports are those supports that facilitate legitimate coping, thereby reducing the need to adopt illegitimate coping strategies.

Instead of looking at juveniles, Tittle and his colleagues assumed social support is relevant to adult offending because individuals' social support networks expand in adulthood as social capital extends across multiple social institutions (Sampson & Laub, 1993). They focused on three specific questions:

1. Does strain predict self-projected criminal behavior, controlling for past self-reported crime?

2. Do negative emotions mediate the relationship between strain and projected crime?

3. Do social support and criminal peers serve as contingencies or mediators for strain in predicting criminality?

The data for this study came from 200 phone interviews done in Raleigh, North Carolina. The interview included questions about the likelihood of different types of offending behavior among the subjects.

> Respondents estimated, using five categories, the likelihood of their committing each of four offenses in the future: (1) "violence, such as assaulting somebody," (2) "a property violation, such as theft of $100 or burglary," (3) "using an illegal drug," and (4) "a minor offense, such as taking something worth less than $5." (Tittle et al., 2008, p. 290)

Respondents were also asked about the frequency of their exposure to unpleasant experiences and loss of positively valued stimuli. The researchers hypothesized that measures of strain should predict criminal behavior among adults but that control of negative emotions, levels of social support, and deviant peer associations may mediate this relationship. In other words, if negative emotions are controlled, there will be less of a relationship between strain and criminal behavior. This study, like others, found that most of the measures of strain were found to affect offending behavior. The researchers conclude that, consistent with other studies, strain is associated with intentions to offend. However, the importance of negative emotions was challenged by the results. This means that the efforts by Agnew to specify an intervening mechanism (negative emotion) within GST may be super-fluous because strain may be directly linked to offending. Questions remain about why strain does not uniformly trigger illegitimate responses.

Tittle and his colleagues (2008) suggest that more attention be paid to understanding how strain affects coping skills in offenders and how different conditions may converge to create strain and ulti-mately lead to crime. While it is not clear why strain does not uniformly trigger illegitimate responses, Tittle and his associates suggest the theory might be augmented by specifying the underlying explan-atory principle about how different conditions that lead to strain may converge, or simultaneously depend on each other, and lead to crime. This is because it appears that negative emotions do not intervene in the strain process, and the process is not contingent on social support or exposure to criminal associates. These findings suggest that the theory may need some rethinking. To date, GST's efforts to specify an intervening mechanism (negative emotion) have not been supported. However, the development of GST suggests something of a revival of interest in causal forces of strain. The main contribution of GST is the extension of possible sources of strain beyond those identified in earlier articulations of the theory.

> **Now that you've read this chapter . . .**consider again how integrated theories could assist efforts to promote the reintegration of those currently incarcerated. Existing integrated theories such as reintegrative shaming theory, social support and coercion theory, and Agnew's integrated theory all suggest that social support programs are crucial to understanding how crime occurs and how it might be confronted. Fergus McNeill (2012) argues that current efforts at prisoner reintegration are insufficient. Instead, a more fully interdisciplinary understanding of offender rehabilitation would integrate approaches that consider psychological, legal, moral, and social aspects to desistence and reintegration. Most important, he suggests that any such integrative effort must involve a more detailed analysis of the relationship between desistance theories and rehabilitation theories and include the knowledge and insights of ex-offenders and practitioners.

 ## Conclusion and Review Questions

In this chapter, we examined integrated theories of crime. Theoretical extensions, cross-fertilization, and integration have advanced our understanding of the causes of crime and offer a novel way to combine existing theories focused on different levels of explanation. For example, some integrated theories combine concepts from three other theories: macro theories, which focus on crime rates or patterns of crime; meso theories, which focus on interactions that give rise to crime or that lead to desistance; and micro theories, which focus on individual behavior. Integrated theories offer a means to create new linkages and advance both theory growth and our overall understanding of crime. The essential challenge for integrated theories is that what makes them potentially more valuable in explanatory terms also makes them more difficult to empirically assess. Different integrated theories combine biological factors, environmental factors, structural factors, education, parental ties, and peer associations to better explain why some engage in criminal behavior while others do not. However, finding or collecting the sort of data that would allow for robust theory testing is difficult.

CHAPTER REVIEW

1. What assumptions do integrated theories make?

2. List the three types of integration and how these integrative efforts operate.

3. Pick four integrated theories. How do these theories build on past theories and research?

4. Why has the complexity of integration led to critiques? What critique do you think is the most important for integration theorists to consider?

5. What are some of the practical approaches and programs suggested by integrated theories?

CHAPTER

14

Biosocial Theories

 ## Chapter Overview and Objectives

In this chapter, we turn to biosocial theories. Although not necessarily new, as biological antecedents have long been connected to criminal behavior, these theories are different because they attempt to account for interactions between biological characteristics and one's physical and social environment. An important distinction made by biosocial criminologists is between antisocial behavior and behavior that is not criminal per se. There is some merit to this approach from a logical point of view because the definition of crime varies based on geographic location and time period. According to this view, certain genetic predispositions or negative environments can produce cognitive deficits that can lead to antisocial behavior and sometimes crime. While some researchers claim a "direct" relationship between biological factors and antisocial behavior, many more consider this claim premature. Instead, these researchers focus on how neuropsychological and cognitive changes that come from biosocial interactions place people at additional risk for antisocial and criminal behavior. Figure 14.1 provides an overview of biosocial theories.

By the end of the chapter, readers should be able to:

- Know the difference between biological and biosocial explanations of antisocial and criminal behavior
- Understand the assumptions of human nature that biosocial theories make
- Explain the role of new technologies in the development and testing of biosocial theories
- Recognize the challenges associated with these theories. Why do some critics suggest biosocial criminology amounts to going back to the future?
- Consider the role of environmental toxins in biosocial criminology. How might this connect to so-called green criminology?

 ## The Biosocial Tradition

Biosocial theories incorporate findings from numerous disciplines and subfields in the life sciences, including developmental biology, psychiatry, cognitive neuroscience, behavioral ecology, and endocrinology

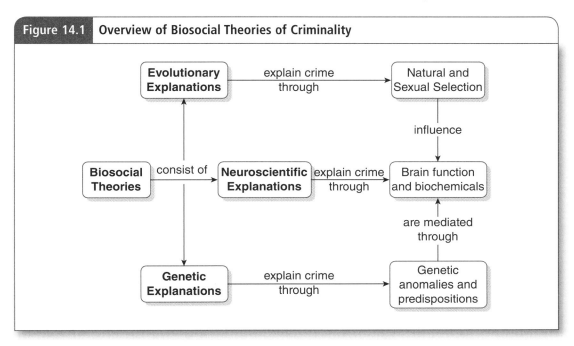

Figure 14.1   Overview of Biosocial Theories of Criminality

(Bohm & Vogel, 2011; Fishbein, 2001). Some criminologists (especially those trained in sociology) remain reluctant to embrace the findings of natural sciences such as biology. This is perhaps understandable given previous issues with Lombroso's early research, social Darwinism, the Nazis' use of eugenics during World War II, and forced sterilizations, as discussed in Chapters 2 and 3 (Bohm & Vogel, 2011; Lilly et al., 2011). However, it is important to recognize biosocial theories are different from earlier biological theories. They are not purely positivist and based on biological factors, they also account for environmental influences (Akers & Sellers, 2013; Beaver & Walsh, 2010). Biosocial criminologists reject the extreme determinist view that biological factors will inevitably lead to crime. Instead, they focus on how neuropsychological and cognitive deficits place people at additional risk for antisocial and criminal behavior and what can be done to reduce this risk.

As you read this chapter, consider. . . how are biological factors connected to other events in a person's development? As you may recall from our chapter on biological theories of crime, brain scans have uncovered differences in the brains of serial killers as compared to other individuals. Yet simply scanning brains for certain markers or functions cannot alone suggest future criminality. Consider the case of neuroscientist James Fallon. Fallon was studying psychopathic minds by using brain scans. One day, he compared a scan of his own brain to scans of serial killers. Much to his surprise, he found that his own brain scan resembled the scans of some serial killers. As you read this chapter, consider why Fallon was different from those who had committed serial murder.

Seven Steps of Criminological Thinking

History and Social Context of Biosocial Theories

In order to fully understand the history of the biosocial perspective, it is necessary to revisit evolutionary theory and explain how it has been updated from its original form. Darwin was aware that traits varied from organism to organism, but he did not correctly identify the reason for this variation (Walsh, 2009). Mendel's work on genetics was able to explain what natural selection could not; scientists eventually came to realize that these two approaches were compatible and complementary. This fusion of knowledge is popularly known as the *modern synthesis*, and it revealed that evolution ultimately causes changes in genes. More recently, E. O. Wilson (1975) proposed a new synthesis of knowledge called *sociobiology*, another key forerunner to the biosocial explanations of criminal behavior. Sociobiology sought to explain social and behavioral phenomena using biological concepts and theories. In spite of some harsh criticism from sociologists and other radical environmentalists, sociobiology proved to be very influential. So, while biosocial theories have only become popular in recent years, the biosocial approach has been emerging for nearly 50 years.

The earliest trace of a biosocial influence on theories of criminality is found in Eysenck's (1964) personality theory of criminality.[1] As Rafter notes,

> No significant change [in criminology] occurred until Eysenck published *Crime and Personality,* with its interactive, biosocial model. *Although Eysenck himself ignored this model's implications until very late in life,* others picked up on it, and today it dominates biocriminology. (2008, p. 246, italics added).

Later in his career, Eysenck and Gudjonsson (1989) advocated a more outwardly biosocial approach. C. R. Jeffery (1977, 1978) was perhaps most responsible for reintroducing the biological approach back into the field of criminology. Essentially, Jeffery's work must be seen as a reaction to the domination of environmental approaches.

Early proponents of biosocial theorizing in criminology were ridiculed and referred to as "neo-Lombrosians" (Jeffery, 1979). In some cases, they were accused of endorsing simplistic theories that led to the eugenics movement (Walsh, 2009; Wright, 2009). Most criminologists have been reluctant to embrace biologically based explanations and are still, by and large, committed to the traditional sociological and related explanations of criminality (e.g., strain, control, and learning theories). This shouldn't be shocking since most criminologists are trained in the social sciences and are unfamiliar with biology and other natural sciences (Ellis & Walsh, 2003). However, some sociological criminologists have started to question this commitment (Hall, 2012). For example, Francis T. Cullen states that

> although I have trumpeted its value, I am equally persuaded that sociological criminology has exhausted itself as a guide for future study on the origins of crime. It is a paradigm for a previous century, not the current one. (2009, p. xvi).

The social context of the 1990s and 2000s also contributed to the development of the biosocial theories. First, during this time period there was a proliferation of television programs focused on

---

[1]See Chapter 4 for an in-depth discussion of this earlier theory.

using natural science approaches to solve crimes. These shows included *CSI, Cold Case Files, Bones*, and *Criminal Minds*, among others (Lilly et al., 2011). It doesn't seem too far-fetched to argue that these television programs helped to buoy the reputation of the biological sciences as a solution to the crime problem. The so-called CSI effect refers to the tendency for people (and especially juries) to overinflate their assumptions and expectations about the value of forensic tools. Second, there were also widespread concerns during this era over superpredators—career criminals and chronic repeat offenders. This led to the emergence of numerous approaches fixated on controlling these individuals at any cost (Blumstein, Cohen, Roth, & Visher, 1986; Bennett, Dilulio, & Walters, 1996). Garland (2001) has referred to this as the "criminology of the other" because it refers to the tendency to distance oneself from criminals and think of some criminals as almost subhuman. The mix of these two potent forces captured the attention of society and likely helped reignite interest in biologically based explanations of criminality.

Finally, several technological advancements have accelerated scientific progress made in the biological sciences (Lilly et al., 2011). In fact, Robinson and Beaver (2008) contend that "the biological sciences have made more contributions to our understanding of behavior in the last 10 years than sociology has in the last 50 years" (p. xvi). A great deal of this progress has resulted from instruments that have provided scientists with more detailed images of the brain, thus allowing them an increased understanding of its various structures and function (Fishbein, 2001; Walsh, 2009). These new technologies for studying the brain include computerized tomography (CT) and magnetic resonance imaging (MRI). Functional aspects of the brain are typically studied using positron emission tomography (PET), regional cerebral blood flow (RCBF), and functional magnetic resonance imaging (fMRI) (Fishbein, 2001; Raine, 1993).

Assumptions of Biosocial Theories

Like evolutionary theorists, biosocial theorists assume that humans are naturally selfish and seek to maximize their own pleasure. In fact, the well-known evolutionary biologist Richard Dawkins claims that this tendency can be traced all the way down to the genetic level:

> Our genes have survived, in some cases for millions of years, in a highly competitive world. This entitles us to expect certain qualities in our genes. . . . A predominant quality to be expected in a successful gene is ruthless selfishness. This gene selfishness will usually give rise to selfishness in individual behavior. (1976, p. 2)

One might wonder how the social contract that we live under is possible if individual behavior is naturally prone to selfishness. E. O. Wilson explains what at first appears be somewhat of a paradox:

> Human beings appear to be sufficiently selfish and calculating to be capable of infinitely greater harmony and social homeostasis. This statement is not self-contradictory. True selfishness, if obedient to the other constraints on mammalian biology, is the key to a nearly perfect social contract. (as cited in Walsh, 2009, pp. 67–68)

In other words, people agree to the social contract because they understand the benefits that come along with living in society. Both Dawkins (1976) and Wilson (1978) claim that altruism is to be expected in some situations as it may ensure survival of one's genes.

Given their connections to the biological sciences, it should come as no surprise that biosocial theorists believe that humans are influenced by factors beyond their control (e.g., genes, physical environments, brain structure and chemistry). Walsh (2009) explains that "*any* trait, characteristic, or behavior of *any* living thing is *always* the result of biological factors intersecting with environmental factors" (p. 9, italics in original). Further, these theories embrace a "soft" determinism and a risk-factor approach to theorizing (Fishbein, 1990, 2001; Lilly et al., 2011). Raine describes his conception of free will in the quote below:

> I might argue for a middle ground between these two extremes. Free will likely lies on a continuum, with some people having almost complete choice in their actions, while others have relatively less. Rather than viewing intent in black-and-white, all-or-nothing terms, as the law does, with a few exceptions, I see shades of gray. Most of us lie between these extremes. Think of the free-will concept like IQ, extraversion, or temperature, which are dimensional in nature. There are degrees of free will, and we all differ on that dimension of agency. (2013, p. 307)

Biosocial theorists also seem to reluctantly grant some agency in the form of active gene–environment interaction (rGE). Active rGE refers to the tendency of individuals to seek out environments that suit their genetic preferences. For example, people with antisocial tendencies and low intelligence will seek out environments containing people with similar characteristics. This acknowledges that people have some degree of free will.

Biosocial theories cannot be easily classified as conflict or consensus. Evolutionary theory is clearly conflict oriented in the sense that it revolves around competition and not cooperation (Dawkins, 1976). With regard to the criminal law, biosocial theorists believe that there is a set of universally condemned acts (e.g., murder, robbery, and rape) and that these acts form the basis for criminal justice systems all over the world (Fishbein, 2001; Walsh & Ellis, 2007). This is in direct opposition to some types of conflict theory that suggest laws serve the elite. However, Marxists and evolutionary theorists are not viewed as natural enemies, and some biosocial theorists have suggested that the two are not necessarily incompatible (Walsh, 2009). Dawkins provides some useful advice on how we ought to structure and manage society:

> My own feeling is that a human society based simply on the gene's law of universal ruthless selfishness would be a very nasty society in which to live. But unfortunately, however much we want to deplore something, it does not stop it being true. This book is mainly intended to be interesting, but if you would extract a moral from it, read it as a warning. Be warned that if you wish, as I do, to build a society in which individuals cooperate generously and unselfishly toward a common good, you can expect little help from biological nature. Let us try to *teach* generosity and altruism, because we are born selfish. Let us understand what our own selfish genes are up to, because we may then at least have the chance to upset their designs, something that no other species has ever aspired to. (1976, p. 3)

Clearly, people's inherent nature is not always altruistic. Instead the question is how this can be encouraged through positive learning, socialization, and social control.

Problem Focus, Scope, and Level of Explanation of Biosocial Theories

Most biosocial theories focus on explaining persistent forms of criminality and antisocial behavior (Fishbein, 2001; Raine, 1993). Wilson and Herrnstein (1985) define criminality as "stable differences across individuals in propensity to commit criminal (or equivalent) acts" (p. 23). Fishbein (2001) advocates an approach that is similar but specifies that criminological theorists should focus on "the measureable dimensions (phenotypes) of antisocial behavior that increase risk for criminal activity and stigmatization" (2001, p. 13). This indicates that there is a clear emphasis on how individual differences give rise to criminality (Bernard & Snipes, 1996).

Recent biosocial theories of criminality have expanded in both scope and focus; specifically, they seek to explain many different types of criminality (Rafter, 2008, pp. 240–241; see also Robinson, 2004). Biosocial theorists distinguish between victimful and victimless forms of crime and tend to focus on the former (Eysenck & Gudjonsson, 1989; Ellis & Hoffman, 1990). However, they caution against using the criminal law to define the object of study because crime is a socio-legal concept and not a true behavioral construct (Eysenck & Gudjonsson, 1989; Ellis & Hoffman, 1990; Fishbein, 2001). While we do know that genes play a role in violent criminal behavior, Raine and his associates (1993) found that a tendency to commit nonviolent crimes seems to be more heritable than one to commit violent crimes. Biosocial theories generally fail to account for most forms of political, white-collar, and corporate crime (for some exceptions, see Ellis, 2005, and Robinson & Beaver, 2008).

Leading evolutionary psychologist David Buss has identified three biological modes of analysis for studying personality and behavioral phenomena:

> Many misunderstandings surround the biological study of personality. One is that there is "a" biological perspective—a single, unified, monolithic approach. This view errs for two reasons (a) There are several distinct levels of biological analysis (e.g., evolutionary, behavioral genetic, and psychophysiological), each with distinct theoretical assumptions, content, and methods, and (b) within each level, there are often competing theories about the same set of observations. (1990, p. 2)

Walsh (2009) has modified this framework and used it to organize biosocial theorizing in criminology. The first branch of theories draws upon the field of **evolutionary psychology**. These explanations explore why criminal behavior may have been adaptive in our distant ancestral environments. The theories on this level of explanation address the larger "why?" questions and account for how environmental factors might impact individuals and alter behavior (Walsh, 2009). The **neuroscientific theories** focus on examining brain dysfunction and chemical imbalances that may lead to criminality. These theories identify various processes associated with abnormal brain functioning, neurochemical imbalances, and hormonal imbalances (Walsh, 2009). **Genetic explanations** are posed at the most basic level. These theories focus on identifying genes that are correlated with traits that make one prone to antisocial behavior and address proximate-level (or "how?") questions (Walsh, 2009).

It is important to note that these three levels are interrelated and have a complementary relationship with one another. Theories originating from evolutionary psychology seek to understand why people are similar to each other. They examine the environmental influences that selected certain traits now represented in human populations. In a sense, this level has much in common with the structural theories described in earlier chapters because they both examine environments. Genetic theories attempt to identify differences that produce unique traits that are associated with antisocial behavior. It should be clear that these explanations seem to have more in common with individual difference theories. The neuroscientific theories mediate or bridge explanations because they focus on brain activity and how various biochemicals may influence behavior. After all, the human brain is really a product of the other two levels of explanation—a combination of genetic influences and evolutionary adaptations to one's environment (Walsh, 2009).

Key Terms and Concepts in Biosocial Theories

Evolutionary Explanations of Criminal Behavior

Evolutionary principles of natural and sexual selection are the glue that holds the biosocial theories together. Recall from Chapter 3 the basic propositions behind natural selection, seen in Figure 14.2.

Darwin's (1871) theory of sexual selection is another important part of evolutionary theory. Some key concepts in sexual selection theory include reproductive success, mating, and parenting effort. Reproductive success refers to an organism's potential for representation in the next gene pool. An instinctual goal of all organisms is to increase their reproductive success so that they can pass on their genes to the next generation; this process is, by nature, a very competitive one (Dawkins, 1976).

In a variety of species, including humans, males will often resort to alternative reproductive strategies that emphasize mating effort over parenting effort in order to maximize their reproductive success. An overemphasis on mating effort may result in a tendency toward antisocial behavior (Ellis, 2003; Raine, 1993). The lack of emphasis on parenting effort also raises the likelihood that children will be at risk for antisocial behavior because they will not be socialized properly and will not learn right from wrong. It should not be hard to see how these evolutionary dynamics could be connected to other theories of criminal

Figure 14.2	Propositions in Natural Selection
Natural Selection	Within a given species, more individuals are produced by reproduction than can survive within the constraints (e.g., food supply) imposed by the species' environment.
	The disparity between the number of individuals produced by reproduction and the number that can survive creates a struggle for existence.
	Individuals within a species show variation, and those with advantageous characteristics have a greater probability of survival and reproduction.
	When advantageous characteristics that promote survival are inherited by offspring, individuals possessing those characteristics will become more common in the population over successive generations.

Source: Adapted from http://www.open.edu/openlearn/nature-environment/natural-history/evolution-through-natural-selection/content-section-2

behavior. For example, many sociological explanations of criminal behavior, such as control and learning theories, also focus on the importance of family, parenting, socialization, and learning.

One challenge for the biosocial theories is to explain how antisocial and criminal behavior can be conceptualized as adaptive responses to one's environment. For example, most people fail to understand how these types of behaviors could possibly be advantageous to survival (Anderson, 2007; Raine, 1993; Walsh, 2009). Many early biological criminologists assumed that criminals were less evolved than law-abiding citizens (Lombroso, 1876). From a modern perspective, law-breaking behavior may seem to lead to more disadvantages since many serious criminals are caught and punished. A criminal conviction can also result in a loss of friends and family and in a reduction in advantages (e.g., job opportunities) critical to survival and reproduction. According to evolutionary theorists, the key is to consider how antisocial and criminal behavior may have provided advantages during earlier phases of human history and why these behaviors might persist in some individuals in modern settings (Walsh, 2009; Beaver & Walsh, 2010).

Belsky's (1980, 1991) theory of conditional adaptation attempts to specify more clearly how sociological factors might fit into an evolutionary theory of criminal behavior. This theory is focused specifically on the relationship between child maltreatment and reproductive strategies. Belsky and his colleagues (1991) claim that humans embrace strategies that encourage reproductive success. The type of strategy adopted depends largely on the experiences in the first 5 to 7 years of life:

> Individuals whose experiences in and around their families of origin lead them to perceive others as untrustworthy, relationships as opportunistic and self-serving, and resources as scarce and/or unpredictable will develop behavior patterns that function to reduce the age of biological maturation (within their range of plasticity), accelerate sexual activity, and orient them toward short-term, as opposed to long-term, pair bonds. (Belsky, Steinberg, & Draper, 1991, p. 650)

So, according to Belsky and his associates (1991), traumatic experiences in childhood can trigger early adolescence. This could be seen as an evolutionary adaptation to a hostile environment meant to maximize one's chances of survival and reproduction.

These theorists identify two types of mating strategies. The first strategy focuses on parenting effort and time spent caring for one's children. Individuals using this strategy tend to be more law-abiding and less aggressive. The second strategy emphasizes mating behavior and results in exhibiting higher levels of antisocial and criminal behavior. To summarize, family context and interaction, coupled with community and cultural factors, may encourage some individuals to pursue a sexual strategy that emphasizes reproduction, thus leading to higher rates of criminal and antisocial behavior in their offspring because of a lack of parenting effort. This theory is somewhat unique when compared to other evolutionary theories of criminality because it attempts to account for female criminality as well as male criminality.

Mealey's (1995) cheater theory also focuses on reproductive strategies and uses them to explain the existence of male sociopaths. She claims that males can be classified as "dads" and "cads" based on their level of parenting effort. Dads exhibit high levels of parenting effort and make good fathers and mates. Cads exhibit low levels of parenting effort and make poor fathers and mates, and they also tend to be sociopaths.

Based on these distinctions, Mealey (1995) posits two types of sociopaths that you may recall from previous chapters. Primary sociopaths (also known as psychopaths) are genetically different from normal people, while secondary sociopaths appear to learn the cad strategy (and other criminal and antisocial behaviors) (Mealey, 1995). Secondary sociopaths normally age out of crime and often abandon the cad strategy after their young adult years (Anderson 2007). Mealey (1995) also predicts that primary sociopaths will commit more crime and will adhere to the cad strategy throughout their lives.

Rowe's (1996) alternative adaptation theory is another theory of criminality inspired by evolutionary theory. He claims that people vary with respect to where they focus their reproductive efforts. At one end of the continuum are those who focus on parenting effort; the other end is composed of those who concentrate on mating effort. He states that the best demographic predictors of where that effort is focused are age and gender. Males and young people emphasize mating effort, while females and older people focus on parenting effort (Walsh, 2009). According to Rowe (1996), traits associated with mating effort, such as deceitfulness, impulsiveness, and hedonism, are also used in the pursuit of criminal activity. The prediction here is that criminal behavior will result as mating effort becomes more pronounced.

Neuroscientific Explanations of Criminal Behavior

In order to understand how the neurosciences help make sense of antisocial and criminal behavior, a basic understanding of the brain and some key biochemicals is required. Neuroscientific theories examine various aspects of the brain, such as levels of cortical arousal, neurotransmitters, and hormonal imbalances, that may affect behavior. At first glance, it may be difficult to see the "social" part of these theories. Indeed, they appear to be mostly inspired by biological explanations and findings. However, it is important to keep in mind that nearly all neuroscientists acknowledge that the human brain has a certain level of plasticity and is shaped by its environment (Jeffery, 1978, 1990; Raine, 1993; Walsh, 2009).

The brain is an incredibly complex organ that is not yet completely understood. Consequently, there are numerous ways to classify and study the many structures and areas of the brain. According to Raine (1993), the brain can be divided into two major areas: the cortex and the subcortex. The cortex contains the most sophisticated portions of the brain in the frontal lobes. The frontal lobes are involved in rational thought, planning, behavioral control, and regulation of emotions (Robinson & Beaver, 2008). The front-most part of the frontal lobes, also known as the prefrontal cortex, is particularly important to understanding criminal behavior. The prefrontal cortex is responsible for complex planning, abstract thinking, and decisions involving morality (Raine, 1993). Psychologists sometimes refer to this as executive function. This is the part of our brain that makes us "human"; this section is much larger in humans than in lower animals, as Figure 14.3 suggests.

The subcortex is also part of the central nervous system and refers to the less evolved sections of the brain. The limbic system is associated with regulation of emotion and expressions of emotion (e.g., trembling, sweating, increased heartbeat and respiration). The amygdala, a key brain structure in the limbic system, plays a particularly important role in our fight-or-flight responses and regulates our reactions to fearful situations (Anderson, 2007). Some think this structure may also serve to inhibit violent responses in humans and other animals (Blair, 1995). The reticular activating system (RAS) and the limbic system are of particular interest to criminologists. The RAS is essentially a bundle of

Figure 14.3	Percentage Prefrontal Cortex in Common Mammals (Raine, 1993, p. 105)
Mammal	**Percentage Prefrontal Cortex**
Humans	29%
Chimpanzees	17%
Gibbons	11.5%
Lemurs	8.5%
Dogs	7%
Cats	3%

Source: Adapted from Raine, A. (1993), p. 105.

neurons located at the base of the brain stem, and it functions as an information-filtering system responsible for controlling arousal and alertness (Walsh, 2009).

As you may recall, in Chapter 4 we reviewed Eysenck's (1964) theory of the criminal personality. According to this theory, less activity in the RAS leads to a lower state of arousal in individuals. People in lower states of arousal tend to feel understimulated and often seek out additional stimulation in their environments to "even" themselves out. Eysenck (1964) also claimed that these individuals are often less responsive to punishment, causing them to condition poorly. This theory illustrates how aspects of brain functioning can help us understand how people learn.

Another example of a theory that illustrates how biological factors may affect learning is Wilson and Herrnstein's (1985) biosocial theory, which is offered in their book *Crime and Human Nature.* This theory suggests that biological predispositions are thought to affect the operant (instrumental) learning process; this is in contrast to Eysenck's (1964) earlier theory that stressed classical (or Pavlovian) conditioning. In other words, one's susceptibility to deterrence is affected by individual differences determined by one's biological makeup.

These theorists posit the existence of two types of reinforcers: primary and secondary. Primary reinforcers are biological rewards based upon innate drives (e.g., sex and hunger), while secondary reinforcers are learned and are often culturally reinforced (e.g., a preference for certain foods). The propositions of this theory can be summarized as follows:

> The larger the ratio of rewards (material and nonmaterial) of noncrime to the rewards (material and nonmaterial) of crime, the weaker the tendency to commit crime. . . . The strength of any reward declines with time, but people differ in the rate at which they discount the future. The strength of a given reward is also affected by the total supply of reinforcers. (Wilson & Herrnstein, 1985, p. 61)

To explain further, classical conditioning functions internally and is connected to one's conscience, while operant conditioning governs actions by influencing one's reactions to stimuli and the perceived consequences of behavior. So, some people will avoid committing crime because they have been socialized against such behavior (i.e., classical conditioning), while other people avoid crime because they fear the consequences of getting caught (i.e., operant conditioning).

According to Wilson and Herrnstein (1985), all actors make rational choices based upon their perceptions of primary and secondary reinforcers. These theorists also point out that various constitutional factors (e.g., gender, age, intelligence, and personality) and some developmental factors (e.g., family, school, and peer experiences) predispose some individuals to involvement with crime.

While the neurosciences contain a wealth of knowledge about the biological causes of criminal behavior, the social and environmental influences are still not completely clear in many of the theories that examine neurotransmitters, hormone levels, and enzyme deficiencies. This is likely due to the fact that research in this area of criminology is still relatively new and underdeveloped. Despite this, there are several important neuroscientific theories that are relevant to criminologists, including the cascade theory of reward (Blum et al., 1990; Blum, Cull, Braverman, & Comings, 1996; Blum et al., 2000; Comings & Blum, 2000); reward dominance theory (Gray, 1970, 1975; Fowles, 1980, 1987); and evolutionary androgenic theory (Ellis, 1986, 1987; Ellis & Walsh, 2003). Because all of these theories use correlations of neurotransmitters, hormone levels, and enzyme deficiencies as a basis for theorizing, it is necessary to be familiar with how these biochemicals are related to antisocial behavior and some forms of criminality.

One can think of the body as having two communication systems, one that uses neural networks to send messages and one that uses hormones to send messages (Anderson, 2007). Nerve cells (or neurons) refer to specialized cells within the nervous system that are responsible for transmitting signals that instruct the body how to act. The cells communicate through the use of chemical messengers, or neurotransmitters, including dopamine, norepinephrine, and serotonin. Neurotransmitter levels are regulated by various enzymes, such as monoamine oxidase (MAO). If one is lacking these enzymes for some reason, levels of neurotransmitters can become unbalanced, causing changes in behavior. Both of these communications systems are determined genetically, but they can also be affected by our environment in many different ways. For example, working out, listening to music, and eating particular types of food can all affect a person's balance of neurotransmitters.

The neurotransmitter most associated with internal biological reward systems is dopamine, and thus it has received a great deal of attention by researchers. Our environment emits cues that alert us to when there are rewards nearby, and when this happens, there is a conditioned response that triggers reward-seeking behavior. The vast majority of research indicates that increased dopamine levels correspond to higher levels of violent and aggressive behavior (Anderson, 2007; Fishbein, 2001; Raine, 1993). Norepinephrine has also received attention from researchers. High levels of norepinephrine seem to create elevated states of arousal and are connected to increased agression; however, there is no direct cause–effect relationship between this neurotransmitter and aggressive or violent behavior (Anderson, 2007). Another neurotransmitter that has been linked to aggression is serotonin. Low levels of this chemical have also been linked to impulsive behaviors, antisocial personality disorder, and depression. So to summarize, higher levels of dopamine and norepinephrine are generally associated with aggression, as are lower levels of serotonin.

Monoamine oxidase (MAO) is an enzyme responsible for breaking down serotonin, norepinephrine, and dopamine neurotransmitters. There are actually two forms of MAO, MAO-A and MAO-B; MAO-A is more directly linked to antisocial behavior. More specifically, inadequate levels of MAO-A have been linked to aggression and loss of self-control (Fishbein, 2001; Anderson, 2007). Brunner (1996) has identified a gene responsible for passing on abnormalities in MAO-A that can eventually lead to violent and antisocial behavior in males. This gene, sometimes referred to as the warrior gene, will receive more discussion later in the section about genetics.

Gray's (1970, 1975) reward dominance theory is one of the early examples of a neuroscientific theory relevant to understanding criminality. This theory is really an extension of Eysenck's (1964, 1967) theory of personality. Gray (1970) uses Eysenck's (1964, 1967) dimensions of personality but proposes rotating the factors of neuroticism (N) and extraversion (E) 45 degrees to understand how internal behavioral regulation systems contribute to behavioral conditioning. This creates new categories of personality types, including the impulsive personality (N+E+) and the anxious personality (N+E-). The individual with an impulsive personality has increased sensitivity to rewards, while anxious individuals have increased sensitivity to punishments. Further, Gray (1970, 1975) posits the existence of two internal regulation systems: the behavioral activation system (BAS) and the behavioral inhibition system (BIS). The BAS is sensitive to rewards and is responsible for activating behavior, while the BIS works to inhibit behavior in anticipation of potential punishments (Raine, 1993; Walsh, 2009). In other words, the BAS is a motivating force and the BIS is the control-oriented or regulating force.

This theory also has some parallels with more mainstream theories of criminal behavior. For example, Reckless's (1973) containment theory posits the existence of inner and outer containments; these work to regulate behavior like the BIS. Recall that this theory also suggests motivating factors in the form of internal pushes and external pulls. The key difference is that Reckless's theory (1973) focuses more on sociological factors than biological factors. These two theories seem to have some compatibility, however.

Another important biosocial theory relevant to understanding criminal behavior is called the cascade theory of reward (CTR) (Blum et al., 1990, 1996, 2000; Comings & Blum, 2000). This theory is associated with what some have called reward deficiency syndrome (Anderson, 2007). Originally, CTR was used to explain alcoholism, and researchers consider alcoholism to be linked to a variant form of a particular dopamine receptor (Blum et al., 1990). Many people misinterpreted this research, assuming that this was proof of an "alcohol gene."

Blum and his colleagues (1996) eventually clarified their findings, explaining that the gene affects much more than alcoholism and is connected to many different patterns of addiction and impulsive behaviors. They claimed that people with this dopamine receptor abnormality experience behavioral rewards differently than normal people because reward centers in the limbic system fail to receive the appropriate neurotransmitters (e.g., dopamine and serotonin). Deficiencies in these neurotransmitters can cause anxiety, anger, and other negative feelings because of an inability to experience pleasure normally (Blum et al., 1996). This problem can lead to a variety of maladaptive behaviors and mental issues, including antisocial personality disorder (or conduct disorder in children), attention deficits, excessive smoking, drug abuse, compulsive gambling, and overeating.

These findings are especially interesting when one compares them to Gottfredson and Hirschi's (1990) low self-control theory. Gottfredson and Hirschi claim that theoretical equivalents of crime, such as substance abuse (i.e., alcoholism and drug abuse), smoking, gambling, speeding, and promiscuous sexual activity, result from low self-control. It seems that there are some logical similarities between these two theories and possibly the potential for some kind of cross-level and cross-disciplinary integration.

There are also several hormones that may be related to criminality and antisocial behavior. Hormones are biochemicals that are secreted into the bloodstream by glands and other organs associated with the endocrine system (Anderson, 2007). Examples include the testes, which are responsible for producing testosterone, and the adrenal glands, which produce cortisol and adrenaline.

Most people are aware that elevated testosterone levels are connected to aggressive behavior. It should come as no surprise then that levels of crime are the highest among young males between the ages of 15 of 24. This is also a time period when testosterone levels are at their highest (Boyd, 2000). Low levels of the stress hormone, cortisol, have also been linked to antisocial behavior; in fact, particularly low levels have been found in many criminal psychopaths. From these findings, one can infer that psychopaths react differently to stressful situations, meaning that they either do not experience stress like normal people or have not been conditioned to avoid stress (Fishbein, 2001; Raine, 1993).

One of the leading hormonal theories of criminality is Ellis's (2005) evolutionary neuroandrogenic theory. This theory attempts to explain why sex is the strongest correlate of crime by examining the effects of testosterone. According to Ellis (2005), unusually high testosterone levels in the womb can impair the development of executive function, may cause hemispheric shifts in brain function, and are often linked to low levels of cortical arousal. The theory consists of two interrelated propositions: one evolutionary and one neuroandrogenic. The evolutionary proposition states that aggressive and selfish behaviors often related to crime evolved as an aspect of human reproduction. In other words, females have mating preferences for higher-status males who they perceive as capable providers. Males with the most resources often exploit others to secure their resources. The theory also predicts that rape will always be more common among males who are unable to be stable providers.

The neuroandrogenic proposition suggests three ways that brain functioning can affect criminal behavior. First, high testosterone levels in the womb may alter brain functioning in ways that produce a tendency toward competitive/victimizing behavior. This is because higher levels of testosterone can affect brain development and may lead to suboptimal arousal levels, may make one prone to seizures, and may cause a rightward shift in neocortical functioning. These correlates all appear frequently in research about serious criminality (see, e.g., Eysenck, 1964; Raine, 1993). Second, one's ability to learn (or IQ) can serve to inhibit criminal behavior; this effect is not necessarily direct. In other words, one's ability to learn could affect school performance, which may lead to poor job prospects and may create some pressure to engage in crime. Third, proper executive functioning (located in the prefrontal cortex) is thought to regulate or inhibit criminal activity. According to Ellis (2005), after adolescence, those with more learning and planning ability will move quickly from "crude" to "sophisticated" forms of behavior. While it is true that this theory relies heavily on biological factors to explain criminality, it does also account for some social factors. For example, the evolutionary aspect of this theory considers the role of social environmental factors relating to sex and social status.

Genetic Explanations of Criminal Behavior

As mentioned previously, genetic explanations of criminality seek to identify different genes associated with traits linked to antisocial behavior. To understand how genetics can offer a better understanding of criminality, it is necessary to familiarize ourselves with a few key terms and concepts. All humans have 46 chromosomes in 23 pairs. Each chromosome consists of strings of genes that are made of deoxyribonucleic acid (DNA). In some cases, two organisms may have similar outward characteristics but actually have different genetic combinations. The underlying genetic makeup of an organism is called a **genotype**, while the outward physical manifestation of traits is referred to as a **phenotype**. Phenotypes can be affected by environmental factors, such as weather and diet.

There are several branches of genetics that are important to understanding how genes influence criminal behavior. These include molecular and behavior genetics and epigenetics and will be discussed in turn below (Walsh & Beaver, 2008). **Molecular genetics** attempts to locate particular genes involved with specific traits. More specifically, molecular geneticists use cheek swabs to gather genetic data and map DNA. In Chapter 3, we discussed the discovery of XYY syndrome and the controversy it created when it was reported to be associated with criminal behavior. Researchers have identified several genetic traits that researchers believe have been connected to criminal behavior; these include low IQ or intelligence (Walsh, 2009) and the underarousal of the autonomic nervous system (ANS) (Eysenck, 1964; Mednick, 1977).

As discussed previously, some neurochemical abnormalities have also been connected to antisocial and aggressive behavior, and some of these abnormalities have been located in the genes. Examples of these abnormalities include MAO-A; promoter polymorphism (Brunner, 1996); the 5HTTLPR serotonin transporter polymorphism (Beaver, Ratchford, & Ferguson, 2009); DRD2 dopamine receptor polymorphism (DeLisi, Beaver, Vaughn, & Wright, 2009); and DAT1 dopamine transporter and 5HTT serotonin transporter polymorphisms (Vaughn, DeLisi, Beaver, & Wright, 2009). It is important to keep in mind that while these discoveries do provide valuable information that aid theorizing, they are not theories themselves. Instead, they should be viewed as examples of how empirical research might specify correlations between various genetic traits and criminality. These findings could be used to inform existing theories or create new ones.

Perhaps more relevant to understanding criminal behavior is the subfield of **behavior (or behavioral) genetics**. Researchers in this area study human personality and behavior by applying aspects of genetics. A key concept in this field is the notion of heritability, or "the extent to which variation in measured phenotypic traits is genetically influenced" (Walsh & Beaver, 2009, p. 10). This area also attempts to gauge how genes are influenced by environmental factors. Gene–environment interaction (GxE) describes how genes and "accumulated experience" (i.e., phenotypes) interact with the environment to produce different behaviors. For example, an impulsive and aggressive child is more vulnerable to environmental opportunities for crime than a less aggressive child with a higher level of self-control (Walsh, 2009, p. 37).

Gene–environment correlations (rGE) are shorthand for genes + accumulated experience/environment correlation. In other words, this means that genes influence the environments in which people find themselves. There are three types of interaction: passive rGE, evocative rGE, and active rGE. **Passive rGE** refers to when the environment exerts influences on the individual; this is usually associated with one's formative years (Walsh & Beaver, 2009). For example, a child with intelligent parents will not only receive related genes that produce higher intelligence but will also likely be exposed to an environment that encourages learning and intellectual pursuits. **Evocative rGE** reveals how an individual's traits elicit positive or negative responses from parents, teachers, and peers. This holds some parallels to certain labeling theories; negative feedback loops can be created by bad reactions to bad behavior, and this may serve to perpetuate the bad behavior. **Active rGE**, also referred to as niche picking, explains how mature individuals seek out environments that are compatible with their underlying genetic traits (Walsh, 2009). As mentioned previously, this grants a certain amount of agency to actors in shaping their own environmental influences. This indicates that these theories are not strictly determinist and also suggests that they have some assumptions in common with other modern criminological theories.

Think You Get It?

Create a table with two columns and put biological theories and biosocial theories at the top of each. Briefly read through both relevant chapters again and make a note of key terms and concepts in each. How are these theories similar? How are they different? Do biosocial theories of crime suggest we are going back to the future?

Research on Biosocial Theories

Caspi and his colleagues (2002) have conducted some important research on the effects of GxE interactions on antisocial behavior. They provided epidemiological evidence that among maltreated children, those with a genotype conferring high levels of MAO-A expression were less likely to develop antisocial problems later in life. Since then, other studies have applied these biosocial explanations to gender and antisocial behavior and have considered other complexities associated with explaining antisocial behavior through reference to GxE (Rutter, Caspi, & Moffitt, 2003; Rutter, Moffitt, & Caspi, 2006).

There are two genetic variants that seem to be very relevant to antisocial cognition and, subsequently, antisocial behavior. These are the 5HTTLPR polymorphism (a serotonin transporter gene) and an MAO-A polymorphism. Low levels of 5HTTLPR have been linked to impulsive behaviors, antisocial personality disorder, depression, and other cognitive and behavioral problems (Canli & Lesch, 2007). Subsequent research has linked genetic variation in the MAO-A gene to variation in brain structure and connectivity and to differences in this effect by gender (Meyer-Lindenberg et al., 2006).

In recent years, advances in neuroscience research have improved our understanding of brain structure and function. In criminology, the relationships between neuropsychological processes and behavioral outcomes have assisted to uncover new ways to make sense of human behavior. Working together, research teams have begun to show that early life experiences such as parenting and SES have effects on brain areas such as the amygdala and prefrontal cortex (Gianaros, Jennings et al., 2007; Gianaros et al., 2011; Hackman, Farah, & Meaney, 2010; Hanson et al., 2013). These areas appear to be linked to higher rates of antisocial behavior (Crowe & Blair, 2008); crime and violence (Hyde, Shaw, & Hariri, 2013); and a number of other relevant outcomes, such as depression, cognition, and drug use.

Recent research in which subjects were studied longitudinally from childhood until adulthood has started to clarify how a child's environment and genetic makeup interact to create a violent adolescent or adult. Males born with a particular allele of the MAO-A gene and who were maltreated as children have a much greater likelihood of manifesting violent, antisocial behavior as adolescents and adults. Others born with particular alleles of the serotonin transporter gene and who have experienced multiple stressful life events are more likely to manifest serious depression and suicidality. Paus (2010, pp. 893–897) discusses four more recent attempts to collect a variety of environmental, behavioral, and cognitive data. Three of these four studies also collected DNA and were designed to offer longitudinal, population-based neuroimaging studies to "identify genetic and environmental factors (exposures) that shape the various structural and functional brain phenotypes (outcomes) (Paus, 2010,

p. 893). Studies based on large and multifaceted datasets can provide the sort of information needed to explore biosocial theories of criminality in greater detail.

The first of these large studies involves a cohort established in the Child Psychiatry Branch of the National Institute of Mental Health (NIMH-CHPB). This project was first conceived in 1989 as a normative study of brain structure during childhood and adolescence conducted in Bethesda, Maryland. This longitudinal study sought to compare normative data (based on what is usual for a defined population) with magnetic resonance (MR) images acquired in parallel studies of psychiatric disorders of childhood, including both common (e.g., attention deficit hyperactivity disorder) and rare (e.g., childhood-onset schizophrenia) conditions. Participants' ages at the time of initial recruitment ranged from 3 to 25 years, and visits were repeated in 2–4 year intervals. The multiethnic sample came primarily from the local community near the Bethesda campus.

The second study was the NIH Pediatric MRI Database (NIH-PD), which was initiated in the mid-2000s as a multicenter, longitudinal study. In this study, MR acquisition took place at six sites in the United States. It complemented the NIH-CHPB cohort by including a large group of infants and young children (age 7 days to 4 years) as well as older children (5 to 18 years). Unlike the NIH-CHPB, the sample was defined through population-based sampling. The six acquisition sites recruited participants using site-specific demographic targets calculated according to US Census 2000 data. The resulting sample was multiethnic and included a wide range of SES characteristics.

The third large study is the Saguenay Youth Study (SYS). Initiated in the mid-2000s, the study seeks to investigate genetic and environmental factors shaping the adolescent brain and body. In this study, MR acquisition takes place at a single site in Canada. Adolescents (12 to 18 years) and their biological parents are recruited from a population of the Saguenay Lac-Saint-Jean (SLSJ) region of Quebec, Canada. At this point, it is a cross-sectional study in which multiple quantitative phenotypes relevant to mental, cardiovascular, and metabolic health are acquired. Based on the study's design, half of the participants have been exposed to maternal cigarette smoking, and the nonexposed half is matched to them by maternal education. Recruitment takes place in high schools across the SLSJ region. The sample is of a single ethnicity (white Caucasians), and samples of DNA are collected from all participating adolescents and their biological parents. Behavioral and cognitive assessments are extensive and include self-reports of psychiatric symptoms and components of positive youth development and personality, as well as a thorough assessment of cognitive abilities.

Fourth and finally, the Imagen Study started in 2007 as a multicenter, cross-sectional study of the genetic and neurobiological bases of individual variability in impulsivity, reinforcer sensitivity, and emotional reactivity. MR acquisition takes place at eight acquisition sites located in the United Kingdom, Ireland, France, and Germany. This is the only large pediatric cohort that includes both structural and functional MRI for all participants. Adolescents (14-year-olds) are recruited primarily through local high schools. The sample is multiethnic, and samples of DNA are collected from all participating adolescents.

Taken together, these studies have and will continue to provide the sort of data that can explore in greater detail biosocial theories of criminality based on the variables listed in Figure 14.4.

Practical Ramifications of Biosocial Theories

Biosocial theories have the potential to offer a science-based alternative to sociologically based theories that meaningfully integrates perspectives and theories from the natural and social

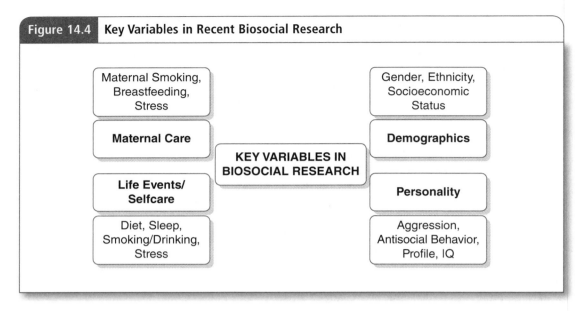

Figure 14.4   Key Variables in Recent Biosocial Research

Maternal Smoking, Breastfeeding, Stress

Maternal Care

Life Events/ Selfcare

Diet, Sleep, Smoking/Drinking, Stress

KEY VARIABLES IN BIOSOCIAL RESEARCH

Gender, Ethnicity, Socioeconomic Status

Demographics

Personality

Aggression, Antisocial Behavior, Profile, IQ

sciences. It is possible to identify three general practical outcomes from biosocial research on criminal behavior. The first strategy is a specific kind of application of the medical model to criminology, and it focuses on how specific treatments or interventions can treat violent offenders (Ellis, 2005; Englander, 2007). Other research suggests that prevention programs focused on improving the diets of at-risk youth offer another way to understand the role of nutrition and crime (Chung & Raine, 2010). Neurosurgery has also been used to remove brain tumors and correct abnormal neurophysiological conditions associated with aggression. Some research suggests that the intersection of brain lesions and criminality offers new neuroscientific perspectives about criminal responsibility (Batts, 2009).

The second, and most common, strategy for dealing with the biological determinants of violent behavior involves the administration of prescription drugs. This approach is based on the idea that just like the genetic codes and inherited traits that cause disease can be treated with medication, pharmacological treatments may prove effective in treating violent offenders with genetic abnormalities. The influence of biosocial criminology can also be connected to the use of drugs that decrease testosterone; the use of hormones to treat sexual offenders (Losel & Schmucker, 2005); and chemical castration used to diminish the threats posed by chronic pedophiles (Lee & Cho, 2013).

Perhaps one of the greatest successes of biosocial science to date has been its role in raising awareness about the importance of adolescent brain development. In outlawing the juvenile death penalty, Supreme Court justice Anthony Kennedy wrote,

Three general differences between juveniles under 18 and adults demonstrate that juvenile offenders cannot with reliability be classified among the worst offenders. First, as any parent knows, youths are more likely to show a lack of maturity and an underdeveloped sense of responsibility [than adults]. . . . These qualities often result in impetuous and ill-considered actions and decisions. . . . The second area of difference is that juveniles are more vulnerable or susceptible to negative influences and outside pressures, including peer pressure. . . . The third broad difference is that the character of a juvenile is not as well formed as that of an adult. The personality traits of juveniles are more transitory.[2]

After Kennedy acknowledged in general terms the recognition that developing brains may impact legal responsibility, the number of judicial opinions that referred to neuroscience evidence tripled between 2005 and 2011. This recent development of *neurolaw* is of particular interest to criminologists. Neurolaw refers to an area of the law that applies to any legal domain in which neuroscience may be relevant. At present, the most common uses of neuroscientific evidence include establishing whether a defendant is competent to stand trial and as part of sentencing once guilt has been proved beyond a reasonable doubt. Another example is when defense attorneys try to convince courts that relevant neuroscience research was overlooked; this might warrant a new trial or dismissal of the case at hand.

Nita Farahany (2012) argues that reliance on neuroscience in the courtroom requires greater attention to the type of evidence that neuroscience and behaviorial genetics represents and the constitutional protections that may apply. Whatever the potential for the criminal justice system, these developments threaten to upend the foundational walls upon which criminal law rests. It will be crucial to consider the doctrine of responsibility and values of liberty and fairness as efforts to incorporate neuroscience responsibly into our criminal justice system continue (Lamparello, 2011). In an increasing number of cases, defendants have argued that even though they committed a crime, they cannot be held responsible because their brains made them impulsive, or violent, or incapable of premeditating a crime. Not all of these claims can easily be dismissed. Can a man truly have free will and be held responsible for his actions if he has a brain abnormality or chemical imbalance that compels him to act criminally?

Consider the case of a middle-aged Virginian man with no history of criminal behavior. He began to collect child pornography and molest his 8-year-old stepdaughter, which led to his arrest (Burns & Swerdlow, 2003). The evening before the man was to be sentenced, he complained of headaches and vertigo and was sent for a brain scan that showed a large tumor in the frontal area of his brain. After removal of the tumor, his sexual interests returned to normal. Months later, his sexual focus on young girls rekindled, and a new scan revealed that bits of tissue missed in the surgery had grown into another sizeable tumor. Surgery once again restored the man to his original behavioral state. An MRI scan at the time of the man's initial neurologic evaluation show the tumor displacing the right orbitofrontal cortex and distorting the dorsolateral prefrontal cortex.

The rise of neurolaw has the potential to result in an interesting paradox. Judges may increasingly accept that certain individuals may have a genetic predisposition to violence and antisocial behavior and apply such a finding in a criminal trial. While this may mitigate criminal responsibility, it may also lead to an increase in civil commitment, as some states have done in cases involving sexual offenders. Civil commitment applies when an individual has served his or her prison sentence but is still judged to be a risk to the community.

---

[2]*Roper v. Simmons* (03-633) 543 U.S. 551 (2005).

Figure 14.5	Seven Steps of Biosocial Theories
Seven Steps	**Biosocial Theories**
1. **Know the History**	Originated in the 1970s with Eysenck's personality theory and Jeffery's learning theory but did not become popular until the 1990s and 2000s
2. **Acknowledge Assumptions**	Humans are thought to be naturally selfish (i.e., selfish genes); free will is acknowledged as one of the many variables important to understanding behavior; conflict is natural in society, but there is a core of laws that represent consensus (violent, expropriative crime)
3. **Problem Focus, Scope, and Level of Explanation**	Many of these theories focus on explaining forms of antisocial behavior rather than crime; address a wide range of problematic behaviors, including white-collar crime; three levels of explanations are addressed, including genetic, neurological/neurochemical, and evolutionary; emphasis is on individual differences
4. **Key Terms and Concepts**	Parenting and mating effort, conditional adaption, alternative adaptation, primary and secondary reinforcers, reward dominance, and passive/evocative/active gene–environment correlation (rGE)
5. **Respect the Research**	Studies use large and multifaceted datasets; examine gene–environment interactions (GxE) and how they function over time; key variables examined include personality, life events/self-care, maternal care, and demographics
6. **Theory/Practice**	Diet and nutrition meant to regulate behavior; neurosurgery to correct behavior; prescription to control behavior; emergence of neurolaw
7. **Mapping the Theory**	See Figure 14.6

Criticisms of Biosocial Theories

Despite their potential for criminology, like with other theories we have covered, critiques of biosocial theories exist. These critiques might be divided into historical, methodological, and ethical categories. Historically, as discussed in previous chapters, biological theorists have been accused of racial and class bias. Those with bigoted views and who propagate race hate have long used "theories" of racial superiority to try and legitimate these prejudices. These critiques remain (Roberts & Gabor, 1990). Indeed, some suggest that natural selection has acted on human populations to open up reproductive niches for individuals and groups who victimize others (Ellis & Hoffman, 1990).

This view has other, perhaps unintended consequences. To argue crime is predominantly a function of genetic variation naturally shifts the focus away from systemic racism, social exclusion, or the strains from the difficulty of attaining the American Dream. If crime is a product of genetic difference, then it would seem that the various social inequalities that persist in countries with high crime rates are irrelevant and need not be challenged. However, just because theories have and may continue to

Figure 14.6   Mapping Biosocial Theories

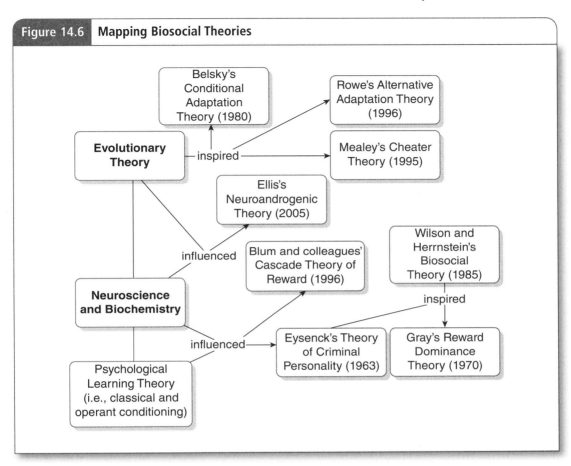

be used for racist ends doesn't mean that we ought to accept the "ignorance that underlies these arguments" (Vila, 1994, p. 329).

Another issue is that biosocial research has in the past been based on small, unrepresentative samples and did not adequately control for the impact of social variables. Biosocial theories also fail to explain regional and temporal differences in violent crime rates. For example, biosocial theories have difficulty addressing why the United States has a much higher rate of violent crime than Canada or most European countries, or why rates of violent behavior appear to have changed over time (Pinker, 2011). In North America, the violent crime rate increased significantly between the 1950s and 1990s and then declined significantly. Did the basic biological makeup of human beings change between the 1950s and the 1990s and then suddenly change back? Very unlikely. Evolution occurs very slowly. Perhaps social conditions altered in ways that addressed the biological basis for the rise of violent crime? To date, very few biosocial theories have tackled this essential question. If the future of biosocial criminology is a minimization of the role of social and environmental factors, then it will fall prey to the same methodological flaws some accuse early sociologists of engaging in by denying biology.

The final issue is ethical. Brain scans cannot predict behavior. The worry expressed by some is that biosocial criminology furthers the risk-based approaches to justice in which economic actuarial approaches are now combined with biomedical imaging used to predict who is most likely to commit crime. Beyond the problems associated with correctly trying to estimate and prevent crime based on assumptions of the role biological predispositions play, other ethical issues abound. For example, imagine that genetic testing could identify a "violence gene." In such a case, should fetuses with this gene be aborted on the assumption that the babies would be destined to do untold social harm? Most would agree forced abortion is a step too far.

What if, instead, we could identify biological markers that increased the risk of violence by 50%? In that case, should individuals with these traits be subject to greater surveillance by the criminal justice system? At what age should this surveillance begin? While some researchers claim a direct link between genetic factors and crime, to date there is no stand-alone genetic basis for crime. Perhaps the most promising work in this area is by those who recognize that brain patterns and genetic makeup are not enough to make anyone a dangerous criminal. Instead, when a child with certain biological predispositions witnesses and/or suffers abuse or violence, these children may represent serious and significant risks to those around them.

Research Example: The Lead–Crime Connection

As discussed throughout this chapter, biosocial criminologists consider how genetic/biological markers as well as more traditional environmental markers may be related to crime. As we have seen, these biological factors include genetic variations, traumatic brain injuries, lesions, and tumors. A recent interesting example of biosocial criminology is the question of interactions between lead exposure and crime. Too much lead is poison for developing brains. We know that if young children or mothers carrying a child are exposed to elevated levels of lead, it can impair formative brain growth, as

> incomplete development of the blood–brain barrier in fetuses and in very young children (up to 36 months of age) increases the risk of lead's entry into the developing nervous system, which can result in prolonged or permanent neurobehavioral disorders. (Agency for Toxic Substances and Disease Registry, 2010, p. 19).

High levels of lead in the blood can negatively affect learning and behavior, may lower IQ scores, and, in some cases, can cause seizures and even death (Canfield et al., 2003; Schwartz, 1994). Needleman et al. (2002) found youth with high levels of lead in their bones are twice as likely to be delinquent, after controlling for other possible variables. Other studies link preschool lead exposure to aggressive and delinquent adolescent behavior and later criminal violence (Denno, 1990).

In 1994, Rick Nevin was a consultant working for the US Department of Housing and Urban Development on the costs and benefits of removing lead paint from old houses. This had been a topic of intense study because of the growing body of research linking lead exposure in small children with a whole raft of complications later in life, including lower IQ, hyperactivity, behavioral problems, and learning disabilities. More precisely, the Centers for Disease Control and Prevention considers 5 micrograms per deciliter of lead in a child's blood to be abnormal. Studies have shown that people who grew up with blood-lead levels at or above this threshold are more likely to have impaired cognition than those who grew up with less lead in their blood. Lead emissions from tailpipes rose steadily from the early 1940s through the early 1970s, nearly quadrupling over that period. Then, as unleaded gasoline began to replace leaded gasoline, emissions plummeted.

In 1976, the average US resident had a blood-lead level of 16 μg/dL, according to the National Health and Nutrition Examination Survey. By 1991, when there was less lead in the air and in housing, the average had dropped to 3 μg/dL (Reyes, 2007). This drop can be attributed to the removal of lead from gasoline under the Clean Air Act and amendments passed in 1972 and 1977. Research suggests reductions in childhood lead exposure in the late 1970s and early 1980s are responsible for significant declines in violent crime in the 1990s and may cause further declines into the future.

One of the first papers to observe this link suggests a 23-year lag between exposure and violent crime (Nevin, 2000). In other words, toddlers exposed to high levels of lead in the 1940s and 1950s were more likely to become violent criminals in the 1960s, 1970s, and 1980s. This is outlined in Figure 14.7.

Of course, correlation does not imply causation. Simply because the two lines in Figure 14.7 fit very well together does not mean that exposure to lead directly and universally leads one to commit crime. However, lead exposure may make the brain more susceptible to inconsistent or antisocial parenting, maltreatment, and abuse. The evidence is mounting that early exposure to lead triggers a higher risk for engaging in aggressive behavior (Wolf, 2014). There are three types of research that all seem to point in this direction. These studies are ecological, longitudinal, and imaging based.

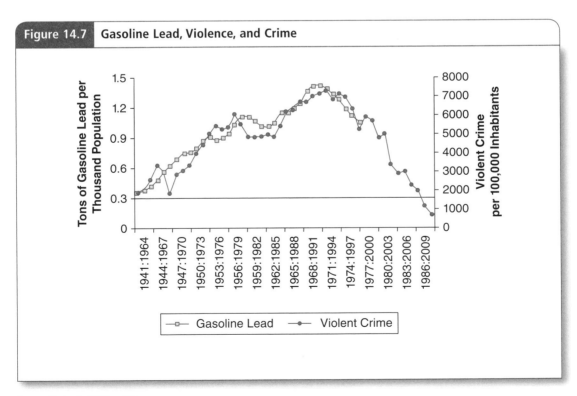

Figure 14.7   Gasoline Lead, Violence, and Crime

Source: Nevin, R. (2000, p. 20).

Ecological studies look at correlations between lead exposure and crime rates at a population level. In addition to Nevin's (2000) research, Stretesky and Lynch (2004) found US counties with high 1990 air lead, mostly from industrial emissions, had murder rates four times higher during the period from 1989 to 1991 than counties with low air lead, after controlling for nine air pollutants and six sociological factors. Later, Stretesky and Lynch (2004) updated their original analysis to investigate the association between air-lead levels and crime rates across 2,772 US counties. They found that air-lead levels and crime rates—property and violent—were strongest in counties that had high levels of resource deprivation and weakest in counties that had low levels of deprivation. Nevin (2007) has since collected lead data and crime data for Australia, Canada, Great Britain, Finland, France, Italy, New Zealand, and West Germany. In all of these countries, high levels of preschool blood lead matched the subsequent crime rate trends over several decades. Of course, population-based studies can't tell us much about individuals.

Longitudinal studies examine the same individuals over a long period of time. For example, in the Cincinnati Lead Study, a University of Cincinnati team began following a group of children starting in the early 1980s. Every 6 months the researchers measured lead levels in the children's blood. Lead exposure was associated with neurobehavioral underdevelopment in early infancy (Dietrich et al., 1987). At age 7, kids with higher lead levels were doing worse in school (Bellinger & Dietrich, 1994). At age 17, they were more heavily involved in juvenile delinquency (Dietrich, Ris, Succop, Berger, & Bornschein, 2001). At age 27, they had higher arrest rates for violent crimes (Wright et al., 2008). Given the high cost of interventions after children have been exposed to lead, this has led to efforts to estimate cost savings over time.

Imaging studies have focused on providing physical proof that lead exposure is linked with various types of brain damage. In one study, researchers tested the possibility that childhood lead exposure might lead to the shrinking (volume loss) of parts of the brain, particularly the parts that are crucial to cognition and behavior. Between 1979 and 1984, using data from the Cincinnati Lead Study, the research involved young children from poor areas of the city where there were many old, lead-contaminated houses. They measured the infants' blood lead levels regularly from birth until they were 78 months old and calculated each child's average blood lead level over this period. They then used MRI brain scans to measure the brain volumes of the participants when they were 19 to 24 years old. The researchers found that exposure to lead as a child was linked with brain volume loss in a region called the anterior cingulate cortex, which is responsible for executive functions and regulating behavior. Lead exposure has a larger effect on brain volumes in men than in women, which might help to explain the higher incidence of antisocial behaviors among men than women.

While the amount of lead in the air has dropped as a result of unleaded fuel, lead paint remains a hazard in more than 50 million homes in America. Levels of lead in the soil may also be relevant. Mielke and Zahran (2012) looked at six major American metropolitan areas over 35 years and found that changing exposure to lead dust explains changing levels of criminality between the cities and within the cities over times, even when controlling for intervention efforts such as education, policing, and incarceration. Zahran, Mielke, and their colleagues (2013) have further examined the city of New Orleans and found that varying levels of lead exposure in neighborhoods there—not economic conditions in neighborhoods—best explain differences in criminality.

The suggestion is that children living in older homes with high concentrations of lead in paint on a wide variety of surfaces or living in areas with higher levels of lead in the soil face some danger of exposure. This will have consequences for many Americans born over the next several decades. Drum

(2013) suggests what is needed is investments designed to reduce future lead exposure. In an article on the Mother Jones Web site, he states that

> we can either attack crime at its root by getting rid of the remaining lead in our environment, or we can continue our current policy of waiting 20 years and then locking up all the lead-poisoned kids who have turned into criminals. There's always an excuse not to spend more money on a policy as tedious-sounding as lead abatement—budgets are tight, and research on a problem as complex as crime will never be definitive—but the association between lead and crime has, in recent years, become pretty overwhelming.

The trouble is that while the end of lead as a gasoline additive is in sight, global demand for lead has more than doubled since the early 1990s to 10 million tons annually. For example, lead-acid batteries are in more than 1 billion vehicles worldwide. They allow for the storage of renewable energy and the stabilization of power grids and provide emergency backup power to most of the world's IT and telecoms infrastructure. Is lead the enemy or is it the way it was used as a fuel additive? What about other environmental toxins? There is at least some evidence that heavy exposure to arsenic, methyl mercury, and a variety of chemicals such as PCBs, dioxins, and pesticides can cause behavior changes, including short attention span, hyperactivity, and impulsive antisocial behavior.

The role of these toxins in crime is not only of interest to biosocial criminologists. Green criminologists, who study not only environmental crimes from a criminological perspective but also the criminological consequences of polluting the planet, have begun to consider the interactions between the environment, criminology, and sociology in new ways (Potter, 2010). While questions remain, the findings to date on lead and crime offer important insight into how the environment shapes developing brains.

A New Direction in Biosocial Theorizing: Epigenetics and Crime

While our underlying DNA is essentially fixed, genes can be expressed in different ways based on environmental circumstances (Beaver & Walsh, 2012). This tendency can actually be passed down over successive generations of offspring in a process referred to as epigenesis. More specifically, epigenetic changes: ". . . afffect the ability of the DNA code to be read and translated into proteins by making the code accessible or inaccessible" (Walsh, Johnston, & Bolen, 2012: 317). While much of this research has been conducted in non-human mammals, similar effects have also been observed in people. To date, few studies have been done that explain how epigenetics might be related to criminal, antisocial, aggressive, or violent behavior in humans (for an example involving drug addiction, see Walsh et al, 2012). If it is possible that epigenetic processes result in different genes being "turned on" or "turned off" in different environments, this line of research may offer an important way to think about the relationships between biology, psychology, social interactions, and criminal behavior (Beaver & Walsh, 2012; Walsh et al., 2012).

Now that you've read this chapter... consider again the case of neuroscientist James Fallon. Recall that Fallon was studying psychopathic minds by using brain scans. One day he compared a scan of his own brain to scans of serial killers. Much to his surprise, he found that his own brain scan resembled the scans of some serial killers. Now that you have read this chapter, how does new research suggest that brain structure, pollution, and early exposure to violence may be linked?

Conclusion and Review Questions

In this chapter, we have discussed biosocial theories. Biological antecedents have long been connected to criminal behavior, but these theories account for interactions between biological characteristics and one's physical and social environment. Theorists in this area suggest certain genetic predispositions interact with negative environments, leading to cognitive deficits that give rise to antisocial behavior and sometimes crime. While some researchers claim a "direct" relationship between biological factors and criminal behavior, many focus on how neuropsychological and cognitive changes that come from biosocial interactions place people at additional risk for antisocial and criminal behavior. While critics of biosocial criminology are right to point to the ways these theories have been used in the past for morally reprehensible purposes, the question for criminologists of all stripes is not whether there is a biological role in crime, but how large a role it plays. How do genetic and other neurological predispositions interact with other sociological and psychological factors? This question has yet to be answered fully.

CHAPTER REVIEW

1. What are some of the differences between biological and biosocial explanations of antisocial and criminal behavior?

2. What assumptions about human nature do biosocial theories make?

3. What role has new technology played in the development and testing of biosocial theories?

4. What are some of the challenges and critiques leveled against these theories?

5. What is the role of environmental toxins in biosocial criminology? How might this connect to so-called green criminology and the study of epigenesis?

C H A P T E R

15

Developmental and Life Course Theories

 ## Chapter Overview and Objectives

In this chapter, we focus on a more recent orientation in criminology. Until the 1990s, most research did not consider how criminal behavior changes over the life course and why people stop committing crime. Developmental and life course (DLC) theories are based on data that examine multiple periods over a lifetime, and they seek to explain why some people start committing crime and why some people desist or stop committing crime. Studies associated with traditional criminological theories, known as cross-sectional research, focuses on differences between groups at one point in time. Longitudinal data is used by DLC theories to examine differences within the same group over a period of time. Longitudinal research helps make sense of the age–crime curve, introduced in Chapter 7, which demonstrates most kinds of crime are likely to be committed by individuals during their teenage years. This activity peaks in the early to late teen years and then drops off significantly. In general, these theories consider how chronological age, common life transitions, and social change shape people's lives from birth to death. They provide a means to understand when most people are most likely to stop committing crime and what approaches are effective to reduce recidivism. Figure 15.1 provides an overview of DLC theories.

By the end of this chapter, readers should be able to:

- Understand how longitudinal research led to DLC theories
- Explain the age–crime curve and what it suggests about patterns of offending
- Be aware of the assumptions, level of explanation, problem focus, and scope of DLC theories
- Describe some practical approaches and programs suggested by these theories
- Consider the critiques leveled against DLC theories

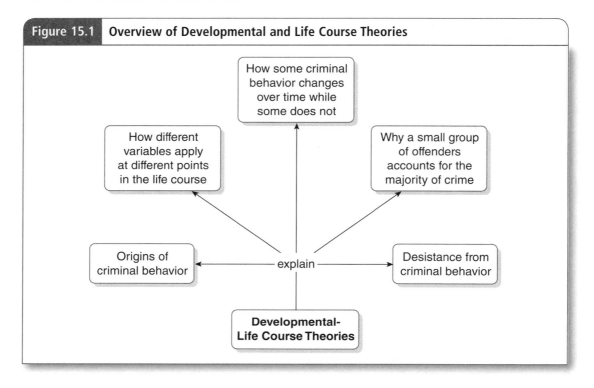

Figure 15.1   **Overview of Developmental and Life Course Theories**

The Developmental and Life Course Tradition

In criminology, the developmental and life course tradition has grown in popularity over the last two decades. However, this approach has been emerging for much longer in numerous disciplines ranging from biology and psychology to sociology, anthropology, and demography. In some ways, these theories represent the best example of the value of collaborative and multidisciplinary criminology to date. David Farrington (2003) first referred to this group of theories as developmental and life course theories. These theories examine change within individuals over time rather than differences between individuals at one point in time. As Hutchinson (2013) suggests, "You could think of the life course as a path. But note that it is not a straight path; it is a path with both continuities and twists and turns" (p. 20).

Studying within-individual change in offenders over time forces criminologists to consider how different variables identified by different disciplines apply (or don't apply) at different points in the life course. More specifically, developmental and life course theorists are interested in why offenders enter into a life of crime, why they continue in a life of crime, and why they abandon a life of crime.

As you read this chapter, consider . . . there is good evidence that a small percentage of offenders (6–7%) is responsible for the vast majority of reported crime. How does this finding correspond to those presented by developmental theorists? If such a small number of offenders commits such a large amount of crime, consider the implications for criminal justice policy. Should the justice system focus more on selective incapacitation of chronic offenders instead of applying the same criminal sanction for the same offense? What are the dangers associated with attempting to prospectively predict these offenders?

Seven Steps of Criminological Thinking

History and Social Context of Developmental and Life Course Theories

DLC theories emerged in the 1990s alongside other integrated theories in criminology. The social explanations of crime had fallen out of favor by this time, but biological theories had also been rejected, and criminologists were looking for a new approach. Up until this point, criminologists had focused on explaining criminal behavior among adolescents (Lilly et al., 2011). Starting in the late 1970s, there was a renewed interest in early childhood development and its connection to criminality (Williams & McShane, 2014). Theorists during this period also started to consider why people stopped committing crime (Sampson & Laub, 1993). These concerns, coupled with the interest in integration, motivated a faction of criminologists to begin to construct a new approach to explaining criminal behavior.

The strain-control paradigm offered by Elliott and his associates (1979, 1985) had a major impact on the formation of developmental and life course theories. One of the key findings in this line of research was that there are multiple pathways to crime. In other words, because offending patterns of different criminals show variation, no individual theory can explain all types of criminal behavior. This doesn't require that a different theory be created for each criminal, but it seems to imply that criminological theorists must open their minds to the possibility that there may be several valid theories that explain different types of criminal behavior (Lilly et al., 2011). It also suggests that a person's life stage is the key to understanding which variables are most relevant. For example, it is not surprising that family factors are very important in childhood. As a person becomes a teenager and young adult, the importance of family is replaced (or at least challenged) by the influence of peers. Later in life (late 20s and 30s), family becomes more important again for many people.

According to Farrington (2003), the DLC theories have four main paradigmatic influences: the risk factor/prevention paradigm, the life course perspective, the criminal career paradigm, and developmental criminology. These are depicted in Figure 15.2.

The **risk factor/prevention** paradigm emerged from the debate about criminological theory integration that took place during the 1980s, and it gained popularity in criminology during the 1990s (Bernard & Snipes, 1996). Bernard and his associates describe this approach below:

The risk factor approach allows for graduated conclusions—the factors identified by some theories explain a whole lot of variation in crime, while the factors identified by others explain only a little . . . where the falsification approach is competitive—if one theory is true, the others are false—the risk factor approach is integrative—many factors may influence crime, some with larger effects than others. (2010, p. 338)

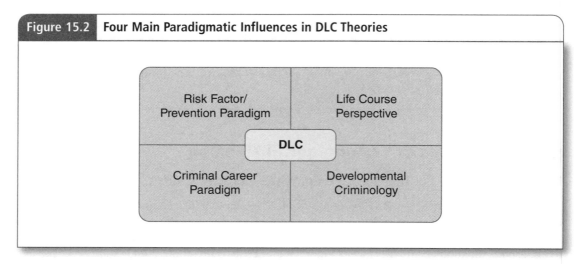

Figure 15.2 Four Main Paradigmatic Influences in DLC Theories

To expand on this statement, the risk factor/prevention paradigm advocates using a variety of motivating and insulating factors to explain criminal behavior. For example, growing up in poverty may put a youth at risk of becoming involved with crime; however, strong family ties may help prevent some people from taking part in criminal activity. When explaining criminal behavior, there are numerous interactions like this that we must consider. Consequently, those working within the risk factor/prevention paradigm incorporate biological, psychological, sociological, and environmental factors into their theories.

Another important aspect to consider is how different factors change in importance as a person progresses through life's different stages; this is the province of the **life course perspective**, another important influence in this area. Life course perspective emerged from sociology (Elder, 1985) but has also influenced psychological theory and research (Baltes, 1987). To clearly understand life course perspective, it is necessary to be familiar with some of its specialized terminology.

The *life course* refers to a set of interconnected trajectories (Benson, 2002). A *trajectory* is a sequence of linked experiences that have something in common. For example, a person could have a work trajectory consisting of the jobs held throughout his or her life. Most trajectories are characterized by frequent changes; some of these are more important than others and are called transitions. Key transitions in a family trajectory might include getting married, having children, or getting a divorce (Elder, 1985, 1993). As we will discuss later, some theorists suggest that people have a criminal trajectory (Sampson & Laub, 1993).

Those using a life course perspective are particularly interested in understanding how factors from different levels of explanations interact with and influence each other (e.g., changes in economies can affect standards of living for particular groups of people, which can influence child-rearing practices that then affect the developmental processes of young children). Elder further explains how this approach connects different levels of explanation to one another:

> Overall the life course can be viewed as a multilevel phenomenon, ranging from structured pathways through social institutions and organizations to the social trajectories of individuals

and their developmental pathways. Though social psychology theories generally exist on one level or another, much of life course study crosses levels, as in the relation between historical change and life experience. (1993, p. 4)

Early versions of the life course perspective from sociology focused primarily on sociological and social psychological factors that influence human behavior. However, criminologists have used this approach as a vehicle for biological factors as well.

The **criminal career paradigm** also impacted the developmental and life course theories. The origins of this approach can be traced back to Wolfgang, Figlio, and Sellin's (1972) study on delinquency in a birth cohort (Bernard et al., 2010). In this study, they found that a very small number of offenders was responsible for committing a very high percentage of crime. This finding indicated that by focusing on chronic offenders, criminologists might be better able to understand crime. The interest in chronic offending grew during the latter part of the 1970s along with the renewed interest in deterrence theory (Blumstein, Cohen, & Nagin, 1978). Eventually, the National Research Council's Panel on Criminal Careers (NRCPCC) was formed to further explore why some criminals were so prolific and how they might be controlled (Blumstein, Cohen, Roth, & Visher, 1986).

Advocates of the criminal career approach argue that two separate theories are required to explain differences between occasional and chronic (or career) criminals. Further, they claim that those who commit criminal acts progress through different stages, each with its own set of relevant factors and variables. For example, it is unlikely that employment opportunities play a major role in youth crime, but unemployment may be an important factor in explaining adult crime (Blumstein, Cohen, Roth, & Visher, 1986).

To truly understand the developmental and life course theories, it is necessary to be familiar with some terminology that has emerged from the NRCPCC. *Onset* (or *emergence*) refers to the origins of criminal behavior (e.g., what ages do people typically start committing crime? Which factors serve to set the stage for criminal behavior?). Participation in crime over an extended period of time is called *maintenance* or *persistence*. For example, in many individuals, associating with delinquent peers is known to play a role in maintaining criminal behavior. Some criminologists have focused on explaining why some people stop committing crime, or *desistance* (Sampson & Laub, 1993; Maruna, 2001). The statistic that expresses the frequency with which a typical offender commits crime is called *lambda*. This is directly relevant to understanding chronic offending and the notion of career criminals. Lambda is measured by calculating the average yearly individual arrest rate (Gottfredson & Hirschi, 1986).

Another key influence in this area is **developmental criminology**; this approach resulted from the intermingling of developmental psychology and criminology (Farrington, 2003). It should come as no surprise that many of the ideas in this area are compatible with the risk factor/prevention and criminal career paradigms as well as the life course perspective. Similar to life course theorists and proponents of the criminal career paradigm, developmental criminologists are interested in understanding how criminal behavior patterns change over time. However, the terminology used in this area is slightly different. For example, developmental criminologists refer to *activation* and *aggravation* instead of onset (or emergence) and maintenance. It should not be difficult to see how this approach could be compatible with the other approaches described previously. Developmental criminologists have also introduced new concepts that focus on changes in offending patterns (Loeber & LeBlanc, 1990).

Assumptions of Developmental and Life Course Theories

DLC theorists make no strict assumptions about human nature and view it as a product of development or an interaction between biological, psychological, and social factors. For example, certain environments may bring out the worst in people; social and historical events may impact how individuals develop in particular geographic areas or time periods. Essentially, this is a complex version of the *tabula rasa* assumption made by earlier psychological process theorists (Agnew, 2011). However, in this view, humans are not merely blank slates but rather that the interaction between individuals and their environments produces motivation for behavior.

Like most other contemporary theories, the DLC theories tend to be characterized by soft determinism, or, as some DLC theorists have called it, indeterminism (Thornberry, 1987). Further, this view corresponds to the approach first suggested by critical criminologists that humans both shape and are shaped by their environments (Agnew, 2011; Taylor et al., 1973). As Elder points out, similar approaches can be found in other theories covered in earlier chapters of this text:

> Theoretical trends in the social sciences favor a constructionist view of individuals in shaping development of the life course. Examples include the cognitive revolution and Bandura's (1986, 1997) pioneering research on personal efficacy. (1993, p. 7)

It is important to note that while all of these theories endorse some brand of soft determinism, many of them vary in their conception of and commitment to free will. For example, Sampson and Laub's (1993) age-graded theory grants greater importance to agency and free will than Moffitt's (1993, 2006) developmental taxonomy, which tends to be more deterministic (Laub & Sampson, 2004). DLC theories tend to be based on a consensus view of society as they focus on explaining acts that most would agree should be illegal.

Problem Focus, Scope, and Level of Explanation of Developmental and Life Course Theories

The problem focus of the DLC theories distinguishes them from all other theories in criminology. Like many of the other formulations reviewed in this text, these theories focus on explaining criminal behavior in individuals, although some also address dynamics of criminal events (c.f. Farrington, 1992). Unlike other earlier criminological theories, DLC theories examine how patterns of criminality change over the course of the lifespan. To put it differently, earlier theories looked at between-individual variations, while the DLC theories examine within-individual changes. This new emphasis requires an entirely different approach to research.

The theories we have covered in previous chapters were generally evaluated by what has come to be called **cross-sectional research**. Cross-sectional research compares a group of individuals at one point in time. Until the 1990s, this accounted for the majority of the research in criminology. By contrast, **longitudinal research** examines the same group of individuals at several points in time, and it has become increasingly popular in recent years (Lilly et al., 2011; Bernard et al., 2010). However, this type of research is expensive, time consuming, and much more difficult to carry out.

The scope of DLC theories is somewhat limited as they focus primarily on explaining crime that is committed by rather serious offenders. Victimless crimes, such as drug use, are important, but these types of acts are of little interest if they do not occur alongside other, more serious forms of crime (e.g., theft, assault, burglary, and robbery). Some theorists also propose explanations for common forms of youth offending (e.g., vandalism, minor theft, underage drinking, and minor drug use) (Moffitt, 1993).

DLC theories are examples of integrated theories of criminal behavior. According to Sampson and Laub (2005), the developmental trend in criminology is toward greater specificity rather than generality. Consequently, end-to-end and side-by-side integrations have been more common than cross-level (multilevel) integrations. In the following passage, Wikstrom describes the ultimate goal of the DLC theorist:

> Our knowledge about how factors at various levels of explanation (genetic, biological, psychological, and social risk factors) might interact in producing acts of crime is not well developed or understood. So it is not only a question about better specifying causal mechanisms at different levels of explanation, but also a question of specifying causal mechanisms that link levels of explanation. (2004, p. 4)

Theories in this area incorporate a variety of both process-oriented and structural theories that were reviewed in earlier chapters of this text (Laub, Sampson, & Sweetin, 2007). Further, they also acknowledge the importance of factors derived from individual difference theories (e.g., impulsivity and self-control).

DLC theorists do not believe that differences in criminal propensity explain stability in criminal activity over the life course. Criminal propensity, and the degree to which it explains the stability of crime, was a hotly debated topic in criminology during the 1980s and 1990s. Some theorists claimed that the presence of some underlying criminal propensity will cause crime to be stable over the life course (c.f., Gottfredson & Hirschi, 1990; Wilson & Herrnstein, 1985). This position is known as **population heterogeneity**, or the "kinds of people" argument, and it is based solely on individual differences (Laub & Sampson, 2003). Most DLC theorists advocate some version of a **state dependence** position, or "kinds of contexts" argument. This position states that observed stability in crime patterns can be explained by the fact that past behavior influences future behavior and shapes events and situational contexts. A third position, known as **cumulative continuity**, states that both population heterogeneity and state dependence can explain stable criminal activity (Laub & Sampson, 2003).

Key Terms and Concepts in Developmental and Life Course Theories

Interactional Theory

Thornberry's (1987) interactional theory is one of the earliest formulations in the DLC program. After examining shortcomings of criminological theories proposed during the 1970s and 1980s, Thornberry claimed that most theories were unidirectional, meaning that variables influenced behavior with no reaction on the part of the actor. Bidirectional or reciprocal effects that account for complex social interactions, such as feedback loops, were ignored or poorly understood. Thornberry (1987) also suggested that most theories were nondevelopmental in the sense that they focused on adolescence at the expense of other key developmental stages that might be important to understanding criminal behavior (e.g., early childhood development, young adulthood, and old age). Finally, he claimed that earlier theories gave little consideration to how a person's location in society influences that person's risk of delinquency.

According to Thornberry (1987), behavior is constantly influenced by social interaction with various groups (e.g., family, peers, and acquaintances). While this may sound similar to social learning theory, interactional theory is actually rooted in control theory. Delinquency and crime result when control is lifted and when the individual is in an interactional setting in which delinquency is learned, performed, and reinforced. This theory posits three primary bonding mechanisms, all derived from Hirschi's (1969) social bonding theory. Under the umbrella of control theory, Thornberry (1987) also incorporates concepts from learning theory to help explain how youth with weak social bonds become involved with crime. For example, if the individual is lacking positive attachments, he or she may become highly attached to delinquent peers.

Thornberry (1987) also connects aspects of Hirschi's (1969) bonding theory to differential association and social learning theory. More specifically, he argues that key concepts from differential association theory, such as delinquent associations and values, have clear parallels to the concepts of involvement and belief offered in Hirschi's (1969) theory. In other words, if a person associates with delinquent peers, the person is "involved" with them in a sense; if a person is exposed to delinquent values, the person's "belief" in delinquent values may increase. Thornberry (1987) also explains the reciprocal effects of these concepts. He claims that while weak social bonds may give rise to delinquent peer associations, these may also help break down bonds to parents and other family members, further freeing up the person for more delinquency in the future. Thornberry further augments his theory by adding developmental and structural dimensions. The developmental aspect of the theory specifies how the model applies to different life stages (e.g., middle and late adolescence), while the structural aspect explains how social location (i.e., age, gender, class, and race) may affect the risks and likelihood of criminal behavior.

Thornberry and Krohn (2001) have proposed an elaboration of this theory containing two important changes. First, life course perspective is more central in this later version as there is a new emphasis on continuity and change in criminal careers. Second, the theory identifies several different patterns of offending. Precocious offenders display antisocial behavior in early childhood (i.e., the first 6 years of life). This type of offending is thought to arise from temperamental traits (e.g., aggressiveness, low self-control) and negative family interactions. Early onset offending occurs from the ages of 6 to 13 and develops as a result of family issues and social structural disadvantages (e.g., social disorganization). The most common pattern takes place after age 13 and is called late onset offending. This type of offending results from the presence of delinquent peers and involves common types of crime committed during one's youth (e.g., petty crimes, drug use, and status offenses).

Think You Get It?

Read the elaborations proposed by Thornberry and Krohn (2001). Can you connect the three patterns they identify to theories and propositions discussed in previous chapters? Make a visual map that identifies patterns, theories, and propositions.

Integrated Cognitive Antisocial Potential Theory

Farrington's (1992) integrated cognitive antisocial potential (ICAP) theory is another important formulation offered by the DLC perspective. The central concept in this theory is the notion of antisocial potential, which assesses the likelihood that a person will become involved with crime. ICAP theory posits that antisocial potential has both long-term and short-term dimensions. **Long-term antisocial potential** refers to factors that help to lay the foundations for a criminal predisposition and set the stage for criminal behavior. Some of these factors include impulsivity, low IQ, lack of empathy, weak conscience, antisocial models, delinquent peers, weak social attachments, and economic problems. These factors should look familiar; they are derived from theories about individual differences, social processes, and structural factors that were covered in previous chapters. This is also a clear example of the influence of the risk-factor paradigm that was discussed previously.

Short-term antisocial potential consists of situational and other factors associated with the immediate physical environment that are thought to be important to understanding crime. This aspect of the ICAP theory focuses on the dynamics of crime and opportunities for crime rather than factors that predispose some people to crime. For example, in order for a crime to take place, an offender not only has to be motivated (by an impulsive personality or delinquent friends or any other element) but also must have an opportunity to commit crime. Opportunity elements in this theory are derived from Cohen and Felson's (1979) routine activities theory, discussed in previous chapters. The decision to commit crime itself is also treated as a variable (e.g., even a highly motivated offender will pass up an opportunity if it will likely result in detection). Decision making is viewed through a cost–benefit model like that used by rational choice theorists (Clarke & Cornish, 1985). Farrington (1992) also attempts to account for mental states and argues that if offenders are intoxicated, angry, bored, or frustrated, they will also be more prone to crime. Figure 15.3 provides an overview of the ICAP theory.

Think You Get It?

Read through the description of the ICAP theory above. Can you connect its short-term and long-term potential to theories from the previous chapters? Make a visual map that identifies elements related to short-term and long-term potential for criminal behavior with other theories discussed in earlier chapters.

The Developmental Taxonomy

Another prominent example of a DLC theory is Moffitt's (1993) developmental taxonomy. This theory can be seen as an attempt to clarify the relationship between age and crime, or what is sometimes called the age–crime curve. As discussed earlier, the age–crime curve refers to the fact that rates of offending peak sharply around the age of 17 and then decline rapidly in young adulthood, with roughly 85% of offenders completely desisting by the age of 28 (Moffitt, 1993).

Moffitt (1993) identifies two categories of offenders in her theory: life-course persistent (LCP) and adolescent-limited (AL) offenders. LCP offenders are much less common, representing only 5% of all offenders. This type of offending emerges in early childhood and continues through adolescence

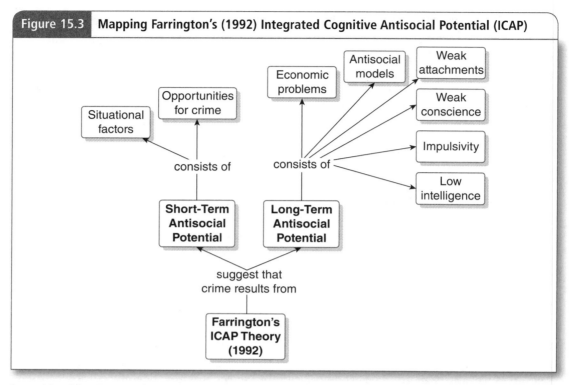

Figure 15.3 | **Mapping Farrington's (1992) Integrated Cognitive Antisocial Potential (ICAP)**

Source: Adapted from Farrington (1992, pp. 253–286).

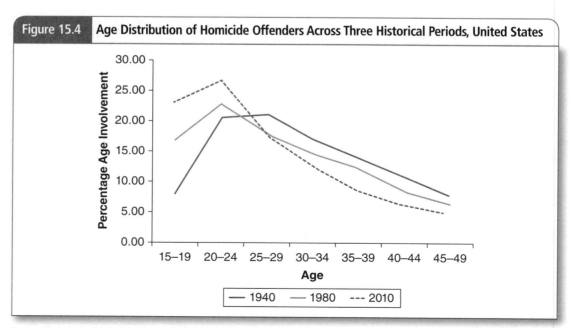

Figure 15.4 | **Age Distribution of Homicide Offenders Across Three Historical Periods, United States**

Source: Ulmer & Steffensmeier (2014, p. 383). Used with permission.

and into adulthood. This persistent antisocial behavior stems from neuropsychological deficits that occur very early in life development and may result from a number of problems, including maternal substance abuse, poor prenatal nutrition, and exposure to toxic agents.

Both verbal and executive functions are disrupted by these neuropsychological deficits, and, according to Moffitt (1993), these types of problems have often been correlated to antisocial behavior. Verbal deficits create problems with reading, writing, expressive speech, and memory; problems in executive functioning often give rise to impulsive behavior and attention deficit problems. To make matters worse, these deficits also create problems with social interaction. Negative interactions with parents, school teachers, and other authority figures may lead to more antisocial behavior because they can erode social bonds and produce negative labeling effects. This mix of problems can put the individual on a life course trajectory in which options for prosocial change become limited, leading to an entrenchment in the criminal lifestyle. This portion of the theory specifies the interactions between traits (i.e., neuropsychological deficits) and the environment (i.e., negative social interactions and labeling) that give rise to criminal behavior.

AL offenders comprise the vast majority of offenders—roughly 95%. Individuals in this category exhibit little to no antisocial behavior in childhood but participate in some crime during adolescence. The initial onset of AL offending is explained by the **maturity gap** that characterizes modern society. According to Moffitt (1993), societal changes occurring in the past century have incrementally delayed activities that were traditionally associated with being a responsible adult (e.g., labor force participation, getting married and having children). Also during this time, dietary and health care shifts helped to lower the age of biological maturity. All of this has served to create what Moffitt (1993) calls a maturity gap.

Moffitt (1993) contends that this maturity gap creates a role vacuum and motivates adolescents to pursue alternative ways to assert their independence. Many of the behaviors of LCP offenders are mimicked because they appear to have the freedom sought by AL offenders. However, many of these desirable behaviors (e.g., underage smoking and drinking, using drugs) are legally prohibited. The crime committed by AL offenders tends to be minor and more socially oriented (e.g., group drug use, vandalism committed with one's friends).

Eventually, AL offenders desist from criminal activity because adult responsibilities (e.g., having a job and family) begin to limit opportunities and motivation for delinquency. Moffitt (1993) is clearly following a life course approach in this portion of the theory as well. Most adolescent offending is viewed as arising from the maturity gap, which is a social structural factor. This is thought to affect the timing of adolescence and also affect the social processes of teenagers. At this point, the proposed interaction between structural, process, and biological elements should be obvious. Figure 15.5 presents one way to visualize Moffitt's theory.

The Age-Graded Theory of Informal Social Control

Sampson and Laub's (1993, 2003) age-graded theory of informal social control is arguably the most influential formulation of the DLC program. In the first version of their theory, Sampson and Laub (1993) introduced a number of concepts originating in the life course perspective (Elder, 1985) into the framework of Hirschi's (1969) theory of social bonding. First, like other advocates of the life course perspective, these theorists emphasized the importance of different interlocking trajectories that are relevant to crime (e.g., family, school, and work) and relevant transitions or life events that are embedded in these trajectories (e.g., getting married, getting a new or better job, having and/or raising a child). These transitions force individuals to reassess their lives and

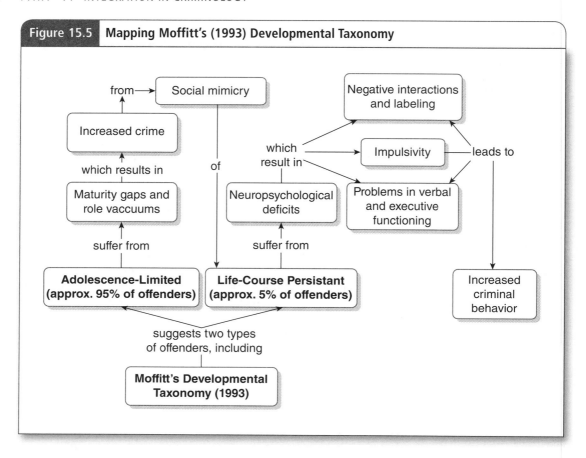

Figure 15.5 | **Mapping Moffitt's (1993) Developmental Taxonomy**

may lead to turning points or substantial changes in one or more of these trajectories (Sampson & Laub, 1993).

These life course concepts readily lend themselves to the control framework within Hirschi's (1969) social bonding theory. For example, a turning point is sometimes caused by an increase in informal social control brought on by the different transitions experienced by an individual; this all can serve to strengthen the connection or bond to society (Sampson & Laub, 1993). Further, the classic institutions of control specified by control theorists (i.e., family and work) correspond to common triggers for turning points in one's life (e.g., marriage, having a child, getting a new job). School attainment and success are also key factors in both control and life course explanations. This theory is essentially an extension of Hirschi's (1969) social bonding theory, inspired by a life course approach.

Sampson and Laub (1993) partition individual difference, social process, and structural variables over the life course. They also consider not only how these variables motivate criminal behavior but how they cause some to desist from criminal behavior. They contend that individual-difference factors are important very early in life but are later mediated by social processes within the family.

As individuals exit childhood and enter early adolescence, school experiences and delinquent peer and sibling attachments become increasingly important. In adulthood, the role of family reemerges with marriage and the experience of becoming of a parent. Work opportunities and responsibilities are also thought to be important in structuring and regulating behavior.

Sampson and Laub have also proposed several extensions of this theory. In their theory of cumulative disadvantage, Sampson and Laub (1997) claim that most forms of labeling theory are developmental in nature and therefore compatible with their framework. They incorporate ideas from Lemert's (1951) principle of secondary deviation and Becker's (1963) notion of master status and argue that efforts to control crime may serve to perpetuate the problem in a few ways. For example, negative labeling can drastically limit opportunities for employment and interpersonal relationships. This creates a situation in which the offender is free to commit more crime because there is little to lose (Laub, Sampson, & Sweeten, 2007). According to Sampson and Laub (1997), these findings prove that the observed stability of criminal behavior is not rooted in one's biological or psychological makeup but rather is, at least in part, maintained by social responses to behavior. In later formulations of the theory, concepts from routine activities theory (Cohen & Felson, 1979) are incorporated to specify how everyday routines can shape criminal behavior (Laub & Sampson, 2003).

Factors derived from individual-difference theories (e.g., self-control and impulsivity) play much less of a role in this theory when compared to Farrington (1992) and Moffitt's (1993) developmental taxonomy. In fact, Sampson and Laub (2005) explicitly caution against theories that claim they can predict future criminal behavior on the basis of early childhood characteristics. The authors seem to imply that criminologists should focus on uncovering important processes involved with criminal behavior and how these interact with structural factors:

> The challenge is that random processes and human agency are ever-present realities, making prediction once again problematic. It further follows that long-term patterns of offending among high-risk populations cannot be divined by individual differences (for example, low verbal IQ, temperament), childhood characteristics (for example, early onset of misbehavior), or even adolescent characteristics (for example, juvenile offending). . . . To more process-oriented, non-reductionist, and generalized accounts of within-individual change, the field of life course criminology might therefore profitably turn. (Sampson & Laub, 2005, pp. 178–180)

Finally, in the most recent formulation of their age-graded theory, Laub and Sampson (2003) emphasize the importance of human agency and introduce a new related concept called **situated choice**. In this view, behavior cannot be predicted or explained by focusing solely on structural factors or individual differences. Instead, we must focus on understanding the interaction between these forces and how this influences choices that people make. Figure 15.6 provides an overview of the age-graded theory.

Situational Action Theory

Wikstrom's (2004) situational action theory is a relatively new, but promising, formulation that has grown out of the DLC tradition. Like Farrington (1992) and Sampson and Laub (1993), Wikstrom identifies a variety of factors from theories that explain both criminal acts (e.g., routine activities and

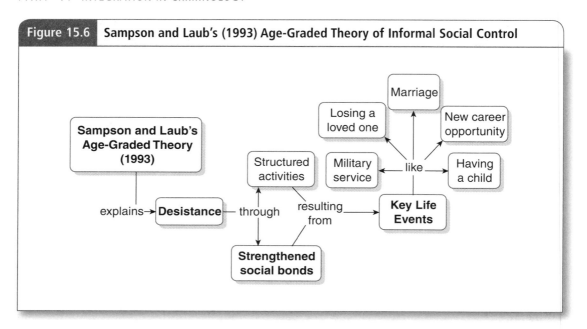

Figure 15.6   **Sampson and Laub's (1993) Age-Graded Theory of Informal Social Control**

rational choice) and criminal behavior (e.g., strain, control, and learning). He then considers how the factors from the different theories fit within different levels of explanation and explains how they relate to each other. This theory is explicitly developmental in nature because it stresses the importance of different variables at different points in the life course and attempts to account for changes in behavior.

Wikstrom's (2004) goal is to identify the underlying mechanisms or processes that explain how factors influence outcomes. He begins by identifying four different levels of explanation, including individual, situational, settings-based, and social mechanisms. After this, he describes the various relevant mechanisms on each level and how they interact with one another. There are two basic individual mechanisms that are thought to determine one's criminal propensity; these are derived, in part, from individual difference theories. The first component is **self-control**; this is slightly different from Gottfredson and Hirschi's (1990) theory of self-control, however. In this theory, self-control refers to a person's ability to make choices in line with his or her moral convictions when presented with temptations or provocations (Wikstrom, 2004). In this view, self-control is inherently linked with executive functioning; this is not surprising considering that executive function is associated with impulse control. So this theory also attempts to account for biological aspects of control.

Morality is the second aspect of criminal propensity. According to Wikstrom (2004), morality is an "*evaluative function of events in the world based on values about what is right and wrong to do (moral values)*" (p. 15, italics in original). He states that this evaluative function includes not only a person's beliefs about right and wrong but also his or her level of commitment to doing the right thing and the level of shame suffered if the right thing is not done. Morals are learned through a combination of socialization, social learning, and observation as well as through key life events (e.g., getting married and having children).

Wikstrom (2004) states that situational-level mechanisms influence how people make choices and perceive alternatives in their environment. These are two key situational mechanisms that link mechanisms on the individual and settings-based levels. Essentially, when an individual encounters a setting, this creates a situation that causes a person to perceive and evaluate choices in the environment. The situation is a product of interaction between the individual mechanisms of self-control, morality, and the settings-based mechanisms described below.

Settings-based mechanisms include temptations, provocations, and deterrence. **Temptations** arise when one encounters opportunities for crime in the environment and may motivate criminal behavior. **Provocations** result from actions that are perceived as attacks on an individual's security, property, or self-respect; they may generate anger or other emotional responses that result in crime. Both temptations and provocations influence the perception of alternative behaviors in one's environment. Based on these two ideas, **deterrence** is defined as "*the perceived risk of intervention (and associated risk of sanction) if acting unlawfully in pursuing a temptation or responding to a provocation*" (Wikstrom, 2004, p. 21, italics in original). The process of choice is shaped by one's perception of deterrence and monitoring. Distribution of settings-based mechanisms is determined by wider social mechanisms.

Social mechanisms refer to systemic factors arising from organizational and structural qualities in one's wider social environment. Wikstrom (2004) identifies **rules**, **resources**, and **routines** as three key social mechanisms that affect crime. Systemic factors, such as segregation and inequality, arise from social norms (or rules) and affect access to resources and people's everyday routines. These shape the presence of temptations, provocations, and deterrence in various ways, which affects how people make choices and perceive alternatives to crime in their environment. This theory is presented in Figure 15.7.

Research on Developmental and Life Course Theories

When discussing research in this area, a useful place to start is Wolfgang, Figlio, and Sellin's (1972) research on chronic offenders. This study examined and analyzed official records to follow the criminal activity of a group of young males from Philadelphia born in 1945. They found that 6% of the juveniles accounted for 50% of all contacts with the police, suggesting the existence of a small group of chronic and prolific offenders (Wolfgang, Figlio, & Sellin, 1972). Based on these findings, the NRCPCC attempted to develop a more consistent terminology to use when studying criminal careers. Specifically, they examined participation in crime by frequency (or lambda) and prevalence (or the fraction of people in a group who committed crime). They also stressed the importance of measuring the onset and duration of crime as well as desistance from crime (Blumstein et al., 1986).

During the early 1970s, researchers launched the Dunedin Study, another key development in this area. This study consisted of longitudinal investigation of both health and behavior based on a cohort of 1,037 children from a mix of social classes on New Zealand's South Island. Moffitt and her associates (Moffitt, Caspi, Harrington, & Milne, 2002) took 79 measures "selected to represent five domains of adult outcome implicated by the theory" (p. 182). The domains included criminal offending (i.e., property crimes, rule violations, drug crimes, and violence); personality; psychopathology (i.e., substance abuse and mental disorders); personal life (i.e., relationships with women and children); and economic life (i.e., education, occupation, income, unemployment, and work problems). These domains were measured through personal interviews and official records or questionnaires completed by informants who were acquainted with the study members.

| Figure 15.7 | **Wikstrom's (2004) Situational Action Theory** |

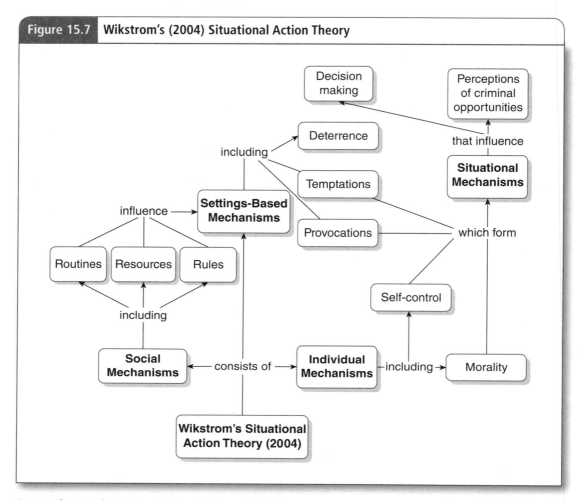

Source: Author created with information from Wikstrom, P-O. (2004).

Moffitt and her colleagues used this data to test her developmental theory. They were also able to elaborate upon her theory by further specifying characteristics of "abstainers." In addition, they were able to refine a category of "recoveries" proposed in earlier research. Recoveries are those who exhibited serious behavioral problems and antisocial behavior early in life but then seemed to reform during adolescence and young adulthood. They concluded that their findings not only support the theory of life-course-persistent and adolescence-limited antisocial behavior but also extend these categories. The findings recommend intervention with all aggressive children and with all delinquent adolescents to prevent a variety of maladjustments in adult life.

The Office of Juvenile Justice and Delinquency Prevention's Program of Research on the Causes and Correlates of Delinquency funded the Rochester Youth Development Study in 1986. This longitudinal research focused on adolescent delinquency and drug use in Rochester, New

York. Over the years it expanded to examine prosocial and antisocial development across the life course. The study was guided, in part, by Thornberry's (1987) interactional theory and has been used to revise and expand the theory based on a sample that consisted of 1,000 students in the 7th and 8th grades and their primary caretakers. Males and those living in high-arrest areas were oversampled because they were assumed to be at a greater risk for offending. Multiple measures of the same variables were taken over time; variables measured included rates of delinquency, parent–child relations, school factors, peer relationships, family socio-demographic characteristics, parental stressors, area characteristics, and individual characteristics. Data for the measures were obtained through a combination of interviews, official statistics, school and social service records, and census data.

The Cambridge Study was started in 1961 by psychiatrist Donald J. West. In 1983, Farrington assumed directorship of the study and it is still ongoing (Farrington, 2003). The study is a longitudinal survey of the development of antisocial and criminal behavior in 411 South London working-class boys born in the early 1950s. The findings of the study have lent support to the criminal career perspective. Farrington (2003) was also able to identify some key risk factors involved in offending and suggests that, in many cases, criminal offending is "part of a larger syndrome of antisocial behavior that tends to persist over time" (p. 155). Finally, researchers have also been able to investigate the importance of life events in one's criminal trajectory. Variables for Farrington's (1992) ICAP theory were derived from early findings of the Cambridge Study. Subsequent findings from the study have also provided support for the theory.

Practical Ramifications of Developmental and Life Course Theories

The DLC theories offer a number of practical solutions and advice to several different areas of the criminal justice system. First, like the integrative and general theories discussed in Chapter 13, DLC theories often recommend programs and early intervention intended to help prevent and control crime (Lilly et al., 2011). These programs might target parenting skills or anger management, or they may be after-school programs targeted at keeping youth off the streets (Tremblay et al., 1992; Laub & Sampson, 2003).

Second, many DLC theorists advocate a risk factor approach, implying that they would support using some risk prediction instruments in the criminal justice system. However, it is important to keep in mind that support for such measures varies among DLC theorists, and some express concerns about overuse of predictive instruments (c.f. Laub & Sampson, 2003). Third, based on the connection to the criminal career paradigm, one might also assume that some DLC theorists would embrace a correctional strategy stressing selective incapacitation. In other words, many DLC theorists suggest that we try to identify and imprison individuals who demonstrate a propensity for chronic offending. However, many warn that such an approach is fraught with difficulties and that it might be better to focus on prevention rather than incapacitation (Laub & Sampson, 2003).

Criticisms of Developmental and Life Course Theories

Critics have identified a number of problems with DLC theories. Gottfredson and Hirschi (1995) have observed that the cross-sectional research used by traditional theories produces the same findings about correlates of crime as the longitudinal research used by DLC theories. Given that longitudinal

Figure 15.8	Seven Steps of Developmental and Life Course Theories
Seven Steps	**Developmental-Life Course Theories**
1. Know the History	Emerged in the 1990s alongside integrated theories; heavily influenced by the risk factor/prevention paradigm, life course perspective, criminal career paradigm, and developmental criminology
2. Acknowledge Assumptions	Humans are both influenced by and interact with their environments (i.e., complex "blank slate"); soft determinist approach; consensus view of society and the law
3. Problem Focus, Scope, and Level of Explanation	Focus is on explaining individual criminal behavior; examine within-individual changes rather than between-individual differences; incorporate individual differences and address both process and structural factors associated with criminal behavior
4. Key Terms and Concepts	Reciprocal causality, short-term/long-term antisocial potential, neuropsychological deficits, maturity gap, adolescent-limited and life-course-persistent offending, trajectory, transition, turning points, desistance, cumulative disadvantage, situated choice, individual/settings-based/social mechanisms, temptations/provocations
5. Respect the Research	Preference for longitudinal over cross-sectional research; large-scale and multifaceted studies that examine changes in offending behavior over time
6. Theory/Practice	Early intervention intended to help prevent and control crime; use of risk prediction instruments; selective incapacitation for serious offenders
7. Mapping the Theory	See Figure 15.9

research is difficult, costly, and time consuming, many believe such research is not required. According to Gottfredson and Hirschi (1995), the causes for crime do not vary with age.

A great deal of criticism of these theories has actually come from internal sources or other DLC theorists. For example, certain DLC theories are accused of being overly committed to the risk factor approach (Caspi et al., 2002; Laub & Sampson, 2003; Wikstrom, 2007). It is also important to note that the risk factor approach has served to justify the use of risk prediction devices in the criminal justice system in the areas of corrections and parole (Feeley & Simon, 1996). Other related approaches, such as the criminal career paradigm, have contributed to an overreliance on simplistic punitive solutions to crime, such as selective incapacitation of chronic offenders.

Another problem is that these theories are very difficult to test. In the past, longitudinal data was hard to come by, expensive, and time consuming. In addition, concepts such as reciprocal and bidirectional causation and situated choice are difficult to measure. These theories also give little consideration to the formation of the criminal law and the activities of the criminal justice system. This emphasis on explaining criminal behavior has provided advantages and methodological nuance. Many research

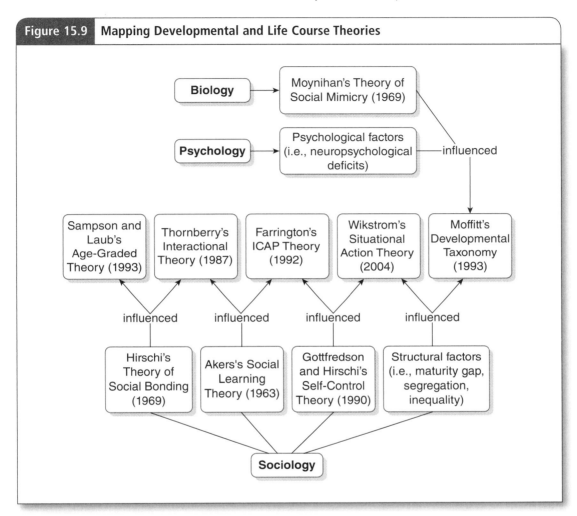

Figure 15.9 Mapping Developmental and Life Course Theories

findings in this area have been important. Some, such as the age–grade curve, are incontrovertible. However, the application of these findings to the criminal justice system would benefit from a more detailed analysis of how findings are implemented. It may be that DLC theorists can best advance theory and practice by considering broader structural, organizational, and practical issues in the operation of criminal justice systems.

Finally, while DLC theories have contributed a great deal to our understanding about within-individual change in offenders, they have not been successful in clarifying relationships between different levels of explanations in criminology. A central tension still exists in this area between more socially oriented theories, such as Sampson and Laub's (1993; Laub & Sampson, 2004) age-graded theory, and theories that emphasize individual differences, such as Moffitt's (1993) developmental taxonomy.

Research Example: Crime and the Life Course

Sampson and Laub's (1993, 2003) studies of crime and desistance are some of the most extensive and important examples of research in the history of criminology. This research started with the multilevel study of Sheldon and Eleanor Glueck that was briefly discussed in Chapter 3. This husband and wife duo started a multifactor research study of juvenile delinquents in 1939. Over the next decade, they interviewed 500 delinquent and nondelinquent boys from the Boston area. The researchers collected data at three points over the life course and examined physical, biological, psychological, and social factors related to criminal behavior. The Gluecks examined body types and took physical measurements of the delinquents. In addition, they did self-report interviews and talked to the delinquent boys' parents and teachers about their behavior. They also examined factors related to the family and socioeconomic status in their study. Their findings were published in 1950.

The first wave of research from Sampson and Laub (1993) was not without its critics. Foremost among these was that they had treated their research subjects as microscopic quantitative tests of hypotheses generated by their age-graded theory. They were also charged with ignoring the inner logic of the lives of offenders (Laub & Sampson, 2003). To address these concerns, Laub and Sampson (2003) embarked on another phase of research, this time embracing a mixed-methods approach. They retained an emphasis on quantitative methods but at the same time introduced a qualitative interviewing technique called life history narratives. Life history narratives are essentially detailed and extended interviews. This required tracking down some of the subjects from the original Glueck study to reinterview them. The researchers managed to find 52 of the original men, who at this point were in their 70s. These men had not been reinterviewed in nearly 40 years!

Laub and Sampson (2003) were able to gather data over a period of almost 70 years—a research design normally associated with large-scale medical studies. This allowed them to examine a number of concepts that were virtually unexplored in criminology. First, they were able to clarify how criminal behavior is maintained in one's later years. Most studies in criminology focus on juvenile delinquency and younger subjects in their 20s, possibly 30s. Very few examine subjects older than this outside of a correctional context. Second, they were able to examine why some offenders desisted and some did not. As predicted in their theory, structured routines (e.g., work, parenting responsibilities) helped many of the men desist. Crime was maintained through a lack of attachments that often resulted from marital disputes. In many of the cases, drinking also played a large role in poorly thought-out, impulsive criminal behavior.

Particularly important were the implications for predicting crime based on early childhood characteristics and past criminal behavior. Developmental psychologists in particular have been supportive of using devices to predict future criminality based on these factors. However, Laub and Sampson's (2003) data indicated that these approaches are fraught with difficulties. They contend that these approaches all fail to account for the power of human agency: Even the most hardened offenders, no matter what their characteristics, can decide at any moment that they will reform. The predictions of psychologists are only applicable on a macro level and cannot currently predict individual behavior accurately (Laub & Sampson, 2003).

To illustrate this inability to predict individual events, consider the act of rolling dice. If you were to roll a set of two six-sided dice 1,000 times, any good statistician could provide a fairly accurate estimate of how many times you would roll snake eyes (i.e., a one on each die). However, if you only roll 100 times, the accuracy of that estimate would be reduced. Once we get down to trying to predict a single roll of the dice, we can no longer make any accurate predictions because it is random event.

To relate this back to crime, think of it this way: Based on some psychological trait or construct, we can predict with reasonable accuracy how many people out of 1,000 will reoffend, but we cannot accurately predict the specific individuals that will reoffend.

Now that you've read this chapter . . . consider research by Nahanni Pollard (2011), who examined sentencing for those identified as chronic offenders. Pollard argues that when sentencing is focused on just deserts, or retribution is based on the gravity of the offense, sentences may not properly consider the length of an individual's criminal record. While many doubt the rehabilitative value of prison, it can serve to selectively incapacitate some offenders and may reduce crime, at least in the short term. This may be especially important for chronic offenders who have committed multiple crimes at numerous points in their lives. What, then, is the point of a prison sentence, theoretically speaking? Many are rethinking the purpose of sentencing, given what appears to be the failure of an overemphasis on retribution. This means finding ways to tailor sentences and ensure that youth who are likely to age out of crime anyway are not sentenced to decades in prison at taxpayer expense. While understanding how youth are more likely to become chronic offenders offers the best means to reduce crime, policymakers must also consider how research can inform sanctions. Smart sentencing means considering the type, nature, and frequency of offending. It means ensuring sentences don't do more harm than good.

Conclusion and Review Questions

In this chapter, we focused on developmental and life course theories. These theories help explain when and why some people desist or stop committing crime. As opposed to cross-sectional research, which looks at differences between groups at one point in time, longitudinal research looks at differences within the same group over a period of time. As a result, we now know most kinds of crime are likely to be committed by individuals during their teenage years. This activity peaks in the early-to-late teen years and then drops off significantly. In general, these theories consider how chronological age, common life transitions, and social change shape people's lives from birth to death. They provide a means to understand when most people are most likely stop committing crime and what approaches are effective to reduce recidivism.

CHAPTER REVIEW

1. How did longitudinal research lead to the development of DLC theories?

2. Explain the age–crime curve and what it suggests about patterns of offending.

3. What are some of the assumptions made by DLC theories, and what kind of crimes do these theories attempt to explain?

4. Describe some practical approaches and programs suggested by DLC theories.

5. What are some of the critiques leveled against DLC theories?

C H A P T E R

16

Conclusion

 ## Chapter Overview

In this book, we have provided what we hope is a comprehensive yet accessible review of the many theories in criminology. By organizing these theories using our seven-step approach, we have shown the similarities and differences between the history and assumptions of these theories and the kinds of criminological problems they attempt to explain. We have also examined how research on these theories depends on specifying the terms and concepts in each theory and applying them through different kinds of research designs. However, as has been suggested, the application of criminological theories depends on more than empirical research. Theories and approaches are more likely to be adopted when they offer a complete view of crime and especially when they offer clear, practical suggestions for agencies, communities, and individuals who work in criminal justice and related fields.

Today, rational choice, biosocial, and developmental and life course theories continue to be popular. In addition, in the past decade, several cross-level and cross-disciplinary approaches have emerged in the field of criminology; these approaches build on the integrated approach to theorizing. They also draw upon a combination of many of the theories reviewed in this textbook, and so it seems appropriate to review them in the concluding chapter. Figure 16.1 provides an overview of these new approaches.

 ## New Directions in Criminological Theory

Integrated Systems Theory and Criminology

Robinson and Beaver's (2008) integrated systems theory is a cross-level integrated theory of criminal behavior. The basis for this theory is Vila's (1994) evolutionary-ecological paradigm, which suggests that a variety of ecological, micro-level, and macro-level factors determine the likelihood of criminal behavior. He also argues that humans are "self-reinforcing systems" and that once they get set on a path of criminal behavior it may become part of their **strategic style**. Robinson and Beaver (2008) liken strategic style to the concept of criminal personality.

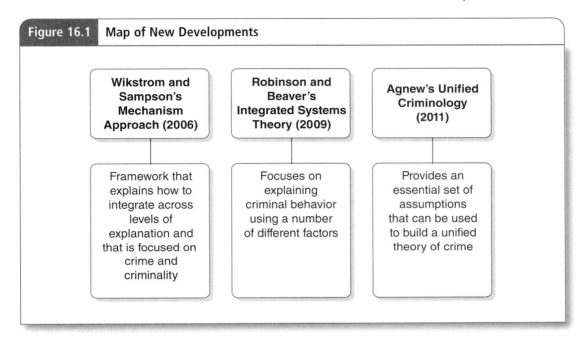

Figure 16.1   Map of New Developments

Wikstrom and Sampson's Mechanism Approach (2006)	Robinson and Beaver's Integrated Systems Theory (2009)	Agnew's Unified Criminology (2011)
Framework that explains how to integrate across levels of explanation and that is focused on crime and criminality	Focuses on explaining criminal behavior using a number of different factors	Provides an essential set of assumptions that can be used to build a unified theory of crime

This theory attempts to explain the formation of a criminal personality by using a number of different factors. It also incorporates ideas from systems theory perspective as the framework for a theory of criminal behavior. Systems theory is an interdisciplinary and integrative approach that attempts to connect findings from numerous disciplines and fields of study. This perspective identifies six levels of analysis: cell, organ, organism, group, organization, and community/society. Each level represents an individual system, but all of the systems interact with and influence their neighboring systems. At this point, Robinson and Beaver (2008) group different variables and factors into the different levels of explanation.

The most basic levels incorporate biological and psychological factors. For example, at the cell level we would examine the impact that genes can have on criminal behavior; the organism level would focus on neuroscientific factors associated with brain function and neurotransmitter levels. To carry the example further, the organism level would look at the formation of personality and how this affects the choices we make about diet and nutrition and drug consumption (gene–environment interactions). Social and environmental factors are located at the higher levels of explanation. Group-level variables include factors derived from social learning and social control theories, while community-level variables are drawn out of disorganization, routine activities, and lifestyle theory, which focus on how certain areas and neighborhoods produce high levels of crime. Labeling and deterrence theory also contribute to community-level factors associated with crime. Finally, larger societal-level variables are derived from more macro theories, such as strain and culture conflict theories.

A Systemic Approach to Criminological Theorizing

In recent years, several criminologists have argued that the field has become stuck in the risk factor mode (Caspi & Moffitt, 2006). In other words, the embrace of the risk factor approach in theory-building has hampered the emergence of fresh, new, and innovative ideas in criminology. Others have questioned the logic of this approach and contend that many risk factors are nothing more than spurious correlations (Wikstrom, 2006). In order to address these problems, Wikstrom and Sampson (2006) have proposed using a systemic approach developed by physicist and social scientist Mario Bunge (2004). This approach identifies a new conceptual framework for criminology that consists of three interrelated concepts: mechanisms, context, and development. The goal of this approach is to identify key mechanisms that produce high levels of crime (in places) and criminal behavior (in people). These mechanisms may be socially, developmentally, or biologically based, and they must be specific and precise.

This mechanistic approach consolidates key insights from a diverse group of criminologists and other social scientists with a specific emphasis on integrating criminological knowledge. Although different disciplines, theories, and methodological approaches contribute to the understanding of crime, the uncoordinated accumulation of ideas confuses and does not assist in the process of theory integration. For example, some traditions in criminology search for the probabilistic causes of crime in characteristics of individuals, while other traditions investigate how social contexts are criminogenic. Wikstrom and Sampson (2006) argue that simplifying different approaches into coherent theories of crime causation would result in better explanations based on the integration of existing approaches that have found support.

This approach is organized around three components to facilitate the integration of criminological knowledge: (1) how social context can be criminogenic, (2) how risk factors influence the individual development of criminal behavior, and (3) mechanisms by which social context and individual development interact to explain crime. **Context** refers to structural, cultural, and situational factors that may be related to crime. This portion of the framework incorporates ideas and variables from macro-level structural theories, such as social disorganization, social strain, and routine activities theory. One may derive underlying social mechanisms from these theories that set the conditions for crime (Sampson, 2006). **Development** consists of developmental and individual-difference factors that may cause a person to commit crime. In this case, biological and psychological characteristics discussed in early chapters may be important, and particular attention is paid to within-individual changes in accordance with the tenets of the developmental and life course theories. **Mechanisms** explain exactly how variables associated with context and individual development interact with each other (Wikstrom & Sampson, 2006).

The ultimate goal of this approach is to better identify causal factors that might lead to high crime rates or high levels of individual criminality. Wikstrom and Sampson (2006), like Robinson and Beaver (2008), hope to specify how different mechanisms from different levels of explanation interact with and influence each other. For example, how can one's environment influence development and produce characteristics that might give rise to high levels of criminality?

Is a Unified Approach to Criminology Possible?

Another important development in modern criminology can be found in Agnew's (2011) *Toward a Unified Criminology*. According to Agnew (2011), many of the base assumptions that criminological theories are based upon are poorly understood and unclear. This should come as no surprise; very few criminologists consider the underlying foundations on which they build their theories. Agnew claims that this has contributed to disharmony in the field and a lack of progress in criminological theorizing. He also contends that most theorists often fail to incorporate modern findings that might be important and relevant to debates that criminologists have about how to define crime, free will and determinism, and the nature of human nature.

Agnew (2011) suggests that a reexamination of assumptions in the field of criminology is in order. He provides some illustrations of how to do this by reviewing a number of recent studies from various disciplines and fields, including biology, psychology, anthropology, and political science. Based on this review, he was able to make suggestions about the scope and problem foci of criminology. According to Agnew (2011), criminologists ought to use a definition of crime that goes beyond simple legal definitions dictated by the criminal justice system and that offers an integrated definition of crime. He says that crime can be defined as acts that cause blameworthy harm, are condemned by the public, and/or are sanctioned by the state.

The hope is that considering these three aspects will cause criminologists to view certain acts in a different light. For example, victimless crimes often cause questionable amounts of harm and yet are often not universally condemned in society. This is complicated by the fact that in some cases these activities are also sanctioned by the state. For example, prostitution is legal in some rural areas of Nevada but not in any other US states. Are people who visit prostitutes in Nevada considered criminals? In some cases of minor drug use, the only crime committed by the individual is the drug use itself. To put it differently, if we consider the fact that the only crime most marijuana users commit is smoking marijuana, it is unclear how studying their behavior will tell us something about crime more generally (Shafer Commission, 1972). Further, the states of Colorado and Washington have both legalized marijuana; this, however, conflicts with federal law prohibiting marijuana. How can we understand criminality in these situations? How should we classify tourists who visit those states and use marijuana? This implies that some acts that are considered criminal may be less important to understanding general criminal behavior because many individuals involved in these behaviors do not commit other types of crime. This also has ramifications for acts that are not considered crimes but that still may cause massive amounts of harm to society. Consider the numerous white-collar and corporate behaviors that are not defined as crimes. What good are theories of crime that omit blameworthy, harmful acts that are condemned by the public?

Agnew (2011) also offers reformulations of several base assumptions in criminology. First, he specifies situations and factors that influence the use of free will and suggests that criminologists view human behavior in terms of bounded agency. This is a more refined version of the soft determinism that many modern theories (e.g., rational choice theory) rely upon. Second, he suggests that criminologists abandon looking at society in either purely consensus or conflict-oriented terms. Instead, he encourages criminologists to further examine the extent and nature of conflicts in society and the different groups whose values give rise to consensus and conflict. Third, he argues that while people often do exhibit high levels of self-interest, they also demonstrate high levels of social concern, especially for members of their intimate groups.

The assumptions offered here are viewed as integrated in nature. Further, Agnew (2011) speculates that both mainstream and critical criminologists will see some value in them since insights from each side have been taken into account. He does not attempt to produce a full-blown integrated theory of crime and criminal behavior, and he cautions that such an endeavor will be a long-term task that will require a great deal of further research to ensure a solid foundation for the theory. Figure 16.2 provides a more detailed overview of contemporary criminological theories.

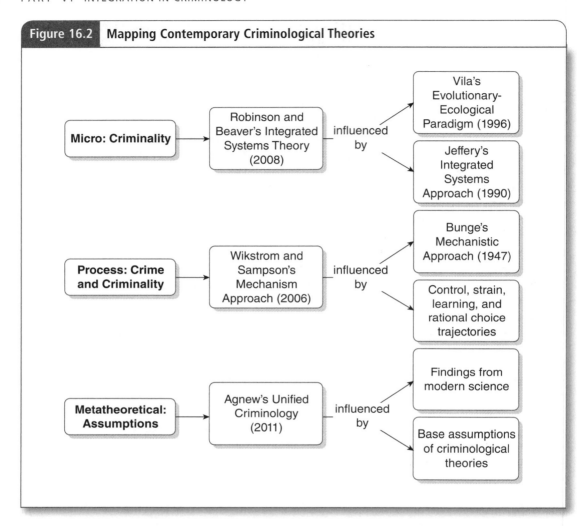

Figure 16.2 | **Mapping Contemporary Criminological Theories**

Toward an Analysis of Criminological Theories

What is the state of contemporary criminological theory? Several criminologists have recently suggested that theory development is lacking or even nonexistent in the field (Laub, 2004; Weisburd & Piquero, 2008; Young, 2011). This is surprising given the number of raw materials that criminologists have to work with—the field is interdisciplinary, drawing from several different disciplines and fields. Others have argued that criminological theory cannot progress until it integrates the understanding that, first and foremost, we are biological organisms and there is the potential that extreme experiences can at least temporarily engrave themselves in our neurological systems, complicating both free will assumptions and belief in the power of society to shape individual behavior. In this view, biosocial criminology must move beyond previous formulations in which "conservative bio-criminologists naturalize vices and culturalize virtues, [while] left-liberal immaterialists culturalize vices and naturalize virtues" (Hall, 2012, p. 253). New theories and formulations of older theories must take neither for granted.

We argue that it is important to analyze theories for a number of different reasons. First, it allows us to understand where theories originate and how they develop over time. Second, it can help clarify the logic behind various criminal justice system practices. Most policies and programs have some sort of theoretical justification either attached to them or that could be attached to them. Third, it helps us create new theories; we can't break new ground without knowing what we have already covered and how we have done so. In recent work, we have proposed three approaches to supplement existing efforts to make criminological theory more accessible, more integrated, and more accountable (Wheeldon, Heidt, & Dooley, 2014).

The first approach taps into the rising interest in visual tools and techniques in criminology (Carrabine, 2012; Lippens & Hardie-Bick, 2013; Sampson et al., 2013). This includes the role of documentary photography to explore punishment, art as a process to understand and experience criminological theorizing phenomenologically, and policy graphs to integrate the theoretical and policy arms of criminology to advance policy translation. Indeed, this book is a part of a broader effort to make better and more nuanced use of visual tools and techniques for the presentation and consideration of data on crime, social control, and public policy. Our focus on criminological theory and the seven steps of criminological theory builds on numerous past efforts to describe data, tell stories, and present information (Wheeldon, 2010b; Heidt, 2008; Harris, 2013; Maltz, 2009; Sampson et al., 2013; Wheeldon, 2011a, 2011b, 2013).

Our effort is based on the assumption that visualization will play an increasingly important role in the social sciences generally and in criminology more specifically. The ubiquity of small, high-powered computing power is already allowing this to occur through tools such as data visualization and infographics. As people increasingly engage visually with phones, tablets, computers, and various forms of entertainment and social media, the expectations about and potential for visual techniques are likely to grow. We believe that visual criminology can best be harnessed to serve future goals for students, researchers, practitioners, and policymakers if existing approaches are organized and key assumptions outlined in criminological theory. This book is one effort toward this larger goal.

The second approach we propose is the view that criminology must move beyond the "method wars," in which some criminologists fervently adhere to either quantitative or qualitative methods to the exclusion of the other. We agree with Agnew, who calls for mixed methods as part of a détente in the method wars:

> The multiple perspectives approach (MPA) therefore draws on both the positivistic and constructionist approaches, incorporating the advantages of each. Drawing on the positivistic approach, it assumes that there is an objective reality. That is, people really do possess certain characteristics, live in certain types of environments, and have certain experiences. Or, in the words of Pinker (2002: 203), "the world really does contain ducks, who really do share properties." And while it may not be possible to measure this reality in a way free of all biases, it is possible to construct reduced-bias measures of it. Drawing on the constructionist approach, it argues that the subjective views of respondents are also important. While such views are affected by a wide range of factors beyond objective reality, they nevertheless guide behavior. So they too affect outcome variables, even after reduced-bias measures of reality are taken into account. (2011, p. 181)

In this book, we have highlighted important mixed-methods research and tried to ensure one methodological orientation has not overwhelmed the others. While quantitative methods remain primary in criminology, there are important voices suggesting a more pragmatic approach. Some "truths" may in fact exist. Pragmatism, however, is far more interested in determining how to ground the various postmodern, antifoundationalist critiques into practical goals. Those interested in pragmatism are suspicious of claims about universal or generalizable truths from which to uniformly proceed. Perhaps criminology can embrace integration by moving beyond efforts to discover one universal truth and instead apply the idea that the solutions to the problems of society require that multiple descriptions of the world be leveraged to focus on real-world problem solving (Rorty, 1998). Rorty's view may have profound implications for criminology (Wheeldon, 2014).

A third approach considers the potential for debate and dialogue as a means to move beyond the stubborn adherence to one set of assumptions about human nature or one approach to data collection and analysis. To answer the call for more practical theorizing and reflexive criminology, we suggest expertise be reconsidered. Instead of allowing scholarship (and scholars) to simply promote one preferred view over all others, true criminological expertise should require weighing and balancing some of the key theories and practices described in this text. Expertise might be best seen as the quality of the debate it sets out. By presenting two competing views, experts are those who don't advocate per se, but who instead organize existing scholarship into credible and accessible arguments based on the needs, interests, and inclinations of the stakeholders involved (Wheeldon et al., 2014, pp. 123–124).

This view may offer a way out of entrenchment in one theoretical, methodological, or professional perspective. It can be applied whatever one's opinion and integrated into the work of students and researchers in a variety of settings (Wheeldon, Chavez, & Cooke, 2013). Expertise should be re-imagined and assessed based on the extent to which individuals take personal responsibility for acknowledging themselves in the research process. This includes considering how interests, interactions, and beliefs may shape and influence specific research decisions (Guba & Lincoln, 1989). We believe that adopting a common means to debate, discuss, and respectfully consider core criminological questions could promote a better quality of criminological conversation.

Together, these three approaches can promote greater accountability. Ensuring that underlying theoretical assumptions are acknowledged, theories are tested based on their stated propositions, and theories are implemented in ways that are cognizant of the historical context in which they arose can allow criminological theory to better inform criminal justice policymaking. Likewise, by ensuring the testing of theories is attempted in ways that consider the value of numeric and narrative data-gathering and analysis, criminologists can avoid myopic either/or conceptions of what good research requires. Finally, science works best when those who contribute do so in modest ways, aware that all results are tentative and all inferences shaped by those who make them. By identifying the strengths and weaknesses within various criminological policies, programs, or practices, we can model a process of more constructive reflection. This can assist students, researchers, and practitioners alike.

Conclusion and Review Questions

In this book, we have reviewed the major theories in criminology. All of these theories are still being used, tested, and reformulated in some capacity by modern criminologists. In order to clearly understand theories, it is not only important to be familiar with their central argument and key concepts but also with their underlying assumptions, scope, level of explanation, problem focus, and relationships with other theories. It is also important to understand the research supporting these theories and the research that these theories have stimulated. Perhaps most important is cultivating in students the ability to theorize and think independently. This can only be done by encouraging people to think critically about criminological theories and the practices employed by criminal justice systems. Ideas matter, and they shape everything around us.

CHAPTER REVIEW

1. Briefly summarize the three approaches to making criminological theories more accessible, integrated, and accountable.

2. Where did the approaches discussed in this chapter originate? How are they similar and what are the differences between them?

3. Why is the analysis and study of theories so important in criminology and criminal justice? List three major ways analyzing and studying theories can help criminologists better understand crime.

References

Abrahamsen, D. (1944). *Crime and the human mind*. New York, NY: Columbia University Press.

Abrahamsen, D. (1960). *The psychology of crime*. New York, NY: Columbia University Press.

Adler, A. (1927). *Understanding human nature*. New York, NY: Greenberg.

Adler, F. (1975). *Sisters in crime: The rise of the new female criminal*. New York, NY: McGraw-Hill.

Adler, P. A., & Adler, P. (1987). *Membership roles in field research*. Newbury Park, CA: Sage.

Adams, J. T. (1931). *The epic of America*. Boston, MA: Little, Brown, and Co.

Agency for Toxic Substances and Disease Registry. (2010). *Case studies in environmental medicine: Lead toxicity*. Washington, DC: U.S. Department of Health and Human Services. Retrieved from http://www.atsdr.cdc.gov/csem/lead/docs/lead.pdf

Agnew, R. (1991). A longitudinal test of social control theory and delinquency. *Journal of Research in Crime and Delinquency, 28*(2), 126–156.

Agnew, R. (1992). Foundation for a general strain theory of crime and delinquency. *Criminology, 30,* 47–87.

Agnew, R. (1995). Determinism, indeterminism, and crime: An empirical exploration. *Criminology, 30,* 83–109.

Agnew, R. (2001). Building on the foundation of general strain theory. *Journal of Research in Crime and Delinquency, 38*(4), 319–361.

Agnew, R. (2005). *Why do criminals offend? A general theory of crime and delinquency*. Boston, MA: Oxford University Press.

Agnew, R. (2006). *Pressured into crime*. Boston, MA: Oxford University Press.

Agnew, R. (2011). *Toward a unified criminology*. New York, NY: New York University Press.

Aharoni, E., Vincent, G., Harenski, C., Calhoun, V., Sinnott-Armstrong, W., Gazzaniga, M., & Kiehl, K. (2013). Neuroprediction of future rearrest. *Proceedings of the National Academy of Sciences, 110*(15), 6223–6228.

Aichhorn, A. (1925). *Wayward youth*. New York, NY: Viking Press.

Aichhorn, A. (1978). *Delinquency and child guidance*. New York, NY: International Universities Press.

Ainsworth, M., Blehar, M., Waters, E., & Wall, S. (1978). *Patterns of attachment*. Hillsdale, NJ: Erlbaum.

Akers, R. L. (1989). A social behaviorist's perspective on integration of theories of crime and deviance. In S. F. Messner, M. D. Krohn, & A. E. Liska (Eds.), *Theoretical integration in the study of deviance and crime: Problems and prospects* (pp. 179–195). Albany, NY: State University of New York Press.

Akers, R. L. (1990). Rational choice, deterrence, and social learning theory in criminology: The path not taken. *The Journal of Criminal Law and Criminology, 81,* 653–676.

Akers, R. L. (1997). *Criminological theories: Introduction and evaluation*. Los Angeles, CA: Roxbury.

Akers, R. L. (1998). *Social structure and social learning: A general theory of crime and deviance*. Boston, MA: Northeastern University Press.

Akers, R. L. (2009). *Social structure and social learning: A general theory of crime and deviance*. Piscataway, New Jersey: Transaction.

Akers, R. L., & Jensen, G. (2006). The empirical status of social learning theory of crime and deviance: The past, present, and future. In F. T. Cullen, J. P. Wright, & K. R. Blevins, *Taking stock: The status of criminological theory* (pp. 37–76). New Brunswick, NJ: Transaction.

Akers, R. L., & Sellers, C. S. (2004). *Criminological theories: Introduction and evaluation* (4th ed.). Los Angeles, CA: Roxbury.

Akers, R. L., & Sellers, C. S. (2013). *Criminological theories: Introduction, evaluation, and application* (6th ed.). New York, NY: Oxford University Press.

Alexander, F., & Healy, W. (1935). *Roots of crime*. Montclair, NJ: Patterson Smith.

Anderson, E. (1999). *Code of the street: Decency, violence, and the moral life of the inner city New York*. London, UK: W. W. Norton.

Anderson, G. (2007). *Biological influences on criminal behavior*. Boca Raton, FL: CRC Press.

Andrews, D. A., & Bonta, J. (2003). *The psychology of criminal conduct*. Cincinnati, OH: Anderson.

Archer, J. (1994). *Male violence*. London and New York: Routledge.

Arrigo, B. A. (1994). Legal discourse and the disordered criminal defendant: Contributions from psychoanalytic semiotics and chaos theory. Legal Studies Forum, 18

Arrigo, B. & Williams, C. (Eds.). (2006). *Philosophy, crime, and criminology*. Urbana, IL: University of Illinois Press.

Austin, J., & Irwin, J. (1997). *It's about time: America's imprisonment binge* (2nd ed.). Belmont, CA: Wadsworth.

Austin, J., & Irwin, J. (1997/2001). *It's about time: America's imprisonment binge* (3rd ed.). Belmont, CA: Wadsworth.

Babiak, P., & Hare, R. D. (2006). *Snakes in suits: When psychopaths go to work.* New York, NY: Regan Books.

Baltes, P. B. (1987). Theoretical propositions of life span developmental psychology: On the dynamics between growth and decline. *Developmental Psychology, 23,* 611–626.

Bandura, A. (1965). Influence of models' reinforcement contingencies on the acquisition of imitative responses. *Journal of Personality and Social Psychology, 1*(6), 589–595.

Bandura, A. (1973). *Aggression: A social learning analysis.* Englewood Cliffs, NJ: Prentice Hall.

Bandura, A. (1977). *Social learning theory.* Englewood Cliffs, NJ: Prentice Hall.

Bandura, A. (1986). *Social foundations of thought and action: A social cognitive theory.* Englewood Cliffs, NJ: Prentice Hall.

Bandura, A. (1990). Mechanisms of moral disengagement. In W. Reich (Ed.), *Origins of terrorism: Psychologies, ideologies, theologies, states of mind* (pp. 161–191). Cambridge, MA: Cambridge University Press.

Bandura, A. (1997). *Self-efficacy: The exercise of control.* New York, NY: W. H. Freeman.

Bandura, A. (2001). Social cognitive theory and clinical psychology. In N. J. Smelser & P. B. Baltes (Eds.), *International encyclopedia of the social and behavioral sciences* (Vol. 21, pp. 14250–14254). Oxford: Elsevier Science.

Bandura, A. (2008). The reconstrual of free will from an agentic perspective of social cognitive theory. In J. Baer, J. C. Kaufman, & R. F. Baumeister (Eds.), *Are we free? Psychology and free will* (pp. 86–127). New York, NY: Oxford University Press.

Bandura, A., Ross, D., & Ross, S. A. (1961). Transmission of aggression through the imitation of aggressive models. *Journal of Abnormal and Social Psychology, 63*(3), 575–582.

Bandura, A., Ross, D., & Ross, S. A. (1963). Imitation of film-mediated aggressive models. *Journal of Abnormal and Social Psychology, 66*(1), 3–11.

Bandura, A., & Walters, R. H. (1963). *Social learning and personality development.* New York, NY: Holt, Rinehart, & Winston.

Barak, G. (1998). *Integrating criminologies.* London, UK: Allyn and Bacon.

Barnes, G. C. (1995). Defining and optimizing displacement. In J. E. Eck and D. Weisburd, (Eds.), *Crime and place.* Monsey, New York: Criminal Justice Press, pp. 95–113.

Barr, R., & Pease, K. (1990). Crime placement, displacement and deflection. In M. Tonry & N. Morris (Eds.), *Crime and justice: A review of research.* Chicago, IL: University of Chicago Press, pp. 277–318.

Barr, R., & Pease, K. (1992). A place for crime and every crime in its place: An alternative perspective on crime displacement. In D. J. Evans & D. T. Herbert (Eds.), *Crime, policing, and place: Essays in environment criminology* (pp. 196–216). London: Routledge.

Bartol, C., & Bartol, A. M. (2011). *Criminal behavior: A psychosocial approach* (9th ed.). Boston, MA: Prentice Hall.

Batts, S. (2009). Brain lesions and their implications in criminal responsibility. *Behavioral Sciences and the Law, 27*(2), 261–272.

Bartusch, C. J., & Matsueda, R. L. (1996). Gender reflected appraisals and labeling: A cross-group test of an interactionist theory of delinquency. *Social Forces, 75*(1), 145–177.

Beaver, K., & Walsh, A. (Eds.). (2010). *Biosocial theories of crime.* Canterbury, UK: Ashgate.

Beaver, K., & Walsh, A. (2012). *Ashgate Research companion to biosocial theories of crime.* Burlington, VT: Ashgate.

Beaver, K. M., Barnes, J., & Boutwell, B. B. (Eds.). (2014). *The nurture versus biosocial debate in criminology: On the origins of criminal behavior and criminality.* Thousand Oaks, CA: Sage, p. 382.

Beaver, K. M., Ratchford, M., & Ferguson, C. J. (2009). Evidence of genetic and environmental effects on the development of low self-control. *Criminal Justice and Behavior, 36*(11), 1158,

Beccaria, C. (1764). An essay on crimes and punishments. Retrieved from http://www.constitution.org/cb/crim_pun.htm

Becker, G. (1974). *The economic approach to human behavior.* Chicago, IL: University of Chicago Press.

Becker, H. (1963). *Outsiders: Studies in the sociology of deviance.* London, UK: Free Press of Glencoe.

Beirne, P., & Messerschmidt, J. (2011). *Criminology: A sociological approach.* New York, NY: Oxford University Press.

Bellinger, D., & Dietrich, K. N. (1994). Low-level lead exposure and cognitive function in children. *Pediatric Annals, 23,* 600–605.

Belsky, J. (1980). Child maltreatment: An ecological integration. *American Psychologist, 35,* 320–335.

Belsky, J., Steinberg, L., & Draper, P. (1991). Childhood experience, interpersonal development, and reproductive strategy: An evolutionary theory of socialization. *Child Development, 62,* 648–670.

Bennett, W. J., DiIulio, J. J., & Walters, J. P. (1996). *Body count: Moral poverty and how to win America's war against crime and drugs.* New York, NY: Simon & Schuster.

Benson, M. (2002). *Crime and the life course: An introduction.* Los Angeles, CA: Roxbury Press.

Bentham, J. (1789). *The principles of morals and legislation.* New York, NY: Hafner.

Berger, J., Fisek, R. Z., Norman, Z., & Wagner, D. G. (1983). The formation of reward expectation in status situations. In D. Messick & K. Cook (Eds.), *Equity theory: Psychological and sociological perspectives* (pp. 126–168). New York, NY: Praeger.

Berger, J., Zelditch, Jr., M., Anderson, B., & Cohen, B. P. (1972). Structural aspects of distributive justice: A status value formulation. In J. Berger, M. Zelditch Jr., and B. Anderson (Eds.), *Sociological theories in progress* (pp. 119–146). Boston, MA: Houghton-Mifflin.

Berger, P., & Luckmann, T. (1966). *The social construction of reality.* Garden City, NY: Doubleday.

Bernanke, B. S. (1995). Macroeconomics of the Great Depression: A comparative approach. *Journal of Money, Credit and Banking, 27*(1), 1–28.

Bernard, T. J., & Snipes, J. B. (1996). Theoretical integration in criminology. *Crime and Justice: A Review of Research, 20,* 301–348.

Bernard, T. J., Snipes, J. B., & Gerould, A. (2010). *Vold's theoretical criminology.* New York, NY: Oxford University Press.

Bernburg, J. G., & Krohn, M. D. (2003). Labeling, life chances, and adult crime: The direct and indirect effects of official intervention in adolescence on crime in early adulthood. *Criminology, 41*(4), 1287–1318.

Bernet, W., Vnencak-Jones, C. L., Farahany, N., & Montgomery, S. A. (2007). Bad nature, bad nurture, and testimony regarding MAOA and SLC6A4 genotyping at murder trials. *Journal of Forensic Science, 52*(6), 1362–1371.

Bishop, J. (2013). The effect of de-individuation of the Internet troller on criminal procedure implementation: An interview with a hater. *International Journal of Cyber Criminology, 7*(1), 28–48.

Black, D. J. (1976). *The behavior of law.* New York, NY: Academic Press.

Black, D. J. (1984). *Towards a general theory of social control.* New York, NY: Academic Press.

Blackburn, R. (1993). *The psychology of criminal conduct.* New York, NY: J. Wiley.

Blattman C., Hartman, A, & Blair, R. (2014). How to promote order and property rights under weak rule of law? An experiment in changing dispute resolution behavior through community education. *American Political Science Review (108)*, pp 100–120.

Blair, R. J. R. (1995) A cognitive developmental approach to mortality: Investigating the psychopathy. *Cognition,* 57, 1–29.

Blair, R. J. R. (2005). *Psychopathy: Emotion and the brain.* Malden, MA: Blackwell.

Blau, J. R., & Blau, P. M. (1982). The cost of inequality: Metropolitan structure and violent crime. *American Sociological Review,* 47, 114–129.

Bloom, B., Owen, B., & Covington, S. (2003). *Gender-responsive strategies: Research practice and guiding principles for women offenders.* Washington, DC: National Institute of Corrections, U.S. Department of Justice.

Blum, K., Braverman, E. R., Holder, J. M., Lubar, J. F., Monastra, V. J., Miller, D., . . . Comings, D. (2000). Reward deficiency syndrome: A biogenetic model for the diagnosis and treatment of impulsive, addictive, and compulsive behaviours. *Journal of Psychoactive Drugs, 32* (Suppl. i–iv), 1–112.

Blum, K., Cull, J., Braverman, E., & Comings, D. (1996). Reward deficiency syndrome. *American Scientist, 84,* 135–145.

Blum, K., Noble, E. P., Sheridan, P. J., Montgomery, A., Ritchie, T., Jagadeeswaran, P. . . . Cohn, J. B. (1990). Allelic association of human dopamine D2 receptor gene in alcoholism. *Journal of the America Medical Association, 263*(15), 2055–2060.

Blumenthal, M. D., Kahn, R. L., Andrews, F. M., & Head, K. B. (1972). Justifying violence: Attitudes of American men. Ann Arbor, MI: Institute for Social Research, University of Michigan.

Blumer, H. (1969). *Symbolic interactionism: Perspective and method.* Englewood Cliffs, NJ: Prentice Hall.

Blumstein, A. (1995). A LEN interview with Professor Alfred Blumstein of Carnegie Mellon University. *Law Enforcement News, 21,* 10–13.

Blumstein, A., Cohen, J., & Nagin, D. (1978). *Deterrence and incapacitation: Estimating the effects of criminal sanctions on crime rates.* Washington, DC: National Academy of Sciences.

Blumstein, A., Cohen, J., Roth, J., & Visher, C. (Eds.). (1986). *Criminal careers and "career criminals."* Washington, DC: National Academy Press.

Bobich, Z. (2006). The general theory of psychopathy. *American Journal of Forensic Psychiatry, 27,* 1–10.

Bohm, R. M. (2001). *A primer on crime and delinquency theory.* Belmont, CA: Wadsworth/Thompson.

Bohm, R. M., & Vogel, B. L. (2011). *A primer on crime and delinquency theory.* Belmont, CA: Wadsworth.

Bonger, W. A. (1916). *Criminality and economic conditions.* New York, NY: Agathon Press.

Bonta, J., & Andrews, D. A. (1993). The level of supervision inventory: An overview. *IARCA Journal, 5*(4), 6–8.

Bowlby, J. (1944). Forty-four juvenile thieves: Their characters and home lives. *International Journal of Psychoanalysis, 25,* 19–52.

Bowlby, J. (1969). *Attachment and loss.* New York, NY: Basic Books.

Boyd, N. (2000). *The beast within: Why men are violent.* Vancouver, BC: Greystone Books.

Braga, A. A. (2005). Hot spots policing and crime prevention: A systematic review of randomized controlled trials. *Journal of Experimental Criminology, 1,* 317–342.

Braga, A. A., & Bond, B. J. (2008). Policing crime and disorder hot spots: A randomized controlled trial. *Criminology, 46,* 577–608.

Braithwaite, J. (1989). *Crime, shame, and reintegration.* Cambridge, UK: Cambridge University Press.

Braithwaite, J. (2001). *Restorative justice and responsive regulation.* Oxford, UK: Oxford University Press.

Braithwaite, J. (2009). Restorative justice for banks through negative licensing. *The British Journal of Criminology, 49*(2), 439–450.

Brantingham, P. J., & Brantingham, P. L. (1978). A theoretical model of crime site selection. In M. D. Krohn & R. L. Akers (Eds.), *Crime, law and sanctions: Theoretical perspectives* (pp. 105–118). Beverly Hills, CA: Sage.

Brantingham, P. J., & Brantingham, P. L. (1984). *Patterns in crime.* New York, NY: Macmillan.

Brantingham, P. J., & Brantingham, P. L. (Eds.). (1991). *Environmental criminology.* Prospect Heights, IL: Waveland Press. (Original work published 1981)

Brantingham, P. J., & Brantingham, P. L. (1995). Criminality of place: Crime generators and crime attractors. *European Journal of Policy and Research, 3,* 1–26.

Brantingham, P. J., & Brantingham, P. L. (2003). Anticipating the displacement of crime using the principles of environmental criminology. In M. Smith & D. Cornish (Eds.), *Theory for practice in situational crime prevention* (pp. 119–148). New York, NY: Criminal Justice Press.

Brantingham, P. J., & Brantingham, P. L. (2008). Crime pattern theory. In R. Wortley & L. Mazerolle (Eds.), *Environmental criminology and crime analysis* (pp. 78–93). Portland, OR: Willan.

Brantingham, P. J., & Faust, F. L. (1976). A conceptual model of crime prevention. *Crime and Delinquency, 22,* 284–296.

Brantingham, P. L., & Brantingham, P. J. (1981). Mobility, notoriety, and crime: A study in the crime pattern of urban nodal points. *Journal of Environmental Systems, 11,* 89–99.

Brantingham, P. L., & Brantingham, P. J. (1993). Environment, routine, and situation: Toward a pattern theory of crime. In R. V. Clarke & M. Felson (Eds.), *Routine activity and rational choice: Advances in criminological theory* (Vol. 5) (pp. 259–294). Piscataway, NJ: Transaction.

Brantingham, P. L., & Brantingham, P. J. (1999). A theoretical model of crime hot spot generation. *Studies on Crime and Crime Prevention, 8,* 7–26.

Brantingham, P. L., & Brantingham, P. J. (2000). Police use of environmental criminology in strategic crime prevention. *Police Practice, 1*(2), 211–238.

Brantingham, P. L., Brantingham, P. J., & Taylor, W. (2005). Situational crime prevention as a key component in embedded crime prevention. *Canadian Journal of Criminology and Criminal Justice, 47,* 271–292.

Brazzell, D., Crayton, A., Mukamal, D., Solomon, A., & Lindahl, N. (2009). *From the classroom to the community: Exploring the role of education during incarceration and reentry.* Washington, DC: Urban Institute.

Brunner, H. G. (1996). *MAOA deficiency and abnormal behavior: Perspectives on an association.* In Ciba Foundation Symposium, Genetics of criminal and antisocial behavior (pp. 155–167). Chichester, UK: Wiley.

Bunge, M. (2004). How does it work? The search for explanatory mechanisms. *Philosophy of the Social Sciences, 34,* 82–110.

Burd, L., Klug, M. G., Martsolf, J. T., & Kerbeshian, J. (2003). Fetal alcohol syndrome: Neuropsychiatric phenomics. *Neurotoxical Teratol, 25*(6), 697–705.

Burgess, E. W. (1925). The growth of a city: An introduction to a research project. In R. Park, E. W. Burgess, & R. D. McKenzie (Comps.), *The city.* Chicago, IL: The University of Chicago Press.

Burgess, R., & Akers, R. (1966). A differential association-reinforcement theory of criminal behavior. *Social Problems, 14*(2), 128–147.

Burns, J. M., & Swerdlow, R. H. (2003). Right orbitofrontal tumor with pedophilia symptom and constructional apraxia sign. *Archives of Neurology, 60,* 437–440.

Burruss, G. W. (2009). Mapping criminological theory. *Journal of Criminal Justice Education, 20*(1), 4–19.

Bursik, R., & Grasmick, H. (1993a). *Neighborhoods and crime: The dimensions of effective community control.* New York, NY: Lexington Books.

Bursik, R., & Grasmick, H. (1993b). Economic deprivation and neighborhood crime rates, 1960–1980. *Law and Society Review,* 27, 263.

Bursik, R., & Webb, J. (1982). Community change and patterns of delinquency. *American Journal of Sociology, 88,* 24–42.

Burton, Jr., V. S., Cullen, F. T., Evans, T. D., Alarid, L. F., & Dunaway, R. G. (1998). Gender, self-control, and crime. *Journal of Research in Crime and Delinquency, 35,* 123–147.

Buss, D. (1990). Toward a biologically informed psychology of personality. *Journal of Personality, 58*(1), 1–16.

Buzan, T. (1974). *Use of your head.* London, UK: BBC Books.

Buzan, T. (1997). *Use of your memory.* London, UK: BBC Books.

Canfield, R. L., Henderson, C. R., Cory-Slechta, D. A., Cox, C., Jusko, T. A., & Lanphear, B. P. (2003). Intellectual impairment in children with blood lead concentrations below 10 microg per deciliter. *New England Journal of Medicine, 348*(16), 1517–1526.

Canli, T., & Lesch, K. P. (2007). Long story short: The serotonin transporter in emotion regulation and social cognition. *Nature Neuroscience, 10,* 1103–1109.

Cao, L. (2004). *Major criminological theories: Concepts and measurement.* Belmont, CA: Wadsworth.

Carrabine, E. (2012). Just images: Aesthetics, ethics, and visual criminology. *British Journal of Criminology, 53*(2), 463–489.

Caspi, A., McClay, J., Moffitt, T. E., Mill, J., Martin, J., Craig, I. W., & Poulton, R. (2002). Role of genotype in the cycle of violence in maltreated children. *Science, 297,* 851–854.

Caspi, A., & Moffitt, T. (2006). Evidence from behavioral genetics for environmental contributions to antisocial conduct. In P. O. Wikstrom & R. J. Sampson (Eds.), *The explanation of crime: Context, mechanisms, and development* (pp. 108–152). Cambridge, MA: Cambridge University Press.

Caulkins, J. P. (1992). Thinking about displacement in drug markets: Why observing change of venue isn't enough. *Journal of Drug Issues, 22,* 17–30.

Cerezo, A. (2013). CCTV and crime displacement: A quasi-experimental evaluation. *European Journal of Criminology, 10*(2), 222–236.

Chambliss, W. J. (1964). A sociological analysis of the law of vagrancy. *Social Problems, 12,* 67–77.

Chambliss, W. J. (1973). The Saints and the Roughnecks. *Society, 11,* 20–44.

Chambliss, W. J., & Seidman, R. (1971). *Law, order, and power.* Reading, MA: Addison-Wesley.

Chamlin, M. B., & Cochran, J. R. (1995). Assessing Messner and Rosenfeld's institutional anomie theory: A partial test. *Criminology, 33,* 411–429.

Chamlin, M. B., & Cochran, J. R. (2007). An evaluation of the assumptions that underlie institutional anomie theory. *Theoretical Criminology, 11,* 39–61.

Chapple, C. (2005). Self-control, peer relations, and delinquency. *Justice Quarterly, 22,* 89–106.

Chiricos, T., Barrick, K., & Bales, W. (2007). The labeling of convicted felons and its consequences for recidivism. *Criminology, 45*(3), 547–581.

Christie, N. (1977). Conflicts as property. *British Journal of Criminology, 17,* 1–15.

Chubb, J. E., & Moe, T. M. (1990). *Politics, markets, and America's schools.* Washington, DC: The Brookings Institute.

Chung, J. Y., & Raine, A. (2010). Crime and nutrition. In F. Cullen & P. Wilcox (Eds.), *The encyclopedia of criminological theory* (pp. 667–670). Thousand Oaks, CA: Sage.

Clarke, R. V. (1983). Situational crime prevention: Its theoretical basis and practical scope. In M. Tonry & N. Morris (Eds.), *Crime and justice: An annual review of research* (Vol. 4) (pp. 225–256). Chicago, IL: University of Chicago.

Clarke, R. V. (1995). Situational crime prevention. In M. Tonry & D. P. Farrington (Eds.), *Building a safer society: Strategic approaches to crime prevention* (pp. 91–150). Chicago, IL: The University of Chicago Press.

Clarke, R. V. (1997). *Situational crime prevention: Successful case studies* (2nd ed.). New York, NY: Harrow & Heston.

Clarke, R. V., & Cornish, D. B. (1985). Modeling offenders' decisions: A framework for research policy. In M. Tonry & N. Morris (Eds.), *Crime and justice: An annual review of research* (Vol. 6) (pp. 147–185). Chicago, IL: University of Chicago.

Cleckley, H. (1941). *The mask of sanity.* Augusta, GA: Emily S. Cleckley.

Cloward, R. A., & Ohlin, L. (1960). *Delinquency and opportunity: A theory of delinquent gangs.* New York, NY: Free Press.

Cohen, A. (1955). *Delinquent boys: The culture of the gang.* New York, NY: Free Press.

Cohen, B. P. (1989). *Developing sociological knowledge.* Chicago, IL: Nelson-Hall.

Cohen, J., Gorr, W., & Singh, P. (2003). Estimating intervention effects in varying risk settings: Do police raids reduce illegal drug dealing at nuisance bars? *Criminology, 41*(2), 257–292.

Cohen, L. E., & Felson, M. (1979). Social change and crime rate trends: A routine activity approach. *American Sociology Review, 44,* 588–608.

Cohen, S. (1971). *Images of deviance.* Harmondsworth, UK: Penguin.

Cohen, S. (1974). Criminology and the sociology of deviance in Britain: A recent history and a current report. In P. Rock & M. McIntosh (Eds.), *Deviance and social control* (pp. 1–40). London, UK: Tavistock.

Cohen, S. (1985). *Visions of social control: Crime, punishment, and classification.* New York, NY: Polity Press.

Cole D. (2007). The umpires strike back: Canadian judicial experience with risk assessment instruments. *Canadian Journal of Criminology 49*(4), 493–519.

Colvin, M. (2000). *Crime and coercion.* New York, NY: St. Martin's Press.

Colvin, M., Cullen, F. T., & Vander Ven, T. (2002). Coercion, social support, and crime: An emerging theoretical consensus. *Criminology, 40,* 19–42.

Comings, D., & Blum, K. (2000). Reward deficiency syndrome: Genetic aspects of behavioral disorders. *Progress in Brain Research, 126,* 325–341.

Conway, K. P., & McCord, J. (2002). A longitudinal examination of the relation between co-offending with violent accomplices and violent crime. *Aggressive Behavior (28),* 97–108.

Cooley, C. H. (1902). *Human nature and the social order.* New York, NY: Scribner's.

Cornish, D. B., & Clarke, R. V. (2001). Rational choice. In R. Paternoster & R. Bachman (Eds.), *Explaining crime and criminals. Essays in contemporary criminological theory* (pp. 23–42). Los Angeles, CA: Roxbury.

Cornish D. B., & Clarke, R. V. (2003). Opportunities, precipitators, and criminal decisions: A reply to Wortley's critique of situational crime prevention. *Crime Prevention Studies, 16,* 41–96.

Covington, S., & Bloom, B. (2006). Gender responsive treatment and services in correctional settings. Inside and out: Women, prison, and therapy. *Women & Therapy, 29*(3/4), 9–33.

Crain, W. C. (1985). *Theories of development.* New York, NY: Prentice Hall.

Cromwell, P. (1995). *In their own words: Criminals on crime.* Los Angeles, CA: Roxbury.

Cromwell, P. F., Killinger, G. G., Kerper, H. B., & Walker, C. (1985). *Probation and parole in the criminal justice system.* St. Paul, MN: West.

Cromwell, P. F., Olson, J. N., & Avary, D. W. (1991). *Breaking and entering: An ethnographic analysis of burglary.* Newbury Park, CA: Sage.

Crowe, S. L., & Blair, R. J. R. (2008). The development of antisocial behavior: What can we learn from functional neuroimaging studies? *Developmental Psychopathology, 20*(4), 1145–1159.

Crowe, T. D. (1991). *Crime prevention through environmental design: Applications of architectural design and space management concepts.* Boston, MA: National Crime Prevention Institute, Butterworth-Heinemann.

Cullen, F. T. (2009). Foreward. In A. Walsh & K. M. Beaver (Eds.), *Biosocial criminology: New directions in theory and research.* New York, NY: Routledge-Taylor Group.

Cullen, F. T., & Agnew, R. (2011). *Criminological theories past to present: Essential readings.* New York, NY: Oxford University Press.

Cullen F. T., & Messner, S. (2007). The making of criminology revisited: An oral history of Merton's anomie paradigm. *Theoretical Criminology, 11,* 5–37.

Currie, E. (1974). [Book review]. The new criminology. *Issues in Criminology (9),* 123–142.

Diagle, L. E., Cullen, F. T., & Wright, J. P. (2007). Gender differences in the predictors of juvenile delinquency. *Youth Violence and Juvenile Justice, 5*(3), 254–286.

Daly, K. (1992). Women's pathways to felony court: Feminist theories of lawbreaking and problems of representation. *Review of Law and Women's Studies, 2,* 11–52.

Darwin, C. (2003) [1859]. *On the origin of species.* New York, NY: Signet.

Darwin, C. (1871). *The descent of man.* New York: D. Appleton and Company.

Davison, S., & Janco, A. (2012). Personality disorder and criminal behavior: What is the nature of the relationship? *Current Opinion in Psychiatry, 25*(1), 39–45.

Dawkins, R. (1976). *The selfish gene.* New York, NY: Oxford University Press.

DeKeseredy, W. S. (2012). History of critical criminology in Canada. In W. S. Dekeseredy & M. Dragiewicz (Eds.), *The Routledge handbook of critical criminology* (pp. 61–69). London, UK: Routledge.

DeKeseredy, W. S., Saunders, D., Schwartz, M. D., & Alvi, S. (1997). The meanings and motives for women's use of violence in Canadian college dating relationships: Results from a national survey. *Sociological Spectrum, 17,* 199–222.

DeLisi, M. (2009). Psychopathy is the unified theory of crime. *Youth Violence and Juvenile Justice, 7*(3), 256–273.

DeLisi, M., Beaver, K. M., Vaughn, M. G., & Wright, J. P. (2009). All in the family: Gene x environment interaction between DRD2 and criminal father is associated with five antisocial phenotypes. *Criminal Justice and Behavior, 36*(11), 1187.

Demetriou, C., & Silke, A. (2003). A criminological Internet "sting." Experimental evidence of illegal and deviant visits to a website trap. *British Journal of Criminology, 44*(1), 213–222.

Denno, D. (1990). *Biology and violence: From birth to adulthood.* New York, NY: Cambridge University Press.

Denton, N. (2013). Great American sociology. *City & Community, 12,* 1–6.

Dickson, E. S., Gordon, S. C., & Huber, G. A. (2013). Institutional sources of legitimate authority: An experimental investigation. Retrieved from http://cniss.wustl.edu/files/cniss/imce/gordon_paper.pdf

Diener, E., Fraser, S. C., Beaman, E. L., & Kelem, R. T. (1976). Effects of deindividuation variables on stealing among Halloween trick-or-treaters. *Journal of Personality and Social Psychology, 33*(2), 178–183.

Dietrich, K. N., Krafft, K. M., Bornschein, R. L., Hammond, P. B., Berger, O., Succop, P. A., & Bier, M. (1987). Low-level fetal lead exposure effect on neurobehavioral development in early infancy. *Pediatrics, 80,* 721–730.

Dietrich, K.N., Ris, D., Succop, P., Berger, O. G., & Bornschein, R. L. (2001). Early exposure to lead and juvenile delinquency. *Neurotoxicology and Teratology, 23,* 511–518.

Dilulio, J. J. (1995). The coming of the super-predators. *The Weekly Standard, 1*(11), 23.

Dodd, D. (1985). Robbers in the classroom: A deindividuation exercise. *Teaching of Psychology Journal, 12*(2), 88–91.

Dollard, J., Miller, N. E., Doob, L. W., Mowrer, O. H., & Sears, R. (1939). *Frustration and aggression.* New Haven, CT: Yale University Press.

Downes, D. (1966). *The delinquent solution.* London, UK: Routledge and Kegan Paul.

Drum, K. (January/February 2013). America's real criminal element: Lead. Mother Jones. Retrieved from http://www.motherjones.com/environment/2013/01/lead-crime-link-gasoline

Dubois, D. L., Holloway, B. E., Valentine, J. C., & Harris, C. (2002). Effectiveness of mentoring programs for youth: A meta-analytic review. *American Journal of Community Psychology, 30*(2), 157–197.

Dugdale, R. (1895). *The Jukes: A study in crime, pauperism, disease, and heredity.* New York, NY: Putnam.

Durkheim, E. (1938) [1895]. *The rules of sociological method.* Translated by S. A. Solovay & J. H. Mueller. New York, NY: Free Press.

Durkheim, E., (1951) [1897]. *Suicide: A study in sociology.* New York, NY: The Free Press.

Durkheim E. (1965). *The division of labor in society.* Translated by G. Simpson. New York, NY: Free Press. (Original work published 1897)

Dutton, D. G., Boyanowsky, E., & Bond, M. H. (2005). Extreme mass homicide: From military massacre to genocide. *Aggression and Violent Behavior, 10,* 437–473.

Eck, J. (1993). The threat of crime displacement. *Problem Solving Quarterly, 6*(3). Retrieved from http://www.popcenter.org/library/psq/1993/summer_1993_vol_6_no_3.pdf

Eck, J., & Weisburd, D. (1995). *Crime and place.* Monsey, NY: Criminal Justice Press.

Einstadter, W. J., & Henry, S. (2006). *Criminological Theory.* Lanham, MD: Rowman and Littlefield.

Ekblom, P., & Tilley, N. (2000). Going equipped: Criminology, situational crime prevention, and the resourceful offender. *British Journal of Criminology, 40,* 376–398.

Elbogen, E. B., Johnson, S. C., Wagner, H. R., Newton, V. M., Timko, C., Vasterling, J. J., & Beckham, J. C. (2002). Protective factors and risk modification of violence in Iraq and Afghanistan War Veterans. *Journal of Clinical Psychology, 76*(3), 767–773.

Elder, G. H. (1985). Perspectives on the life course. In G. H. Elder (Ed.), *Life course dynamics* (pp. 23–46). Ithaca, NY: Cornell University Press.

Elder, G. H. (1993). Time, agency, and social change. *Social Psychology, 57,* 4–15.

Eley, T. C., Lichtenstein, P., & Stevenson, J. (1999). Sex differences in the etiology of aggressive and nonaggressive antisocial behavior: Results from two twin studies. *Child Development, 70*(1), 155–168.

Elliot, D. S., Ageton, S. S., & Cantor, R. J. (1979). An integrated theoretical perspective on delinquent behavior. *Journal of Research in Crime and Delinquency, 16,* 3–27.

Elliott, D. S., Huizinga, D., & Ageton, S. S. (1985). *Explaining delinquency and drug use.* Beverly Hills, CA: Sage.

Elliott, L. (2002). Con game and restorative justice: Inventing the truth about Canada's prisons (commentary). *Canadian Journal of Criminology, 44*(4), pp. 459–474.

Elliott, L. (2011). *Security, with care: Restorative justice and healthy societies.* Halifax, Nova Scotia: Fernwood.

Ellis, L. (1986). Evidence of neuroandrogenic etiology of sex roles from a combined analysis of human, nonhuman primate, and nonprimate mammalian studies. *Personality and Individual Differences, 7*(4), 519–552.

Ellis, L. (1987). Criminal behavior and r/K selection: An extension of gene-based evolutionary theory. *Deviant Behavior, 8*(2), 149–176.

Ellis, L. (2003). Genes, criminality, and the evolutionary neuroandrogenic theory. In A. Walsh and L. Ellis (Eds.), *Biosocialcriminology: Challenging environmentalism's supremacy* (pp. 13–34). Hauppauge, NY: Nova Science.

Ellis, L. (2005). Theory explaining the biological correlates of criminality. *European Journal of Criminology, 2*(3), 287–314.

Ellis, L., & Hoffmann, H. (1990). *Crime in biological, social and moral contexts.* New York, NY: Praeger.

Ellis, L., & Walsh, A. (Eds.). (2003). *Biosocial criminology: Challenging environmentalism's supremacy.* New York, NY: Nova Science.

Empey, L. T. (1978). *American delinquency: Its meaning and construction.* Homewood, IL: Dorsey Press.

Empey, L. T. (1982). American delinquency, its meaning and construction. Florence, KY: Dorsey Press.

Englander, E. (2007). *Understanding violence* (3rd ed.). Mahwah, NJ: Lawrence Erlbaum Associates.

Erikson, E. (1950). *Childhood and society* (1st ed.). New York, NY: Norton.

Eysenck, H. J. (1964). *Crime and personality.* London, UK: Methuen.

Eysenck, H. J. (1967). *The biological basis of personality.* Springfield, IL: Thomas.

Eysenck, H. J. (1977). *You and neurosis.* London, UK: Temple Smith.

Eysenck, H. J. (1978). Superfactors, P, E, and N in a comprehensive factor space. *Multivariate Behavioral Research, 13*(4), 475–481.

Eysenck, H. J., & Gudjonsson, G. H. (1989). *The causes and cures of criminality.* New York, NY: Plenum.

Farahanay, N. (2012). Incriminating thoughts. *Stanford Law Review, 64*(2), 351–408.

Farrar, T. J., Frost, R. B, & Hedges, D. W. (2013). Prevalence of traumatic brain injury in juvenile offenders: A meta-analysis. *Child Neuropsychology, 19*(3), 225–234.

Farrington, D. P. (1986). Age and crime. In M. Tonry & N. Morris (Eds.), *Crime and justice: An annual review of research* (pp. 189–250). Chicago, IL: University of Chicago Press.

Farrington, D. P. (1992). Explaining the beginning, progress, and ending of antisocial behavior from birth to adulthood. In J. McCord (Ed.), *Facts, frameworks, and forecasts: Advances in criminology theory* (Vol. 3) (pp. 253–286). New Brunswick, NJ: Transaction.

Farrington, D. P. (2003). Key results from the first forty years of the Cambridge Study in delinquent development. In T. Thornberry & M. D. Krohn (Eds.), *Taking stock of delinquency: An overview of findings from contemporary longitudinal studies.* (pp. 137–183). New York, NY: Kluwer Academic/Plenum Publishers.

Farrington, D. P., & Welsh, B. (2007). *Saving children from a life of crime.* New York, NY: Oxford University Press.

Fast, D., & Conry, J. (2004). The challenge of fetal alcohol syndrome in the criminal legal system. *Addiction Biology, 9*(2), 161–166.

Fazel, S., & Danesh, J. (2002). Serious mental disorder in 23,000 prisoners: A systematic review of 62 surveys. *Lancet, 359*(9306), 545–550.

Fazel, S. & Seewalk, K. (2012). Severe mental illness in 33,588 prisoners worldwide: Systematic review and meta-regression analysis. *British Journal of Psychiatry, 200*(5), 364–373.

Federal Bureau of Investigation. (2005). *Financial crimes report to the public.* Department of Justice, Washington, DC. Retrieved from http://www.fbi.gov/stats-services/publications/fcs_report2005/financial-crimes-report-to-the-public-2005-pdf

Feeley, M., & Simon, J. (1992). The new penology: Notes on the emerging strategy of corrections and its implications. *Criminology, 30*(4), 449–474.

Felson, M. (1998). *Crime and everyday life.* Thousand Oaks, CA: Sage.

Felson, M. (2002). *Crime and everyday life* (3rd ed.). Thousand Oaks, CA: Sage.

Felson, M. (2005). *Crime and nature.* Thousand Oaks, CA: Sage.

Felson, M., & Clarke, R. V. (1998). *Opportunity makes the thief: Practical theory for crime prevention.* Paper No. 98, Police Research Series. London, UK: British Home Office Research Publications.

Ferrell, J. (1995). Culture, crime, and cultural criminology. *Journal of Criminal Justice and Popular Culture, 3*(2), 25–42.

Ferrell, J., & Weide, R. D. (2010). Spot theory. *City, 14*(1), 48–62.

Ferri. E. (1896). *Criminal sociology.* New York, NY: D. Appleton and Company. (Original work published 1896)

Ferri, E. (1917). *Criminal sociology.* Boston, MA: Little, Brown.

Ferguson, P. L., Pickelsimer, E. E., Corrigan, J. D., & Bogner, J. (2012). Prevalence of traumatic brain injury among prisoners in South Carolina. *Journal of Head Trauma Rehabilitationm, 27,* 11–20.

Festinger, L., Pepitone, A., & Newcomb, T. (1952). Some consequences of deindividuation in a group. *Journal of Abnormal and Social Psychology, 47,* 382–389.

Figueira-McDonough, J. (1991). Community structure and delinquency: A typology. *Social Service Review, 65,* 68–91.

Firebaugh, G. (2008). *Seven rules for social research.* Princeton, NJ: Princeton University Press.

Fishbein, D. (1990). Biological perspectives in criminology. *Criminology, 28,* 27–72.

Fishbein, D. (2001). *Biobehavioral perspectives in criminology.* Belmont, CA: Wadsworth.

Foucault, M. (1977). *Discipline and punish: The birth of the prison.* New York, NY: Pantheon Books.

Fowles, D. C. (1980). The three arousal model: Implication of Gray's two-factor theory for heart rate, electrodermal activity, and psychopathy. *Psychophysiology, 17,* 87–104.

Fowles, D. C. (1987). Psychophysiology and psychopath: A motivational approach. *Psychophysiology, 25,* 373–391.

Fratello, F., Rengifo, A., & Trone, J. (2013). *Coming of age with stop and frisk: Experiences, self-perceptions, and public safety implications.* New York: Vera Institute. Available at http://www.vera.org/sites/default/files/resources/downloads/stop-and-frisk-summary-report-v2.pdf

Freud, S. (1920). *A general introduction to psychoanalysis.* New York, NY: Boney and Liveright.

Freud, S. (1923). *The ego and the id.* New York, NY: Norton.

Freud, S. (1930). *Civilization and its discontents.* New York, NY: Norton.

Fromm, E. (1942). *The fear of freedom.* London, UK: Paul Trench.

Fullbright-Anderson, K., & Auspos, P. (2006). *Community change: Theories, practice, and evidence.* Washington, DC: Aspen Institute.

Galton, F. (1833). *Hereditary genius.* London, UK: Macmillan.

Gardiner, R. (1978). *Design for safe neighborhoods: The environmental security planning and design process.* Washington, DC: U.S. National Institute of Law Enforcement and Criminal Justice.

Garland, D. (1997). "Governmentality" and the problem of crime: Foucault, criminology, and sociology. *Theoretical Criminology, 1*(2), 173–214.

Garland, D. (2001). *The culture of control: Crime and social order in contemporary society.* Chicago, IL: University of Chicago Press.

Garofalo, R. (1914). *Criminology.* Translated by R. W. Millar. Montclair, NJ: Patterson Smith.

Gendreau, P., Goggin, C., & Cullen, F. T. (1999). *The effects of prison sentences on recidivism.* Ottawa: Solicitor General of Canada.

Gendreau, P., Goggin, C. E., & Law, M. A. (1997). Predicting prison misconducts. *Criminal Justice and Behavior, 24,* 414–431.

Gendreau, P., Little, T., & Goggin, C. E. (1996). A meta-analysis of the predictors of adult offender recidivism: What works! *Criminology, 34,* 575–607.

Gianaros, P. J., Horenstein, J. A., Cohen, S., Matthews, K. A., Brown, S. M., Flory, J. D., Critchley, H. D., . . . Hariri, H. R. (2007). Perigenual anterior cingulate morphology covaries with perceived social standing. *Social Cognition & Affective Neuroscience, 2*(3), 161–173.

Gianaros, P. J., Jennings, J. R., Sheu, L. K., Greer, P. J., Kuller, L. H., & Matthews, K. A. (2007). Prospective reports of chronic life stress predict decreased grey matter volume in the hippocampus. *Neuroimage, 35*(2), 795–803.

Gianaros, P. J., Manuck, S. B., Sheu, L. K., Kuan, D. C., Votruba-Drzal, E., Craig, A. E., & Hariri, A. R. (2011). Parental education predicts corticostriatal functionality in adulthood. *Cerebral Cortex, 21*(4), 896–910.

Gibbons, D. C. (1985). The assumption of efficacy of middle-range explanation: Typologies. In R. F. Meier (Ed.), *Theoretical methods* (pp.151–174). Beverly Hills, CA: Sage.

Gibbons, D. C. (1992). *Society, crime, and criminal behavior.* Englewood Cliffs, NJ: Prentice-Hall.

Gibbs, J. J., & Giever, D. (1995). Self-control and its manifestations among university students: An empirical test of Gottfredson and Hirschi's general theory. *Justice Quarterly, 12*(2), 231–256.

Gibbons, D. C. (1979). *The criminological enterprise: Theories and perspectives.* Englewood Cliffs: Prentice Hall.

Gibbons, D. C. (1985). The assumption of efficacy of middle-range explanation: Typologies. In R. F. Meier (Ed.), *Theoretical methods* (pp.151–174). Beverly Hills, CA: Sage.

Gibbons, D. C. (1992). *Society, crime, and criminal behavior.* Englewood Cliffs, NJ: Prentice Hall.

Gibbons, D. C. (1994). *Talking about crime and criminals: Problems and issues in theory development in criminology.* Englewood Cliffs, NJ: Prentice Hall.

Gibson, M., & Rafter, N. H. (2006). [Translation: Lombroso, C., 1876]. *Criminal man.* Durham, NC: Duke University Press, pp. 44–45.

Giordano, P., Cherkovich, S. A., & Rudolf, J. (2002). Gender, crime and desistance: Toward a theory of cognitive transformation. *American Journal of Sociology, 107,* 990–1064.

Glueck, S., & Glueck, E. (1950). *Unraveling juvenile delinquency.* New York: Commonwealth Fund.

Goddard, H. H. (1913). *The Kallikak family.* New York, NY: Macmillan.

Goddard, H. H. (1914). *Feeblemindness: Its causes and consequences.* New York, NY: Macmillan.

Goldstein, H. (1977). *Policing a free society.* Cambridge, MA: Ballinger.

Goring, C. (1913). *The English convict: A statistical study.* London, UK: Her Majesty's Stationery Office.

Gottfredson, M. R. (2006). The empirical status of control theory in criminology. In F. T. Cullen, J. P. Wright, & K. Blevins (Eds.), *Taking stock: The status of criminological theory* (pp. 419–446). New Brunswick, NJ: Transaction.

Gottfredson, M., & Hirschi, T. (1986). The true value of lambda would appear to be zero. *Criminology* (24), 213–234.

Gottfredson, M. R., & Hirschi, T. (1990). *A general theory of crime.* Stanford, CA: Stanford University Press.

Gottfredson, M. R., & Hirschi, T. (1995). National crime control policies. *Society, 32*(2), 30–36.

Graham, J., & Bennett, T. (1995). *Crime prevention strategies in Europe and North America.* Helsinki, Finland: European Institute for Crime Prevention and Control.

Grasmick, H. G., Tittle, C. R., Bursik, R. J. Jr., & Arneklev, B. J. (1993). Testing the core empirical implications of Gottfredson and Hirschi's general theory of crime. *Journal of Research in Crime and Delinquency, 30*(1), 5–29.

Gray, J. A. (1970). The psychophysiological basis of introversion-extraversion. *Behavior Research & Therapy, 8*(3), 249–266.

Gray, J. A. (1975). *Elements of a two-process theory of learning.* New York, NY: Academic Press.

Greenwood, P. (2006). *Changing lives: Delinquency prevention as crime-control policy.* Chicago, IL: University of Chicago Press.

Griffiths, C. T. (2010). *Canadian criminal justice: A primer.* Toronto, Ontario: Nelson Education, Ltd.

Griffiths, C. T. (2011). *Canadian corrections.* Toronto, Ontario: Thomson-Nelson.

Guba, E. G., & Lincoln, Y. S. (1989). Fourth generation evaluation. Newbury Park, CA: Sage.

Guerette, R. T., & Bowers, K. J. (2009), Assessing the extent of crime displacement and diffusion of benefits: A review of situational crime prevention evaluations. *Criminology, 47,* 1331–1368.

Guerry, A. M. (1833). *Essai sur la statistique morale de la France.* Paris, France: Crochard.

Hacking. I. (1990). *The taming of chance.* Cambridge, UK: Cambridge University Press.

Hackman, D. A., Farah, M. J., & Meaney, M. J. (2010). Socioeconomic status and the brain: Mechanistic insights from human and animal research. *National Review of Neuroscience, 11*(9), 651–659.

Hagan, J. (1989). *Structural criminology.* New Brunswick, NJ: Rutgers University Press.

Hagan, J., Boehnke, K., & Merkens, H. (2004). Gender differences in capitalization processes and the delinquency of siblings in Toronto and Berlin. *British Journal of Criminology, 44,* 659–676.

Hall, J. (1952). *Theft, law, and society.* Indianapolis, IN: Bobbs-Merrill.

Hall, S. (2012). *Theorizing crime and deviance: A new perspective.* London, UK: Sage.

Halleck, S. L. (1967). *Psychiatry and the dilemmas of crime.* New York, NY: Harper & Row.

Halleck, S. L. (1967). *Psychiatry and the dilemmas of crime* (6th ed.). New York, NY: Harper & Row.

Haney, C. (1982). Psychological theory and criminal justice policy: Law and psychology in the "Formative Era." *Law and Human Behavior, 6,* 191–235.

Haney, C. (2002). Making law modern: Toward a contextual model of justice. *Psychology, Public Policy, and Law, 8,* 3–63.

Haney, C., & Zimbardo, P. (1998). The past and future of U.S. prison policy. *American Psychology, 53*(7), 709–727.

Hanson, J., Hair, N., Chandra, A., Moss, E., Bhattacharya, J., Pollak, S. D., & Wolfe, B. (2013). Brain development and poverty: A first look. In B. Wolfe, W. Evans, & T. E. Seeman (Eds.), *The biological consequences of socioeconomic inequalities* (pp. 187–214). New York, NY: Russell Sage Foundation.

Hanson, J. D., & Yosifon, D. (2003). The situation: An introduction to the situational character, critical realism, power economics, and deep capture. *University of Pennsylvania Law Review, 152,* 129–348.

Harcourt, B. E. (2001). *Illusion of order: The false promise of broken windows policing.* Cambridge, MA: Harvard University Press.

Harcourt, B. E. (2007). *Against prediction: Profiling, policing, and punishing in an actuarial age.* Chicago, IL: University of Chicago Press.

Harcourt, B. E. (2007). *Against prediction: Profiling, policing, and punishing in an actuarial age.* Chicago, IL: University of Chicago Press.

Harcourt, B. E., & Ludwig, J. (2007). Reefer madness: Broken windows policing and misdemeanor marijuana arrests in New York City, 1989–2000. *Criminology and Public Policy, 6*(1), 165–182.

Hare, R. D. (1970). *Psychopathy: Theory and practice.* New York, NY: Wiley.

Hare, R. D. (1996). Psychopathy: A clinical construct whose time has come. *Criminal Justice and Behavior, 23,* 25–54.

Hare, R. D. (2003). *Manual for revised psychopathy checklist revised* (2nd ed.). Toronto, Ontario: Multi-Health Systems.

Hare, R. D., & Cox, D. N. (1978). Clinical and empirical conceptions of psychopathy, and the selection of subjects for research. In R. D. Hare & D. Schalling (Eds.), *Psychopathic behavior: Approaches to research* (pp. 107–144). Chichester, UK: Wiley.

Harrison, P. M., & Beck, A. J. (2006). *Prisoners in 2005: A Bureau of Justice statistics bulletin.* Washington, DC: Department of Justice.

Hartwell, S. (2003). Deviance over the life course: The case of homeless substance abusers. *Substance Use & Misuse, 38*(3–6), 475–502.

Hawley, A. H. (1950). *Human ecology: A theory of community structure.* New York, NY: The Ronald Press Company.

Haynie, D. L. (2001). Delinquent peers revisited: Does network structure matter? *American Journal of Sociology, 106,* 1013–1057.

Hayward, K. (2012). Five spaces of cultural criminology. *British Journal of Criminology, 52*(3), 441–462.

Healy, W. (1915). *The individual delinquent.* Boston, MA: Little, Brown.

Healy, W., & Bronner, A. (1926). *Delinquents and criminals: Their making and unmaking; Studies in two American cities.* New York, NY: AMS Press.

Heidt, J. (2008). *The growth of criminological theories.* Germany: VDM Verlag.

Henry, B., & Moffitt, T. E. (1997). Neuropsychological and neuro-imaging studies of juvenile delinquency and adult criminal behavior. In D. Stoff, J. Breiling, & J. D. Maser (Eds.), *Handbook of antisocial behavior* (pp. 280–288). New York, NY: John Wiley.

Hertz, D. (2014). Homicide inequality in Chicago. *The New Republic.* Retrieved from http://www.newrepublic.com/article/118003/maps-crime-chicago-crime-different-neighborhoods

Higgins, G. E. (2004). Gender and self-control theory: Are there differences in the measures and the theory's causal model? *Criminal Justice Studies, 17,* 33–55.

Hirschfield, P. J. (2008). The declining significance of delinquent labels in disadvantaged urban communities. *Sociological Forum, 23*(3), 575–601.

Hirschi, T. (1969). *Causes of delinquency.* Berkeley: University of California Press.

Hirschi, T. (1979). Separate and unequal is better. *Journal of Research in Crime and Delinquency, 16,* 34–38.

Hirschi, T. (1989). Exploring alternatives to integrated theory. In S. F. Messner, M. D. Krohn, & A. E. Liska (Eds.), *Theoretical integration in the study of deviance and crime: Problems and prospects,* pp. 37–50. Albany, NY: State University of New York Press.

Hirschi, T. (2004). Self-control and crime. In R. F. Baumeister & K. D. Vohs (Eds.), *Handbook of self-regulation: Research, theory, and applications* (pp. 537–552). New York, NY: Guildford.

Hirschi, T., & Gottfredson, M. R. (1994). The generality of deviance. In T. Hirschi & M. R. Gottfredson (Eds.), *The generality of deviance* (pp. 1–22). New Brunswick, NJ: Transaction.

Hobbes, T. (1651). *Leviathan.* Retrieved from Project Gutenberg, http://www.gutenberg.org/files/3207/3207-h/3207-h.htm

Home Office. (1993). *A practical guide to crime prevention for local partnerships.* London, UK: Home Office.

Hooton, E. A. (1939). *Crime and the man.* Cambridge, MA: Harvard University Press.

Hopkins-Burke, R. (2005). *An introduction to criminology theory* (2nd ed.). Devon, Willan Publishing.

Hotton, T. (2003). *Childhood aggression and exposure to violence in the home.* Ottawa: Canadian Centre for Justice Statistics.

Huesmann, L. R., & Taylor, L. D. (2006). The role of media violence in violent behavior. *Annual Review of Public Health, 27*(1), 1–23.

Hughes, E. C. (1945). Dilemmas and contradictions of status. *The American Journal of Sociology, 50,* 353–359.

Hull, C. L. (1943). *Principles of behavior: An introduction to behavior theory.* New York, NY: Appleton-Century-Crofts.

Hutchinson, E. (2013). *Essentials of human behavior: Integrating person, environment, and the life course.* Thousand Oaks, CA: Sage.

Hyde, L. W., Shaw, D. S., & Hariri, A. R. (2013). Neuroscience, developmental psychopathology, and youth antisocial behavior: Review, integration, and directions for research. *Developmental Review, 33,* 168–223.

Ignatieff, M. (1978). *A just measure of pain.* London, UK: Macmillan.

Insel, T. (2013). Director's blog: Transforming diagnosis. National Institute of Mental Health. Retrieved from http://www.nimh.nih.gov/about/director/2013/transforming-diagnosis.shtml

Intrator, J., Hare, R., Stritzke, P., Brichtswein, K., Dorfman, D., Harpur, T., . . . Machac, J. (1997). A brain imaging (single photon emission computerized tomography) study of semantic and affective processing in psychopaths. *Biological Psychiatry, 45*(2), 96–103.

Jackson-Jacobs, C. (2004). Taking a beating: The narrative gratifications of fighting as an underdog. In K. J. Hayward, J. Ferrell, W. Morrison, & M. Presdee (Eds.), *Cultural criminology unleashed* (pp. 231–244). London, UK: Glasshouse Press.

Jacobs, J. (1961). *The life and death of great American cities.* New York, NY: Vintage.

James, W. (1907). *Pragmatism, a new name for some old ways of thinking; popular lectures on philosophy.* New York, NY: Longmans, Green.

Jang, S. J. (1999). Age-varying effects of family, school, and peers on delinquency: A multilevel modeling test of interactional theory. *Criminology, 37,* 643–685.

Jeffery, C. R. (1971). *Crime prevention through environmental design.* Beverly Hills, CA: Sage.

Jeffery C. R. (1977). Criminology: Whither or wither? *Criminology, 15*(3), 283–286.

Jeffery, C.R. (1978). *Biology and crime.* Beverly Hills, CA: Sage.

Jeffery, C. R. (1990) *Criminology: An interdisciplinary approach.* Englewood Cliffs, NJ: Prentice Hall.

Jeffery, C. R., & Zahm, D. L. (1993). Crime prevention through environmental design, opportunity theory, and rational choice models. In R. V. Clarke & M. Felson (Eds.), *Advances in criminological theory* (Vol. 5) (pp. 323–350). New Brunswick, NJ: Transaction.

Jensen, G. F. (1996). Comment on Chamlin and Cochran. *Criminology, 34,* 129–131.

Johns Hopkins University. (2013). *Guns, public health, and mental illness: An evidence-based approach for federal policy.* Baltimore, MD: Consortium for Risk-Based Firearm Policy. Retrieved from http://www.hopkinsmedicine.org/healthlibrary/conditions/mental_health_disorders/personality_disorders_85,p00760/

Johns, J. H., & Quay, H. C. (1962). The effect of social reward on verbal conditioning in psychopathic and neurotic military offenders. *Journal of Consulting and Clinical Psychology, 26,* 217–220.

Johnson, S. D., & Bowers, K. J. (2004). The burglary as clue to the future: The beginnings of prospective hot-spotting. *The European Journal of Criminology, 1*(2), 237–255.

Jung, C. (1971) [1921]. *Psychological types.* Princeton, NJ: Princeton University Press.

Kamerman, S. B., & Kahn, A. J. (1989). *Social services for children, youth, and families in the United States.* Greenwich, CT: The Annie E. Casey Foundation.

Kandel, D., & Davies, M. (1991). Friendship networks, intimacy, and illicit drug use in young adulthood: A comparison on two competing theories. *Criminology, 29,* 441–469.

Katz, J. (1988). *Seductions of crime: Moral and sensual attractions of doing evil.* New York, NY: Basic Books.

Katz, R. (1999). Building the foundation for a side-by-side explanatory model: A general theory of crime, the age-graded life course theory, and attachment theory. *Western Criminology Review, 1*(2). Retrieved from http://wcr.sonoma.edu/v1n2/katz.html

Katz, R. (2002). Re-examining the social capital theory of crime. *Western Criminology Review, 4*(1), 30–54.

Keen, M. F. (1999). *Stalking the sociological imagination: J. Edgar Hoover's FBI surveillance of American sociology.* Westport, CT: Greenwood Press.

Kemshall, H. (1995). Risk in probation practice: The hazards and dangers of supervision. *Probation Journal, 42*(2), 67–72.

Kick E. L., & LaFree, G. (1985). Development and the social context of murder and theft. *Comparative Social Research, 8,* 37–56.

Kiehl, K. A. (2014). *The psychopath whisperer: The science of those without a conscience.* New York, NY: Crown.

Kim, S. W., & Pridemore, W. A. (2005). Poverty, social change, institutional anomie, and homicide. *Social Science Quarterly, 86,* 1377–1398.

Kitsuse, J. I., & Dietrick, D. (1958). The delinquent subculture: An alternative formulation. *The Pacific Sociological Review, 1,* 85–93.

Kitsuse, J. I., & Dietrick, D. C. (1959). Delinquent boys: A critique. *American Sociological Review, 24*(2), 208–215.

Kornhauser, R. (1978). *Social sources of delinquency.* Chicago, IL: University of Chicago Press.

Kretschmer, E. (1925). *Physique and character: An investigation of the nature of constitution and of the theory of temperament.* New York, NY: Cooper Square.

Kuhn, T. (1962). *The structure of scientific revolution.* Chicago, IL: University of Chicago Press.

Kumpfer, K., & Alvarado, R. (2003). Family-strengthening approaches for the prevention of youth problem behaviors. *American Psychologist, 58,* 457–465.

Kurtz, D. L., Linnemann, T., & Green, E. (2013). Support, coercion, and delinquency: Testing aspects of an emerging theory. *Journal of Crime and Justice* (Pre-print), 1–18.

Kuruoglu, A. C., Arikan, Z., Vural, G., Karatas, M., Arac, M., & Isik, E. (1996). Single photo emission computerized tomography in chronic alcoholism: Antisocial personality disorder may be associated with decreased frontal perfusion. *British Journal of Psychiatry, 169,* 348–354.

LaFree, G., & Kick E. L. (1986). Development and the social context of murder and theft. *Comparative Social Research, 8,* 37–56.

Lamparello, A. (2011). Using cognitive neuroscience to predict future dangerousness. *Columbia Human Rights Law Review, 42*(2), 481–540.

Laub, J. (2004). The life course of criminology in the United States: The American Society of Criminology Presidential Address, 2003. *Criminology, 42,* 1–25.

Laub, J. H., & Sampson, R. J. (2004). *Shared beginnings, divergent lives: Delinquent boys to age 70.* Cambridge, MA: Harvard University Press.

Laub, J. H., Sampson, R. J., & Allen, L. C. (2001). Explaining crime over the life course: Toward a theory of age-graded informal social control. In R. Paternoster & R. Bachman (Eds.), *Explaining criminals and crime* (pp. 97–112). Los Angeles, CA: Roxbury.

Laub, J. H., Sampson, R. J., & Sweeten, G. A. (2006). Assessing Sampson and Laub's life-course theory of crime. In F. T. Cullen, J. P. Wright, & K. Blevins (Eds.), *Taking stock: The status of criminological theory* (Vol. 15) (pp. 313–333). New Brunswick, NJ: Transaction.

Le Bon, G. (1960) [1895]. *The crowd: A study of the popular mind.* New York, NY: Viking Press.

Lee, J. Y., & Cho, K. S. (2013). Chemical castration for sexual offenders: Physicians' views. *Journal of Korean Medical Science, 28*(2), 171–172.

Lemert, E. (1951). *Social pathology.* New York, NY: McGraw-Hill.

Lester, D. (1989). Neurotransmitter bases for Eysenck's theory of personality. *Psychological Reports, 64*(1), 189–190.

Levine, H. G., & Small, D. P. (2008). Marijuana arrest crusade: Racial bias and police policy in New York City, 1997–2007. New York, NY: New York Civil Liberties Union.

Levitt, S. D. (1997). Using electoral cycles in police hiring to estimate the effect of police on crime. *The American Economic Review, 87*(3), 270–290.

Lewis, M. (2014). *Flash boys: A Wall Street revolt.* New York, NY: Norton.

Lilly, R. J., Cullen, F. T., & Ball, R. A. (2011). *Criminological theory: Context and consequences* (4th ed.). Thousand Oaks, CA: Sage.

Lindqvist, P., & Allebeck, P. (1990). Schizophrenia and crime. A longitudinal follow-up of 644 schizophrenics in Stockholm. *British Journal of Psychiatry, 157,* 345–50.

Lippens, R., & Hardie-Bick, J. (2013). Can one paint criminology? *Journal of Theoretical & Philosophical Criminology, 5*(1), 64–73.

Liska, A., Krohn, M. D., & Messner, S. (1989). Strategies and requisites for theoretical integration in the study of crime and deviance. In S. Messner, M. D. Krohn, & A. Liska (Eds.), *Theoretical integration in the study of deviance and crime: Problems and prospects* (pp. 1–19) Albany, NY: SUNY Press.

Liska, A. E., Lawrence, J. J., & Sanchirico, A. (1982). Fear of crime as a social fact. *Social Forces, 60,* 760–770.

Liska, A. E., Messner, S. F., & Krohn, M. D. (Eds.). (1989). Strategies and requisites for theoretical integration in the study of crime and deviance. In S. F. Messner & M. D. Krohn (Eds.), *Theoretical integration in the study of deviance and crime: Problems and prospects* (pp. 1–19). Albany: State University of New York Press.

Lodhi, A. Q., & Tilly, C. (1973). Urbanization, crime, and collective violence in nineteenth-century France. *American Journal of Sociology, 79*(2), 196–218.

Loeber, R., & LeBlanc, M. (1990). Toward a developmental criminology. In M. Tonry & N. Morris (Eds.), *Crime and justice* (Vol. 12) (pp. 375–437). Chicago, IL: University of Chicago Press.

Losel, F., Bliesener, T., & Bender, D. (2007). Social information processing, experiences in social contexts, and aggressive behavior in adolescents. *Criminal Justice and Behavior, 34,* 330–347.

Losel, F., & Schmucker, M. (2005). The effectiveness of treatment for sexual offenders: A comprehensive meta-analysis. *Journal of Experimental Criminology, 1,* 117–146.

Lutters, W. G., & Ackerman, M. S. (1996.) *Social relations in complex environments: An introduction to the Chicago school of sociology.* UCI-ICS Social Worlds Lab #96-1. Retrieved from http://userpages.umbc.edu/~lutters/pubs/1996_SWLNote96-1_Lutters,Ackerman.pdf

Lyman, D. R., Milich, R., Zimmerman, R., Novak, S. P., Logan, T. K., Martin, C., & Clayton, R. (1999). Project DARE: No effects at ten-year follow-up. *Journal of Consulting and Clinical Psychology, 67*(4), 590–593.

Lynch, M. J., & Michalowski, R. (2010). *A primer in radical criminology.* New York, NY: Harrow and Heston.

Maltz, M. D. (2009). Look before you analyze: Visualizing data in criminal justice. In A. Piquero and D. Weisburd (Eds.), *Handbook of quantitative criminology* (pp. 25–52). New York, NY: Springer.

Martinson, R. (1974). What works? Questions and answers about prison reform. *The Public Interest, 35,* 22–54.

Maruna, S. (2001). *Making good: How ex-convicts reform and rebuild their lives.* Washington, DC: American Psychological Association.

Maruna, S. (2010). Mixed method research in criminology: Why not go both ways? In A. R. Piquero & D. Weisburd (Eds.), *Handbook of quantitative criminology, part 1* (pp. 123–140). New York, NY: Springer.

Maruna, S., & Copes, H. (2005). What have we learned in five decades of neutralization research? *Crime and Justice: A Review of Research, 32,* 221–320.

Marvell, T. B., & Moody, C. E. (1996). Specification problems, police levels, and crime rates. *Criminology, 34*(4), 609–646.

Matsueda, R. L. (1988). The current state of differential association theory. *Crime and Delinquency* (34), 277–306.

Matsueda, R. L. (1992). Reflected appraisals, parental labeling, and delinquency: Specifying a symbolic interactionist theory. *American Journal of Sociology, 97*(6), 1577–1611.

Matza, D. (1964). *Delinquency and drift.* New York, NY: Wiley.

Matza, D. (1969). *Becoming deviant.* Englewood Cliffs, NJ: Prentice Hall.

Maume, M. O., & Lee, M. R. (2003). Social institutions and violence: A sub-national test of institutional anomie theory. *Criminology, 41,* 1137–1172.

McNeill, F. (2012). Four forms of 'offender' rehabilitation: Towards an interdisciplinary perspective. *Legal and Criminological Psychology, 17,* 18–36.

Mead, G. H. (1934). *Mind, self, and society.* Chicago, IL: University of Chicago Press.

Mealey, L. (1995). The sociobiology of sociopathy: An integrated evolutionary model. *Behavioral and Brain Sciences, 18,* 523–599.

Mednick, S. A. (1977). A biological theory of the learning of law-abiding behavior. In S. A. Mednick & K. O. Christiansen (Eds.), *Biosocial bases of criminal behavior* (pp. 1–8). New York, NY: Gardiner.

Meier, R. S., Kennedy, L., & Sacco, V. (2001). *The process and structure of crime: Criminal events and crime analysis.* New Brunswick, NJ: Transaction.

Merton, R. K. (1938). Social structure and anomie. *American Sociological Review, 22,* 635–659.

Merton, R. K. (1949). *Social theory and social structure.* New York, NY: The Free Press.

Merton, R. K. (1960). Introduction: The ambivalences of Le Bon's *The Crowd.* In G. Le Bon, *The crowd: A study of the popular mind* (pp. ix–xv). New York, NY: Viking Press.

Merton, R. K. (1968). *Social theory and social structure* (enlarged edition). New York, NY: Free Press.

Merton, R. K. (1995). Opportunity structure: The emergence, diffusion, and differentiation of a sociological concept, 1930s–1950s. In F. Adler & W. S. Laufer (Eds.), The legacy of anomie theory: Advances in criminological theory (pp. 3–78). New Brunswick, NJ: Transaction.

Merton, R. K., & Ashley-Montagu, M. F. (1940). Crime and the anthropologist. *American Anthropologist, 42,* 384–408.

Messerschimdt, J. W. (1986). *Capitalism, patriarchy, and crime: Towards a Socialist-Feminist Criminology.* Totowa, NJ: Rowman & Littlefield.

Messerschimdt, J. W. (2000). *Nine lives: Adolescent masculinities, the body, and violence.* Boulder, CO: Westview Press.

Messner, S. F., Krohn, M. D., & Liska, A. E. (1989). *Theoretical integration in the study of deviance and crime.* Albany: State University of New York Press.

Messner, S. F., & Rosenfeld, R. (1994). *Crime and the American dream.* Belmont, CA: Wadsworth.

Messner, S. F., & Rosenfeld, R. (2012). *Crime and the American dream* (3rd ed.). Belmont, CA: Wadsworth.

Meyer-Lindenberg, A., Buckholtz, J. W., Kolachana, B., Hariri, A. R., Pezawas, L., Blasi, G., . . . Weinberger, D. R. (2006). Neural mechanisms of genetic risk for impulsivity and violence in humans. *Proceedings of the National Academy of Sciences, 103,* 6269–6274.

Michalowski, R. (2012). The history of critical criminology in the United States. In W. DeKeseredy & M. Dragiewicz (Eds.), *The Routledge handbook of critical criminology* (pp. 32–45), London, UK: Routledge.

Michalowski, R., & Bohlander, E. (1976). Repression and criminal justice in capitalist America. *Sociological Inquiry, 46,* 95–106.

Mielke, H. W., & Zahran, S. (2012). The urban rise and fall of air lead (Pb) and the latent surge and retreat of societal violence. *Environment International, 43,* 48–55.

Milgram, S. (1963). Behavioral study of obedience. *Journal of Abnormal and Social Psychology, 67*(4), 371–378.

Milgram, S. (1974). *Obedience to authority: An experimental view.* New York, NY: Harper Collins.

Miller, J. (2005). *The status of qualitative research in criminology: Proceedings from the National Science Foundation's workshop on interdisciplinary standards for systematic qualitative research.* Retrieved from http://www.wjh.harvard.edu/nsfqual/ Miller%20Paper.pdf

Miller, J. M., Schreck, C. J., & Tewksbury, R. (2011). *Criminological theory: A brief introduction.* Boston, MA: Prentice Hall.

Miller, N. E., & Dollard, J. (1941). *Social learning and imitation.* New Haven, CT: Yale University Press.

Miller, W. (1958). Lower-class culture as a generating milieu of gang delinquency. *Journal of Social Issues, 14,* 5–14.

Minor, K., & Morrison, J. T. (1996). A theoretical study and critique of restorative justice. In: B. Galaway & J. Hudson (Eds.), *Restorative justice: International perspectives* (pp. 117–133). Monsey, NY: Criminal Justice Press.

Moffitt, T. (1993). Adolescence-limited and life-course-persistent antisocial behaviour: A developmental taxonomy. *Psychological Review, 100,* 674–701.

Moffitt, T. (2006). A review of research on the taxonomy of life-course persistent and adolescence-limited offending. In F. T. Cullen, J. P. Wright, & M. Coleman (Eds.), *Taking stock: The status of criminological theory* (pp. 502–521). New Brunswick, NJ: Transaction.

Moffitt, T. (2012). Self-control theory then and now. In R. Loeber & B. Welsh (Eds.), *The future of criminology* (pp. 40–45). New York, NY: Oxford University Press.

Moffitt, T., Caspi, A., Harrington, H., & Milne, B. J. (2002). Males on the life-course-persistent and adolescence-limited antisocial pathways. *Development and Psychopathology, 14,* 179–207.

Mooney, J. (2012). Finding a political voice: The emergence of critical criminology in Britain. In W. Dekeseredy & M. Dragiewicz (Eds.), *The Routledge handbook of critical criminology.* London: Routledge.

Moore, J. (1991). *Going down to the barrio: Homeboys and homegirls in change.* Philadelphia, PA: Temple University Press.

Morenoff, J. D., Sampson, R. J., & Raudenbush, S. W. (2006). Neighborhood inequality, collective efficacy, and the spatial dynamics of urban violence. *Criminology, 39*(3), 517–558.

Morrison, B. (2007). *Restoring safe school communities: A whole school response to bullying, violence and alienation.* Annandale, Australia: Federation Press.

Morse, G. (October 2004). Executive psychopaths. *Harvard Business Review.* Retrieved from http://hbr.org/2004/10/executive-psychopaths/ar/1

Mosher, C. J., Miethe, T., & Hart, T. C. (2011). *The mismeasure of crime* (2nd ed.). Los Angeles, CA: Sage.

Moynihan, D. P. (1969). *Maximum feasible misunderstanding: Community action in the war on poverty.* New York, NY: Free Press.

Murphy, D. S., & Robinson, M. B. (2008). The maximizer: Clarifying Merton's theories of anomie and strain. *Theoretical Criminology, 12*(4), 501–521.

Murphy, K., & Harris, N. (2007). Shaming, shame and recidivism: A test of reintegrative shaming theory in the white-collar crime context. *British Journal of Criminology, 47*(6), 900–917.

Nadler, A., Goldberg, M., & Jaffe, Y. (1982). Effects of self differentiation and anonymity in group on deindividuation. *Journal of Personality and Social Psychology, 39,* 449–459.

National Institute of Justice. (2012). *Drug courts: An overview.* Retrieved from http://www.nij.gov/topics/courts/drug-courts/welcome.htm

Needleman H. L., McFarland C., Ness R. B., Fienberg, S. E., & Tobin, M. J. (2002). Bone lead levels in adjudicated delinquents: A case control study. *Neurotoxicology and Teratology* (24), 711–717.

Nelson, K., Landsman, M. J., & Deutelman, W. (1990). Three models of family-centered placement prevention services. *Child Welfare, 69,* 3–21.

Nevin, R. (2000). How lead exposure relates to temporal changes in IQ, violent crime, and unwed pregnancy. *Environmental Research, 83*(1), 1–22.

Nevin, R. (2007). Understanding international crime trends: The legacy of preschool lead exposure. *Environmental Research* (104), 315–336.

New York State Division of Criminal Justice Services, Computerized Criminal History system. Cited in Levine, H. G. & Small, D. P. (2008). *Marijuana arrest crusade: Racial bias and police policy in New York City, 1997 to 2007.* NY: New York Civil Liberties Union.

Newman, G. (1983). *Just and painful: A case for corporal punishment of criminals.* New York, NY: Macmillan Publishing Co.

Newman, O. (1972). *Defensible space.* New York, NY: Macmillian.

Novak, J. D. (1981). Applying learning psychology and philosophy of science to biology teaching. *The American Biology Teacher, 43*(1), 12–20.

Novak, J. D., & Gowin, J. B. (1984). *Learning how to learn.* Cambridge, UK: Cambridge University Press.

Nye, I. F. (1958). *Family relationships and delinquent behavior.* New York, NY: Wiley.

Ogburn, W. F. (1964). *On culture and social change: Selected papers of William F. Ogburn.* Chicago, IL: University of Chicago Press.

Palys, T. (1997). *Research decisions.* Toronto: Harcourt Canada.

Park, R. E. (1936). Succession: An ecological concept. *American Sociological Review, 1,* 171–179.

Park, R. E., & Burgess, E. W. (1921). *Introduction to the science of sociology.* Chicago, IL: University of Chicago Press.

Park, R. E., Burgess, E. W., & McKenzie, R. D. (1925). *The city.* Chicago, IL: The University of Chicago Press.

Passas, N. (1990). Anomie and corporate crime. *Contemporary Crises, 14,* 157–178.

Passas, N. (2000). Global anomie, dysnomie, and economic crime: Hidden consequences of neoliberalism and globalization in Russia and around the world. *Social Justice, 27,* 16–44.

Passas, N. (2010). Anomie and white-collar crime. In F. T. Cullen & P. Wilcox (Eds.), *Encyclopedia of criminological theory* (pp. 57–59). Thousand Oaks, CA: Sage.

Paternoster, R., & Bachman, R. (2001). *Explaining crime and criminals: Essays in contemporary criminological theory.* Los Angeles, CA: Roxbury.

Paus, T. (2010). Population neuroscience: Why and how. *Human Brain Mapping, 31*(6), 891–903.

Pavlov, I. (1897). *Conditioned reflexes: An investigation of the physiological activity of the cerebral cortex.* New York, NY: Dover.

Pearson, F. S., & Weiner, N. A. (1985). Toward an integration of criminological theories. *Journal of Criminal Law and Criminology, 76,* 116–165.

Pepinsky, H. (1991). The peacemaking choice. Peacemaking in criminology and criminal justice. In H. E. Pepinsky & R. Quinney (Eds.), *Criminology as peacemaking* (pp. 300–304). Chicago, IL: Illinois University Press.

Pepinsky, H. E., & Quinney, R. (Eds.). (1991). *Criminology as peacemaking.* Chicago, IL: Illinois University Press.

Pew Research Center. (2012). *Religion in prisons: A 50-state survey of prison chaplains.* Washington, DC: The Pew Forum on Religious and Public Life.

Phillips, C. (2011). *Situational crime prevention and crime displacement: Myths and miracles?* (Unpublished doctoral dissertation). Nottingham Trent University, Nottingham, UK.

Phillips, M. R., Wolf, A. S., & Coons, D. J. (1988). Psychiatry and the criminal justice system: Testing the methods. *American Journal of Psychiatry, 145,* 605–610.

Pichot, P. (1978). Psychopathic behavior: A historical overview. In R. D. Hare & D. Schalling (Eds.), *Psychopathic behavior: Approaches to research* (pp. 55–70). New York, NY: Wiley.

Piliavin, I., Gartner, R., Thornton, C., & Matsueda, R. L. (1986). Crime, deterrence, and rational choice. *American Sociological Review, 51,* 101–119.

Pinker, S. (2011). *The better angels of our nature: Why violence has declined.* New York, NY: Viking Books.

Piquero, A., & Hickman, M. J. (1999). An empirical test of Tittle's control balance theory. *Criminology, 37*(2), 319–342.

Piquero, A., & Piquero, N. L. (1998). On testing institutional anomie theory with varying specifications. *Studies on Crime and Crime Prevention, 7,* 61–84.

Pollard, N. (2011). *Sentencing chronic offenders: 30 strikes and you're out?* (Unpublished doctoral dissertation). Simon Fraser University: Burnaby, BC.

Pollock, G. (1999). *Differencing the canon: Feminism and the histories of art.* London, UK: Routledge.

Pollak, O. (1950). *The criminality of women.* Philadelphia: University of Pennsylvania Press.

Popper, K. (1962). *Conjectures and refutations.* New York, NY: Basics Books.

Postmes, T., & Spears, R. (1998). Deindividuation and antinormative behavior: A meta-analysis. *Psychological Bulletin, 123*(3), 238–259.

Potter, G. R. (2010). What is green criminology? *Sociology Review 20*(2). Retrieved from http://www.greencriminology.org/monthly/WhatIsGreenCriminology.pdf

Pound, R. (1942). *Social control through law.* New Brunswick, NY: Transaction.

Pratt, T. C., & Cullen, F. T. (2000). The empirical status of Gottfredson and Hirschi's general theory of crime: A meta-analysis. *Criminology, 38*(1), 931–964.

Pratt, T. C., & Cullen, F. T. (2005). Assessing macro-level predictors and theories of crime: A meta-analysis. *Crime and Justice, 32,* 373–450.

Pratt, T. C., Cullen, F. T., Sellers, C. S., & Thomas Winfree, L. (2010). The empirical status of social learning theory: A meta-analysis. *Justice Quarterly, 27*(6), 765–802.

Pratt, T. C., & Godsey, T. W. (2003). Social support, inequality, and homicide: A cross-national test of an integrated theoretical model. *Criminology, 41,* 611–644.

Puzzanchera, C. (2013). *Juvenile arrests 2011.* Washington, DC: Office of Juvenile Justice and Delinquency Prevention.

Quay, H. C., & Johns, J. H. (1962). The effect of social reward on verbal conditioning in psychopathic and neurotic military offenders. *Journal of Consulting and Clinical Psychology, 26,* 217–220.

Quetelet, A. (1831). *Research on the propensity for crime at different ages.* Brussels, Belgium: M. Hayez.

Quinney, R. (1970). *The social reality of crime.* Boston, MA: Little, Brown.

R. v. Gladue (1999) 1 S.C.R. 688.

Radzinowicz, L. (1999). *Adventures in criminology.* London, UK: Routledge.

Rafter, N. H. (1997). *Creating born criminals.* Urbana, IL: University of Illinois Press.

Rafter, N. H. (2008). *The criminal brain: Understanding biological theories of crime.* New York, NY: New York University Press.

Raine, A. (1993). *The psychopathology of crime: Criminal behavior as a clinical disorder.* San Diego, CA: Academic Press.

Raine, A. (2002). Biosocial studies of antisocial and violent behavior in children and adults: A review. *Journal of Abnormal Child Psychology 30*(4), 311–326.

Raine, A. (2013). *The anatomy of violence: Biological roots of crime.* New York, NY: Pantheon Books.

Raine, A., & Buschbaum, M. S. (1996). Violence, brain imaging, and neuropsychology. In D. M. Stoff and R. B. Cairns (Eds.), *Aggression and violence: Genetic, neurobiological, and biological perspectives* (pp. 195–218). New York, NY: Psychology Press.

Raine, A., Buchsbaum, M. S., Stanley, J., Lottenburg, S., Abel, L., & Stoddard, J. (1994). Selective reductions in pre-frontal glucose metabolism assessed with positron emission tomography in accused murderers pleading not guilty by reason of insanity. *Biological Psychiatry* (36), 365–373.

Ratcliffe, J. (2004). The hotspot matrix: A framework for the spatio-temporal targeting of crime reduction. *Police Practice and Research, 5*(1), 5–23.

Reckless, W. (1961). A new theory of delinquency and crime. *Federal Probation, 25,* 42–46.

Reckless, W. (1973). *The crime problem.* New York, NY: Appleton-Century-Crofts.

Redl, F., & Toch, H. (1979). Psychoanalytic perspective. In H. Toch (Ed.), *Psychology of crime and criminal justice* (pp. 183–197). New York, NY: Holt, Rinehart, & Winston.

Redl, F., & Wineman, D. (1951). *Children who hate: The disorganization and breakdown of behavior controls.* New York, NY: Free Press.

Reiman, J. (1979). *The rich get richer and the poor get prison.* New York, NY: Wiley.

Reiss, A. (1951). Delinquency as a failure of personal and social controls. *American Sociological Review, 16,* 196–207.

Rengert, G. F. (1990). *Drug purchasing as a routine activity of drug-dependent property criminals and the spatial concentration of crime.* Paper presented at the annual meeting of the American Society of Criminology, Baltimore, MD.

Reyes, J. W. (2007). *Environmental policy as social policy? The impact of childhood lead exposure on crime.* NBER Working Paper No. 13097. Retrieved from http://www.nber.org/papers/w13097

Roberts, J. R., & Gabor, T. (1990). Lombrosian wine in a new bottle: Research on race and crime. *Canadian Journal of Criminology, 32,* 34–54.

Robinson, M. (2004). *Why crime? An integrated systems theory of antisocial behavior.* Upper Saddle River, NJ: Pearson/Prentice Hall.

Robinson, M. B. (1996). The theoretical development of 'CPTED': 25 years of responses to C. Ray Jeffery. *Advances in Criminological Theory* (8).

Robinson, M. B., & Beaver, K. M. (2008). *Why crime? An interdisciplinary approach to explaining criminal behavior.* Durham, NC: Carolina Academic Press.

Robinson, W. S. (1950). Ecological correlations and the behavior of individuals. *American Sociological Review, 15*(3), 351–357.

Rorty, R. (1998). *Truth and progress: Philosophical papers* (Vol. 3). Cambridge, MA: Cambridge University Press.

Rose, D. R., & Clear, T. R. (1998). Incarceration, social capital, and crime: Implications for social disorganization theory. *Criminology, 36*(3), 441–479.

Rosenfeld, R., & Fornango, R. (2011). *The impact of police stops on precinct crime rates in New York City, 2003–2010.* Prepared for presentation at the Understanding the Crime Decline in NYC conference, John Jay College of Criminal Justice, New York (September 22–23).

Ross, L., & Shestowsky, D. (2003). Contemporary psychology's challenges to traditional legal theory and practice. *Northwestern University Law Review, 97*(3), 1081–1113.

Ross, R. R., & Ross, R. D. (1995). *Thinking straight: The reasoning and rehabilitation program for delinquency prevention and offender rehabilitation.* Ottawa, Ontario: Air Training Publications.

Rowe, D. C. (1996). An adaptive strategy theory of crime and delinquency. In J. D. Hawkins (Ed.), *Delinquency and crime: Current theories* (pp. 268–314). New York, NY: Cambridge University Press.

Rusche, G., & Kirchheimer, O. (1939). *Punishment and social structure.* New York, NY: Columbia University Press.

Rushowy, K. (April 30, 2007). Canada is failing its kids, MD says. *Toronto Star.* Retrieved from http://www.thestar.com/news/2007/04/30/canada_is_failing_its_kids_md_says.html

Rushton, J. P. (1985). Differential K theory: The sociobiology of individual and group differences. *Personality and Individual Differences, 4,* 441–452.

Rushton, J. P. (1988). Race differences in behavior: A review and evolutionary analysis. *Personality and Individual Differences, 9,* 1009–1024.

Rutter, M., Caspi, A., & Moffitt, T. E. (2003). Using sex differences in psychopathology to study causal mechanisms: Unifying issues and research strategies. *Journal of Child Psychology and Psychiatry, 44,* 1092–1115.

Rutter, M., Moffitt, T. E., & Caspi, A. (2006). Gene-environment interplay and psychopathology: Multiple varieties but real effects. *Journal of Child Psychology and Psychiatry, 47,* 226–261.

Sampson, R. J. (1986). Neighborhood family structure and the risk of criminal victimization. In J. Byrne and R. J. Sampson (Eds.), *The social ecology of crime* (pp. 25–46). New York, NY: Springer-Verlag.

Sampson, R. J. (1988). Local friendship ties and community attachment in mass society: A multi-level systemic model. *American Sociological Review, 53,* 766–779.

Sampson, R. J. (2006). How does community context matter? Social mechanisms and the explanation of crime rates. In P. O. Wikstrom & R. J. Sampson (Eds.), *The explanation of crime: Contexts, mechanisms, and development* (pp. 31–60). Cambridge, MA: Cambridge University Press.

Sampson, R. J. (2012). *Great American city.* Chicago, IL: University of Chicago Press.

Sampson, R. J., & Groves, B. (1989). Community structure and crime: Testing social disorganization theory. *American Journal of Sociology, 94,* 774–802.

Sampson, R. J., & Laub, J. H. (1993). *Crime in the making: Pathways and turning points through life.* Cambridge, MA: Harvard University Press.

Sampson, R. J., & Laub, J. H. (1997). A life-course theory of cumulative disadvantage and the stability of delinquency. In T. P. Thornberry (Ed.), *Developmental theories of crime and delinquency. Advances in criminological theory* (Vol. 7) (pp. 131–166). New Brunswick, NJ: Transaction.

Sampson, R. J., & Laub, J. H. (2005). A general age-graded theory of crime: Lessons learned and the future of life-course criminology. In D. P. Farrington (Ed.), *Integrated developmental and life-course theories of offending* (Vol. 14). (pp. 165–181). Piscataway, NJ: Transaction.

Sampson, R. J, Morenoff, J. D., & Gannon-Rowley, T. (2002). Assessing "neighborhood effects": Social processes and new directions in research. *Annual Review of Sociology, 28,* 443–478.

Sampson R. J., & Raudenbush, S. (1999). Systematic observation of public places: A new look at disorder in urban neighborhoods. *American Journal of Sociology, 105,* 603–651.

Sampson, R. J., Raudenbush, S., & Earls, F. J. (1997). Neighborhoods and violent crime: A multi-level study of collective efficacy. *Science, 277,* 918–924.

Sampson, R. J., Winship, C., & Knight, C. (2013). Overview of: "Translating causal claims: Principles and strategies for poli-cy-relevant criminology." *Criminology and Public Policy, 12*(4), 1–30.

Samuels, J. F., Nestadt, G., Romanoski, A. J., Folstein, M. F., & McHugh, P. R. (1994). DSM-III personality disorders in the community. *American Journal of Psychiatry, 151,* 1055–1062.

Savelsberg, J. J., King, R., & Cleveland, L. (2002). Politicized scholarship: Science on crime and the state. *Social Problems, 49,* 327–348.

Savitz, L., Turner, S. H., & Dickman, T. (1977). The origin of scientific criminology: Franz Joseph Gall as the first criminologist. In R. S. Meier (Ed.), *Theory and criminology* (pp. 41–56). Beverly Hills, CA: Sage.

Savolainen, J. (2000). Inequality, welfare state, and homicide: Further support for the institutional anomie theory. *Criminology, 38,* 1021–1042.

Schur, E. (1971). *Labeling deviant behavior: Its sociological implications.* New York, NY: Harper and Row.

Schur, E. (1973). *Radical non-intervention.* Englewood Cliffs, NJ: Prentice Hall.

Schwartz, J. (1994). Low-level lead exposure and children's IQ: A meta-analysis and search for a threshold. Environmental Research, 65, 42–55.

Seidenwurm, D., Pounds, T. R., Globus, A., & Valk, P. E. (1997). Temporal lobe metabolism in violent subjects: Correlation of imaging and neuropsychiatric findings. *American Journal of Neuroradiology, 18*(4), 625–631.

Sellers, C. S., Cochran, J. K., & Winfree, L. T. Jr. (2003). Social learning theory and courtship violence. In R. L. Akers & G. F. Jensen (Eds.), *Social learning theory and the explanation of crime: Advances in criminological theory* (pp. 109–127). New Brunswick, NJ: Transaction.

Sellin, T. (1938). *Culture, conflict and crime.* New York, NY: Social Science Research Council.

Serin, R., Forth, A., Brown, S., Nunes, K., Bennell, C., & Pozzulo, J. (2011). *Psychology of Criminal Behavior.* Toronto, Ontario: Pearson.

Shafer Commission. (1972). Marihuana: A signal of misunderstanding. Retrieved from http://www.druglibrary.org/schaffer/library/studies/nc/ncmenu.htm

Shaw, C. (1930). *The jack-roller: A delinquent boy's story.* Chicago, IL: University of Chicago Press.

Shaw, C., & McKay, H. (1969). *Juvenile delinquency in urban areas.* Chicago, IL: University of Chicago Press. (Original work published 1942)

Sheldon, W. H. (1940). *The varieties of human physique: An introduction to constitutional psychology.* New York, NY: Harper & Bros.

Sheldon, W. H. (1942). *The varieties of temperament: A psychology of constitutional differences.* New York, NY: Harper & Bros.

Sheldon, W. H. (1949). *Varieties of delinquent youth.* New York: Harper and Row.

Sherman, L. W. (1990). Police crackdowns: Initial and residual deterrence. In M. Tonry & N. Morris (Eds.), *Crime and justice: A review of research* (Vol. 12) (pp. 1–48). Chicago, IL: University of Chicago Press.

Sherman, L. W., Gartin, P. R., & Buerger, M. E. (1989). Hot spots of predatory crime: Routine activities and the criminology of place. *Criminology, 27,* 27–55.

Sherman, L., Gottfredson, D., MacKenzie, D. L., Eck, J., Reuter, P., & Bushway, S. (1998). *Preventing crime: What works, what doesn't, what's promising.* Washington, DC: National Institute of Justice.

Sherman, L., & Weisburd, D. L. (1995). General deterrent effects of police patrol in crime hot spots: A randomized controlled trial. *Justice Quarterly, 12,* 625–48.

Shestowsky, D., & Ross, L. (2003). Contemporary psychology's challenges to legal theory and practice. *Northwestern University Law Review, 97*(3), 1081–1115.

Short, J. F. (1985). The level of explanation problem in sociology. In R. Meier (Ed.), *Theoretical Methods in Criminology* (pp. 51–74). Beverly Hills, CA: Sage.

Skinner, B. F. (1953). *Science and human behavior.* New York, NY: Macmillan.

Skogan, W. G. (1990). *Disorder and decline: Crime and the spiral of decay in American neighborhoods.* New York, NY: Free Press.

Skolnick, J. H. (1966). *Justice without trial: Law enforcement in democratic society.* New York, NY: Wiley.

Slutske, W., Heath, A., Dinwiddie, S., Madden, P., Bucholz, K., Dunne, M., . . . Martin, N. (1997). Modeling genetic and environmental influences in the etiology of conduct disorder: A study of 2,682 adult twin pairs. *Journal of Abnormal Psychology, 106*(2), 266–279.

Smith, D. C., & Purtell, R. (2008). *Does stop and frisk stop crime?* Paper presented at the Annual Research Conference of the Association of Public Policy and Management, Los Angeles, CA.

Soderstrom, H., Hultin, L., Tullberg, M., Wikkelso, C., Eckholm, S., & Forsman, A. (2002). Reduced frontotemporal perfusion in psychopathic personality. *Psychiatry Research Neuroimaging, 114*(2), 81–94.

Sorg, E. T., Haberman, C. P., Ratcliffe, J. H., & Groff, E. R. (2013). Foot patrol in violent crime hot spots: The longitudinal impact of deterrence and posttreatment effects of displacement. *Criminology, 51,* 65–101.

Sprott, J. B., Jenkins, J. M., & Doob, A. N. (2005). The importance of school: Protecting at-risk youth from early offending. *Youth Violence and Juvenile Justice, 3*(1), 59–77.

Stahura, J. M., & Sloan, J. J. (1988). Urban stratification of places, routine activities, and suburban crime rates. *Social Forces, 66,* 1102–1118.

Stark, R. (1987). Deviant places: A theory of the ecology of crime. *Criminology, 25,* 893–910.

Steffensmeier, D., & Ulmer, J. T. (2003). Confessions of a dying thief: A tutorial on differential association/social learning theory. In R. Akers and G. Jensen (Eds.), Social Learning Theory and the Explanation of Crime (pp. 227–264). New Brunswick, NJ: Transaction.

Stochholm, K., Bojesen, A., Jensen, A. S., Juul, S., Gravholt, C. H. (2012). Criminality in men with Klinefelter's syndrome and XYY syndrome: A cohort study. *BMJ Open, 2*(1), http://bmjopen.bmj.com/content/2/1/e000650.full.

Strang, H., Woods, D., Sherman, L. W., Mayo-Wilson, E., & Ariel, B. (November 2013). Restorative justice conferencing (RJC) using face-to-face meetings of offenders and victims: Effects on offender recidivism and victim satisfaction. A systematic review. *Campbell Systematic Reviews.* Retrieved from http://www.crim.cam.ac.uk/people/academic_research/heather_strang/rj_strang_review.pdf

Stretesky, P. B., & Lynch, M. J. (2004). The relationship between lead and crime. *Journal of Health and Social Behavior, 45,* 214–229.

Sutherland, E. (1939). *Principles of criminology* (3rd ed.). Chicago: J. B. Lippincott (Original work published 1924).

Sutherland, E. (1942). Development of the theory. In K. Schuessler (Ed.), *Edwin H. Sutherland on analyzing crime* (pp. 13–29). Chicago: University of Chicago Press.

Sutherland, E. (1949). *White collar crime.* New York, NY: Dryden.

Sutherland, E. (1973). *On analyzing crime.* Chicago: University of Chicago Press.

Sutherland, E., & Conwell, C. (1937). *The professional thief.* Chicago, IL: University of Chicago Press.

Sutherland, E., & Cressey, D. (1974). *Principles of criminology* (9th ed.). New York, NY: J. P. Lippincott (Original work published 1924).

Sutton, J. R. (2004). The political economy of imprisonment in affluent Western democracies, *American Sociological Review, 69,* 170–189.

Sykes, G. M., & Matza, D. (1957). Techniques of neutralization: A theory of delinquency. *American Sociological Review, 22,* 664–670.

Talentino, A. K. (2007). Perceptions of peacebuilding: The dynamic of imposer and imposed upon. *International Studies Perspectives, 8*(2), 152–171.

Tannenbaum, F. (1938). *Crime and community.* Boston, MA: Ginn.

Tarde, G. (1962). *The laws of imitation.* Glouster, MA: P. Smith. (Original work published 1903)

Taylor, I., Walton, P., & Young, J. (1973). *The new criminology: For a social theory of deviance.* Boston, MA: Routledge & Kegan Paul.

Teddlie, C. B., & Tashakkori, A. (2009). *Foundations of mixed methods research: Integrating quantitative and qualitative approaches in the social and behavioral sciences.* Thousand Oaks, CA: Sage.

Thornberry, T. (1987). Toward an interactional theory of delinquency. *Criminology, 25,* 863–891.

Thornberry, T. (1989). Reflections on advantages and disadvantages of theoretical integration. In S. F. Messner, M. D. Krohn, & A. E. Liska (Eds.), *Theoretical integration in the study of deviance and crime: Problems and prospects* (pp. 37–50). Albany, NY: State University of New York Press.

Thornberry, T., & Krohn, M. D. (2001). The development of delinquency: An interactional perspective. In S. O. White (Ed.), *Handbook of youth justice* (pp. 289–307). New York, NY: Plenum.

Thorndike, E. (1898). *Animal intelligence: An experimental study of the associative processes in animals.* New York and London: Macmillan Co.

Thrasher, F. (1927). *The Gang: A study of 1,313 gangs in Chicago.* Chicago, IL: University of Chicago Press.

Tittle, C. (1995). *Control balance: Toward a general theory of deviance.* Boulder, CO: Westview Press.

Tittle, C., Broidy, L., & Gertz, M. (2008). Strain, crime, and contingencies. *Justice Quarterly, 25,* 283–312.

Toby, J. (1957). Social disorganization and stake in conformity: Complementary factors in the predatory behavior of hoodlums. *Journal of Criminal Law and Criminology, 48*(1), 12–17.

Tonry, M. (2008). Learning from the limitations of deterrence theory. *Crime and Justice, 37*(1), 279–311.

Tonry, M., & Farrington, D. P. (1995). Strategic approaches to crime prevention. *Crime and Justice, 19,* 1–20.

Tremblay, R. E., Vitaro, F., Bertrand, L., LeBlanc, M., Beauchesne, H., Boileau, H., & David, L. (1992). Parent and child training to prevent early onset of delinquency: The Montreal longitudinal-experimental study. In J. McCord and R. E. Tremblay (Eds.), *Preventing antisocial behavior: Interventions from birth through adolescence* (pp. 117–138). New York, NY: Guilford Press.

Tunnell, K. D. (1990). Choosing crime: Close your eyes and take your chances. *Justice Quarterly, 7*(4), 673–690.

Tunnell, K. D. (1992). *Choosing crime: The criminal calculus of property offenders.* Chicago, IL: Nelson-Hall.

Turk, A. T. (1966). Conflict and criminality. *American Sociological Review, 3,* 338–352.

Turk, A. T. (1969). *Criminality and the legal order.* Chicago, IL: Rand McNally.

Turner, J. (2013). *Contemporary sociological theory.* Thousand Oaks, CA: Sage.

Tyler, T., Fagan, J., & Geller, A. (2014). *Street stops and police legitimacy: Teachable moments in young urban men's legal socialization.* Public Law & Legal Theory Working Paper Group, Columbia Law School, Paper Number 14–380, 3–66.

Tyler, T., Sherman, L., Strang, H., Barnes, G. C., & Woods, D. (2007). Reintegrative shaming, procedural justice, and recidivism: The engagement of offenders' psychological mechanisms in the Canberra RISE drinking-and-driving experiment. *Law & Society Review, 41*(3), 553–586.

Ulmer, J. T., & Steffensmeier, D. (2014). The age and crime relationship: Social variation, social explanations. In K. Beaver, B. Boutwell, & J. C. Barnes (Eds.), *The nurture versus biosocial debate in criminology* (pp. 377–396). Thousand Oaks, CA: Sage.

Unnever, J. D., Cullen, F. T., Mathers, S. A., McClure, T. E., & Allison, M. C. (2009). Racial discrimination and Hirschi's criminological classic: A chapter in the sociology of knowledge. *Justice Quarterly, 26*(3), 377–409.

U.S. Department of Health and Human Services. Substance Abuse and Mental Health Services Administration. Office of Applied Studies. *2005 National Survey on Drug Use & Health: Detailed Tables. Table 1.80B: Marijuana Use in Lifetime, Past Year, and Past Month Among Persons Aged 18 to 25.* Retrieved from http://www.samhsa.gov/data/NSDUH/2k5NSDUH/tabs/Sect1peTabs67t0132.htm

Van Den Haag, E. (1975). *Punishing criminals: Concerning a very old and painful question.* New York, NY: Basic Books.

Van Dijk, J. J. M., & de Waard, J. (1991). A two-dimensional typology of crime prevention projects. *British Journal of Criminology, 37,* 46–63.

Van Ness, D., & Strong, K. H. (1997). *Restoring justice.* Cincinnati, OH: Anderson.

Vaughn, M., Delisi, M., Beaver, K., & Wright, J. P. (2009). DAT1 and 5HTT are associated with pathological criminal behavior in a nationally representative sample of youth. *Criminal Justice and Behavior* (3), 1113.

Vila, B. J. (1994). A general paradigm for understanding criminal behavior: Extending evolutionary ecological theory. *Criminology, 32,* 501–549.

Vold, G. (1958). *Theoretical criminology.* New York, NY: Oxford University Press.

Vold, G. B, & Bernard, T. J. (1986). *Theoretical criminology.* (3rd ed.). New York, NY: Oxford University Press.

Wagner, D. G. (1984). *The growth of sociological theories.* Beverly Hills, CA: Sage.

Walsh, A. (2009). *Biology and criminology: The biosocial synthesis.* New York, NY: Routledge.

Walsh, A., & Beaver, K. (2009). *Biosocial criminology: New directions in theory and research.* New York: Routledge.

Walsh, A., & Ellis, L. (2007). *Criminology: An interdisciplinary approach.* Thousand Oaks, CA: Sage/Pine Forge Press.

Walsh, A., Johnston, H., & Bolen, J. D. (2012). Drugs, crime, and epigenetics of hedonic allostasis. *Journal of Contemporary Criminal Justice, 283,* 14–330.

Wedlock, E. (2006). Crime and cohesive communities. Home Office online report. Retrieved from http://www.bucksdaat.co.uk/attachments/093_crime_cohesive_communities.pdf

Weisburd, D., Bushway, S., Lum, C., & Yang, S-M. (2004). Crime trajectories at places: A longitudinal study of street segments in the city of Seattle. *Criminology, 42*(2), 283–322.

Weisburd, D., Wyckoff, L., Ready, J., Eck, J., Hinkle, J., & Gajewski, F. (2006). Does crime just move around the corner? A controlled study of spatial displacement and diffusion of crime control benefits. *Criminology, 44,* 549–592.

Weisburd, D. L., & Green, L. (1995). Policing drug hot spots: The Jersey City DMA experiment. *Justice Quarterly, 12,* 711–736.

Weisburd, D. L., & Piquero, A. (2008). How well do criminologists explain crime? Statistical modeling in published studies. *Crime and Justice, 37,* 453–502.

Weisburd, D., & Telep, C. (2014). Hot spots policing: What we know and what we need to know. *Journal of Contemporary Criminal Justice, 30*(2), 200–220.

Wenzel, M. (2006). A letter from the tax office: Compliance effects of informational and interpersonal justice. *Social Justice Research, 19*(3), 345–364.

Western, B. (2006). *Punishment and inequality in America.* New York, NY: Russell Sage.

Wheeldon, J. (2007). Bridging the gap: A pragmatic approach to understanding critical criminologies and policy influence. *Critical Criminology, 15*(4), 313–325.

Wheeldon, J. (2009a). Between pedagogy and practice: Developing and delivering international criminal justice coursework. *Crime, Law and Social Change, 52*(5), 427–539.

Wheeldon, J. (2009b). Toward common ground: Restorative justice and its theoretical construction(s). *Contemporary Justice Review, 12*(1), 91–100.

Wheeldon, J. (2010a). Learning from Latvia: Adoption, adaptation, and evidence-based justice reform. *The Journal of Baltic Studies, 41*(4), 507–530.

Wheeldon, J. (2010b). Mapping mixed methods research: Methods, measures, and meaning. *Journal of Mixed Methods Research, 4*(2), 87–102.

Wheeldon, J. (2011a). Is a picture worth a thousand words? Using mind maps to facilitate participant recall in qualitative research. *The Qualitative Report, 16*(2), 509–522.

Wheeldon, J. (2011b). Visualizing the future of post secondary correctional education: Designs, data, and deliverables. *The Journal of Correctional Education, 62*(2), 94–116.

Wheeldon, J. (2013). To guide or provoke? Maps, pedagogy, and the value(s) of teaching criminal justice ethics. *Journal of Criminal Justice Education, 24*(1), 97–121.

Wheeldon, J. (2014). Ontology, epistemology, and irony: Richard Rorty and re-imagining pragmatic criminology. *Theoretical Criminology* (Pre Print).

Wheeldon, J., & Åhlberg, M. (2012). *Visualizing social science research.* Thousand Oaks, CA: Sage.

Wheeldon, J., & Burruss, G. (2013). Employing visual techniques to teach in criminology and criminal justice classrooms: Notes from the field. *The Criminologist, 38*(1), 32–34.

Wheeldon, J., Chavez, R., & Cooke, J. (2013). *Debate and dialogue in correctional settings: Maps, models, and materials.* New York, NY: IDEA Press/Open Society Foundation.

Wheeldon, J., & Faubert, J. (2009). Framing experience: Concept maps, mind maps, and data collection in qualitative research. *International Journal of Qualitative Methods, 8*(3), 68–83.

Wheeldon, J., & Heidt, J. (2007). Bridging the gap: A pragmatic approach to understanding critical criminologies and policy influence. *Critical Criminology, 15*(4), 313–325.

Wheeldon, J., Heidt, J., & Dooley, B. (2014). The trouble(s) with unification: Assumptions, methods, and expertise in criminology. *Journal of Theoretical and Philosophic Criminology, 6*(2), 111–131.

Wikstrom P-O. (2004). Crime as alternative: Towards a cross-level situational action theory of crime causation. In J. McCord (Ed.), *Beyond empiricism: Institutions and intentions in the study of crime* (pp. 1–37). New Brunswick, NJ: Transaction.

Wikstrom, P-O. (2008). In search of causes and explanations of crime. In R. D. King & E. Wincup (Eds.), *Doing research on crime and justice* (pp., 117–139). Oxford, NY: Oxford Press.

Wikstrom, P-O. (2006). Individuals, settings, and acts of crime: Situational mechanisms and the explanation of crime. In P.-O. Wikstrom & R. J. Sampson (Eds.), *The explanation of crime: Context, mechanisms, and development* (pp. 61–107). Cambridge: Cambridge University Press.

Wikstrom, P-O., & Sampson, R. J. (2006). *The explanation of crime: Contexts, mechanisms, and development.* Cambridge, MA: Cambridge University Press.

Williams III, F. P., & McShane, M. D. (1994). *Criminological theory* (2nd ed.). Upper Saddle River, NJ: Prentice Hall.

Williams III, F. P., & McShane, M. D. (1999). *Criminological theory* (3rd ed.). Upper Saddle River, NJ: Prentice Hall.

Williams III, F. P., & McShane, M. D. (2010). *Criminological theory* (5th ed.). Upper Saddle River, NJ: Prentice Hall.

Williams III, F. P., & McShane, M. D. (2014). *Criminological theory* (6th ed.). Upper Saddle River, NJ: Prentice Hall.

Williams, J. (2000). *Unbending gender: Why family and work conflict and what to do about it.* New York, NY: Oxford University Press.

Wilson, E. O. (1975). *Sociobiology.* Cambridge, MA: Cambridge University Press.

Wilson, E. O. (1978). *On human nature.* Boston, MA: Harvard University Press.

Wilson, J. Q. (1975). *Thinking about crime.* New York, NY: Basic Books.

Wilson, J. Q., & Herrnstein, R. (1985). *Crime and human nature.* New York, NY: Simon and Schuster.

Wilson, J. Q., & Kelling, G. (March 1, 1982). Broken windows: The police and neighborhood safety. *Atlantic Monthly.* Retrieved from http://www.theatlantic.com/magazine/archive/1982/03/broken-windows/304465/

Wolf, L. K. (2014). The crimes of lead. *Chemical and Engineering News, 92*(5), 27–29.

Wolfgang, M. E., & Ferracuti, F. (1967). *The subculture of violence: Towards an integrated theory in criminology.* London, UK: Sage.

Wolfgang, M. E., Figlio, R. M., & Sellin, T. (1972). *Delinquency in a birth cohort.* Chicago, IL: University of Chicago Press.

Wolin, S. S. (2008). *Democracy incorporated: Managed democracy and the specter of inverted totalitarianism.* Princeton, NJ: Princeton University Press.

Wortman, C. B., & Loftus, E. F. (1992). *Psychology* (4th ed.). NY, New York: McGraw Hill.

Wright, J. P. (2009). Inconvenient truths: Science, race, and crime. In A. Walsh & K. Beaver (Eds.), *Biosocial criminology: New directions in theory and research* (pp. 137–153). New York, NY: Routledge.

Wright, J. P., Dietrich, K. N., Ris, M. D., Hornung, R. W., Wessel, S. D., Lanphear, B. P., . . . Rae, M. N. (2008). The association of prenatal and childhood blood lead concentrations with arrests in early adulthood: A prospective cohort study. *PLOS Medicine, 5,* 732–740.

Wright, R., & Decker, D. (1994). *Burglars on the job: Street life and residential break-ins.* Boston, MA: Northeastern University Press.

Yeager, M. (2011). Frank Tannenbaum: The making of a convict criminologist. *The Prison Journal, 91,* 177–197.

Yochelson, S., & Samenow, S. E. (1976). *The criminal personality: Vol. I: A profile for change.* New York, NY: Jason Aronson.

Young, J. (1971). *The drugtakers.* London, UK: Paladin.

Young, J. (1981). Thinking seriously about crime: Some models of criminology. In M. Fitzgerald, G. McLennon, & J. Pawson (Comps.), *Crime and society: Readings in history and theory* (pp. 248–309). London, UK: Routledge and K. Paul Walton.

Young, J. (1987). The tasks facing realist criminology. *Contemporary Crises, 2*(4): 337–356.

Young, J. (1988). Radical criminology in Britain: The emergence of a competing paradigm. In P. Rock (Ed.), *A history of British criminology* (pp. 159–183). Oxford, UK: Clarendon Press.

Young, J. (2011). *The criminological imagination.* Malden, MA: Polity Press.

Young, J., & Matthews, R. (1992). *Issues in realist criminology.* Thousand Oaks, CA: Sage.

Zahn, M. A., Day, C. D., Mihalic, S. F., & Tichavsky, L. (2009). Determining what works for girls in the juvenile justice system: A summary of evaluation evidence. *Crime and Delinquincy, 55*(2), 266–293.

Zahran, S., Mielke, H. W., McElmurry, S. P., Filippelli, G. M., Laidlaw, M. A. S., & Taylor, M. P. (2013). Determining the relative importance of soil sample locations to predict risk of child lead exposure. *Environment International, 60,* 7–14.

Zaplin, R. T. (1998). Female offenders: Critical perspectives and effective interventions. Gaithersburg, MD: Aspen Publishers.

Zimbardo, P. (1970). The human choice: Individuation, reason, and order versus deindividuation, impulse and chaos. In W. J. Arnold & D. Levine (Eds.), *Nebraska symposium on motivation, 1969* (pp. 237–307) Lincoln, NE: University of Nebraska Press.

Zimbardo, P. (2007). *The Lucifer effect: Understanding how good people turn evil.* New York, NY: Random House.

Zimbardo, P. G. (1971). The power and pathology of imprisonment. *Congressional Record* (Serial No. 15, October 25, 1971). Hearings before subcommittee No. 3, of the committee on the Judiciary, House of Representatives, 92nd Congress, first session on corrections, part II, prisons, prison reform and prisoners' rights: California. Washington, DC: U.S. Government Printing Office.

Zimring, F. E., & Hawkins, G. (1995). *Incapacitation: Penal confinement and the restraint of crime.* New York, NY: Oxford University Press.

Ziskin, L. (Producer), & Fincher, D. (Director). (1999). *Fight club.* [Motion picture]. United States: Fox 2000 Pictures.

Index

Reward deficiency syndrome, 297
Rewards, 94
Rich Get Richer and the Poor Get Prison, The, 224
Risk factor/prevention paradigm, 313
Ritualism, 193
Robertson, K., Jr., 150
Robinson 1950, 182
Robinson 2004, 181, 198
Robinson, M., 56, 176, 289, 332–333
Rochester Youth Development Study, 326–327
Rosenfeld, R., 197–199, 204, 227
Rousseau, J.-J., 18, 214
Routine activities theory, 243–244, 245 (figure), 319
Rowe, D. C., 294
Rules, resources, and routines as social mechanisms, 325
Rusche, G., 223
Rush, B., 62

Saguenay Youth Study (SYS), 301
Saints and the Roughnecks, 163–164
Samenow, S. E., 77
Sampson, R. J., 170, 172, 175–176, 178, 182, 185–186, 316, 317, 321–323, 322, 329, 330, 334
Sanchirico, A., 271
Sandy Hook Elementary School, 61
Savolainen, J., 199
Schizoid personality disorder, 82 (figure), 84 (figure)
Schizophrenia, 81–82
Schizotypal personality disorder, 82 (figure)
Schneiderman, E., 205
Schreck, C. J., 30, 32
Schur, E., 161
Scope, theory, 20–21
    biological positivism, 43
    biosocial theories, 291–292
    conflict theories, 215–216
    control theories, 132
    developmental and life course theories, 316–317
    differential association and social learning theories, 111
    integrated theories, 267–268
    labeling theories, 155–156
    psychological positivism, 66
    psychological process perspective, 93
    rational choice theories, 240–241
    social disorganization theories, 173
    social strain and anomie (SSA) theories, 192–193
Sears, R., 93
Seau, J., 53
Secondary conflict, 110
Secondary deviation, theory of, 157

Secondary drives, 94
Secondary prevention strategies, 253
Secondary psychopaths, 73
Seidman, R., 218
Self-control, 324
    low, 138–143
Self-efficacy, 97, 181 (figure)
Self-identification, deviant, 67, 159
Sellers, C. S., 3, 125, 141
Sellin, T., 110
Serotonin transporter gene, 300
Seven step model, 6–8, 12
    assumptions in, 17–19, 42–43, 65–66, 91–92, 110–111, 131, 153–154, 155 (figure), 172, 191–192, 214–215, 239–240, 267, 289–292, 316
    biological positivism in, 40–53
    biosocial theories, 288–303, 304 (figure)
    conflict theories, 210–227
    control theories, 130–144, 144–145 (figure)
    developmental and life course theories, 313–327
    differential association and social learning theories, 109–122, 122–123 (figure)
    history and social context in, 13–17, 40–42, 62–65, 90–91, 109–110, 130–131, 151–153, 190–191, 210–214, 237–239, 266–267
    integrated theories, 266–281
    key terms and concepts in, 21–24, 43–48, 66–75, 93–98, 111–119, 120 (figure), 132–140, 156–158, 173–176, 177 (figure), 193–198, 216–222, 241–250, 268, 317–325
    labeling theory, 151–161
    mapping in, 30, 55 (figure), 80 (figure), 104 (figure), 145 (figure), 155 (figure), 162 (figure), 181 (figure), 197 (figure), 203 (figure), 230 (figure), 242 (figure), 257 (figure), 270 (figure), 274 (figure), 282 (figure), 305 (figure), 320 (figure), 322 (figure), 329 (figure)
    practical ramifications in, 29, 52–53, 77–79, 101–102, 121–122, 143–144, 160–161, 179–180, 181 (figure), 200–202, 225–227, 252–256, 257 (figure), 280–281, 301–303, 327
    problem focus, scope, and level of explanation in, 20–21, 43, 66, 93, 111, 132, 155–156, 173, 215–216, 240–241, 267–268, 316–317
    psychological positivism in, 61–79
    psychological process perspective in, 90–102, 103 (figure)
    rational choice theories, 237–256, 257 (figure)
    research and, 24–29, 48–53, 75–77, 98–101, 120–121, 140–143, 158–160, 177–179, 198–200, 222–225, 250–252, 278–280, 300–301, 325–327

About the Authors

Jon Heidt is an assistant professor of criminology at the University of the Fraser Valley in British Columbia, Canada. He received his BA in sociology from the University of Montana and his PhD from Simon Fraser University in 2011. He has been studying theories for 15 years and has taught theory and methods courses at several different institutions. His work has appeared in *Critical Criminology, The Journal of Theoretical and Philosophical Criminology,* and *The Encyclopedia of Criminology and Criminal Justice.* Dr. Heidt was also involved with research on the supervised injection site in Vancouver's Downtown Eastside. His other interests include corrections, ethnography, and drug policy legislation.

Johannes P. Wheeldon is an assistant professor at the School of Justice Studies and Sociology at Norwich University in Vermont. He received his BA from Dalhousie University, an LLM from Durham University, and a PhD from Simon Fraser University. He has published three books and more than 20 journal articles. Recent work has appeared in *Theoretical Criminology, Journal of Criminal Justice Education,* and *the Journal of Theoretical and Philosophical Criminology.* The Open Society Foundation funds his current work on correctional education, moral development, and debate and dialogue.

SAGE researchmethods

The essential online tool for researchers from the world's leading methods publisher

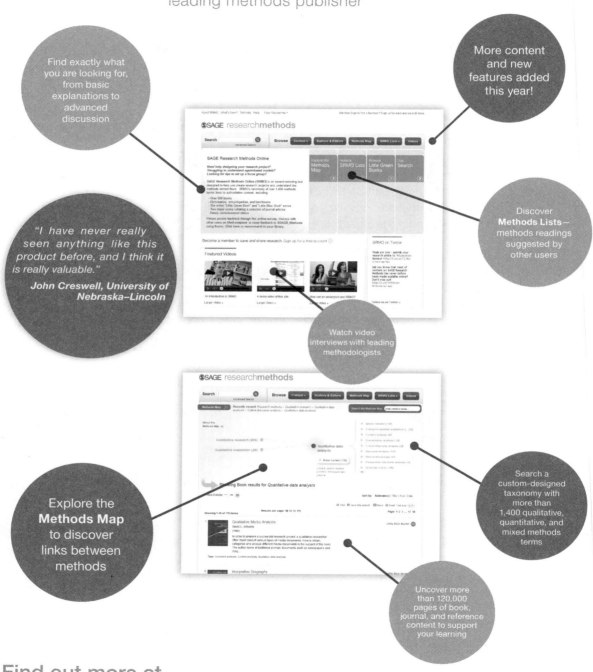

Find exactly what you are looking for, from basic explanations to advanced discussion

More content and new features added this year!

"I have never really seen anything like this product before, and I think it is really valuable."

John Creswell, University of Nebraska–Lincoln

Discover **Methods Lists**—methods readings suggested by other users

Watch video interviews with leading methodologists

Explore the **Methods Map** to discover links between methods

Search a custom-designed taxonomy with more than 1,400 qualitative, quantitative, and mixed methods terms

Uncover more than 120,000 pages of book, journal, and reference content to support your learning

Find out more at
www.sageresearchmethods.com